Major Problems in
American Popular Culture

MAJOR PROBLEMS IN AMERICAN HISTORY SERIES

GENERAL EDITOR

THOMAS G. PATERSON

Major Problems in American Popular Culture

Documents and Essays

EDITED BY

KATHLEEN FRANZ
Department of History
American University

SUSAN SMULYAN
Department of American Civilization
Brown University

WADSWORTH
CENGAGE Learning

Australia • Brazil • Japan • Korea • Mexico • Singapore • Spain • United Kingdom • United States

WADSWORTH
CENGAGE Learning

Major Problems in American Popular Culture
Kathleen Franz and Susan Smulyan

Senior Publisher: Suzanne Jeans

Acquisitions Editor: Jeffrey Greene

Development Editor: Terri Wise

Assistant Editor: Megan Chrisman

Editorial Assistant: Patrick Roach

Senior Media Editor: Lisa Ciccolo

Senior Marketing Manager: Katherine Bates

Manufacturing Manager: Martha Wallace

Marketing Coordinator: Lorreen R. Towle

Marketing Communications Manager: Caitlin Green

Project Management: PreMediaGlobal

Senior Art Director: Cate Rickard Barr

Senior Print Buyer: Sandra Milewski

Rights Acquisition Specialist, Text: Shalice Shah-Caldwell

Senior Rights Acquisition Specialist, Images: Jennifer Meyer Dare

Cover Designer: Gary Ragaglia

Cover Image: Smithsonian American Art Museum, Washington, DC/Art Resource, NY

Author photo (Kathleen Franz) on the back cover: Petrina Foti, National Museum of American History

Compositor: PreMediaGlobal

Library of Congress Control Number: 2011921644

ISBN-13: 978-0-618-47481-3

ISBN-10: 0-618-47481-1

Wadsworth
20 Channel Center Street
Boston, MA, 02210
USA

Cengage Learning is a leading provider of customized learning solutions with office locations around the globe, including Singapore, the United Kingdom, Australia, Mexico, Brazil, and Japan. Locate your local office at **international.cengage.com/ region.**

Cengage Learning products are represented in Canada by Nelson Education, Ltd.

For your course and learning solutions, visit **www.cengage.com.**

Purchase any of our products at your local college store or at our preferred online store **www.cengagebrain.com.**

Instructors: Please visit **login.cengage.com** and log in to access instructor-specific resources.

Printed in the United States of America
1 2 3 4 5 6 7 15 14 13 12 11

Dedicated to the memories of Robert Griffith and Roy Rosenzweig, historians who never saw history as past and who taught as much by their lives as by their scholarship.

Contents

Preface

Popular culture presents a critical group of players, texts, and activities for examining the history of everyday life in the United States. Particularly since the 1970s, the study of popular culture has opened new doors for understanding how the ideologies and identities that shape daily life in the United States have been constituted and contested. The essayists in this volume treat popular culture as a site of conflict where audiences, producers, and vested interests work out cultural meanings. Although vibrant work on popular culture has grown out of film studies, cultural studies, ethnomusicology, and literature, popular culture remains of particular interest to historians. Case studies of popular culture genres have provided a vocabulary for and examples of the material forms on which our collective memories of an American past have been imagined, made material, and transmitted. Cultural historians have seen the realm of the popular as an arena for forming, maintaining, and testing racial, class, gender, and national identities from the early nineteenth century to the present day. This volume contributes to the ongoing study of the ubiquitous, often commercial, and sometimes difficult-to-understand artifacts of popular culture.

The documents and essays in this volume address four major problems that historians encounter in studying and interpreting popular culture: defining our object of study, the role of audiences, the relationship between popular culture and society, and how to think about the globalization of cultures. As the readings take up these questions, they also pay attention to issues of identity (gender, class, and race in particular), changing technologies, increasing commercialization, and the role of the nation-state in the formation of the economic and political structure of the popular culture industries.

Perhaps the most important issue facing scholars in this field remains how to define what we study. For this volume, we have chosen *popular culture* as our primary terminology and our object of study, because we think it connects the newly industrialized versions of leisure found in the nineteenth century such as circuses with the more commodified forms of the mid-twentieth century such as radio and television to the information-based genres just taking hold in the twenty-first century; Facebook, for example. In addition, the term *popular culture* helps raise the idea that audiences, despite the power of the commercial entertainment industry, might possess some power to modify, enjoy, and use the forms handed to them. Others, in the essays and the documents included in this volume, call the same forms *mass culture* or *mass media; commodified* or *commercial culture; low culture; sub-cultures; and hybrid* or *glocalized cultures.*

The issues around the naming of the field raise our second question. What role do audiences play? At least one important scholar, John Fiske, contends that popular culture is made by the complex interactions among producers, forms, and audiences and doesn't exist unless those interactions happen. Others find audiences increasingly passive and oppressed as commercialized entertainment grows. Can audiences change the meaning of the commercial culture they are handed? What role does technology play in how audiences are constructed and think about themselves? Are audiences for minstrel shows the same as those on Facebook?

The third major issue we examine is how popular culture relates to society. Most of us see popular culture as either shaping or reflecting the society of which it is a part. Many contemporary critics, as well as scholars, make the case that popular culture is worth studying to understand the bigger society. Others insist that popular culture has so much power that we must understand it changes the culture. Questions such as, "Why aren't there more women starring in video games/comic books/films/television?" imply that the lack of strong female characters both shows and shapes the culture's sexism. In the end, it may be that popular forms are not only shapers and reflectors of deeply held cultural ideologies; they are, rather, the shifting and highly commercialized territory on which critical social issues, identities, and memories have been, and still are, formed and debated.

Our fourth issue, globalization, raises some of the most interesting and still current debates in the field. American culture has traveled around the world since circuses and minstrel shows took their expertise in scheduling and moving large groups of people (and animals) across the United States to a bigger stage. But the question of whether a definable American culture exists and whether it has been imposed on other countries remains a matter of debate. Is cultural imperialism different or are all forms of imperialism the same? Are products such as blue jeans part of an American empire or do cultural commodities flow across the globe, adapted and used by audiences in their own way? Is the McDonald's where Beijing parents celebrate their children's birthdays an American place, a Chinese place, or a mixture of the two? Does it matter from where the popular culture originates and can we even know? Given wars, harsh economic realities, and political influence, such things do matter, but what role does the popular culture play in a continually expanding global marketplace?

Beginning in the nineteenth century, this volume proceeds chronologically by genre. Each chapter takes up a different form of popular culture, ending in the present, with chapters on the globalized popular culture and on new media. Each chapter has a focus but also, more important, mirrors the ways in which historians have worked. Social and cultural historians often use the "case study" approach that allows for in-depth examination of one relatively small event that explains larger issues. In this volume, we've chosen case studies that explore the political, ideological, and cultural work of popular forms in a particular time period. These case studies introduce the history of important popular culture forms at particular moments, from minstrelsy and the circus to television and social networking sites. At the same time, they address what popular culture is and how popular culture became a cultural space for the construction and contestation of audience and identities.

As with other volumes in the Major Problems in American History series, each chapter opens with a brief introduction to the topic that situates the cultural form and larger questions within a historical context. Following the headnotes, which identify speakers and their approaches, each chapter presents eye–witness accounts that give readers a sense of the great variety of perspectives on popular culture grounded in particular times and places. These primary sources present the opinions of different historical actors, including producers, civic officials, advertisers, performers, journalists, fans, reformers, and critics. The documents also illustrate the rich and diverse types of evidence historians work with, including visual, textual, and audio documents. Sometimes the documents present both the popular culture itself and a critique of it at the same time. Taken together the documents often articulate the sharp concerns and debates that go into making popular culture and prove the point that popular culture lies at the heart of cultural and social discussions that address these problems. Students are encouraged to assess the various ideas presented and consider how the writers' social position may have influenced their comments.

In addition to the primary sources, each chapter has essays written by experts in the particular popular culture genre. Sometimes these essays provide differing viewpoints on the same topic, but more often they complement each other. Demonstrating the breadth and diversity of popular culture studies, the essays provide historical background and theoretical frameworks, and address some of the abstract questions and debates regarding historical interpretation for each of these forms. Some of the essays are classics, while others present more recent, cutting-edge scholarship.

We hope those who seek more information on the issues will consult the Further Readings list at the end of each chapter. In addition, a website supplements the volume and includes links to multimedia archives, further visual images, and music files chosen to illuminate the readings and expand the primary sources. You can find the website at *www.cengagebrain.com*. At the CengageBrain .com home page, enter the ISBN of this title (from the back cover of this book). This will take you to the product page where these resources can be found.

Many studies of popular culture take place within the sub-specialty of cultural history. Cultural historians of the United States often train and teach in Departments of American Studies. Students who want to learn more about American Studies can consult the American Studies Association website "Crossroads" at *http://crossroads.georgetown.edu* or look for the latest scholarship in the organization's journal, *American Quarterly*. Other countries and regions maintain their own American Studies associations (some of the most active include the European American Studies Association, the Japanese Association of American Studies, and the Australian/New Zealand American Studies Association), and each of these organizations has their own journals, which often take up the history of American culture outside the United States. In addition, the Popular Culture Association/American Culture Association *(www.pcaaca.org)*, founded at Bowling Green University, sponsors regional and national conferences and two journals, the *Journal of Popular Culture* and the *Journal of American Culture*.

Collaboration is often at the heart of successful scholarly work, and this project benefited from the insights and advice of many people. The editors wish to thank Thomas G. Paterson, the general editor for the series, for asking them to consider the project and for increasing their files by tenfold with good ideas. For their thoughtful comments on the initial ideas, outline, and drafts of chapters, we thank Richard Butsch, Rider University; Daniel Cavicci, Rhode Island School of Design; Nan Enstad, University of Wisconsin; Lewis Erenburg, Loyola University, Chicago; Briann Greenfield, Central Connecticut State University; David Goodman, University of Melbourne; Phoebe Kropp, University of Pennsylvania; Alex Russo, Catholic University of America; Michael Trotti, Ithaca College; and Jeff Wiltse, University of Montana. Undergraduate Teaching and Research Assistant (UTRA) funds at Brown University paid for the time and talent of undergraduate researchers. For their long hours in the collections at the Library of Congress, the Smithsonian Institution, the New York Historical Society, and the John Hay Library at Brown University, we thank UTRAs Katie Meyers, Billy O'Neill, and Chelsea Miro, all of whom have gone on to even bigger and better things. For his intellectual contributions and tireless efforts on large pieces of this project, including the chapter on the blues, we especially want to acknowledge Chris Suh. We remain moved that Chris has decided to become a historian and wish him well in his own scholarship. We hope he is as fortunate in his research assistants as we were in ours. We are also deeply grateful for the guidance, patience, and thoroughness of the editors at Cengage, Jeff Greene, sponsoring editor, and Terri Wise, development editor.

K.F.

S.S.

Major Problems in
American Popular Culture

CHAPTER 1

Why Study Popular Culture?

Why study popular culture? Our families, like yours, ask this question all the time. Looking at the debates over popular culture studies might help all of us explain the importance of popular culture to our families, friends, and colleagues. The study of popular culture as a subfield of history came about at the same time as a larger set of changes within the humanities and social sciences in the 1970s and 1980s. The exploration of interdisciplinary methods, the adoption of literary theories as new means of analysis, and the reworking of an academic canon of great books and thinkers sparked discussions among scholars and public intellectuals. Traditionalists defended conventional college curricula and continued a long, surprisingly resilient, tradition of suspicion about the effects of commercial media on civil society and on the minds of young people. Bringing television, Elvis, and comic books into the classroom lowered academic standards by examining things that were common and commodified rather than arcane and high-minded. In 1988, Jonathan Yardley, a writer for the Washington Post *and staunch critic of the emerging popular culture studies movement, wrote, "'popular culture' is not an academic course but a form of escape: from the obligation to ground oneself in the rich, complex intellectual legacy of the past, and from the not inconsiderable difficulties of self-discipline." He ended with the sobering charge that anyone who claimed popular culture as an academic discipline was "either self-deluded or a fool." To many, popular culture had always seemed ephemeral, empty, commercial, and "low," and suddenly it sought entrance to the university, the last preserve of high culture.*

Cultural historians, the main proponents of popular culture studies, met these criticisms by doing what they did best: digging deep into the granular details of the past to provide both empirical and theoretical arguments for the historical significance of popular culture. Theater, sports, dime novels, and saloons provided rich territory in which to understand everyday life in the United States, especially for communities that left few written records. The study of popular culture provided another way to learn about people's history from the bottom up and to move the questions of social historians about gender, race, class, and politics into new arenas of inquiry. Yet, cultural historians became intrigued not just by what people did but by what they thought about these activities, what popular culture meant. These historians argued that popular culture provided a space in which people without much formal political power could make social

1

and political change. For instance, historian George Lipsitz, in his essay, states that popular culture is not the sideshow of history but rather the main event. He argues, "for all their triviality and frivolity, the messages of popular culture circulate in a network of production and reception that is quite serious. At their worst, they perform the dirty work of the economy and the state. At their best, they retain memories of the past and contain hopes for the future that rebuke the injustices and inequalities of the present."

The essays in this chapter explain popular culture as political: as a place where ordinary people think about their lives and their society; as a site where the government intervenes in everyday life; as a primary form of consumption in a consumer culture; as a series of technological changes that have influenced how we live and imagine social relationships; and as a set of ideas about how the United States should interact with the rest of the world. We also understand popular culture as fun and as a form of escape, but we continually ask why we have fun or escape in these particular ways and how fun has changed over time.

 # ESSAYS

The following three foundational essays frame the field of popular culture for historians and answer the questions: What is popular culture and why is it important? George Lipsitz, professor of Black Studies at the University of California, Santa Barbara, asks readers to think about the powerful role of popular culture in forging identity and historical memory. Lipsitz argues that identity is not fixed but contested, manipulated, and re-created in the realm of popular culture. He notes that historians can learn a lot about the process of identity and memory creation in the past by deciphering the messages contained in popular culture forms such as the blues. Lipsitz demonstrates that popular culture is not peripheral to the workings of society but rather, as Stuart Hall says, the ground on which cultural and social transformations are worked. Hall, professor emeritus of sociology at the Open University, London, and founding member of the Birmingham School of Social Research in Great Britain, provides critical definitions for, and approaches to, deconstructing the political and social meanings of popular culture. We find his ideas about the dialectical nature of popular culture, the concepts of resistance and containment and the relationship of popular culture to the "institutions of dominant culture of production," particularly important in providing a theoretical basis from which to study popular forms. Finally, John Clarke, dean of the Faculty of Social Sciences at the Open University, London, addresses one of the critical debates among scholars about whether popular culture manipulates audiences or allows them to express themselves. His work defines terms and critiques the arguments on both sides of this debate as well as providing an important context for the other documents and essays collected here, and a starting point for original research in the field.

The Case for Studying Popular Culture

GEORGE LIPSITZ

In this great future, you can't forget your past.

Bob Marley

The late jazz musician Rahsaan Roland Kirk used to preface his performances with an unusual word of advice for the audience. A burly black man who often wore a stovepipe hat with a feather in it, and who frequently carried two saxophones (which he sometimes played simultaneously), Kirk would peer out at the crowd through dark sunglasses and growl, "This ain't no sideshow." Invariably people would laugh at the incongruity of this consummately theatrical individual denying his theatricality. Yet once Kirk began to play, discerning listeners grasped his point.

There was a show going on when Roland Kirk played music, but it was not a sideshow. Nearly everything that Kirk did and said, nearly everything that he played and sang called attention to his role as a black musician in a society controlled by whites. With bitingly satiric renditions of hymns like "The Old Rugged Cross," Kirk related the forms and conventions of popular music to their origins within the historical struggles of the Afro-American past. With mischievous wordplay his song "Blacknuss" called attention to the unequal relationship between the black keys and the white keys on the piano. Kirk's attire and stage behavior subverted conventional expectations about performance, and his aggressive humor exposed the tension between music as a commodity and music as an expression of lived experience.

What distinguished Rahsaan Roland Kirk's "show" from a "side show" was history. All his eccentricities called attention to his identity as a historical subject, a descendant of slaves and a victim of white racism, a human being forced to disguise his pain and anger within the outward appearances of a sideshow. In songs like "The Old Rugged Cross" and "Blacknuss," Kirk translated his experiences and aspirations into art, just as his ancestors had done when they fashioned spirituals, blues, and jazz out of the clash between Afro-American values and Euro-American racism. His stage antics played against the expectations of the audience because they revealed a sedimented layer of historical knowledge and historical critique beneath the surface appearance of novelty and performance. Within the commercial context of commodified mass culture, Rahsaan Roland Kirk created a history that could be hummed, a story of the past that relied on sharps and flats instead of on footnotes, and one that testified to the historicity of experience even while avoiding the linearity and teleology generally associated with historical narratives.

The elements of historical inquiry and explanation encapsulated in Rahsaan Roland Kirk's stage performance present both possibilities and problems. They testify to the importance of historical thinking as an organic and necessary way of understanding human experience, a mode of organizing ideas and

George Lipsitz, "Popular Culture: This Ain't No Sideshow" in *Critical Studies in Mass Communications* 5.2 (June 1988). Speech Communication Association, 1988. Copyright © 1988 by George Lipsitz. Reproduced by permission of the author.

interpretations that is as indispensable in everyday life as it is in scholarly research. Yet its location within popular culture gives Kirk's "history" an impressionistic, interpretive, and allegorical aspect. His art contained multilayered and heavily coded covert messages about the past, but for a large part of his audience, Kirk's music inevitably appeared as just another novelty and diversion within the seemingly autonomous realms of commercialized leisure.

Kirk's problem is our problem. The powerful apparatuses of contemporary commercial electronic mass communications dominate discourse in the modern world. They supply us with endless diversion and distraction mobilized to direct our minds toward advertising messages. They colonize the most intimate and personal aspects of our lives, seizing upon every possible flaw in our bodies, minds, and psyches to increase our anxieties and augment our appetites for consumer goods. Culture itself comes to us as a commodity. The artistry and historical consciousness of a Rahsaan Roland Kirk becomes obscured by our contexts of reception. We buy records and attend concerts, watch films and television commercials as a matter of course. Rarely do we ask about the origins and intentions of the messages we encounter through the mass media; sometimes we forget that artists have origins or intentions at all, so pervasive are the stimuli around us.

Yet mass communications also embody some of our deepest hopes and engage some of our most profound sympathies. People ingeniously enter those discourses to which they have access; the saxophone or the guitar, the stage or the camera can offer precious and unique opportunities for expression. For some populations at some times, commercialized leisure is history—a repository of collective memory that places immediate experience in the context of change over time. The very same media that trivialize and distort culture, that turn art into commodities, and that obscure the origins and intentions of artists also provide meaningful connection to our own pasts and to the pasts of others. But they do so only indirectly, constrained by the nonlinear biases of the electronic media as well as by a commercial matrix hostile to the kinds of empathy, inquiry, and analysis basic to historical thinking.

The presence of sedimented historical currents within popular culture illumines the paradoxical relationship between history and commercialized leisure. Time, history, and memory become qualitatively different concepts in a world where electronic mass communication is possible. Instead of relating to the past through a shared sense of place or ancestry, consumers of electronic mass media can experience a common heritage with people they have never seen; they can acquire memories of a past to which they have no geographic or biological connection. This capacity of electronic mass communication to transcend time and space creates instability by disconnecting people from past traditions, but it also liberates people by making the past less determinate of experiences in the present.

History and commercialized leisure appear to be polar opposites—the former concerned with continuities that unite the totality of human experience, the latter with immediate sense gratifications that divide society into atomized consumers. But both the variants of history and the forms of commercialized leisure familiar to us originated at the same time and for the same reasons. Both developed in the nineteenth century in response to extraordinary technological and social changes. Recognition of the common origins of history and commercialized leisure can explain the seemingly paradoxical tensions within Roland Kirk's music, while also helping to explain how the "remembering" of history and the "forgetting" of commercialized leisure form parts of a dialectical totality....

As literary critic Richard Terdiman has demonstrated, nineteenth century industrialization and state-building entailed a massive disruption of traditional forms of memory. The instrumental mentality capable of building the political and industrial machines of that century had to countenance the destruction of tradition—the enclosure of farm lands, massive migrations to industrial cities, the construction of an interchangeable work force, and a consumer market free from the constraints of tradition. A sense of disconnection from the past united an otherwise fragmented and stratified polity, and consequently the study of the past took on new meaning. Terdiman notes that "history became the discipline of memory," whose task was to uncover "the crisis which inevitably entailed disconnection with the past as a referent." ...

The beginnings of the electronic mass media in the form of the telegraph exacerbated the nineteenth-century crisis of memory. The telegraph enabled simultaneous communication for the first time, dissolving previous barriers of time and space. But that very simultaneity favored the agenda of ascendant industrial capitalism. The telegraph innately privileged the transmission of isolated facts like prices or recent events; it did little to convey context or continuity. Newspapers took on a new role with the stimulus of the telegraph, but it was a role geared toward commerce and change rather than to the preservation of cultural memory. The daily newspaper naturalized a kind of confusion in which the world seemed structured by isolated and discrete events; news became synonymous with change and more important than tradition.

A new kind of commercialized leisure emerged as a corollary to the telegraph in the United States during the late nineteenth century. Previously, churches, lodge halls, and community centers had served as sites for theatrical productions designed to mark festive occasions like weddings and holidays. But urban taverns, dance halls, amusement parks, and theaters brought new meanings to culture. The new commercial theaters, and later variety, vaudeville, and motion-picture halls, needed no special occasions and no association with ritualized activities to justify plays, skits, and music. They carved away a new kind of social space for working-class people—buildings devoted exclusively to leisure activities. Theatrical performances became commodities sold to strangers for an agreed-upon price rather than collective creations by communities enacting rituals essential to group identity and solidarity....

Along with the telegraph and the daily newspaper, the theater helped reshape cultural memory and consciousness. Its role on behalf of the emergent industrial order helped mold a diverse population into a unified working and consuming force, but it also raised anxieties about the moral costs of disconnection from the past. To many critics, the "dissembling" of theater presented a challenge to established order and morality. These critics feared that nothing genuine or refined could come from a sphere of activity devoted to false representations and masked identities. Furthermore, they recognized that theatrical "time" presented an alternative to work time, pitting the pleasures of leisure against the responsibilities of labor. Theater attendance enabled individuals to play out fictive scenarios of changed identities, to escape from the surveillance and supervision of moral authorities and institutions. The fantasy world of the theatrical stage encouraged audiences to pursue personal desires and passions at the expense of their socially prescribed responsibilities....

Melodramas, vaudeville and variety shows, and motion pictures also taught Americans to make a break with the discipline, sobriety, thrift, and sexual repression that formed the core of Victorian culture. Appropriate to an industrializing economy, Victorian values provided necessary preconditions for economic growth during the nineteenth century. They stressed the work ethic, personal responsibility, punctuality, and willingness to defer gratification necessary for life as an industrial worker. But by the 1890s, it appeared that Victorian culture had done its work all too well. The hard-working Americans who internalized Victorian values helped build a powerful industrial economy that produced more products than the domestic market could consume. Overproduction and underconsumption threatened the very survival of industrial capitalism in the 1880s and 1890s, as business failures led to massive unemployment and repeated financial panics. The "false promise" of the Victorian code, that sober self-management would lead to upward mobility, helped provoke general strikes and other forms of "aggressive festivity" among workers. To solve their many problems, business leaders had to move away from the production of capital goods like railroads and locomotives and start producing consumer goods for the domestic market. But as long as Victorian repressions inhibited desires for immediate gratification, consumers lacked the psychological makeup necessary for an economy oriented around ever-increasing purchases of commodities by individuals.

Commercialized leisure evolved out of the contradictions in late nineteenth-century capitalism. For instance motion pictures not only served as renewable commodities in themselves, but they also helped legitimate the consciousness necessary for purchasing other renewable commodities.... Between 1890 and 1930 American society underwent extraordinary changes, from a Victorian culture of thrift to a consumer-oriented culture of spending. By the 1920s, production of renewable commodities like automobiles and appliances played a more important role in the U.S. economy than production of nonrenewable capital goods like heavy equipment and machinery. Economic historians have long understood the logic of this change for the interests of capital; building factories and locomotive engines brought enormous immediate profits, but the market for them became saturated rather quickly. Consumer goods did not need to last—indeed advertisers worked very diligently to see to it that considerations of fashion and style would render old goods obsolete and engender a demand for new ones.

Scholars examining the transition from Victorianism to consumerism in the U.S. have concentrated on the idea of leisure as contested terrain. Drawing upon the research of E. P. Thompson and Herbert Gutman, they have emphasized the ways in which the transition from agrarian to industrial life gave new meanings to work and play....

Commercialized leisure both facilitated the triumphs of industrial capitalism and focused attention on their psychic and emotional costs. Commercial culture sought credibility with its audiences by promising at least the illusion of connec-tion with the past. But the gap between lived experience and the false promises of popular culture always created the possibility for counter-memories, for ethnic, class, and regional music, art, speech, and theater. Culture itself contributed to retraining and reshaping the masses to serve the interests of capital, but also to articulating unfilled desires and expressing disconnection from the past. British cultural studies theorist Stuart Hall notes the contradictions in this process as well as the centrality of tradition as a contested category in the nineteenth century....

The transformations in behavior and collective memory fueled by the con-tradictions of the nineteenth century have passed through three major stages in the United States. The first involved the establishment and codification of com-mercialized leisure from the invention of the telegraph to the 1890s. The second involved the transition from Victorian to consumer-hedonist values between 1890 and 1945. The third and most important stage, from World War II to the 1980s, involved extraordinary expansion in both the distribution of consumer purchasing power and in the reach and scope of the electronic mass media. The dislocations of urban renewal, suburbanization, and deindustrialization accelerated the demise of tradition in America, while the worldwide pace of change undermined stability elsewhere. The period from World War II to the 1980s marks the final triumph of commercialized leisure, and with it an aug-mented crisis over the loss of connection to the past. Popular culture has played an important role in creating this crisis of memory, but it has also been one of the main vehicles for the expression of loss and the projection of hopes for reconnection to the past....

As historian Ramon Gutierrez observes, the term "popular culture" is a description crafted exclusively from the outside. The creators of popular culture do not think of themselves as operating within an endeavor called "popular cul-ture"; they see themselves merely creating signs and symbols appropriate to their audiences and to themselves. It is only from the vantage point of Enlightenment ideals of "high culture" that something called popular culture can be seen to exist. In recent years, scholars have increasingly challenged the divisions between "high" and popular culture, and rightly so. Yet it is also clear that what we call popular culture differs markedly in its aims and intentions from the Enlightenment culture of "beauty and truth" idealized in the nineteenth century by Matthew Arnold, as well as from the isolated "folk" cultures studied by anthropologists and folklorists. In general, we have a better idea of what commercial culture *is not* (high art and folklore) than what it is. But we can identify some aspects of commercialized lei-sure that have come to define its conditions of possibility.

Popular culture has no fixed forms: the historical circumstances of reception and appropriation determine whether novels or motion pictures or videos belong to a sphere called popular culture. Similarly, individual artifacts of popular culture have no fixed meanings. It is impossible to say whether any one combi-nation of sounds or set of images or grouping of words innately expresses one unified political position. Images and icons compete for dominance within a multiplicity of discourse; consumers of popular culture move in and out of subject positions in a way that allows the same message to have widely varying meanings at the point of reception. Although cultural products generally reflect the dominant ideology of any given period, no cultural moment exists within a hermetically sealed cultural present; all cultural expressions speak to both residual memories of the past and emergent hopes for the future.

Rather than looking for innately emancipatory or hegemonic forms and meanings within popular culture, we would do better to study its "transformations," which Stuart Hall defines as

> the active work on existing traditions and activities, their active re-working so that they come out a different way: they appear to 'persist'—yet, from one period to another, they come to stand in a different relation to the ways working people live and the ways they define their relations to each other, to 'the others' and to the conditions of life.

In the United States since World War II, these transformations have coalesced around identifiable conditions of possibility. These conditions are not an "aesthetic," or a finite set of rules guiding artistic production and reception; they are not inherently "progressive" practices guaranteed to advance struggles against exploitation and hierarchy wherever they appear; they are not pure, authentic, or transcendent by themselves. They are historically specific elements within commercial culture that allow for the expression of collective popular memory and the reworking of tradition. Participation and investment, carnival, and a struggle for hegemony have provided significant conditions of possibility within American commercial culture since World War II. At times, all of these have created frames of reception consistent with dominant ideology, but they have also worked to hone and sharpen collective popular memory....

Cultural forms create conditions of possibility, they expand the present by informing it with memories of the past and hopes for the future; but they also engender accommodation with prevailing power realities, separating art from life, and internalizing the dominant culture's norms and values as necessary and inevitable. Politics and culture maintain a paradoxical relationship in which only effective political action can win breathing room for a new culture, but only a revolution in culture can make people capable of political action. Culture can seem like a substitute for politics, a way of posing only imaginary solutions to real problems, but under other circumstances culture can become a rehearsal for politics, trying out values and beliefs permissible in art but forbidden in social life. Most often, however, culture exists as a form of politics, as a means of re-shaping individual and collective practice for specified interests, and as long as individuals perceive their interests as unfilled, culture retains an oppositional potential. Fredric Jameson argues that the dominant culture can only presume to ease anxieties like disconnection from the past by calling attention to them in the first place, thereby running the risk of re-opening the very ruptures it seeks to close. For Jameson, the best cultural creations present contemporary social contradictions in such a way as to suggest eventual resolutions of them, but even works that fall short of that goal retain the potential to play a role in the struggle for hegemony....

For all of their triviality and frivolity, the messages of popular culture circulate in a network of production and reception that is quite serious. At their worst, they perform the dirty work of the economy and the state. At their best, they retain memories of the past and contain hopes for the future that rebuke the injustices and inequities of the present. It might be thought a measure of the inescapable irony of our time that the most profound intellectual questions emerge out of what seem to be ordinary and commonplace objects of study. It may well be that such a paradox exposes the decline of intellectual work and the eclipse of historical reason. But there is another possibility. Perhaps the most important facts about people and about societies have always been encoded within the ordinary and the commonplace. Rahsaan Roland Kirk had an eminently serious agenda, but little access to the arenas in which "serious" decisions about power and resources are contested. However, every time he picked up the saxophone (or saxophones), he made a statement about the past, present, and future. By examining the relationship between collective popular memory and commercial culture, we may be on the threshhold of a new kind of knowledge, one sensitive to contestations over meaning and capable of teaching us that a sideshow can sometimes be the main event.

Deconstructing Popular Culture as Political

STUART HALL

...Throughout the long transition into agrarian capitalism and then in the formation and development of industrial capitalism, there is a more or less continuous struggle over the culture of working people, the labouring classes and the poor. This fact must be the starting point for any study, both of the basis for and of the transformations of popular culture. The changing balance and relations of social forces throughout that history reveal themselves, time and again, in struggles over the forms of the culture, traditions and ways of life of the popular classes. Capital had a stake in the culture of the popular classes because the constitution of a whole new social order around capital required a more or less continuous, if intermittent, process of re-education, in the broadest sense. And one of the principal sites of resistance to the forms through which this "reformation" of the people was pursued lay in popular tradition. That is why popular culture is linked, for so long, to questions of tradition, of traditional forms of life—and why its "traditionalism" has been so often misinterpreted as a product of a merely conservative impulse, backward looking and anachronistic. Struggle and resistance—but also, of course, appropriation and ex-propriation. Time and again, what we are really looking at is the active destruction of particular ways of life, and their transformation into something new. "Cultural change" is a polite euphemism for the process by which some cultural forms and practices are driven out of the centre of popular life, actively marginalised. Rather than simply "falling into disuse" through the Long March to modernisation, things are actively pushed aside, so that something else can take their place. The magistrate and the evangelical police have, or ought to have, a more "honoured" place in the history of popular culture than they have usually been accorded. Even more important than ban and proscription is that subtle and slippery customer—"reform" (with all the positive and unambiguous overtones it carries today). One way or another, "the people" are frequently the object of "reform," often for their own good, of course—"in their best interests." We understand struggle and resistance, nowadays, rather better than we do reform and transformation. Yet "transformations" are at the heart of the study of popular culture. I mean the active work on existing traditions and activities, their active re-working, so that they come out a different way: they appear to "persist"—yet, from one period to another, they come to stand in a different relation to the ways working people live and the ways they define their relations to each other, to "the others" and to their conditions of life. Transformation is the key to the long and protracted process of the "moralisation" of the labouring classes, and the "demoralisation" of the poor, and the "re-education" of the people. Popular culture is neither, in a "pure" sense, the popular traditions of resistance to these processes; nor is it the forms which are superimposed on and over them. It is the ground on which the transformations are worked.

In the study of popular culture, we should always start here: with the double–stake in popular culture, the double movement of containment and resistance, which is always inevitably inside it....

Next, I want to say something about "popular." The term can have a number of different meanings: not all of them useful. Take the most common-sense meaning: the things which are said to be "popular" because masses of people listen to them, buy them, read them, consume them, and seem to enjoy them to the full. This is the "market" or commercial definition of the term: the one which brings socialists out in spots. It is quite rightly associated with the manipulation and debasement of the culture of the people. In one sense, it is the direct opposite of the way I have been using the word earlier. I have, though, two reservations about entirely dispensing with this meaning, unsatisfactory as it is.

First, if it is true that, in the twentieth century, vast numbers of people do consume and even indeed enjoy the cultural products of our modern cultural industry, then it follows that very substantial numbers of working people must be included within the audiences for such products. Now, if the forms and relationships, on which participation in this sort of commercially provided "culture" depend are purely manipulative and debased, then the people who consume and enjoy them must either be themselves debased by these activities or else living in a permanent state of "false consciousness." They must be "cultural dopes" who can't tell that what they are being fed is an updated form of the opium of the people. That judgment may make us feel right, decent and self-satisfied about our denunciations of the agents of mass manipulation and deception—the capitalist cultural industries—but I don't know that it is a view which can survive for long as an adequate account of cultural relationships, and even less as a socialist perspective on the culture and nature of the working class. Ultimately, the notion of the people as a purely *passive*, outline force is a deeply unsocialist perspective.

Second, then: can we get around this problem without dropping the inevitable and necessary attention to the manipulative aspect of a great deal of commercial popular culture? There are a number of strategies for doing so, adopted by radical critical and theorists of popular culture, which, I think are highly dubious. One is to counterpose to it another whole, "alternative" culture—the authentic "popular culture"; and to suggest that the "real" working class (whatever that is) isn't taken in by the commercial substitutes. This is a *heroic* alternative, but not a very convincing one. Basically what is wrong with it is that it neglects the absolutely essential relations of cultural power—of domination and subordination—which is an intrinsic feature of cultural relations. I want to assert on the contrary that there is no whole, authentic, autonomous "popular culture" which lies outside the field of force of the relations of cultural power and domination. Second, it greatly underestimates the power of cultural implantation. This is a tricky point to make, for, as soon as it is made, one opens oneself to the charge that one is subscribing to the thesis of cultural incorporation. The study of popular culture keeps shifting between these two, quite unacceptable, poles: pure "autonomy" or total incapsulation.

Actually, I don't think it is necessary or right to subscribe to either. Since ordinary people are not cultural dopes, they are perfectly capable of recognising the way the realities of working-class life are reorganised, reconstructed and re-shaped by the way they are represented (i.e. re-presented), in, say, *Coronation Street*. The cultural industries do have the power constantly to rework and re-shape what they represent, and, by repetition and selection, to impose and im-plant such definitions of ourselves as fit more easily the descriptions of the dominant or preferred culture. That is what the concentrations of the cultural power—the means of culture-making in the heads of the few—actually means. These definitions don't have the power to occupy our minds: they don't func-tion on us as if we are blank screens. But they do occupy and rework the interior contradictions of feeling and perception in the dominated classes; they do find or clear a space of recognition in those who respond to them. Cultural domination has real effects—even if these are neither all-powerful nor all-inclusive. If we were to argue that these imposed forms have no influence, it would be tanta-mount to arguing that the culture of the people can exist as a separate enclave, outside the distribution of cultural power and the relations of cultural force. I do not believe that. Rather, I think there is a continuous and necessarily uneven and unequal struggle by the dominant culture, constantly to disorganize and reorga-nize popular culture; to enclose and confine its definitions and forms within a more inclusive range of dominant forms. There are points of resistance; there are also moments of supersession. This is the dialectic of cultural struggle. In our times, it goes on continuously, in the complex lines of resistance and accep-tance, refusal and capitulation, which make the field of culture a sort of constant battlefield. A battlefield where no once-for-all victories are obtained but where there are always strategic positions to be won and lost.

This first definition, then, is not a useful one for our purposes; but it might force us to think more deeply about the complexity of cultural relations, about the reality of cultural power and about the nature of cultural implantation. If the forms of provided commercial popular culture are not purely manipulative, then it is because, alongside the false appeals, the foreshortenings, the trivialisation and shortcircuits, there are also elements of recognition and identification, something approaching a recreation of recognisable experiences and attitudes, to which people are responding. The danger arises because we tend to think of cultural forms as whole and coherent: either wholly corrupt or wholly authentic. Whereas they are deeply contradictory; they play on contradictions, especially when they function in the domain of the "popular.". . .

The second definition of "popular" is easier to live with. This is the descriptive one. Popular culture is all those things that "the people" do or have done. This is close to an "anthropological" definition of the term: the culture, mores, customs and folkways of "the people." What defines their "distinctive way of life." I have two difficulties with this definition, too.

First, I am suspicious of it precisely because it is too descriptive. This is putting it mildly. Actually, it is based on an infinitely expanding inventory. Virtually anything which "the people" have ever done can fall into the list. Pigeon-fancying and stamp-collecting, flying ducks on the wall and garden gnomes. The problem is how to distinguish this infinite list in any but a descriptive way, from what popular culture is *not*.

But the second difficulty is more important—and relates to a point made earlier. We can't simply collect into one category all the things which "the people" do, without observing that the real analytic distinction arises, not from the list itself—an inert category of things and activities—but from the key opposition: the people/not of the people. That is to say, the structuring principle of "the popular" in this sense is the tensions and oppositions between what belongs to the central domain of elite or dominant culture, and the culture of the "periphery." It is this opposition which constantly structures the domain of culture into the "popular" and the "non-popular." But you cannot construct these oppositions in a purely descriptive way. For, from period to period, the contents of each category changes. Popular forms become enhanced in cultural value, go up the cultural escalator—and find themselves on the opposite side. Others things cease to have high cultural value, and are appropriated into the popular, becoming transformed in the process. The structuring principle does not consist of the contents of each category—which, I insist, will after from one period to another. Rather it consists of the forces and relations which sustain the distinction the difference: roughly, between what, at any time, counts as an elite cultural activity or form, and what does not. These categories remain, though the inventories change. What is more a whole set of institutions and institutional processes are required to sustain each—and to continually mark the difference between them. The school and the education system is one such institution—distinguishing the valued part of the culture, the cultural heritage, the history to be transmitted, from the "value-less" part. The literary and scholarly apparatus is another—marking-off certain kinds of valued knowledge from others. The important fact, then, is not a mere descriptive inventory—which may have the negative effect of freezing popular culture into some timeless descriptive mould—but the relations of power which are constantly punctuating and dividing the domain of culture into its preferred and its residual categories.

So I settle for a third definition of "popular" though it is a rather uneasy one. This looks, in any particular period, at those forms and activities which have their roots in the social and material conditions of particular classes; which have been embodied in popular traditions and practices. In this sense, it retains what is valuable in the descriptive definition. But it goes on to insist that what is essential to the definition of popular culture is the relations which define "popular culture" in a continuing tension (relationship, influence and antagonism) to the dominant culture. It is a conception of culture which is polarised around this cultural dialectic. It treats the domain of cultural forms and activities as a constantly changing field. Then it looks at the relations which constantly structure this field into dominant and subordinate formations. It looks at the process by which these relations of dominance and subordination are articulated. It treats them as a process: the process by means of which some things are actively preferred so that others can be dethroned. It has at its centre the changing and uneven relations of force which define the field of culture—that is, the question of cultural struggle and its many forms. Its main focus of attention is the relation between culture and questions of hegemony.

What we have to be concerned with, in this definition, is not the question of the "authenticity" or organic wholeness of popular culture. Actually, it recognises that almost *all* cultural forms will be contradictory in this sense, composed of antagonistic and unstable elements. The meaning of a cultural form and its place or position in the cultural field is not inscribed inside its form. Nor is its position fixed once and forever. This year's radical symbol or slogan will be neutralised into next year's fashion; the year after, it will be the object of a profound cultural nostalgia. Today's rebel folksinger ends up, tomorrow, on the cover of *The Observer* colour magazine. The meaning of a cultural symbol is given in part by the social field into which it is incorporated, the practices with which it articulates and is made to resonate. What matters is not the intrinsic or historically fixed objects of culture, but the state of play in cultural relations: to put it bluntly and in an over simplified form—what counts is the class struggle in and over culture.

Almost every fixed inventory will betray us. Is the novel a "bourgeois" form? The answer can only be historically provisional: when? Which novels? For whom? Under what conditions? ...

Cultural struggle, of course, takes many forms: incorporation, distortion, resistance, negotiation, recuperation. Raymond Williams has done us a great deal of service by outlining some of these processes with his distinction between emergent, residual and incorporated moments. We need to expand and develop this rudimentary schema. The important thing is to look at it dynamically: as an historical process. Emergent forces reappear in ancient historical disguise: emergent forces, pointing to the future, lose their anticipatory power, and become merely backward looking; today's cultural breaks can be recuperated as a support to tomorrow's dominant system of values and meanings. The struggle continues, but it is almost never in the same place, over the same meaning or value. It seems to me that the cultural process—cultural power—in our society depends, in the first instance, on this drawing of the line, always in each period in a different place, as to what is to be incorporated into the great tradition and what is not. Educational and cultural institutions, along with the many positive things they do, also help to discipline and police this boundary.

This should make us think again about that tricky term in popular culture, "tradition." Tradition is a vital element in culture, but it has little to do with the mere persistence of old forms. It has much more to do with the way elements have been linked together or articulated. These arrangements in a national-popular culture have no fixed or inscribed position, and certainly no meaning which is carried along, so to speak, in the stream of historical tradition, unchanged. Not only can the elements of "tradition" be rearranged, so that they articulate with different practices and positions, and take on a new meaning and relevance. It is also often the case that cultural struggle arises in its sharpest form just at the point where different opposed traditions meet, intersect. They seek to detach a cultural form from its implantation in one tradition, and to give it a new cultural resonance or accent. Traditions are not fixed forever, certainly not in any universal position in relation to a single class. Cultures conceived not as separate "ways of life" but as "ways of struggle" constantly intersect: the pertinent cultural struggles arise at the points of intersection…. This is the terrain of national-popular culture and tradition as a battlefield.

This provides us with a warning against those self-enclosed approaches to popular culture which, valuing "tradition" for its own sake, and treating it in an a historical manner, analyse popular cultural forms as if they contained within themselves, from their moment of origin, some fixed and unchanging meaning or value. The relationship between historical position and aesthetic value is an important and difficult question in popular culture. But the attempt to develop some universal popular aesthetic, founded on the moment of origin of cultural forms and practices, is almost certainly profoundly mistaken. What could be more eclectic and random than that assemblage of dead symbols and bric-a-brac, ransacked from yesterday's dressing up box, in which, just now, many young people have chosen to adorn themselves? These symbols and bits and pieces are profoundly ambiguous. A thousand lost cultural causes could be summoned up through them. Every now and then, amongst the other trinkets, we find that sign which, above all other signs, ought to be fixed—solidified—in its cultural meaning and connotation forever: the swastika. And yet there it dangles, partly—but not entirely—out loose from its profound cultural reference in twentieth-century history. What does it mean? What is it signifying? It's signification is rich, and richly ambiguous: certainly unstable. This terrifying sign may delimit a range of meanings but it carries no guarantee of a single meaning within itself. The streets are full of kids who are not "fascist" because they may wear a swastika on a chain. On the other hand, perhaps they could be … what this sign means will ultimately depend, in the politics of youth culture, less on the intrinsic cultural symbolism of the thing in itself, and more on the balance of forces between, say, the National Front and the Anti-Nazi League, between White Rock and the Two Tone Sound.

Not only is there no intrinsic guarantee within the cultural sign or form itself. There is no guarantee that, because at one time it was linked with a pertinent struggle, that it will always be the living expression of a class: so that every time you give it an airing it will "speak the language of socialism." If cultural expressions register for socialism, it is because they have been linked as the practices, the forms and organisation of a living struggle, which has succeeded in appropriating those symbols and giving them a socialist connotation. Culture is not already permanently inscribed with the conditions of a class before that struggle begins. The struggle consists in the success or failure to give "the cultural" a socialist accent.

The term "popular" has very complex relations to the term "class." We know this, but are often at pains to forget it. We speak of particular forms of working-class culture, but we use more inclusive term, "popular culture" to refer to the general field of enquiry. It's perfectly clear that what I've been saying would make little sense without reference to a class perspective and to class struggle. But it is also clear that there is one-to-one relationship between a class and a particular cultural form or practice. The terms "class" and "popular" are deeply related but they are not absolutely interchangeable. The reason for that is obvious. There are no wholly separate "cultures" paradigmatically attached, in a relation of historical fixity, to specific "whole" classes—although there are clearly distinct and variable class-cultural formations. Class cultures tend to intersect and overlap in the same field of struggle. The term "popular" indicates this somewhat displaced relationship of culture to classes. More accurately, it refers to that alliance of classes and forces which constitute the "popular classes." The culture of the oppressed, the excluded classes: this is the area to which the term "popular" refers us. And the opposite side to that—the side with the cultural power to decide what belongs and what does not—is, by definition, not another "whole" class, but that other alliance of classes, strata and social forces which constitute what is not "the people" and not the "popular classes": the culture of the power-bloc.

The people versus the power-bloc: this, rather than "class-against-class," is the central line of contradiction around which the terrain of culture is polarised. Popular culture, especially, is organised around the contradiction: the popular forces versus the power-bloc. This gives to the terrain of cultural struggle its own kind of specifically. But the term "popular," and even more, the collective subject to which it must refer—"the people"—is highly problematic. It is made problematic by, say, the ability of Mrs Thatcher to pronounce a sentence like, "We have to limit the power of the trade unions because that is what the people want." That suggests to me that, just as there is no fixed content to the category of "popular culture," so there is no fixed subject to attach to it—"the people." The people are not always back there, where they have always been, their culture untouched, their liberties and their instincts intact, still struggling on against the Norman yoke or whatever, as if, if only we can "discover" them and bring them back on stage. They will always stand up in the right, appointed place and be counted. The capacity to constitute classes and individuals as a popular force—that is the nature of political and cultural struggle: to make the divided classes and the separated peoples—divided and separated by culture as much as by other factors—into a popular-democratic cultural force.

We can be certain that other forces also have a stake in defining "the people" as something else: "the people" who need to be disciplined more, ruled better, more effectively policed, whose way of life needs to be protected from "alien cultures," and so on. There is some part of both those alternatives inside each of us. Sometimes we can be constituted as a force against the power-bloc: that is the historical opening in which it is possible to construct a culture which is genuinely popular. But, in our society, if we are not constituted like that, we will be constituted into its opposite: an effective populist force, saying "Yes" to power. Popular culture is one of the sites where this struggle for and against a culture of the powerful is engaged: it is also the stake to be won or lost in that struggle. It is the arena of consent and resistance. It is partly where hegemony arises and where it is secured. It is not a sphere where socialism, a socialist culture—already fully formed—might be simply "expressed." But it is one of the places where socialism might be constituted. That is why "popular culture" matters. Otherwise, to tell you the truth, I don't give a damn about it.

Approaches to Interpreting Popular Culture

JOHN CLARKE

... "Culture" represents a wider framework within which the analysis of leisure can be situated. "Culture" designates the social field of meaning production (sometimes called ideological struggle, signifying practice or processes of representation). It refers to the processes through which people make sense of themselves and their lives within the frame of possibilities offered by the society of which they are members. It is within culture that individual and collective identities and projects are formed. In Britain, "culture"—and the set of approaches known as "cultural studies"—has been the focus for analyses of ideological power, patterns of domination and subordination, and struggles to mobilize meaning around the social divisions of class, race, and gender.

The view of culture as the site of struggle over meaning illuminates many issues concerning the historical and cultural specificity of "leisure" itself, not least the historical development of the spatial, temporal, and cultural separation of "work" (defined as wage labor) and "leisure" (defined as "free time"). A cultural history of leisure, for example, casts light not only on the struggles to "win" free time which accompanied the development of industrial capitalism but also the struggles to control the uses to which such free time could be put. Cultural analysis, then, enables us to think about both the meaning of leisure and the meaning of activities or social practices within leisure.

... Investigations of contemporary culture have had to take account of the ways in which the means of cultural production and distribution have been both commercialized and centralized over the last century. By itself, this does not mean that social groups have become the passive recipients of centrally produced meanings, any more than the commercialization of leisure necessarily implies that

John Clarke, "Pessimism Versus Populism: The Problematic Politics of Popular Culture" in *For Fun and Profit: The Transformation of Leisure into Consumption*, ed. Richard Butsch. Used by permission of Temple University Press. Copyright © 1990 by Temple University. All rights reserved.

groups do not choose how to "spend" their free time. But it does mean that the conditions under which social groups choose and create meanings are overshadowed by the concentrations of economic, cultural, and political power that the "cultural industries" represent.

The consequences for popular culture of these economic and political developments have been the subject of continuing debates. I outline here two major—and very different—assessments of the significance of those changes. The most obvious starting point is the ambiguity embedded in the very idea of what popular culture is.

In one definition, "popular" refers to cultures that arise from and "belong to" the people (the popular masses, the subordinate classes, or subordinated social groups). This is a historically derived reference, drawing on the distinction between "high" and "low" "elite" and "folk" cultures. This concept of the popular carries an implicitly (and sometimes explicitly) positive political affirmation of the validity of popular culture, relative to the dominant views and standards expressed in "high" or "official" culture. The most resonant expression of this view of popular (class-based) culture was provided by Edward Thompson in his introduction to *The Making of the English Working Class*: "I am seeking to rescue the poor stockinger, the Luddite cropper, the 'obsolete' handloom weaver, the 'utopain' artisan, and even the deluded follower of Joanna Southcott from the enormous condescension of posterity."

In a contrasting definition, "popular" describes a culture provided for the people but not produced or distributed by them. The first view sees popular cultures as produced by the people; the second sees it as consumed by them. The first carries a positive validation of the "popular"; the second stresses the more passive implications of consumption as opposed to production. It opens up suspicion of the motives and intentions of the producers of popular culture and questions the political effects of cultures that do not arise from and belong to "the people."

Clearly, the tension between these two views is intensified in the study of contemporary popular culture, precisely because of the domination of culture by the institutions of mass cultural production and distribution, of which the mass media are the most striking example. The rise of mass cultural institutions means that the task of the political assessment of popular culture has moved away from the rescue and celebration of "popular" forms into the much more ambiguous issue of the "popular" in an era of mass cultural production. Political evaluation now has to confront the consequences of a culture whose dominant forms are mass produced and distributed and in which "popular" participation is primarily defined by the act of consumption rather than of production.

The analysis of contemporary popular culture has become increasingly polarized between two assessments of its political significance, whose proponents I characterize as the "cultural pessimists" and the "cultural populists." This chapter explores the focal points of these two positions before considering how they might be reconciled. I should confess that in discussing these as "polar" positions and emphasizing the ways in which they are opposed, I am undoubtedly less than just to some of their subtleties. Nevertheless, I think this "hardening up" of the positions does no injustice to the main direction of the arguments....

The pessimistic evaluation of contemporary popular culture focuses on the primacy of cultural production. It emphasizes the insertion of popular culture into a system where production is concentrated in a limited number of centers and where consumption takes place among a disaggregate populace at the periphery. In these broad terms, this pessimism carries more than a few echoes of earlier, culturally conservative analyses of "mass culture" and "mass society." It differs in the way that it locates the economic, political, and ideological impulses of contemporary cultural production within the processes of economic and cultural power in advanced capitalism. The imperatives of popular culture derive from the tendencies of the dominant classes toward economic concentration and ideological incorporation in contemporary capitalist societies.

"Culture" in capitalism has been commodified: that is, it has been brought into the realm of objects that are produced and exchanged under capitalist social relations of production. From being a practice "of the people"—a self-creating process—cultural production has been taken into the centers of economic power. Culture is profitable. For the cultural pessimists, this is the decisive shift. The "alienation" of cultural production from the people locates it decisively in the heart of the capitalist domination of the social world. Information, entertainment, the pleasures of leisure have all been subordinated to the processes of what Harry Braverman called "the universal market." Access to and participation in them has been increasingly dominated by exchange relationships. People have to buy their way into popular culture, through the direct purchase of clothes, music, and sporting goods, for example, and through such indirect means as buying television sets. Popular culture now demands an entrance price.

The starting point of this pessimistic evaluation is the massive concentration of cultural power that the "cultural industries" represent. Culture is not a marginal aspect of capitalist economies but a central object of investment and production. The enterprises involved in cultural production and distribution have followed the characteristic economic logics of capitalist organization: the process of concentration (the absorption and elimination of competition); the process of diversification (both horizontal and vertical); and the creation of new markets. What is more, they have followed those logics successfully, becoming not merely corporate giants in the fields of communications and culture but also dominant enterprises in the larger realm of multinational capitalism.

But these enterprises also represent a distinctive aspect of the capitalist economy in that they combine concentrations of economic power with concentrations of cultural power. They stand at the intersection of "the economy" and "daily life" (as it is represented by popular culture), linking the logics of capitalism to the realms of play, fantasy, imagination, and pleasure. Needs and desires are directed into the world of commodities, and each new need fuels the fires of capitalist expansion. But the logic at work here is not merely an economic logic—the drive to reproduce the ideologies of domination that serve to hold the subordinate classes in their places.

This issue needs to be addressed in two rather different ways. The first concerns the way in which the "industrialization" of popular culture reproduces the social relations of capitalism: the second, the reproduction of specific ideologies. In the first, the transposition of popular culture into "consumer culture" moves cultural production into the cultural industries and changes the participation of subordinate social groups into the act (and relationships) of exchange and consumption. In this sense, the conditions of popular culture reproduce the dominant economic relations of capitalism and extend them to new spheres of life....

This new popular culture individualizes social relationships; turns social interactions into the impersonal act of exchange; and transposes relations between people into relations between things:

> It is a world defined by the retail (individualized) consumption of goods and services: a world in which social relations are often disciplined by the exchange of money; a world where it increasingly makes sense that if there are solutions to be had, they can be bought.

A consumption-based popular culture both reproduces and reinforces the social relations of capitalism: it works through them in the sense that participation in popular culture increasingly rests on the exchange relationship, and its messages reinforce the "normality" of the presumption that life is like that. This point opens up the second sense in which the pessimistic reading of popular culture links economic and ideological domination, this time in its content rather that its relationships.

Popular culture is a field in which dominant ideological meanings are reproduced and relayed.... [O]ne aspect of this is the insistence that satisfactions are to be gained through the act of consumption. Both in mass advertising (and its promises of fulfillment through the use of specific products) and the many forms of popular entertainment that celebrate the equation of success with ownership..., the reassertion of the promises of capitalism is a dominant theme of popular culture. Similarly, many forms of popular culture celebrate the "naturalness" of competitive individualism as the elemental human condition.

Equally, popular culture is involved in the reproduction of specific sets of relationships within capitalist societies: forms of domination and subordination between classes, genders, and ethnic groups. It validates and recuperates existing forms of social divisions, rendering them invisible and naturalizing them.... Popular culture is enmeshed in the recirculation and revitalization of structures of social inequality. And in the process of revitalization, alternative possibilities are marginalized and demobilized.

This is a very truncated representation of arguments about the place of ideological domination in popular culture, and many discussions of it are considerably more complex than my summary suggests. Nevertheless, the range of view—from those that stress direct "reflection" of dominant ideologies to those that see popular culture as a ground in which dominance is "recuperated" against challenges to it—share a common view about the production of cultural meaning. It is one that stresses the dominance of the moment of production as against the structured secondariness of the moment of consumption. Meanings are inscribed and fixed in the act of cultural production and are presented to the consumers. Popular culture as mass consumption fuses the economic and ideological logics of contemporary capitalism and positions the "popular audience" both through its social relations and through the cultural meanings it relays.

The production of dominant meanings and the secondariness of consumption is the point of sharpest contrast between cultural pessimism and cultural populism. In the arguments of the cultural populists, the reproduction of dominant ideologies is an altogether more elusive process....

Whereas cultural pessimism sees the production of meaning as relatively closed at the point of production and therefore thinks of consumption as a relatively passive process, cultural populism starts from a more complex view of signification. It regards the production of meaning as an unstable process, drawing heavily on those analyses of signification that have stressed the arbitrary quality of signs. In particular, the arguments derived from semiology, and expanded in "poststructuralist" writing, that all signs are polysemic—that is, capable of multiple meanings—have been particularly influential. The emphasis of cultural populism is thus on the instability, or even volatility, of meaning: the same cultural object or social practice can be "read" [or invested with meaning] in different ways.

This approach has been influential in studies of youth subcultures and of the creation of subcultural styles, studies that have examined the processes by which the original meanings of commodities have been subverted or reworked in the creation of subcultural identities.... In this view, consumption is an active, rather than a passive process. It involves the investment of the object being consumed with new significance: it plays upon the possible meanings of the object rather than merely receiving the meaning inscribed within it in the act of production. Meanings are constantly being re-created....

Where cultural pessimism sees consumption as an act that is subordinated to the conditions of production, cultural populism sees it as a distinct and separate social practice that takes place after the act of exchange. The "consumer" appropriates the commodity and then consumes it, investing it with meaning in the process. Allied to this separation of exchange and consumption is a theory of social difference that provides the cultural motivation for such subversive consumption. The "difference" here is the difference of a multiplicity of "social audiences" or groups of cultural consumers—differentiated by class, gender, ethnicity, sexuality, locality, and age. These social positionings provide the possibility of different "readings" of the same cultural practice or object....

Two things are worth emphasizing about the view of popular culture offered here. One is a growing concern with the form as much as the content of popular culture, which has led to analyses of the "spaces" left open in its texts for readers to create their own meanings. Such arguments give further emphasis to the polysemic character of culture (suggesting that the reproduction of dominant ideologies is far from unproblematic), paralleled by a view of the audience as "knowing"—understanding the codes and conventions of the cultural forms it consumes and able to engage with them in a distanced and critical way.... [P]opular culture is a field in which we are all "experts."

In effect, then, the cultural populists have turned many of the central propositions of the pessimists on their heads. Rather than regarding the creation of meaning as limited to the moment of cultural production, they insist that the practice of consumption is also a process of signification. Where cultural pessimism identifies consumption as a passive position of structured secondariness, populism finds it an autonomous moment of active cultural creativity. Where pessimism tends to see the "consumer" as the dominant social role, populism sees "consumers" as differentially socially located, "reading" from their distinctive experiences. And where pessimism stresses the reproduction of dominant social relationships and ideology, populism celebrates the existence of difference, critical distance, and knowing creativity….

Weighing the merits of these two assessments of popular culture is a difficult task, as is trying to reconcile them. In comparing what seem to be their relative strengths and weaknesses for understanding popular culture, let me begin by raising two problems about the pessimistic evaluation.

First, a central strand of cultural pessimism is its emphasis on the integration of economic and cultural power achieved through linking the economic structures of the cultural industries with the reproduction of cultural domination. However this position is qualified, it nevertheless points to a structural tendency of popular culture to be a field in which domination is reproduced. The pessimistic "readings" of popular cultural forms, practices, and objects tend to emphasize the ways in which these work to insert subordinate groups into dominant relations and ideologies. The effect is to make popular culture a more or less "unproblematic" field and, in the "hardest" variants of this position, to stress incorporation as a functional quality of popular culture. Doing so minimizes some of the contradictory processes and consequences of popular cultural practice, and marginalizes the problems of how the "people" are inserted into popular culture.

This stress on incorporation or domination through popular culture overestimates the unity of economic and cultural logics in advanced capitalism. The movement beyond the nineteenth-century bourgeois commitment to "improve" the masses, through rational recreation and rational reproduction, to a more "multicultural" commercialized popular culture suggests that the economic and cultural logics may not combine so directly. Indeed, the narrow economic logic of maximizing audiences and markets may run counter to the "political-cultural" interests of capital. The discovery of new "needs," new markets, and new ways to mobilize consumers may drive sections of capital to "market" cultures of protest and opposition: the counterculture, reggae, feminism, and so on. This raises a question about the sources of popular culture. It has constantly been revitalized not just (not even primarily) by the greater circulation of bourgeois cultural forms ("high culture") but by the adoption and adaptation of popular pleasures and practices from subordinate groups, of which the most consistent example has been the relationship between "pop" music and black musics. Similarly, the processes described by Stuart Hall as cultural "ventriloquism" in the popular media suggest that popular culture cannot be viewed as a field of monolithic domination and incorporation through the imposition of bourgeois forms and meanings.

Second, I take issue with the tendency of the pessimistic view to elide the processes of exchange and consumption. There is rightly a concern with the historical subjugation of popular culture to the processes of the market and the growing domination of the exchange relationship. But cultural pessimism tends to assume a unity of production, exchange, and consumption that links consumption too lightly with the act of exchange. Purchase is not the same as use; exchange needs to be differentiated from consumption. Hence, cultural populism points to a significant weakness in the pessimistic view that the meaning of consumption is inscribed (and cirucumscribed) by the relations of production and exchange. The pessimistic view of the "passive" consumer is a direct consequences of this elision. I want to hold open the spaces between production, exchange, and consumption as allowing the possibility of difference in the social practices of consumption. Viewed abstractly, "consumption" designates social practice that takes place *after* the act of exchange and outside the exchange relation—a differentiation of time and place. In terms of the processes of capitalist economies, it is a "private" rather than a "public" practice and is subject to all the varied social conditions that characterize civil society (and all the forms of social differentiation and division therein).

Together, these two points suggest that cultural pessimism collapses the "economic" and the "cultural" too readily into a single unified system of domination. It closes the space in which it makes sense to talk about difference and resistance, which are the central themes of cultural populism....

This leads me to some of the problems that surround cultural populism in spite of its attention to the questions of resistance and refusal. The radical reevaluation of popular culture that cultural populism represents has both challenged some of the presumptions of cultural pessimism and set aside some of the central issues. I begin by returning to the intersection of the economic and the cultural in popular culture. Many of arguments I have drawn together as "cultural populism" have taken the separation of the economic and the cultural to its extreme conclusion—which is to focus on cultural as an "autonomous" sphere. This extreme is reflected in the study of popular culture as a domain of texts, signs, objects, forms, codes, and the like, that are radically decontextualized from the economic relations within which they are produced, exchanged, and consumed.

Briefly, there are three significant consequences of such decontextualization. First, it separates cultural texts from their conditions at production within the cultural industries, and thus from the economic, political, and cultural imperatives that those industries condense (ranging from censorship through selection to construction). Second, it leaves to one side the whole issue of the dominance of the exchange relationship. By focusing on consumption, it allows the conditions of consumption (exchange) to remain an unexamined (and uncriticized) "backdrop" to the practices of consuming. In that sense, it has lowered its horizons to what happens within "actually existing" popular culture, rather than keeping open the question of how popular culture is socially and historically constituted. Third, and as a consequence of the second point, it fails to engage with the economic inequalities that govern "access" to popular culture. The "entrance price" created by the dominance of exchange relationships cannot be paid by all. The unequal distribution of "disposable income" (both in the wider society and within households) unevenly conditions access to the consumption of popular culture by class, gender, race, and age.

My second area of concern about cultural populism centers more specifically on the "cultural" and the processes of the creation of meaning. I argued earlier that a central theme was the idea of the polysemic quality of the sign—its availability to carry multiple meanings. Populism has stressed this volatility of meaning and has used it to define the theoretical "space" within which diverse audience "readings" of the same text are seen as possible. The corollary to such an insistence on the diversity of meanings that can be generated at the point of consumption is that the meanings inscribed in production are seen as less than monolithic or fixed. The "original" meanings (or those created in cultural production) are decentered, displaced by the meanings generated in the practices of consumption. This celebration of the volatility of meaning seems to me to be overstated. By decentering the question of cultural production, it leaves out of account the power of cultural industries to limit the range of meanings/ideologies that are in public circulation.

Equally, it underestimates the effectivity of the production or "preferred" or "dominant" meanings within the range of possible meanings of a particular practice, object, or sign. Although cultural production may not involve the power to fix a unidimensional or invariant meaning absolutely, it does involve the power to attempt closure and to narrow the range of possible readings or uses. This suggests that audience "readings" take place within a field of cultural struggle, which might be crudely characterized as reading "with or against the grain" of the preferred meanings inscribed in production. While I do not argue against the possibility that alternative meanings may be constructed in the social practices of consumption, I do see these as having a secondary quality: they are readings/uses of texts or objects already produced with meanings inscribed in them. They are "readings of" cultural products rather than cultural production: they are dependent rather than originating....

Further, the construction of a "subversive" or "critical" reading is not a matter just of a position of "social difference" but of having cultural resources that can be mobilized to support and sustain such alternatives. By itself, "difference" is merely a positional precondition for alternative practices. To be realized as an active principle, such difference needs to be associated with a culture of difference: the availability of meanings that can be put to work in the active construction of alternatives "against the grain" of dominant meanings. To talk, of social differentiation as the basis of alternatives is to collapse the space between social position and cultural formation and, implicitly, to present a new essentialism that equates social position with cultural practice. In practice, what emerges is a speculative—rather than a grounded—defense of "resistance." Because it is gestural rather than material, it lapses into the "heroic" celebration of resistance of which [scholars like Elizabeth & Stuart Ewen] are so critical.

One further point needs to be made about "difference" and "resistance." While the fact of resistance (in terms of the continuation of social distancing, alternative meanings, and so on) demands our attention in the study of popular culture, it is not necessarily a cause for political celebration. Most studies of cultures of resistance also reveal their partial, uneven, and contradictory character— and the limits of their political horizons. Subcultural resistances also need to be viewed as ways of "living subordination." Such a view is an important counterweight to the tendency of cultural pessimism to stress the passive incorporation of subordinated groups, but it is also important not to overestimate resistances by treating them as if they are self-evidently counterhegemonic....

Finally, I want to draw together the implications of my comments for a view of popular culture which treats it as a field of cultural power and struggle, and which might allow political analyses that do not lapse into the oscillation between pessimism and populism (and their different forms of political immobilization). I do not claim that any of what I have to say is particularly new, simply that confronted by an unattractive choice between pessimism and populism, I think the arguments are worth restating.

Any analysis of contemporary popular culture must come to terms with the massive economic dominance of the cultural industries. The bulk of popular cultural texts, objects, and activities is produced, supplied, and delivered by these agencies, even though there remain areas of private and semicommercial cultural practice. On the one hand, that dominance poses issues about the concentration of cultural power; on the other, it makes popular cultural practice predominantly a practice of consumption....

The significance of [this] argument is not that it equates the economic domination of popular culture with a passive and incorporated "people" but that it registers how that economic (and ideological) dominance limits the spaces and forms available for alternative or oppositional cultural practice.

A similar argument needs to be made about the contradictory character of popular culture, which would recognize it as a field of conflict rather than representing it either as a monolithic reproduction of dominant ideology or as an unstructured array of endlessly volatile meanings. Against the former, the constant revitalizing of popular culture by the appropriation of subordinate cultural practices, meanings, and forms needs to be recognized. But this "appropriation of the vernacular" is conditional, involving struggles to conform and conventionalize subordinate meanings. And quite often it looks like the selective appropriation of the "bad sense" of "common sense" (its racism and its sexism, for example) rather than of its progressive elements. In these ways, we need to recognize the ways in which popular culture, although it may be a field of conflict, is tendentially "structured in dominance," tending toward the reproduction of domination.

None of this is intended to deny the continuing existence of forms of cultural practice involving critical distance, subversion, resistance, and opposition. But it is to insist on two qualifications to that view. On the one hand, the structural conditions of popular culture need to be recognized. On the other, the social and cultural conditions of "resistance" need to be considered....

The resources for realizing such possibilities are harder to identify. For example, the concept of the "knowing" consumer creator of social meanings contains two problems. One concerns what it is that this "knowing" consumer knows. A thorough expertise in the codes, conventions, and forms of popular culture (and thus the ability to "play" with them) is rather different from the knowledge and ability to transform them. The Ewens provide this reminder about the accomplishments of mass culture: "Its successes have been founded in the ability to define the realm of popular literacy, the terms of that literacy." The difficulty in analyzing the political implications of alternative and subversive "readings" is recognizing the points at which they subvert the terms of that "popular literacy."

The idea of a "knowing" audience for popular culture also involves questions about what the political effects of "critical distance" from its products might be. Cultural populism has been right to argue against the notion of the people as cultural dupes, but the alternative is not necessarily a population of cultural activists conducting a cultural guerilla war. Mundanely, the critical distance from the institutions of popular culture and their products registers itself as skepticism: "it's only entertainment"; "nobody takes it seriously"; "well, they would say that, wouldn't they?" Skeptical distance may be a foundation for oppositional and subversive practices but is by itself an inert force, a state of "passive dissent." It is a dissent that can lead nowhere unless it is connected to systematic sets of alternative meanings, oppositional practices of control, and subversive vocabularies of "popular literacy." To read and practice "against the grain" requires access to cultural resources that can transform passive dissent into an active move in new directions. That is both the political problem and the prospect of popular culture.

FURTHER READING

Buhle, Paul, ed. *Popular Culture in America* (Minneapolis, MN: University of Minnesota Press, 1987).

Butsch, Richard. *For Fun and Profit: The Transformation of Leisure into Consumption* (Philadelphia: Temple University Press, 1990).

Collins, Jim. *Uncommon Cultures: Popular Culture and Post-Modernism* (New York: Routledge, 1989).

Cullen, Jim. *The Art of Democracy: A Concise History of Popular Culture in the United States* (New York: Monthly Review Press, 2002).

Cullen, Jim. ed. *Popular Culture in American History* (Malden, MA: Wiley-Blackwell, 2001).

Fiske, John. *Understanding Popular Culture* (Boston: Unwin Hyman, 1989).

Gans, Herbert J. *Popular Culture and High Culture: An Analysis and Evaluation of Taste.* (New York: Basic Books, 1999).

Guins, Raiford, and Omayra Zaragoza Cruz, eds. *Popular Culture: A Reader* (London: Sage, 2005).

Kammen, Michael G. *American Culture, American Tastes: Social Change and the Twentieth Century* (New York: Knopf, 1999).

Lears, T.J. Jackson. "AHR Forum: Making Fun of Popular Culture." *American Historical Review* 97 (*December* 1992): 1417–26.

Mukerji, Chandra, and Michael Schudson, eds. *Rethinking Popular Culture: Contemporary Perspectives in Cultural Studies*, (Berkeley, CA: University of California Press, 1991).

Ohmann, Richard, and Gage Averill. *Making and Selling Culture* (Hanover, NH: University Press of New England, 1996).

Storey, John. *Inventing Popular Culture: From Folklore to Globalization* (Malden, MA: Blackwell Publishing, 2003).

Storey, John, ed. *Popular Culture and Cultural Theory: A Reader* (New York: Harvester Wheatsheaf, 1994).

CHAPTER 2

Popular Culture Expresses and Constructs Race

Minstrel Shows Across Two Centuries, 1850–1950

The volume begins with minstrel shows, one of the earliest nationalized forms of entertainment, in order to anchor the development of popular culture in the mid-nineteenth century and in a discussion of the social construction of race. Minstrel shows featured white actors wearing black makeup and odd clothing to ridicule African Americans. Some black people also earned money as minstrels, finding the racist form their only chance to work as actors. This chapter illustrates the historical longevity of minstrelsy and its part in the formation of not only racial but also class and national identities.

Industrialization, the nineteenth-century move from an economy based on agriculture to one based on manufacturing, became intertwined with minstrelsy in three ways: the differentiation between leisure and work brought by industrialization made commodified entertainment possible; racism, as expressed in minstrel shows, became one method white workers used to face their unease about new working conditions; and minstrel shows employed the new industrial transportation and communication networks, such as railroads and the telegraph, to organize national and international tours.

As part of industrialization, life on the farm where leisure and work were intertwined changed to city life where work and fun were separated. Minstrel shows soon spread from cities to enter the experiences and thoughts of all Americans who increasingly spent money for leisure entertainment. Some scholars, such as Eric Lott, see minstrel shows as deeply psychological, presenting a vision of American racism as personal and evil, a way for individual white Americans to work out their conflicting feelings about race. Historians

David Roediger and Alexander Saxton, on the other hand, trace the racism of minstrel shows to a form of class solidarity as the white working class came to a grudging acceptance of their own oppression by ensuring there was a group below them, African Americans.

Minstrel shows, with a rigid format performed by professional actors and musicians, traveled the country throughout the nineteenth century. The content shifted but the main feature—white people pretending to be black people to show African Americans as stupid and not deserving of equality—stayed the same. The organization necessary for the minstrel troupes to cover the United States (and to travel internationally) was a product of the coming of the railroads and the kind of synchronization necessary for industrialized production. As popular culture expanded into other genres (circuses and vaudeville, for example), the concept of the "circuit," a set of theaters and sponsors, first organized by the minstrel show producers, became an important feature of nineteenth-century entertainment. Radio and television networks, combining local outlets into a national entertainment system, worked in exactly the same way.

The history of commodified popular entertainment began with a story about race. But minstrel shows remained popular through the twentieth century when students on college campuses often got in trouble for staging them. Spike Lee's film Bamboozled *(2000) tells of an African American television executive who produces a hugely popular contemporary minstrel show. Lee ends the film with a montage of television and film images that stereotype African Americans and are derived from nineteenth-century minstrel shows. Have your ideas about race been formed by minstrel images?*

DOCUMENTS

These documents illustrate minstrelsy's content and images, the way of life for professional minstrels, and the protests against minstrel shows. Document 1 demonstrates what audiences heard when they went to a nineteenth-century minstrel show and illustrates the exact nature of the racism inherent in such productions. This speech parodies one by Abraham Lincoln in the 1858 Lincoln-Douglas debates in which Lincoln describes his ideas about race as much like those of "any other man." In the images of Documents 2 and 3, the stereotypes of both African Americans and Asian Americans are shown in horrifying detail. Document 4 provides a glimpse of the life of a professional minstrel, more concerned with audience response than with the racist content of the materials he performed. Document 5 represents the kinds of resources provided for the twentieth-century amateurs who take over the minstrel form to present community programs featuring minstrel stereotypes. Documents 6 and 7 bring the minstrel story closer to the present and illustrate the protests against minstrel shows (by this time presented by amateurs in small towns). Such protests against minstrelsy probably existed from the beginning, but evidence of them is often difficult to find until the civil rights movement of the 1950s and 1960s made protesting against racism slightly easier and more public.

1. Minstrel Stump Speech, 1868

Feller citizens:—Correspondin' to your unanimous call I shall now hab de pleasure ob ondressin' ebery one of you; and I'm gwine to stick to de pints and de confluence where by I am myself annihilated.

When in de course ob human events it becomes necessary for the colored portion of dis pop'lation to look into and inquire into dis inexpressible conflict. It is—it is—it is—to return to our subject....

What do de folks mean talkin' 'bout de Norf and de Souf? Do dey want to separate us from our brederin' in de sunshiney Souf? Do dey? Eh? umph? Do dese people (what's roamin' around like hungry lions seekin' whom dey may devour) want more? Eh? umph? If dey do let 'em hab New Jersey, Hardscrabble, or—or—or any other man.

Do dese people want to tear up dat magnificent and magniglorious American flag what's ravelin' out in de breezes ob de atmosphere on the top ob de St. Nicholas Hotel? Eh? umph? Do dey want to strip it up and gib de *stars* to de *Souf,* and de *stripes* to de *Norf!* I answer you in clarion tones dat I hope may be heard from de risin' place ob de sun to de cheer in which he sets down. *Dey* can't do it. nor—nor any other man....

Whar is our progressiveness—ness—ness—is not our—is not our—our—our—to return to our subject.

I ask you in de name ob de shaggy-headed eagle, what's flyin' ober de cloud-capped sommits of de rookyganey mountains; be we gwine to be so extemporaneously bigoted in dis yer fashion? Eh? Answer me, as Shakspeare says: "Do not let me blush in ignorance," nor—nor—any other man.

What does our glorious constitution say on referrin' to dis lamentable subject? Does not our glorious constitution—*shun*—*shun*—TUTION! Don't it? Eh? umph? I'll bet two dollars and a half it does.

Now, den, feller citizens, I've got a question to ask you all; I don't want you to go one side ob it, nor on the toder side of side of it, but I want you all to keep huddled up togedder as you be. If de Democrats; de Aristocrats, de Autocrats, or any other *rats*, will elect ME to be dere president, I'll tell you what I'll do for you; I shall hab de Japanese Embassy and the Prince ob Whales here once a week fur to look at you, and Johnny Heenan, de Magnesia Boy, *shall* hab de champion belt, or—or—any other man....

What did my friend General Grant say when he signed de Deoliolumption ob Dependence. I was dar—I seed him sign it. He said to me (as he laid his right hand on my head), "Clem, my boy, who knows but what you might wake up

John F. Scott, ed. "Stump Speech: Or 'Any Other Man,'" in *Brudder Bones' Book of Stump Speeches and Burlesque Orations* (New York: Dick & Fitzgerald, 1868).

some fine mornin' and find yourself de President ob dis glorious Unicorn; you might, or—or—any other man."

2. Minstrelsy Creates Racist Stereotypes, 1896

Ernest Hogan, *All Coons Look Alike to Me* (Chicago: M. Witmark and Sons, 1896). Courtesy Brown University.

3. Minstrel Sheet Music Extends
Racist Stereotypes from African Americans
to Asian Americans, 1907

Bob Cole, *The Wedding of the Chinee and the Coon* (New York: Howley, Haviland and Company, 1907). The Library of Congress.

4. Edward LeRoy Rice Remembers
Minstrelsy, 1911

Let me begin by saying that I am not a "Monarch of Minstrelsy," not even, a duke or prince; as a matter of fact I am a mere subject, perhaps it would be more exact to say I am a slave, for I cannot recall the time when the curtain having been rung up on the first part, the interlocutor saying, "Gentlemen, be seated," that it did not thrill me through and through; in all probability they would have been seated without his invitation, but still, disappointment would have been keen had he not have done so. Then the overture accompanied by the bones and tambos; but that part of the performance seems to be obsolete now; and how I yearn for it. The second son of the late Wm. Henry Rice, who put on cork for nearly fifty years, I was born in New York City, August 24, 1871, on Fourteenth Street, nearly opposite the Armory, above Sixth Avenue. If you happen to see a crowd around there at any time, you will know it is part of the excited populace trying to carry away portions of the building which housed me on my first appearance in any country.

I can remember, as a youngster even before my school days began, my father asking me if I wanted to be a minstrel? I knew that my mother was averse to it and, as they both looked at me awaiting my reply, I vehemently said NO; that was the first lie I ever told. I have done better subsequently, but they have no bearing on this matter. When I was about six or eight years of age, my father, wishing to celebrate the occasion in a fitting manner, took me down town (Philadelphia) and giving me my choice to go in one direction and see "Jack the Giant Killer," or take another route and see the minstrels. I had heard a whole lot about the youthful prodigy who made a business of trimming big husky gents for the sake of getting an appetite that he might better enjoy his meals, and confess to a feeling of curiosity; but it was the "nigger singers" for mine, and it was there that I obtained my first recollection of any individual performer. It was Bobby Newcomb doing Topsy. Whether it was an "Uncle Tom" show, with which the late minstrel was prominently identified at one time, or whether it was a burletta on Mrs. Stowe's immortal work, I never learned, but Newcomb's dress, a ragbag affair, I remember distinctly, subsequently, one made from an American flag, finishing with the well-known suit of white duck in knee-breeches. That was the beginning. I decided then that a minstrel's life was the life for me, and for years I importuned my father to take me on the road with him, finally obtaining a promise to go the next time he took a show out. This was somewhat hazy, but I clung to it tenaciously, and when in July, 1890, he organized the World's Fair Minstrels, my happiness was unbounded....

Old minstrel *habitues* will recall that nigger–act wherein one of the performers declares loudly to his friends that he is boss in his own home, how he rules the ranch and so on; and just as he is saying if his wife would show up then he would inflict dire punishment upon her, she comes running down the aisle from

Edward LeRoy Rice, "Sketch of the Author, with Personal Recollections," in *Monarchs of Minstrelsy* (New York: Kenny Publishing Company, 1911).

the front of the house saying, "Where's my husband?" gathers her lesser half by the ear and amidst the jeers of his companions, carries him away.

At the second performance, at Morristown, N. J., I was cast for the enraged spouse. I believe I was made up for the part fully an hour before the house opened. How nervous I was awaiting my cue, but when it came, my ears seemed to hear nothing but wife, wife, wife, and instead of saying, "Where's my husband?" I said, "Where's my wife?" ★ ★ ★ I won't repeat what my father said, but what with the tears of mortification that flowed from my eyes and the perspiration from the pores of my face, almost made washing-up a superfluity.

After that awful first night I got away with the part without any trouble, and even indulged in conversations while awaiting my cue, which I had always thought to be a physical impossibility....

The company closed early in November and a couple of weeks before Christmas I consented to wrap parcels at Wanamaker's store in Philadelphia for a small weekly stipend. It was hard to work for wages after having received a salary....

In the fall of 1898 I was a member of one of the many California Minstrel organizations that have invaded the country in the past fifty years. The Spring and Summer of 1900 found me selling pasteboards to the Southerners while with the Primrose & Dockstader Minstrels; in the Fall of 1900 I was agent for Andrew Robson in "The Royal Box;" 1901–02, agent for "Pud'dn-head Wilson," with William S. Gill in the name part, Walker Whiteside, and a return to Primrose & Dockstader; 1902–03, manager, Western Alphonse & Gaston Co.; 1903–04, treasurer, Great Lafayette Company.

At various times I acted as usher and lithographer at the Park, Walnut and Arch Street Theatres in Philadelphia; Columbus Theatre, New York City, and the Park in Brooklyn....

5. Instructions for Twentieth Century Amateur Minstrels Reinforce Earlier Racist Ideas, 1938

The lure of burnt cork entertainment never seems to fade. Combining as it does the three major elements of comedy, music, and drama it is the form of entertainment most readily adaptable to the presentation of a variety of talents. The ballad singer, the eccentric dancer, and the man who can play a tune on a jug all find a hearty welcome in the minstrel.

Because of this fact and because of the comparative ease with which a minstrel may be produced, organizations such as American Legion posts and local chapters of clubs and lodges have found it a convenient way of providing entertainment and of raising money....

The real minstrel is a blend of the old and the new. The songs of yesteryear blend with the songs of today. The comedy, though new, carries with it some of the aroma of the pleasant past. Thus does the minstrel live up to its name as entertainment both for old and young....

LeRoy Stahl, *The Five Star Minstrel Book* (Minneapolis, MN: The Northwestern Press, 1938).

There is considerable latitude in the choice of costumes for a minstrel. They need not be expensive. The use of bright, cheerful colors is preferable.

In the traditional minstrel show, the interlocutor wears an elaborate Colonial-type costume of satin, with lace and ruffles and a white wig, but nowadays, he is more likely to be discovered wearing an ordinary Tuxedo or a full-dress suit. If there is any choice, the full-dress suit with "tails" is to be preferred. It has more distinction....

The end men usually wear a burlesqued version of the full-dress suit with long, flowing tails behind. They are brightly colored, purple or green with a contrasting trim in either white or yellow. Frequently, the trousers and the coats are of contrasting colors. In other cases, the entire costume is sometimes made of material in a colorful pattern of checks or plaids....

The minstrel collar, a large tie of paper cambric, and a huge paper flower in the button-hole completes the costume. White cotton gloves are worn on the hands of both the end men and the vocalists to obviate the necessity of making them up, and each performer carries the traditional tambourine....

Burnt cork is to be preferred over grease paint as the make-up for the minstrel show....

Burnt cork is applied as follows: the face is slightly dampened with water. Then, a small dab of the burnt cork is placed in the palm of the left hand and moistened with water. It is then worked with the middle finger of the right hand until it attains the consistency of a thick paste. When this consistency has been achieved it is applied to the face with long, smooth strokes of the finger. Before laying in the principal areas of the face, it is advisable to outline the mouth and the eyes with small quantities of burnt cork on the little finger. A white space of about one eighth inch left around the lids of the eyes adds to the comedy effect and prevents the possibility of getting burnt cork in the eyes. When the make-up is thoroughly dry any excess particles of the burnt cork can be removed by brushing the face lightly with a rabbit's foot or small cosmetic brush. The area around the lips is usually left in its natural white. Some performers feel that the lips must be painted a vivid red, but this is a favorite predilection of the amateur black-face entertainer. No professional burnt cork comedian ever paints his lips. At best, the effect is very unhappy and complicates considerably the removal of the make-up.

In a financial emergency, acceptable minstrel wigs can be manufactured from large, black stockings, but the genuine article may be obtained at so reasonable a price that this is seldom necessary....

The producer of a minstrel show is not obligated to preserve in its entirety the traditional form. Of late years, numerous attempts have been made to freshen the minstrel show by using backgrounds other than the deep South. These have led to the production of Spanish minstrels, gypsy minstrels, collegiate minstrels, and so on. There is no objection to this practice provided the material selected has the true flavor of the form in which it is presented. The material in this book is designed for the traditional black-face minstrel as the form most easily presented by the average amateur. However, with changes here and there, it may easily be adapted to almost any type of production.

6. The Urban League Objects to Amateur Minstrel Shows, 1950

The Urban League of Portland. Oregon is to be commended for having launched a publicity campaign calling for the banning of the outmoded and offensive minstrel show. It is encouraging to observe that a number of magazines and papers in different parts of the country are also taking a vigorous stand. We believe that publicity and public education will bring the downfall of this ignoble kind of theatre.

For many years it has become increasingly evident to fair-minded Americans that the minstrel show—a popular form of amateur theatricals—is lacking in good taste and understandably offensive and objectionable to the American Negro. The gist of the minstrel show was the cheap comedy and the laughter that came from depicting the Negro as the general laughing-stock. He was characterized as a buffoon, a boob and the butt of humor. He was given lines to show the Negro as crude ignorant and utterly lacking in common sense. The time has come to outlaw this lampooning of a racial group.

While it is true that there is little of malicious intent and purpose in the minds of amateurs who choose the minstrel show as requiring the least skill and experience, certainly these thespians should be constantly reminded that the minstrel is by its very nature an insult to Negro citizen and causes well-justified resentment.

Thoughtful Americans recognize that the time has come to call for the final demise of the minstrel show which is an unwanted relic of the days when too many Americans gave little thought to the seriousness, the consequences and the grave moral wrong of prejudice.

We believe that Catholic leaders, aided by the Catholic press should take an active part in condemning and discouraging the minstrel show. The minstrel show must go!

7. A Catholic Newspaper Confronts Minstrelsy's Racism, 1950

1. The Stereotypes. The blackface minstrel tags a whole group of our fellow men as buffoons and clowns. A typical minstrel is shiftless, ignorant, uncouth, and ill-mannered. By invariably portraying the Negro in these roles, the minstrels brand a whole people with the inferior mentality, the degraded morals and the gaudy taste of a few.

2. The Slang. The minstrels use and perpetuate the racial slang offensive to our fellow citizens. They insult the American Negro by referring to him as "nigger," "pickaninny," "coon," "jig," and the like....

"Minstrel Shows Must Go," *Interracial Review* (May 1950), 68.

S.J. Albert Foley, "Blackface Minstrels: Ten Reasons Why They Are Not So Funny," *Catholic Interracialist* (April 1952), 1–2.

3. The Trifling with Tragedies. The minstrel shows … laugh at the tragic effects of the crime of enslavement. They mock the marks of enduring oppression. They ridicule the results of systematic deprivation of civil and social rights. They perpetuate the white man's hardheaded refusal to recognize the serious claims of his Negro fellow citizen to equal justice under God and before the law.

4. The Dulling of Conscience. The racial humor of the minstrel show is a cunning device. White supremacists use it as a way out of their feeling of guilt for the sins of caste. By presenting the Negro as a happy contented, carefree, singing dancing-jigging ne'er-do-well, it creates a smug sense of satisfaction on the part of the on lookers. The white Bilbo … continues in his process of underpaying, ill-treating, disfranchising, and segregating his fellow colored citizens…

5. The Eighth Commandment. The blackface minstrels bear false witness against our colored neighbors. They present the typical Negro as a chicken stealing, wife-beating, razor slashing, and generally immoral person. The cheap songs vilify the entire group. They slander colored saints, Negro bishops, priests, sisters, and seminarians. They humiliate the thousands of holy, God-fearing, upright Negro Christians. They grossly violate the Eighth Commandment.

6. The Effect on Youth. Young people present at, or participating in, minstrels are wrongly educated in a whole series of unChristian attitudes toward their fellow men. Early impressions of the Negro gathered from experience in the minstrels remain as the basis for lasting, almost ineradicable prejudices….

7. Damage to Souls. Religious organizations sponsoring minstrel shows can be the cause of further estrangement of souls from the Church. Eight million Negroes in the country are unchurched…. They become infuriated against all organized religion upon seeing this utter disregard for their plight on the part of church members and clergy who sponsor minstrels.

8. The Golden Rule. No minority likes to have its members caricatured in a farce that embarrasses and disgraces their whole nation or ethnic group…. We should respect the rights, achievements, and characteristics of the colored minority as we also expect to be allowed to live in dignity and honor among our fellow men.

9. "With Liberty and Justice for All." The allegiance we swear to the flag of our country binds us to support the freedoms for which it stands. Freedom from vilification, and the right to a good name, both demand that we cease from these offenses against our fellow Americans. Their sons and brothers have fought and died for the country. The blood of heroes cries for liberty and justice for all.

10. The Global Aspect. Our country has assumed leadership in a world that is two-thirds colored. It is unpatriotic to perpetuate through minstrels the color-consciousness and color complex of a dead and buried past. These create divisions, schisms, unnatural barriers, and disunity within our country that hamper our cause before the nations of the world…. Only thus can we secure the triumph of our ideals in a world threatened with atomic extinction if we fail.

ESSAYS

The essays raise questions about the ways in which different groups, at different times, use popular culture to form racial identities, not just black and white, but Asian American as well. Robert Toll, in his early and classic work on minstrel shows, traces the history of the nineteenth-century form, paying close attention to changes in content and production before and after the Civil War. Robert Lee, associate professor of American Civilization at Brown University, makes an important contribution by looking closely at minstrel show materials about Chinese Americans to contend that minstrelsy constructed not only what it meant to be white or black, but also what it meant to be Chinese or Asian in the United States. Susan Smulyan, professor of American Studies at Brown University and co-editor of this volume, shows that the stereotypes set up by nineteenth-century minstrels were continued and reinforced in the twentieth century as local community groups chose minstrelsy for their fundraising performances. An elaborate industry grew up to provide minstrel materials to these amateurs, who ranged from women's groups to Rotary Clubs to high school clubs, and a reading of these how-to books shows how racist stereotypes continued from the nineteenth century to the twentieth century.

Minstrels and African Americans in the Nineteenth Century

ROBERT TOLL

... To some mid-nineteenth-century Americans, it was "The only true American drama" or an "American National Opera." But to most people it was simply "nigger minstrelsy." Performed by white men in blackface make-up, using what they claimed were Negro dialects, songs, dances, and jokes, minstrelsy literally swept the nation in the 1840's, from the White House to the California gold fields, from New Orleans to New England, from riverboats and saloons to 2500-seat theaters. For over half a century it remained the most popular entertainment form in the country.

With its images of Negroes shaped by white expectations and desires and not by black realities, minstrelsy and its latter-day successors, like "Uncle Remus" and "Amos and Andy," deeply embedded caricatures of blacks into American popular culture. (Besides its portrayals of Negroes, minstrelsy also "informed" its patrons about a wide range of important subjects, from plantations to cities, from fashions to morality, and from Indians to immigrants). Furthermore, as the first American popular entertainment form to become a national institution, it set many precedents and trends that strongly influenced its successors, especially burlesque and vaudeville. Thus, minstrelsy helped shape the way Americans conceived of and

Robert Toll, "The Evolution of the Minstrel Show," in *Blacking Up: The Minstrel Show in Nineteenth Century America* (New York: Oxford University Press, 1974).

thought about each other and their country, as well as playing a formative role in the evolution of American show business....

As the first new popular entertainment form to grow out of the turbulent 1830's and 1840's, the minstrel show escaped most of the problems that plagued other stage entertainment. It was unabashedly popular in appeal, housed in its own show places, performed by middling Americans, focused on humble characters, and dominated by earthy, vital, song, dance, and humor. Every part of the minstrel show—its features, form, and content—was hammered out in the interaction between performers and the vocal audiences they sought only to please....

By addressing themselves to race in the decades when white Americans first had to come to grips with what the position of blacks would be in America, while at the same time producing captivating, unique entertainment, blackfaced performers quickly established the minstrel show as a national institution, one that more than any other of its time was truly shaped by and for the masses of average Americans. Even though it was always extremely flexible, minstrelsy gradually evolved standard patterns and features that crystallized as audiences came to expect and demand their favorites and as performers found it increasingly necessary to plan their shows, which rapidly grew in size and complexity as well as popularity. The minstrel form and conventions that emerged in its formative first decade not only restructured American popular stage entertainment, they also revealed its huge audiences' central concerns, needs, and desires....

In February 1843, four blackfaced white men, wearing ill-fitting, ragtag clothing, took the stage in New York City to perform for the first time an entire evening of the "oddities, peculiarities, eccentricities, and comicalities of that Sable Genus of Humanity." The four men, Billy Whitlock, Frank Pelham, Dan Emmett, and Frank Brower, who billed themselves as the Virginia Minstrels, each had had experience as blackfaced entertainers with circuses, but they had no idea how popular blackface minstrelsy would be as a separate entertainment form. Having found themselves out of work in New York City during the disastrous 1842-43 entertainment season, they merely hoped that by increasing their numbers they would improve their box office. Their choice of name fits the same opportunistic pattern. Besides taking the name of a famous Southern state to enhance their claims of authenticity, they called themselves "minstrels" instead of the more common "delineators" because of the great success of the Tyrolese Minstrel Family which had recently toured America. Even though by accident, the Virginia Minstrels appeared at the right time. They were instant sensations. In late 1843 the company left for a successful English tour, during which it dissolved for basically personal reasons, but also because the performers still thought of themselves as singles, not as a troupe. What they left behind, however, was a minstrel-mad public and a bevy of imitators that reshaped American popular entertainment....

Minstrelsy swept the nation in the mid-1840's.... In response to the seemingly insatiable public demand, innumerable minstrel troupes appeared.... [D]evelopments occurred wherever people were concentrated and transportation was available, especially along the Mississippi River, the rapidly expanding rail lines into the North-west, and in the burgeoning cities of the Northeast.

Antebellum minstrelsy enjoyed great popularity throughout the nation, but few famous troupes, in fact, traveled widely before the Civil War....

Although blackface entertainment was born in the Mid-West and South, the minstrel show itself began and matured in the cities of the Northeast....

New York City, the birthplace of the minstrel show, was by far its greatest stronghold until after the Civil War. Virtually all the major developments in minstrelsy began there, primarily because the intense competition eliminated poor performers and forced innovations. From mid-1840 to mid-1850, five or six major companies regularly played there; during the 1850's, ten mayor minstrel houses thrived and three famous troupes played in the same block on Broadway....

But why was minstrelsy a national sensation? What gave it such great appeal for Northern white common people of all ages? As it evolved into an entertainment institution over the years, it became a major vehicle through which Northern whites conceptualized and coped with many of their problems....

But, first of all, minstrelsy had to establish itself as an amusement that masses of people would pay to see. Although blackface makeup and portrayal of Negro characters were synonymous with minstrelsy from its inception, the form had enough other attractions to have made it at least a temporary success. It offered antebellum Americans an irresistible entertainment package. Like Davy Crockett's tall tales and Mose's braggadocio stunts, minstrelsy brought the vitality and vigor of the folk into popular culture. Furthermore, minstrelsy was not only responsive to its audiences, it was very much like them. It was immediate, unpretentious, and direct. It had no characterization to develop, no plot to evolve, no musical score, no set speeches, no subsidiary dialogue—indeed no fixed script at all. Each act—song, dance, joke, or skit—was a self-contained performance that strived to be a highlight of the show. This meant that minstrels could adapt to their specific audience while the show was in process.

To these general entertainment appeals, minstrelsy added the promise of satisfying white Northerners' growing curiosity about blacks and especially slaves at a time when slavery was becoming a major national controversy....

Because early minstrels created plausible black characters, some Northerners, probably a substantial number of the gullible public that had seen few Negroes and were still unfamiliar with minstrel conventions, mistook minstrels for real Negroes.... Furthermore, after the Civil War, when black people first became minstrels, whites were astonished at the diversity of Negroes' skin color. Realizing that some audience members believed that they were Negroes, early minstrels tried to make it quite clear that only their makeup and some of their material was black....

Minstrels ... put material into their shows to stress the point. "Why am I like a young widow?" a comedian asked. After the line was slowly repeated, he fired back: "Because I do not stay long in black." With such devices, minstrels established their identities as professional entertainers—and as white men.

Although primarily Northern and white, the Virginia Minstrels and their many successors claimed to be authentic delineators of black life. But were they? In one important sense, the question is easily answerable. Blackface minstrels were not authentic, even in intention. They were not ethnographers, but professional entertainers whose major concern was to create stage acts that would please their audiences. The issue then, is where the minstrels obtained the material they transformed into blackfaced stage acts. Did they draw on Afro-Americans for more than color?

Like other antebellum entertainers, minstrels drew on Anglo-American folklore, especially on the volatile frontiersman who was better suited to minstrels' flamboyant style than the understated Yankee....

Like the literature of the frontier, minstrelsy also made extensive use of tall tales.... In portraying ... incredible exploits, which were typical of the Western lore that played such an important part in the emergence of American popular culture, minstrels used familiar material guaranteed to please their audiences.

But what was so striking about early minstrelsy was that it seemed unique. Although minstrels' strange and exaggerated gestures and makeup account for part of this appearance of distinctiveness, strong evidence exists that as part of their effort to capture the native vitality of America and to establish themselves as authentic delineators of Negroes, white minstrels selectively adapted elements of black as well as white folk culture. Even though early blackface entertainers were almost all Northern white men, they had ample opportunity to learn about black music, dance, and lore while traveling widely in the South and West before minstrelsy became a sedentary, urban form. They were constantly on the lookout for material to construct unique stage acts with a strong folk appeal. And since they could shape the lore they adapted into nonthreatening images of Negroes as harmless curiosities, there was no reason for them not to ... "borrow" material from Negroes....

[B]lendings of black and white dances pervaded early minstrelsy and help account for its appearance of uniqueness. The normal direction of the adaption, however, was from blacks to blackface, and the "borrowers" were white men who consciously learned from blacks. Thomas D. Rice's "Jump Jim Crow," the first blackface act to win widespread fame, was also the first clear instance of a minstrel using an Afro-American dance. Since the melody to "Jim Crow" was a familiar English tune and the words were neither unusual or especially clever, it must have been the dance that made Rice's performance such a public rage. Descriptions of the "hop," the rhythms, and the peculiar shoulder and arm movements involved in the dance strongly suggest that it was a variation of a characteristically Negro shuffle in which the feet remain close to the ground and upper-body movements predominate. "Jump Jim Crow" was, thus, probably the first of many Afro-American dances to become a worldwide success....

Although blackface performers rarely credited specific material to blacks because they wanted to be known as creative artists as well as entertainers, many early minstrels claimed that they did "field work" among Southern Negroes while they were traveling. The individual claims are rarely ... confirmable ... but since these performers had both the opportunities and the motives to do it, and since Afro-American culture did influence minstrelsy, these claims probably represent what at least some minstrels did to find new material....

Lending further credence to the argument that they did draw material from blacks, early minstrels incorporated elements of Afro-American folklore and beliefs into their shows....

Minstrels made extensive use of nonsense humor, fantasy, and animal fables that they almost certainly derived from Afro-American folk song and narrative, which relied heavily on animal symbolism, used indirection and guile to voice protests or attack adversaries, and featured victories for the weak over the strong. Anglo-American tradition, on the other hand, was direct and "realistic," employed overt protest, and presented direct conflicts, in which the strong always won out. Minstrel songs reveal traits of both traditions, which again reinforces the point that minstrels eclectically selected their material with their eyes on its entertainment value, not on its origins. Since minstrels' early songs were often little more than series of unconnected fragments held together only by a common chorus, it was quite easy for them to add any items, themes, or verses that they liked to their repertoires....

Besides confirming the folk origins of American popular entertainment, minstrelsy's borrowing of Afro-American culture is of great significance because it was the first indication of the powerful influence Afro-American culture would have on the performing arts in America. It does not mean that early minstrels accurately portrayed Negro life or even the cultural elements that they used. They did neither. In the process of creating their stage images of Negroes, Northern white professional entertainers selectively adapted elements of Afro-American folk culture into caricatures and stereotypes of Negroes. These negative images of blacks did have some elements of black culture in them, however twisted and distorted the overall effect was. Thus, when white Americans later came in contact with Afro-Americans, whites who were disposed to confirm the caricatures could do it by focusing on the familiar elements, like superstition, love of music and dance, and the "childish" belief in "silly" animal fables and by ignoring everything else about blacks. Minstrelsy was the first example of the way American popular culture would exploit and manipulate Afro-Americans and their culture to please and benefit white Americans....

By the mid-1850's, minstrel companies had grown larger, performers had become more specialized, featured roles had emerged, and minstrelsy had arrived at the basic three-part structure that it thereafter retained. The basic minstrel format, which resulted from audience-performer interaction and extensive experimentation, reveals a great deal about the entertainment appeal of minstrelsy. In the first part, the entire company appeared in a semicircle and followed a standard pattern that included jokes and comic songs interspersed between "serious" songs and dances performed by individuals with the full cast often singing the choruses. Besides the humor and songs done in dialect, there were nondialect songs and material that commented on current events and social problems. The first part regularly closed with a lively group song and dance number....

[T]he greatest stars of most companies [were] the comedians, Brudder Tambo and Brudder Bones—named for their instruments. Made up to give the appearance of large eyes and gaping mouths with huge lips, set apart by brighter, more flamboyant dress, and using heavier, more ludicrous dialects, the endmen contorted their bodies in exaggerated gestures and twisted their words in endless puns in order to keep the audience laughing. An endman caught in a shipwreck in the Erie Canal pulled out a bar of soap and washed himself ashore. The chicken crossed the road to get to the other side. Firemen wore red suspenders to hold up their pants. And the audience howled. "The pun and the conundrum were mighty popular with our grandfathers," Lew Dockstader, himself a great minstrel comedian, recalled. "They screamed-over both." At the same time that they laughed down at the stupid blackface characters, audience members also learned the intricacies of the language and the staccato pace of urban life. Endmen also delighted audiences with their physically funny performances of comedy songs....

The second part of the show, the variety section, or olio, offered a wide range of entertainment to the audience.... Other than diversity, its distinctive feature was the stump speech. Usually given by one of the endmen, it was a discourse as much on the infinite possibilities for malaprops as on the chosen subject....

The typical stump speech was considered a "marvel of grotesque humor" that was "just such an oration as a pompous darkey, better stocked with words that Judgement" might give.

Over the years, the stump speaker became one of the major minstrel comedy specialists. Each of these stars had his own special style and topics. While some limited themselves to "nonsense," others used their ludicrous verbosity to express "serious" social criticism. Ad Ryman, for example, regularly "lectured" on education, temperance, and women's rights. But whatever their content, stump speakers regularly got laughs by combining the physical comedy of endmen with their verbal pomposity. While discoursing on education with "mock dignity and absurd seriousness," Ryman, on one occasion, concluded by "diving under the table and standing rigidly upon his head with heels in the air, sending the audience into screams of laughter." If the stump speaker did not fall off the podium onto the floor to punctuate his oration, one fan reminisced, the audience felt cheated. They were rarely disappointed....

By 1860 minstrelsy had been transformed. It had gone from unorganized individual acts to a structured entertainment form, from primarily musical to heavily comical, from a concentration on plantation material to a more diversified show. But its basic appeal remained the same. The reason minstrels drew so much better then *Othello,* although both were dark, the editor of the *Clipper* explained in November 1860, was that "people favor mirth more than melancholy" and are "more ready to laugh over the oddities of a darkie on a Virginia plantation than to weep over the solemnity of a noble Moor." Minstrelsy provided common Americans with folk-based earthy songs, vital dances, and robust humor as well as with beautiful ballads and fine singing that they could enjoy at reasonable prices. It also provided a nonthreatening way for white Americans to cope with questions about the nature and proper place of black people in America. In this regard, as in almost every other, the editor of the *Clipper* properly concluded that minstrelsy had "truly democratic associations."...

It was no accident that the incredible popularity of minstrelsy coincided with public concern about slavery and the proper position of Negroes in America.

Precisely because people could always just laugh off the performance, because viewers did not have to take the show seriously, minstrelsy served as a "safe" vehicle through which its primarily Northern, urban audiences could work out their feelings about even the most sensitive and volatile issues. During the sectional crisis, minstrels shaped white Americans' vague notions and amorphous beliefs about Negroes into vivid, eye-catching caricatures as they literally acted out images of blacks and plantation life that satisfied their huge audiences....

During minstrelsy's first decade, roughly from 1843 to 1853, its Northern urban audiences could at the same time cry over the destruction of black families and over the beauty of the loving, interracial plantation family; bemoan the cruelty to slaves and also the forlorn fate of runaways; respect the bondsman's intense feelings and desire for freedom and the contented slave's love for his master; and laugh *with* black tricksters making fools of white aristocrats and also *at* foolish black characters. Because the minstrel show's structure did not require continuity or consistency and because minstrelsy's antislavery sentiments contained no call to action, audiences could do all of this on the same night without feeling that Negroes were their equals or that they had to reconcile their contradictory feelings about slavery. For a decade, Northern audiences could view slavery as little more than part of the minstrel show.

Most white Americans act out their need for racial subordination only when they feel that their own interests and values are challenged. The 1850's were just such a time. The accelerating agitation of black and white abolitionists for full exercise of Northern Negroes' rights, the intensified pitch of the propaganda battle over slavery, the enforcement of the fugitive slave law in the North, the increased use of race as a political issue, the controversy over *Uncle Tom's Cabin,* and finally the outbreak of a virtual civil war in Kansas—all combined to make slavery and race seem real and immediate threats to white Northerners. By the mid-1850's, everything Northerners were committed to—national destiny, social order, their own status, the plantation myth, and the Union itself—seemed at stake....

After the mid-1850's the tone of minstrelsy sharply changed as its folk and antislavery content virtually disappeared. Romantic and sentimentalized images of happy, contented slaves and nostalgic old Negroes looking back to the good old days on the plantation completely dominated minstrel portrayals of slaves. In drawing these images, white Americans rejected the humanizing content of folklore and the complexity of human diversity for the comforting façade of romanticized, folksy caricatures. They thrust aside wily black tricksters and antislavery protesters for loyal, grinning darkies who loved their white folks and were contented and indeed fulfilled by working all day and singing and dancing all night.

Minstrels repeatedly contrasted these simplified images of Southern Negroes to their caricatures of Northern blacks who were either pretentious dandies, ridiculous failures even in the useless world of fashion, or foolish and inept low-comedy types that minstrels prominently featured in their increasingly popular slapstick farces. Minstrels also expanded the role of ex-plantation Negroes who were unhappy in the North and longed for the comfort and security of their "place" on the plantation. With all indications that slaves were unhappy or mistreated purged from the shows, minstrels in the late 1850's incessantly hammered out their simplified rationalization: on the plantation Negroes were happy, contented, and fulfilled; off it, they were ludicrous and/or helpless incompetents. Blacks *needed* the plantation. Racial subordination did not conflict with the American Creed. It was the nation's gift to Negroes....

The mounting horror of the war that was striking down young soldiers in their prime and devastating their families at home forced minstrels to take a harder, more critical look at the Northern society for which the sacrifices were being made. Beginning during the war, the emphasis of minstrelsy began to shift from romantic fantasy to social criticism, from Southern plantations to Northern cities, from blacks to whites. Reflecting their egalitarian orientation, minstrels focused first on the glaring gap between rich and poor. They lambasted corrupt businessmen, who seemed to minstrels to be prolonging the war in order to make more money for themselves....

...Even though black people suffered greatly from the fighting, minstrels did not include them in their sentimental songs about the anguish of the war. To them, Negroes were merely pawns in the struggle for Union.

Throughout the war, minstrels, with few exceptions, continued to portray blacks as happy and contented inferiors. The genius of minstrelsy was that, unlike the vitriolic anti-Negro propaganda that bluntly advocated repression of blacks, minstrelsy phrased racial subordination in terms of benevolent paternalism.... Minstrels took threatening images of blacks and softened them into those of good-natured children or at the very worst of ludicrous incompetents who required supervision for their own good....

In the late nineteenth century, the minstrel show underwent a fundamental reorganization. Like other institutions, minstrelsy felt the general effects of the powerful new developments which were profoundly altering the quality of American life: the completion of a national transportation system, the emergence of national businesses demanding standardization and uniformity, the development of more sophisticated marketing and promotional techniques, the westward population shift, the influx of immigrants, and the accelerated growth of the size and influence of cities, but minstrelsy faced new problems of its own. Most immediately, minstrels lost their virtual monopoly on popular stage entertainment. Variety shows, purified of their earlier off-color image, offered an even broader entertainment kaleidoscope than minstrelsy and began to win acceptance as wholesome family outings. Lavishly produced musical comedies, featuring partially undraped women and truly spectacular staging, became common.... Furthermore, white minstrels were even challenged in the area of their supposed expertise when black people became minstrels and earned reputations as the authentic "delineators of Negro life."

Minstrels responded to these challenges in the decades after the Civil War by making substantial changes in their format and repertoire. To broaden their audience base and to reach new markets, troupes traveled widely. To enhance their appeal, they increased the size of their companies, expanded their olios, added new speciality features, staged much more lavish production numbers, and featured more "refined" acts—guaranteed to offend no one. And to avoid black competition, they even moved away from "Negro Subjects." In the process, minstrelsy almost completely transformed itself. It went from small troupes concentrating on portrayals of Negroes to huge companies staging lavish extravaganzas and virtually ignoring blacks, from resident troupes with a Northeastern, urban base to truly national traveling companies whose greatest strength was in the Midwest and South. In many ways, the changes in minstrel form reflect the basic restructuring of American society in the late nineteenth century....

As it underwent such fundamental changes, minstrelsy became nostalgic about its own past. As early as 1857, in fact, Christy and Wood's Minstrels "in answer to many requests" devoted one night a week to a first part composed of songs of the "olden time." ... Like the rest of the nation, the raucous, vital antebellum form had grown larger, slicker, and more concerned with a respectable appearance as it matured. Its original form had become just a quaint relic suitable only for nostalgia....

Although troupes of black minstrels appeared as early as 1855, it was a decade before blacks had established themselves in minstrelsy, their first large-scale entrance into American show business....

Emphasizing their authenticity as Negroes and claiming to be ex-slaves, black minstrels became the acknowledged minstrel experts at portraying plantation material. But since they inherited the white-created stereotypes and could make only minor modifications in them, black minstrels in effect added credibility to these images by making it seem that Negroes actually behaved like minstrelsy's black caricatures. This negative aspect of their shows was balanced, perhaps even outweighed, by the fact that black people had their first chance to become entertainers, which not only gave many Negroes a rare opportunity for mobility but also eventually put blacks in a position to modify and then correct these stereotypes....

[I]ts success in England helped black minstrels establish themselves as entertainers in America, something they devoted considerable attention and ink to in these early years.

Black minstrels tried to legitimize themselves in two ways. In their advertisements, they quoted extensively from favorable reviews stressing that they were at least the equal of whites as minstrels. But realizing that their greatest appeal was their race, they repeatedly stressed that they were "genuine" "real," "bona-fide" Negroes....

Because the notion that blacks were inherently musical was already deeply embedded in the public's images of Negroes and because these performers stressed their authenticity, they were thought of as natural, spontaneous people on exhibit rather than as professional entertainers.... Again and again, critics noted that black minstrelsy was not a show; it was a display of natural impulses....

Black minstrelsy matured in the 1870's. By early in the decade, several companies regularly toured, primarily in the East and Midwest....

Although black men had to struggle against great odds to own their own companies, black performers inevitably became big stars. The highest paid black minstrel was Kersands, whose fame was based on the comic contortions of his gigantic mouth. Besides such "feats" as dancing with a cup and saucer or several billiard balls in his mouth, he acted out the caricatured role of the ignorant, slow-witted black man. But many other celebrated black minstrel stars did not perform such heavily stereotyped roles. The second highest paid performer with the famous 1882 Callender troupe, Wallace King, was a "Sweet Singing Tenor" noted for his moving renditions of romantic ballads. James and George Bohee and Horace Weston won renown in both England and America as banjo virtuosos. The S. S. Stewart Banjo company even used Weston to endorse its product in a tasteful ad, complete with a dignified photograph of him in formal wear. Black minstrels also won plaudits for "refined" dancing and for song writing, In fact, although within a heavily stereotyped framework, black minstrels clearly demonstrated the diverse talents of black people. In the nineteenth century, minstrelsy was their only chance to make a regular living as entertainers, musicians, actors, or composers....

By 1890, because of minstrelsy, blacks had established themselves in American show business. They had made clear to their large black audiences that it was possible for common blacks to become entertainers. And minstrelsy produced all sorts of black artists: Ernest Hogan, an influential ragtime and musical comedy composer and singer; Gussie L. Davis, composer of sentimental songs and the first black man to succeed in Tin Pan Alley; Bert Williams, a star of musicals, vaudeville, and the Ziegfeld Follies; W. C. Handy, one of the first popularizers of blues; Dewey "Pigmeat" Markham, a veteran of fifty years as a comedian; and the Queens of the Blues, Gertrude "Ma" Rainey and Bessie Smith. But black people also had to pay a great price for entering show business. They had to act out white caricatures of Negroes. But since whites had already created and spread these images, it was really less a question of *what* minstrel images of blacks would be than of *who* would portray them. Given the circumstances, participation at least gave blacks a chance to modify these caricatures....

Perhaps most important of all its social and psychological functions, minstrelsy provided a nonthreatening way for vast numbers of white Americans to work out their ambivalence about race at a time when that issue was paramount. Consistent with their nationalism, egalitarianism, and commitment to the status of whites, minstrels ultimately evolved a rationalization of racial caste.... If Negroes were to share in America's bounty of happiness, minstrels asserted, they needed whites to take care of them. To confirm this, minstrels created and repeatedly portrayed the contrasting caricatures of inept, ludicrous Northern blacks and contented, fulfilled Southern Negroes. Besides providing "living" proof that whites need not feel guilty about racial caste, the minstrel plantation also furnished romanticized images of a simpler, happier time when society was properly ordered and the loving bonds of home and family were completely secure. Minstrelsy, in short, was one of the few comforting and reassuring experiences that nineteenth-century white Americans shared.

Beginning with early blackface entertainers who adapted aspects of Afro-American music, dance, and humor to suit white audiences, minstrelsy also brought blacks and at least part of their culture into American popular culture for the first time. The enthralling vitality of this material, even as adapted by white performers, accounted in large part for minstrelsy's great initial impact. Although minstrel use of black culture declined in the late 1850's as white minstrels concentrated on caricatures of blacks, when Negroes themselves became minstrels after the Civil War, they brought a transfusion of their culture with them. Again, Afro-American culture intrigued white Americans. But black minstrels had to work within narrow limits because they performed for audiences that expected them to act out well-established minstrel stereotypes of Negroes. Within these restrictions, however, black minstrels began to modify plantation caricatures and first attracted large numbers of black people to American popular entertainment....

Despite its great impact and extensive influence on both popular thought and popular culture, minstrelsy lost its dominance of the entertainment business in the 1890's. From its inception, its portrayals of the plantation and of Negroes, especially Southern Negroes, had been its greatest asset and its distinguishing characteristic. Its popularity directly coincided with public curiosity, concern, and interest in these subjects. When these waned, minstrelsy was doomed.... Vaudeville ... absorb[ed] the blackface act and [took] minstrelsy's place as the most popular and therefore the most significant entertainment form in the country. But like the Cheshire Cat in the topsy-turvy world through the looking glass where appearances offered few clues to reality, the minstrel show, long after it had disappeared, left its central image—the grinning black mask—lingering on, deeply embedded in American consciousness.

Chinese American Stereotypes in Nineteenth-Century Minstrelsy

ROBERT LEE

Minstrelsy was a powerful vehicle for constructing the Chinaman as a polluting racial Other in the popular imagination. From the 1850s onward, the character of John Chinaman and, to a somewhat lesser extent, Japanese characters were played in yellowface on the minstrel stage. Dozens of songs, comedy skits, and stump speeches (monologues that featured caricatured languages and "dialects," including spurious Chinese, Irish, Dutch, Hebrew, and African American) featured "John Chinaman." So prominent was the Chinese theme in comedy theater and minstrelsy that the famed Buckley Family minstrels (originally the Buckley Ethiopian Melodists) made their home stage in New York at the Chinese Theater.

In 1849, only a year after the discovery of gold at Sutter's mill, minstrel theater arrived in San Francisco, where it met immediate success. By the mid-1850s San Francisco had become a destination for all the major minstrel companies in the country. It was such a center for minstrelsy that E. P. Christie's already famous Christie Minstrels changed their name to Christie's San Francisco Minstrels to add to their luster when traveling around the country....

Robert Lee, "The 'Heathen Chinee' on God's Free Soil," in *Orientals: Asian Americans in Popular Culture*. Used by permission of Temple University Press. Copyright © 1999 by Temple University. All rights reserved.

[T]he minstrel show began as an entertainment for the new urban working class. Blackface minstrelsy made a place for itself on the American stage in the 1820s and '30s when production was shifting from workshop to factory and proletarianization of labor was in full swing. These were decades of deep economic and social insecurity for small producers and a new class of wage earners, both in the cities and on the farm. Blackface minstrelsy attended to the class anxieties and animosities of this nascent and stratified working class, unsure of its position and prospects. Alexander Saxton has shown that most of the major minstrel performers had come from artisan or petty bourgeois families in the urban Northeast. Reflecting their own class background as well as an affinity for the class interests of their audience, many of the most prominent minstrel performers—Daniel Emmett, E. P. Christie, Stephen Foster—were all prominent in the Northern wing of the Democratic Party....

For its audience of urban workers who were being shaped into a working class, the minstrel show constructed and displayed a line-up of racial and ethnic characters. Blacks, Jim Crow, and Zip Coon, Indians and John Chinaman were compared and contrasted with European Americans, Tommy the English Sailor, Mose the Irish fireman, Siegal the German. Even as these characters interacted on the stage, the minstrel show drew sharp boundaries around racial difference and made clear the unacceptablity of racial amalgamation. By distinguishing between funny but acceptable behavior among various white characters and ridiculous and punishable behavior among colored characters, these minstrel shows enacted the bounds of acceptable working-class behavior and resistance. In this regard, minstrelsy can be understood as a ritual response to boundary crisis. As such, minstrelsy was called upon to distinguish a category of anomalous and polluting (hence non-assimilable) racial difference from a category of normal and nonpolluting (and hence amalgamable) ethnic difference.

The power of the minstrel show as a ritual of race-making lay in the ambiguity of laughing with and laughing at Zip Coon, Jim Crow, and John Chinaman. Although in the 1850s blackface minstrelsy would mount a nostalgic defense of slavery in the face of the abolition movement, in its beginning decades of the 1830s and '40s, it made the urban free person of color, in the caricatures of Zip Coon and Jim Crow, its principal object of ridicule. Constructed as a trickster, the citified dandy Zip Coon represented freedom without the self-control needed for republican virtue. The tricks that Zip Coon played on his always pompous oppressors could be appreciated for their spirit of resistance by the "b'hoy boy," the epitome of a newly emergent white working-class urban youth culture whose brash behavior and style in many ways mirrored the dandified, urban, free black. At the same lime, the white journeyman turned factory worker might be nostalgic for the sense of freedom from restraint that Jim Crow was depicted as enjoying. While Zip Coon's or Jim Crow's antics could be applauded, their ambitions to move outside the boundaries of their black world had to be sharply thwarted through ridicule.

The ideological effect of the blackface minstrel show lay in its dual message to a nascent working class consolidating its own white racial identity. The minstrel show featured Zip Coon's stump speeches, parodies of political campaign speeches, academic lectures, or sermons, replete with exaggerated elocution and littered with malapropisms to emphasize that, however "free," the African American could only masquerade as a citizen. While the malapropism of the hilarious stump speech warned that the anomalous freedom of persons of color represented a danger to the republic, it served to remind its working-class and immigrant audiences of the utter seriousness and responsibilities of citizenship.

The minstrel representation of the Chinese immigrant as a racial Other relied on a trope of insurmountable cultural difference. Unlike the minstrel characterization of free blacks, who were represented as fraudulent citizens because they were supposed to lack culture, the Chinese were seen as having an excess of culture.... The minstrel construction of Chinese racial difference around cultural excess focused on three natural symbolic systems, each closely related to boundary crises: language, food, and hair.

Chinese "pidgin" fascinated white Americans and was widely imitated on the minstrel stage....

Canton English was only one of many languages spoken in nineteenth century California. This pidgin English attributed to Chinese speakers in California was in actuality a trade language, with its own linguistic and symbolic codes, syntax and vocabulary rules. The origin of this language dates back to early English-Chinese trade relations in the late seventeenth century; some of its vocabulary had even earlier antecedents in Arab, Portuguese, and Spanish trade relations with China from the fifteenth and sixteenth centuries....

Minstrelsy's response to ... a crisis was to reinforce the hegemonic power of standard English, setting the linguistic standard for participation in citizenship. Comedic skits centered around miscommunication based on ethnic accents, dialects, and creoles. Malapropism and the exaggerated elocution of the "Nigger stump speech or gag" were commonly used to ridicule the ambitions of African Americans for full participation in social or political life. On the minstrel stage, Canton English and nonsense words were often deployed together in the construction of John Chinaman.... The conjoining of pidgin with nonsense simultaneously diminished the status of Canton English as an important commercial language and infantilized its speakers....

Minstrel songs paid great attention to Chinese foodways; indeed it is uncommon not to find some reference to Chinese eating habits in a minstrel song. Food habits, customs, and rules are central symbolic structures through which societies articulate identity; you are symbolically at least, what you eat....

The consumption of dogs and cats is the most common image of Chinese foodways....

The Chinese are also identified as eating mice and rats, animals considered filthy and disease-carrying and therefore dangerous and polluting....

A third focus of minstrel attention was the braided plait of hair or queue worn by Chinese men. The length and manner in which hair is cut and groomed has been a central marker of gender, age, and class in many cultures.... In California, ... the queue presented a cultural anomaly and a source of ambiguity. In an age when middle-class white men had shorn their hair, and among so-called civilized people only women wore their hair long (although Native

American men also often wore their hair long and in a braids), the Chinese males' practice of wearing their hair long and in a braid was perceived as sexually and racially ambiguous, and therefore dangerous.

The Chinaman's queue thus became a principal target for the victimization of the Chinese by every bigot, old and young....

The queue may have been the most public target of the attack on the Chinaman, but it was not the cause of his victimization. In fact, there was little that the Chinaman did to occasion such an assault on his person, and there was little the Chinese could do to deter such attacks. The presence of the Chinese, as anomalous, ambiguous, and hence representative of a dangerous pollution, was itself sufficient to require punishment. Although physical attacks, robbery, and murder were a frequent occurrence, the mode of punishment most celebrated in the song was the cuckolding of the Chinese....

The arrival in California of Chinese women "among [whom] good morals are unknown, [and who] have no regard whatever for chastity or virtue," was no solace ... only the presence of true (white) womanhood could provide the moral nurturing required by a new republic of virtue in California. Indeed, the fashion among Chinese women of wearing trousered suits of cotton or silk caused [confusion] about the gender difference between Chinese immigrants....

"The Days of '49," a song published by E. Zimmer in 1876, lamented the late pioneers of the gold rush days.... The last stanza mourns the "loss" of the white republic.

> Since that time how things have changed In this land of liberty,
> Darkies didn't vote nor plead in court, Nor rule this country,
> But the Chinese question, the worst of all In those days did not shine,
> For the country was right and the boys all white,
> In the days of '49.

Twentieth-Century Amateur Minstrels

SUSAN SMULYAN

During the first sixty years of the twentieth century, white middle-class men, women, and children across the United States joined together to put on minstrel shows. A large industry supported these amateur minstrels with books of instructions, music, and jokes; costumes, wigs, "bones," and burnt cork makeup; and sometimes professional directors to organize the amateur productions. One of the most prolific writers of amateur minstrel materials, Arthur LeRoy Kaser, wrote that amateur minstrel shows had become "so very popular" that "if one is not given occasionally in a community everybody wonders why."...

In local minstrel productions, everyday people enacted racial otherness, performed class solidarity, and took their place in a newly commodified, and increasingly mass produced, world of leisure activities.

Susan Smulyan, "Minstrel Laughs," in *Popular Ideologies: Mass Culture at Mid-Century*. Copyright © 2007 by University of Pennsylvania Press. Reprinted with permission of the University of Pennsylvania Press.

The instruction books often reported that community groups found minstrel shows "easy" to produce. The audience agreed about the ideas being promulgated in the shows and found further ease in the racial masking during which white middle-class people constructed, expressed, and reinforced their racialized class positions while not taking responsibility for their actions....

The shows provided a common space to express and work out ideas that might not have been so "easy," "fun," or nonoffensive with other performers or audiences....

The amateur minstrel shows borrowed from nineteenth-century professional minstrelsy but with important differences. A nineteenth-century minstrel evening was divided into three acts, the first a series of jokes and songs delivered by a small group of performers seated in a semicircle, the second an "olio," which resembled a vaudeville show with a variety of acts, and the third a short play. The twentieth-century books explained the tradition and offered help with the first and third parts, generally leaving local groups on their own for the variety acts. Communities found it easy to fill the variety section with individual performers, who rehearsed on their own and appeared for the performance. Groups found it more difficult to envision, practice, and perform the first parts and the plays. The instruction manuals focused on the popular minstrel "first parts" and showed community groups how to produce them easily. Performers sat together on the stage, in a semicircle, with individuals standing up to deliver an occasional joke, story, or song (all provided by the textbooks) while the master of ceremonies ran the show. Minstrel "first parts," according to the twentieth-century books, always included "end-men" in blackface and a master of ceremonies, often called by his nineteenth-century name, "the interlocutor."...

The cultural history of amateur minstrelsy is relatively easy to discover, although its social history remains hidden. By the turn of the century, publishers offered books of minstrel songs, jokes, and plays for community groups who wanted to put on a minstrel show, and an examination of these texts provides a cultural history of the form. These minstrel books, along with materials prepared for other amateur theater groups, appeared in the catalogs of major play publishing companies. The publication of amateur minstrel show books peaked in the 1920s and 1930s, but it began about 1900 and continued into the 1950s. While it is a bit difficult to get a good count of amateur minstrel show materials, there are plenty to examine....

The social historian is not so lucky.... While amateur minstrel shows occurred often around the country, the records are scattered throughout local historical societies. Also, amateur minstrelsy was part of a shameful history of racial oppression, and many communities believe that such activities are best forgotten. While historians may disagree about how to approach the histories of oppression (African slavery and Japanese American internment, for two other examples), keepers of local records agree that such recent, and disturbing, historical materials should not be made available to outsiders....

Amateur minstrelsy may be the perfect example of the strengths of cultural history, not only because the social history record proves difficult to access, but because the audience, performers, and even authors were the same. Amateur performances thus provide special insight into ideological formation. Since actors and audience members swapped places in the middle of performances, we don't have to wonder whether audiences agreed with what happened on stage. Amateur minstrel shows perpetuated a "common sense," taken-for-granted ideology and provide excellent historical evidence of the construction and consideration of such ideology. In addition, amateur theatricals were widely popular in the early twentieth century, as huge numbers of Americans participated, and deserve study in their own right....

Twentieth-century amateur minstrel shows helped the middle class see itself both as white and as able to purchase leisure activities. With these productions, middle-class, small-town whites announced a position of economic superiority (since many performances raised money for charity), and the performers signaled that they could afford to buy things to amuse themselves (because the performances depended on instruction books and other purchased products). By tying the middle class to consumption, amateur minstrel shows also served as a crucial bridge between popular and mass culture. Amateur productions showed how amusements became further commodified, codified, and national as publishing companies sold a "system" that provided everything needed for a minstrel show production. Finally, the move from participatory shows, given by and for communities, to standardized performances, taken from a book written by a professional producer, illustrated the beginnings of the change from popular to mass culture.

But the lengthiest directions in any amateur minstrel book concerned how to black up. Any explanation of amateur minstrels as creating a consuming middle class, ready to be part of a mass audience, must always return to the ways in which race structured and expressed these processes. In chillingly racist detail, the books described the preparation and use of either actual burnt cork or commercial makeup....

Most of the books also included elaborate descriptions of how to remove the makeup. Books disagreed on the "proper" minstrel way to make up lips and eyes to look more or less grotesque....

Minstrels who hated the mess of blackface could choose other forms of racial masks also offered by minstrelsy. Wigs played important roles, with the books advising, "always use a black kinkly wig...."

While much of the material in the amateur minstrel shows came straight from vaudeville—punning, jokes about families, male-female relationships, and city life—most shows also contained stories, jokes, or running commentaries on the stupidity of African Americans. These stories provided additional ways for the performers to create, teach, and reinforce racial hierarchy....

If many of the jokes and songs found in amateur minstrel shows came from vaudeville, the concept and format came from nineteenth-century professional minstrelsy. The historical authority conferred by nostalgic references to minstrel shows' beginnings helped make the shows popular, but the ways in which the two centuries of minstrelsy operated connected them on deeper levels as well. Historians David Roediger and Alexander Saxton have carefully outlined how working-class whites used professional minstrelsy in the nineteenth century to construct their racialized class positions, while Eric Lott has explained the ways such performances psychologically assisted whites in perpetuating racial hierarchy. Just as professional minstrels played a part in working-class formation in the nineteenth century, amateur minstrels assisted in solidifying the self-identification of the middle class in the twentieth.

Professional minstrel shows flourished in nineteenth-century America, whether as traveling troupes visiting small towns or as permanent shows located in big cities.... Historians have long contended that professional minstrelsy died with the nineteenth century.... In part, newer forms (burlesque, vaudeville, and eventually film and radio) superseded the minstrel show; in part, the form may have run its course, with minstrels finding it difficult to innovate enough to satisfy an ever restless commercial audience.

At the end of professional minstrelsy, the black performers and their shows and the white performers and theirs took different directions. Black minstrels influenced Broadway musicals as well as small traveling blues shows. White minstrelsy continued on in vaudeville (and from there moved into film and radio) as well as among amateurs....

Amateur minstrel shows may have begun on college campuses, with male students imitating a form that was already on its way out and thus provided little professional competition to the college minstrels....

[A]s industrialization continued, college students (training to become new managers) had a particular interest in securing, extending, and shoring up their middle-class positions and were among the first to see how minstrel shows could help....

The instruction books and articles about amateur minstrels ... always described their relationship to the older tradition of professional minstrelsy....

The twentieth century's nostalgia about minstrelsy, like the nineteenth century's ... interest in the form's origins and history, also operated as an explanation of racial politics that posited benevolent whites and passive African Americans. In addition, the twentieth-century interest in the origins of minstrelsy helped explain that all commodified cultural forms have origins in "authentic" and more personal expressions of an earlier age....

The amateur minstrels knew that they operated in a newly commodified culture with the beginnings of a cult of celebrity. Yet their historicity, which allowed the mass culture to hide while making significant inroads, remained one of the reasons for the popularity of amateur minstrel shows and another reason they operated so well as a site of ideological expression. The amateur productions, while expressing and constructing a range of ideological positions on race and class, also served as a bridge between popular and mass culture....

Despite their local and participatory nature, the amateur minstrel shows used nationally marketed books that explained how to produce a minstrel show and provided the content of the shows in excruciating detail. Most of the content came from vaudeville, that ultimately middle-class form of entertainment carved out of burlesque and variety. The amateur shows drew on vaudeville rather than minstrelsy for their materials, because vaudeville had incorporated much of minstrelsy, including blackface acts. In addition, vaudeville was an intrinsically middle-class and respectable entertainment, while minstrel shows carried a tinge of the risqué and working class. Amateurs would be reassured by the vaudeville, and thus highly respectable, materials found in the instruction books. At the same time, minstrel shows provided the historicity and nostalgic aura that allowed for an exploration and construction of race that so fascinated white Americans....

One could ... make the case that all American popular, and mass, culture was born in race, in the minstrel show, including broadcasting (with "Amos n' Andy") and music (drawing from black sacred music and the blues). Historians Eric Lott, David Roediger, and Alexander Saxton have explored nineteenth-century professional minstrel shows as a site where members of the white working class investigated African American culture while expressing racial difference and class solidarity. In the amateur minstrel shows of the twentieth century, the middle class, working through both the implications of a newly created mass culture and their own identity in the emerging culture of consumption, returned to racial formation as the central trope in American culture. Participating in amateur minstrelsy, local communities both moved toward a mass culture and resisted it and created themselves as white by masquerading as black. As they participated in the move toward a mass culture, amateur minstrels cared deeply about their middle-class positions and worked to identify the middle class as racialized and consuming....

The charitable goals of most amateur minstrel shows remained one of the simplest ways to view them as expressions of the middle-class positions of the participants. Examining clippings and letters kept by the publishers, one article explained that amateur productions came together for economic reasons because "putting on a show ... remains one of the surest methods of raising funds for almost anything," including "instruments for the school band, a new rug for the minister's study, or woolen bed socks for the deserving Eskimo."...

Middle-class people wanted to express their economic status publicly, and amateur performances allowed them to do so.

Middle-class ideology also expressed itself in terms of taste and gentility, often seen as the provenance of women.... As a culture of production lost ground to a culture of consumption, the middle class eagerly sought to become the consuming class with a favored place for women in the consumption process, just as they had previously held a special role in matters of gentility and taste.

Publishers of minstrel show books often boasted that they provided clean and nonoffensive material, joining with other purveyors of amusements who believed that they could change their class position by including women in their audiences, in part by managing what appeared on stage....

Amateur minstrel shows helped begin the transformation of popular culture into mass culture for the white middle class, suitable for men, women, and children from a variety of groups....

Whites heard little criticism of the minstrel show until the Civil Rights movement began in the early 1950s.

Only when race and nation began to clash, when the nation's racial attitudes had an impact on foreign policy, and when middle-class people began to believe that racial tolerance might help secure economic advantages in the world did minstrel shows become problematic. As the Cold War deepened and the

United States sought the allegiance of developing countries, particularly in Africa and the Middle East, the oppression and stereotyping of African Americans became a foreign policy issue…. [T]he individual complaints that actually stopped local minstrel shows came from African Americans and integrated antiracist organizations.

Divided by class and region, African Americans had long found it difficult to unite against representations of themselves in entertainment. Many African Americans hated minstrel shows throughout the two centuries they were a mainstay of American entertainment, but others found them either amusing and authentic tributes to African American culture or of little importance in the landscape of American racial oppression. As a target, amateur minstrel shows presented problems. The amateurs presented shows for only a few nights each year, sometimes in small towns with few black residents, and the most powerful members of the white community were performers and audiences for the shows. The ephemeral nature of the amateur shows, their widespread presentation, and the local and immediate power of their producers over the protestors made them difficult to organize against.

When African Americans did target minstrel shows, they did it on the basis of their own intertwined middle-class status and national interests. The early Civil Rights Movement, with its emphasis on representation, schooling, church-based action, and the importance of U.S. presentation of a good example to the rest of the world, saw amateur minstrel shows as a useful target and used a middle-class approach to protest them. Beginning in 1950, local chapters of the National Association for the Advancement of Colored People (NAACP), Urban League, and Catholic Interracial Council attacked particular amateur minstrel performances as well as minstrel shows in general….

By the 1960s many people had decided that objections to blackface minstrel shows merited consideration, and amateur minstrelsy died out. Amateur groups presented minstrel shows sporadically, throughout the next thirty-five years, but organized protests followed most performances. Ironically, college campuses, where amateur minstrelsy was born, presented some of the last amateur shows. As college populations and racial attitudes changed, students used minstrel shows as a form of rebellion against "political correctness" rather than as the status-affirming entertainments of earlier generations.

During the first half of the twentieth century, amateur minstrelsy served as a way for the middle-class white men, women, and children who participated to construct the racial, gender, and national aspects of their class positions….

The racist stereotypes played out by middle-class white people on the amateur stage implanted constructions of racial inferiority deep in the middle-class consciousness and proved to be one of the bases for the reformation of the middle class in the twentieth century. Amateur minstrel shows became one way for the middle class to articulate and understand its class positions. College students, with their ongoing investment in the status hierarchy, early used minstrel shows ideologically to express and construct a middle-class consciousness. The amateur minstrel instruction books that drew primarily on vaudeville writers and materials also illustrated the interest of the amateur minstrels in their class positions…. In choosing to produce an amateur minstrel show, rather than another form of theater, middle-class whites aligned racial stereotyping with good taste and gentility…. The use of minstrelsy to raise money for good causes, at the same time requiring the purchase of materials to use for entertainment, aligned the middle class with the newly emerging culture of consumption. Finally, the nationalism expressed in the minstrel shows helped make the middle class congruent with the nation, reexpressing the United States as a middle-class preserve where class lines were unimportant since all white citizens shared the same class position.

FURTHER READING

Abbott Lynn, and Doug Seroff. *Ragged but Right: Black Traveling Shows, Coon Songs, and the Dark Pathway to Blues and Jazz* (2007).

Bailey, Ben. "The Minstrel Show in Mississippi," *Journal of Mississippi History* 57 (Summer 1995): 139–52.

Bean, Annemarie, James V. Hatch, and Brooks McNamara, eds. *Inside the Minstrel Mask: Readings in Nineteenth-Century Blackface Minstrelsy* (1996).

Boskin, Joseph. *Sambo: The Rise and Demise of an American Jester* (1986).

Ely, Melvin Patrick. *The Adventures of Amos n' Andy: A Social History of an American Phenomenon* (1991).

Engle, Gary D. *This Grotesque Essence: Plays from the American Minstrel Stage* (1978).

Gates, Henry Louis. "The Chitlin Circuit," *New Yorker* 72 (3 February 1997): 44–50.

Lee, Spike. *Bamboozled* (2000).

Lhamon, W.T. *Raising Cain: Blackface Performance from Jim Crow to Hip Hop* (1998).

Lott, Eric. *Love and Theft: Blackface Minstrelsy and the Working Class* (1993).

Manring, M.M. *Slave in a Box: The Strange Career of Aunt Jemima* (1998).

Moon, Krystyn R. *Yellowface: Creating the Chinese in American Popular Music and Performance, 1850s–1920s* (2005).

Riggs, Marlon. *Ethnic Notions* (1986).

Riis, Thomas L. *More Than Just Minstrel Shows: The Rise of Black Musical Theatre at the Turn of the Century* (1992).

Roediger, David. *The Wages of Whiteness: Race and the Making of the American Working Class* (1999).

Saxton, Alexander. *The Rise and Fall of the White Republic: Class Politics and Mass Culture in Nineteenth-Century American* (2003).

Tosches, Nick. *Where Dead Voices Gather* (2001).

Woll, Allan. *Black Musical Theatre: From Coontown to Dreamgirls* (1989).

CHAPTER 3

Nineteenth-Century Audiences Contribute to Popular Culture, 1849–1880

This chapter addresses the invention and fracturing of audiences (particularly by class) in the nineteenth century. It also explores the tension between creating a larger, national audience and separating high culture from low culture during the industrial revolution. Finally, how were these first "industrialized" audiences understood by actors, producers, theater owners, and theatergoers?

Industrialization, the change from an agricultural economy to one based on manufacturing, involved a strict split between home and factory, between work and leisure time. The distinction we now recognize between fun and work is also the result of nineteenth-century industrial revolution. Industrialization in the United States brought with it a market economy, the idea that everything, including people's labor, can be bought and sold. People began to buy things that they or their neighbors had previously made—even entertainment. Drinking in saloons was different than brewing your own beer (or trading for it with your next-door neighbor) and then drinking it at home or at the shop where you worked. Industrialization also brought changes in interpersonal relationships and interactions between individuals and technology as more people moved to impersonal cities and began work with new machines.

The increasing work/leisure split and the commercialization of everyday life contributed to a solidifying of different social classes. There had been rich and poor folks in America before the industrial revolution, but in many ways people thought of themselves as part of community united around various activities. The rise of a middle class (the managers needed to run the factories) contributed to a shift in how people thought of their class positions. Working together in large groups and then playing together brought working people into more frequent contact with each other and brought them some consciousness of their particular interests and concerns. The middle class often used leisure pursuits to express their different, and higher, class positions: "we don't go to saloons, we go for walks in the park." The wealthy also needed markers to show that they weren't workers, but rather bought workers' labor.

The best example of this increasing class stratification occurred in the Astor Place Riot in 1849 where 22 people died in a protest over which Shakespearean actor should appear as Macbeth in New York City. Class separation in entertainment practices acquired a spatial reality in growing cities. Different classes began to go to different theaters rather than simply sitting in different places within the same theaters, as they had earlier. Upper-class theaters introduced decorum among the audience as a class marker, while in the theaters of the working class, the audiences interacted with what happened, intending to control what happened on the stage. This theater riot is a place to see the conflict that existed in American society at the time. The riot doesn't reflect the social tensions but presents a central ground for the struggle. Arguments over who controls the theater, who controls leisure, who gets to say what is fun result from, and present a way of working out, class formation in the nineteenth century. Other popular culture forms helped audiences think about urban living, the new technologies crowding into their lives, and who to trust in the complex web of industrial life. Issues of what plays get produced, how actors interpret roles, which presentations were true and which fake, and proper audience behavior may seem like questions with no relevance for bigger historical issues but, in making these decisions, nineteenth-century people began to understand and enact their new roles in an industrialized economy.

DOCUMENTS

These documents show how audiences interacted with, sometimes controlling and sometimes acquiescing in, nineteenth-century popular culture. The nineteenth century saw the invention of the audience and these reports illustrate that process. Document 1 excerpts a rare diary of a participant in the Astor Place Riot, during which theatergoers expressed their opinions of how Shakespeare should be performed, while Document 2 presents an image of the riot. Documents 3 and 4 show how newspapers covered one of P.T. Barnum's hoaxes, the Feejee Mermaid, and how Barnum himself thought of his actions in presenting the Mermaid to the public. Olive Logan, in Document 5, describes theater audiences and their high level of activity, proving that standards of decorum in theater behavior, introduced by the wealthy, had not become widespread. Document 6 gives an idea of the forms of Shakespeare that were widely popular in the nineteenth century and reminds us that minstrelsy and Shakespeare were often intertwined. What does it mean for audiences to be active? Is passive bad and active good when it comes to popular culture? Do you have to participate in a riot or can you simply be engaged in order to be called an "active participant"?

1. An Eyewitness Details the Class Conflict of the Astor Place Riot, 1849

(Monday May 7th) The dark, gloomy, and disagreeable weather of Sunday still prevails, and as yet there is but little prospect of a change. During the day,

Edward Neufville Tailer, *Diary*, (7–16, May 1849), in the collections of the New York Historical Society, New York, NY.

however, there was very little rain, but the wind was cold, and piercing, and every countenance seemed to wear a melancholy look. The previous beautiful and pleasant weather only seems to make it more disagreeable….

(Tuesday May 8th) … Mr. Macready will appear on Thursday evening for the second time in the character of "Macbeth" at the Astor Place Opera House, he was prevailed upon to perform again, and to finish his engagement, by a petition, which was sent to him, signed by a great number of the most influential citizens of New York, who disowned and discountenanced the manner in which he had been treated and promised to support him with the aid of the friends of order, upon this night and would by their presence put a stop to the disgraceful and ungentlemanly conduct, which had met him upon his appearance on last Monday evening.

(Wednesday May 9th) For the first time since Saturday last, the sun and clear sky were visible, and their appearance was hailed with delight by all the people of this great metropolis, and the thousands now congregated in it…. We were very busy all day … and when the shades of evening came, I was heartily glad to leave the store for the pleasanter associations of home. I called and spent the evening with H Franklin as he had not been very well for the last few days…. Mother, and Aunt Eliza, called on Mrs. Robson, and remained until half after ten o'clock.

(Thursday May 10th) … After tea in the evening, I walked up to the Astor Place Opera House, and found that there was already congregated there, an immense crowd, who had assembled from all parts of the city, to witness a contemplated riot, which had been got up, by parties of organized ruffians whose ultimate intention, and object, was not only to prevent Macready from playing, but to destroy if possible this classic and beautiful structure. As early as half past six o'clock, persons began to assemble around the theater, and, at about seven, crowds were seen wending their way to the theater from all parts of the city. By half past seven, there were several hundreds in the streets in front of the Opera House, and the rush to get admittance was tremendous. The house itself was filled to the dome. A great portion of the assemblage in the theater consisted of policemen, who had been distributed in different portions of the house, in detached parties. When the curtain arose, Macready was met by a shower of hisses, which was soon silenced, and those who disturbed the peace of the theater, by their ungentlemanly voices, were placed in irons … and marched to the station house, early the next morning. About eight o'clock, the mob commenced to stone the edifice, and in a few moments shower after shower of stones assailed the windows of the theater. Soon after Edward Z.C. Judson, who was heading the mob outside, and calling upon them to stone the buildings, was arrested by the orders of the Chief of the Police. In the mean time the assault upon the doors and windows continued, volley after volley of large paving stones was discharged against the widows. The glass was, of course, in a few moments all smashed to atoms, the windows resisted the attack for some minutes; at last yielding, however, the fragments were carried into the body of the house, causing great alarm to the audience. At nine o'clock I went to Ninth St and remained there during a few minutes, happily for me I did not return to the principal theater of the riot, in Astor Place, but went to Jones' bar room in Broadway. In the mean time, however, unknown to me, a corps of the National guard were ordered out and had fired on the mob, with blank cartridges, but this only appeared to excite them the more, until finally they went so far as to seriously wound several of the Members of the National guard with stones and other missiles, and as a last resort, to save themselves from further injury, and to disperse the mob, they fired three successive vollies upon the people. The first intimation that I had of this occurrence; was upon a sudden, a rush was made into Jones', bringing with them a dead body of an aged gentlemen, who was unfortunately shot in the breast. Bill Woodcock attended him, and had him carried into a back room, where medical aid was in attendance, although then, I think it was useless. This sickening and heart rending scene served to wind up the adventure of this evening which will ever be remembered in New York, as one of the saddest most terrible occurrences, that this city has ever witnessed. When I got home, Father felt quite relieved, to find that I was well and had not received any injury but he still thought of Henry, who was about and drew sad inferences, from the story which I gave him, of what was going on. 11 o'clock however, relieved him from all his anxieties, and we all were thankful to find that our numerous family were not in any manner injured, in the conflicts of the evening.

(Friday, May 11th) I got up at half past four, A.M. and my first movements after dressing were to visit the scene of last night's conflict. The first object, which attracted my attention, was a corps of the National guard, who were returning from the Astor Place Opera House, fatigued and sorrowful at what had occurred. The Opera House has the appearance of a fortress, which has withstood a vigorous siege, the windows and doors have almost entirely been broken in, and everything has an appearance of destruction and wanton sacrifice, to satisfy the pleasures and whims of an enraged bewildered populace. The side of Mr. Langdon's house, shows plainly in nine places, where as many random bullets have struck, and in the inside of the railing, there are three pools of blood, and upon his side walk, there are but two, crossing Lafayette Place, you will find another, and one, which surpasses the rest of them in size, will be found behind, the sewer in L.P. and contains a compound of the poor victim's blood, brains, and skull. The excitement had not subsided, and at that early hour in the morning, crowds of men and boys were again congregating, upon the field, which had been the theater of the previous evening's conflict, marks of which had not yet been erased from the pavements of both side walk and street. From this scene of slaughter, I went to the Fifteenth ward Station House, and there the scene was truly tragical. On a bench at the end of the room lay the dead body of a tall, genteel looking man whose name I believe is George W. Gedney (?), brother to a broker in Wall st, he had been shot through the brain. Next to him was a man of middle stature, with the whole of the cap of his skull blown off, then came a man, who had a throat wound. Besides those victims on the floor, lay the body of a young man, and then one with dark whiskers shot in the right breast, a thin faced man apparently a mechanic, shot in the neck; a man of somewhat similar appearance, shot in the abdomen, and an elderly man, shot in the right cheek, who had been conveyed from the street to the theater, and thence to the station house, making eight bodies in all. There was also another body of a common looking man, and never in my life, do I remember of having seen such as awful and tragical scene, and I pray never to behold another and perhaps I never shall, as such a tragical transaction, as this, had never occurred in the N. York before.

2. Viewing the Violent Astor Place Riot, 1843

ASTOR PLACE OPERA-HOUSE RIOTS.

3. *Charleston Courier* Reports on an Exhibition of the Fejee Mermaid, 1843

The exhibition of the wonders of nature and art, now in progress, at the Masonic Hall, corner of King and Wentworth streets, is one of the most attractive, in variety, beauty, curiosity, and comic effect we have ever witnessed. Ingenuity and taste convert the ductile glass into shapes and forms of surpassing elegance and beauty; the dancing figures exhibit the most extraordinary and most exquisite mechanism, conferring on inanimate matter seeming life, and displaying the viscomica of motion in the highest perfection; the colloquies of the ventriloquist [sic] are complete in illusion, and furnish a succession of most laughable and amusing farces; and the feats of legerdemain are performed with an adroitness rarely if ever surpassed. The natural curiosities too

Picture Collection, *The New York Public Library*, Astor, Lenox and Tilden Foundations.

"The Exhibition at the Masonic Hall," *Charleston Courier* (21 January 1843), http://chnm.gmu.edu/lostmuseum/lm/181/.

are well worthy a visit from the curious and scientific—and most curious among them is the Fee-jee beauty—the mermaid, hitherto believed to be of fabulous existence. We, of course, cannot undertake to say whether this seeming wonder of nature be real or not, it not being in our power to apply to it any scientific test of truth; but this we deem it but just to say, that we were permitted to handle and examine it as closely as could be effected by touch and sight, and that if there be any deception, it is beyond the discovery of both those senses. The appearance is in every respect that of a natural and not an artificial object—it is certainly no compound or combination, as has been supposed, of ape and fish—but is either altogether nature's handiwork, or altogether the production of art—and if it be indeed artificial, it is the very perfection of art, imitating nature in the closest similitude. We are rather inclined to have faith on the occasion, for the connection, which this curious object establishes between fish and women, is only in analogy with that which every body knows to exist between monkey and man. Of one allusion, however, the sight of the wonder has forever robbed us—we shall never again discourse, even in poesy of mermaid beauty, nor woo a mermaid even in our dreams—for the Fee-jee lady is the very incarnation of ugliness.

The entire entertainment is an eminently successful one, it amuses the grave and heightens the gayety of the gay—and the delight it ministers to children is literally uproarious—and exhilarating to all who own a sympathy with the innocent enjoyments of childhood. A special exhibition, for the entertainment of children exclusively and their parental and other attendants, will be given, and commence at 3 o'clock this afternoon.

4. P.T. Barnum Explains the Appeal of the FeJee Mermaid, 1855

Early in the summer of 1842, Moses Kimball, Esq., the popular proprietor of the Boston Museum, came to New-York and exhibited to me what purported to be a mermaid. He stated that he had bought it of a sailor whose father, while in Calcutta in 1817 as captain of a Boston ship, had purchased it, believing it to be a preserved specimen of a veritable mermaid, obtained, as he was assured, from Japanese sailors. Not doubting that it would prove as surprising to others as it had been to himself, and hoping to make a rare speculation of it as an extraordinary curiosity, he appropriated $6000 of the ship's money to the purchase of it, left the ship in charge of the mate, and went to London.

He did not realize his expectations, and returned to Boston. Still believing that his curiosity was a genuine animal and therefore highly valuable, he preserved it with great care, not stinting himself in the expense of keeping it insured, though re-engaged as ship's captain under his former employers to reimburse the sum taken from their funds to pay for the mermaid. He died possessing no other property, and his only son and heir, who placed a low estimate on his father's purchase, sold it to Mr. Kimball, who brought it to New-York for my inspection.

_____
"Barnum on the Fejee Mermaid," *The Life of P.T. Barnum, Written by Himself, 1855*.
http://chnm.gmu.edu/lostmuseum/lm/182/

Such was the story. Not trusting my own acuteness on such matters, I requested my naturalist's opinion of the *genuineness* of the animal. He replied that he could not conceive how it was manufactured; for he never knew a monkey with such peculiar teeth, arms, hands etc., nor had he knowledge of a fish with such peculiar fins.

"Then why do you suppose it is manufactured?" I inquired.

"Because I don't believe in mermaids," replied the naturalist.

"That is no reason at all," said I, "and therefore I'll believe in the mermaid, and hire it."

This was the easiest part of the experiment. How to modify general incredulity in the existence of mermaids, so far as to awaken curiosity to see and examine the specimen, was now the all-important question. Some extraordinary means must be resorted to, and I saw no better method than to "start the ball a-rolling" at some distance from the centre of attraction.

In due time a communication appeared in the New-York Herald, dated and mailed in Montgomery, Ala., giving the news of the day, trade, the crops, political gossip, etc., and also an incidental paragraph about a certain Dr. Griffin, agent of the Lyceum of Natural History in London, recently from Pernambuco, who had in his possession a most remarkable curiosity, being nothing less than a veritable mermaid taken among the Fejee Islands, and preserved in China, where the Doctor had bought it at a high figure for the Lyceum of Natural History.

A week or ten days afterwards, a letter of similar tenor, dated and mailed in Charleston, S.C., varying of course in the items of local news, was published in another New-York paper.

This was followed by a third letter, dated and mailed in Washington city, published in still another New-York paper—there being in addition the expressed hope that the editors of the Empire City would beg a sight of the extraordinary curiosity before Dr. Griffin took ship for England.

A few days subsequently to the publication of this thrice-repeated announcement, Mr. Lyman (who was my employee in the case of Joice Heth) was duly registered at one of the principal hotels in Philadelphia as Dr. Griffin of Pernambuco for London. His gentlemanly, dignified, yet social manners and liberality gained him a fine reputation for a few days, and when he paid his bill one afternoon, preparatory to leaving for New-York the next day, he expressed his thanks to the landlord for special attention and courtesy. "If you will step to my room," said Lyman, alias Griffin, "I will permit you to see something that will surprise you." Whereupon the landlord was shown the most extraordinary curiosity in the world—a mermaid. He was so highly gratified and interested that he earnestly begged permission to introduce certain friends of his, including several editors, to view the wonderful specimen.

…The result might easily be gathered from the editorial columns of the Philadelphia papers a day or two subsequently to that interview with the mermaid. Suffice it to say, that the plan worked admirably, and the Philadelphia press aided the press of New-York in awakening a wide-reaching and increasing curiosity to see the mermaid.

I may as well confess that those three communications from the South were written by myself, and forwarded to friends of mine, with instructions respectively to mail them, each on the day of its date. This fact and the corresponding post-marks did much to prevent suspicion of a hoax, and the New-York editors thus unconsciously contributed to my arrangements for bringing the mermaid into public notice.

5. Observer Olive Logan Describes Active Theater Audiences, 1878

To the general play-goer, it is presumed that the most interesting part of a theater is behind the scenes.

To actors and actresses, naturally enough, the chief interest lies with the audience—Before the Footlights.

At least, it has always been and is so with me.

I am never tired of studying that many-headed animal—the Audience. I love to take it up in its different elements, and ponder it—looking out from a cozy corner in a stage-box, myself unobserved.

The doors are thrown open, and now comes in the promiscuous crowd—that sea of human nothings which makes up a "good house" at the theater. Kitty and her beau, who don't care a pin for the play, but have only come for a long conversation, in which they indulge during the entire evening....

There is the school-girl of fifteen, who worships the walking gentleman, and refuses to believe that his moustache is painted....

There is the habitual theater-goer, who remembers seeing this piece, or something very like it, at least thirty years ago, and according to whose statements theatricals, theaters and stage appointments of the present day are in a complete state of degeneracy....

There is the man who laughs at everything. There is the universal fault-finder....

Four times the curtain comes down, and four times there is gossip, and flirting, and scandal, and hypocrisy of all sorts.

Mrs. X comments on her neighbor, and calls her a "horrid creature." They kiss, nevertheless, each time they meet....

But at last the curtain comes down for good, or bad perhaps, and Kitty gets her dress trod upon, and young Larkins loses his umbrella, and Pa leaves his overcoat on the seat, and a sweet-scented billet-doux passes from a small neatly gloved hand into one which is larger and not gloved, and P. lights a cigar, and Mrs. P. says the smoke makes her sick, and the swells take carriages, and the mediocrity take the omnibuses, and the plebeians walk, and the gas is turned off, and there is a damp smell in the theater, and in an hour or two, critics, and criticized, swells, mediocrities, plebeians and artistes are in that happy sleepy land where criticism comes not, and newspapers are unknown....

In these days of battle for "equal rights," it seems to me that something ought to be said in behalf of the rights of audiences.

Olive Logan, *The Mimic World and Public Exhibitions: Their History, Their Morals and Effects* (Philadelphia, PA: New World Publishing Company, 1878).

Among these, unquestionably, is the right to hiss. It is difficult to say just where the limits of this right are to be drawn; but that an audience has a right to express disapprobation is a thing which must be freely conceded.

I would urge all audience to be generous in the exercise of this right, however. I would have them lenient toward the poor player who does his best, and does it honestly, however poor that best may be. But I would have every audience hiss, and vigorously hiss, exhibitions of vulgarity, indecency and drunkenness in actors—for these are insults to an audience, and it ought to resent them promptly....

A manager in a Western theater adopted [a] ... sensible plan of quelling expressions of displeasure. During the performance of "Hamlet," the actor who should have played the "Ghost" was prevented by illness from making his appearance. An ambitious supernumerary volunteered his services, which were gladly accepted. His execrable performance aroused the ire of the audience, who hissed him from the stage. The disapproval being marked by further acts of violence, the manager came forward and said: "Ladies and gentlemen, Mr. Smith has given up the 'Ghost.'" This sally diverted the popular indignation, and the play continued....

Another nuisance ... is that of excessive and repeated *encores*. A critic remarks: "We have frequently seen artists called out to repeat a dance when they have been so exhausted that they could scarcely stand.... We have frequently seen dancers ... after having been compelled to repeat a dance on a warm evening, come off the stage so tired that they have fainted and fallen to the floor, while others have resorted to drinking freely of ice water, which has thrown them into fits. This is no fancy sketch, but truthful. Some will say that it is their own fault. But would such things occur if the public, instead of compelling them to repeat, would be satisfied with their answering the call with a bow? ...

For many years past it has been the custom when an actor or actress was "called out," as the phrase is, that they should come out before the curtain; the great wooden roller having to be dragged out of their way, while they crushed out through the narrow pathway thus afforded them....

The practice of calling performers before the curtain began with the appearance in this country of the elder Kean; and a Philadelphia manager under whom Kean played an engagement thus refers to the practice: "The absurdity of dragging out before the curtain a deceased *Hamlet, Macbeth* or *Richard* in an exhausted state, merely to make a bow, or to attempt an asthmatic address in defiance of all good taste, and solely for the gratification of a few unthinking partisans, or a few lovers of noise and tumult, is one which we date with us from this time. It has always been a matter of wonder with me that the better part of the audience should tolerate these fooleries. Can anything be more ridiculous, than that an actor, after laboring through an arduous character—a protracted combat, and the whole series of simulated, expiring agonies, should instantly revive, and appear panting before the curtain to look and feel like a fool, and to destroy the little illusion he has been endeavoring to create?" ...

Among the bad habits of audiences may be enumerated the habit of chewing tobacco and expectoration; the habit of profane and vulgar talk; the fashionably vulgar habit of going late to the theater or concert, after things are in progress, and thus disturbing that part of the audience which is in season; the habit of creating an uproar by rushing for the door at the efective closing parts of the performance; the habit of stamping for applause and raising a shocking and choking dust, while the hands should be sufficient for the polite expression of approbation.

Some of these habits are far too common, and I hope all good people who read this will resolve to discountenance them....

A lady in whom I have the fullest confidence relates, as an actual fact, the story of Jenny Lind and the Hoosier ... Jenny Lind found herself one evening in the (then) small town of Madison, Indiana. Mr. Barnum had made an arrangement with the captain of the mail steamer which plies between Cincinnati and Louisville, to have the boat lie by on the Indiana shore long enough for the divine Jenny to give a concert at Madison....

"Comin' thro' the Rye" was given first. This was followed by "Home, Sweet Home;" and who can describe the marvelous effect of that song, as rendered by Jenny Lind? The famous "Bird Song" was then the popular air of the country, and it was given as a concluding piece on the evening in question. The last line of the song runs thus, "I know not, I know not why I am singing," and Jenny gave it with her full power. At this moment, a genuine Hoosier, indigenous to the soil, rose up in the auditorium, and thus delivered himself:

"You don't know why you are singin', eh" Gosh! I know if you don't! You're singin' to the tune of five dollars a head, and I reckon dad's hogs will have to suffer for my ticket!"...

Mr. John Hollingshead, the dramatic critic of the London *Times,* was in this country some two years ago....

"With the exception of the Bowery," he says, "the New York theaters, considered as edifices, furnish models which the London architect would do well to imitate, as they are light, commodious, and so arranged as to allow nearly the whole of the audience a good view of the stage.... The New York audiences are, for the most part, extremely sedate and decorous, and, save at the Bowery, seem devoid of the decidedly plebeian element. This deficiency, which, perhaps, more than any other peculiarity, renders an American audience remarkable to an English visitor, may be attributed partly to the architectural arrangement by which the gallery, with its low-priced seats, is kept out of sight, partly to a disposition among the operative classes to make as good a figure as their fellow-citizens. It is quite probable that a workingman may be among the aristocrats of the house, a contingency which is scarcely possible at a fashionable London theater....

With all their ardent love for theatrical amusement, I have no hesitation in saying that the Americans care much more for the actors than for the merits of the play itself. This predilection is consistently accompanied by a regard less to a perfect *ensemble* than to the excellency of the 'star' of the evening.... Youth and personal appearance have much to do with the success of a female artist, and, I fear, are allowed to overbalance the proper estimation of talent....

The story of the Astor Place riot, in 1849, is one of the most interesting in the history of the American stage. It is stated that there was a feud between certain partisans of Edwin Forrest ... and the adherents of Macready, the English tragedian....

It is very interesting to read the newspaper accounts of this celebrated riot, as printed at the time. The following account is compiled from various journals:

On Wednesday night, on the first appearance of Mr. Macready on the stage, he was received with the most vociferous groaning, hisses, and cries of "Off! Off!" A portion of the audience were warm in their plaudits, and waved their handkerchiefs, but they were overborne by the horrid and uncouth noises which continued almost without intermission … until the end of so much of the tragedy as was performed. Mr. Macready walked down to the footlights, and abode "the pelting of the pitiless storm" of groans and shouts of derision and contumely with wonderful firmness. A placard was hung over the upper box, on which was inscribed, "You have been proved A LIAR!" Then arose louder yells, and these were accompanied with showers of rotten eggs, apples, and a bottle of asafœtida, which diffused a most repulsive stench throughout the house.… This over, the rioters slowly left the house.

Early in the morning of the following day, placards were posted up through the city, stating that the crew of the British steamer had threatened violence to all who "dared express their opinions at the English Aristocratic Opera House," and calling on all working men to "stand by their lawful rights." In consequence of this and similar threats, a large body of police was ordered to attend at the Opera House … In anticipation of a riot, the rush for tickets was very great, and before night none were to be had.… The entrance of Mr. Macready, in the third act, was the signal for a perfect storm of cheers, groans, and hisses. The whole audience rose, and the nine-tenths of it who were friendly to Macready cheered, waving their hats and handkerchiefs. A large body in the parquette, with others of the second tier and amphitheater hissed and groaned with equal zeal. The tumult lasted for ten or fifteen minutes, when an attempt was made to restore order by a board being thrown upon the stage, upon which was written, "The friends of order will remain quiet." This silenced all but the rioters, who continued to drown all sound of what was said upon the stage.… One by one, the rioters were taken and carried out, the greater part of the audience applauding as they disappeared.… As the parquet and gallery were cleared of the noisiest rioters, the crowds without grew more violent, and stones were hurled against the windows on the Astor place side. As one window cracked after another, and pieces of bricks and paving stones rattled against the terrace and lobbies, the confusion increased, till the Opera House resembled a fortress besieged by an invading army, rather than a place meant for the peaceful amusement of a civilized community.…

After the play was over, the noise being apparently diminished somewhat, the audience was allowed to go out quietly by the door nearest Broadway.…

The crowd refusing to disperse after the reading of the riot act, a volley was fired by the troops, the quick, scattering flashes throwing a sudden gleam over the crowd, the gas-lights in the streets having all been extinguished. The crowd seemed taken by surprise, as, on account of the incessant noises, very few could have heard the reading of the Riot Act.… Presently a second volley was fired, followed, almost without pause, by three or four others. A part of the crowd came rushing down Lafayette place, but there was no shout nor noise except the deadly report of the muskets. After this horrid sound had ceased, groups of people came along, bearing away the bodies of the dead and dying....

I need make no further comment on this disgraceful event than to say that while it was nominally a theatrical riot, it was in reality nothing more nor less than a *political* disturbance, with foreign actor as the scapegoat....

It is curious, in these days when the reserved seat system is so universal at all places of amusement, to read an account given by manager Wood in his "Recollections," of the troubles following the introduction of private boxes into the Philadelphia theater. The difficulty attaching to this innovation, he relates, came to him with the very opening of the theater in 1793. "Mrs. Bingham, a lady, in her day the chief leader in the fashion of Philadelphia, the wife of an early and valued friend of Wignell himself, a lady of great social and family influence, and very extensively connected, proposed for the purchase of a box *at any price to be fixed by the manager....* [B]eing a woman of exclusive and elegant tastes, [she] was desirous to have the privileges which were allowed in the theaters with which she had been familiar abroad. She offered to furnish and decorate the box at her own expense; but it was an absolute condition that the key should be kept by herself, and no admission to it allowed to any one except on her assent. Mr. Wignell had many strong inducements to accept this offer.... He looked at the matter, however, with much more comprehensive and philosophic regards. He knew that the theater in a country like ours must depend entirely for permanent success, not upon individuals, however powerful, not upon clubs, cliques, factions or parties, but upon THE PUBLIC alone; that in a country where the spirit of liberty is so fierce as in ours, such a privilege would excite from an immense class a feeling of positive hostility.... He saw that it must be a cardinal maxim of any American manager to act on the principles of his country's government, and on the recognition of feelings deeply pervading the structure of its society; to hold, in short, all men 'free' to come into his house, and 'equal' while they continued to be and behave themselves in it.

6. Playwright G.W.H. Griffin Rewrites Hamlet for Nineteenth-Century Audiences, 1880

SCENE I

A Street

Enter *Hamlet, Horatio* and *Marcellus, Hamlet* is dressed in black tights, with tight fitting swallow-tailed dress coat.... The other characters are dressed in any comical wardrobe they may choose.

HAMLET. The air bites shrewdly—it is very cold.

HORATIO. I never saw a darky half so bold.

G.W.H. Griffin, *Hamlet the Dainty: An Ethiopian Burlesque on Shakespeare's Hamlet Performed by Griffin & Christy's Minstrels* (New York: Happy Hours Co., 1880).

HAMLET.   What is't o'clock?

HORATIO.   (*Draws out very large tin watch.*)—Half past eleven, at most.
(*Winds up his watch.*)

MARCELLUS.   (*Drawing out large round turnip.*)—My watch says twelve.
(*Clock strikes twelve.*)

HAMLET.   Dry up! here comes the ghost.
Enter *Ghost*, dressed in shabby, ragged uniform, his face perfectly white with flour; he is smoking a long segar, and reading a newspaper. *Horatio* and *Marcellus* are very much frightened. They fall against each other, then on the stage, rolling over and doing all sorts of comic bus.

HAMLET.   He's from the South! Oh, grace defend us!
Prythee! no more such frightful specters send us!
Be thou blacked up, or goblin damned!
Be thou with whisky puffed, or old cheese cramm'd!
Be thy intents indifferent, good or bad,
I'll speak to thee, thou look'st so like my dad—
In a trim box so snugly was't thou lain.
Say! what the deuce e'er brought you out again?
I like a joke myself—but 'tis not right,
To come and frighten us to death at night,
Say, why is this, will you the reason tell us?
Why come to frighten me, Horatio and Marcellus?
(Ghost *puts his finger on his nose, then motions* Hamlet *to follow him.*)

HORATIO.   He wants to speak a word with you alone!

HAMLET.   Does he? Here goes then! Now, old pap, lead on!

MARCELLUS.   You shall not go!
(*They take hold of him.*)

HORATIO.   Perhaps he means to kill you!

HAMLET.   You'd better hold your jaw—be quiet, will you?

HORATIO.   No, sweetness, you shall not go.

HAMLET.   My fate cries out and gives me pluck—so mind
What you're about—(Ghost *motions him.*)—Still am I called.
Paws off! The time does fly!
Let go your hold—or else I'll black your eye.
Hop off, I say! (*Breaks from them. To* Ghost.) Lead on!
I closely follow.
(*To* Horatio *and* Marcellus.)—Wait here! If I want you, boys,
I'll holler.
[*Exeunt* Ghost *and* Hamlet, R., Horatio *and* Marcellus, L.

SCENE II

A Wood
Enter *Ghost* and *Hamlet*, R.

HAMLET. Look here, Mr. Ghost, this is played out—I'll go no further!

GHOST. You had better.

HAMLET. No!

GHOST. Then hold your tongue and hear what I declare—
I'm pressed for time—we keep good hours down there.
Soon I must go and get an oyster roast;
Then list! Oh, list!

HAMLET. Alas, poor ghost!

GHOST. I am thy father's ghost,
Doomed for a certain time to walk the night.
I could such a dismal tale unfold—

HAMLET. I knew he had a tail. Oh, lord!

GHOST. As would make your precious blood run cold.
★ ★ ★ ★ ★
One afternoon, as was my use,
I went to a gin mill to take a snooze—
When your uncle into my mouth did pour
A gallon of brandy smash, or more.
★ ★ ★ ★ ★
Torment your uncle, for my sake—
Let him never have a drink, asleep or awake.
Your mother's plague, let her consolence be;
Adieu! adieu! remember me!   *(Vanishes.)*
Enter *Horatio* and *Marcellus*, running....

SCENE III

Interior of Palace—throne, chairs, &c.
Enter *Hamlet* and *Horatio*.

HAMLET. Horatio, I've not seen such scenes,
Since I was in Boston eating pork and beans.

Enter *Osrick,* dressed extravagantly, as a fop.

OSRICK. *(To Hamlet.)*—His majesty has made a match for you
To spar with young Laertes, a rummy bruiser—
And betted him the contents of his purse
That you—young Hamlet—that you'll bust his crust.
Laertes is quite ready to set to;
They're all assembled, and but wait for you.

HAMLET. I'll fight him, sir. I ne'er felt bolder—

HORATIO. I'll be your second.

OSRICK. And I'll be bottle holder.

(Flourish of trumpets and drums.)

Enter *King, Queen, Laertes*, and others, and take seats to witness the contest.

KING. To put an end to all this muss and noise,
(*To* Hamlet *and* Laertes.) Shake hands, and make it up, my jolly boys.
(They shake hands, and the gloves are all brought in.)
If in the two first rounds, Hamlet hit most blows,
Or 'scape the third without a bloody nose—
Let all the guns we've got make the discovery *(Drum)*,
The king shall drink to Hamlet's quick recovery.
(They put on gloves and make a comical fight.)

HAMLET. A hit!

LAERTES. No hit!

OSRICK. An 'it. I'll bet a dollar.

HAMLET. A hit or not, 'twas something made him holler!

KING. Give me the beer. (*To* Hamlet.)—This Stoughton is for you.
(Pours poison.)
Hamlet, your health. *(Pretends to drink.)*—You'd better drink some too.

HAMLET. Let's have this round—when I want drink I'll ask it.
I had him then, right in the bread basket.

QUEEN. Hamlet, your health. *(Drinks.)*—Ha! this is famous stingo!

KING. Don't drink!

QUEEN. I have!

KING. The poisoned cup, by jingo!

HAMLET. Another hit, Laertes, in the stomach.
(Laertes down.)

LAERTES. Then it's below the belt, you great big lummox,
(Queen *screams and faints.*)

OSRICK. Look to the Queen! (*To* Laertes.)—How is't, my lord?

LAERTES. I'm dished! I'm whipped as neatly as I have have wished.

HAMLET. How does the Queen?

KING. To see your bloody noses, her stomach slightly indisposes.

QUEEN. No, no! I'm poisoned! Your old uncle, here,
Has mixed a deadly poison with the beer.
It's now too late—I took too many swigs—
He put the poison in, to kill off all you nigs.
(Dies.)

(They all attack the King *with stuffed clubs, brooms, &c.; while they are all fighting* Ghost *appears; they all fall back upon the stage, and tremble with fright. Curtain.)*

THE END

ESSAYS

These two essays present somewhat different visions of nineteenth-century audiences. In his highly influential article, the late Lawrence W. Levine, professor of history at George Mason University, describes the popularity of Shakespeare in the nineteenth century to argue that the labels applied to culture, such as "high" and "popular," don't relate to the inherent worth of the production but are constructions and shift over time. The continuing interaction between the audience and the Shakespeare plays presented to them helped make Shakespeare fit into the normal theatrical experience in the nineteenth century, but Levine clearly states that it isn't that nineteenth-century audiences don't understand Shakespeare or saw poorly presented plays that made him popular. Nineteenth-century audiences simply saw nothing difficult or off-putting about Shakespeare, which allows us to question a hierarchical view of culture in which popular culture is trash and high culture is art. The active audiences described by Levine take a different form in the essay by the late Neil Harris, professor of history at the University of Chicago. Harris argues that despite the fact that those who went to see P.T. Barnum's shows seemed easily fooled, even stupid, in accepting hoaxes such as the Feejee Mermaid, their acceptance was part of a complex "operational aesthetic" that kept audiences interested and connected to Barnum's world. In learning how Barnum fooled them, audience members considered and replayed their roles in a new and complex industrialized society. Both authors make historical audiences come alive and explain their thoughts and actions as deriving from complicated motivations and understandings of what they saw.

Audiences Riot Over Interpretations of Shakespeare

LAWRENCE W. LEVINE

The humor of a people affords important insights into the nature of their culture. Thus Mark Twain's treatment of Shakespeare in his novel *Huckleberry Finn* helps us place the Elizabethan playwright in nineteenth-century American culture. Shortly after the two rogues, who pass themselves off as a duke and a king, invade the raft of Huck and Jim, they decide to raise funds by performing scenes from Shakespeare's *Romeo and Juliet* and *Richard III*. That the presentation of Shakespeare in small Mississippi River towns could be conceived of as potentially lucrative tells us much about the position of Shakespeare in the nineteenth century. The specific nature of Twain's humor tells us even more. Realizing that

Lawrence W. Levine, "William Shakespeare and the American People: A Study in Cultural Transformation," *American Historical Review*, 89 (1, 1984), 34–66.

they would need material for encores, the "duke" starts to teach the "king" Hamlet's soliloquy, which he recites from memory:

> To be, or not to be; that is the bare bodkin
> That makes calamity of so long life;
> For who would fardels bear, till Birnam Wood do come to Dunsinane,
> But that the fear of something after death Murders the innocent sleep,
> Great nature's second course,
> And makes us rather sling arrows of outrageous fortune
> Than fly to others that we know not of.

Twain's humor relies on his audience's familiarity with *Hamlet* and its ability to recognize the duke's improbable coupling of lines from a variety of Shakespeare's plays. Twain was employing one of the most popular forms of humor in nineteenth-century America. Everywhere in the nation burlesques and parodies of Shakespeare constituted a prominent form of entertainment....

Not until the nineteenth century, however, did Shakespeare come into his own—presented and recognized almost everywhere in the country. In the cities of the Northeast and Southeast, Shakespeare's plays dominated the theater. During the 1810–11 season in Philadelphia, for example, Shakespearean plays accounted for twenty-two of eighty-eight performances. The following season lasted 108 nights, of which again one-quarter—27—were devoted to Shakespeare. From 1800 to 1835, Philadelphians had the opportunity to see twenty-one of Shakespeare's thirty-seven plays. The Philadelphia theater was not exceptional; one student of the American stage concluded that in cities on the Eastern Seaboard at least one-fifth of all plays offered in a season were likely to be by Shakespeare....

It is important to understand that their journey did not end with big cities or the Eastern Seaboard.... The theater, like the church, was one of the earliest and most important cultural institutions established in frontier cities. And almost everywhere the theater blossomed Shakespeare was a paramount force.... Beginning in the early 1830s, the rivers themselves became the site of Shakespearean productions, with floating theaters in the form first of flatboats and then steamboats bringing drama to small river towns.

By mid-century, Shakespeare was taken across the Great Plains and over the Rocky Mountains and soon became a staple of theaters in the Far West. During the decade following the arrival of the Forty-niners, at least twenty-two of Shakespeare's plays were performed on California stages, with *Richard III* retaining the predominance it had gained in the East and South....

But Shakespeare could not be confined to the major population centers in the Far West any more than he had been in the East. If miners could not always come to San Francisco to see theater, the theater came to them. Stark, Buchanan, Edwin Booth, and their peers performed on makeshift stages in mining camps around Sacramento and crossed the border into Nevada, where they brought characterizations of Hamlet, Iago, Macbeth, Kate, Lear, and Othello to miners in Virginia City, Silver City, Dayton, and Carson City....

Shakespeare's popularity can be determined not only by the frequency of Shakespearean productions and the size of the audiences for them but also by the nature of the productions and the manner in which they were presented. Shakespeare was performed not merely alongside popular entertainment as an elite supplement to it; Shakespeare was performed as an integral part of it. Shakespeare *was* popular entertainment in nineteenth-century America. The theater in the first half of the nineteenth century played the role that movies played in the first half of the twentieth: it was a kaleidoscopic, democratic institution presenting a widely varying bill of fare to all classes and socioeconomic groups.

During the first two-thirds of the nineteenth century, the play may have been the thing, but it was not the only thing. It was the centerpiece, the main attraction, but an entire evening generally consisted of a long play, an afterpiece (usually a farce), and a variety of between-act specialities....

Thus Shakespeare was presented amid a full range of contemporary entertainment....

These afterpieces and *divertissements* most often are seen as having diluted or denigrated Shakespeare. I suggest that they may be understood more meaningfully as having *integrated* him into American culture. Shakespeare was presented as part of the same milieu inhabited by magicians, dancers, singers, acrobats, minstrels, and comics. He appeared on the same playbills and was advertised in the same spirit. This does not mean that theatergoers were unable to make distinctions between Shakespearean productions and the accompanying entertainment. Of course they were. Shakespeare, after all, was what most of them came to see. But it was a Shakespeare presented as part of the culture they enjoyed, a Shakespeare rendered familiar and intimate by virtue of his context....

Nineteenth-century America swallowed Shakespeare, digested him and his plays, and made them part of the cultural body. If Shakespeare originally came to America as *Culture* in the libraries of the educated, he existed in pre-Civil War America as *culture*. The nature of his reception by nineteenth-century audiences confirms this conclusion....

One of Shakespeare's contemporaries commented that the theater was "frequented by all sorts of people old and younge, rich and poore, masters and servants, papists and puritans, wise men etc., churchmen and statesmen." The nineteenth-century American audience was equally heterogeneous. In both eras the various classes saw the same plays in the same theaters—though not necessarily from the same vantage point. Until mid-century, at least, American theaters generally had a tripartite seating arrangement: the pit (orchestra), the boxes, and the gallery (balcony). Although theater prices fell substantially from 1800 to 1850, seating arrangements continued to dovetail with class and economic divisions. In the boxes sat, as one spectator put it, "the dandies, and people of the first respectability and fashion." The gallery was inhabited largely by those—apprentices, servants, poor workingmen—who could not afford better seats or by those—Negroes and often prostitutes—who were not allowed to sit elsewhere. The pit was dominated by what were rather vaguely called the "middling classes"—a "mixed multitude" that some contemporaries praised as the "honest folks" or "the sterling part of the audience."

All observers agreed that the nineteenth-century theater housed under one roof a microcosm of American society....

[A]n understanding of the American theater in our own time is not adequate grounding for a comprehension of American theater in the nineteenth century. To envision nineteenth-century theater audiences correctly, one might do well to visit a contemporary sporting event in which the spectators not only are similarly heterogeneous but are also—in the manner of both the nineteenth century and the Elizabethan era—more than an audience; they are participants who can enter into the action on the field, who feel a sense of immediacy and at times even of control, who articulate their opinions and feelings vocally and unmistakably…. The audience's vociferousness continued during the play itself, which was punctuated by expressions of disapproval in the form of hisses or groans and of approval in the form of applause, whistles, and stamping to the point that a Virginia editor felt called upon to remind his readers in 1829 that it was not "a duty to applaud at the conclusion of every sentence.".… Audiences frequently demanded—and got—instant encores from performers who particularly pleased them. "Perhaps," a New York editor wrote sarcastically in 1846, "we'll flatter Mr. Kean by making him take position twice." …

These frenetic displays of approval and disapproval were signs of engagement in what was happening on the stage—an engagement that on occasion could blur the line between audience and actors…. Frequently, members of the audience became so involved in the action on stage that they interfered in order to dispense charity to the sick and destitute, advice to the indecisive, and, as one man did during a Baltimore production of *Coriolanus* and another during a New York production of *Othello*, protection to someone involved in an unfair fight.

These descriptions should make it clear how difficult it is to draw arbitrary lines between popular and folk culture. Here was professional entertainment containing numerous folkish elements, including a knowledgeable, participatory audience exerting important degrees of control. The integration of Shakespeare into the culture as a whole should bring into serious question our tendency to see culture on a vertical plane, neatly divided into a hierarchy of inclusive adjectival categories such as "high," "low," "pop," "mass," "folk," and the like. If the phenomenon of Shakespeare was not an abberation—and the diverse audiences for such art forms as Italian opera, such performers as singer Jenny Lind, and such writers as Longfellow, Dickens, and Mark Twain indicate it was not—then the study of Shakespeare's relationship to the American people helps reveal the existence of a shared public culture to which we have not paid enough attention. It has been obscured by the practice of employing such categories as "popular" aesthetically rather then literally. That is, the adjective "popular" has been utilized to describe not only those creations of expressive culture that actually had a large audience (which is the way I have tried to use it in this essay), but also, and often primarily, those that had questionable artistic merit. Thus, a banal play or a poorly written romantic novel has been categorized as popular culture, even if it had a tiny audience, while the recognized artistic attributes of a Shakespearean play have prevented it from being included in popular culture, regardless of its high degree of popularity. The use of such arbitrary and imprecise cultural categories has helped obscure the dynamic complexity of American culture in the nineteenth century.

Our difficulty also proceeds from the historical fallacy of reading the present into the past. By the middle of the twentieth century, Shakespearean drama did not occupy the place it had in the nineteenth century....

Although in the mid-twentieth century there was no more widely known, respected, or quoted dramatist in our culture than Shakespeare, the nature of his relationship to the American people had changed: he was no longer their familiar, no longer part of their culture, no longer at home in their theaters or on the movie and television screens that had become the twentieth-century equivalents of the stage. If Shakespeare had been an integral part of mainstream culture in the nineteenth century, in the twentieth he had become part of "polite" culture—an essential ingredient in a complex we call, significantly, "legitimate" theater. He had become the possession of the educated portions of society who disseminated his plays for the enlightenment of the average folk who were to swallow him not for their entertainment but for their education, as a respite from—not as a normal part of—their usual cultural diet. Recalling his youthful experiences with Shakespeare, the columnist Gerald Nachman wrote in 1979 that in the schools of America "Shakespeare become theatrical spinach: He's good for you. If you digest enough of his plays, you'll grow up big and strong intellectually like teacher." ...

Culture is a process, not a fixed condition; it is the product of unremitting interaction between the past and the present. Thus, Shakespeare's relationship to the American people was always in flux, always changing. Still, it is possible to isolate a period during which the increasing separation of Shakespeare from "every-day people" becomes more evident.... There is no precise date, but everywhere in the United States during the final decades of the nineteenth century the same transformation was evidently taking place; Shakespeare was being divorced from the broader world of everyday culture. Gone were the entre-act diversions: the singers, jugglers, dancers, acrobats, orators. Gone, too, was the purple prose trumpeting the sensational events and pageantry that were part of the Shakespearean plays themselves. Those who wanted their Shakespeare had to take him alone, lured to his plays by stark playbills promising no frills or enhancements.... Once again, William Shakespeare had become *Culture*.

It is easier to describe this transformation than to explain it, since the transformation itself has clouded our vision of the past. So completely have twentieth-century Americans learned to accept as natural and timeless Shakespeare's status as an elite, classic dramatist, to whose plays the bulk of the populace do not or cannot relate, that we have found it difficult to comprehend nineteenth-century conceptions of Shakespeare. Too frequently, modern historians of the theater have spent less time and energy understanding Shakespeare's nineteenth-century popularity than in explaining it away. The formula is simple: how to account for the indisputable popularity of a great master in a frontier society with an "overwhelmingly uneducated" public. The consensus seems to be that Shakespeare was popular for all the wrong reasons: because of the afterpieces and *divertissements* that surrounded his plays; because the people wanted to see great actors who in turn insisted on performing Shakespeare to demonstrate their abilities; because his plays were presented in altered, simplified versions; because of his bombast, crudities, and sexual allusions rather than his poetry or sophistication; because of almost anything but his dramatic genius. "Shakespeare," we are told in a conclusion that would not be important if it were not so typical, "could communicate with the unsophisticated at the level of action and oratory while appealing to the small refined element at the level of dramatic and poetic artistry."

Again and again, historians and critics have arbitrarily separated the "action and oratory" of Shakespeare's plays from the "dramatic and poetic artistry" with which they were, in reality, so intricately connected. We are asked to believe that the average member of the audience saw only violence, lewdness, and sensationalism in such plays as *Richard III, Hamlet, King Lear, Othello,* and *Macbeth* and was incapable of understanding the moral and ethical dilemmas, the generational strains between parents and children, the crude ambition of Richard III or Lady Macbeth, the haunting guilt of Macbeth, the paralyzing introspection and doubts of Hamlet, the envy of Iago, the insecurities of Othello. We have been asked to believe that such human conditions and situations were beyond the powers of most of the audience and touched only a "refined element" who understood the "subtleties of Shakespeare's art."

Certainly, the relationship of an audience to the object of its focus—be it a sermon, political speech, newspaper, musical composition, or play—is a complex one and constitutes a problem for the historian who would reconstruct it. But the problem cannot be resolved through the use of such ahistorical devices as dividing both the audience and the object into crude categories and then coming to conclusions that have more to do with the culture of the writer than that of the subject. In fact, the way to understand the popularity of Shakespeare is to enter into the spirit of the nineteenth century. Shakespeare was popular, first and foremost, because he was integrated into the culture and presented within its context. Nineteenth-century Americans were able to fit Shakespeare into their culture so easily because he *seemed* to fit—because so many of his values and tastes were, or at least appeared to be, close to their own, and were presented through figures that seemed real and came to matter to the audience....

Both worlds enshrined the art of oratory. The same Americans who found diversion and pleasure in lengthy political debates, who sought joy and God in the sermons of church and camp meeting, who had, in short, a seemingly inexhaustible appetite for the spoken word, thrilled to Shakespeare's eloquence, memorized his soliloquies, delighted in his dialogues. Although nineteenth-century Americans stressed the importance of literacy and built an impressive system of public education, theirs remained an oral world in which the spoken word was central. In such a world, Shakespeare had no difficulty finding a place.... Shakespeare was taught in nineteenth-century schools and colleges as declamation or rhetoric, not literature. For many youngsters Shakespeare was first encountered in schoolbooks as texts to be recited aloud and memorized.

Through such means, Shakespearean phrases, aphorisms, ideas, and language helped shape American speech and became so integral a part of the nineteenth-century imagination that it is a futile exercise to separate Americans' love of Shakespeare's oratory from their appreciation for his subtle use of language.

It was not merely Shakespeare's language but his style that recommended itself to nineteenth-century audiences. In a period when melodrama became one of the mainstays of the American stage, Shakespearean plays easily lent themselves to the melodramatic style. Shakespearean drama featured heroes and villains who communicated directly with the audience and left little doubt about the nature of their character or their intentions. In a series of asides during the opening scenes of the first act, Macbeth shares his "horrible imaginings" and "vaulting ambition" with the audience.... Iago, even as he plots against Othello, admits that "The Moor—howbeit that I endure him not—Is of a constant, loving, noble nature."

Lines like these, which so easily fit the melodramatic mode, were delivered in appropriately melodramatic style. The actors who dominated the stage during the first half of the nineteenth century were vigorous, tempestuous, emotional. To describe these men, contemporaries reached for words like "hurricane," "maelstrom," "avalanche," "earthquake," "monsoon," and "whirlwind." Edmund Kean's acting, one of them noted, was "just on the edge, sometimes quite over the edge of madness."... The first great American-born Shakespearean actor, Edwin Forrest, carried this romantic tradition to its logical culmination. William Rounseville Alger, who saw Forrest perform, described his portrayal of Lear after Goneril rebuffs him:

> His eyes flashed and faded and reflashed. He beat his breast as if not knowing what he did. His hands clutched wildly at the air as though struggling with something invisible. Then, sinking on his knees, with upturned look and hands straight outstretched towards his unnatural daughter, he poured out, in frenzied tones of mingled shriek and sob, his withering curse, half adjuration, half malediction.

As in melodrama itself, language and style in American productions of Shakespeare were not utilized randomly; they were used to inculcate values, to express ideas and attitudes.... Shakespeare's attraction for nineteenth-century audiences was due in no small part to the fact that he was—or at least was taken to be—in tune with much of nineteenth-century American consciousness. From the beginning, Shakespeare's American admirers and promoters maintained that he was pre-eminently a *moral* playwright. To overcome the general prejudice against the theater in the eighteenth-century, Shakespeare's plays were frequently presented as "moral dialogues" or "moral lectures." ...

Whatever Shakespeare's own designs, philosophy, and concept of humanity were, his plays had meaning to a nation that placed the individual at the center of the universe and personalized the large questions of the day. The actor Joseph Jefferson held Shakespeare responsible for the star system that prevailed for so much of the nineteenth century since "his tragedies almost without exception contain one great character on whom the interest of the play turns, and upon whom the attention of the audience is centered." Shakespeare's characters—like the Davy Crocketts and Mike Finks that dominated American folklore and the Jacksons, Websters, Clays, and Calhouns who dominated American politics—were larger than life: their passions, appetites, and dilemmas were of epic proportions. Here were forceful, meaningful people who faced, on a larger scale, the same questions as those that filled the pages of schoolbooks: the duties of children and parents, husbands and wives, governed and governors to one another. In their lives the problems of jealousy, morality, and ambition were all writ large. However flawed some of Shakespeare's central figures were, they at least acted—even the indecisive Hamlet—and bore responsibility for their own fate. If they failed, they did so because ultimately they lacked sufficient inner control. Thus Othello was undone by his jealousy and gullibility, Coriolanus by his pride, Macbeth and Richard III by their ambition. All of them could be seen as the architects of their own fortunes, masters of their own fate....

This ideological equation, this ability of Shakespeare to connect with Americans' underlying beliefs, is crucial to an understanding of his role in nineteenth-century America. Much has been made of the adaptations of Shakespeare as instruments that made him somehow more understandable to American audiences. Certainly, the adaptations did work this way—but not primarily, as has been so widely claimed, by vulgarizing or simplifying him to the point of utter distortion but rather by heightening those qualities in Shakespeare that American audiences were particularly drawn to....

The profound and longstanding nineteenth-century American experience with Shakespeare, then, was neither accidental nor aberrant. It was based upon the language and eloquence, the artistry and humor, the excitement and action, the moral sense and worldview that Americans found in Shakespearean drama. The more firmly based Shakespeare was in nineteenth-century culture, of course, the more difficult it is to understand why he lost so much of his audience so quickly....

So long as the theater was under attack on moral grounds, as it was in the eighteenth and early nineteenth centuries, Shakespeare, because of his immense reputation, could be presented more easily and could be used to help make the theater itself legitimate. Shakespearean drama also lent itself to the prevalent star system. Only the existence of a small repertory of well-known plays, in which Shakespeare's were central, made it feasible for the towering stars of England and America to travel throughout the United States acting with resident stock companies wherever they went. The relative dearth of native dramatists and the relative scarcity of competing forms of theatrical entertainment also figured in Shakespeare's popularity. As these conditions were altered, Shakespeare's popularity and centrality were affected. As important as factors peculiar to the theater were, the theater did not exist in a vacuum; it was an integral part of American culture—of interest to the historian precisely because it so frequently and so accurately indicated the conditions surrounding it. A fuller explanation must therefore be sought in the larger culture itself.

Among the salient cultural changes at the turn of the century were those in language and rhetorical style. The oratorical mode, which so dominated the nineteenth century and which helped make Shakespeare popular, hardly survived into the twentieth century. No longer did Americans tolerate speeches of several hour's duration…. The surprisingly rapid decline of oratory as a force in national life has not received the study it deserves, but certainly it was affected by the influx of millions of non-English-speaking people. The more than one thousand foreign-language newspapers and magazines published in the United States by 1910 testify graphically to the existence of a substantial group for whom Shakespeare, at least in his original language, was less familiar and less accessible. These immigrant folk helped constitute a ready audience for the rise of the more visual entertainments such as baseball, boxing, vaudeville, burlesque, and especially the new silent movies, which could be enjoyed by a larger and often more marginal audience less steeped in the language and the culture….

These language-related changes were accompanied by changes in taste and style. John Higham has argued that from the 1860s through the 1880s romantic idealism declined in the United States. The melodramatic mode, to which Shakespeare lent himself so well and in which he was performed so frequently, went into a related decline….

These gradual and decisive changes in language, style, and taste are important but by themselves do not constitute a totally satisfying explanation for the diminished popularity of Shakespeare. As important as changes in language were, they did not prevent the development of radio as a central entertainment medium at the beginning of the 1920s or the emergence of talking movies at the end of that decade. Nor was there anything inherent in the new popular media that necessarily relegated Shakespeare to a smaller, elite audience: on the contrary, he was quite well suited to the new forms of presentation that came to dominate. His comedies had an abundance of slapstick and contrived happy endings, his tragedies and historical plays had more than their share of action. Most importantly, having written for a stage devoid of scenery, Shakespeare could and did incorporate as much spatial mobility as he desired into his plays—twenty-five scene changes in *Macbeth,* one of his shortest plays, and forty-two in *Antony and Cleopatra*, where the action gravitated from Alexandria to such locales as Rome, Messina, Athens, and Syria. This fluidity—which caused innumerable problems for the stagecraft of the nineteenth century—was particularly appropriate to the movies, which could visually reproduce whatever Shakespeare had in mind, and to radio, which, like the Elizabethan stage itself, could rely upon the imagination of its audience. That these new media did not take full advantage of so recently a popular source of entertainment as Shakespearean drama demands further explanation.

Shakespeare did not, of course, disappear from American culture after the turn of the century; he was transformed from a playwright for the general public into one for a specific audience. This metamorphosis from popular culture to polite culture, from entertainment to erudition, from the property of "Everyman" to the possession of a more elite circle needs to be seen with the perspective of other transformations that took place in nineteenth-century America.

At the beginning of the century, as we have seen, the theater was a micro-cosm; it housed both the entire spectrum of the population and the complete range of entertainment from tragedy to farce, juggling to ballet, opera to minstrelsy....

In the theater, people not only sat under one roof, they interacted. In this sense, the theater in the first half of the nineteenth century constituted a micro-cosm of still another sort: a microcosm of the relations between the various socioeconomic groups in America....

Not only was there an increasing segregation of audiences but ultimately of actors and styles as well....

In 1810 John Howard Payne complained, "The judicious few are very few indeed. They are always to be found in a Theater, like flowers in a desert, but they are nowhere sufficiently numerous to *fill* one." By the second half of the century this was evidently no longer the case. Separate theaters, often called *legit-imate* theaters, catering to the "judicious," appeared in city after city, leaving the other theaters to those whom Payne called "the idle, profligate, and vulgar."...
As the traditional spatial distinctions among pit, gallery, and boxes within the theater were undermined by the aggressive behavior of audiences caught up in the egalitarian exhuberance of the period and freed in the atmosphere of the theater from many of the demands of normative behavior, this urge gradually led to the creation of separate theaters catering to distinct audiences and shattered for good the phenomenon of theater as a social microcosm of the entire society.

This dramatic split in the American theater was part of more important bifurcations that were taking place in American culture and society. How closely the theater registered societal dissonance can be seen in the audiences' volatile reaction to anything they considered condescending behavior, out of keeping with a democratic society. The tension created by hierarchical seating arrange-ments helps explain the periodic rain of objects that the gallery unleashed upon those in more privileged parts of the theater....

English actors, who were *ipso facto* suspected of aristocratic leanings, had to tread with particular caution....

The full extent of class feeling and divisions existing in egalitarian America was revealed on a bloody Thursday in May 1849 at and around the Astor Place Opera House in New York City. The immediate catalyst was a longstanding feud between two leading actors, the Englishman William Charles Macready and the American Edwin Forrest, who had become symbols of antithetical values. Forrest's vigorous acting style, his militant love of his country, his outspo-ken belief in its citizenry, and his frequent articulation of the possibilities of self-improvement and social mobility endeared him to the American people, while Macready's cerebral acting style, his aristocratic demeanor, and his identification with the wealthy gentry made him appear Forrest's diametric opposite. On May 7, Macready and Forrest appeared against one another in separate productions of *Macbeth*. Forrest's performance was a triumph; Macready's was never heard—he was silenced by a storm of boos and cries of "Down with the codfish aristocracy," which drowned out appeals for order from those in the boxes, and by an avalanche of eggs, apples, potatoes, lemons, and, ultimately, chairs hurled from the gallery, which forced him to leave the stage in the third act.

Macready was now prepared to leave the country as well, but he was dissuaded by persons of "highest respectability," including Washington Irving and Herman Melville, who urged him not to encourage the mob by giving in to it and assured him "that the good sense and respect for order prevailing in this community will sustain you." Eighteen hundred people filled the Astor Place Opera House on the evening of May 10, with some ten thousand more on the streets outside. Assisted by the quick arrest of the most voluble opponents inside the theater, Macready completed his performance of *Macbeth*, but only under great duress. Those outside—stirred by orators' shouts of "Burn the damned den of the aristocracy!" and "You can't go in there without ... kid gloves and a white vest, damn 'em!"—bombarded the theater with paving stones, attempted to storm the entrances, and were stopped only after detachments of militia fired point blank into the crowd. In the end at least twenty-two people were killed, and over one hundred and fifty were wounded or injured.

If the eighty-six men arrested were at all typical, the crowd had been composed of workingmen—coopers, printers, butchers, carpenters, servants, sail makers, machinists, clerks, masons, bakers, plumbers, laborers—whose feelings were probably reflected in a speech given at a rally the next day: "Fellow citizens, for what—for whom was this murder committed? ... To please the aristocracy of the city, at the expense of the lives of unoffending citizens ... to revenge the aristocrats of this city against the working classes." Although such observers as the New York *Tribune* saw the riot as the "absurd and incredible" result of a petty quarrel, the role of class was not ignored. The *Home Journal* viewed the riot as a protest against "aristocratizing the pit" in such new and exclusive theaters as the Astor Place Opera House and warned that in the future the republic's rich would have to "be mindful where its luxuries offend." The New York *Herald* asserted that the riot had introduced a "new aspect in the minds of many, ... nothing short of a controversy and collision between those who have been styled the 'exclusives.' or 'upper ten,' and the great popular masses." The New York correspondent for the Philadelphia *Public Ledger* lamented a few days after the riot, "It leaves behind a feeling to which this community has hitherto been a stranger—an opposition of classes—the rich and poor, ... a feeling that there is now in our country, in New York City, what every good patriot hitherto has considered it his duty to deny—*a high and a low class."*

The purpose of acting, Shakespeare had Hamlet say in his charge to the players, "was and is to hold, as 'twere, the mirror up to nature; to show virtue her own feature, scorn her own image, and the very age and body of time his form and pressure." The functions of the nineteenth-century American stage were even broader. As a central institution, the theater not only mirrored the sweep of events in the larger society but presented an arena in which those events could unfold. The Astor Place Riot was both an indication of and a catalyst for the cultural changes that came to characterize the United States at the end of the century. Theater no longer functioned as a cultural form that embodied all classes within a shared public space, nor did Shakespeare much longer remain the common property of all Americans. The changes were not cataclysmic; they were gradual and took place in rough stages: physical or spatial bifurcation, with different socioeconomic groups becoming associated with different theaters in large urban centers, was followed inevitably by the stylistic bifurcation described by George William Curtis and ultimately culminated in a content bifurcation, which saw a growing chasm between "serious" and "popular" culture.

Increasingly in the second half of the nineteenth century, as public life became everywhere more fragmented, the concept of culture took on hierarchical connotations along the lines of Matthew Arnold's definition—"the best that has been thought and known in the world …, the study and pursuit of perfection."… This practice of distinguishing "culture" from lesser forms of expression became so common that by 1915 Van Wyck Brooks found it necessary to incorporate the terms "highbrow" and "lowbrow" to express the chasm between which "there is no community, no genial middle ground." "What side of American life is not touched by this antithesis?" Brooks asked. "What explanation of American life is more central or more illuminating?"…

The emergence of new middle and upper-middle classes, created by rapid industrialization in the nineteenth century, seems to have accelerated rather than inhibited the growing distinctions between elite and mass culture…. "Culture" became something refined, ideal, removed from and elevated above the mundane events of everyday life….

It also helps explain the transformation of Shakespeare, who fit the new cultural equation so well. His plays had survived the test of time and were therefore immortal; his language was archaic and therefore too complex for ordinary people; his poetry was sublime and therefore elevating—especially if his plays could be seen in a theater and a style of one's own choice, devoid of constant reminders that they contained earthier elements and more universal appeals as well. The point is not that there was a conspiracy to remove Shakespeare from the American people but that a cultural development occurred which produced the same result—a result that was compounded by the fact during these years American entertainment was shaped by many of the same forces of consolidation and centralization that molded other businesses.

If the managers of the new theater chains and huge booking agencies approached their tasks with a hierarchical concept of culture, with the conviction that an unbridgeable gulf separated the tastes and predilections of the various socioeconomic groups, and with the belief that Shakespeare was "highbrow" culture, then we have isolated another decisive factor in his transformation.

The transformation of Shakespeare is important precisely because it was not unique. It was part of a larger transformation … in which public culture fractured into a series of discrete private cultures that had less and less to do with one another. The audience that had been heterogeneous, interactive, and participatory became homogeneous, atomized, and passive….

This is not to suggest the existence of an idyllic era when the American people experienced a cultural unity devoid of tensions…. Still, America in the first half of the nineteenth century did experience greater cultural sharing in the sense that cultural lines were more fluid, cultural spaces less rigidly subdivided than they were to become. Certainly, what I have called a shared public culture did not disappear with the nineteenth century. Twentieth-century Americans, especially in the places they built to the movies and in their sporting arenas, continued to share public space and public culture. But with a difference. Cultural space became more sharply defined, more circumscribed, and less fluid than it had been. Americans might sit together to watch the same films and athletic contests, but those who also desired to experience "legitimate" theater or hear "serious" music went to segregated temples devoted to "high" or "classical" art. Cultural lines are generally porous, and there were important exceptions—Toscanini was featured on commercial radio and television, and Shakespeare's works were offered on the movie screen. But these were conscious exceptions to what normally prevailed. The cultural fare that was actively and regularly shared by all segments of the population belonged to the lower rungs of the cultural hierarchy.

As we gradually come to the realization that Fred Astaire was one of this century's fine dancers, Louis Armstrong one of its important musicians, Charlie Chaplin one of its acute social commentators, we must remember that they could be shared by all of the people only when they were devalued as "popular" art, only when they were rendered nonthreatening by being relegated to the nether regions of the cultural complex. By the twentieth century, art could not have it both ways: no longer could it simultaneously enjoy high cultural status and mass popularity. Shakespeare is a prime example. He retained his lofty position only by being limited and confined to audiences whose space was no longer shared with, and whose sensibilities no longer violated by, the bulk of the populace.

Audiences Enjoy Being Fooled by P.T. Barnum

NEIL HARRIS

At the end of August 1843, New York newspaper advertisements announced a "Grand Buffalo Hunt, Free of Charge," to take place on a Thursday afternoon in Hoboken. A Mr. C. D. French, "one of the most daring and experienced hunters of the West," had captured the animals near Santa Fe at considerable risk to life and limb. Strong fences would protect the public from the savage beasts, who would be lassoed and hunted as part of the entertainment. What the newspaper advertisements did not say was that the buffaloes were feeble, docile beasts, hardly capable of movement, much less of violence. Barnum had purchased the herd for seven hundred dollars when he saw it earlier that summer in Massachusetts and had stowed it away for several weeks in New Jersey. Knowing that the spectacle might not be all the audience anticipated, Barnum wisely decided to make admission free. What he did not disclose was an

Neil Harris, "The Operational Aesthetic," in *Humbug: The Art of P.T. Barnum* (Chicago: University of Chicago Press, 1973). Reprinted by permission from the author.

arrangement with the ferryboat owners who would transport the public from Manhattan to New Jersey; his profits were to come from a percentage of the fares.

The great day finally arrived, and boatloads of spectators crossed to New Jersey. There were to be several shows, and by the time the first batch of spectators had seen the hunt, a second batch was passing them on the Hudson. The returnees called out from their boats that the hunt—a debacle in which the frightened animals fled to a nearby swamp—was the biggest humbug imaginable. Instead of being disappointed, however, the expectant audience, in the words of a witness, "Instantly gave three cheers for the author of the humbug, whoever he might be."

Barnum told the whole story in his autobiography. He understood that American audiences did not mind cries of trickery; in fact, they delighted in debate. Amusement and deceit could coexist; people would come to see something they suspected might be exaggeration or even a masquerade. Any publicity was better than none at all, and if the audiences did not get all they anticipated, they had a pleasant outing in New Jersey for the price of a boat ride.

The principles of the Hoboken hunt—the national tolerance for clever imposture—was one Barnum relied on again and again in his early museum days. As he was building up his cabinet of natural curiosities, he couldn't resist making his exhibits a bit more enticing than literal truth permitted….

The most famous put-on of all, or the one on which Barnum exercised his most vigorous ingenuity, was the "Fejee Mermaid." The origin of the mermaid is shrouded in mystery, but according to Barnum—not the most reliable but the only witness—he encountered this oddity in the summer of 1842. Moses Kimball owned the mermaid, having purchased it from a sailor, and he offered to share exhibition profits (and costs) with Barnum. Before parting with any money Barman referred the matter to a naturalist, who pronounced the object manufactured. When Barnum asked the naturalist why he gave this verdict, he replied, "Because I don't believe in mermaids." With only faith at stake, Barnum decided to ignore the advice. But he realized that more objective observers might take a bit more convincing.

On June 18, 1842, Barnum and Kimball signed an agreement. For twelve dollars and fifty cents a week Barnum was to lease the mermaid and hire a manager for it (at no more than eight dollars a week, or one quarter of the net profits). Promising "to take all proper and possible care of said curiosity and not allow it to be handled or in any manner injured or abused," and agreeing "to exert himself to the atmost without regard to trouble or expense to bring it before the public," Barnum would share the profits with Kimball. Thus, Barnum never became literally the owner of the mermaid, a fact he would use to advantage in the controversy that followed.

The campaign of preparation was long and tortuous. In the early summer of 1842 letters were sent to New York newspapers from various southern cities— Montgomery. Charleston, Washington—mentioning a British naturalist who had with him a remarkable mermaid owned by the Lyceum of Natural History in London and said to have originated in the "Fejee [Fiji] Islands."…

The mermaid itself, as Barnum agreed, was hardly an object of beauty. It consisted of the body of a fish and the head and hands of a monkey. "The animal was an ugly, dried-up, black-looking, and diminutive specimen, about three feet long. Its mouth was open, its tail turned over, and its arms thrown up, giving it the appearance of having died in great agony." Even if it had been manufactured, as Barnum suspected, the object was a superb piece of craftsmanship, for it seemed impossible to see where the fish and the monkey had been "joined." For the moment, however, emphasis was on its natural origins, ... Barnum arranged for reporters to call and examine the curiosity. They were convinced it was genuine.... Barnum then made the rounds of the New York papers, offering free use of a mermaid woodcut, explaining that he had it made in hopes of exhibiting the mermaid.... On Sunday, July 17, 1842, each editor, convinced he had an exclusive, printed the woodcut, and Barnum distributed ten thousand copies of the pamphlet on mermaids through the city.... And then, ... the mermaid was brought to the American Museum and therein presented "without extra charge."

At the time, Barnum was well pleased with his coup. In the first four weeks of the mermaid's exhibition, museum receipts almost tripled. Obviously, the careful campaign of publicity... the reports from other cities, the transparencies, pamphlets, and newspaper puffs had produced results. Moreover, promoted in part by the growth of racism, debates about the immutability of species and the divine plan were vigorous. A number of Americans, arguing for the perpetuation of black slavery, challenged belief in the unity of mankind. The races of mankind, men like Dr. Josiah Nott insisted, had been created at separate times and formed distinctive species. The Mossic description in Genesis was ignorant and incorrect, said Nott, and belief in the equality of man, an assumption of Jefferson's generation, was ill-founded. Into this atmosphere of controversy, any bizarre product of Nature that might bear on biblical narrative or the relationship among species was bound to find a large audience.

In later years, as dignity and philanthropy figured more importantly among Barnum's objectives, he grew reticent about the mermaid episode. The fraud was so transparent, no matter who had originally manufactured the article, and the campaign of deception was so elaborate, that it took the most artful rationalizations to justify it. Even then, Barnum had to take care. Faced with newspaper indignation and a certain level of public clamor, he curbed his publicity plans.... And the advertising changed in tone. In 1843 Barnum suggested a more cautiously worded description of the mermaid, emphasizing the problematic rather than the assured.... "Who is to decide," an advertisement asked piously, "when *doctors* disagree?" But whether the mermaid was "the work of *nature* or art it is decidedly the most stupendous curiosity ever submitted to the public for inspection. If it is artificial the senses of sight and touch are ineffectual—if it is natural then all concur in declaring it *the greatest Curiosity in the World*."...

Barnum had realized the values of disagreement earlier ... [and] [h]e acted on it again when he arranged for someone to prosecute him for imposture on the grounds that the American Museum's bearded lady was a man. With great unwillingness, or so it seemed, Barnum arranged for a medical examination, and crowds poured in for a closer look. This time his triumph was total, as he had both truth and profits on his side. But as usual, truth was more expendable than cash receipts.

The frequency with which Barnum repeated this pattern of planted objections, denials, and countercharges raises some questions concerning his audience. Barnum's success was so great and so long-lasting … that there had to be more to it than the simple collection of curiosities on which other entrepreneurs had already given up. To explain it, at least two questions must be answered. First, why were Americans apparently so credulous, why could they be fooled so easily, why did they flock to see mermaids, woolly horses, and other anatomical monstrosities that seem in later days to be so patently false? Why did they accept commonplace objects—wooden legs, articles of clothing, minerals and weapons— as sacred relics associated with famous men and historic events? And second, why did Americans enjoy watching shows and visiting exhibits that they suspected might be contrived, why did they flock to witness impostures that they knew about? In other words, why the apparent naïtivé about deception, and why the pleasure in experiencing deception after knowledge of it had been gained? …

Edgar Allan Poe … [I]n "Diddling Considered as One of the Exact Sciences," noted the prevalence of deception on both a large and a small scale. "A crow thieves; a fox cheats; a weasel outwits; a man diddles." The successful diddler was ingenious, audacious, persevering, original, and entirely self-interested. Poe described some of the successful variations. A camp meeting would be held near a free bridge. "A diddler stations himself upon this bridge, respectfully informs all passers-by of the new country law which establishes a toll of one cent for foot passengers, two for horses and donkeys, and so forth and so forth. Some grumble but all submit, and the diddler goes home a wealthier man by some $50 or $60 well earned." This scene was not the product of Poe's imagination but actually took place, one of the innumerable devices by which Americans tricked each other.

At first glance, America appeared an unlikely setting for either the successful hoaxer or the successful diddler. According to foreign travelers and native critics alike, one of America's besetting vices was an aggressive individualism that disinclined the citizen to trust anyone or anything, a cynical suspicion of idealism and pure motives. Frances Trollope, Harriet Martineau, and Charles Dickens found the typical American a hardheaded, hard-bitten realist, shrewd, cautious, suspicious, sparing in speech, narrow in sentiment, refusing to credit surface appearances and demanding proof for any statement, particularly any statement impugning American greatness….

One explanation for the prevalence of hoaxes in the competitive materialism of American life focused on the proximity of the frontier—an untamed natural world fraught with obstacles and dangers. Constance Rourke, Richard Chase, and Kenneth Lynn have pointed to the relationship between the hoax and the western tall take, with its characteristic boasting and exaggeration….

But this explanation does not account for the popularity and effectiveness of practical joking in eastern cities, physically and spiritually hundreds of miles away from the frontier. A full explanation for the effectiveness of the pranksters must take account of the advanced technical and material conditions of American life. By the 1830s and 1840s portions of the United States were as advanced in those areas as any part of the Old World; innovations like the railroad and the telegraphs were greeted with enthusiasm and constructed with rapidity. American mechanics and toolmakers competed with European rivals. There was widespread interest in and support for scientific progress. Physical improvement had become inextricably connected with the genius of American civilization....

American experiences with science and technology was crucial to the hoaxing attempts, but this ... led not to less credulity but to more. A vital factor in the success of the hoaxes was national skepticism itself. Men accustomed to examining the truth or validity of every person, idea, object or act presented to them—as Americans proverbially were—became easy targets for pseudoscientific explanation, for detailed descriptions of fictional machinery, for any fantasy that was couched in the bland neutrality of a technological vocabulary. Men priding themselves on their rationalistic, scientific bent, familiar with the operation of novel machines, aware of the variety of nature, tended to accept as true anything which seemed to work—or seemed likely to work. The coming of steam, of railroads, of telegraphs indicated the futility of declaring anything impossible or incredible Nothing mechanical was beyond the range of Nature's imagination....

Not only was the predisposition to accept the mechanically probable or the organically possible a result of changing technology and the growth of natural science, it was also a peculiarly patriotic portion in Jacksonism America. At a time when the advantages of a common school education were being extolled by reformers, when the common sense of the average citizen was proposed as a guarantee for the republic's future, many democrats assumed that any problem could be expressed clearly, concisely, and comprehensibly enough for the ordinary man to resolve it. Secret information and private learning were anathema. All knowledge was meant to be shared. Contemporary pamphleteers delighted in ridiculing experts and specialists; the expert turned out frequently to be a pedantic ignoramus, easily fooled himself; the learned doctor was often a victim of scientific nonsense and deserved to be overruled by intelligent laymen. "When *doctors* disagree," Barnum had phrased it in his mermaid advertisement, then it was up to ordinary men to decide for themselves.

This emphasis on individual learning and confidence in popular majorities made Americans inveterate lecturers and lecture-goers....

The American was eager to import whatever he knew, politically but volubly....

Technological progress and egalitarian self-confidence combined to make many Americans certain of their own opinions—and so, easy prey for the hoaxers. And these traits were supplemented by the sheer exhilaration of debate, the utter fun of the opportunity to learn and evaluate, whether the subject was an ancient slave, an exotic mermaid, or a politician's honor. Barnum's audience found the encounter with potential frauds exciting. It was a form of intellectual exercise, stimulating even when literal truth could not be determined. Machinery was beginning to accustom the public not merely to a belief in the continual appearance of new marvels but to a jargon that concentrated on methods of operation, on aspects of mechanical organization and construction, on horsepower, gears, pulleys, and safety valves....

This delight in learning explains why the experience of deceit was enjoyable even after the hoax had been penetrated, or at least during the period of doubt and suspicion. Experiencing a complicated hoax was pleasurable because of the competition between victim and hoaxer, each seeking to outmaneuver the other, to catch him off-balance and detect the critical weakness. Barnum, Poe, ... and other hoaxers didn't fear public suspicion; they invited it. They understood, most particularly Barnum understood, that the opportunity to debate the issue of falsity, to discover how deception had been practiced, was even more exciting than the discovery of fraud itself. The manipulation of a prank, after all, was as interesting a technique in its own right as the presentation of genuine curiosities. Therefore, when people paid to see frauds, thinking they were true, they paid again to hear how the frauds were committed. Barnum reprinted his own ticket-seller's analysis. "First he humbugs them, and then they pay to hear him tell how he did it. I believe if he should swindle a man out of twenty dollars, the man would give a quarter to hear him tell about it."...

There is one final reason why American audiences responded to Barnum's techniques and so enjoyed practical joking. The practice of humbugging solved some special problems of the mass sensibility, problems particularly acute in America, where cultural ambitions outstripped cultural achievements. Concentration on whether a particular show, exhibit, or event was real or false, genuine or contrived, narrowed the task of judgment for the multitude of spectators. It structured problems of experiencing the exotic and unfamiliar by reducing that experience to a simple evaluation.

Many Americans, however much they admired and respected the realm of art, feared its mysteries. They were uncomfortable encountering masterpieces because they could neither analyze nor justify their reactions. Art exhibitions, when they were organized with theatrical settings and sentimental appeals—Hiram Power's sensationally popular "Greek Slave," for example—were crowded with onlookers. And patriotic appeals aided the art unions of the forties and fifties in distributing thousands of lithographs of landscapes and genre paintings. But these were, on the whole, exceptional experiences. No great public galleries existed for the public to stroll through; no historic buildings featured ancient murals and statuary. Instead, painting and sculpture stood alongside mummies, mastodon bones and stuffed animals. American museums were not, in the antebellum period, segregated temples of the fine arts, but repositories of information, collections of strange or doubtful data. Such indiscriminate assemblages made artistic objects take on the innocent yet familiar shape of exhibition curiosities. Contemplating a painting or a statue was not so different from studying Napoleon's cane or wood from Noah's ark; in every instance, a momentary brush with a historical artifact stimulating reflections on its cost, age, detail, and rarity.

The American Museum then, as well as Barnum's elaborate hoaxes, trained Americans to absorb knowledge. This was an aesthetic of the operational, a delight in observing process and examining for literal truth. In place of intensive spiritual absorption, Barnum's exhibitions concentrated on information and the problem of deception. Onlookers were relieved from the burden of coping with more abstract problems. Beauty, significance, spiritual values could be bypassed in favor of seeing what was odd, or what worked, or was genuine.

FURTHER READING

Agnew, Jean-Christophe. *Worlds Apart: The Market and the Theater in Anglo-American Throught, 1550–1750* (1988).

Ahlquist, Karen. *Democracy at the Opera: Music, Theater, and Culture in New York City, 1815–1860* (1997).

Allen, Robert. *Horrible Prettiness* (1991).

Bogdan, Robert. *Freak Show: Presenting Human Oddities for Amusement and Profit* (1988).

Butsch, Richard. *The Citizen Audience* (2008).

———. *The Making of American Audiences* (2000).

Cook, Jay W. *The Arts of Deception: Playing with Fraud in the Age of Barnum* (2001).

Crary, Jonathan. *Techniques of the Observer* (1992).

Gilje, Paul A. *The Road to Mobocracy: Popular Disorder in New York City*, 1763–1834 (1987).

Grimsted, David. *Melodrama Unveiled* (1987).

Gutman, Herbert. *Work, Culture and Society in Industrializing America* (1976).

Orvell, Miles. *The Real Thing: Imitation and Authenticity in American Culture, 1880–1940* (1989).

Reiss, Benjamin. *The Showman and the Slave: Race, Death, and Memory in Barnum's America* (2001).

Snyder, Robert. *The Voice of the City: Vaudeville and Popular Culture in New York* (1989).

Thomson, Rosemarie Garland, ed. *Freakery: Cultural Spectacles of the Extraordinary Body* (1996).

Toll, Robert. *The Entertainment Machine: Show Business in Twentieth-Century America* (1982).

CHAPTER 4

World's Fairs, Circuses, and Wild West Shows Express Ideas about U.S. Imperialism, 1876–1918

Even as historian Frederick Jackson Turner declared the American frontier closed in his famous speech at the 1893 World's Columbian Exposition in Chicago, American leaders in politics, business, and entertainment expanded the territorial and economic boundaries of the United States. The United States gained control of new territories during the Spanish-American War of 1898, including Puerto Rico, Cuba, and Hawaii, increasing America's political power and economic reach. Popular culture played a critical role in the economic expansion of the United States; it provided places where Americans could make sense of the colossal changes underway; satisfied their curiosity about new territories, peoples, and products; and provided a rationale for American imperialism. As historians and sociologists such as Janet Davis, Robert Rydell, and Tony Bennett have shown, world's fairs, wild west shows, and circuses offered critical frameworks for understanding the benefits of expansion. World's fairs and circuses, in particular, imported and exhibited goods and people from places such as Hawaii and the Philippines to the United States and, in turn, exported political mythologies of American exceptionalism along with a host of new consumer products. As grand spectacles, these popular forms fed American interest in new technologies, racial difference, and national distinctions. All three forms presented industrialization and technological innovation as social progress and they affirmed national unity at a moment of extreme social disunity in the wake of Reconstruction and at the height of immigration. They also provided Americans with models of racialized social hierarchies as seen in the exhibition of various races at world's fairs and what scholars have referred to as powerful "object lessons" in American exceptionalism because they relied so heavily on material displays and performances. In other words, popular culture underscored the idea of American expansion as part of the moral mission of the United States to aid and uplift less-civilized or less-advanced societies.

With the growth of corporate capitalism in the United States, popular entertainments such as the railroad circus and wild west shows became big businesses, aided by innovations in transportation, communication, business organization, and advertising. For their part, world's fairs, which began with London's Crystal Palace exhibition in 1851, offered a way for businesses and manufacturers to show off and promote their wares to huge crowds both in the United States and Western Europe. Hundreds of fairs, large and small, were produced in the decades between 1876 and World War I, through collaboration among leaders in business, politics, and intellectual life. Taken together, all of these forms emphasized the progress of western civilization, a progress staked on innovations in technology and business. Where the national circus rode the rails and was a wonder of industrial organization, and wild west shows demonstrated military technology, fairs introduced American consumers to a host of new products from exotic fruits to bicycles.

Historians of popular culture have been interested in how cultural commodities and performances articulated and complicated the goals of U.S. expansion at this critical moment in American history; they have examined how commercial performances and entertainments, even in their earliest forms, were part of the circulation of commodities and cultural imperialsim in the nineteenth century. How did popular culture support and sometimes critique expansion? How did commercial leisure spread ideas of American exceptionalism, white supremacy, and technological innovation as social progress? How did audiences in the United States and abroad receive these messages?

 # DOCUMENTS

The following primary sources illustrate how popular culture forms played critical roles in the intense debates about American expansion in this period. The first two documents exemplify the global reach and visual power of these entertainments. Advances in printing technology made inexpensive color reproductions possible in the late nineteenth century and advance men literally papered towns with broadsides, or posters, advertising the eye-popping and educational spectacles at circuses and wild west shows. In particular, advertising touted the educational value of such entertainments, including historical reenactments of the discovery of America and maritime battles during the recently concluded Spanish-American War. Document 3 provides a detailed schedule and description of performances for Ringling Brothers' circus during 1898, the same year as the Spanish-American War, that shows the incorporation of reenactments and nationalistic fare among the standard circus performances. Document 4 illustrates the political nature of circuses with this popular re-enactment of scenes from the Spanish American War. Document 5 traces the experiences of Jules Turnour, a professional clown who traveled across continents to perform in the circus. Turnour speaks to the international origins of circus performers and documents many of the hardships of being a traveling performer. Document 6 compares Buffalo Bill to Napoleon.

1. British Journalist Fred A. McKenzie
Notes the Americanization of the United
Kingdom, 1901
All American

In the domestic life we have got to this: The average man rises in the morning from his New England sheets, he shaves with "Williams'" soap and a Yankee safety razor, pulls on his Boston boots over his socks from North Carolina, fastens his Connecticut braces, slips his Waltham or Waterbury watch in his pocket, and sits down to breakfast. There he congratulates his wife on the way her Illinois straight-front corset sets off her Massachusetts blouse, and he tackles his breakfast, where he eats bread made from prairie flour (possibly doctored at the special establishments on the lakes), tinned oysters from Baltimore, and a little Kansas City bacon, while his wife plays with a slice of Chicago ox-tongue. The children are given "Quaker" oats. At the same time he reads his morning paper printed by American machines, on American paper with American ink, and, possibly, edited by a smart journalist from New York City.

He rushes out, catches the electric tram (New York) to Shepherd's Bush; where he gets in a Yankee elevator to take him on to the American-fitted electric railway to the city.

At his office, of course, everything is American. He sits on a Nebraskan swivel chair, before a Michigan roll-top desk, writes his letters on a Syracuse typewriter, signing them with a New York fountain pen, and drying them with a blotting-sheet from New England. The letter copies are put away in files manufactured in Grand Rapids.

At lunch time he hastily swallows some cold roast beef that comes from the Mid-West cow, and flavors it with Pittsburg pickles, followed by a few Delaware tinned peaches, and then soothes his mind with a couple of Virginia cigarettes.

To follow his course all day would be wearisome. But when evening comes he seeks relaxation at the latest American musical comedy, drinks a cocktail or some California wine, and finished up with a couple of "little liver pills" "made in America."

2. *Literary Digest* Sees World's
Fairs as Educational, 1904
Educational Value of The World's Fair

... President William F. Slocum, of Colorado College, pays a remarkable tribute ... to the World's Fair as an educative force, declaring that the Exposition is in all essential points "as perfect an illustration as has been seen of the method of the 'University of the Future,' which is to exchange pictures and living objects

Fred A. McKenzie, *The American Invaders: Their Plans, Tactics and Progress* (New York: Smith Street Publishers, 1901).

"The Educational Value of the World's Fair," *Literary Digest*, 13(August 1904), 192.

for text-books, and to make these, with the aid of laboratory work, the means whereby instruction is [to be] given and individual development to be obtained." He says further:

> One need only recall what the other great fairs have done to enlighten and educate the masses of people who have flocked to them to be sure that this, too, will have its own definite and direct results, tho it may be too early now to tell what these are to be, with the same certainty with which we note the specific outcome of each of the others....

President Slocum is hardly willing to contend, as some have done, that "a ramble through a World's Fair is an equivalent for a liberal education." But he thinks that "too much emphasis can not be laid on the value of such a ramble to the open-eyed and open-souled thousands who have waited for this event to gain their first vital knowledge of the way other workers do their work." He continues:...

> So thoroughly does it represent the world's civilization that if all man's other works were by some unspeakable catastrophe blotted out, the records here established by the assembled nations would offer all necessary standards for the rebuilding of our entire civilization.

... It is significant of the place that social science and educational work have taken in the thought of the world that, for the first time, an entire building in a great exposition has been set apart for their exhibits; and yet the demand for space, both from foreign nations and the United States, was so great that it was impossible to provide for them all in this building, with its more than seven acres of floor space. Here, perhaps more than anywhere else, the parent or teacher with the most limited training stands side by side with the traveled expert, and both carry away the best the Exposition has for them.

Mr. Walter H. Page, writing in *The World's Work* on "The People as an Exhibit," has this to say:

> The people are in a holiday, communicative, inquisitive mood; but it is not an idle mood. They are very much in earnest. If you stand a moment, for example, at the German exhibit of artistic rooms, you will hear one woman say to another, 'I see how I can make my dining-room much prettier.' Everywhere they are learning something. Wherever an idea may be got, there is a crowd. They ask questions frankly and directly. 'I wish to know how to do this.' 'I want this.' It may be a typewriter that will write with two colors of ink; it may be a new kitchen utensil; it may be a new idea in education.

> "You may discuss great fairs—their advantages or disadvantages to the cities in which they are held, the losses they cause stockholders, the wisdom or the unwisdom of the appropriation of public money to them—the fact remains that they play an important part in the education of the people. And they reveal the eagerness of the people to learn. The

unrestricted opportunity of our democracy has brought an unrestricted ambition to know both useful and beautiful things. The people are at school here; and the wise exhibitor is the exhibitor who teaches something."

3. The Circus Encounters the Spanish-American War in the United States, 1898
Ringling Brothers' Official Program

A1. Ringling, Equestrienne Director

Ringmasters: Fred Clarke, John Slater, John Rooney, Dan. Leon

Ringling Brothers' Military Band

Geo. Ganweiler, Conductor

Popular Concert preceding each performance. Numbers rendered from the following repertoire, and announced by placard displayed from band stand, corresponding with numbers of selections as below.

1. March
2. Overture, The Hermit's Bell—Mallard
3. Scotch Melodies—Bonnisseau
4. Paraphrase: Sweet Alice, Ben Bolt—Luck; The Bride Elect (March)—Sousa
5. Scenes from Carmen—Bizet's
6. Invocation to Battle (Rienzi)—R. Wagner; Dance des Sultanes—Polak Daniels
7. Overture, Hunting for Luck—Suppe
8. Descriptive Piece, Columbus—Herman. Synopsis: Torchlight Dance, The Sorrow of Departure, Fealty to the Flag, Anchors Weighed, On the Vast Waters, Chorus and Dance of the Sailors, Storm, The Storm Gradually Abates, Prayer, Melancholy, Mutiny, Columbus Quells the Disturbance, Land Ho! Salute of the Guns, Hail Columbia....
28. **Popular American Airs—Theo. Coates. Hail Columbia, Our Army and Navy Forever, Yankee Doodle, Star Spangled Banner.**
29. Tone Pictures of the North and South—Bendix

Display No. 1—Dazzling Introductory Pageant, presenting the Inaugural Ceremonies of the Grand Fetes of Ancient Olympus. A Brilliant Kaleidoscopic Panorama of Regal Magnificence, completely filling all the Rings, Stages and Immense Hippodrome Concourse.

Red Wagon Annual. *A Route Book of Ringling Brothers World's Greatest Shows* (Chicago: Central Printing and Engraving Co. Program, Season 1898). www.circushistory.org/History/Ringling1898.htm

The Tour of 1898

Containing an Account of Events of More or Less Importance.

St. Louis, Mo. April 11th to 20th. The season of 1898 marks the fifteenth annual milestone in the history of the World's Greatest Shows.

It was fourteen years ago last spring that the original nine wagons upon which everything comprising what was then called the "Old Yankee Robinson and Ringling Bros.' Great Double Shows" were first hauled from town to town by a very "measly" lot of horses.

Fourteen years is not a long time when reckoned by years, but when computed by days and all by all the events crowded into those days, a great long panorama of past history and events unfolds itself to the memory and makes those few years seem like an age. Circus life is brimful of these events, and each season has enough of them to fill a book. Therefore, almost every show publishes a volume at the end of each season known as a route book, which chronicles the events of the season, and that is the apology for the publication of this volume. To tell the most important happenings and many of the minor ones and to incidentally leave a memento of one of the most important seasons in the history of the great show in the hands of the hundreds of employees who each in his or her way contributed by personal effort toward the success of the season of 1898, is the mission of this little book. To many out of the profession, there may be much of interest in the following pages. And then again, there may not be. It rests entirely with the disposition of the reader, whether he interests himself in the world as it exists outside his own immediate sphere, or not. To cut what might become a long introduction short and avoid unnecessary and perhaps tiresome digression, the Ringling Brothers' World's Greatest Shows opened the season of 1898 in St. Louis Mo....

Opening day, April 11th dawned bright and clear. For almost two weeks previous the trainloads of circus paraphernalia had been arriving, and preparatory to the event rehearsals by the army of artists, performers, musicians, etc., had been given. The preparation of aerial and other acts requiring apparatuses to be adjusted to the dome of the Coliseum had been completed....

The parade was advertised to leave … at 8:30, and promptly at that hour it started. The entire route was lined with dense throngs that filled every available point of vantage, windows, balconies, doorsteps and sidewalks.... The street cars of the entire downtown district were in a condition of chaos and for over four hours the entire city was given over to the circus. Though the 400 horses in the parade were green from winter quarters, and the score of elephants had not seen street cars in five months, the casualties, aside from one, were few and insignificant....

Although our engagement here was filled with "war" and "rumors of war," the notable "Declaration of War" being made while here, and public excitement was at its highest tension, yet it seemed in no way to affect the large crowds..., and public interest never lagged from the opening to the close. It was from this city, April 14th, the telegram was sent to the secretary of war, Russell A. Alger, which received universal commendation and showed the patriotism of "The Famous Five." The appended extract from the St. Louis Post-Dispatch will fully explain:

Elephants for Cuba

Ringling Brothers Make a Tender of Their Herd to the War Department.

For the Artillery Service....

Ringling Brothers have decided to offer the government the use of a herd of twenty-five trained elephants for light artillery service in Cuba when war shall have been declared.

The value of the elephant in such service has been fully demonstrated in India, Burmah and elsewhere in the East. Its great strength, endurance, docility and sagacity make it almost invaluable in places where horses and other methods of transportation are unavailable. Elephants are not only useful in hauling heavy artillery over rough roads, underbrush and fresh trails, but guns of lighter caliber can be strapped to their backs and they can be trained so that they can be fired from that vantage, and the elephants remain perfectly still, unfrightened by the noise and concussion.

Alfred Ringling, who originated the plan, thinks the animals can be utilized in various other ways. They are great swimmers, and they could be used to transport troops and supplies over unbridged streams in the interior.

The animals could be equipped with coats of mail, as they are in India, and a herd so armored would form a movable fort of great utility in the open field, and would be a shelter behind which a considerable force could operate at considerable advantage....

The Ringlings have elephant keepers and trainers who are willing to enlist to direct their movements, they think their herd would prove a valuable addition to the American forces in Cuba, should that country be occupied in carrying out the plan of armed intervention.

With the approval of his brothers and partners, Alfred Ringling made a formal tender of the herd Thursday ... to the Secretary of War....

Belleville, Ill, Friday, April 22. The road season of 1898 was formally opened here. Of course there was the usual hand-shaking of old friends of former seasons; the pleasures and hardships of the past winter discussed; the sizing up of new forces, etc.; the spread of canvas examined by critical eyes and compared with other shows, and former seasons; the band, parade and performance receiving its share of attention from the employees—thus in its baptism of criticism, favorable and unfavorable, the World's Greatest Shows inaugurated its fifteenth road season. The side show people began their season here as the "Museum of Wonders."...

Washington, D.C. Monday and Tuesday. May 2 and 3. The National Capitol, situated on the banks of the Potomac river, and surrounded by places of interest dear to the heart of every American citizen. It is here the laws are made and upheld that control the destinies of a great nation, which is now battling for the freedom of a weak country which has thrown off the yoke of tyranny which has oppressed it so long, and the city is full of war talk and the cry of "War Extra" is heard on every hand. We arrived late Sunday night, but Monday, bright and early, found us on the lot on East Capitol avenue. The parade was out on time, and was an innovation to many who did not believe the circus bill boards. The majority of "troupers" spend all their spare time in viewing the many public buildings and other places of interest the Capital building, Congressional Library, Treasury, and the Washington Monument receiving the greatest percentage of "tourists," many of whom contributed umbrellas and small parcels that they left with the door tenders and under the excitement of the occasion came away without them. Ed. Brady and Van Cleve each contributed umbrellas to the hungry horde of government clerks. Joe Le Fluer left for his home in Providence, R. I., to give his knee proper rest. This city is the home of the Carrolls, who spent the time pleasantly visiting relatives and friends. This is where the hen said she had been "laying for them," and they had eggs for breakfast. **Very tough and saucy negroes here. News of the victory of Manila, in which Commodore Dewey placed the entire Spanish fleet hors de combat, received here and the populace are wild with excitement and delight....**

4. The Circus Re-Enacts the Spanish–American War, 1899

5. Circus Clown Jules Turnour Comments on His International Travels, 1910

... I had been traveling all over Europe, first with one circus and then, another. My work as clown developed. Of course, in passing from one country to the

Library of Congress Prints and Photographs Division Washington, D.C.
[LC-USZC4-5232]

Isaac Marcosson, *The Autobiography of a Clown* (New York: Mead and Co., 1910).

other I picked up the different Continental languages. This was highly important, because I had often to carry on a sort of running conversation with the spectators.

Like every other circus performer I had many escapes from death. My body and arms were soon covered with scars, each one a souvenir of some accident. At the Circus Cliniselli in Berlin I was knocked down by a horse, which walked on my face. One hoof laid my cheek open. The crowd thought it was part of the show, and laughed, while I suffered tortures, not knowing what the animal would do next....

We went on an elaborate tour, and reached Mexico. There we played many small towns. It was hard traveling, for Mexico was a rude country with few cities. We had to journey by donkey and by stage; the roads were bad and the land infested with brigands. All the men in our troupe were heavily armed....

We traveled through Mexico and some of the Central American countries. Finally we reached the Pacific coast. The Combination was headed for South America and wanted me to go along, but I declined. I was in the New World, and I wanted to see something of it. Besides, my mother had come to New York to live. She had married for the second time, her new husband being a manufacturer of fireworks.

I took the first boat for San Francisco. It gave me a sort of thrill to step ashore there, for the United States had always beckoned to me. I felt that there could be no hardship here. The land was smiling and the sky was as blue as Italy's.

I crossed the continent to New York and went straight to my mother's. She lived in a little flat on Third Avenue. You must remember that I had not seen her for nineteen years. Almost tremblingly I mounted the steps and rang the bell at her door. It seemed an age before the knob turned and the door opened. In the doorway I saw a stout woman, who stared at me curiously. I saw that she did not recognize me....

But I was glad to be back even in the pretense of a home. I inquired eagerly of my sisters. One of them, Millie, had become a great balancing trapeze artist, and was with the Forepaugh circus. Another sister, Jennie, was a noted bareback rider with the Sells show; my brother Tom had developed into a famous acrobat and pantomimist, and was with the Hanlons. I felt proud of all of them. They had done honor and dignity to the family's circus name, and maintained its best traditions. I alone felt that it was up to me to do something great in my line.

I wanted to remain near my mother for a little while, so I went on as juggler at a variety show on the Bowery, which was then the most famous amusement highway in New York. But the call of the circus was always in my ears.... I played the part of a Spanish clown in a circus at Havana, and then returned to the United States, this time to stay....

In Europe we had heard various kinds of reports about the American circus from performers who had gone over. Some seemed incredible. It was said that the shows in this country had hundreds of horses and as many attendants. This seemed so huge alongside our smaller Continental circuses that I refused to believe it. But when I did come over and saw an American circus in all its glory I realized that half of the truth about it had not been told. When I came back from Havana the old circus kings were coming into their own. W. C. Coup ... had the "United Monster Shows" out. He lured P. T. Barnum from the museum business to the circus game, and they formed what was undoubtedly the first great combination of showmen. "Yankee" Robinson, who had been a circus autocrat as far back as the sixties, the Sells Brothers, Adam Forepaugh, the Mabies, Dan Costello, and John Robinson, all had shows on the road, and were getting bigger and stronger all the time. It was about that time that the Ringling Brothers were having their first circus thrills, and were laying the foundation of a knowledge and experience that have made them leaders of their world to-day....

... I have had many odd experiences, but none more memorable than my first appearance under canvas in America. I felt as if I had been transported to a different show world and was moving and breathing under a sea of canvas. The arena was much bigger than those of the European circuses, and I found that you had to strain every effort to be seen and heard and appreciated.

I found, among other things, that the average American circus–goer was not so responsive to the clown as the European.... One reason for this is that the average American, even in the smaller towns, has more diversions than his foreign cousin. Besides, Europe had seen many generations of clowns, and had witnessed the whole evolution of his art. The American had to be educated up to him.

I stayed with the Robbins show for a number of years. I found the wagon life very alluring. There was an odd sort of democracy among the circus people. I found various countrymen of mine, for the average circus performer is a great nomad.

6. Wild West Shows Take American Culture Outside the United States, 1896

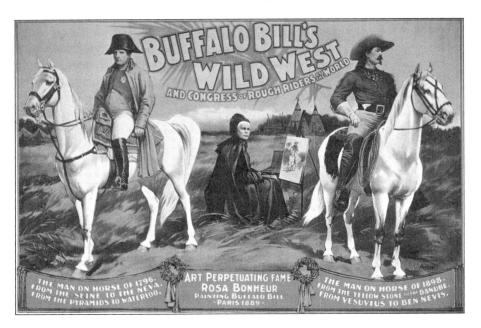

ESSAYS

In the first essay, Robert W. Rydell, professor of history at Montana State University–Bozeman, and Rob Kroes, professor of American studies and director of the Amerika Instituut at the University of Amsterdam, examine the influence of American commercialized leisure on Western Europe. They argue, among other things, that the era of American expansionism also saw the early use of spectacles as "weapons for accomplishing specific US foreign policy objectives." The deployment of popular culture as a tool of American foreign policy reached its apex during the cold war, as explored by a later chapter in this volume. But, as Rydell and Kroes point out, wild west shows, fairs, and circuses were early examples. Considering American exhibitions at fairs, particularly the display of technology and industrial products, and the diplomacy of Buffalo Bill Cody's wild west show, the authors also ask: Were these object lessons in American technological supremacy and exceptionalism "passively absorbed and unthinkingly used"? In doing so, they state one of the defining questions of popular culture studies, and one that historians have asked most recently with regard to the globalization of American popular culture. Were these forms a kind of cultural imperialism that eclipsed more authentic cultural practices? In the second essay, Janet M. Davis, cultural historian at the University of Texas at Austin, explores how the circus and wild west shows framed expansion and benefits of empire for American audiences. She explores the educational intent and value of circuses at the turn of the twentieth century, a moment when circus producers began to emphasize the "moral, political, and economic dominance of the United States in world affairs" and the only time that they included elaborate reenactments of battles and other foreign encounters that made expansion into a salable and educational spectacle. Davis argues that these performances as "sites of fun making" had an even greater didactic impact than official messages about U.S. foreign policy because they made the idea of American superiority and imperialism seem natural. How did performances turn territorial expansion into fun and make it seem natural? How did showmen such as Buffalo Bill Cody or Barnum and Bailey become promoters of U.S. imperialism? What did U.S. and European audiences think? How did they respond to these messages? What historical evidence might one examine to think about audience reception?

Fairs Take the United States to Europe

ROBERT W. RYDELL AND ROB KROES

… By the beginning of the twentieth century, European and British audiences had been exposed to American exhibits at dozens of international exhibitions that had followed in the wake of London's fabled 1851 Crystal Palace Exhibition. At

Robert W. Rydell and Rob Kroes, "The Americanization of the World," in *Buffalo Bill in Bologna: The Americanization of the World, 1869–1922.* Copyright © 2005 by The University of Chicago Press. Reproduced by permission.

that fair, American exhibitors knocked British government officials, industrialists, and the broader public back on their collective heels with displays of Colt revolvers and McCormick reapers. Almost overnight, the United States established itself as an industrial and commercial power worthy of note that also gave every appearance of lacking the artistic heft expected of a truly civilized nation…. American representations at England's and Europe's world's fairs between 1851 and 1900 only sharpened that image, especially at the 1900 Paris Universal Exposition.

"Until the Great Exposition of 1900 closed its doors in November, Adams haunted it, aching to absorb knowledge, and helpless to find it." With these words, American historian Henry Adams opened the "Dynamo and the Virgin," the most famous chapter of his autobiography, *The Education of Henry Adams*. Captivated by the Paris exposition's displays of automobiles and dynamos, radium and x-rays, cinematography and chromophotography, Adams reflected on the distance the world had traveled since the Middle Ages. On the Paris exposition grounds, as he described his feelings, he "entered a supersensual world, in which he could measure nothing except by chance collisions of movements…" Awestruck by "physics stark mad in metaphysics," he proceeded to reflect on the symbols of power on view at the fair and concluded: "All the steam in the world could not, like the Virgin, build Chartres."

Whether Adams was right about steam and Chartres, or about dynamos and virgins for that matter, he certainly captured the lure that the Paris Universal Exposition held for anyone interested in the meaning of modernity. And Adams was not alone. Some fifty million people visited this fair, making it the most highly attended event of its kind since the world's fair movement had begun with London's 1851 Crystal Palace Exhibition. To be sure, not all of these visitors "felt the forty-foot dynamos as a moral force" and most, while fatigued, probably derived more pleasure than anguish from the stunning array of exhibits divided between the Trocadero, the banks of the Seine, and the Bois de Vincennes. But Adams's account, while exceptional, should not be discounted. He did, after all, recognize the Paris Universal Exposition for what it was—a cultural powerhouse.

In late 1899, a U.S. ship arrived in France carrying the bulk of the American displays for the fair. Full of cargo, the *U.S.S. Prairie* bore a name that was full of meaning. Nine years earlier, the U.S. Census had proclaimed the end of the frontier period in American life; three years after that, at the 1893 Chicago fair, historian Frederick Jackson Turner had read his famous paper on the significance of the frontier in American life, in which he had cautioned: "He would be a rash prophet who should assert that the expansive character of American life has now entirely ceased."…

When they arrived in Paris, the nearly 7,000 exhibits, which had already been fit into the exposition's classification scheme, were dispersed to pavilions and annexes spread around the expositions various sites. Unlike many world's fairs that had a central site, the Paris Universal Exposition, like many European universities both then and now, occupied diverse sites around the city….

The core ideas of the exposition, … were saturated with ideas of racial hierarchy and the deep-seated conviction that "civilization" had triumphed over "savagery."

These broad racialized zones of the exposition were linked by exhibition avenues that ran along both sides of the Seine. On the Left Bank, foreign pavilions joined the Champ-de-Mars (site of the tower Gustave Eiffel had erected for the 1889 exposition) and the Esplanade des Invalides. On the Right Bank, a mélange of commercialized entertainments and official exposition structures stretched between the Trocadero and the Champs Elysées. Even with these exhibition areas, French exposition officials had concluded long before the fair opened that additional space would be required to accommodate the quantity of domestic and foreign exhibit material....

Even this expansion of the exposition grounds left American officials wanting more. A year and a half before the fair opened, the French director-general had tried to put a stop to U.S. demands by reminding the U.S. commissioner-general, Ferdinand Peck: "You know the old saying, 'The prettiest girl in the world can only give what she has.'" But American officials refused to take the hint. By the time the fair opened, they had persuaded French authorities to accommodate the desires of several American corporations, including the McCormick Harvester and Southern Railway companies, to build their own pavilions and to provide additional annexes to major exposition palaces to satisfy the demands of American business and agricultural interests.

Exactly why French authorities conceded so much to the American commission is not hard to explain. The Paris Universal Exposition, like all world's fairs, reflected the intrigues of international politics. Increasing the exhibit space of the United States to the levels enjoyed by Britain and Germany had the not-so-subtle effect of diminishing the stature of France's European rivals at the Universal Exposition. But the decision to inflate the American presence at the fair had this unintended consequence: it gave the United States a commanding port of entry to French and European markets.

In retrospect, it might seem as if the strength of the U.S. presence at the Paris fair was diluted because American exhibits were scattered around various exposition sites. But the breadth of the U.S. presence across the fair's expanses made it difficult to find a sector of the fair without an American element.

For instance, in the major exhibition palaces near the Eiffel Tower that were dedicated to outfitting visitors with lasting lessons about the meaning of "civilization," the United States developed displays devoted to mining and metallurgy, education and liberal arts, civil engineering and transportation, chemical industries, and textiles....

Across from the Champ-de-Mars, in the area of the exposition set aside for colonial exhibits, the U.S. government, despite its formal denials of having colonies, requested and received space in the Trocadero Palace for exhibits from Cuba and Hawaii. Because of an outbreak of plague in Hawaii, the Hawaiian displays were relatively small. But the Cuban exhibit, housed in a Renaissance-style pavilion built within the Trocadero Palace, more than made up for the limited Hawaiian showing. For these displays, the U.S. War Department allocated $25,000 and detailed its military liaison to the U.S. Commission to Cuba to help Gonzalo de Quesada, Cuba's future minister to Washington, D.C., assemble displays of natural resources from more than 400 exhibitors that would "illustrate the opportunities that capital now has in the development of the island."

As vital as they were to the American representation in Paris, the Cuban exhibits also posed a dilemma. As Peck explained the situation to U.S. secretary of state John Hay, French exposition authorities had decided that, since Cuba was not technically a colony or an independent nation, exhibits from Cuba "would have to be received from Cuban exhibitors as American citizens" thus granting "recognition on the part of the Commission that Cubans are American citizens." Given the divisive debates in the U.S. Congress over the annexation of Cuba, the secretary of state was unwilling to open a back door to Cubans wanting to claim U.S. citizenship on a technicality. Consequently, Peck had to persuade French exposition authorities to make an exception to their rules of classification to allow the Cuban exhibits to appear in a niche by themselves. But having negotiated this concession, the question came up as to whether the United States flag could be flown over the Cuban exhibits. This too required delicate diplomacy and apparently was resolved with a decision to drape the Cuban pavilion in red, white, and blue bunting....

But beneath its neoclassical facade [of the U.S. National Pavilion] signs of a modern American mass culture abounded. As one senior U.S. official wrote of the building's interior: Here "the American will be at home with his friends, his newspapers, his guides, his facilities for stenography and typewriting, his post-office and his telegraph station, his money exchange, his bureau of public comfort and even his ice-water...."

One of the primary underpinnings of this new [American] civilization was on view across the Alexander Bridge from the Grand Palais in the U.S. Publisher's Building. Inside this building, it was not so much Culture as the commercialization of Culture—what cultural critic Walter Benjamin would term "art in the age of mechanical reproduction"—that was on view. The centerpiece of the exhibit was the enormous Goss Press that, each hour, printed and folded 50,000 copies of the sixteen-page Paris edition of the *New York Times*.... [The press] captured an important European perception about American "civilization at the dawn of the new century—namely that, since mass production and mass culture had already become its defining features, American culture really could be reduced to its technology and mechanical reproducibility.

Further examples of America's industrially and technologically based culture were on view at ... the fair, where displays of automobiles, bicycles, railroads, elevators, revolvers, and machine tools were featured in the American sections of Machinery Hall and where the McCormick Company erected its own separate exhibition hall. Inaugurated with ceremonies that featured John Philip Sousa's band, these exhibits lent visible support to the proposition offered by the American exhibit as a whole that "the Republic is rapidly developing a highly perfected as well as a soundly organized civilization, and particularly that it promises fair to solve, to the satisfaction of all, that problem which has so long annoyed Europe and the world.... To be sure, ... expositions were not the only way American mass cultural forms infiltrated Europe. Europeans also gained insights into American "civilization" from the multiple treks of Buffalo Bill's Wild West performers across England and the Continent....

In 1886, William Cody received an offer that seemed too good to be true. Thanks to the skill of his manager, Nate Salsbury, Buffalo Bill received an invitation from the organizers of London's American Exhibition to perform as part of their show in the Earls Court exhibition complex…. The results were simply incredible. Not since P. T. Barnum had paraded General Tom Thumb around the sitting rooms of British aristocracy had there been a comparable American production in England.

The scale of Cody's undertaking amazed the press on both shores of the Atlantic. When the show's company boarded the *State of Nebraska* steamship for London, its entourage included "83 saloon passengers, 38 steerage passengers, 97 Indians, 180 horses, 18 buffalo, 10 elk, 5 Texan steers, 4 donkeys, and 2 deer." As the ship steamed across the ocean, Major John Burke (one of the show's managers) and an advance party plastered London with posters and drummed up anticipation in the press….

Several weeks prior to the show's opening, Buffalo Bill's encampment became a veritable Mecca for England's upper crust. Among the many notables to visit the site was the former prime minister, William Gladstone, who toured the grounds in the company of the American consul general and, amidst great fanfare, met the Indian chief Red Shirt. Over lunch, Gladstone lifted a glass to the future of Anglo-American relations. Then, on May 5, just four days before the show opened to the public, the Prince of Wales, the future King Edward VII and a notable rake, accepted an invitation from Cody to bring his wife and daughters to attend a special preview of the Wild West performance. Afterwards, he met all of the performers, including Annie Oakley, who, in an episode widely reported in the press, ignored proper etiquette and shook hands with the Princess of Wales, whom she later described as a "wonderful little girl." Neither the prince nor princess took offense; to the contrary, the prince made a point of telling his mother, Queen Victoria, about the performance and urged her to attend one. With remarkable speed, proper arrangements were made for a command performance of the Wild West on May 11, and, for the first time since her husband's death a quarter of a century before, Queen Victoria appeared in person at a public performance.

Her attendance at the Wild West show was news everywhere in the English-speaking world, and the fact that she made her appearance in the context of the celebrations that marked the Jubilee Year of her reign only added more weight to the occasion. And what an occasion it was. When the show began and a rider entered the arena carrying the American flag, Queen Victoria stood and bowed. The rest of the audience followed suit, while British soldiers and officers saluted….

Over the course of the next century, it would become fairly routine practice for American mass cultural exports to serve as weapons for accomplishing specific U.S. foreign policy objectives. In the Victorian era, this use of mass culture was still being nurtured and the Wild West was one of the key incubators….

During the Wild West's run at the American Exhibition, Cody's managers rarely missed a beat. They organized twice-a-day performances that played to crowds that averaged around 30,000. This meant that, … the show played to standing-room only crowds who thrilled to the performances based on "The Drama of Civilization.".…

Looking at European responses to American mass culture, whether in its early forms like Buffalo Bill's Wild West show touring Europe, or in later forms like Hollywood movies, or advertisements for American consumer products, they have always been of two kinds. Some have been on the level of articulate reflection producing a repertoire of critical views; others have consisted of selective appropriation, redirecting the impact of American cultural exports, sometimes Europeanizing them as well.

To take the example of Buffalo Bill in Europe, we need to answer two questions. First, at the level of articulate, specific responses, the question is what did Europeans choose to read in what they saw? What did they make of it? Did they enjoy it as pure entertainment, a display of American exoticism? Were they impressed by the Wild West's showmanship, its mastery of a form of popular entertainment? And, if so, did they recognize a typical American flair in it, far surpassing anything they had seen so far? Or was it rather a matter of affiliation with a historical narrative of conquest and imperial expansion that they could meaningfully relate to the world they lived in? The intention of Buffalo Bill's staging was certainly to make the story of the American West merge with the story of European expansion at a time when European colonization reached the far frontiers of its own empires. European audiences may have been aware of this larger connection and may have seen the show as confirming views of Western superiority and the White Man's civilizing mission. Yet, when we conceive of response in terms of reception and appropriation, we need to take a longer view. We need to ask ourselves to what extent the Wild West intersected with ideas about the American West that had already been formed by earlier carriers of imagery, in novels by the likes of François René de Châteaubriand and James Fenimore Cooper, through journalism, travelogues, immigrant letters, or visual materials such as paintings, drawings, prints, and photographs. In fact, the European fantasy of the American West had already spawned its own popular authors.… The American West had already been appropriated and made to serve as a projection screen for European fantasies, for instance of White-Indian male bonding in a setting reminiscent of German dreams of pristine nature … or the guise of a quasi-anthropological exoticism.… To put it in slightly different terms, the Wild West made a splash in a pond already filled with images of the American West.

Equally important to remember is that Europe was never just one homogeneous setting for the reception of Buffalo Bill's Wild West show as an accomplished form of American mass culture. Each European country had at the time its own specific history in fictionalizing the American West. For instance, among European countries, Germany offers the clearest case of a longtime infatuation with the American Indian. This may have had to do with a romantic, if not nostalgic, affiliation with peoples threatened by the onward march of civilization, an affiliation that had the marks of a projection of feelings of loss of cultural bearings prevalent in a Germany undergoing rapid modernization itself.…

Exotic and intriguing the Indians may have been to Europeans. Yet, at the same time, there was the sense that, here on display, reenacting their historical defeat at the hands of whites, were literally the last of the Mohicans, the representatives of a vanishing race. Such, white Europeans and Americans agreed, was the course of history. This tragic dimension may have actually heightened interest in Buffalo Bill's Indians as living representatives of a different race. Much of the European press gave equal if not more space to the Indian living quarters, with their tipis pitched on the show's grounds, than to the historical drama that made up the Wild West show.... Yet, their image as bloodthirsty savages, well established in Europe at the time, also permeated much of the press reports. It was further disseminated by European equivalents of American dime novels and pulp magazines with names like *Buffalo Bill, the Wild West Hero*. The show did nothing to alter these impressions, with its central drama always portraying the Indians as savage aggressors who were eventually defeated by Buffalo Bill and other such heroes.

Infatuation with the Indian, though, was not the only romance that engaged Europeans. Before Buffalo Bill appeared in Europe, Europeans had also become fascinated by the cowboy. The appeal of Buffalo Bill's Wild West lay as much in the heroism of the pioneer and frontiersman—tales that Cody restaged through his performers' stunning mastery of everything having to do with horses. As a result of the Wild West, the two romances became interlinked, and children growing up in Europe would play Cowboys *and* Indians for generations to come.

Buffalo Bill, then, clearly encountered in Europe a world already alive with images of the American West. While Cody may have been more catching than others in his showmanship, in other words more "American," it is important to ask, did European audiences notice this difference? Or was the Wild West just another touring show, turning the American West into a pageant, only better than rival shows? As it turns out, there were clear moments in the European response that spoke of an awareness of the Americanness of Buffalo Bill's Wild West....

... [A]s much as the show may have succeeded in embodying the "wildness" or the West, the show was as much a display of the products of nineteenth-century industrial civilization as it was of the savage life of the frontier. The key to the whole affair was not the wild men and animals..., but the revolver and the repeating rifles, two of the most innovative products of nineteenth-century industrial civilization in the United States.... Both types of firearms, as used in the show, were seen as mediators between a world of increasing technological precision and the freewheeling life of the frontier. The heart of the show was a display of shooting which ritualized the practical and symbolic role of guns in American culture. In Europe, for a number of historical reasons, the gun had never become a significant symbol in popular culture and folklore....

The Americans ... certainly satisfied a German, and more generally European, need for authenticity. The "Wild West fever" caused by Buffalo Bill's show in Europe had centrally to do with the show's claim to represent "the real thing" that people in Europe had read about and dreamed about for years. The Wild West show was fast, exciting entertainment that competed with the big circuses that emerged at about the same time in the United States and a little later in Europe as well, but offered something the circuses did not: authenticity....

Here was an experience of the real thing, of living history that had just passed. These are critical words when it comes to exploring the appeal of forms of American mass culture. No sales pitch has more powerfully drawn publics around the world toward forms of American mass culture than the claim of authenticity. It was a lesson that others would learn and apply in the not so distant future. For instance, Coca-Cola would be advertised as being "the real thing." Levi's jeans would for many years be advertised as being "the original Levi's," an American original. This is exactly what Buffalo Bill had promised as well by bringing real Indians, real buffaloes, real cowboys, and the West as it really was or had been, to Europe. Like their American counterparts, Europeans, for the most part, fell for this ploy. They loved it and never sat back to call Buffalo Bill's bluff in that respect....

Circuses Educate Americans about Nationalism and Imperialism

JANET M. DAVIS

The circus and Wild West gave their vast audiences an immediate, intimate look at America's new position in world affairs with live translations of abstract foreign relations ideologies. A program for Buffalo Bill's Wild West in 1899 beckoned American audiences to meet "Strange People from Our New Possessions." Tightly packed together by the thousands, spectators could share a cosmopolitan experience of the new empire that offered more than the purely visual sensation of reading about foreign affairs in a newspaper: they could smell the acrid odor of gunpowder during a battle reenactment, or hear the soft sounds of Hawaiian grass skirts rustling during a hula demonstration. Tody Hamilton, a press agent for Barnum & Bailey, recognized the circus's power to make America's military prowess intimate to its audiences when he advertised Barnum & Bailey's exhibition of model battleships from the Spanish–American War in 1903: "Many in the interior of America, who have their money voted yearly in vast appropriation for naval defense, have never even seen a battleship. It will be a pleasure to give them their first sight of the ships that defend them in times of war" providing people with their "first sight," the circus ... had tremendous power to help shape audiences' ideas about the expanding nation-slate and its changing position in world affairs. Because the circus and Wild West also performed profitably across Europe, these popular imports were especially powerful promulgators of the nation's rising the world.

Circus and Wild West spectacles framed the new empire within the American exceptionalist tradition. However inaccurately, these amusements defined U.S. expansion as a distinct counterpoint to European formulations of formal empire solely characterized by colonization and military domination, because the nation's acquisition of noncontiguous territory was predicated on an abiding sense of moral "uplift" through economic intervention…. As moral cheerleaders of expansionism, circus and Wild West owners echoed these paradoxical convictions in their staged spectacles. They also participated in the new empire in a complementary way, through the physical procurement of people and animals from other countries. American circus proprietors engaged in a form of diplomacy that should be characterized as informal because these showmen were nongovernmental actors. As sites of fun making, the circus and Wild West show had even greater ideological significance because their instructive messages were blanketed and thus naturalized in hair-raising fun….

From its inception in 1793, the American circus and related amusements like the museum and menagerie capitalized on exotic animals, people, and artifacts from colonized areas. Early examples of the outlandish included "Iranistan," the mansion in Bridgeport, Connecticut, of the future circus proprietor P. T. Barnum, erected in 1846. Costing over $150,000 at the time, the palace was based upon the architecture of the Brighton Pavilion (home of the British prince regent), which in turn was inspired by colonial Indo-Saracenic architecture of British India. In New York City, roving sea captains and other collectors provided Barnum's profitable American Museum with an enormous international hodgepodge of extraordinary living and dead creatures, and historical relics….

However, these early images paled in comparison to the railroad circus's full-blown imperial scenes at the end of the nineteenth century. By the 1890s showmen had transmogrified happenstance foreign objects into teleological exhibitions of American nationalism. Huge circus [spectacles] transformed what the British historian John Springhall has called "little wars of empire" into entertaining proof of the growing influence of the United States on the world stage. These widely circulating performances promoted broad support for American military activity, using selective scenes from generally "popular" wars like the Spanish-American War and the Indian Wars. Collectively, these specs portrayed the United States as a democratic republic whose style of government, economic system, and "way of life" spread worldwide would herald a Utopian age of unprecedented prosperity. These specs reiterated the theme in different ways: as narratives of national origins, as frontier stories, as au courant reenactments of contemporary events, and as crusading, missionary-style narratives of Christian progress.

The wars that the circus and Wild West chose to ignore were as significant as the ones they reenacted. Scenes from the Mexican War and the American Civil War—wars that reminded the nation of its slavery past—were virtually absent. Although individual amusement proprietors toured urban areas during the Mexican War with bulky moving panoramas (vast paintings on canvas panels sewn together and wound from one huge roller to another to simulate a moving landscape), circus owners did not incorporate these scenes into their exhibitions given the escalating sectional crisis that followed. The Civil War itself, moreover, could not be easily watered down so as to be palatable on both sides of the Mason-Dixon Line....

Just as world's fairs commemorated seminal historical occasions like the Louisiana Purchase of 1803, the circus and Wild West used the past to substantiate contemporary nationalist celebrations of the new empire. The Hungarian immigrant brothers Imre and Bolossy Kiralfy created several spectacles, notably "Columbus And the Discovery of America," an expensive production that linked the arrival of Columbus on North American soil to later nation building....

At the onset of the Spanish-American War, William F. Cody publicly expressed his desire to send "30,000 braves" to Cuba. His Wild West opened the 1898 season with a Color Guard of Cuban Veterans who marched around the arena. The program noted that all were "on leave of absence in order to give their various wounds time to heal, all have fought for the flag of Cuba and will soon return to that country to act as scouts and guides, for which their familiarity with the topography of the island especially commends them." When the war ended on August 12, audience members at the Forepaugh & Sells Brothers circus in Beloit, Kansas, erupted after a worker interrupted the performance to read a telegram announcing the big news. The circus route book noted: "[This] was the occasion for a mighty ovation, the entire audience rising to their feet and cheering the stars and stripes. Merrick's Military band struck up the air of 'Star Spangled Banner, and again the audience burst into an uproar. It was surely a memorable occasion." The national mood was jubilant after a four-month war that resulted in—few U.S. casualties (385 battle deaths, 2,061 deaths from other causes, and 1,662 nonmortal wounds) and the acquisition of overseas territories that remapped the nation's position in world affairs.

The circus and Wild West portrayed the Spanish-American War not in terms of colonial conquest but as evidence of liberal progress and democratic equality. Subsequent U.S. actions, however, clearly belied such lofty aims. Relations with the Philippines quickly spiraled into a protracted guerrilla war after McKinley annexed the islands with the Treaty of Paris in February 1899. More than 200,000 Filipinos died from battle wounds, famine, and disease from 1899 to 1902, and sporadic fighting continued there-rafter. In Cuba, U.S. intervention soon turned into a military occupation that transformed the newly liberated nation into a virtual U.S. colony under the auspices of the Piatt Amendment of 1901. In Puerto Rico, U.S. financial policies prompted local elites to consolidate landholdings so that they could grow crops primarily for export.... But even the U.S. ideal of economic development and free markets, [historian] William Appleman Williams contends, contained the seeds of formal empire.... Despite the contradictions between the rhetoric of self-determination and actual military domination, many prominent Americans like William E Cody supported expansion by the United States. Cody, for instance, voiced his support for its rule of the Philippines in his correspondence with his friend Theodore Roosevelt.

Artifacts of war saturated the circus and Wild West to such an extent that one newspaper writer was prompted to compare the war in the Philippines to the Wild West show: "The theory of the Administration is that the trouble in the Philippines is like the Wild West show. It isn't war, but it looks a good deal like it." In 1899 Barnum & Bailey fashioned "America's Great Naval Victory at Santiago" while touring Europe.... The spectacle was "Presented on a Miniature Ocean of Real Water, with real War Ships, Guns, and Explosives," and ended with the annihilation of the Spanish fleet while "The Star Spangled Banner" played in the background. Viewed by countless thousands of Europeans, the circus announced to British, French, and German rivals America's new position on the world stage and the power of its expanding navy.

Upon returning to the United States in 1903, Barnum & Bailey exhibited official models of U.S. warships (based on plans from Secretary of the Navy John D. Long), ranging in length from three to nine feet. The 1904 Barnum & Bailey program announced: "These models were built as an expression of the appreciation of the management of this exhibition of the power and glory of the American navy as so magnificently manifested during the late Spanish-American war. [Because the circus was traveling in England] ... the people with the ... show realize, perhaps, more fully than their fellow-Americans who have remained at home, the magic potency of the name 'American' that has been given to it by its splendid navy." The presence of miniature battleships, government-sanctioned objects, enhanced Barnum & Bailey's credibility as a respectable source of information about current events.... The battleships were powerful fetish objects, linking an abstract, faraway war to an intimate material reality, a riveting "first sight" that could be inspected and touched by curious circus-goers, thereby giving Americans a concrete sense of how the government was spending their excise tax dollars.

A year after the Spanish-American War, Buffalo Bill's production "Battle of San Juan Hill" exhibited the multiracial Congress of Rough Riders doing battle with the Spanish. The artists playing Theodore Roosevelt's regiment of Rough Riders' included Euroamericans, Cubans, African Americans, and, in a twist of intentional racial disguise, Native Americans as the Spanish villains. In the second act, "The Rough Riders' Immortal Charge," Roosevelt's "virile" regiment defeated the "wine-soaked" Spanish through "manly" courage and discipline: "There is a frantic yell of admiration and approval as the soldiers—*white, red and black*—spring from their cowering position of utter helplessness and follow Roosevelt and the flag. On and ever onward they leap, struggle and crawl.... The Spaniards cannot believe that so small a force would dare an assault so forlorn of all hope. They erroneously infer that an army is charging close behind it, and as it breathlessly comes closely on for a hand-to-hand death grapple, they pale, they flinch, and at last they turn and fly in panic. Their gold and crimson emblem of ruthless oppression is torn from the ramparts, and Old Glory streams on the breeze, triumphant in its place" (emphasis in original).

Showmen's seamless spectacles of the Spanish-American War dramatized a racially and economically diverse American military destroying the "decrepit" and "effete" Spanish colonial empire and (ostensibly) replacing it with a democratic American empire of liberty and free markets. African American soldiers played a crucial role in the Rough Riders' victory, and show programs acknowledged their presence. In 1900 Buffalo Bill featured Negro Cavalrymen in a new act. Programs for the "Battle of San Juan Hill" celebrated the presence of multiracial American troops in the Spanish-American War as evidence of the readiness of the United States to "guide" the rest of the world by its own multicultural model….

As a whole, showmen predicted that the benefits of an American empire of liberty would soon be felt worldwide. Peter Sells, proprietor of the Adam Forepaugh & Sells Brothers circus, proclaimed: "The building of the Nicaragua canal, enlargement of our standing army, a navy that will equal, if not surpass that of any other nation on earth, a wise and just supervision over Cuba and Porto Rico, the acquisition of ports at several points in Asia for coaling and resting stations for our commercial and war ships, are all essential to the future welfare of this nation."… In an address to the American Historical Association at the 1893 Columbian Exposition in Chicago, Frederick Jackson Turner set forth his frontier thesis, which linked the nation's future prosperity to its ability to solve the crisis of overproduction by establishing (and protecting) new overseas markets. But as the co-owner of a vastly popular live, nomadic show, Peter Sells advanced expansionist ideology in a far more accessible medium than print. The circus, a national entertainment, projected an ostensibly unifying patriotic consensus to a diverse audiences of immigrants, African Americans, Native Americans, and native-born whites—although those same audiences often used Circus Day and Buffalo Bill Day as opportunities to engage in fractious, racially charged altercations with each other….

Circus and Wild West scenes of triumphal empire building flourished in a society that largely supported overseas expansion: the pro-imperialist presidential candidate William McKinley, for one, handily defeated his anti-imperialist opponent William Jennings Bryan in 1896 and 1900. Theodore Roosevelt, an ardent expansionist, easily won the presidency in 1904, and William Howard Taft, an architect of "dollar diplomacy," beat Bryan in 1908. A wide range of ordinary Americans—from farmers and industrial workers to urban businessmen—supported expansion, which particularly in the wake of the devastating panics of 1873 and 1893 was seen as a necessary antidote to overproduction and a failing economy.

But a small group of citizens rejected the new empire's utopian promise. Discrete, dystopic groups of anti-imperialists argued that the dawning of U.S. globalism signaled the nation's constitutional and cultural demise. Charles Towne, a former congressman from Michigan, gloomily forecast the rapid decline of the United States within a year of the Spanish-American War, "from the moral leadership of mankind into the common brigandage of the robber nations of the world." …

Within a year after it was founded in 1898, the Boston-based Anti-Imperialist League claimed 70,000 members, the highest number in its history. Although virtually all anti-imperialists supported participation by the United States in the global economy, they were mightily concerned with the boundaries of its expansion…. Still, anti-imperialist ideology was often contradictory. While some anti-imperialists, including Mark Twain, W. E. B. Du Bois, and Jane Addams, disavowed the establishment of a formal empire on humanitarian antiracist and constitutional grounds, others like Senator "Pitchfork" Ben Tillman of South Carolina, a vice-president of the Anti-Imperialist League, maintained that imperialism would inevitably "mongrelize" American racial identity. Accordingly, anti-imperialist debates were interconnected with the explosive racial tensions of the period. White supremacists expressed their outrage when President Theodore Roosevelt in 1901 invited the black leader Booker T. Washington to the White House. In some respects, Roosevelt's position as a vigorous expansionist and advocate of domestic civil rights (a position similar to that of his friend William F. Cody) might seem paradoxical, but like other politicians and showmen of the Progressive Era, Roosevelt was a paternalistic believer in the "white man's burden." He asserted that people of color throughout the world could become "civilized" through "proper" education and "moral uplift," of the sort provided by Washington's Tuskegee program of "Thrift, Patience, and Industrial Training for the masses."

Anti-imperialist white supremacists dreaded the specter of racial amalgamation. After the United States ratified the Treaty of Paris, which sanctioned its annexation of the Philippines, the U.S. Senate passed the McEnery Resolution, which stipulated that the Filipinos would never become U.S. citizens. However, many anti-imperialists argued that inevitably, people of color from "America's possessions" *would* become U.S. citizens—just as African Americans had done so as a result of the Thirteenth, Fourteenth, and Fifteenth Amendments. Linking the racial identity of African Americans to that of so-called mongrel people of color throughout the world, the editor of the *Jackson* (Miss.) *Clarion-Ledger* announced that only racial segregation—at home and abroad—would preserve the social order: "The surest step to joint degradation and deterioration is amalgamation."…

In this social context, it would seem that the presence of Cuban "brown-skinned American revolutionaries" and of Filipino, Hawaiian, and black Rough Riders would unsettle certain Euroamerican audiences. Those from the southern United States, where racially based anti-imperialism was fierce, might have found these exhibits particularly disturbing. "The Battle of San Juan Hill," for one, freely displayed armed African Americans and Native Americans fighting for the independence of another people of color.…

Still, southern newspapers made no connection between multiracial circus acts, armed people of color, and anti-imperialist racial ideologies. In fact, articles praising circus scenes of multiracial athletic wizardry existed alongside the above-mentioned diatribes against the supposed "intractability" of African American soldiers in Cuba and Filipinos' "inability" to become "civilized." What accounts for this disjuncture? What made the circus and Wild West a seemingly safe social space for exhibiting anti-imperialists' worst fears concerning racial amalgamation and claims to citizenship? This absence of protest is especially striking because the circus and Wild West were traveling communities whose nomadic multiracial members lived and performed in close proximity to one another. Given these logistical realities of a traveling outfit, certain audiences might have been even more likely to read pro-imperialist exhibits of U.S. expansionism as socially ominous. But they did not make such explicit connections. For that matter, African American newspapers did not comment on these displays either.

Perhaps the fanfare of the racial other at the freak show helped offset the subversive implications of the pro-imperialist displays. The range of professional

African and Asian "savages," "missing links," and legless, armless, conjoined, and hirsute people of color collectively reified racial distinctions through bodily exhibition, similar to the evolutionary juxtaposition of humans and animals at the "Ethnological Congress of Strange and Savage Tribes." Perhaps the performance of racial "savagery" helped diminish the potentially transgressive claims to equality found in other parts of the exhibition. To some audiences, the players might have served as examples of inassimilable racial difference, living proof of the prevailing "wisdom" of racial segregation. The literary scholar Amy Kaplan points out that Roosevelt himself diffused the disturbing implications of his multiracial Rough Riders by rewriting the course of the battle shortly after it took place: in several accounts, he minimized African American accomplishments, instead characterizing black soldiers as comical, lazy, shiftless, freakish, and impotent without white commanders—despite the critical role that African Americans actually played in storming Kettle Hill.

Burlesque also may have played a role in diminishing these potentially jarring displays. As much as circuses and Wild West proprietors earnestly took pride in their shows' verisimilitude, they also poked fun at international affairs. As Emilio Aguinaldo triumphantly returned from exile to his native Philippines on the U.S. gunboat *McCulloch* to draft a new constitution fashioned along American lines, the Ringling Bros, circus menagerie displayed its big Philippine boa constrictor named "Emilio Aguinaldo." In September 1898 Aguinaldo supposedly swallowed himself....

Yet ... Circus Day and "Buffalo Bill Day" *were* sites of real racial and ethnic anxiety. One can turn to the behavior of the enormous multiethnic crowds—sometimes more than 20,000 milled around the show grounds—as another barometer of the ways in which this amusement served to "instruct the minds of all classes." Circus workers observed countless examples of racial violence on Circus Day. For example, on October 25, 1890, in Navasota, Texas, a white man named James Whitfield shot and killed an African American man at the Sells Brothers' sideshow door after supposedly being insulted by him. After a white man and a black man scuffled at the circus grounds at Falls City, Nebraska, in 1898, the Adam Forepaugh & Sells Brothers route book reported that "there was talk of lynching the negro." Despite its fleeting presence, the circus and Wild West provided a moment of community articulation, bringing dystopian racial anxieties into sharp relief just as much as it highlighted unifying national narratives of modernization, global power, and prosperity.

With U.S. participation in World War I looming in 1916, the circus and Wild West plugged the readiness of U.S. troops. In 1916 Buffalo Bill and Miller Brothers 101 Ranch Wild West Combined produced a new military pageant, "Preparedness," designed not only to entertain with its colorful pageantry and athleticism, "but also to arouse public interest in the enlargement of the army and in 'Preparedness' for defense in case of possible attack." On the eve of U.S. entry into the war, the War Department granted furloughs to scores of soldiers to allow them to participate in "Preparedness." The soldiers demonstrated the dangers of trench warfare and the work of the scout and sharpshooter in an effort to arouse public support for the war effort. Circus posters during the war exhorted Americans to buy Liberty Bonds, and the aerialist Bird Millman personally sold war bonds to fellow workers and audience members; other circus members sewed socks for soldiers volunteered for the Red Cross. Working with the federal government, the circus and Wild West actively supported the war.

Yet circus spectacles of World War I were limited to military exercises before the advent of actual American fighting. In the context of contemporary anti-German hysteria, xenophobia, and bloodshed, battles from World War I— unlike those of the Spanish-American War—were never recreated at the circus and Wild West....

The age of the great circus and Wild West foreign affairs spectacle, then, ended with World War I. Although the victory of the United States marked the start of its clear-cut economic (and later military) domination on the world stage, this same period was also marked by extraordinary global unrest. Amid the Bolshevik Revolution and its aftermath, a devastating influenza epidemic, massive strikes, the Palmer Raids, and heated debates about isolationism versus internationalism, circus owners avoided controversy by choosing fictive, erotic, ahistorical pageants set in the Middle East, Africa, and Asia, devoid of any references to the concurrent demise of the Ottoman empire. The geographic interchangeability of such orientalist programs was constant.... These circus pageants contained lecherous "oriental" despots, scores of "oriental dancing girls," and military stunts on elephants and camels. Furthermore, with the growing popularity of movies and radio (media that also chronicled up-to-date foreign affairs), circus proprietors no longer emphasized their specs' verisimilitude as a way to draw the crowds. However, the ideological thrust of the turn-of-the-century circus and Wild West spec—characterized by a triumphant, Disneylike emphasis on America's moral and economic stewardship—remained a critical component of the nation's foreign relations "mission" during the rest of what Henry Luce later termed the "American Century." According to William Appleman Williams, this ideology manifested itself as "a firm conviction, even dogmatic belief, that America's domestic well-being depends upon such sustained, ever increasing overseas economic expansion."

FURTHER READING

Bennett, Tony. *The Birth of the Museum: History, Theory, Politics* (1995).

De Grazia, Victoria. *Irresistible Empire: America's Advance through 20th Century Europe* (2005).

Drinnon, Richard. *Facing West* (1980).

Jacobson, Matthew Frye. *Barbarian Virtues: The United States Encounters Foreign Peoples at Home and Abroad, 1876–1917* (2001).

Kasson, Joy. *Buffalo Bill's Wild West: Celebrity, Memory and Popular Culture* (2000).

Rosenberg, Emily S., and Eric Foner. *Spreading the American Dream: American Economic and Cultural Expansion, 1890–1945* (1982).

Rydell, Robert. *All the World's a Fair: Visions of Empire at American International Expositions* (1984).

———. *World of Fairs: The Century-of-Progress Expositions* (1993).

Rydell, Robert, and Rob Kroess. *Buffalo Bill in Bologna: The Americanization of the World, 1869–1922* (2005).

Rydell, Robert., et al. *Fair America: World's Fairs in the United States* (1993).

Schwartz, Vanessa R., and Jeannene M. Przyblyski, eds. *The Nineteenth-Century Visual Culture Reader* (2004).

Zeiler, Thomas. *Ambassadors in Pinstripes: The Spalding World Baseball Tour and the Birth of American Empire* (2006).

CHAPTER 5

Workers Demand Leisure Time, 1866–1914

In the later half of the nineteenth century, as the United States became an industrial power, working-class Americans demanded more time for leisure and found respite from work in a range of new, commercial amusements. The push for a shorter workday, known as the "eight hour movement," got underway in the 1870s and became a key issue for labor unions such as the Knights of Labor and later the American Federation of Labor (AFL). In the 1880s, a factory worker could expect to be on the job, often doing repetitive and monotonous work, for 12 to 14 hours a day, a jarring change for those who came from farms or had been pushed out of skilled crafts by mechanization. In addition to repetitive work, workers had to adjust to a schedule set not by tasks or by the seasons, but by the clock and the demands of managers who sought to maximize efficiency by running machines on a 24-hour schedule. Many industrial laborers characterized their plight as "wage slavery" because they had so little control over their time and their lives. Leaders of the eight-hour movement claimed that a workday divided into time for work, rest, and personal pursuits reflected a more natural and humane cycle of labor. This push for a shorter and more humane use of time fueled union membership and a number of strikes in this period, the bloodiest of which in 1886 ended with eight dead in Chicago's Haymarket Square. Although industrial workers would not be guaranteed an eight-hour day by national law until the passage of the Fair Labor Standards Act in the late 1930s, unions made modest gains and the work week shortened slightly to about 50 hours a week at the turn of the century, giving the majority of American workers more time for recreation.

By the 1890s, members of the expanding middle class—office clerks, managers, and white-collar professionals—along with Progressive reformers also advocated for the necessity of leisure to the health and well-being of Americans. In particular they endorsed not only shorter workdays but the idea of an annual vacation that would allow many Americans to escape the monotony and stultifying routine of the office and restore themselves physically and mentally. While the middle classes wanted less time at the office, they had a vision of leisure that contrasted sharply with that of the working class. For the middle classes, feared idleness and believed leisure time should be a form of self-improvement that would make one more productive. For working-class Americans and recent immigrants, a day off and the pleasures to be had during that time were often ends in themselves.

Historians such as Roy Rosenzweig have studied popular culture as an arena of political and social conflict by examining the contests over leisure time and space at the turn of the century. He argued that the eight-hour movement, and the leisure time it afforded, allowed workers to preserve their autonomy and carve out space for themselves within the changing urban landscape and in relation to industrial capitalism. In his classic book, Eight Hours for What We Will, *he examined struggles over saloons and Fourth of July celebrations where immigrant workers resisted attempts by middle-class and elite reformers to quash rowdy, distinctly working-class forms of relaxation. Although native-born elites sought to impose a sense of reverence and "sane and safe" celebrations for the Fourth of July, workers in the same cities and towns resisted attempts to curb their more raucous celebrations of the national holiday.*

More time for leisure, higher wages, and a substantial population of unmarried city dwellers also created new markets for commercial entertainment. By the turn of the century, mass entertainment had become a lucrative business. Older forms of pleasure such as drinking continued to thrive in cities, even while they drew the ire and considerable attention of middle-class reformers. Although saloons remained a staple of working-class leisure and a place for political organization, the proliferation of new pastimes appealed to much broader audiences that crossed gender, ethnic, and class lines. In Chicago, New York, Boston, or almost any city or large town, workers could enjoy the newfound pleasures of dance halls, vaudeville performances, amusement parks, nickelodeons, and spectator sports. Although leisure spaces could become contested terrain that defined class and racial inequality, the popular cultures created from these cheap amusements also forged a sense of national identity, tested traditional notions of gender and public propriety, turned the technologies of the industrial revolution on their head at places such as Coney Island, and eventually eroded Victorian expectations about public decorum and respectable behavior.

Sports, and especially baseball, had national and democratic appeal. As the game evolved from men's clubs to a more commercialized spectator sport, some national leagues attempted to quell the rowdy, working-class atmosphere at games and reach out to more "respectable" classes of fans. At the same time, players-turned-entrepreneurs such as Albert Spalding set rules and invented new ways to capitalize on baseball's popularity by producing official equipment and constructing stadiums. While the professionalization of baseball made the sport commerically viable, it also served to racially segregate the game.

As the classic essays in this chapter reveal, popular culture first captured the attention of American historians in the 1970s and 1980s. Social and labor historians turned their attention to leisure time as a way to document and understand more fully the everyday lives of working-class Americans and their relationship to industrial capitalism, work, and urbanization. Influenced by European scholars working in cultural history, cultural anthropologists, and Marxist critics such as Antonio Gramsci, these historians argued for the political and social importance of studying popular culture and addressed questions of class-based power and hegemony, arguing that workers used popular culture as a way to make time and space for themselves within the existing social and economic structures of industrial America. In addition, the first generation of women's historians addressed these questions from the perspective of gender, finding that young, working-class women at the turn of the century played significant roles in shaping a gendered experience of leisure time at dance halls and other public venues and in extending women's place in the public sphere.

 # DOCUMENTS

All of these documents illustrate the close relationship between labor and leisure in turn-of-the-century America. Documents 1 and 2 articulate the central tenets of the eight-hour movement through a popular song and a lecture. Jesse Henry Jones's song "Eight Hours" was reproduced and sung widely by union members and advocates of the movement. The next three documents illustrate the business, popular pleasure, and the cultural critique of commercialized leisure at Coney Island. The reporter for the *Independent* observes that businessmen at Coney Island expanded their customer base in 1904 by reforming the once unseemly, raucous, working-class activities at the amusement park and appealing to more respectable middle-class patrons. He also provides a comprehensive and detailed view of the various commercial and non-commercial entertainments at the park. The photograph of masses of people enjoying the beach at Coney Island under-scores John Kasson's argument that such spaces challenged and eventually dissolved older, Victorian notions of public behavior, particularly ones related to class-based decorum and gender roles. In Document 4, Maxim Gorky, a Russian novelist and cultural critic, declaims Coney Island as a soul-destroying wasteland that diverted people from higher, intellectual pursuits and nurtured a sense of "false consciousness" among the working class. The final three documents explore the emergence of baseball as a national pastime, one that drew mixed crowds, embodied middle-class desires for healthy leisure activities, and also facilitated middle-class women's entrance into the public sphere. Why did workers want more leisure time and why did they have to struggle to achieve their goals? Who frequented Coney Island and baseball games? Did these amusements blur or sharpen the social distinctions, such as class, gender, and race in American society in the 1900s? What can historians learn from photographs about how audiences used and made sense of these new commercial leisure environments?

1. Songwriter Jesse Henry Addresses Workers' Demands, c. 1866

Eight Hours
Words by I.G. Blanchard
Music by Rev. Jesse H. Jones, c. 1866 or later

Jesse Henry Jones, "Eight Hours." Lyrics: I. G. Blanchard. Music: Rev. Jesse H. Jones, n.d. [1866 or later]. The music for "Eight Hours" was printed in Philip S. Foner, *American Labor Songs of the Nineteenth Century* (Urbana: University of Illinois Press, 1975).

We mean to make things over, we are tired of toil for naught,
With but bare enough to live upon, and never an hour for thought;
We want to feel the sunshine, and we want to smell the flowers,
We are sure that God has will'd it, and we mean to have eight hours
We're summoning our forces from the shipyard, shop and mill,

Chorus:
Eight hours for work, eight hours for rest, eight hours for what we will!
Eight hours for work, eight hours for rest, eight hours for what we will!

The beasts that graze the hillside, and the birds that wander free,
In the life that God has meted have a better lot than we.
Oh! hands and hearts are weary, and homes are heavy with dole;
If our life's to be filled with drudgery, what need of a human soul!
Shout, shout the lusty rally from shipyard, shop and mill,

Chorus …

Hurrah, hurrah, for Labor! for it shall arise in might;
It has filled the world with plenty, it shall fill the world with light;
Hurrah, hurrah, for Labor! it is mustering all its powers,
And shall march along to victory with the banner of Eight Hours!
Shout, shout the echoing rally till all the welkin thrill,

Chorus

2. Activist Edward H. Rogers Struggles for an Eight-Hour Day, 1872

This lecture has had five readings before audiences of workingmen. Its main point, that productive power is compelling leisure, has commended their approval.
My thanks are due to the Boston Eight Hour League, and to personal friends for pecuniary aid in publishing; and also for the assistance growing out of debate; and social intercourse. The League, however, is not responsible for the views expressed.

E. H. R.

Chelsea, Mass., 1872.

A Lecture

Your thoughtful interest is requested, as the effort is made to present a statement of facts, and principles, which underlie the demand for a Reduction of the Hours of Labor.

The distinction of questions of industry, has extended the domain of spiritual law into affairs hitherto deemed commonplace. My convictions require me to urge the application of religious obligation to the use of time.

Edward H. Rogers, "Eight Hour a Day's Work: A Lecture" (Boston Printed at the Office of the "Weekly American Workman," 1872).

Misconception

It will appear quite evident that, there is a marked misconception of some of the aspects of this demand. A visitor to the mill or the forge, even though he be a laborer, finds it difficult to realize of appreciate the irksome, and often painful exercise of force and endurance, which precedes and accompanies the graceful and apparently easy movements of the toilers. This is one of our most subtle illusions, in connection with an erroneous public sentiment, it operates with great power in the prevention or equitable adjustments.

Sophistry

Mrs. Stowe shall speak for me in exposing the largely prevalent sophistry respecting the dignity of labor, which pervades the circles of refined society. "Let anyone observe the conversation in good society for an hour or two, and hear the tone in which servant girls, seamstresses, mechanics, and all who work for their living are mentioned, and he will see, that while every one of the speakers professes to regard useful labor as respectable, she is yet deeply imbued with the leaven of aristocratic ideas." Objectionable as these sentiments appear, when viewed solely from their moral side, I am free to express the opinion that the effort to reform then by moral means alone is hopeless. It may be assumed without fear of effective denial, that, as certain conditions of daily culture always in exercise, by the favored classes, tend with irresistible power in the direction of refinement, and all that it implies, so, on the other hand, conditions and circumstances directly reversed in their nature, but similarly operative, tend inevitably to widen the existing gap between labor and culture. So marked, and so controlling are these influences, that every element of reform is united in opinion on this point; that the present daily duration of labor is of itself sufficient to continue the disastrous tendencies of society, into two antagonistic classes.

The familiar anecdote which comes to be across the water, has in it a volume of satire on all gospels and philosophies which propose to elevate the people, while neglecting their surroundings. A party of travellers descended one of the English mines. They were discourteously received. When they came up, they reported the fact to the proprietors complaining that they had been treated in an ungentlemanly manner. The mine owners excused themselves on the ground that they had made every effort to obtain gentlemen to engage in the labor of mining, but so far, they had been unsuccessful.

Assumptions of Ignorance Refuted

A writer of ability, in a recent discussion of industrial questions, says of the representative workman, that "Over the whole field of industry in which he is a laborer, be never raises his eyes; be works like a mole in the darkness and underground. Artillery horses do not stand more helplessly in the rear of their guns to be pelted by the pitiless fire of the enemy, than the working classes in the battle of industry behind the great manufacturing chiefs. If all goes well, they drag the cannon forward to new positions and fresh triumphs in a glorious gallop; if things go wrong they leave their bones on the ground, but why and wherefore they cannot tell. A striking illustration of their ignorance of the things of all others which it most concerns them to understand—the causes of production, and the relations of production to wages—has just been afforded in the Eight-Hour agitation. A vast number even of the most intelligent joined in it, and carry it on to this hour, in the belief that an Act of the Legislature can secure a workingman the same amount of the results of labor in return for less labor."

The latter portion of this statement admits of an explicit denial. The working men who are active in the Eight-Hour movement, have always confined their requests to the regulation of the hours of labor in public works. It is no fault of ours, if, at a later stage of proceedings, all the employees of the government, whatever may be their opinion upon the duration of labor, unite, and successfully resist the effort to reduce their wages pro-rata.

With some reservations, which blunt the point of the charge of ignorance, we concede that industrial reform, so far as its inception is concerned, depends mainly upon crude simultaneous impulses proceeding from the people. But a demand so radical as that for the Eight-Hour day, is not necessarily unreasonable, because in its initiation, and in much of its advocacy, it has been characterized by the impulsive peculiarities of the masses.

It is hardly possible to conceive that the working people of a country so extensive as ours, could unite in this claim unless potent causes had been for a long time operative in such a manner as to impress their minds....

Benefits of Reduction

Having shown some of the tendencies of excess of production, in the prostration of industry, which results from the unintelligent and exclusive devotion of labor to the great staples, an outlined allusion to the benefits of a different course, will be appropriate.

The common conception which has attached itself to the idea of leisure, as demanded by the masses, has been that of idleness, or at best of rest. A fair construction would read differently. It deserves to be respected as protest of the human mind and soul, against the monotonous routine which could only have been initiated in a barbarons age, and among classes of laborers ranking little higher in their range of faculties than the beasts that perish. We should shudder, and instinctively recoil from the brutal serfs, who, in Edward 2d's time, began the modern industrial contest, by a bloody march on London. They uttered however, no protest against the duration of daily toil. Its absolutely unrequited character, was as appropriate for them to rectify, as it is for the workmen of the present day, urged by all the necessities of an advanced state of society, to claim as an undoubted right, such liberation of time as is evidently required by the manifold obligations and privileges which are ours.

Benjamin Franklin's example has often been quoted as an instance proving that the ordinary hours of labor allow sufficient time for intellectual improvement. The fact, as started by himself in Weld's Biography, is that at some time before 1730, when he could not have been more than twenty-four, he adopted the eight hour day. Franklin's brain and temperament however, even with twelve hours work would have elevated hours of laborers, who in their mediocrity of ability, fail in the effort to meet even ordinary demands.

A vast and much needed element of power, will be developed among large classes of intelligent men and women, in all their relations, by reductions. The ordinary calls to personal service in connection with our social obligations, meet for the most part with blunt declination, or with inefficient compliance, for lack of time, which is drawn worse than uselessly toward unprofitable production.

Suppose the fifty thousand boot and shoe makers of the State should repeat the ten hour reduction, and extend the yearly season of activity by a further restriction of two hours each day, doing as much each year as they do now, and getting of course as much for it, devoting the leisure thus acquired, to a system of well matured garden industry, working about their own homes with the pleasure which such labor inspires, receiving the help of their elder children of both sexes, by the general adoption of reduced hours of schooling; would not such a course, generously extend the incomes now we scant for all the higher calls of the times.

We do not urge our idea because it is humane, but we are not without war- rant for doing so. Many of our offensive or laborions trades involve each efflu- vial, or such elemental or physical exposures as to rank them with the miners' plea; and even it this were not the case, the general tendency of our race to advance in average longevity, because weakly persons lived longer than they did, should prompt an easement of toil for their sake. The sternest advocate of lengthy labor, as essential to the manhood of our yeomanry, should be ashamed of our present usages in our factory and metropolitan industry in the control of females. Even the London *Times* has come down to nine hours, so clear is the physiological argument in its application to those who would the future genera- tions. How marked the incidental, but yet important benefits. What relief would be experienced by the young man struggling in his preparatory studies, while he labors, and what large opening for evening schools of the highest grade, and to carry along into mature life, the instruction in refined arts, and elevating natural sciences now almost wholly neglected. The partial and imperfect development of the inventive, or as we might almost turn it, the creative faculty, is not the least of the losses entailed upon us by the traditional hours of labor. To a very large extent, inventions in mechanism originate among professional or cultivated men. All improvements in machinery, which abate the exercise of manual force, all reductions of working time, all spiritual, intellectual and ideal culture, opening broadly upon the classes, which by the circumstances of their callings, stand in natural relations to the constructive faculty, lift and throw aside the clods which cover their exalted capacity.

Incessant toil, anxious solicitude for a living, the whole force of training thrown upon perceptive intellect by machinery and specialization, so tent to dwarf and benumb every quick and original susceptibility, and lower the condi- tion of the working classes, that it is not too much to say that this noble function is practically buried under the burdens imposed by excessive toil.

Opposition

The demand which is made by labor for a new adjustment of working time, is met with the objection that capital will be withdrawn to be employed in more lucrative business. This statement cannot be fully answered without exposing the defects of our banking system. Its large issues, and the profits which they brings, affect injuriously legitimate demands for capital. All parties who have the management of investments, being under an ever present pressure to bring their dividends up to the standard of profit which satisfies the greed of speculation and usury. But there are purely industrial aspects of our question, suggested by this objection, which we are at liberty to discuss at sufficient length to allow their momentous character to be discerned.

The threat of capital to close its mills if reduction should be insisted on, finds a parallel in the assertion which has been freely uttered, that the great cost of machinery requires that more, instead of less, time should be devoted to production. Ridiculous as this last position appears, it is nevertheless the real attitude of capital toward labor as further statements will show.

A modern sewing machine increases production from three to five times. A seamstress engaged upon one of them receives for plain sewing in our families, one dollar and fifty cents per day. She is fortunate if she is not expected to labor more than ten hours. I am safe in saying, that if the sewing machine had required by the circumstances of its construction, the aid of steam, so as preclude its use in private residences, the wages of the women sewing by hand in our homes, would from general causes have been the same, she would not have been asked to work any longer, and she would have escaped the severe strain upon her health of the unnatural use of her lower limbs. I think that this illustration leads as directly to the obstacles which impede our industrial progress.

Obstacles

At a nearly nominal cost of machinery, the seamstress is doing three or four times as much as she could do by hand, with no reduction of her hours, and no increase of pay comparing with the increased product. If we can ascertain where her surplus of production goes, and how it goes, we shall solve the mystery why inventions has not lessened toil, and we shall also learn the principal reason why the manufacturers in dispensing with intelligent and well paid, labor find themselves burdened with wares they cannot sell, just as the venders of counterfeit honey were, when they attempted to supersede the bee.

The results of our toil are tending by all the influences governing their distribution, to develop as fixed capital in the form of mille, ships, railroads, banks, the higher educational institutions, costly public buildings and private residences, warehouses etc., under such conditions as regards the dividends expected, and the expenses incurred, as to render justice to labor, both in regard to its payment or its continuous employment, impossible.

The laboring classes of this country and of Europe are engaged in the hopeless effort to make profitable returns for immense sums of money, which ought to be in their own hands, so far, at least, as their first division and expenditure is concerned. It is the intelligent perception of this relation of labor to capital; in connection with their deprivation of the ballot, and their despair of aid from the church, which gives tremendous momentum to the Internationals of the continent. They see plainly, what we are beginning to see, that wages and excessive labor, united; are a true cancer upon the body politic, and that national death must ensue to all of our civilizations which do not succeed in throwing them off....

Moral Aspects

It is impossible to reach sound conclusions on these questions, while neglecting or undervaluing their moral aspects. The writers of both the Old and New Testaments, are all radical Industrial Reformers. In His contemptuous allusions to hirelings, the Saviour reprobates wages, and in His choice of the Apostles, His preference for fishermen, indecates his appreciation of the vital character of the co-operative ideas and customs which the precarious nature of that calling necessitates.

The Book of Exodus introduces us to the first direct intercourse of the Supreme Being with a whole people. It is a point of great interest, that the awe inspiring circumstances which attended the annunciation of the primary laws of morals, should also be associated with the promulgation of an ordinance requiring the cessation of all labor every seventh year. Three reasons are given for this regulation, viz:—"But the seventh year thou shalt let it rest, and lie still; that the poor of thy people may eat: and what they leave, the beasts of the field shall eat."—Ex. xxiii, 11th. "But in the seventh year, shall be a sabbath of rest note the land."—Lev. xxv-4. We have in the first of these reasons "that the poor of thy people may eat," a corroboration of our present claim, that the elevation of the depressed masses of Christendom, is to come by the way of less, rather than more labor....

Adjustment

Having shown the moral weakness of the opposition to our movement, a few remarks relative to its adjustment, are pertinent.

One fact in the history of the ten hour crisis is quite suggestive, repeating itself, as it does, at the present time. Labor was not then, nor is it now, permitted to take the risk upon itself of introducing the shorter day. It is well known as a matter of history, and equally well understood, as a present condition of the contest, that even piece or job workers, are not at liberty to regulate their own time. This aspect of our situation, has compelled us to make an open issue. In appealing, as we are doing, to the moral sense and intelligent judgment of the community, we are confronted with a truth of the greatest interest, namely. That the Human will enters as a controlling power into the complicated interests involved in this discussion.

From the moment when the demand for the Eight Hour Day was projected into our active life, opinion has pronounced itself, for, or against, the new idea. Its influential utterance, has come for the most part, from those who are somewhat advanced in line, and has been adverse. But from a very large number, the verdict has been favorable. In the simple utterance, eight hours is enough for a day's work, millions of the youthful, and unbiassed have ranged themselves on the side of justice, and of progress. Nor am I dealing in this statement with an substantial conception. Death is a sublime and universal moralist. When he removes from among men, those who are full of years and honor, he makes room for the advanced ideas of a more complete culture, as rank after rank, the generations advances toward perfection. Seen by this light, the apparently confused and tumultuous movement of the masses, appears orderly and symmetrical. We are prepared by it to recognize the fact, that the will of the working classes, chastened, and adapted, in the great debate we have forced, may properly enter the arena of the world's industry, with the force of economic law....

Final Remarks

The impediments which lie in the way of the deliverance of the masses from their extreme toil, are of human origin, and transient in their duration. The true course is to compel their removal by constant, earnest and powerful appeals to the reason and the conscience.

The preposition sometimes heard, for an hour or two's remission on Saturday, does not meet the merits of the question, or the needs of the people. It is of little consequence whether as much can be done in the ten or the eight hour day, as is at present. It is puerile for capital to put itself angrily on its defense, at the possibility of reduced dividends on investments, made in manifest ignorance or neglect of industrial, as well as spiritual law.

The depth and volume of the productive forces of our laborious people, our mechanical powers, and our fertile soil, is underrated. We have convincing proof of this in the absence of injury and the plenitude of benefit which has attended accomplished reductions. The fear that somebody will starve, if laboring time is limited, though finding very respectable utterance, vanishes in view of the reduction of factory time in this State from thirteen to eleven hours, without the slightest detriment. In the course of my reading, I have found an item which illustrates somewhat ludicrously the distorted state of the public mind on this subject. An examiner in our Patent Office has volunteered the statement, in an exact computation of the relative cost of steam as a motor, compared with animals—that an ox does not, and cannot, healthfully labor more than eight hours out of the twenty-four. This estimate takes into account all natural momentary pauses. The thought occurred to me that if oxen had the ballot, we should not have been favored with such an official opinion as this. The fear of being called a demagogue would have ensured silence.

In view of facts so evident, and motives so powerful, as have been presented, I would emulate the sound sense of our English brethren in throwing a larger portion of our interest upon this unprepossessing but most vital element of our grand reform.

It is useless to urge that a possible slight advance in the price of necessaries can offset the benefits we shall derive. One point alone—evident tendencies to steadier employ—ought to case our minds in this respect.

With the clear evidence we have that so large a reduction as four hours from the summer day has not lowered wages, increased the cost of commodities, or injured capital, why should we continue by excessive toil to glut markets, and by spasmodic and disastrous reductions of prices to augment the numbers of a monied aristocracy, who have the power by a delusive currency, to divert the ample product of our stolid endurance of toil to their own aggrandizement.

We are at liberty to make all proper admissions in respect to any relief which may come from reform in Revenue, or Taxation, or from the united influence of these, and other beneficial agencies which are being pressed. When we have done all this, we are still securely intrenched in the position, that the condition of the working classes cannot be permanently improved by continuing their excessive toil, because it defeats co-operation, by preventing culture; and also, because the terms of competition which control their wages, absolutely prevent a permanent increase of their income by overwork.

The facts of over-production, and of enforced leisure in consequence, are facts of to-day. Their full adjustment, by a broad and equitable distribution of labor, and its reward, will be the work of one or two generations.

The dictates of Religion, the deductions of Philosophy, and the conclusions of vast numbers of sagacious and practical workingmen, unite in pointing to the radical Reduction of the Hours of Labor, as the initiative step in bringing about this grand result.

The capitalist and economist may ridicule these views, and point their sarcasm by general statements of public and private necessities for increased production. Controlling as they do, public opinion through the press, we shall find it impossible by argument, or the clearest statement of truth, to obtain a just verdict. It is the nature of conservatism, however, to recognize and maintain established customs; this is its present position toward the ten-hour-day.

The conclusion is obvious, that our success lies in our own hands, and depends upon the discretion, energy, and perseverance with which we continue to press our claim.

3. Reporter Edwin E. Slosson
Explains the Business of Leisure, 1904

"A trip up the Hudson, or down the bay,
A trolley to Coney or Far Rockaway,
On a Sunday afternoon."

… Coney Island has reformed. Even a naturally incredulous public must be convinced of that. Coney Island is no Sunday school yet, but it is probable that nowhere else in the world can be found so great a variety of popular amusement with so little of the essentially vicious as on this little strip of sand which for two centuries has been a pleasure ground to the metropolis…. [J]ust 60 years ago, when it was reported that the enormous number of 300 vehicles had paid toll on old Shell Road, people all over the country have been shocked, both at its sinfulness and popularity. Men went to the seaside resort to be free, as they said, from the conventionalities of the city; the said conventionalities being, apparently, the Ten Commandments….

The reform of Coney Island was effected not so much by the pressure of public opinion of the respectable people who did not go there, or internal conviction of sin on the part of the dive keepers, or by the strong arm of the law, altho some courageous police action wiped out the most disreputable of the

Edwin W. Slosson, "The Amusement Business," *The Independent*, July 1904, 131–139.

gambling hells, but primarily because it was discovered that vice does not pay as well as decency. It was learned that decent people have in the aggregate more money to spend than the dissipated, even tho they spend it more sparingly … and that a show which can take in the whole family pays better than a show where only one would go. A reform based on financial advantage is likely to prove lasting. People sought the vicious amusements, not so much for the vice as for the amusement, and when they found they could get the latter without the former they flocked to Coney Island at the rate of 100,000 a day.

Important factors in the development of the new Coney Island are the syndicated amusements; first, Steeplechase Park, last year Luna Park, this year Dreamland. The proprietors of Dreamland claim that $3,500,000 was spent before its gates were opened, and the owners of Luna Park state that $750,000 was paid out this year on additional attractions. Just as in manufactures it has been found advantageous to combine all the interdependent industries, so in the amusement business it was found profitable to bring together into one inclosure all the popular forms of entertainment and exclude fraudulent and offensive features and objectionable characters.

The admission is only 10 or 15 cents and a view of the "park" itself, with its holiday thousands, its free shows, and its illuminated palaces of staff, is sufficient in itself to repay the trip. It is a development of the medieval street fair, a twentieth century Corso in carnival time. On every side are offered enticing entertainments, always just about to begin…. In general, only soft drinks are sold in the park, and it is very rare that one sees a drunken or disorderly person. Policemen are chiefly for ornament, and the arrests reported after 200,000 pleasure seekers have spent the day at the island are very few; a marked contrast with the record of old Coney. Your pocket-book is not safe there yet, but it is not likely to be opened by another than yourself. It is the ordinary American crowd, the best natured, best dressed, best behaving and best smelling crowd in the world….

In the popular amusements is most strikingly manifested that curious disposition of people to make their amusements so like their daily life. Like the power horse which was driven around the ring from left to right every day, and so on Sunday, to rest himself, went around all day from right to left, so human beings in their hours of recreation merely modify their daily treadmill…. So these city people, tired by the jar and noise and glare and crowds of the streets, go for recreation where all these are intensified, instead of to the quiet country. The switchbacks, scenic railways and toy trains are merely trolley cars, a little more uneven in roadbed, jerky in motion and cramped in the seat than the ordinary means of transportation, but not much. The burning building is one of the most popular of attractions, because, it is most like what they have all seen and know about and, therefore, are most interested in. The Ferris wheel and the gigantic see-saw are but exaggerations of the ordinary elevator, and the towers are not unlike office buildings….

At night, when the shams and incongruities are hidden and the architectural features are outlined by hundreds of thousands of electric lights, the spectacle of the Dreamland tower, 375 feet high, as seen from the water, and of the court of

Luna Park, is quite fairy-like and enchanting…. Now, line by line, as we watch in the twilight, as if lit by an unseen taper, as if drawn by the architect on the darkness by a pen of fire, the building slowly appears, until with a final flash it stands like a glorified ghost of itself in the night….

After all, the social feature is the important one in popular amusements. Does any one go to Coney Island alone? To get away for a holiday, to "go some place," is the common desire. Hospitality and visiting in the country sense being impossible in city flats people must meet in public, and little trips by sea or land afford this opportunity. The reference to "dear little Coney Isle" in the folk love songs show what a part it has played as a matchmaker. Many a young couple have been so well satisfied with each other in this short journey that they have decided to continue traveling together through life…. The young man who takes his girl to Coney has also a chance to find out whether she is economical or extravagant in her tastes. A little more thoughtfulness of her escort's pocketbook would, therefore, often pay the girl in the long run. Since time is money, some girls think that the more money is spent the better time they have had. As I stepped off the steamer at the conclusion of the arduous investigations involved in the preparation of this article, I overheard the scrap of a conversation between two girls, temporarily parted from their escorts. Said the girl in the red hat to the girl in the white one:

"What sort of a time did you have?"

"Great. He blew … $5.00 on the blow out."

"You beat me again. My chump only spent $2.55."

4. Russian Novelist Maxim Gorky Criticizes Commercialized Leisure, 1907

This is Coney Island.

On Monday the metropolitan newspapers triumphantly announce:

"Three Hundred Thousand People in Coney Island Yesterday. Twenty-three Children Lost."

"There's something doing there" the reader thinks.

First a long ride by trolley thru Brooklyn and Long Island amid the dust and noise of the streets. Then the gaze is met by the sight of dazzling, magnificent Coney Island. From the very first moment of arrival at this city of fire, the eye is blinded…. Everything whirls and dazzles, and blends into a tempestuous ferment of fiery foam. The visitor is stunned: his consciousness is withered by the intense gleam; his thoughts are routed from his mind; he becomes a particle in the crowd. People wander about in the flashing, blinding fire intoxicated and devoid of will. A dull-white mist penetrates their brains, greedy expectation envelopes their souls. Dazed by the brilliancy the throngs wind about like dark bands in the surging sea of light, pressed upon all sides by the black bournes of night.

Maxim Gorky, "Boredom," *The Independent*, 8 August 1907, 309–317.

Everywhere electric bulbs shed their cold, garish gleam. They shine on posts and walls, on window casings and cornices: they stretch in an even line along the high tubes of the power-house: they burn on all the roofs, and prick the eye with the sharp needles of their dead, indifferent sparkle. The people screw up their eyes, and smiling disconcertedly crawl along the ground like the heavy line of a tangled chain.

A man must make a great effort not to lose himself in the crowd, not to be overwhelmed by his amazement—an amazement in which there is neither transport nor joy. But if he succeeds in individualizing himself, he finds that these millions of fires produce a dismal, all-revealing light. Tho they hint at the possibility of beauty, they everywhere discover a dull, gloomy ugliness. The city, magic and fantastic from afar, now appears an absurd jumble of straight lines of wood, a cheap, hastily constructed toy-house for the amusement of children. Dozens of white buildings, monstrously diverse, not one with even the suggestion of beauty. They are built of wood, and smeared over with peeling white paint, which gives them the appearance of suffering with the same skin disease…. Inside is a cloud of smoke and the dark figures of the people. The people eat, drink and smoke.

But no human voice is heard. The monotonous hissing of the arc lights fills the air, the sounds of music, the cheap notes of the orchestrions, and the thin, continuous sputtering of the sausage-frying counters. All these sounds mingle in an importunate hum, as of some thick, taut chord. And if the human voice breaks into this ceaseless resonance, it is like a frightened whisper. Everything round about glitters insolently and reveals its own dismal ugliness.

The soul is seized with a desire for a living, beautiful fire, a sublime fire, which should free the people from the slavery of a varied boredom. For this boredom deafens their ears and blinds their eyes. The soul would burn away all this allurement, all this mad frenzy, this dead magnificence and spiritual penury. It would have a merry dancing and shouting and singing; it would see a passionate play of the motley tongues of fire; it would have joyousness and life.

The people huddled together in this city actually number hundreds of thousands. They swarm into the cages like black flies. Children walk about, silent, with gaping mouths and dazzled eyes. They look around with such intensity, such seriousness, that the sight of them feeding their little souls upon this hideousness, which they mistake for beauty, inspires a pained sense of pity. The men's faces, shaven even to the mustache, all strangely like one another, are grave and immobile. The majority bring their wives and children along, and feel that they are benefactors of their families, because they provide not only bread, but also magnificent shows. They enjoy the tinsel, but, too serious to betray their pleasure, they keep their thin lips pressed together, and look from the corners of their screwed-up eyes, like people whom nothing can astonish. Yet, under the mask of indifference simulated by the man of mature experience, a strained desire can be detected to take in all the delights of the city….

They are filled with contented *ennui*, their nerves are racked by an intricate maze of motion and dazzling fire. Bright eyes grow still brighter, as if the brain paled and lost blood in the strange turmoil of the white, glittering wood. The *ennui*, which issues from under the pressure of self-disgust, seems to turn and turn in a slow circle of agony. It drags tens of thousands of uniformly dark people into its somber dance, and sweeps them into a will-less heap, as the wind sweeps the rubbish of the street. Then it scatters them apart and sweeps them together again....

Thus, when night comes, a fantastic magic city, all of fire, suddenly blazes up from the ocean. Without consuming, it burns long against the dark background of the sky, its beauty mirrored in the broad, gleaming bosom of the sea.

In the glittering gossamer of its fantastic buildings, tens of thousands of gray people, like patches on the ragged clothes of a beggar, creep along with weary faces and colorless eyes.

Mean panderers to debased tastes unfold the disgusting nakedness of their falsehood, the *naïveté* of their shrewdness, the hypocrisy and insatiable force of their greed. The cold gleam of the dead fire bares the stupidity of it all. Its pompous glitter rests upon everything round about the people.

But the precaution has been taken to blind the people, and they drink in the vile poison with silent rapture. The poison contaminates their souls. Boredom whirls about in an idle dance, expiring in the agony of its inanition....

CAPRI. ITALY.

5. Ordinary People Challenge Propriety at the Beach, 1903–1909

6. The *New York Sun* Portrays a Typical Baseball Crowd, 1884

The first thing that impresses one on a visit to the Polo Grounds on any day of the week is the number of spectators. It makes no difference what day it is or which clubs are to compete; there are always crowds on hand to witness a match. On Fridays and Saturdays there are more persons than on other days. But a match between two of the more prominent nines of the League will call out 7,000 or 8,000 persons, no matter what the day may be. The wonder to a man who works for his living is how so many people can spare the time for the sport. They are obliged to leave their offices down town at 2 or 3 o'clock in order to get to the Polo Grounds in time, and very many of them are constant attendants on the field. The next thing that impresses the visitor is the absolute and perfect knowledge of base-ball which every visitor at the grounds possesses. Nearly every boy and man keeps his own score, registering base hits, runs and errors as the game goes along, and the slightest hint of unfairness on the part of the umpire will bring a yell from thousands of throats instantaneously. The third notable characteristic … is the good nature, affability, and friendliness of the crowd. The slim schoolboy ten years of age, and the fat, lager-beer saloon proprietor of fifty talk gracefully about the game as it progresses as though they had known each other for years. Men exchange opinions freely about the game with persons they never saw before and everybody seems good-natured and happy.

The Majority of the Men

[The majority of men] are intensely interested in the game. Most of them come well provided with their own cigars, and sedulously evade the eye of the man who peddles "sody-water, sarss-a-parilla lemonade, pea-nuts and seegars." There is little drinking of any sort and much smoking…. At times when the umpire renders a decision that does not meet with popular approval, there will be a terrific outbreak, and for the next ten minutes the offending one is guyed unmercifully. Every decision he renders is received with jeers, and sarcastic comments are made upon the play. The good sense of the crowd gets the better of this boyishness, however, and unless the umpire is decidedly biased, which rarely occurs, the crowd soon settles back into its accustomed condition of contentment.

Perhaps the most enthusiastic and expert spectators at the Polo Grounds are the stockily built young Irishmen. They may be bartenders, light porters, expressmen, clerks, loungers, policemen off duty, or merchants out on a holiday. One of them is a type of a thousand others. He is usually square shouldered and well built. Probably he has had a taste of athletics himself and plays….

It has often been remarked that there are at the Polo Grounds every day AN EXTRAORDINARY NUMBER OF FAT MEN. No one can tell why this is. It is said that men of extraordinary avoirdupois who find it impractical, inelegant,

From *New York Sun*, 16 June 1884.

and more or less sensational to throw hand-springs, steal base, and run swiftly at 250 pounds weight, enjoy the spectacle of the cat-like and rapid movements of the athletes on the field....

A good many gray heads and gray beards are to be seen on the grand stand. They belong to men who have been base-ball enthusiasts from boyhood up. They enjoy the sport more than they would any play, horse or boat race, and they are full of reminiscences of the game. Scattered in among them are bright-face boys, who are well dressed, well mannered and intelligent. They are looked upon by the men as of enough importance to warrant sober treatment, and their opinions are as gravely accepted as those of men. Another pronounced type is the young business man. Hundreds of spruce, well-dressed and wide-awake young men who are apparently clerks, brokers or business men from downtown are to be seen about the grounds. They talk balls and strike, but principally ball. They do not know as much about it as ... the solid young Irishmen, but they make up in enthusiasm what they lack in knowledge. Their interest in the game consists largely in the money they have on it. They always bet freely among themselves, and return home happy or crestfallen, according to their winnings.

There are among the ladies who attend ball matches a few, perhaps a dozen in all, who thoroughly understand the game and are actually and warmly interested in the sport. Most of them, however have such a superficial knowledge of the game that they grow tired before the ninth inning is reached, and conceal their weariness when they leave early, by expressing a desire to avoid the crowd.

7. Anne O'Hagan Describes the Athletic American Girl, 1901

To whomsoever the athletic woman owes her existence, to him or her the whole world of women owes a debt incomparably great. Absolutely no other social achievement in the behalf of women is so important and so far reaching in its results.... With the single exception of the improvement in the legal status of women, their entrance into the realm of sports is the most cheering thing that has happened to them in the century just past.

The Benefit to Body and Mind

In the first place, there is the question of health. The general adoption of athletic sports by women meant the gradual disappearance of the swooning damsel of old romance, and of that very real creature, the lady who delighted, a decade or so ago, to describe herself as "high strung," which, being properly interpreted, meant uncontrolled and difficult to live with. Women who didn't like athletics were forced to take them up in self defense; and exercise meant firmer muscles, better circulation, a more equable temper, and the dethronement of the "nervous headache" from its high place in feminine regard.

Anne O'Hagan, "The Athletic Girl," *Munsey's Magazine* 25 (August 1901), 729–738.

The revolution meant as much psychologically as it did physically.... In dress, ... no boon has been granted to woman so great as the privilege of wearing shirt waists and short skirts. When the tennis players of ten or fifteen years ago first popularized that boneless, free chested, loose armed bodice they struck a blow for feminine freedom.... The woman who plays golf has made it possible for the woman who cannot distinguish between a cleek and a broom handle to go about her marketing in a short skirt; she has given the working girl, who never saw a golf course, freedom from the tyranny of braids and bindings....

To have improved half the race in health, disposition, and dress would seem almost enough for one movement to have accomplished. But athletics have done more than this. They have robbed old age of some of its terrors for women, and they promise to rob it of more....

When "Play" Was "Wisely Banished"

Twenty five years ago a woman so fortunate as to live in the country probably rode on horseback—primarily as a means of locomotion, however. She could also play croquet. The city woman might walk, and she too might play croquet, if she had a large enough lawn; but that was about the sum of the sports permitted.

The change began with the gradual introduction of physical training into the schools. Today there is not a girls' school of any standing that does not include in its curriculum a course in gymnastics, and encourage or insist upon some sort of outdoor exercise.... Boards of education require that the newer school buildings shall be properly equipped with gymnasiums....

The Growth of College Sports

From being the chief factor in the athletic life of the women's colleges, the gymnasiums have grown to be distinctly subsidiary. They supplement the outdoor exercises which the location of most of the institutions for higher education makes so natural and attractive. Each has its specialty in the line of sport, and the young woman who wins a championship in rowing, swimming, track events, basket ball, bicycling, or whatever it may be, is a lionized creature who tastes for once the sweets of the cup of utter adulation.

At Wellesley, where the distinctive sport is rowing, Float Day is the banner festival of the year. No girl is allowed to row upon the crews who is not able to swim, but, ... the only contest permitted is in rowing form, not in speed. Bryn Mawr has by far the most complete and elaborate of the gymnasiums connected with the women's colleges, and its basket ball is famous wherever college women, past, present, or to be, are gathered together....

There are many reasons why college athletics for women are the most important of all. In the first place, a girl who, while struggling for a degree, develops a taste for outdoor sports, never loses it. The chances are ten to one that as a grandmother, she will be an active pedestrian or mountain climber.... Moreover, it is college athletics that have the greatest effect upon the physique of women. Once they have attained their full growth, exercise may keep them well, or make them stout or thin, but it will not have the marked effect upon their bodily development that it has upon that of a growing girl.

Physical Culture in the Cities

Once upon a time the young woman who came out of college was somewhat at a loss how to expend her energy and to keep up her sports. Bicycles, golf, and the country clubs have altered that. Moreover, ... there are, in the large cities at any rate, excellent gymnasiums. In New York, for instance, apart from the gymnasiums in all the schools, in the working girls' clubs, and in the various branches of the Young Women's Christian Association, there are at least six well known private gymnasiums where women may pursue physical culture to their hearts' content and the good of their bodies....

Between three and four hundred women are enrolled as pupils of the Savage Gymnasium, which, both in attendance and equipment, is the largest in New York. There are classes and there is individual work. Fencing and boxing, both of which have many ardent disciples, are taught privately. Girls of five and women of fifty and sixty are among the patrons....

The cost of being a gymnast in New York varies. There is one gymnasium with pillowed couches about the room, soft, lovely lights, and walls that rest weary eyes; where a crisp capped maid brings the exerciser a cup of milk during her rest upon the divan, where her boots are laced or buttoned by deft fingers other than her own. For these privileges and the ordinary ones of gymnastic training the charge is a hundred dollars a year.

Forty dollars covers the cost in less Sybaritic circles, and if one has the distinction of being a working woman, ten dollars will pay for gymnastic instruction and privileges. The gymnasiums connected with the Christian Associations, the working girls' clubs, the settlements, and the like are even less expensive.

8. H. Addington Bruce Analyzes Baseball and the National Life, 1913

... Veritably baseball is something more than the great American game—it is an American institution having a significant place in the life of the people, and consequently worthy of close and careful analysis.

Fully to grasp its significance, however, it is necessary to study it, in the first place, as merely a game, and seek to determine wherein lie its peculiar qualities of fascination. As a game, as something that is "playable," it of course must serve the ordinary ends of play. These, according to the best authorities on the physiology and psychology of play, are threefold: the expenditure of surplus nervous energy in a way that will not be harmful to the organism, but on the contrary, will give needed exercise to growing muscles; the development of traits and

H. Addington Bruce, "Baseball and the National Life," *Outlook*, 104(May 1913), 104–170.

abilities that will afterwards aid the player in the serious business of life; and the attainment of mental rest through pleasurable occupation....

... Success and progress depend chiefly on the presence of certain personal characteristics. Physical fitness, courage, honesty, patience, the spirit of initiative combined with due respect for lawful authority, soundness and quickness of judgment, self-confidence, self-control, cheeriness, fair-mindedness, and appreciation of the importance of social solidarity, of "team play"—these are traits requisite as never before for success in the life of an individual and of a nation.... But it is safe to say that no other game—not even excepting football—develops them as does baseball.

One need attend only a few games, whether played by untrained schoolboys or by the most expert professionals, to appreciate the great value of baseball as a developmental agent. Habits of sobriety and self-control are established in the players if only from the necessity of keeping in good condition in order to acquit one's self creditably and hold a place on the team. Patience, dogged persistence, the pluck that refuses to acknowledge either weariness or defeat, are essential to the mastery of the fine points of batting, fielding, or pitching—a mastery which in turn brings with it a feeling of self-confidence that eventually will go far in helping its possessor to achieve success off as well as on the "diamond."

So, too, courage, and plenty of it, is needed at the bat—courage not simply to face the swiftly moving ball, but to "crowd" the "plate" so as to handicap the pitcher in his efforts to perform successfully and expeditiously the work of elimination.... The courage of the batsman ... had no small share in winning for the "Giants" the National League honors in 1911 and again last year.

As an agent in the development of the "team spirit" baseball is no less notable. The term "sacrifice hit" eloquently expresses one phase of the game which must leave on all playing it an indelible impression of the importance in all affairs of life of unselfish co-operation....

... Baseball is also a splendid mind-builder. The ability to think, and to think quickly, is fostered by the duties of its every position as well as by the complicated problems that are constantly arising in its swiftly changing course of events. Time and again games have been won, or the way has been cleared to victory, by the quickness of a player or a manager in appreciating the possibilities of a critical situation and planning a definite plan of campaign to meet the emergency....

So incessant and so varied are the demands made on the ball-player's intelligence that any one who really knows the game will be inclined to indorse unreservedly the published declaration of that most successful baseball-player and most successful business man, Mr. Albert G. Spalding:

> "I never struck anything in business that did not seem a simple matter when compared with complications I have faced on the baseball field. A young man playing baseball gets into the habit of quick thinking in most adverse circumstances and under the most merciless criticism in the world—the criticism from the 'bleachers.' ... "

... With the passage of time the technique of the game has been improved to an extent that makes it more of a developmental agent than it was even ten years ago. Lacking the strength, skill, and experience of the professional player, the schoolboy whose efforts are confined to the "diamond" of the vacant lot or public park plays the game under precisely the same rules as the professional, and with no less zest and earnestness, and profits correspondingly. To be sure, in playing it he does not dream for an instant that he is thereby helping to prepare himself for the important struggles of maturity. He plays it merely because he finds it "good fun"—merely because, in its variety and rapidity of action, in the comparative ease with which its fundamental principles may be learned, and in its essentially co-operative yet competitive character, it affords an intensely pleasurable occupation. It is, in truth, a game which makes an irresistible appeal to the instincts of youth precisely because it so admirably meets the principal objects of play— mental rest through enjoyment, exercise for the muscles, the healthy expenditure of surplus nervous energy, and practice and preparation for life's work....

... An instinctive resort to sport [is] a method of gaining momentary relief from the strain of an intolerable burden, and at the same time finding a harmless outlet for pent-up emotions which, unless thus gaining expression, might discharge themselves in a dangerous way.... It is no mere coincidence that the great sport-loving peoples of the world—the Americans, the English, the Canadians, and the Australians—have been pre-eminent in the art of achieving progress by peaceful and orderly reform....

Baseball, then, from the spectator's standpoint, is to be regarded as a means of catharsis, or, perhaps better, as a safety-valve. And it performs this service the more readily because of the appeal it makes to the basic instincts, with resultant removal of the inhibitions that ordinarily cause tenseness and restraint. For exactly the same reason it has a democratizing value no less important to the welfare of society than is its value as a developmental and tension-relieving agent. The spectator at a ball game is no longer a statesman, lawyer, broker, doctor, merchant, or artisan, but just a plain every-day man, with a heart full of fraternity and good will to all his fellow-men—except perhaps the umpire. The oftener he sits in grand stand or "bleachers," the broader, kindlier, better man and citizen he must tend to become.

Finally, it is to be observed that the mere watching of a game of baseball, as of football, lacrosse, hockey, or any other game of swift action, has a certain beneficial physical effect. It is a psychological commonplace that pleasurable emotions, especially if they find expression in laughter, shouts, cheers, and other muscle-expanding noises, have a tonic value to the whole bodily system. So that it is quite possible to get exercise vicariously, as it were; and the more stimulating the spectacle that excites feelings of happiness and enjoyment, the greater will be the resultant good. Most decidedly baseball is a game well designed to render this excellent service....

 # ESSAYS

The essays by John F. Kasson, professor of history at Chapel Hill, and Stephen Riess, professor of history at Northeastern Illinois University, represent the vanguard of early historical scholarship on commercial leisure and spectator sports as

sites of peoples' culture, or culture created from the bottom up.
lar culture express the desires of working people and overturn (
ceptions of public life at a critical moment of change in A
Kasson studies the success of Coney Island, as opposed to high c__
porating "immigrants and working-class groups into their forms and values" (42)
and posing a challenge to sexual and social mores in public culture. Coney Island
turned business culture and the mechanization of work on their heads; the
amusement park was a carnivalesque playground where Americans could let
loose, quite literally, of work routines and gentile behavior and use machines,
such as the rollercoaster, to temporarily reconfigure their relationship to industrial
work, the city, and American society. Although sports history is often seen as a
distinct subfield within history, historians such as Riess have addressed questions
that overlap with and inform studies of popular culture in urban–industrial
America in this period. Did Coney Island and spectator sports perform similar cultural work in terms of redefining the relationship of immigrant workers to the
city, work, and capitalism? Who attended sporting events and why did baseball
become known as the national pastime? How did both amusement parks and
sports help redefine public life for women?

Workers Seek Leisure Time and Space

JOHN F. KASSON

Although the subway did not extend all the way to Coney Island until 1920,
turn-of-the-century visitors made their way by a variety of routes and often a
combination of conveyances. These included excursion boats, ferryboats, railroads, elevated trains, electric trolleys, subway trains, horsecars, hackney carriages,
automobiles, and bicycles. The cheapest fare to the resort in the early 1890s had
been forty cents, fifty for a steamer; but improvements in rapid transit beginning
with the nickel trolley ride to Coney in 1895 forced these prices down and
brought the excursion within the means of the great multitude. The time
required for the journey obviously varied greatly depending upon the route
and means one took, but the construction of new bridges and tunnels linking
New York's boroughs combined with the speed of elevated trains, railroads,
and subways all made Coney's amusement parks widely accessible. Express trains
from Brooklyn Bridge, for example, reportedly reached the gates of Luna Park in
only thirty-two minutes.

Coney Island's amusement parks were open from May until early September,
and in the heat of the summer the crush of visitors reached staggering proportions.
Hordes of pleasure seekers flocked to the resort whenever they had leisure, often in
hours snatched after work during the week and especially on Sundays and holidays.
Coney no longer reckoned its customers merely in the thousands. Press agents
declared the multitudes numbered as many as 200,000 on a single day, and Luna

Park claimed five million paid admissions in a season. In the proud phrase of Luna's manager, Frederic Thompson, Coney Island was in the business of "amusing the million." The resort offered amusement on a scale unprecedented in American history. Here the new mass culture was not a vague abstraction but a tangible reality.

Impressed by the extraordinary size of the crowds at Coney, turn-of-the-century observers were equally struck by their diversity. Readers accustomed to the more informal standards of dress of our own time may mistake the jackets, ties, hats, dresses, and parasols in old photographs as evidence of an elite clientele. However, these constituted the public fashion of the day observed by all classes, particularly on special outings. Closer inspection indicates what various observers confirm: Coney Island drew upon all social classes and especially upon the rising middle class and the more prosperous working-class visitors, salesmen, clerks, tradesmen, secretaries, shop attendants, laborers, and the like....

In addition to families, young men and women came by themselves to Coney, saving whatever spending money they could, sometimes skipping lunches and walking to work in order to have enough for a trip to the resort. Coney offered pleasures infinitely more thrilling than the dominant youthful pastimes of sitting on the front steps or hanging around on the street. Young working-class women in particular could plan to spend no more than the cost of their transportation, since they quickly attracted escorts to "treat."

Increasingly, too, Coney Island reflected the changing ethnic character of Brooklyn, Manhattan, and the greater New York area. Led by newcomers from Italy and Eastern Europe, immigration mounted to unprecedented proportions during this period.... Coney Island provided attractions and generated a sense of festivity in many respects familiar to frequenters of, say, New York's Italian street festivals, band concerts, and theaters, or to celebrants of Purim and patrons of the Yiddish theater. At the same time, the resort lifted visitors beyond the confines of home and neighborhood, of foreign languages and folkways. For immigrants and especially for their children, notoriously eager to assimilate, Coney Island provided a means to participate in mainstream American culture on an equal footing. Far more immediately and successfully than agents of the genteel culture, Coney's amusements parks and other institutions of the new mass culture incorporated immigrants and working-class groups into their forms and values....

The relaxation of conventional proprieties made Coney Island especially popular with young men and women. The middle-class ideal as described in etiquette books of the period placed severe restraints on the circumstances under which a man might presume even to tip his hat to a woman in public; and certainly such books would never approve a gentleman intruding himself upon a lady with whom he was unacquainted. The social codes of the working class were less formal, but many families observed a strict etiquette of courting, monitoring the activities of their daughters especially and insisting upon the presence of a chaperon, if need be a child, when male callers came to the home. In such circumstances, as one New Yorker from an immigrant working-class family later recalled, for the young, ironically, "privacy could be had only in public." Sidewalks, public parks, dance halls, and amusement parks offered opportunities to meet and enjoy the company of the opposite sex away from familial scrutiny.

At Coney Island in particular, unattached young men and women easily struck up acquaintanceships for the day or evening. According to Coney Island folk-lore, some couples even married on the spot. The freedom of anonymity together with the holiday atmosphere of the resort encouraged intimacy and an easing of inhibitions and permitted couples to display their affections in public....

Coney Island thus offered strikingly visible expression of major shifts in sexual mores ... traditionally associated with the 1920s but beginning to take place at this time.... Various amusements contrived to lift women's skirts and reveal their legs and underclothing, while numerous others provided opportunities for intimate physical contact. Slow, scenic rides through tunnels and caves offered abundant occasions for "spooning" and "petting" to use the language of the day. Other, more vigorous rides worked less subtly, throwing couples into each other's arms....

One may gather additional hints of the way Coney Island loosened the rigors of a structured society simply by contrasting scenes at the resort with city street scenes of the same period. In turn-of-the-century photographs of urban life, we see people of all classes proceeding quickly and unostentatiously about their business.... Keenly interested in the social drama about them and their potential part in it, they nonetheless held themselves in check and assumed fairly rigid postures. Not simply their dress but their whole demeanor remained formal.

From the beginning of Coney Island's history as a resort a strong element of its appeal lay in the way it permitted a respite from such formal, highly regulated social situations. Coney's initial attraction, the beach, furnished an occasion for a relaxation of proprieties. The most obvious aspect of this "looseness," the lack of social rigidity and situational "presence", was clothing. Notions of propriety of dress have clearly changed enormously since the turn of the century, so that to a modern reader the fashion of dress visitors wore even on Coney Island's beaches may appear rather formal. But it is important to look at the photographs of turn-of-the-century Coney Island, not according to present conventions, but in light of the prevailing standards of the day. Modest as they may appear to our eyes, the bathing suits of the time were in every sense looser than customary street wear. Not only did they expose more of the wearer's body, but they also encouraged freer deportment in general....

The analogy of carnival and similar festivals is an extremely illuminating one. It helps explain the special appeal of Coney Island for Americans at the turn of the century and offers important clues to the resort's cultural significance. Carnivals and other seasonal feasts and festivals ... have served in a number of pre-industrial cultures as occasions in which customary roles are reversed, hierarchies overturned, and penalties suspended.... Coney Island appeared to have institutionalized the carnival spirit for a culture that lacked a carnival tradition, but Coney located its festivity not in time as a special moment on the calendar but in space as a special place on the map. By creating its own version of carnival, Coney Island tested and transformed accustomed social roles and values. It attracted people because of the way in which it mocked the established social order. Coney Island in effect declared a moral holiday for all who entered its gates. Against the values of thrift, sobriety, industry, and ambition, it encouraged extravagance, gaiety, abandon, revelry. Coney Island signaled the rise of a new mass culture no longer deferential to genteel tastes and values, which demanded a democratic resort of its own. It served as a Feast of Fools for an urban-industrial society....

Steeplechase, Luna Park, Dreamland, the three great enclosed amusement parks that sprang up at the turn of the century, were elaborate constructions designed to heighten Coney Island's own version of carnival. Like the "Streets of Cairo" and other attractions but on a much grander scale, they borrowed freely from the Columbian Exposition and other fairs to create, in effect, a White City for the multitude, a fantastic fair for the common man. They formed the heart of the "New Coney Island" that became a center of cultural expression and of critical debate....

[W]hile critics themselves responded to the carnival spirit, they often scrutinized the crowds about them carefully. Coney Island offered a case study in collective behavior for observers to ponder, one which many regarded as a significant harbinger of the emergent American culture. Some returned with reassuring messages for their readership. In contrast to the unsavory Coney Island of [an earlier] era, the crowds appeared orderly and thoroughly decent in their merrymaking.... Coney Island, these observers appeared to suggest with sighs of relief, did not mark any basic departure from the traditional values of American middle-class culture.

However, a few critics, more openly critical of the genteel tradition, insisted that Coney Island did indeed signal a cultural innovation and a welcome one at that. In their judgment the spirit of carnival appeared to be leavening native American seriousness with a sense of joyfulness. They applauded Coney Island as a crucible of democratic freedom and equality, a cultural melting pot mingling individuals and races from all segments of society. If this emergent culture was crude in some respects, it was irresistibly genial....

Nonetheless, the unrepressed new culture of Coney Island deeply troubled other observers—not all of whom were "hardened aristocrats or bigoted-esthetes." The spectacle of "bare human nature" crying out "Brother" repelled them more than it pleased; they heartily wished he would check his fraternal affections and get dressed. The response of James Gibbons Huneker is especially interesting in this respect. An enthusiastic and iconoclastic critic, Huneker ranged freely over music, literature, art, and other subjects from the 1890s to the 1920s, often in vigorous defense of artistic novelty. But when he ventured to Coney Island in the 1910s to see this new cultural institution and aesthetic in action, most of what he saw moved him to despair. He denounced the whole complex as "a disgrace to our civilisation" and urged its immediate abolition. Not that he didn't enjoy himself, he admitted, "for when you are at Coney you cast aside your hampering reason and become a plain lunatic." ...

In articulating these opinions, Huneker was not merely voicing idiosyncratic fears, but expressing concerns frequently advanced by leading behavioral scientists of the period. According to the dominant school of American psychiatry in the late nineteenth and early twentieth centuries, the genteel virtues of sobriety, diligence, thrift, and self-mastery safeguarded not only family and society but sanity itself. By encouraging sensuous self-abandon, then, Coney Island in a very real sense promoted lunacy. In addition, beginning in the 1890s a number of influential social psychologists, both European and American, focused on crowds as a topic for special study. In the works of these scholars, the presence of the crowd brought a lessening of customary restraints and an explosion of repressed impulses.... Such theories cast the exaggerated behavior of Coney Island in a most disturbing light. The spectacle of masses of people anonymously congregating to participate in intensely emotional amusements seemed like social dynamite....

If the propensity of the crowd was inherently primitive, some observers believed this tendency was exacerbated by the growing proportion of immigrants from Southern and Eastern Europe. Shuddering at the vulgar multitude of Coney even as he sought it out, Huneker fondly recalled the day when New York had not yet become "the dumping-ground of the cosmos."... [These men] wrote not as a carping aristocrat[s] but as [part] of a large number of progressive intellectuals and reformers in the early twentieth century concerned with the character of American recreation, for Coney Island raised issues that were central to progressive reform. Coney held up a mirror to the larger society albeit the grotesque distorting mirror of a fun house—and reflected a general crisis in American culture. Progressive reformers repeatedly lamented the fact that modern American cities were organized only in the service of work and profit; no provision had been made for the organization of community life and leisure. As a result, they believed, society had become dangerously unbalanced. The social restraints that had traditionally prevailed in small towns had collapsed in modern cities with nothing to take their place....

Adding to these concerns, ... a number of social critics feared the demands of industrial work invited debauchery. As the liberal cleric and reformer Walter Rauschenbusch observed, "The long hours and the high speed and pressure of industry use up the vitality of all except the most capable. An exhausted body craves rest, change, and stimulus, but it responds only to strong and coarse stimulation." From the fatigue of modern work and the frustrations of urban industrial life in general individuals demanded relief. In the absence of wholesome public recreation, they turned to commercialized forms, dance halls, music halls, cheap theaters, brothels, saloons, and amusement parks like Coney Island.

Such entertainments, reformers contended, provided escape rather than renewal. As Jane Addams warned, "'Looping the loop' amid shrieks of stimulated terror or dancing in disorderly saloon halls, are perhaps the natural reactions to a day spent in noisy factories and in trolley cars whirling through the distracting streets, but the city which permits them to be the acme of pleasure and recreation to its young people, commits a grievous mistake." Some urban reformers sharing Addams's convictions itched to tear down Coney Island's cheap commercial entertainments and to convert the site to a public park.... From this vantage point, the very popularity of Coney Island testified to the double debasement of American culture—in both work and play environments. It represented, in the phrase of one writer, "an artificial distraction for an artificial life."

For progressive reformers, then, attractions such as Coney Island were essentially frauds, perversions of play. Special interests, they charged, had discovered "the natural resource of the play instinct and [were] exploiting it for gain as they have exploited other great natural resources." In their cynical pursuit of gain, amusement promoters resorted to sensational appeals. They worked up the "carnival spirit" for maximum financial profit. Unsophisticated customers, caught up in the spirit of revelry of the crowd, surrendered not only their money but in many cases their virtue as well: "the innocent under multiplied and insistent suggestions can be reduced into intoxication and immorality in the space of a few hours, and the whole gamut of illicit relations foisted on them." ...

While encouraging the revelry of the crowd, Coney Island's managers aimed always to shape and control it. Not only did they have to winnow out undesirables; they also needed to engineer the environment so as to keep customers in the role of active consumers. Amusement parks thus pioneered merchandising techniques that designers of shopping malls would later adopt: dramatizing objects of desire, elevating goods and attractions to fetishes, they made spending a pageant.

As the cultural upheaval of the early twentieth century has solidified, these characteristics of amusement parks have grown increasingly pronounced. Offended by the tawdriness of amusement parks such as Coney Island, Walt Disney sanitized them for the solidly middle class. California's Disneyland, Florida's Disney World, and the myriad "theme" parks that dot the country have perfected the administration of amusement in a way at which Tilyou and Thompson would have marveled. In the process these new parks have also stripped amusement of the vulgar exuberance that gave Coney Island its vitality. With the genteel culture no longer a real opponent, the elements of farce, clowning, and nonsense have given way to the canned reverence and robotized responses of Disney's "Hall of the Presidents." Sexual symbolism has been supplanted by technological perfectionism; urban heterogeneity has yielded to the clean cut corporate homogeneity of "The American way."

What, then, was ultimately the function of Coney Island and the type of amusement it represented? If the popular resort appeared to symbolize revolt from genteel cultural standards, in what direction did this revolt lead? While Coney Island indeed helped to displace genteel culture with a new mass culture, this was not the subversive development conservative critics feared. Rather it represented cultural accommodation to the developing urban–industrial society in a tighter integration of work and leisure than ever before....

With the 1920s this new economy and culture of consumption would expand enormously, although its salient characteristics had already been determined. Mass production, mass distribution, and installment buying allowed people of moderate means to acquire products similar to those of the rich, from automobiles to electric ranges and toasters. The advertising industry took as its mission the stimulation of consumption and the creation of new wants by quickening public appetite for alluring accouterments of the Good Life. As movies and radio swelled into major entertainment industries, they reinforced these consumer values and aspirations. The mass culture which had first emerged in the cities was now disseminated nationwide. The result was to endow a new middle-class ideal of consumption with as much if not more authority than the genteel culture had ever been able to command.

To what degree Coney Island and the new mass culture it represented marked an increase in freedom obviously depends upon one's perspective. For many middle-class writers, Coney represented a loss of deference to older genteel standards, a vulgar and disorderly pursuit of sensation rather than the cultivation of sensibility they stood for. The result, to their minds, was a dangerous loss of social controls, an increase not of freedom but of license. However, for Coney's lower-middle- and working-class visitors and particularly for the foreign-born and their children, the amusement parks and the emergent mass culture offered an opportunity to participate in American life on a new basis, outside traditional forms and proscriptions. Though class divisions clearly remained, the success of the commercial mass culture depended on its ability to be inclusive rather than exclusive, to encourage a sense of access on a variety of levels.

From a third perspective, nonetheless, Coney Island and the new mass culture generally signified not liberation but a new form of subjection. Various critics and reformers raised this issue when they noted how visitors to Coney sought escape from the demands of urban-industrial life, yet were so totally creatures of their environment that they turned for recreation to a fantastic replication of that life. Amusement thus became an extension of work; a mechanized, standardized character pervaded both experiences. To counteract weariness and boredom, Coney Island prescribed a homeopathic remedy of intense, frenetic physical activity without imaginative demands.

The visitor who most fully perceived this aspect of Coney Island was not an American at all, but the Russian writer and revolutionary Maxim Gorky, who visited the resort in 1906. Viewing the amusement complex at night from a distance, Gorky responded enthusiastically to its promise. But as he scrutinized the resort and its visitors more closely, he was dismayed to discover not joy or transport but a "contented *ennui.*" Entertainers and customers alike appeared to be wearily going through the motions of amusement, quickening their interest only at the prospect of cruelty or danger. The whole scene Gorky pronounced a "marsh of glittering boredom,' particularly pernicious because it stupefied the working people, poisoned their souls, and reinforced their subjection. Concluded Gorky, "Life is made for the people to work six days in the week, sin on the seventh, and pay for their sins, confess their sins, and pay for the confession." In an age of mass culture, amusement emerged as the new opiate of the people.

Gorky's view was an extreme one, which the editor of the American magazine that printed it suggested revealed more about Gorky than his subject. Yet while Gorky minimized the pleasures Coney Island provided, he raised forcefully if crudely the point other critics had only suggested: Coney Island did not lead to true cultural revolt, but served to affirm the existing culture. Rather than suggesting alternatives to the prevailing economic and social order, as carnivals have often done in other cultures, Coney acted as a safety valve, a mechanism of social release and control that ultimately protected existing society. Its fantasy led not to a new apprehension of social possibilities, but toward passive acceptance of the cycle of production and consumption. The egalitarian spirit it fostered paradoxically served to reconcile visitors to the inequalities of society at large.

The difficulty Coney Island's entrepreneurs faced was to continue to offer pleasure without effort on the part of consumers while keeping the experience from hardening into conscious boredom. The owners and managers of the three great amusement parks were well aware of this need and sought to meet it as best they could. While "manufacturing the carnival spirit," in Frederic Thompson's phrase, they aimed to give their products at least a superficial variety. The success of their entire venture depended upon maintaining the appearance of freshness, in sustaining the sense of contrast between Coney Island and society at large....

The problem Coney Island entrepreneurs faced by the 1920s was that the rest of the culture was catching up. The authority of the older genteel order that the amusement capital had challenged was now crumbling rapidly, and opportunities for mass entertainment were more abundant than ever. A long-time Coney Island resident would later observe, "Once upon a time Coney Island was the greatest amusement resort in the world. The radio and the movies killed it. The movies killed illusions." More accurately, radio and movies made amusement ubiquitous, and the movies in particular presented elaborate, convincing illusions at a price Coney Island could not match.... The experience of the city and the experience of the resort increasingly blurred. Coney declined most markedly in the power to astound, and cultural critics stopped paying attention. A harbinger of the new mass culture, Coney Island lost its distinctiveness by the very triumph of its values.

Sports Change Urban Leisure

STEVEN RIESS

The development of the industrial radial city had a crucial impact upon the sporting pleasures of all urban social classes. The greatest impact was economic: the rise of industrial capitalism enriched a small number of people, improved the standard of living for the nonmanual middle class, weakened the position of the artisan class, and gave rise to a huge pool of poorly paid, semiskilled and unskilled industrial workers who worked long hours at a backbreaking pace. As widening income levels, substantial differences in discretionary time, and diverse social values resulted in different leisure options for different social classes, sport came to mark social boundaries and to define status communities. Spatial and demographic changes in the radial city also influenced the development of urban sport along class lines. The enormous physical growth of cities, accompanied by extraordinary increases in population, had major impacts on historic patterns of land use, which in turn influenced each class's sporting opportunities. In the era of the walking city, the countryside had been relatively accessible to most urbanites, who could enjoy there a wide variety of outdoor sports, but after the 1870s, empty lots, the woods, and unpolluted streams were harder to reach,

Steven A. Riess, "Sport and the Urban Social Structure," in *City Games: The Evolution of American Urban Society and the Rise of Sports*. Copyright © 1989 by the Board of Trustees of the University of Illinois. Used with permission of the University of Illinois Press.

especially for lower-class men who could not afford costly transportation fees. Furthermore, traditional playing fields and sports centers in the old urban core were displaced to make way for more valuable development, and consequently workingmen lost many traditional recreational sites. But the changing spatial patterns were far less of a problem for middle- and upper-income groups, who were more likely to live near sports facilities and could afford the cost of transportation to their favorite athletic sites....

In the antebellum era the development of a positive sports ideology that justified and encouraged participation in respectable sports, and the increased middle-class participation in those sports paved the way for the great postwar boom in bourgeois athletics.... Middle-class sportsmen had sufficient discretionary income and free time, and were psychologically prepared to take advantage of the social changes wrought by urbanization to enhance their athletic prospects. By the late nineteenth century, office workers were down to a forty-four hour week, including a half-day on Saturday. Although they could not afford expensive elite sports staged at private resorts, they could utilize the new mass transit facilities to travel to respectable semipublic sporting sites and the new public parks located on the suburban fringe beyond the old boundaries of the walking city. This enabled them to physically separate themselves from the lower orders of society.

The rising middle-class interest in sport reflected a desire by workers in sedentary jobs to demonstrate physical prowess and manliness and to gain recognition which bureaucratic occupations did not always supply. The enormous changes underway with urbanization, industrialization, and the rise of big business and the corporate state were blamed for a loss of individuality.... These white-collar workers were now subordinates, no longer independent workers or entrepreneurs, and they did not enjoy the same sense of creativity and accomplishment previously enjoyed by the old middle class. Middle-class men were also concerned about their courage, about becoming "overcivilized," about losing their sexual identity, and about the feminization of culture. New terms like "sissy," "stuffed shirt," and "mollycoddle" entered the English language. Manliness became less the opposite of childishness and more the opposite of femininity. Vigorous physical activity was seen as one possible antidote to the loss of masculinity. A strenuous life and a return to nature would invigorate the body and revitalize the spirit of a young man. Many new middle- and upper-middle-class magazines devoted to field sports, like *Field and Stream, Sports Afield*, and *Outing*, lauded the outdoor life, and competitive athletic sport became a staple topic in all the major newspapers and periodicals that catered to the bourgeoisie.

Middle-class participation in sports ranging from noncompetitive coeducational leisure sports to highly competitive team sports was facilitated by voluntary athletic organizations and by ready access to public space. Middle-class athletic associations performed many of the same functions as more elite sports clubs in securing private space, purchasing equipment, and organizing competition, as well as providing status and opportunities to communicate with other individuals with similar backgrounds and values. Members of these organizations and other middle-class folk living in the radial city did not have to go far from their homes to enjoy sports; their residential communities were the least developed and most likely to still have empty lots, and the new municipal parks were primarily established in the suburban fringe. After the invention of the bicycle even such basic public space as streets became a locus for middle-class athletic pleasure....

Baseball was the most important sport played by the middle classes in the period from 1870 to 1920. Despite its pastoral mythology, baseball was very much an urban game, first played in cities, and the best players were mainly urbanites. The first fully modernized American team game, the sport was rationalized and bureaucratized in cities, where its spirit of nationalism, wholesomeness, excitement, and drama made it the national pastime. The character of the team game was congruent with the work experience of bureaucrats. But in one important way the sport did not fit in with industrialized urban society: baseball was not controlled by the clock. The length of games was determined not by a fixed time or distance but by innings, which in theory could be timeless. However, games normally took two hours or less, an important factor in a society where time was money.

In the post-Civil War period baseball was a democratic sport which lacked social prestige, but the ideology of the sport fit in nicely with the bourgeoisie's prevailing value system as well as their social experiences. The baseball creed—an extension of the positive sports ideology developed in the antebellum era in response to modernization and urbanization—fully touched base with the beliefs, values, and social needs of middle America, reassuring old-stock folk that their traditional small-town values were still relevant to the increasingly impersonalized, bureaucratized, and urbanized society....

While there is little evidence that baseball actually built character or provided a social catharsis, the baseball creed had a strong influence on contemporary thought and behavior because people perceived the ideology to be accurate. They regarded baseball as a rural game played on large verdant lots and through it identified with the values of a simple, pristine world. They believed that baseball provided the means to prevent or at least alleviate many urban social problems, particularly those that affected the indigent children of recent immigrants living in slums, as well as youngsters living in more affluent neighborhoods. The creed convinced middle-class Americans, regardless of where they lived, that playing and watching the game made better citizens, but in the Gilded Age and the Progressive era, it seemed that primarily urban folk needed such socialization....

White-collar workers not only played baseball, but had the time, money, access, and interest to attend professional games and appreciate the high quality of play on the field. They could afford the cost of public transportation to ballparks located on the suburban fringe as well as the cost of admission....

Fans became part of a community of like-minded spectators who rooted for the local club in a collective demonstration of hometown pride and boosterism. Baseball competition became a metaphor for interurban rivalries, and a victory over other towns in the league symbolized the superiority of your city. The presence of a person at a ball game, particularly on Opening Day, became a means of publicly displaying civic-mindedness.... Since players on professional nines were mercenaries recruited from out-of-town, the local pride exhibited in sports teams was hardly rational: a victory by the Braves over the Giants did not prove Boston's superiority over New York any more than an East German sprinter defeating an American in the Olympics would demonstrate the ascendancy of communism over capitalism. Nevertheless, journalists believed that if a city deficient in self-pride developed a positive spirit because of baseball, then localism was good and proper....

Working-class attendance at spectator sports was limited by time, discretionary income, and access. In the days before cheap mass transit the easiest sites to reach were indoor gymnasiums located in slums or arenas in the Central Business District. Boxing matches that attracted a working-class clientele were usually held in neighborhood gymnasiums, often known as "athletic clubs"—firetraps that were "nothing more than a loft, with tiers of wooden benches to the ceiling." Occasionally a higher-priced match was staged at an armory or multipurpose arena like Madison Square Garden. These semipublic facilities also attracted working-class fans who could afford the modest twenty-five cent admission to a six-day marathon race in the 1880s or six-day bicycle races a decade later....

Outdoor sporting events like thoroughbred racing or baseball were more difficult to attend because of the cost and time. These events were held at distant sites that required public transportation. Professional baseball did not gear itself as much for the poor urban masses as for the middle classes, who paid higher admission fees and lent the sport an aura of respectability. Games were scheduled for times when most employed blue-collar men were on the job, the general admission ticket to a National League game was set at fifty cents in 1876, and the fields were far from the inner city. Thus lower-class urbanites were underrepresented in the stands in most large cities until the 1920s. Manual workers who attended were mainly artisans who worked half-days on Saturday or city workers and other employees like butchers and bakers who worked unusual shifts and had free time in mid-afternoon.

Unlike the NL, the American Association, the second major league, did try to cater to working-class fans. Founded in 1882, the AA charged just twenty-five cents for admission, sold alcoholic beverages, and scheduled Sunday games wherever possible. When the two leagues merged in 1892, the new NL adopted the AA policy of Sunday ball and gave each team the option to sell bleacher seats for a quarter to build up attendance, a pricing policy later adopted for one season by the new American League (AL) in 1901. In the early 1900s major league teams usually set aside about 2,000 cheap seats in distant bleachers, and in 1910 one-fourth of all admissions were in those sections. The franchise with the greatest number of working-class spectators was probably the Chicago White Sox, who had 7,000 quarter seats, played on Sunday, and was the only team located in a working-class neighborhood....

The glamor, fame, and earnings of top professional athletes encouraged athletically gifted lower-class urban youth who lacked traditional alternate avenues to success to become professional sportsmen.... However, these earnings were made by just a select few; most competitors earned far more modest incomes during brief careers before they faded away.

Participation and success in professional sport were functions of class ethnicity, size, and urban space. Prizefighters, for example, were nearly always the products of urban slums, where they had learned to fight to protect themselves and their turf from rival ethnic groups. Boxing could be readily learned in the streets or in neighborhood gymnasiums.... Baseball, on the other hand was more appropriate for youths living in more prosperous communities where there was sufficient outdoor space to play regularly and achieve high level of proficiency.

American-born players in the National Association (NA), the first major league (1871–75), were predominantly urban in origin (83 percent). Two-fifths came from Philadelphia, Brooklyn, Baltimore, and New York—among the most important sites of franchises. Adelman found that three-fifths (61.8 percent) of the Brooklyn and New York amateurs active in the 1860s who later played in the NA were artisans and the rest were white-collar workers. They were attracted by high salaries, which averaged from $1,300 to $1,600, or triple an average worker's wages. Despite the good pay, the occupation then had little social prestige—baseball players were placed on the same unfavorable social level as actors and prize fighters—and because of that and a lack of education, marketable skills, or savings, many players found it difficult to secure good positions after leaving the diamond.

Most major leaguers in the late nineteenth century were from blue-collar backgrounds, but that changed after the turn of the century when the status of the sport—especially the prestige and wages of ballplayers—improved considerably. The standing of the national pastime was never higher as it touched base with prevailing middle-class attitudes, beliefs, and values, was applauded for its character-building qualities, and drew large middle-class audiences. At the same time, players' unions and management both encouraged greater decorum and proper attire on and off the field to secure respectability and acceptance for the athletes.... By 1910 salaries had risen to an average of about $3,000, which lured young men whose social and educational backgrounds were well above the national norm.... Particularly significant was the near total absence of players from the poorest sectors of urban society; just 3.3 percent of the big leaguers had unskilled fathers.

Once baseball expanded nationally, beyond its urban origins in the northeast, fewer players (58.4 percent in 1900–19) came from cities. But this number still far exceeded the national urban proportion, which did not reach 50 percent until the 1920 census. Players continued to come in disproportionate numbers from large cities; one-fourth (24.4 percent) of big leaguers active between 1900 and 1919 came from cities with over 100,000 residents. Because of spatial variables the big cities were unevenly represented. Densely populated New York (Manhattan) and Boston, severely underrepresented, contributed just one-half their proportionate share compared to Cincinnati, Cleveland, and St. Louis, which overproduced by 300 percent, and Chicago, by 150 percent. Chicago had done even better in the past, but as it became more crowded in the late nineteenth century, there was less space than before for diamonds.... Close-in suburbs were potentially good sources for recruitment (Boston was outproduced by Cambridge by 250 percent) because of the available space, their acculturated populations, and community support for sport in the schools and at public spaces.

The proportion of urban-born American players declined over the next forty years. Between 1920 and 1939, 53.7 percent came from cities—below the American urban population in 1940 (56.5 percent). Between 1940 and 1959 the number of active players of urban origin rose to 62.4 percent, but that was still below the country as a whole (70.6 percent in 1960). These trends further reflected the nationalization of baseball and the continued importance of space as a condition for the preparation of future top-flight ballplayers. Still, the proportion of recruits from large cities was about the same between the wars as in the early 1900s, and the fifty-two largest cities produced 19 percent more players than their share of the white population. Productivity improved markedly in warm-weather cities that had a lot of space and a longer playing season and declined in colder eastern and midwestern cities. Newark failed to produce a single major leaguer between 1920 and 1939, while Oakland produced 6.2 times more players than its share of the population, followed by San Francisco (4.5) and Los Angeles (3.9). This trend continued over the next twenty years, when one-third of major leaguers (32.8 percent) came from big cities, where competition to make high school teams was especially fierce.

In the 1920s and 1930s, when there were 400 spots available on major league rosters, just a minority came from impoverished inner-city backgrounds. Nearly half (48 percent) of the players active in the 1920s and 1930s had white-collar fathers; just three out of ten (30 percent) had blue-collar fathers. However, this pattern changed in the 1940s, when white-collar players (35.5 percent) were outnumbered by their blue-collar peers (38.9 percent), a result of the Depression drying up alternate routes of mobility and the increased presence of acculturated inner-city ethnic youths in professional baseball....

Even if a lower-class athlete made the majors, his tenure was short—four years is generally accepted as the average—and consequently he had to secure other employment at a time when most men were well into their lifelong occupations. The first professionals, active in the period from 1871 to 1882, had a difficult time obtaining white-collar positions after baseball; over one-third (35.6 percent) skidded down into a blue-collar occupation, an unusually sharp intergenerational decline that reflected their low status and lack of education, savings, or marketable skills. Nearly half (48.4 percent) ended up in low-level white-collar jobs as clerks, salesmen, petty shopkeepers, or managers of baseball teams—jobs in which they hoped to utilize their fame or expertise. One out of eight worked at a position tied to saloons, billiard parlors, or bookmaking—low-status enterprises intimately involved with local politics and the male bachelor subculture. There were a few instances of rags-to-riches tales like store clerk A. G. Spalding, who utilized his pitching talents to become owner of the Chicago White Stockings and head of the nation's leading sporting goods company. Spalding got in at the ground floor of the sports boom, but few players ever duplicated his success.

Ballplayers active after the turn of the century fared considerably better. While one-third of the retirees who played in the early days of major league baseball ended up with blue-collar jobs, the ratio was one out of seven (14.0 percent) for men active between 1900 and 1919, one out of five (18.3 percent) for those active in the interwar decades, and one out of nine (11.8 percent) for those in the 1950s. They ended up mainly in low white-collar jobs, particularly in sports (24.6 percent for players active in the 1950s) or positions which required a lot of direct contact with clients, such as sales, real estate, and insurance, which presumably enabled them to utilize their fame.

In the long run retirees succeeded largely because of their educational and social backgrounds. Fame was crucial in determining a player's initial retirement occupation, but thereafter receded into the background. Among players active in the early 1900s, for example, nearly all college attendees became white-collar workers (93 percent) compared to two-thirds (67.5 percent) of the noncollege men. In that era the overwhelming majority of players with nonmanual fathers secured white-collar work (85 percent), but barely a majority of manual fathers' sons did (58 percent). Social background was important because of its correlation to educational and cultural values. Middle-class sons were encouraged to have a strong self-image, high expectations, and such traditional bourgeois values as thrift and deferred gratification. Players from blue-collar families did not get the same kind of positive reinforcement as youths and were not socialized to plan for the future. Lower-class players who were insecure and lacked experience in saving money often engaged in conspicuous consumption to demonstrate their success to friends, teammates, and themselves. When the time for retirement arrived, they had no skills, no connections, and no money in the bank....

The nature of the urban social structure and its dynamic interaction with such elements of urbanization as space, demography, economic development, social institutions, political structures, and ideology had an important bearing on the development of sport and sporting institutions in the industrialized radial city. Because of different economic situations, social and cultural environments, neighborhoods, and value systems, members of different social classes did not have the same opportunities or options to partake of sports. However, over time sporting choices did become more democratic, especially by the 1920s and 1930s as the standard of living improved and municipal and private institutions increased their sponsorship of mass sport.

FURTHER READING

Cohen, Lizabeth. *Making a New Deal: Industrial Workers in Chicago, 1919–1939* (1990).

Denning, Michael. *Mechanic Accents: Dime Novels and Working Class Culture in America* (1998).

Enstad, Nan. *Ladies of Labor, Girls of Adventure: Working Women, Popular Culture, and Labor Politics at the Turn of the Twentieth Century* (1999).

Erenberg, Lewis A. *Steppin' Out: New York Nightlife and the Transformation of American Culture* (1984).

Greeky, Andrew M. William C. McCready, and Gary Theisen. *Ethnic Drinking Subcultures* (1980).

Kasson, John F. *Rudeness and Civility: Manners and Nineteenth Century America* (1991).

McBee, Randy. *Dance Hall Days; Intimacy and Leisure among Working-Class Immigrants in the United States* (2000).

Nasaw, David. *Going Out: The Rise and Fall of Public Amusements* (1999).

Peiss, Kathy. *Cheap Amusements: Working Women and Leisure in Turn-of-the-Century New York* (1986).

Powers, Madelon. *Faces Along the Bar: Lore and Order in the Workingman's Saloon, 1870–1920* (1999).

Rosenzweig, Roy. *Eight Hours for What We Will* (reprint 2002).

Rosenzweig, Roy, and Elizabeth Blackmar. *The Park and the People: A History of Central Park* (1998).

Ross, Steven J. *Working-Class Hollywood* (1999).

Rubin, Rachel, and Jeffrey Melnick. *Immigration and American Popular Culture* (2007).

Sterngass, John. *First Resorts: Pursuing Pleasure at Saratoga Springs, Newport, and Coney Island* (2001).

CHAPTER 6

Movies, Gender, and the Making
of Fans, 1910–1935

This chapter examines the growth of movie culture at the turn of the century and returns to the critical role of audiences in making popular culture. Since this volume is focused on the history of American popular culture rather than communications or film theory, this chapter provides some background on the development of movies as a commercial entertainment and an industry, and also uses them to explore the historical emergence of fan culture and censorship. Movies had their historical roots in what historian Daniel Czitrom calls "the gritty cauldron of urban amusements," the same environment that produced Coney Island, dance halls, and vaudeville in the 1890s. Like these venues, early movie theaters became a staple of the urban scene and catered to large audiences of working-class immigrants. As technological developments improved the quality, length, and viewing experience, movie theaters sprang up everywhere and audiences expanded to include almost every community within the United States.

Although inventors on both sides of the Atlantic worked on the problem of recording moving pictures on film, W.K.L. Dickson, working in Thomas Edison's laborartory, successfully produced a viable motion picture camera and viewing device by 1893. The peephole kinetoscope debuted at the 1893 World's Columbian Exposition in Chicago, capturing the interest of the public and inventors alike. Soon after the fair, kino parlors appeared in cities and offered the public the chance to view short, 15-second films of everything from animal acts to prize fighters. The thrill of seeing moving pictures through peepholes did not last, but it convinced Edison and several rivals that there was a large market for films. With the refinement of film technology, and the development of first narrative and then feature films, movies evolved into a bona fide industry by the 1910s, and audiences expanded exponentially between 1910 and 1918.

Movies eclipsed every other kind of entertainment by the early 1920s. According to Czitrom, movie houses became part of the "physical and psychic space of urban street life." By World War I, the social ritual of watching movies had infiltrated the daily routines of Americans, young and old, female and male, working class and middle class. Movies also quickly produced a new kind of audience—fanatics or fans—who watched more than the average number of films per week, followed the industry and their favorite actors and ac-tresses through movie magazines such as Photoplay, *and sometimes aspired to become stars themselves.*

Censorship developed simultaneously with fans, as city officials, religious authorities, secu-lar reformers, and cultural critics worried that movies proved too powerful an influence on young audiences. Censors worried about the viewing practices of children and teens who watched movies in groups, often without the supervision of parents. These young fans created new youth sub-cultures seemingly unmoored from traditional centers of authority and control in the home. Censorship began early at the municipal and state levels, as officials responded to various refor-mers and religious groups. After World War I, sociologists embarked on a massive study of the effects of media—including music, radio, and movies—on children. The first report from the Payne Fund Studies, entitled Motion Pictures and Youth, appeared in 1933. Giving in to pressure and hoping to ward off government regulation, the industry adopted a censorship code, known as the Motion Picture Production Code, in 1934. Written by Postmaster General Will Hays, the code set rules for the display of sex and violence in films.

Where historians such as Daniel Czitrom, Robert Sklar, and Paul Buhle, have charted the development of the movie industry, recent historical work on movies has taken a closer look at audiences, particularly historical practices of moviegoing and the creation of fan cultures. These studies reflect a larger interest in fan culture among scho-lars who study music, science fiction, and the Internet. Cultural historians are part of this larger movement to ask questions about audience reception and have added their work to that of film theorists and anthropologists who think about consumers as active creators of culture.

 # DOCUMENTS

The documents in this chapter highlight social debates about fans and the influ-ence of film on youth. Document 1 provides an early description of fans by a writer for a movie magazine. Document 2 is a piece of fan literature aimed at avid moviegoers who wanted to break into the business and write for serials, or movies that came in series. The advice illustrates that fans could take an active part in shaping characters and, indeed, films. Documents 3 and 4 provide an excerpt from a play about a male fan, Merton, whose life was consumed by the movies, and a review of the play. "Merton of the Movies" quickly made its way from the stage to the silver screen, where it was recycled in the 1920s, 1930s, and 1940s, a sign of its popularity and the tendency of Hollywood to turn the camera lens on itself. Merton provides an interesting twist on the idea of fans, who most American media and advertisers imagined as women. Does the play argue for the active or passive nature of fans? Does it play to the claims of censors that movies had too much influence over young people? Lastly, Document 5 comes from one of the Payne Study reports issued in 1933 and details the concerns of censors about the power of movies to manipulate behavior.

1. Early Writer W.W. Winters Defines Movie Fanatics, 1910

... When one says five-cent theater the first thought is that they are for the poorer people, those who cannot afford even to pay 50 cents for a seat in the "peanut" at one of the other theaters. But is this so? To a certain extent, yes; but only to a certain extent. No matter what time you take to visit these theaters you are sure to find among the motley throng some who are of your station almost, no matter what that station may be. You can, for instance, see plenty of Chinamen there, but whether or not—and from the immobile expression I should say not—they are enjoying it can only be a conjecture. And right here it can be said, and with praise, that one set that they appeal to is the soldier.... Then, too, there are the children. They can surely find no more harmless amusement, and few less expensive. And last, but not by any means least, are the men and women who drop in for a while to be amused, or to fill up a spare moment, or even out of courtesy. This only brings us to the cleanness of the performance. It can be truly said that, as a general rule, there is nothing to offend the most fastidious. Taken as a whole, they present amusements that are good, bad, and—worse, the pictures of which the same may be said at times, but which are at least clean. This, too, is a fact worthy of praise, and more—of continuance.

★ ★ ★

How different it must seem to a man or woman who has not visited the city for, say, five years—nay, even less—to come here, and in the evening stroll down the avenues and streets. To see tall buildings outlined with lights, huge doorways filled with lighted figures, brilliant paintings, and the ever-present pho- nograph. But to see the outlay of lights and noise and color is to go back to the Midway at a fair.... You go there to see moving pictures and vaudeville acts, and not to comment upon the wall decorations. You go there for amusement. And you can surely get it. No matter how crude the acting, or how far fetched the pictures, there is always sure to be some one who thinks they are "perfectly lovely," and so amusement is assured. For if you cannot enjoy the performance it is pretty safe to say it is because you have been used to better acting, etc., but unless you are an absolute pessimist you cannot fail to be amused by those around you who do enjoy it.

★ ★ ★

One of the most noticeable habits of the patrons of those theaters is that of reading out loud what is flashed upon the screen. "The Capture of the Outlaws." Ah-h-h-h-h. Everybody sits up and "takes notice." "Love Triumphant." Another long-drawn-out "Ah-h-h-h-!" and some more notice. Then comes an act a la vaudeville. Somebody in the exurberance of their spirits yells "Get the hook!" whether or not the act is bad, whereat everybody laughs. There are times when the whole audience is so pleased with itself and everybody else that let any one accidentally, quite accidentally, sneeze, why, the whole house re- echoes with laughter.... Somehow you all enter into the spirit of the thing.

W.W. Winters, "With the Picture Fans," *The Nickelodeon* (1 September 1910), 123.

Armed with a few stray nickels, a bag of peanuts, a good supply of patience and good humor, and oh! What a time we did have!...

★ ★ ★

And when you come out, this is particularly so of a Saturday night, you wander up and down and find yourself brushing shoulders with goodness knows who.... And, of course, it is understood that you had not only no idea of ever going in the "Cheap" places, but, when you were finally inveigled in, that you would go once, but never again. But what's the use? Why not submit gracefully and admit that the five-cent theaters have a place all their own and that, after all, you are going again....

2. William Lewis Gordon Advises Fans on How to Script Movies, 1914

... Photoplays are more popular today than ever before. They have come to stay. The highest class of legitimate stage productions are restricted for the rich, to the exclusion of the poor. Motion pictures have filled this vacancy, making it the international amusement from one side of the world to the other, extending to the rich, poor, and middle class its irresistible invitation.

It is approximated that over three thousand photoplays are produced every year, more stories than contained in all of the standard monthly magazines combined for the same period. Then, to what source must producers look to supply this enormous demand? A staff of two or three salaried writers for each company could never do it; but if such a task were even possible, originality would suffer, and there would exist a volume of sameness to each writer's work. The answer is THE PUBLIC MUST COME TO THE RESCUE; and film-producers care not whether the writer is a clergyman, teacher, banker, stenographer, shop-girl, farmer, housewife, or invalid.

How many of us, among the millions of people interested in moving pictures, have not felt at some time or another the ambition to write photoplays? How many of us, upon witnessing some crude motion picture play, have not said to ourselves, "I am quite sure that I could write a better picture story than that?" Then, WHY have you not tried? Others are making a success in the work, and there is certainly room for you. If there is one field of work in this wide country where everyone is cordially welcomed, it is that of photoplay writing.

This work is now a recognized art. Film-producers are spending millions of dollars to meet increasing demands of the public, and one of the chief problems today is the scarcity of good plays. The constant and rapid growth of this immense industry should serve as an incentive to the aspiring photoplaywright when once convinced that fortunes are being spent annually towards the betterment of the motion picture, and that a liberal amount awaits him or her who can submit a good play worthy of production. It has opened a new field of work to

William Lewis Gordon, *How to Write Moving Picture Plays* (Cincinnati: Atlas Publishing Company, 1914).

every bright, imaginative mind with foresight to grasp the opportunity and gain prestige as a photoplaywright before the thousands who will eventually seek entrance have awakened to the call....

A photoplay is a story told in photographic action. Dialogue or conversation cannot be used. Therefore, the entire story must be unfolded to the audience by the "scene action" alone....

The photoplay is therefore WRITTEN IN ACTION instead of dialogue or story form. Picturesque descriptions and clever conversation are essential to the magazine story, but are NOT WANTED in the photoplay.

The technical form of the written photoplay, required by the film-producing companies, embraces the Title, Synopsis, Cast of Characters, and Scenario. These four features are fully explained in the following pages....

Try to emphasize acts of honest, faithfulness, perseverance, courage, truthfulness, charity, devotion, ... true friendship, self-sacrifice, thoughtfulness, worthy and ambitious struggles for success, love and business. However, just as good are the stories portraying the foully and penalties of dishonesty, unfaithfulness, cowardice, untruthfulness, lack of devotion, weakness of character, selfishness, haughtiness, carelessness, waywardness, unworthy struggles for success, and similar themes.

In practicality every story there should be an element of rivalry with one or more obstacles to overcome whether it be a tale of war, business, or love. The public likes a struggle, where there are difficulties to master, regardless of ultimate conquest or defeat; and is more interested in stories of modern life than the heroic tales of past ages.

When possible, have some moral to your story, and you may be preparing an effective sermon for someone, a sermon that will be illustrated before millions of people. It is best to give your story a happy ending. Life contains enough real tragedy, and it is far better to have John marry Helen and live happily ever afterwards than to send your audience out of the theater after witnessing John hurl the villain down a hundred foot embankment, only to find that Helen was untrue and had eloped with a former suitor.

Comedy is in greatest demand and brings the higher prices; this is because real good comedy is the most difficult to prepare. But should your inclination run towards drama, pathos, romance, historical, melodrama, Western, cowboy, Indian, or biblical, direct your work in the channel you prefer, giving it your very best efforts, and you are more likely to succeed than were you to attempt something not suited to your taste or ability....

If you are writing a story involving a courtroom scene, you must know just how such a scene would be conducted; if you are not posted, you must inquire from someone, otherwise some of your scene action will appear ridiculous to any attorneys in the audience.... The moral is—KNOW YOUR SUBJECT.

If you want to write a dramatic story, do not think that you must have a man burnt at the stake, or that you must kill an actor in every scene to bring the thrills. Our hero is tied to the stake, the Indian is about to apply the torch, and you know that a company of soldiers are due to arrive, is not the suspense more dramatic and thrilling than it would be to witness the poor, tortured hero in flames?

Do not mix comedy with tragedy; you have only a few minutes in which to tell your story, and you cannot do justice to both in this short time.

Above all, try to be original and build plays from our own imagination, taking some incident that you have seen, read, or heard as the basis for your plot....

Avoid any scenes or suggestive complications that say offend good taste or morals. Avoid scenes of murder, suicide, robbery, kidnapping, harrowing deathbeds, horrible accidents, persons being tortured, scenes attending an electrocution or hanging, violent fights showing strangling, shooting, or stabbing, staggering drunkards, depraved or wayward women, rioting strikers, funerals, and all such scenes of a depressing or unpleasant nature. Do not make a hero of a highwayman or escaped convict. Do not reflect upon any religious belief, nationality, or physical deformity. Thousands of men, women, and CHILDREN of all classes, nationalities, and creeds witness these pictures daily. We may occasionally see some play depicted which is contrary to the above advice, but they are the exceptions, and are to be avoided. Give your story clean, wholesome, pleasant tone, leaving the morbid tales for others to write. These tales of crime are growing less every day, and consequently the photoplay is growing better.

Do not copy your story from any book, magazine, or other moving picture play that you have read or seen. These are all protected by copyright, and you would make yourself liable to prosecution. I do not mean that you may not get your inspiration from some book, magazine story, or photocopy, but you must build your own story around this idea.

Do not try to write "trick" plays, where a beautiful maiden emerges from a vase of flowers, or a villain vanishes in a cloud of smoke. Only the producers at the studies are capable of devising these scenes.

Try to avoid using children and animals in your play. Animals are "bad actors," and many studios have no capable children....

Do not write a story of your life; this would no doubt be of interest to Uncle Charlie and Aunt Martha and all of your cousins and friends, but would hold no interest for the other ninety million people throughout the country....

Wild-west stories are difficult to write unless you are familiar with the life of cowboys, Indians, and Western customs.

Avoid military stories or plays requiring a full regiment of people. They are very expensive to produce....

Avoid "rough comedy" of the slapstick variety, where everybody is fighting, falling, running. This class of play is bought by a few companies, but very few....

If you are writing comedy, do not try to make your story "read funny." Your words will not be shown on screen. It is the ACTION that must make the audience laugh. The most humorous story you ever read might make the poorest photoplay comedy....

After reviewing these restrictions, it may occur to the student that "there is nothing left to write about." ...There is not a daily paper that does not contain a dozen ideas; there is not a day of our life but what some incident we see or item we read will suggest a theme, provided we are observant.

There is now a National Board of Censorship that passes upon every photo-play from the standpoint of public morals before a permit for production is granted; and they condemn practically every story that could have a demoralizing effect upon the mind—murder, suicide, kidnaping, hanging, unlawful destruction of property, etc. There are many morbid people to whom such a suggestion would prove a temptation not to be resisted.

A play will often pass if it is clearly shown that the crime in question is invariably punished by law or conscience. Then the crime should be shown only by suggestion, not the actual deed....

In many cities there is often a local censorship board which passes upon all plays. Thus a questionable story might pass the National Board and then be rejected by the city board. The moral is—MAKE YOUR STORY CLEAN, WHOLESOME, and out of reach of ANY censorship. There are too many happy inspirations to necessitate writing of murders and suicides....

3. Playwrights George S. Kaufman and Marc Connelly Explain Male Film Fans in "Merton of the Movies," 1925

ACT I

SCENE: *The rear of the Gashwiler General Store. Ten o'clock on a Saturday night.... MERTON'S bed and trunk are concealed in the counter down* R....

AT RISE: GASHWILER *back of counter, busy.* ELMER *enters* R., *sees* GASHWILER— *starts to exit, as* GASHWILER *speaks....*

GASHWILER. I suppose you want to see Merton?

ELMER. Well, as long as I'm here, I did think I'd drop in on him....

GASHWILER. Elmer?...

ELMER. Yes, sir.

GASHWILER. I—I don't want you to get Merton in no bad habits.

ELMER. Me?—why—

GASHWILER. Now hold on. I don't mean this personal—exactly—but Merton's different from most of you boys. He's—funny, sort of. But he's got the makings of a fine boy, and I don't want to see him get started *wrong*.

ELMER. I'm not going to do anything to him. (*Sits on edge of table.*)

GASHWILER. You see, it ain't as thought he had any parents—I been sort of looking after him ever since he came to work here.... Besides, if he goes out nights, he ain't no good in the store mornings.

ELMER. But honest, Mr. Gashwiler, I'm only going to *talk* to him.

George S. Kaufman and Marc Connelly, "Merton of the Movies," in *Four Acts: A Dramati-zation of Harry Leon Wilson's Story of the Same Name* (New York: Samuel French, 1925).

GASHWILER. I wish I knew what you and him talk about all the time.... Merton's been awful dreamy lately—can't keep his mind on things a bit.

ELMER. (*To counter*) It ain't me, Mr. Gashwiler. I can't get him to come out with us or northing....

GASHWILER. Oh, then you *do try?*

ELMER. ... Well—well, anyhow, he *won't.*

GASHWILER. You're telling me—the truth, Elmer?

ELMER. ... Yes, sir. Why, he hasn't even played poker with us for months.... He don't go anywhere—...

GASHWILER. ... Yes. I know what you're going to say.... Moving pictures.

ELMER. Yes, sir. That's all he'll talk about to *anybody.*

GASHWILER. I hope they ain't going to his head. Merton's an awful sensitive boy.

ELMER. Just the same, he goes to them all the time, Mr. Gashwiler, and I think you ought to know it. Why, he—he imitates the *people* in em, too.

GASHWILER. I don't know what he's coming to. (*He looks around to see if* MERTON *is coming; then brings up a magazine from under the counter.*) I—I found this underneath the counter a while ago. Know what it is?

ELMER. ... "Cameraland." It's a moving picture magazine.

GASHWILER. Yes, I know it is.... Even got magazines about 'em. Got a lot of pictures in it about bungalows and—Japanese hired help. I hope Merton don't get all worked up by it....

ELMER. Charley Harper seen him down in Ford's meadow at five o'clock yesterday morning. He had your horse there.

GASHWILER. My Dexter? (*Comes to* ELMER.)

ELMER. Yes, sir.

GASHWILER. Are you *sure?*

ELMER. Pretty sure. Lem Hardy was there with his picture camera, and Merton had his arm around the horse's neck one time, and was talking to it.

GASHWILER. Did Charley hear what he said?

ELMER. He wasn't close enough. At first he didn't know what to make of it, and then he remembered there'd been a William S. Hart picture at the Bijou Palace the night before.

GASHWILER. You mean—Merton was *imitating* him?...

ELMER. That's what.

GASHWILER. You think—he might want to be a picture actor?

ELMER. It certainly looks like it.
(GASHWILER *hesitates a second and then crosses determinedly to* L.)

GASHWILER. Merton! … Merton!

MERTON. … Yes, sir.

GASHWILER. Leave off whatever you're doing and look here a minute.

MERTON. … Yes, sir…. Oh, hello, Elmer.

ELMER. …'Lo, Merton….

MERTON. … It's—ten o'clock.

GASHWILER. You can close up in a minute. First I want to ask you a question.

MERTON. Yes, sir.

GASHWILER. Was it you down in the meadow—yesterday morning?

MERTON. … Yes, sir….

GASHWILER. With—the horse. *Again*?

MERTON. Yes, sir.

GASHWILER. You couldn't have been–hitching him up—before six—could you?

MERTON. No—sir, I just—wanted to see if he was all right. (R.)

GASHWILER. I don't know as I understand you lately—Merton.

MERTON. I'm—just the same….

GASHWILER. No, you ain't—you're different…. And I know what it is.

MERTON. It's not anything.

GASHWILER. Yes, it is. It's moving pictures. You just keep on working steady and you'll get there much faster than if you was always running out to picture shows.

MERTON. Yes, sir.

GASHWILER. Here! Here's your money….

MERTON. Thank you.

GASHWILER. Hope you're saving it….

MERTON. … Well, I can't save the whole fifteen, each week.

GASHWILER. If you wasn't to flighty, I'd say you had the makin's of a wealthy man.

MERTON. I don't think I'm flighty….

GASHWILER. Well, you seem to moon around a lot….

MERTON. Good-night!

GASHWILER. *(Looks up at window)* Don't forget to lock that window. *(Sharply.)*

MERTON. No, sir….

ELMER. How about a little session with My Lady Luck?

MERTON. No, I can't….

ELMER. Oh, why can't you? Gee whiz, that's the third time this month you've stayed away.... sore at anybody?

MERTON. No!

ELMER. ... I thought maybe it was because Dan Turner kidded you about buying that cowboy outfit.

MERTON. Nobody got me sore about anything.... That's right, Elmer, I'm not sore.

ELMER. Then what's the reason you don't meet up with the crowd any more? I'd think you'd want *some* relaxation.

MERTON. Well, I'll put it frankly to you, Elmer. I can't afford to run around with the crowd. I've got other *interests*.

ELMER. *What other interests?*

MERTON. Well, I have them ... that's all.

ELMER. ... You're not in love with some girl?

MERTON. ... Is that what they think?

ELMER. No, but——— ... Is that it, Merton? Are you in love with some girl?

MERTON. Why, how rid——— *(He is about to say "ridiculous" when a realization of the truth makes him change his statement.)* Well, maybe I am, in a way.

ELMER. ... Who is she?

MERTON. ... I don't think you have the honor of her acquaintance, Elmer.

ELMER. ... Where does she live?

MERTON. In a place far away.

ELMER. ... Oh——— Where did *you* ever meet anybody in a place far away? You've never *been* anywhere's——— except like when you went to Peoria last month....

MERTON. She could be *visitor* here in Simsbury, *couldn't she?*

ELMER. ... No, *she couldn't!* I've seen everybody that ever visited here.... It ain't that girl that come over from Masonville to help at the restaurant. She's terrible. Why, she's———

MERTON. ... That isn't the person. Really, you don't know her. And as for this lady being a mere restaurant girl———Why, she's on a mountain peak!

ELMER. ... Oh, boy!

MERTON. ... This thing's all pretty sacred to me, Elmer....

ELMER. Well, it's your funeral. But I certainly think a man ought to have a *little* amusement. Here———...

MERTON. No, thanks, Elmer....

ELMER. Don't you even *smoke* any more?

MERTON. No. *(He turns away from adjusting the last cover on counter.)* I guess you think I must be nutty, don't you, Elmer?

ELMER. No, I don't, no matter *what* people say.

MERTON. How do you mean ———— what they say?

ELMER. Oh, about ———— things you do. You can trust *me,* Merton ———— tell me, *were* you in the pasture this morning, talking to the horse?

MERTON. What horse?

ELMER. Gashwiler's horse. Charlie Harper said he saw you with your arms around his neck.

MERTON. What would I be talking to a horse for?...

ELMER. Of course, I can understand ———— I mean, if you were ————*lonesome.*

MERTON. It isn't ———— that ———— I never said I was ———— *(Knock on door. To* ELMER*)* It's Tessie Kearns. *(Crosses to door* R.I.*)* Hello!

(Enter MISS KEARNS.*)*

MISS KEARNS. Hello, Merton. I thought I'd come and tell you about the picture.

MERTON. Thanks.

*(*MISS KEARNS *carries a movie magazine and an envelope containing photographs.)*

MISS KEARNS. Good evening, Elmer.

ELMER. ... H'llo, Miss Kearns. *(To* MERTON*)* Well, I guess I'll meander ————...

MISS KEARNS. *(*C.*)* I hope I'm not interrupting you, gentlemen!

MERTON. ... Oh, no!

ELMER. ... We were just talking. I gotta get down to a *meeting,* anyway. Sorry you can't come, Mert. G'night, Miss Kearns. G'night, Mert. *(*ELMER *exits as* MERTON *murmurs a good-night.)*

MISS KEARNS. Are you sure I didn't *interrupts?*

MERTON. *(Crosses to* TESSIE, *front of counter)* No, I was glad you come. I want to hear about the picture. He only wanted me to go to a pocker game.

MISS KEARNS. ... Maybe you wanted to go.

MERTON. No! You see, with me it's either idle pleasure or a career, and I'm going to have the career. Was the picture good to-night?

MISS KEARNS. It was great! Oh, here are some prints Mr. Hardy, the photographer, asked me to give you.———— I nearly forgot.

MERTON.   Thanks…. You know what they are?

MISS KEARNS.   You, ain't they!

MERTON   … They're ———— *stills* of me ———— in different characters.

MISS KEARNS.   … Oh, Merton! Can I see them?

MERTON.   Would you really like to?

MISS KEARNS.   I'd be delighted…. And oh, yes! Mr. Hardy said to tell you he'd meet you at two-thirty tomorrow just as you said.

MERTON.   … On the Lot.

MISS KEARNS.   … Uh-huh.

MERTON.   He's ————…———— a great help to a man like me who is studying.

MISS KEARNS.   Oh, this is fine! You look wonderful in evening dress. Merton, why, you just seem to be an actor already.

MERTON.   *(Abandoning the consideration of the photograph in his hand to go over and examine the one he has given* MISS KEARNS.*)* That's a society man type. *(He draws back a pacc and looks at it from a distance.)* Notice anything particular about it?

MISS KEARNS.   *(After a moment)* Well, you look very refined and dignified….

MISS KEARNS.   Have you made up your mind yet when you're going?

MERTON.   *(Back of couch* C.*)* Pretty soon now. I've got two hundred and seventy dollars. I figure in another month or so I'll have a clear three hundred.

MISS KEARNS.   And then you'll go out to California?

MERTON.   The minute I get three hundred. *(He crosses* L. *to* TESSIE.*)* I've got about all the clothes I need now. They can't say I haven't the equipment. I've got Western suits, automobile clothes, a suit for polo everything!

MISS KEARNS.   *(Depressed)* I'll be sorry to see you go———— in a way. Merton. But I know you're going to be a big success as an actor….

4. *Chicago Daily Tribune* Reports Positive Audience Reaction to Movie about Fans, 1924

… To those who have read the story by Harry Leon Wilson—and didn't see the play—the picture will drag a little at first. You will be inclined to wish, as I did, that Mr. Wilson were there to introduce his Merton. James Cruze, however, does the honors pretty well. It isn't so long before the film gains momentum—and when it does it swings you right along with it.

"Merton Makes People Laugh Through Tears" *Chicago Daily Tribune* (12 August 1924), Section 2, 17.

"Ah, little girl," says Merton, the movie-mad clerk in the village store to the wax lady he dresses in the latest market down models. "I have come in the nick of time. Hereafter our lives shall be linked together!" And he gives the wax gentleman also in his charge—a dirty look.

That's Merton before he goes to Hollywood. Just swamped in dreams and his admiration for a certain Harold Parmalee—shiek of the cinema—whom Merton without a doubt resembles. The story makes him exceedingly funny during this period. The picture—not so much so. Where he shines in the photoplay version, is in sunny California. As a lonely, broke, earnest, game, conceited and finally successful in a way he never dreamed or wanted to be successful aspirant to film fame, Glenn Hunter gives an unforgettable impersonation.

He wrings a laugh from you at moments when you are so fiercely sorry for him that you kick yourselves for laughing.... And he gets across his boyishness and an illusion of innocence in a fashion that sure enough, will make every woman who sees him want to give him a bear hug—as Miss Dana does most convincingly on various occasions.

That little lady is far from bad herself as the hard boiled, but tender-hearted, always understanding "Montague girl," ingénue in slapstick comedies....

De Witt Jennings as a bluff, merry, humorous director does the next best bit of work. He has one scene where he laughs for about five minutes—but he doesn't laugh alone. You'll laugh with him—heartily and loudly.

Lots of "atmosphere" to "Merton of the Movies." Lots of good "dope" for YOU—who write in and ask me, ask me:

"Is there a chance for me in the movies? What will I do to become a star?" See you tomorrow!

5. W.W. Charters, Educational Researcher, Reports the Effects of Movies on Boys and Girls, 1933

Motion pictures are not understood by the present generation of adults. They are new; they make an enormous appeal to children; and they present ideas and situations which parents may not like. Consequently when parents think of the welfare of their children who are exposed to these compelling situations, they wonder about the effect of the pictures upon the ideals and behavior of the children. Do the pictures really influence children in any direction? Are their conduct, ideals, and attitudes affected by the movies? Are the scenes which are objectionable to adults understood by children, or at least by very young children? Do children eventually become sophisticated and grow superior to pictures? Are the emotions of children harmfully excited? In short, just what effect do motion pictures have upon children of different ages?

Each individual has his answer to these questions. He knows of this or that incident in his own experience, and upon these he bases his conclusions.

W.W. Charters, *Motion Pictures and Youth: A Summary* (New York: Macmillan, 1933).

Consequently opinions differ widely. No one in this country up to the present time has known in any general and impersonal manner just what effect motion pictures have upon children. Meanwhile children clamor to attend the movies as often as they are allowed to go. Moving pictures make a profound appeal to children of all ages. In such a situation it is obvious that a comprehensive study of the influence of motion pictures upon children and youth is appropriate.

To measure these influences the investigators who cooperated to make this series of studies analyzed the problem to discover the most significant questions involved. They set up individual studies to ascertain the answer to the questions and to provide a composite answer to the central question of the nature and extent of these influences. In using this technique the answers must inevitably be sketches without all the details filled in; but when the details are added the picture will not be changed in any essential manner. Parents, educators, and physicians will have little difficulty in fitting concrete details of their own into the outlines which these studies supply.

Specifically, the studies were designed to form a series to answer the following questions: What sorts of scenes do the children of America see when they attend the theaters? How do the mores depicted in these scenes compare with those of the community? How often do children attend? How much of what they see do they remember? What effect does what they witness have upon their ideals and attitudes? ... Do motion pictures directly or indirectly affect the conduct of children? Are they related to delinquency and crime, and, finally, how can we teach children to discriminate between movies that are artistically and morally good and bad?

... In 1928 William H. Short, Executive Director of the Motion Picture Research Council, invited a group of university psychologists, sociologists, and educators to meet with the members of the Council to confer about the possibility of discovering just what effect motion pictures have upon children, a subject, as has been indicated, upon which many conflicting opinions and few substantial facts were in existence. The university men proposed a program of study. When Mr. Short appealed to The Payne Fund for a grant to support such an investigation, he found the foundation receptive because of its well-known interest in motion pictures as one of the major influences in the lives of modern youth....

The committee's work is an illustration of an interesting technique for studying any social problem.... Such a program yields a skeleton framework, which, while somewhat lacking in detail, is substantially correct if the contributing investigations have been validly conducted. To provide this framework or outline is the task of research. To fill in the detail and to provide the interpretations are the natural and easy tasks of those who use the data.

W. W. C.

Ohio State University
September, 1933

Because a close relationship between the attitude of an individual and his actions may be assumed, the study of the effect of motion pictures upon the attitude of children toward important social values is central in importance.... May and Shuttleworth conducted two studies: one on the correlation between movie attendance and character and another on the relation of attendance to attitudes toward objects of social interest.

In the first study they selected in three communities 102 children who attended the movies from four to five times a week and 101 other children who attended about twice a month. Each group was about equally divided between boys and girls. The groups were equated for age, sex, school grade, intelligence, occupational level of the father, and cultural home background.

The "movie" and "non-movie" children were compared as to reputation in school among teachers and classmates....

The investigators report: "We have found that the movie children average lower deportment records, do on the average poorer work in their school subjects, are rated lower in reputation by teachers on two rating forms, are rated lower by their classmates ... are less cooperative and less controlled as measured both by ratings and conduct tests, are slightly more deceptive in school situations, are slightly less skillful in judging what is the most useful and helpful and sensible thing to do, and are slightly less emotionally stable. Against this long record, the movie children are superior on only two measures: They are mentioned more frequently on the 'Guess Who' test as a whole and are named more frequently as best friends by their classmates. Tests showing no differences also need cataloging. These include honesty rating and honesty as measured in out-of-school situations, persistence, suggestibility, and moral knowledge."

Cressey and Thrasher in their study of a congested area in New York City found conditions of similar import. Of 949 boys studied in the area about one quarter were retarded and another quarter were accelerated in school. Of those who attended the movies 4 times a week or more 19 per cent were accelerated in school, 24 per cent were normal, and 57 per cent were retarded. Of those, however, who attended once a week or less 35 per cent were accelerated, 33 per cent were normal, and 32 per cent were retarded. The movie group contained nearly twice as many retarded pupils and half as many accelerated pupils as the non-movie children.

Cressey and Thrasher also discovered in this area that among 1,356 boys 109 were delinquents. Of these 22 per cent attended the movies 3 times or more a week and 6 per cent attended less than once a week, while among those who were not delinquent 14 per cent attended 3 times or more a week and 6 per cent attended less than once a week. These figures indicate that for this population there is a positive relationship between truancy and delinquency and frequent movie attendance.

An important question arises at this point. Does extreme movie attendance lead to conduct which harms reputation or do children of low reputation go frequently to the movies? It rises also at other points. Thrasher and Blumer and their associates as they present their cases are faced by the same question and discuss it. The authors who raise the question express the general conclusion that a simple cause and effect relationship does not prevail. To say that the movies are solely responsible for anti-social conduct, delinquency, or crime is not valid. To assert contrariwise that delinquents and criminals happen to frequent the movies and are not affected by them is clearly indefensible. Validity probably rests with a combination of the two—tendencies toward unapproved conduct and movie influence work together to produce more movie interest on the one hand and more anti-social conduct on the other. The two factors drive toward progressive aggravation of unhealthful conditions.

Turning from their conduct study to their attitudes study, we find that May and Shuttleworth searched diligently for specific criticisms of the movies in literature, in conversation, and the like, and divided them into twelve classes: heroes and boobs of the movies, the people of other lands, prohibition, crime and criminals, sex attitudes, attitude toward schools, clothing, militarism, personal attitude, escape from threatening danger, special dislikes, and a miscellaneous group. For each of the first eleven classes an hypothesis was advanced concerning the effect of the movies upon that particular area. The responsibility of the investigators was to find out whether or not this hypothesis was true. For instance, for the class, heroes and boobs of the movies, the investigators selected the hypothesis that there is a tendency for the movies to place certain characters in a favorable light and to hold up others to ridicule. Their task was to discover whether or not this hypothesis was correct; that is, whether movie and non-movie children showed significant differences in their attitudes toward characters shown in the movies, athletes, Protestant ministers, actors, cowboys, college professors, policemen, and the like.

To explore the eleven hypotheses of which the foregoing is an illustration approximately 250 questions were prepared, making an average of about 22 questions in each area. They thus covered by this procedure all the statements that they could discover about the influence of the movies upon attitudes.

The investigators then selected from large populations of children groups which attended the movies frequently and others which attended them infrequently. The movie groups attended the theater nearly three times a week while the non-movie groups attended less than once a month. Unfortunately, enough children could not be found for their uses who had never attended the movies. The investigators were compelled, therefore, to use children in the groups who had gone to the movies twice a month or less. But the movie group had attended twelve times as often as the other group.… These groups were equated for age, school grade, intelligence, socio-economic-educational background, and a few other special factors in individual localities. Equal proportions of boys and girls were included. To each of the groups, movie and non-movie, were given series of statements upon which it was thought there might be discernible differences which might possibly be attributed to movie attendance. These statements occurred usually in the form: "All Most Many Some Few No Chinese are cunning and underhand." Each child was then required to underline one word which best expressed his attitude toward the Chinese. Questions were also used such as, "Which would you rather be, a college professor or a cowboy?"… The replies were then tabulated for the movie and the non-movie groups and the differences were observed to see whether or not they were statistically significant.

On the basis of the questions and statements used, no significant differences in attitude were discovered between the movie and non-movie groups on a number of objects including athletics, the Chinese, robbers, gang leaders, rum runners, prohibition agents, prohibition enforcement, the success of marriage, sex attitudes, and the like. Significant differences were found in that movie children admire cowboys, popular actors, dancers, and chorus girls while non-movie children are more interested in such types as the medical student and the college professor. Movie children are more inclined to believe that much drinking and violation of the prohibition laws exist. Movie children set special value on smart clothes and dressing well. They are also more sensitive about parental control. The movie children go to more dances and read more, but the quality of their reading is not high.

They say in conclusion: "That the movies exert an influence there can be no doubt. But it is our opinion that this influence is specific for a given child and a given movie. The same picture may influence different children in distinctly opposite directions. Thus in a general survey such as we have made, the net effect appears small. We are also convinced that among the most frequent attendants the movies are drawing children who are in some way maladjusted and whose difficulties are relieved only in the most temporary manner and are, in fact, much aggravated. In other words, the movies tend to fix and further establish the behavior patterns and types of attitudes which already exist among those who attend most frequently."

This attitude study ... is of peculiar interest because it is the only one in which the influence of the motion picture is not clearly apparent either as cause or effect or as an aggravation of precedent conditions. Superficially one might claim that this study indicates that motion pictures have no influence upon boys and girls. That position May and Shuttleworth do not take. They say that movies do exert an influence upon children and indicate that this influence is greater than appears on the surface. The studies of Stoddard, Thurstone, Blumer, Thrasher, and their associates support this position with a huge mass of specific data....

ESSAYS

The essays provide some social historical background on movies and moviegoing practices, as well as the early development of fans. In a path-breaking essay on the history of movies, Daniel Czitrom, professor of history at Mount Holyoke College, charts the development of movies as part of the social realm of urban America in the late nineteenth and early twentieth centuries. Kathryn Fuller, associate professor of moving image studies at Georgia State University, examines the origins of fans in an essay from her book on small-town audiences. Like other historians of film, she grapples methodological and evidentiary problems in searching for fans and how they interacted with films. Both essays demonstrate the dialectical nature of popular culture—that fans helped create the culture of movies, practices of viewing, and even influenced the form of serial films by writing scripts—and offer models for understanding movie culture within a broader historical context of urbanization, changing gender roles, and the rise of censorship.

Movies as Popular Culture

DANIEL CZITROM

… Movies introduced more than a new communication technology; they quickly became the principal new (and most popular) art form of the twentieth century. Films communicated not with coded messages but with familiar idioms of photography and narrative. They brought people together in public exhibitions, and the most successful entrepreneurs of these exhibitions soon won control of the entire industry. With origins deep in the gritty cauldron of urban amusements, motion pictures found their first audiences and showmen mainly in the immigrant and working class districts of the large cities.

Insofar as contemporary popular culture has become inextricably linked to modern media of communication, the birth of the movies marked a crucial cultural turning point. The motion picture's curious amalgam of technology, commercial entertainment, art, and spectacle set it off as something quite unfamiliar and threatening to the old cultural elite. But this strange blend of elements also produced a peculiarly American alloy, one that ironically recalled and perhaps even fulfilled one of the oldest dreams of America's cultural nationalists.…

… Between 1895 and 1905, prior to the nickelodeon boom, films were presented mainly in vaudeville performances, traveling shows, and penny arcades. Movies fit naturally into vaudeville; at first they were merely another novelty act. Audiences literally cheered the first exhibitions of the vitascope, biograph, and cinematograph in the years 1895 to 1897. But the triteness and poor quality of these early films soon dimmed the novelty and by 1900 or so vaudeville shows used films mainly as chasers that were calculated to clear the house for the next performance. Itinerant film exhibitors also became active in these years, as different inventors leased the territorial rights to projectors or sold them outright to enterprising showmen. From rural New England and upstate New York to Louisiana and Alaska, numerous visitors made movies a profitable attraction in theaters and tent shows. Finally, the penny arcades provided the third means of exposure for the infant cinema. Aside from their use of kinetoscopes, arcade owners quickly seized on other possibilities. Arcade patrons included a hard core of devoted movie fans, who wandered from place to place in search of films they had not seen yet. Some arcade owners bought, rented, or built their own projectors; they then partitioned off part of the arcade for screening movies. They acquired films from vaudeville managers who discarded them.…

Of all the facets of motion picture history, none is so stunning as the extraordinarily rapid growth in the audience during the brief period between 1905 and 1918. Two key factors, closely connected, made this boom possible. First, the introduction and refinement of the story film liberated the moving picture from its previous length of a minute or two, allowing exhibitors to present a longer program of films. One-reel westerns, comedies, melodramas, and

Daniel Czitrom, "American Motion Pictures and the New Popular Culture, 1893–1918," in *Media and the American Mind*. Copyright © 1982 by the University of North Carolina Press. Used by permission of the publisher. www.uncpress.unc.edu.

travelogues, lasting ten to fifteen minutes each, became the staple of film programs until they were replaced by feature pictures around World War I. George Melies, Edwin S. Porter *(The Great Train Robbery, 1903)*, and D. W. Griffith, in his early work with Biograph (1908 to 1913), all set the pace for transforming the motion picture from a novelty into an art.

Secondly, the emergence of the nickelodeon as a place devoted to screening motion pictures meant that movies could now stand on their own as an entertainment. These store theaters, presenting a continuous show of moving pictures, may have begun as early as 1896 in New Orleans and Chicago. In 1902 Thomas Tally closed down his penny arcade in Los Angeles and opened the Electric Theater, charging ten cents for "Up to Date High Class Moving Picture Entertainment, Especially for Ladies and Children." But the first to use the term *nickelodeon* were John P. Harris and Harry Davis, who converted a vacant store front in Pittsburgh in late 1905.

News of their success spread quickly and spawned imitators everywhere. All over America adventurous exhibitors converted penny arcades, empty store rooms, tenement lofts, and almost any available space into movie theaters. Because no official statistics remain from those years, we must rely on contemporary estimates. By 1907 between three and five thousand nickelodeons had been established, with over two million admissions a day. In 1911 the Patents Company reported 11,500 theaters across America devoted solely to showing motion pictures, with hundreds more showing them occasionally; daily attendance that year probably reached five million. By 1914 the figures reached about 18,000 theaters, with more than seven million daily admissions totaling about $300 million.

Perhaps more graphic (and accurate) than these national statistics, local surveys revealed the terrific popularity of movies, especially in the larger cities. Table 1 summarizes data from a number of contemporary estimates of movie attendance in eight cities during these years.

Although data for smaller cities and towns is more scarce, what little we have suggests that the "nickel madness" was not limited to large urban centers. For example, in Ipswich, Massachusetts, an industrial town of six thousand in 1914,

T A B L E   1   Urban Movie Attendance, 1911–1918

City	Population (1910)	Year	Weekly Attendance	Number Theaters
New York	4,766,883	1911	1,500,000	400
Cleveland	560,663	1913	890,000	131
Detroit	465,766	1912	400,000	
San Francisco	416,912	1913	327,500	
Milwaukee	373,857	1911	210,630	50
Kansas City	248,381	1912	449,064	81
Indianapolis	233,650	1914	320,000	70
Toledo	187,840 (1915)	1918	316,000	58

movie attendance was substantial among school children. Of 127 children in grades five through eight, 69 percent of the boys went once a week or more to the movies, as did 55 percent of the girls. Among 179 high school students, 81 percent attended moving picture shows, on the average of 1.23 times per week for boys and 1.08 for girls....

This sudden and staggering boom in movie attendance evoked strenuous reactions from the nation's cultural traditionalists, those whose values and sensibilities had been shaped largely by some version of the doctrine of culture. Although the motion picture held out great promise for many of the traditionalists in the abstract, few of them could accept as positive advance the new popular culture and all it implied. Their consideration of motion pictures centered on three points, all interrelated: the context of exhibition, the nature of audience, and the content of the films themselves.

★

All of the surveys of motion picture popularity, and indeed a large fraction of all discussions of the new medium, placed movies in a larger context of urban commercial amusements. Movies represented "the most spectacular single feature of the amusement situation in recent years," a situation that included penny arcades, dance academies and dance halls, vaudeville and burlesque theaters, pool rooms, amusement parks, and even saloons. Motion pictures inhabited the physical and psychic space of the urban street life. Standing opposite these commercial amusements, in the minds of the cultural traditionalists, were municipal parks, playgrounds, libraries, museums, school recreation centers, YMCAs, and church-sponsored recreation.... The mushrooming growth of movies and other commercial amusements thus signaled a weakness and perhaps a fundamental shifts in the values of American civilization....

For those who spoke about "the moral significance of play" and preferred the literal meaning of the term *recreation*, the flood of commercial amusements posed a grave cultural threat. Most identified the amusement situation as inseparable from the expansion of the city and factory labor. Referring to the enormous vogue of the movies in Providence, Rhode Island before World War I, Francis R. North noted the "great alluring power in an amusement which for a few cents ... can make a humdrum mill hand become an absorbed witness of stirring scenes otherwise unattainable, a quick transference from the real to the unreal."

Commercial amusements tempted rural folk as well, and some writers argued that "the young people coming from the country form the mainstay of the amusement resorts." Frederick C. Howe warned in 1914 that "commercialized leisure is moulding our civilization—not as it should be moulded but as commerce dictates.... And leisure must be controlled by the community, if it is to become an agency of civilization rather than the reverse."

A scientific assessment of the situation, as attempted by the myriad of recreation and amusement surveys of the early twentieth century, seemed a logical first step. Beyond this, the drive for municipal supervision of public recreation and commercial amusements fit comfortably into the progressive ethos of philanthropists, social workers, and urban reformers all over America. "In a word," asserted Michael M. Davis of the Russell Sage Foundation in 1912, "recreation within the modern city has become a matter of public concern; laissez faire, in recreation as in industry, can no longer be the policy of the state."

What actually transpired in and around the early nickelodeons varied from theater to theater and city to city. On the whole they do not seem to have been an especially pleasant place to watch a show. A 1911 report made on moving picture shows by New York City authorities disclosed that "the conditions found to exist are such as to attach to cheap and impermanent places of amusement, to wit: poor sanitation, dangerous overcrowding, and inadequate protection from fire or panic." Despite the foul smells, poor ventilation, and frequent breakdowns in projection, investigators found overflow crowds in a majority of theaters. Managers scurried around their halls, halfheartedly spraying the fetid air with deodorizers and vainly trying to calm the quarrels and shoving matches that commonly broke out over attempts to better one's view. The overall atmosphere was perhaps no more rowdy or squalid than the tenement home life endured by much of the audience; but the nickelodeons offered a place of escape for its eager patrons.

The darkness of the nickelodeon theater, argued some doctors and social workers, caused eye strain and related disorders: "Intense ocular and cerebral weariness, a sort of dazed 'good-for-nothing' feeling, lack of energy, or appetite, etc.," as one physician put it. The health problem melted into a moral one, as critics condemned the darkness. Declared John Collier at a child welfare conference, "It is an evil pure and simple, destructive of social interchange, and of artistic effect." Jane Addams observed that "the very darkness of the theater is an added attraction to many young people, for whom the space is filled with the glamour of love-making." Darkness in the nickelodeon reinforced old fears of theaters as havens for prostitutes and places where innocent girls could be taken advantage of. John Collier asked: "Must moving picture shows be given in a dark auditorium, with all the lack of social spirit and the tendency to careless conduct which a dark auditorium leads to?"

If the inside of the theaters was seamy, the immediate space outside could be severely jolting. Gaudy architecture and lurid, exaggerated posters were literally "a psychological blow in the face," as one writer put it. Sensational handbills, passed out among school children, vividly described movies such as *Temptations of a Great City*.... Phonographs or live barkers would often be placed just outside the theater, exhorting passers-by to come in. Inside, the nickelodeon program varied from theater to theater. An hour-long show might include illustrated song slides accompanying a singer, one or more vaudeville acts, and an illustrated lecture, in addition to several one-reelers. But movies were the prime attraction....

Nickelodeon vaudeville was usually cheap, almost impossible to regulate, and socially objectionable—to the authorities, if not to the audience. As a result, police harassment and stricter theater regulations were employed all over the country to exclude vaudeville from movie houses. By 1918 nearly all movie exhibitors had responded to external pressure and internal trade opinion by eliminating vaudeville. They were forced to concede what one exhibitor had written in a trade paper in 1909, that "a properly managed exclusive picture show is in a higher class than a show comprised partly of vaudeville."...

On Christmas day exhibitors, film producers, and distributors responded by meeting and forming the Moving Picture Exhibitors Association, with William Fox as their leader. The movie men successfully fought the order with injunctions, but the message was clear: some form of regulation was necessary. Marcus Loew bagan to ask various civic bodies for names of potential inspectors to investigate the theaters. It took several years, however, for New York to enact the first comprehensive law in the United States regulating movie theaters. The 1913 legislation included provisions for fire protection, ventilation, sanitation, exits, and structural requirements. Seating limits increased from three hundred to six hundred to provide exhibitors more funds for making improvements. Significantly, all vaudevillae acts were banned from movie houses unless they met the stiffer requirements of regular stage theaters.

Although movies contributed to the new web of commercial amusements, they obviously stood apart from them as well. Motion pictures presented a troubling paradox: they clearly departed from traditional forms of recreation, yet they were undoubtedly superior to dance halls and pool rooms. Their potential for uplift was enormous, especially when one considered the makeup of the audience. Contemporary observers never tired of stressing the strong appeal motion pictures held for the working classes and new immigrants. Vigorous movie-phobes thought it impossible to exaggerate "the disintegrating effect of the sensational moving picture." Those more sanguine about its possibilities agreed with publisher Joseph M. Patterson: "The sentient life of the half-civilized beings at the bottoms has been enlarged and altered by the introduction of the dramatic motif, to resemble more closely the sentient life of the civilized beings at the top." Both sides agreed that precisely because of the special appeal movies had for these groups, as well as for children, one had an obligation to discover how and why the motion picture captured its enormous audience.

The 1911 Russell Sage study of New York theaters estimated movie audiences in that city to be 72 percent working class. A 1914 study of how one thousand working men spent their leisure time concluded that the popularity of moving pictures was the one outstanding fact of the survey. Sixty percent of those questioned attended movies regularly; those working the longest hours spent the most time at the shows; and those who earned less than ten dollars per week went the most often....

Even before the rise of the feature film and the wave of new movie palaces built after 1914, two developments usually cited as correlative with the winning of the middle-class audience, movie men actively sought to leave the slums behind.... Trade papers were filled with advice on how to improve the reputation of movies through higher prices, more attractive and carefully located theaters, and better films.

The presence of large numbers of "undeveloped minds" in the nickelodeons— immigrants and children—evoked endless assertions about movies as a potential agent of Americanization and moral suasion. The notion that movies served to Americanize immigrants had more to do with wish fulfillment than reality. For one thing, perhaps a majority of films screened in early years were produced in

Europe. The Americanization argument seems to have been largely another piece of ammunition in the battle to establish a censorship of films.

The image of ignorant immigrants and incorrigible youth uplifted by movies was a potent and reassuring one for social workers and civic leaders sympathetic to film. An anonymous poem entitled "A Newsboy's Point of View," written about 1910, typified this sentimental attitude. It purported to describe how a newsboy witnesses the father of his girlfriend giving up drink after they all see a film about the evils of alcohol....

A far more significant effect of the motion picture, particularly for children, was in the area of peer socialization. The act of moviegoing created an important new subculture centered outside of the home. Jane Addams astutely recognized this development. Although she actively involved herself in the community supervision of movies and theaters, Addams always looked upon this work as only a holding action. To the end of her life she remained ambivalent about the implications of motion pictures. Her response to the motion picture's growth in Chicago reflected the uneasiness of even the most sympathetic traditionalists....

Although both the exhibition milieu and the nature of the audience continued to trouble the cultural traditionalists, they realized that movies were here to stay. Municipal regulation of the theaters, along with the elimination of vaudeville, might improve the moral atmosphere of shows. However, in no way could the size of the audience and the intensity of its devotion be diminished by substituting alternative forms of cheap amusement. Regulation of the films themselves thus remained the focal point for social control.

The 1908 nickelodeon licensing struggle in New York City led directly to the first attempt at a comprehensive censorship of motion pictures, and this attempt was spearheaded by the movie industry itself. In March 1909 the movie exhibitors and producers in New York City requested the People's Institute, a civic and educational foundation, to organize the National Board of Censorship of Motion Pictures. Although administered by the People's Institute, the board was a self-regulating body; it comprised a general committee (electing its own members and an executive board) that formally elected people to the actual censoring committee. Essentially, the NBC was the first of several methods of voluntary trade regulation for the movie industry, with the exhibitors and producers footing the bill. The movie men clearly wanted to counter public criticism of their business, for the standing of each exhibitor and producer depended on every other. The creation of the board may also be viewed as another important method by which the industry could make motion pictures more palatable to the upper and middle classes, "to improve the average quality of the films in order that a larger and larger number of the total population [would] patronize motion pictures."

Here the commercial realities of the movies forced the industry to seek the cooperation of the cultural traditionalists. The board continually defined its mission as the uplifting of both the film and the taste of the audience; it claimed that its goal was the elimination of any need for censorship. It began with the premise that "the motion picture has become a public power and a moral and cultural influence which must be brought under social control." Hence it made sure that "these censors [were] cultured men and women, trained to look on the activities of life from the broad view of their social significance; … persons of culture and more or less prominent in social and other public life in New York—doctors, lawyers, clergymen, and, in fact, men and women of all kinds of activities."

The board presumed a very simple psychology at the core of the moviegoer's experience: "Those who are educated by the movies are educated through their hearts and their sense impressions and that sort of education sticks. Every person in an audience has paid admission and for that reason gives his attention willingly…. Therefore be gives it his confidence and opens the window of his mind. And what the movie says sinks in." The board's standards of judgment mostly concerned elimination of excesses in scenes dealing with sex, drugs, and crime, particularly prostitution. While keeping in mind the differences in local standards, it tried "to act on behalf of the general conscience and intelligence of the country in permitting or prohibiting a given scene on film." By 1914 the National Board of Censorship claimed to be reviewing 95 percent of the total film output in the United States; it either passed a film, suggested changes, or condemned a movie entirely. Mayors, police chiefs, some four hundred civic groups, and local censoring committees from all over the country subscribed to the board's weekly bulletin.

Local censorship arrangements remained active despite the work of the national board. Compared to the national board, local censors felt a greater confidence in their absolute right and ability to distinguish between moral and immoral films. Local boards often attacked the national board as too lenient, and they fiercely defended the necessity for community control of the censorship power. They tended to judge films solely as an endless succession of potential morality plays….

Compared to the large number of people interested mainly in the social effects of motion pictures, writers who approached movies as an art form were a small circle before World War I. They stand out as a prophetic minority in their efforts to treat the new popular culture from an aesthetic perspective, but they frequently revealed the same assumptions as the traditionalists about the nature of "true culture." At first most critics assessed movies in relation to the art form to which they seemed closest: drama. Indeed, there was a great deal of cross-fertilization between movies and the theater in these early years, both in terms of personnel and in the stylistic fusion of realism and romanticism. But this insistence on judging motion pictures as merely another category of drama blinded many critics to the early achievements of film artists such as Griffith, Chaplin, Sennett, Pickford, Ince, and others. The motion picture, argued Brander Matthews in 1917, can improve on standard theatrical melodrama and farce, but "comedy and tragedy are wholly beyond its reach, and equally unattainable by it are the social drama and the problem play."…

As the movie industry turned away from the simple one- and two-reelers produced by the Patents Company members and moved toward full-length features and spectacles, so too did film slowly achieve an independent critical status. By World War I more and more newspapers, magazines, and trade publications began to employ full-time reviewers to consider the latest in film art. Aside from professional critics, though, increasing numbers of intellectuals and artists began to contemplate seriously the aesthetic possibilities that movies offered. They were excited because film seemed a truly popular art, one that entered to an amazing extent "into the daily thought of the masses." As a new medium of expression, movies had advantages over the drama. It liberated the narrative from constraints of time and space and gave the artist a greater ability to alter his point of view. Robert Coady, writing in the avant-grade little magazine *Soil*, defended the motion picture as "a medium of visual motion." Aesthetic censorship, the attempt to make movies simply imitate drama, would prove just as crippling as the legal kind. "There is a world of visual motion yet to be explored, a world the motion picture is opening up to us."...

By the end of the Great War, the medium of motion pictures had established a new popular culture; a postprint confluence of entertainment, big business, art, and modern technology that catered to and drew its strength from popular taste. The new popular culture *combined product and process,* neither of which fit within the matrix of the old doctrine of culture. The achievements of film art could not be measured by traditional critical standards; they demanded their own aesthetic. The act of moviegoing became a powerful social ritual for millions, a new way of experiencing and defining the shared values of peer and family....

Studying Movie Audiences

KATHRYN FULLER

Movie fan culture was created through a dialogue between the film industry and viewers. On one side of the dialogue were the commercial practices and promotional efforts of the film producers to publicize films and stars, as well as the exhibitors' efforts to attract the public to movie theaters though local advertising and other on-site activities. On the other side of the dialogue, audience members absorbed the publicity materials provided by the studios, read fan publications, and shared Hollywood gossip with like-minded friends. What they created was a truly popular culture of film. Movie fan culture started with material provided by the film industry and then was re-created as scrapbooks, poems, fan letters to the magazines and the stars, and fan-written film scripts—all created by moviegoers for their own enjoyment. Movie fan culture consisted not only of tangible items and gossip swapped at the lunch table, but it was also present in the fantasies the fans generated from the movies, the movie-influenced attitudes, behaviors, and identities that moviegoers experimented with....

About Movie Fans

... The movie fan has always been a breed apart from the average person who occasionally drops in at a theater; fans are the most visible and most passionately engaged segment of the film audience. In the "classical Hollywood cinema" period, from the mid-1910s to the 1960s, movie fans were depicted in films, books, plays, and popular song as eccentric, even obsessive people who spent too much time in theaters, who thought and talked incessantly about celebrities, and who perhaps dreamed of "going Hollywood" themselves and becoming movie stars. Since the late 1910s, this depiction of movie fans as deluded dreamers has been considered feminine, but this was not always so.

The usual depiction of movie fans in the silent era featured starstruck, teenaged girls mobbing movies stars at film premieres, hysterically fainting at Rudolph Valentino's funeral, or mooning over photos and Hollywood gossip in the fan magazines. The few males among the dedicated movie fans were ridiculous figures—antisocial, emasculated dimwits—like the title character of a popular 1923 novel, *Merton of the Movies*, which became a successful play and film. Merton was a movie-crazed, small-town simpleton who became a Hollywood celebrity only because of dumb luck and the fact that he physically resembled a popular film actor.

Popular culture in the 1920s helped reinforce the image of movie fandom as feminine and obscured the fact that there had existed an era of negotiation over the identity and role of the fan. In the nickelodeon era, both male and female hobbyists experimented with various modes of interaction with the growing film industry. While fans eagerly sought a dialogue with the film studios and film publications, the industry was eventually successful in establishing boundaries of fan participation in the creation of films, scripts, and fan magazines. The new limits truncated most avenues of amateur participation in script production and direct lines of contact between fans and film actors. Much previously acceptable "masculine" interest in the movies—such as the interest in the optics of projection and in the technical aspects of the film production—also became marginalized. These boundaries nevertheless encouraged the growth of a rich and multilayered movie fan culture that provided a mediated link between viewers and the glamorous fantasy of movie stars and the film industry. Movie fan culture brought new pleasures and meanings to the experience of moviegoing for women and men in the largest cities and smallest towns in the golden age of Hollywood film.

The male movie fan's marginalization occurred in movie fan maganines soon after the close of the nickelodeon period, between 1915 and the United States' entry into the First World War. Despite the male movie fan's disappearance from fan discourse, men and boys continued to have an equal presence with women in the movie audience. After the shift, male enjoyment of the movies was considered to the more detached than female enjoyment, which included absorption in Hollywood gossip; men supposedly reserved their fanlike enthusiasms for more "masculine" interests such as sporting events, wireless radio, and war news.

The subject of media fandom has received increasing attention as scholars employing reader-, viewer-, and listener-reception theories have moved beyond the critical position of audiences as passive spectators and have explored how audiences have used mass media to shape their identities, attitudes, and behavior.... These studies have substantially increased our understanding of how viewers, listeners, and readers appropriate elements of popular texts to create pleasurable and meaningful narratives of romance and adventure for their own personal fulfillment.

Men and boys have often been absent from these pathbreaking studies of fandom, which have focused primarily on the intersections of mass media and feminine culture. In media fan research, it is assumed either that men actively denigrate or have little interest in the subject matter (such as romance novels), or like the legions of male science fiction and rock music fans, they form the dominant audience group from which women and girls differentiate themselves through their fannish activities....

The rise of movie fan culture and of the roles it afforded male movie fans to some extent paralleled the radio enthusiasts' model. Motion picture film cameras and projectors were more complex and expensive to fabricate than broadcasting apparatus, and movie production never offered amateurs the level of accessibility that crystal sets gave to the radio boys. Nevertheless, it was not inevitable that becoming a devotee of motion pictures or reading fan magazines would be seen by the public as primarily a passive, leisure activity for young women or that movie fan culture would seem so inhospitable to the professed interests of male movie fans....

Origins of the Fan

The evolution of the term *movie fan* occurred in the context of long existing ideas about celebrity, spectatorship, and gender roles in European and American culture.... The term *fan* itself has two origins; one comes from the world of sports and masculinity, the other from discourse on aberrant psychological behaviors that were often labeled feminine....

By the middle of the nineteenth century, the term *fan* had gained side usage in the United States to describe ardent male supporters of baseball. Sports fans loyally rooted for teams with which they shared common geographical or institutional bonds. Spurred by newspapers' coverage of individual performer's efforts, fans began to single out favorite players for admiration. Increased newspaper publicity about heroic sports personalities across the country opened the way for baseball fans to gain interest in teams outside their localities. Being a "sports fan" carried a certain cachet, as the physical exertion on the baseball field and unwavering support in the stands for one's team and community was deemed admirable, masculine, and patriotic.

American middle- and working-class women of the nineteenth century, although representing only a small proportion of the spectators at sporting events, were nevertheless eager participants in the growing fascination with fame. Women and girls were widely criticized for their frivolous addiction to novel reading; indeed, they were disparaged more often for their "fanatical" interests in books and authors than were men with similar interests. Women were prominent in the crowds who thronged the engagements of touring celebrities such as composers, opera singers, statesmen, and literary lions like Charles Dickens, Mark Twain, and Oscar Wilde. Female audience members also participated in the creation of the "matinee idol" of the legitimate stage. Although American women and girls of the Victorian era were increasingly engaged in fanlike behavior, the term *fan* was then rarely applied to them.

By 1900, American theatrical entertainment was firmly entrenched in the cult of personality. Famous actors and actresses toured the country, performing roles geared to exploit their attractiveness and personal magnetism, such as Joseph Jefferson's Rip

Van Winkle and Edwin Booth's Hamlet. However, few admirers saw the great stars in person more than once or twice in their lives if they lived outside the major theatrical centers. They often had only photographs, newspaper clippings, or other thirdhand evidence to connect them to flesh-and-blood celebrities. Theatrical promoters began to introduce the stars' names and faces into many areas of consumer culture. Stage performers started to define standards of beauty and sell cosmetics, perfume, shirts, and cigars through testimonial advertisements.

Motion pictures of the prenickelodeon era did not initially contribute much to the growing national obsession with celebrity; presidents, generals, and sports heroes occasionally appeared before the camera while cutting ceremonial ribbons or marching in parades. A few years later, when motion picture producers began to shift the bulk of their production from scenics to story pictures, moviegoers saw theatrical performers more often on film. With a few exceptions, however, these actors were not famous stars of the stage, but journeyman performers. Most film studios operated with stock companies, utilizing the same band of actors and actresses over and over in the roles ingenue, hero, child, mother. Certain frequently cast actors soon became recognized, and moviegoers across the country became interested in learning the identities of the individuals who played in their favorite film releases each week.

The anonymity of film performers maintained by the major American film producers tantalized and frustrated movie audiences; probably it was a shrewd move by film producers, for it increased moviegoers' clamor to know more. Exhibitors and film industry trade journal reporters began to notice that men and women were seeking out copies of film exhibitor's professional trade journals at newsstands to secure more information about current films and players. Moviegoers wrote to the film studios seeking information on film casts and began to pester their local exhibitors to obtain the names of actors and photo souvenirs of performers they admired....

Despite the roadblocks thrown up by film producers, some moviegoers, not content with merely uncovering the identities of their favorites, began to attempt to contact the players directly. Viewers wrote to actors they knew only as the "Biograph girl" or "Vitagraph girl" in care of their film studios; others located the studio addresses and haunted the production facilities in Manhattan, Brooklyn, and Chicago. Scornful commentators in the exhibitors' trade press criticized moviegoers who overstepped what they considered the boundaries of propriety. Film studios were flooded with letters from both urban and small-town men bearing marriage proposals to movie actresses. Stage actresses had encountered these unsolicited attentions for many years, and the married lives of stage performers were often kept secret to save the illusion of their availability; few in the film industry realized initially that the flicking, soundless, black-and-white images could provoke equally passionate responses in movie viewers. Proposals to film actresses from male admirers soon became expected, though deemed ludicrous by trade press critics; the volume of marriage offers from "forward" female viewers to male film actors, however, shocked them.

At the same time, some American film producers began to publicize the names of their actors and to address movie audiences' interests more directly in advertising campaigns. J. Stuart Blackton, head of the Vitagraph studio, drew on his promotional experience with newspapers and vaudeville to become one of the most enthusiastic proponents of increased producers' contact with audiences. In 1910, Vitagraph and other film production companies began to offer souvenir photographs of film performers and other trinkets for sale to movie theater managers, who could either give or resell them to their movie patrons. Trading cards, art prints, cigarette cards, and other customer premiums and bits of advertising had long proven successful in American retailing to promote customer loyalty to particular product brands and stores. Grocery store and department store retailers alike distributed these items for their patrons to collect. Product manufacturers had also participated in premium programs, including spoons, towels, or souvenir cards inside their product packaging.... This overlapping of advertising and motion pictures increased the number of faces on the screen recognizable to movie fans.

The film industry was not unanimous in its support for this new publicity.... But by November, even the trade journals acknowledged that the machinery of movie stardom had set in motion.... Even so, only the identities of a few leading players were yet publicized, and the performers themselves were beginning to call for complete cast credits to introduce each reel.

While film performers garnered more attention in 1910, their increasingly devoted, vocal supporters in the movie audience were also gathering notice. During the same year, a newly coined term, *movie fan,* began to be applied to the men and women who regularly and enthusiastically attended nickelodeon shows. Some cultural critics used the term as a sign of their enmity toward working-class film audiences. In a 1910 trade journal article, W.W.Winters wrote of his pleasure-seeking, middle-class friends feeling "deliciously low" while slumming in big-city nickelodeons, but he also chronicled how quickly middle-class people were becoming "fans" themselves. The term gained rapid acceptance in American popular speech. Unlike the association of the term *fan* with baseball spectators, however, *movie fan* from the start accommodated both male and female moviegoers. The designation *movie fan* was flexible enough to apply to a nationwide audience of enthusiastic men, women, and children, blurring many of the class, ethnic, regional, and gender distinctions that had separated audiences for earlier amusements....

The spread of cameras and phonographs into middle-class homes across the United States at the turn of the century made new forms of mass communication and entertainment accessible to hobbyists. Motion pictures, like other Edison inventions, piqued the curiosity of amateur tinkerers as well as business people. *Scientific American* and *Popular Mechanics* magazines published numerous articles on the technology of motion picture photography and projection for the legions of middle- and working-class men and boys fascinated by new mechanical and electrical technology. While it was difficult to build a movie camera from spare parts, by 1898 cameras and projectors could be purchased from several manufacturers or ordered through the Sears catalog. Between 1897 and 1910, Sears's entertainment department outfitted entrepreneurial young men with complete moving picture kits. The relatively easy availability of this new invention started many hobbyists on the road as itinerant motion picture exhibitors....

In the film trade journals of the day, exhibitors noted with bemusement that members of their audiences sought participation in the production of films as well as consumption. They also felt some disquietude that their customers wanted to embrace a role contrary to that of passive film spectator.... Across the nation movie enthusiasts wanted to become involved in the movies by writing their own scripts, or scenarios, and marketing them to the studios, by learning the mechanical mysteries of film projection, and by reading novelizations and briefer plot synopses of current film releases.

One of the most popular and widely available opportunities for audience participation in the production of films was the writing of photoplay scenarios, as the brief movie scripts of the nickelodeon era were called. Scenario writing provided one way for fans to create their own "fan literature" based on film characters and situations. Tens of thousands of eager amateur writers across the country, middle-class and working-class men, women, and children, joined the silent film scenario-writing craze, which rivaled only the writing of advertising jingles for contests as a national passion during the 1910s and early 1920s. A columnist for *Moving Picture World* reported in 1913 that "the number of scenario writers is estimated at about fifteen hundred. If a census were made of all who had written one or two scenarios the number would approximate twenty thousand."

Among the many appeals of photoplay writing were its ease and quickness; all one had to compose was a synopsis no longer than a few paragraphs of short-story length. Plot formulas were easy to pick up at the nickelodeon show and from the pulp-fiction magazines. One could live anywhere in the nation and mail scenarios to the film studios.... The financial rewards of scenario writing could be inviting. The studios offered anywhere from five to fifty dollars for each scenario they accepted. These factors made scenario writing especially attractive to audience members who wanted to get into the movies but who did not posses physical beauty or acting talent, or who lived far from the film production centers of New York, Chicago, and California. Scenario writing also allowed thousands of movie fans a creative outlet for their film-inspired fantasies....

Company studio scenario editor Giles Warren received five thousand manuscripts over a period of several months in 1910 after advertising for submissions in the *Saturday Evening Post, Collier's, Munsey's,* and other middle-class publications. Warren claimed that only fifty of the scenarios were original enough for consideration. Scores of fly-by-night "photo-play-writing schools" and publishers of scriptwriting advice manuals sprang up in such "literary centers" as Fergus Falls, Minnesota, and Everett, Washington, to capitalize on the public's fascination with the movies. The Library of Congress still holds over eighty books on how to write photoplay scenarios from this era.

While one report estimated that perhaps one hundred freelancers, only ten of them untrained writers, earned substantial income from scenario writing, enough amateurs succeeded for American popular culture to support the idea that anyone could write for the movies. The scenario-writing field was especially popular with women, who would be notably successful both as amateur and professional scriptwriters and story editors in the silent era film industry.... As feature films lengthened and their plots became more complicated, however, studios hired professional writing staffs and adapted famous books and plays for the screen. Still, in 1920, Stephen Bush reported that eight thousand unsolicited scenarios were arriving at California studios each week. A series of damaging court decisions on plagiarized scenarios in the mid-1920s greatly curtailed the movie studios' consideration of outside scripts....

The film, the theater, the audience members who cavorted before the camera—almost all vestiges of that day, which was billed as "an added summer attraction, without extra charge," are long gone. What seems especially remote, when we think about the disengagement of far-flung mass-media audiences from the creation of the product, is the possibility that at least some individuals in the movie audience could have participated in various aspects of the movie show, or could have seen themselves up on the screen, performing and mugging just like their beloved Mary and Charlie. With the end of the nickelodeon era and the rise of feature-length films, however, extraordinary high salaries and fame had become associated with top movie actors like Mary Pickford and Charlie Chaplin. Many of the film production studios had relocated away from the easily accessible East to the West Coast, and the process of film industry professionalization was well underway. Consequently, opportunities for movie audience member's participation after the initial period of novelty and experimentation in the nickelodeon era became increasingly slim.

FURTHER READING

Bean, Jennifer, ed. *A Feminist Reader in Early Cinema* (2002).

Bhule, Paul. *From the Lower East Side to Hollywood: Jews in American Popular Culture* (2004).

Charney, Leo, and Vanessa R. Schwartz, eds. *Cinema and the Invention of Modern Life* (1996).

Czitrom, Daniel. *Media and then American Mind: From Morse to McLuhan* (1982).

Fregosa, Rosa Linda. *The Bronze Screen: Chicana and Chicano Film Culture* (1993).

Fuller-Seeley, Kathryn H. ed. *Hollywood in the Neighborhood: Historical Case Studies of Local Movie Going* (2008).

Gray, Johnathan, Cornel Sandvoss, and C. Lee Harrington, eds. *Fandom: Identities and Communities in a Mediated World* (2007).

Hansen, Miriam. *Babel in Babylon: Spectatorship in American Silent Film* (2006).

Hills, Matthew. *Fan Cultures* (2002).

Jowett, Garth. *Film the Democratic Art: A Social History of American Film* (1976).

Lewis, Lisa A. *The Adoring Audience: Fan Culture and Popular Media* (1992).

May, Larry. *Screening Out the Past: The Birth of Mass Culture and the Motion Picture Industry* (1980).

Musser, Charles. *The Emergence of Cinema: The American Screen to 1907* (1990).

Rabinovitz, Lauren. *For the Love of Pleasure: Women, Movies and Culture in Turn-of-the-Century Chicago* (1988).

Ross, Steven. *Working-Class Hollywood: Silent Film and the Shaping of Class in America* (1988).

Ruiz, Vicki. *Producing Dreams, Consuming Youth: Mexican Americans and Mass Media* (2003).

Sklar, Robert. *Movie-Made America: A Cultural History of American Movies* (1994).

Stamp, Shelley. *Movie-Struck Girls* (2000).

CHAPTER 7

Advertising and the Culture
of Consumption, 1880–1930

Advertising both formed and funded modern media, from magazines to radio and from commercial television to the Internet. The growth of popular culture was married to advertising, but advertising also existed as a cultural form in its own right. In addition, historians have seen the "culture of consumption" as a defining paradigm of the twentieth century and advertising serves as consumption's language. While some scholars focus on the advertisements themselves, most historians look at the economic system of which advertising is a part, the consumers, and the advertising industry that produces the ads, as well as the advertisements, to uncover the complex role advertising plays in a consumer culture.

Advertising changed more between 1880 and 1920 than it has since 1920. Before 1880, most advertisements were announcements of goods available, factual descriptions of merchandise offered by local shopkeepers and artisans. Advertising looked more like classified notices than the product promotion we see today. In 1897, Harper's Weekly summarized the new ads beginning to appear: "Once we skipped [advertisements] unless some want compelled us to read, while now we read to find out what we really want." The shift that pushed American advertising into the remarkable change between the nineteenth and twentieth centuries was, according to historian Susan Strasser, "the development of national markets for the branded, standardized, products of large scale manufacturers." Technological and economic innovations brought mass production, which used advertising to sell the goods to consumers. By 1920, advertising expenditures had passed a billion dollars annually with the biggest advertisers (like Proctor and Gamble, Goodyear Tire, and Quaker Oats) each spending over a million dollars on magazine advertising alone. Advertising agencies worked much like they do today with advertisements as elements in campaigns based on marketing strategies. Among leading national advertisers there was far more turnover in the twenty-five years before World War I than in the years since then. The current top ten advertisers and the top ten ad categories of today would be quite familiar to advertisers of the 1920s.

For advertising to succeed, it needed more than a national apparatus of marketing and distribution. The acceptance of advertising required a cultural change, a change in thinking. Consumers had to learn to read ads and to think about consumption as a way of 1ife. How did consumption became a cultural ideal, an all powerful, hegemonic "way of seeing" in twentieth century America? In a consumer culture, everything, including people themselves, is and must be subject to the market, able to be bought and sold. People see themselves as consumers and people look to the goods they can buy—consume—for more than just their physical properties. Historian Jackson Lears explored how consumers came to believe they could buy products that would provide emotional or spiritual sustenance, in a form we've learned to call therapy.

Most contemporary Americans both love and hate advertising and the culture of consumption. At the same time, as with most forms of hegemonic culture, we have also learned to ignore it. The fact that all of entertainment, leisure activities, media, and social life exists only because, and within, a web of advertising causes hardly a ripple of concern. Would media be different if advertising didn't exist? Examining the history of advertising shows its naturalness as a façade—things could have developed differently.

 # DOCUMENTS

These documents show that throughout the twentieth century, there have been critiques of advertising; a fascination with it as a fictional subject; and a spirited defense of advertising's necessity, despite its widespread acceptance. The documents also address the contradictions inherent in advertising's growth just before and during the Great Depression. Document 1 illustrates the advertising available in 1872. In Document 2, an advertisement appearing only 28 years after those in Document 1, we see a new form of communication and realize that readers needed to be fluent in the language of consumption to understand this ad. The excerpts from a play in Document 3 present an early critique of advertising as well as a cultural fascination with its power and inner workings. In Document 4, one of the first advertising professionals, Bruce Barton, explains how advertising forms the basis of Christianity, as a way of defending both. Document 5 shows how women became a particularly important audience for advertising, constructed as the ultimate consumers. Critiques of advertising peaked during the hard economic times of the 1930s. In Document 6, James Rorty points to the importance and evils of an advertising-supported media. *Ballyhoo* magazine, appearing during the Depression, took advertising as its subject and in Document 7, a spoof ad raised the ultimate question. Do we need advertising to sell products? Are there any products or ideas that should stand outside the culture of consumption?

1. Early Magazine Advertisements
Crowd the Page, 1880

Harper's Weekly (10 March 1872), The Library of Congress.

2. Advertising Changes Visually, 1900

"Put a Kodak in Your Pocket," Kodak Ad, *Century* (April 1900), Courtesy of George Eastman House, International Museum of Photography and Film.

3. Playwrights Roi Cooper Megrue and Walter Hackett Make Fun of Advertising and Consumers, 1917

It Pays to Advertise

Old Cyrus Martin, the soap king, sat in his library in no very contented frame of mind. There was a thorn in his flesh and he began to feel it more and more. It was not an agreeable sensation, a thorn in the flesh, for a soap king whose cuticle was not accustomed to it.

The fact was that Mr. Cyrus Martin, sixty-five years old, richer than it is wholesome for most people to be, in fairly good health, except for a touch of real or imaginary gout now and then, enjoying his semi-retirement from an old established and lucrative business, was nevertheless conscious this afternoon of a distinct subcurrent of irritation....

What was the matter with rich men's sons anyway? thought Cyrus Martin. Rodney's father had not spoiled him: his father's conscience was clear on that point at least....

The boy was attractive too; his father had always liked him. Perhaps that was one of the chief troubles. Even as a little child he had never flown into tempers or had hateful ways. His own winning and non-combative disposition had been the chief means, no doubt, of warding off the disciplines of life. He was amiable and good-looking in an obtrusive way, and everybody liked him.... he had never done so much, and in college he had got fairly good marks, as nearly as his father could make out, and had won his degree of A. B. without too obvious difficulty.... Cyrus Martin had been credibly informed that you could not actually graduate from Harvard or Yale or Princeton without some portion of mentality. Where did it show itself in Rodney?...

He rang the bell sharply for Johnson, his butler, prepared to have a pretty sharp twinge of gout if the summons was not promptly answered....

"... has she been here, Miss Grayson?"

"Yes, sir, she's been here since four o'clock, sir, doing some typing. She's still waiting for you."

"Why the devil didn't you say so, then?"

"I was coming to her presently, sir."

"Tell her to come in, then, to the library....

... Old Martin sat and thought.

Mary Grayson! Well, what made young men work? Love, sometimes, and poverty and necessity. The first might stir Rodney up, if not the second and third. But why not all three?

"She stoops to conquer," he muttered to himself.... Rodney might be made to stoop to be conquered—to conquer himself and his laziness of a rich man's son. On Mary Grayson's part it was not really stooping if you considered Rodney's mentality and character; he admitted it sourly. If Rodney could find

Roi Cooper Megrue and Walter Hackett, *It Pays to Advertise: A Farcical Fact in Three Acts* (New York: S. French, 1917).

an incentive in Mary Grayson, the stenographer, what did old man Martin care? He knew her for a good girl, as she was a pretty one....

Rodney Martin himself, as luck would have it, opened the front door with his pass key and came in just as Mary was descending into the lower hall from his father's library....

"I want to talk to you," said Rodney, coming towards her. "I've been wanting this opportunity for days...."

Rodney had come over to her, and now stood facing her, his eyes eager and full of light.

"I want to talk to you," he said impetuously.

"Mary, will you marry me?"

"Why, really," began Mary shyly, looking sidewise and enjoying herself curiously well.

"You love me, don't you?" queried the boy warmly.

"I don't know what to say," hesitated the girl, feeling her ground.

"Say yes," cried Rodney, waiting feverishly to hear her answer.

It came at last shyly, "Yes," whereupon Rodney cried, "You angel," joyfully, and tried to grab her....

"No, no; wait a moment," she said, eluding him.

"We'll be married right away," went on Rodney unabashed.

"But suppose your father disapproves," said Mary....

"Don't you bother ...," cried Rodney.

"We'll be married tomorrow, and then come home for the parental blessing."

"No, I couldn't do that," said Mary. "It wouldn't be right. I'm his private secretary. He trusts me, and brings me here to his home, and then to find I'd married his son on the sly—No, Rodney, we couldn't do that."...

"But suppose he does object?" Rodney argued, seeing his light of happiness grow dim.

"Even then I wouldn't give you up," said his sweetheart.

"Mary!"

"You could go into business," she went on; "make a big man of yourself; make me proud of you—."...

"Don't you want to work?" asked Mary anxiously.

"I should say not," Rodney answered quite seriously. "Imagine going to bed every night, knowing you'd got to get up in the morning and go to business."

"You'd be happier, wouldn't you?" queried Mary, "if you had a job?"

"Please don't talk like father," protested Rodney. "He's preached a job at me ever since I left college. Why should I work? Father made millions out of soap, and is forever complaining that he's always had his nose to the grindstone, that he's never known what fun was, that it's all made him old before his time. I can't see the sense of following an example like that—I really can't...."

He leaned hungrily toward her, stretching out his arms to her, and finished on a note of genuine appeal: "Come, kiss me, Mary."

But Mary drew back from him quickly. "No, you mustn't," she said firmly. "Not till you've spoken to your father."

"You won't even kiss me till I tell him?"

"No."

"And you will when I do?"

"Yes."

"Then I'll tell him right away," cried the valiant lover, striding to the door.

"Oh, Rodney, you're splendid," applauded Mary, "and don't be afraid."…

Rodney stood a moment with his hand on the knob, plucking up resolution. As he lingered there, a violent knocking sounded on the other side, and his father's voice could be distinctly heard crying "Ouch" in an extra loud tone in the hall….

… Martin painfully limped to a chair by a small table and sank into it, his foot giving him another twinge.

"Ouch! Oh, my poor foot!" he moaned.

Rodney hastily picked up a footstool and came with it to his father.

"I wanted to have a talk with you—an important talk—"

"Curious! That's just what I wanted to have with you. I've wanted it all day. And now we'll have it…."

Mary looked from father to son with an elaborately assumed air of innocence, and inquired:

"You wanted me, Mr. Martin?"…

"My precious son," he told her, "has just informed me that you and he intend to get married. Is that right?"…

"Because I wish to tell you," he began again, "that if he marries you he'll not get one penny of my money. And that means he'll starve. I suppose you realize that?"…

"Then at least we'll starve together."…

"Well, what can you do to keep from starving?" demanded his father. "You're not a producer. You never will be. You're just an idler. You couldn't earn five dollars a week. But you'll have a chance to try. You'll get out of my house to-night, or I'll have you thrown out."…

"Oh, Rodney, Rodney, what have I done? I'm so, so sorry," snivelled Mary.

"You haven't done anything," Rodney answered. "Neither of us has. Father didn't seem to give us a chance to; he did it all—"…

"What are you going to do?" she asked him excitedly.

"I'm going to work."

"You are—really?"

"Yes, indeed—Father couldn't make me do it, but you can. I'll work for you."

"Oh, you are splendid," Mary cried. "Shall you get a position?"

"I should say not! Work for someone else? No! I'm going in business for myself—for you. I'm going to show the stuff that's in me. Of course we can't get married till I've made good. Will you wait?"

"Yes, dear," said Mary shyly….

"Mary, sweetheart!" he cried.

He held her away from him a moment to regard her face.

"The pater's upstairs dressing for dinner," he rattled on. "I shan't even say good-by to him. Serve him right. I'm going to take a stage down to the Harvard Club this very night. Can't afford cabs now."…

Of course the old man was throwing a kind of bluff, thought Rodney; he wouldn't really allow his son to land in the workhouse, or starve to death. But the old man would carry things through with a high hand, too, and in the end it would come to the same net result in discomfort and the long wait for Mary. He must work very, very hard:—oh, so hard. He took out a cigarette, and lit it, finding a quiet seat near the 44th Street window to sit down and think things over.... He armed himself with a newspaper, so that he could occasionally hold it up and ward off unwelcome chatterers who might disturb his train of thought. The armament was not modern enough, however, to repel the attack of the alert young man who presently came and peered over the top of his *Sun*.

"Well, Ambrose Peale," said Rodney, looking up.

"That's me absolutely," said Mr. Peale. "The same, at your service. So you remember me, eh?"...

"Well, if you'll excuse me, I've been looking for you to talk business with you. Shall I blaze away?" asked Peale.

"Business? Surely, surely," rejoined Rodney, with an inward wink. "I'm a business man now. Blaze away, as you say."

Ambrose Peale was one of those young Americans for whom a special series of new words has been minted. He was a hustler and he certainly was breezy; he was a live wire and he had the gift of the gab. He was not born yesterday and he would never really grow old. He turned up everywhere, like a bad penny, which nevertheless rang true. He had even taken a special course at Harvard for a time—to get next to "that college stuff," he had explained, and he occupied the seat next to the soap king's son ... now in his own divine right....

"Oh, you're one of those wise guys who don't believe in advertising, are you?" said Peale, expostulating and expounding. "Now don't get me talking advertising. That's where I live, where I have my town house and country estate, my yacht and motors.—That's my home. Maybe you think love is important. Piffle! Advertising, my boy; the power of suggestion, the psychology of print. Say a thing often enough—hard enough—and the other chap'll not only believe you, he'll think it's his own idea; and he'll fight for it.—Some old gink, a professor of psychology, showed forty Vassar girls, the other day, two samples of satin, one blue, one pink same grade—same value—same artistic worth. One he described as a delicate warm old rose—the other he called a faded blue. He asked them to choose their favorite. Girls picked the old rose. Why? Because they'd been told it was warm and delicate—no faded blue for theirs. What did it? Power of suggestion—advertising."...

"When you see a thing in print about something you don't really know anything about, you come pretty near believing it. And all the advertiser has to do is to tell you right and you'll fall—"

"But I never read advertisements," said Rodney.

"Oh, you don't eh? If I say fifty-seven varieties you know it means pickles. I guess you've got some idea that 'His Master's Voice' advertises a phonograph. You're on to what soap 'It floats' refers to. There's a Reason—Uneeda—All the News That's Fit to Print....

The offices of the Soap Company were finally located about half way down Broadway. There was a waiting-room, and a private office—as private as could be expected with three people using it. It was a rather commonplace room, furnished comfortable but not elaborately. The walls were hung with posters extolling the virtues of 13 Soap, such as,

---

DO YOU BELIEVE IN SIGNS?

13 Soap is Unlucky for Dirt

Isn't it funny, though, that nobody's tried to buy any soap from us yet?" asked Rodney with some anxiety.

This was a very tender point with the soap company. Mary and Rodney worried over it, and Rodney dreamed at night about it. An occasional small order that might filter in from some remote outlying district, or some small merchant whose credit was doubtful, was gazed upon as parents gaze at their first baby. Peale was the bachelor of the crowd, and seemed not to care whether they were productive or not. "It takes time to create a demand," he would say; but admitted that the two hundred cakes of pink castile they had bought looked swell in their old rose wrappers.

Peale explained,… "The 13 Soap—it's great—it's got imagination—Soap— a fact—13, unlucky—unlucky for what? Why, dirt. Imagination, superstition, humor. Cleanliness, soap—all associated in one phrase. Plus buncombe, good old bunk for the pinheads—the most expensive soap in the world. And think of the advantage we have that we're selling soap. People know whether automobiles go or not—if clothes wear well, or collars crack, or soups taste good, or furniture falls apart, or roofs leak, or phonographs can't talk. There you have to deliver the goods;—but soap or dental cream, or tooth powder or cold cream, who really knows anything about 'em? Who can tell anything about 'em? Can you? I can't. All you have to do is to make 'em smell nice."

Rodney began to take fire again from this enthusiasm.

"By George, it's wonderful, colossal, I never realized it," he began.

"Neither did I," assented Mary.

"Kind of beginning to believe in advertising?" buzzed Peale.…

If only they had just made soap, Mary couldn't help thinking sometimes, as all this talk rang in her ears. If only they had just made soap, and made it good. Good wine needs no bush, was an ancient proverb she came to believe in. By the same token good soap would need no ads.…

Ambrose Peale, the advertising expert, was cynical enough to maintain it did not matter. First create your demand, he would say, then make your soap.… It took six months to get any returns from advertising any way. In the end, for lack of funds, he carried the day.… In truth the orders were very, very few. The whole question was the old one of which came first, the chicken or the egg. Their cakes of soap were the eggs and their advertising was the mother chicken that was to hatch out the plentiful brood, if you put it that way; but it was all too metaphysical for Mary, who felt somehow that metaphysics wouldn't help her much with 13 Soap.…

The darkest hour comes just before the dawn, and dawn came with a sudden burst of glory one morning when Ambrose Peale flew into the office in great excitement, interrupting Mary and Rodney in a long embrace. Always discreet and tactful, he coughed and scraped his feet, as a signal to them to break away....

"A telegram," said Peale, "it's the first we've ever had—I was afraid to open it."...

So … Mary opened it and read: …

"Ship at once, collect, fifty thousand cakes 13 Soap.

"Signed: Marshall Field, Chicago."

A profound silence fell upon the trio: the colossal number of fifty thousand, and the magic name of Marshall Field had overpowered them. It was far too good to be true.

"Somebody really wants to buy some of our soap," echoed Rodney stupidly.

"I don't believe it," said Peale....

Then Peale burst out joyfully; the tide had turned.

"We've started—we've begun!" he yelled; "we're actually going to sell some soap."

"The tide's turned," said Rodney; "didn't I tell you advertising pays? We'll sweep the country—Europe—Asia—Africa."...

"I'll wire Marshall Field right away," said Peale briskly.

"Go ahead, do," said Rodney.

But an exclamation from Mary made them both turn.

"What is it?" asked Peale nervously.

"What's happened?" asked Rodney.

"That order is no good," Mary said sadly.

"What!"

"Why?"

"We can't fill it—we've never made any soap," said Mary with a sinking heart.

They stood staring at each other aghast.

"What shall we do?" quavered Rodney.

"Let's think," said Peale hopefully.

They sat staring straight ahead dolefully, till finally Rodney remarked slowly:

"We must get some soap."

"Yes, I thought of that," said Peale.

"Where can we get it?" Mary asked them deliberately.

"From a soap factory!" Peale suggested.

"But they all belong to your father," Mary reminded him.

Meanwhile Rodney had a ray of dawning hope.

"But he can't know about this Marshall Field order—maybe we could buy some soap before he'd have a chance to stop them selling to us—"...

They could hardly wait till the soap came in and was shipped out again to Chicago. All three of them were as excited as children waiting before the doors that open on a Christmas tree. Fifty thousand cakes! It was an inestimable, an infinite, an incredible, number. Rodney had not an idea whether a row of fifty thousand cakes of 13 Soap would reach from our earth to the moon, or only from the Plaza to the Pennsylvania Terminal. They came and came, an endless chain. But when the influx stopped and had been carefully counted by Mary,

Miss Burke and the office boy, pro tem., it totaled, not fifty thousand, though it seemed a million, but only five thousand altogether....

The company's three officers made a dash for their telephones.... only to be told that there was no more soap in stock. In each instance the news was conveyed in a cool and uncordial tone that gave them to understand there was nothing more doing in that quarter. What was the matter? ...

Rodney was the most crestfallen of them all, for an idea had come to him of the true reason of things.

"It's the pater," he said in a quiet tone that carried conviction. "He's shut down on us." ...

Rodney ... looked as if something were working in his mind, and no wonder, Mary thought, with their situation what it was. Mary knew him like a book, but this time she would ask no questions and keep her own counsel. She was going straight up to Mr. Martin's on Fifth Avenue and have a long talk and argument with him. He simply *must* let them have those extra forty-five thousand cakes of soap for Marshall Field....

If there is any time in the day when a retired business man should be allowed to enjoy himself in his own mature and self chosen way, it is the hour between five and six.... Disgruntlement still swayed his paternal heart when he thought of Rodney—he was torn between love and irritation where that boy was concerned....

It was a relief when Johnson presently appeared and announced a caller, though a great surprise to hear the caller's name. Mary Grayson!...

"... what are you here for?" he demanded, really curious.

"To make you a business proposition," said Mary stoutly.

"Why doesn't Rodney make it himself?" asked his father.

"He doesn't know what it is," explained Mary.

"That's something in his favor," Martin conceded; "I can't see much use in women tying up in men's business. Somehow I love the scallawag, and, damn it, I miss him around here." ...

His reflections and Mary's business were interrupted, however, by Johnson's entering a second time and announcing the last two people in the world that Mary had counted on, namely, Mr. Rodney Martin and Mr. Ambrose Peale.

"Oh, the whole firm, eh?" said Mr. Martin, eyeing Mary sharply....

"You see, my boy," said Martin senior, "even if you did nearly trim me, I've got a sort of sneaking fondness for you. Look here, son, why not quit? There's no market for dollar soap."

"But how do you know?" Rodney objected bravely.

"How do I know?" asked his father. "Because I had a letter from Marshall Field a few days ago asking me what to do with the soap. They hadn't sold a cake. I told 'em to dump it in the Chicago river. It might help the drainage canal."

"But you didn't give our advertising a chance," objected Rodney.

"Yes," said Peale eagerly. "We only finished a great big advertising campaign in Chicago two days ago."

"I know the soap would have made good," insisted Rodney, "with that trademark." ...

In the meantime Peale had grown more and more discouraged.

"Oh, what's the use? He doesn't believe in advertising," he said pathetically.

"Oh yes, I do," Mr. Martin objected; "sound conservative advertising, but not the crazy, sensational stuff you go in for."

Mary decided she would try another tack.

"Oh, you're just mad because the soap trust didn't think of 13 Soap itself," she said, half mischievously.

"Why, we wouldn't touch a fool thing like that," said Mr. Martin. "If you deliver the goods, your goods will advertise you; that's always been our policy."

This was an unfortunate lead for the old soap king to have made. To doubt the efficiency of his ads was to strike at the vitals of Ambrose Peale, to challenge him and draw his fire every time. And now Rodney was his enthusiastic squire and second.

Both boys drew good long breaths and began on their favorite themes. Poor Mary felt that she too was being swept along with them in the flood of Peale's enthusiasm.

"I'm sorry, father," Rodney led off, "but you are too old fashioned to know the modern way of advertising. Why, do you know the National Biscuit Company was on the verge of failing until they hit on the title Uneeda Biscuit?"

Mary took a hand, too.

"And since then, they have had over four hundred law-suits to protect it," quoted Mary.

"Their trademark made 'em," Rodney went on. "They value that trademark now at six million dollars." …

"And did you ever hear of the Gillette Safety Razor?" asked Mary. "Tell him about it, Rodney."

"It costs you five dollars," said Rodney; "don't you know there's a mighty good safety razor for a quarter and dozens at a dollar? But you use the Gillette because Gillette was there first. You buy his razor at a high price simply because of its trademark."

"Advertising," said Mary, with a gesture she had learned from Rodney.

"Absolutely," said Rodney, with a word he had learned from Peale.

Peale himself went on:

"And Ivory soap in the magazines alone used four hundred and fifty thousand dollars' worth of space in 1913; and at three cents a cake wholesale that represents fifteen million cakes for magazine advertising alone."

"I don't believe it," old Martin interrupted.

"Yes," said Peale irreverently, "and a lot of other guys didn't believe that iron ships would float, or that machines heavier than air would fly, or that you could talk to Chicago on a wire, or send a message across the Atlantic without a wire. Pardon me, sir, but you want to get on to yourself."

"Yes, father, you certainly do," said Rodney.

"And you'd better hurry up," added Mary.

Mr. Martin laughed grimly.

"You've got a fine lot of theories, but what have they done for those five thousand cakes of 13 Soap out at Marshall Field's?"

"Why, we haven't really spent enough money advertising," said Peale, true to his faith.

"That's the trouble."…

"Yes, … let's show him our list," said Mary.

Rodney and Peale each grabbed a long typewritten sheet out of his breast pocket….

"Sure," Rodney said. "It's an absolutely accurate list of what some of the big advertisers spent in the thirty-one leading magazines last year. Eastman Kodak," he began to read off: "four hundred thousand. Postum Coffee, one hundred and twenty-five thousand, Arrow Collars, four hundred thousand, Philip Morris Cigarettes, one hundred thousand, Welch's Grape Juice, one hundred thousand."

"Grape Juice, my friend," put in Peale, winking.

"Uneeda Biscuit one hundred and fifty thousand, Spearmint Gum one hundred and forty thousand," pursued Rodney.

"That's enough; that's enough," protested his father.

"Oh, I've only just begun," Rodney laughed. "Grape Nuts two hundred and twenty-eight thousand."

"Colgate's Dental Cream, two hundred and thirty thousand," mentioned Mary.

"Campbell's Soups, one hundred and eighty-six thousand," said Peale.

"Kellogg's Toasted Cornflakes, two hundred thousand," said Mary.

"Quaker Oats, three hundred sixty-seven thousand, and these are only a few," said Rodney. "You can't see how it pays, but you do know that it must pay or they wouldn't do it."

"Doesn't all that mean anything to you?" inquired Mary anxiously.

"Yes, doesn't it?" Peale persisted….

"It won't be long before there are twenty-five million people buying magazines, and you can reach all of them by advertising—get a new market, a new population to deal with. Think what national advertising is accomplishing. It sells automobiles, vacuum cleaners, talking machines, rubber heels, kodaks, washing machines, foods, clothes, shoes, paints, houses, plumbing, electric irons, fireless cookers, mostly to a lot of people who'd never even hear of 'em if it weren't for advertisements."

Peale took up the refrain next.

"But nowadays it isn't only people who have stoves to sell or tooth brushes that are spending money on publicity," he began. "Banks are advertising for money, nations for immigrants, colleges for students, cities for citizens and churches for congregations; and you sit there thinking it doesn't pay to advertise."

"Six hundred and sixteen million dollars were spent last year in magazines and newspapers, billboards and electric signs," recited Mary.

"Bringing education and comfort and fun and luxury to the people of the United States," said Rodney. "It's romance, father, the romance of printing presses, of steel rails, of the wireless, of trains and competition, the romance of modern business, and it's all built on advertising. Why, advertising is the biggest thing in this country, and it's only just begun."…

"Well," said Mr. Martin, "when you boys get through talking, and you're flat broke and down and out, come around and see me; I'll show you an old business that has a lot of money, that isn't radical, and that manages to keep going without wasting a fortune in fool advertising.".…

Meanwhile, in far away Chicago, something of importance to the little company had taken place. The soap had begun to sell. One demand after another had come in, and finally made an impression. It was as if a stone had been dropped in the puddle and the circles had widened out and out. The last ripple reached New York and Mr. Martin when Johnson came one day to the library and announced:

"I beg pardon. A gentleman to see you, sir," handing his master a card on a silver tray.

"Mr. Charles Bronson," read Martin; "what's he want?"

"He says he's from Marshall Field, Chicago," said Johnson.…

[T]o-day, with Mr. Martin, this Mr. Bronson seemed very full of business and his business, it seemed, was about 13 Soap.

"Well, what about it?" Mr. Martin demanded, not too graciously.…

"Through some error we received only five thousand cakes," explained Bronson, "instead of fifty thousand; but that's all gone."

"All gone? What happened to it?"

"We've sold it."

Mr. Martin could not believe his ears.

"Sold it!" he ejaculated.…

Mr. Bronson laughed.

"I know, I know," he said. "We felt at first that of course there could be no popular market for a dollar soap—we weren't as far sighted as you were.".…

"But of course, when those extraordinary advertisements appeared, so different from your usual conservative publicity, well, the sales began immediately; we sold the five thousand cakes in two days."

"And the advertising did it?" Mr. Martin ventured to inquire.

"Of course, what else?" said Bronson.…

"[N]ow what's your proposition?" demanded the soap king.

"A quarter of a million cash just for the trademark," said Bronson.

"A quarter of a million?" said Martin scornfully to the quailing Bronson. "Why, you ought to be ashamed of yourself to try to trim these poor boys like that."

The events of his busy and momentous morning had been gradually mounting to old Mr. Martin's head. The excitement of putting through an important deal, … the reclamation of his boy Rodney, and finally Rodney's marriage with Mary Grayson, something he had always wanted, exhilarated him; and as wine boils up unaccustomed things in one's brain, so this last speech by Bronson caused the soap king to pour forth all the bits of advertising talk that had been flowing round him for the last six months. He squared away like Ambrose Peale, for all the world, and let Bronson have a full blast.

"You know that 13 Soap is worth half a million in Chicago alone," he shouted. "And you try to take advantage of these kids' ignorance. Why, it's outrageous; but you can't trim me.—No, sir—we wouldn't take a million. Do you know that the Uneeda trademark is valued at six million, the Gold Dust Twins at ten million and our trademark is better than theirs? We're going to advertise all over the world—That's what advertising means—the power of suggestion—the psychology of print. All you have to do is to say a thing often enough and hard enough and ninety-seven per cent of the public'll fall. Get 'em talking about you—don't let 'em be quiet—mention your name—argue about it—be a hero or a villain—but don't be a dub....

"Well, father, father," laughed Mary, hearing this torrent of advertising talk from these erstwhile "conservative" lips. "You've got religion."

"And you need it, Missy," cried the delighted soap king, turning on her.

"Mrs., if you please," laughed Mary.

"Mrs. Rodney Martin, eh?" he chuckled.

"Tell me all about it all over again. When were you married? Where did you go? Where do you live? I'll tell you one thing, anyway. You've got to come and live here now, both of you."

"It's a good thing I never took away my trunk after all," said Rodney, putting one arm around Mary's waist and shaking his father's hand with the other.

Mr. Martin took out a large silk handkerchief and blew his nose quite loudly.

"I'll settle a hundred thousand dollars on the first grandchild," he said, "just for luck."

"Well, well," said Ambrose Peale, with a suspicious twinkle in his eye. "Believe me, it pays to advertise."

THE END

4. A Pioneer Ad Man, Bruce Barton, Defends the Need for Advertising, 1925

... I propose ... to speak of the advertisements of Jesus which have survived for twenty centuries and are still the most potent influence in the world.

Let us begin by asking why he was so successful in mastering public attention.... The answer is twofold. In the first place he recognized the basic principle that all good advertising is news. He was never trite or commonplace; he had no routine. If there had been newspapers in those days, no city editor could have said, "No need to visit him to-day; he will be doing just what he did last Sunday." Reporters would have followed him every single hour, for it was impossible to predict what he would say or do; every action and word were news....

One of those who had been attracted by the excitement was a tax-collector named Matthew. Being a man of business he could not stay through the argument, but slipped away early and was hard at work when Jesus passed by a few minutes before noon.

"Matthew, I want you," said Jesus.

Bruce Barton, *The Man Nobody Knows* (Indianapolis, IN: Bobbs-Merrill, 1925).

That was all. No argument; no offer of inducements; no promise of rewards. Merely "I want you;" and the prosperous tax-collector closed his office, made a feast for the brilliant young teacher and forthwith announced himself a disciple.

★★★

PROMINENT TAX COLLECTOR JOINS
NAZARETH FORCES
MATTHEW ABANDONS BUSINESS TO PROMOTE
NEW CULT

★★★

GIVES LARGE LUNCHEON

Front page story....

If he were to live again, in these modern days, he would find a way ... to be advertised by his service, not merely by his sermons. One thing is certain: he would not neglect the market-place. Few of his sermons were delivered in synagogues. For the most part he was in the crowded places, the Temple Court, the city squares, the centers where goods were bought and sold....

[T]he present day market-place is the newspaper and the magazine. Printed columns are the modern thoroughfares; published advertisements are the cross-roads where the sellers and the buyers meet. Any issue of a national magazine is a world's fair, a bazaar filled with the products of the world's work. Clothes and clocks and candle-sticks; soup and soap and cigarettes; lingerie and limousines— the best of all of them are there, proclaimed by their makers in persuasive tones. That every other voice should be raised in such great market–places, and the voice of Jesus of Nazareth be still—this is a vital omission which he would find a way to correct. He would be a national advertiser today, I am sure, as he was the great advertiser of his own day. To the minds of those who hurry through the bristling pages, he too would send his call:

> What shall it profit a man if he shall gain the whole world and lose his own soul; or **what shall a man give in exchange for his soul**?

This would be his challenge in every newspaper and magazine; and with it would be coupled an invitation to share in the joyous enterprise of his work....

One of the most revealing of all verses to those who would understand the secret of his power is this: "All these things spake Jesus unto the multitude *in parables;* and without a parable spake he not unto them." A parable is a story. He told them stories, stories about people, and let the stories carry his message....

Take any one of the parables, no matter which—you will find that it exemplifies all the principles on which advertising text books are written. Always a picture in the very first sentence; crisp, graphic language and a message so clear that even the dullest can not escape it.

TEN VIRGINS WENT FORTH TO MEET A BRIDEGROOM

A striking picture and a striking head-line....

Every advertising man ought to study the parables of Jesus in the same fashion, schooling himself in their language and learning these four big elements of their power.

1. First of all they are marvelously condensed, as all good advertising must be...

2. His language was marvelously simple—a second great essential. There is hardly a sentence in his teaching which a child can not understand. His illustrations were all drawn from the commonest experiences of life; "a sower went forth to sow"; "a certain man had two sons"; "a man built his house on the sands"; "the kingdom of heaven is like a grain of mustard seed."...

3. Sincerity glistened like sunshine through every sentence he uttered; sincerity is the third essential.... The public has a sixth sense for detecting insincerity; they know instinctively when words ring true....

   Much brass has been sounded and many cymbals tinkled in the name of advertising; but the advertisements which persuade people to act are written by men who have an abiding respect for the intelligence of their readers, and a deep sincerity regarding the merits of the goods they have to sell.

4. Finally he knew the necessity for repetition and practised it....

It has been said that "reputation is repetition." No important truth can be impressed upon the minds of any large number of people by being said only once. The thoughts which Jesus had to give the world were revolutionary, but they were few in number. "God is your father," he said, "caring more for the welfare of every one of you than any human father can possibly care for his children. His Kingdom is happiness! his rule is love." This is what he had to teach, but he knew the necessity of driving it home from every possible angle. So in one of his stories God is the shepherd searching the wilds for one wandering sheep; in another, the Father welcoming home a prodigal boy; in another a King who forgives his debtors large amounts and expects them to be forgiving in turn—*many* stories, *many* advertisements, but the same big Idea.

Because the advertisements were unforgettable, the Idea lived, and is to-day the one most powerful influence on human action and thought. To be sure the work of the advertisements is far from complete. The Idea that God is the Father of *all* men—not merely of a specially selected few—has still to penetrate some creeds, and to establish its dominance in society....

And whoever feels an impulse to make his own life count in this grand process of human betterment, can have no surer guide for his activities than the advertisements of Jesus. Let him learn their lesson, that if you would teach people you first must capture their interest with news; that your service rather than your sermons must be your claim upon their attention; that what you say must be simple, and brief, an above all *sincere*—the unmistakable voice of true regard and affection....

5. Home Economist Christine Frederick
Explains How to Advertise to Women, 1929

... **The High Status of American Women in Family Spending**—The American male himself often testifies that he labors in order that his wife and children should enjoy luxury and comfort. He seems to enjoy himself most *at earning*, while content to leave the pleasure of spending to his women. It has therefore become a male American tradition that the wife is the purchasing agent of the family, and on lower income levels men actually turn over intact, their pay envelopes to their wives. Such a condition puts buying power into women's hands on a tremendously broad scale—so broad indeed that in a research made by Dr. H. L. Hollingworth of Columbia University, the only item that men bought entirely by themselves, without consultation with women, was their own collars! The purchase of not another article of apparel was free from the coöperating purchasing influence of women; and now that men are wearing shirts with attached collars so extensively, even that little island of isolation is being taken from man!

Every article of family use, even those beginning with exclusively male interest, like automobiles and radio, have slowly come into woman's purchasing fold, and their design, distribution, sales and advertising vitally affected by the fact of woman's purchasing standards. Since all but a mere small fraction of income goes for family purposes, it is of course inevitable that woman should dominate family expenditure. The percentage of this domination is a matter of dispute, but the minimum that students of the subject name is 80%.

I am not able to agree with this, and I place it at 90% if we include, as I think we must, woman's increasing voice in investments, savings and the general types of expenditure. The reasonableness of this high percentage is further demonstrated in the chapter on women's wealth and property in the U.S., a wealth which is astounding our bankers.

Surely such a staggering percentage of spending power as 80% or 90% in the hands of woman is something of the deepest importance to analyze. It is apparent that women have developed a very special faculty and ability for spending....

Any number of American men are brilliant money makers and yet very untrustworthy custodians of their earnings. They are safe if they have wives who can conserve these earnings, but if not they live on a very erratic economic plane.

Women are by nature conservers of values. It is their oldest instinct next to mother love. For millions of years they have had to make sure that seeds were planted and harvested and that there was food and shelter and supplies, while man lived in his world of ideas and adventure and even disdained to cut up the animal he shot for food. Woman's economic, and even political and social dignity and status, *has always been high wherever she had an important share in the domestic arrangements*. The American Indian squaw has always fed and clothed and housed and taken care of the Indian and the family, and because of this enjoyed a greater

Christine Frederick, *Selling Mrs. Consumer* (New York: Business Bourse, 1929).

degree of liberty and equality than even her civilized white sister did until recent years.

In drawing this picture of woman's status and buying power in America I do not mean to overvalue her or make her out a prodigy, but merely to get the facts in a true focus. Woman is of course powerful in buying largely because of her *secondary* position to man. She is not man's equal in earning and doing and building, therefore she gravitates toward the position of quartermaster rather than general in their mutual organization. She takes charge of supplies largely for the very reason that she can't lead the forces in the field....

Having now presented the psychological picture of the basis for Mrs. Consumer's great buying power in America, I want to discuss some of its exact measurements and extent.

The 1928 pay envelope of the American people totaled approximately $92,000,000,000. Of this, as admitted by the Director of the U.S. Bureau of Standards, $52,000,000,000 is spent by women for food, clothing, shelter and other services. Taking this figure as representing the most conservative estimate of what women buy, we have *one billion dollars a week* passed out from the hands of Mrs. Consumer. This is 166 millions per business day, or almost about $21,000,000 for each of eight hours per day. Twenty-one millions of dollars per hour, or $350,000 per minute, or almost $6,000 *per second* is the breathtaking speed with which Mrs. Consumer spends money in America....

I believe it is worthwhile to try here to visualize Mrs. Consumer in a more personal manner. It is extremely easy for a seller of goods to suffer from mirages about Mrs. Consumer. I have found innumerable advertising men and marketing executives who carry in their minds completely erroneous pictures of Mrs. Consumer in the mass. Unconsciously they tend to think of her (because they would *like* so to think of her) as a woman of their own class or nearly so. The executive higher up in business is guilty of the same thing, only more so! Neither make as a rule an accurate study of just what levels of Mrs. Consumer they must address, and what she is like on those levels. They are often as a matter of fact, somewhat romantic in their point of view about Mrs. Consumer, their customer. They gild her and embroider her and doll her up for their own delectation....

What, then, can be told about Mrs. Consumer? I have already elsewhere described her buying psychology. Here we should deal with her education, and literacy, vocabulary, social status, her physical characteristics, etc....

From college education, Mrs. Average Consumer is of course ... removed. There are only about 2,500,000 women in the country who are college graduates or have taken some college work. Mrs. Average Consumer's education consists approximately of a sixth grade school education. 95 or 96% of Mrs. Consumers know only what the grade schools taught them, and many have forgotten much of that!...

Mrs. Consumer habitually proceeds more along the lines of instinct than upon theory or reason, and accommodates herself more readily to practical realities. Man is more stubbornly theoretical. She is adept at matching one desire against another and evaluating her emotional and instinctive reactions. The logical-minded social worker who severely criticizes a woman of a very poor family when she "blows herself" to some cut glass for her sideboard is entirely forgetful of the fact that the cut glass bowl may make the woman's hard life bearable through the pleasure it gives her. Without it, she might "break" under the severe economic pressure. She knows life "in the round" better, perhaps, than the social worker.

On a higher plane many Mrs. Consumers do equally "illogical" or "unreasonable" things in their spending. Women understand such acts, but only a few men ever do. They often revive their spirits and youthfulness and their zest in life with such "foolish" purchases. One reason why so many women have failed to get a thrill out of scientific training in home economics or budget-keeping is because it is too strictly logical. It is mechanistic, and women have never felt much in common with mechanics. They live emotionally on a pulsating rhythm, not a on flat plateau, such as is more characteristic of men. Their moods are of shifting hues, not of one set color. The emotional consideration is to them always the vital consideration....

Naturally an effort to classify women consumers is largely guesswork. A former president of the Illinois Federation of Women's Clubs made such a general classification some time ago, as follows:

20% of American wives are of the jazz or "can-opener type."

15% are of the nagging type.

20% are of the drudge type.

15% are of the "baby doll" type.

30% are of the home-maker or ideal type.

This, coming from a woman, indicating that 70% of American married women, or nearly 17,000,000 wives, are of a kind that is below an admirable standard, is certainly frank and a bit devastating. It leaves only about 7,200,000 wives is the admirable class....

More important for purposes of classification is the seggregation of women into more practically useful types for the seller. This has been done for the guidance of textile and fashion goods sellers, but it is useful for any seller. Here they are:

Youthful	Middle Aged	Matured
The Flapper Type	The Vivacious Type	The Vivacious Type
The Boyish Type	The Conservative Type	The Matronly Type
The Demure Type	The Dignified Type	The Conservative Type
The Vivacious Type	The Feminine Type	The Feminine Type
The Conservative Type	The Sophisticated Type	The Uninteresting Type
The Statuesque Type	The Uninteresting Type	
The Feminine Type		
The Sophisticated Type		
The Uninteresting Type		

Naturally the youthful or unmarried type indicates a wider variety; Mrs. Consumer tends to mould herself more to a pattern after she is married—but not even then until she has children; often not until she has two or three. It is one of the marked characteristics of Mrs. Consumer of today, that she insists on being somewhat girlish even until past 35. She "dies hard" so far as her youthfulness is concerned. Women in other countries settle down to matronliness as early as 25, but there are grandmothers in America who belong to the "jazz" type, and since weight is such a tell-tale, they have violently concentrated on holding down their figures. There are any number of mothers who are less serious and more playful and girlish than their own daughters, who so often at 18 or 20 are in a "serious" or intellectual mood....

Another curious bit of interesting sub-division of women into arbitrary classes has been made by *Needlecraft Magazine*. It attempted no percentage or statistical grouping, but it presented, with photographs four "types" (1) the Indolent Rich, (2) the Overworked Poor, (3) the Clinging Vine, (4) the Creative Woman. I regard this as a shrewd classification, and shall make so bold as to submit my percentage estimate, based on these types:

1. The Indolent Rich Woman, 1%, 360,000 women.
2. The Overworked Poor Woman, 20%, 7,200,000 women.
3. The Clinging Vine Woman, 5%, 1,800,000 women.
4. The Creative Woman, 74%, 26,640,000 women.

These classes overlap, of course. The "clinging vine" type is often also an "indolent rich" type—but she may also be in other classes. The creative woman, as I see her, is any woman who works, whether at home or elsewhere. I do not attach any importance to the above—it is merely interesting speculation. As a matter of fact one might profitably enter into some deepgoing discussions as to the greater ultimate usefulness of these various types of women. It seems that many "feminists" of today are somewhat disillusioned over working. There is something profound to be said of the relative effects on man of the creative and the indolent types of women. It is a philosophical problem as to whether men are spurred to their utmost in accomplishment by one or the other type; also whether we wish a civilization in which women work and create, or one in which women merely consume. In my own opinion this depends on how well women solve their work and personal problems; how well they are able to maintain the male sex tension by working. If they fail in this, we may move toward the more savage standard, where only women work.

6. Radical Critic James Rorty Attacks
Radio Advertising, 1934

The conception of "Truth in Advertising" is at once *the least tenable* and the *most necessary* tenet of the ad-man's doctrine. This contradiction arises from the fact that the advertising business is essentially an enterprise in the exploitation of belief.

It is untenable because profit-motivated business, in its relations with the consumer, is necessarily exploitative—not moderately and reasonably exploitative, but exploitative up to the tolerance limit of the traffic. This tolerance limit is determined not by ethical considerations, which are strictly irrelevant, but by the ability of the buyer to detect and penalize dishonesty and deception. This ability varies with the individual, but in general reaches its minimum in the case of the isolated ultimate consumer.

No manufacturer, in buying his raw materials or his mechanical equipment, trusts the integrity of the seller except in so far as he is obliged to do so. So far as possible, he protects himself by specifications, inspections and tests, and by legally enforceable contracts that penalize double-dealing.

But when the manufacturer or retailer turns to selling his finished product to the ultimate consumer, the situation is reversed and the elements are sharply different. In his natural state the ultimate consumer is ignorant enough in all conscience. But he is not permitted to remain in his natural state. It would be unprofitable, unbusinesslike, to leave him in his natural state. Hence business has developed the apparatus of advertising, which, as the editor of the leading advertising trade publication has pointed out, is scarcely a thing in itself, but merely a function of business management.

That function is not merely to sell customers, but to manufacture customers....

What has honesty or truth to do with this business? A great deal, because the *idea* of truth is a highly exploitable asset. Always, the customer must be made to feel that the seller is honest and truthful and that he needs or wants the product offered for sale. Hence the advertising business becomes an enterprise in the coincident manufacture and exploitation of reader-confidence and reader-acceptance. In this respect the ad-man's technique is not essentially different from that of any vulgar confidence man whose stock in trade is invariably a plausible line of chatter about his alleged "trustfulness" and "honesty." ...

... [T]he writer permitted an oil stock salesman to give him transportation form Los Angeles to the oil well, and to lead him through the successive steps by which the "sucker" is noosed, thrown and shorn. Later, on the basis of our professional kinship, I got to know him sufficiently so that, warmed by a little liquor, he became approximately confidential.

"Brother," I remember his saying (He always insisted on calling me "brother"), "the technique of this racket is simple. Always tell the truth. Tell a lot of the truth. Tell a lot more of the truth than anybody expects you to tell. Never tell the whole truth."

James Rorty, *Our Master's Voice: Advertising* (New York: The John Day Company, 1934).

My colleague omitted one important element from his formula, the element of emotional conviction, which I had seen him manipulate with devastating effectiveness. It is observable that most charlatans, like the best advertising men, are always more than half sincere and honest according to their lights. Sincerity is indeed a great virtue in an ad-man, and if one has it not, one must at least feign it....

The possession of a personal code of ethics is a handicap in the practice of advertising-as-usual, the business being above all else impersonal, and in fact so far as possible de-humanized. One must be loyal to the process, which is a necessary part of the total economic process of competitive acquisition. The god of advertising is a jealous god and tolerates no competing loyalties, no human compunctions, no private impurities of will and judgment.

The yoke of this jealous god chafes. How could it be otherwise, unless one were to suppose that advertising men are a selected class of knaves and rascals? They are, of course, nothing of the sort. They are average middle-class Americans, a bit more honest, I suspect, than the average banker or lawyer. In their personal lives they are likely to be kindly, truthful, just and generous. They would doubtless like to be equally truthful and just in the conduct of their business. But this, in the nature of the case, is impossible. The alternatives are either a cynical, realistic acceptance, or heroic gestures of rationalization. Hence the tremendous pother that advertising men make about "truth in advertising"; or at least, that is half of the explanation. The other half lies in the business-like necessity of keeping advertising in good repute; of nursing the health of that estimable goose, reader-confidence. Are they sincere, these advertising men who conduct this "truth-in-advertising" propaganda which is echoed and re-echoed by editors, publicists, economists, sociologists, preachers, politicians? How can one tell, and does it really matter? ...

[T]he cynics retort somewhat after this fashion: "You fellows prate a great deal about 'truth in advertising.' What do you mean, truth, and what has the truth got to do with this racket? You say we are killing that estimable goose, reader-confidence, the goose that lays the golden eggs of advertising profits. Nonsense. It wasn't the goose that squawked. It was you. And the reason you squawked was not because you really give a whoop about 'truth,' but because we, with our more sophisticated, more scientific practice, have been chiselling into your business. We can prove and have proved that bought-and-paid-for testimonials sell two to one as compared to your inept cozenage, your primitive appeals to fear, greed and emulation. Furthermore, the ethics of advertising communications is relative and must be flexible. You have to take into account both the audience to which such communications are addressed and the object which these communications are intended to achieve, and demonstrably do achieve.

"The audience, by and large, is composed of 14-year-old intelligences that have no capacity for weighing evidence, no experience in doing so, and no desire to do so. That goes equally for the readers of *Vogue* and the readers of *True Romances*. They are effectively gulled by bought-and-paid for testimonials and even appear to take some pleasure in being gulled. They buy on the basis of such corrupt, false and misleading evidence, and this way of selling them cost less than any other way we have discovered. It is, you will grant, our duty as advertisers and as advertising agencies acting in behalf of our clients, to advertise as efficiently as possible, thereby reducing the sales overhead which must ultimately be charged to the consumer: thereby, incidentally safeguarding and increasing the profits of the companies in which hundreds of thousands of widows and orphans, directly or indirectly, have invested their all. It is our duty to use every means we can devise, truthful or untruthful, ethical or unethical, to persuade consumers to buy, since only by increased buying can the country be pulled out of this depression. Our is the higher morality. The burden of restoring prosperity on our shoulders. We have seen our duty and we are doing it."...

[C]onsider the recent advertising of Gimbles department store in New York. Mr. Collins is Gimbels' advertising manager, having recently transferred his talents from Macy's across the street, where he had achieved a notable success by exploiting the slogan "It's smart to be thrifty."

Mr. Collins, judged by his writings in the trade press, is something of a realist. One can only conclude therefore, that when he assumed his new duties, his survey of the situation convinced him that radical measures were needed for the effective exploitation of belief. Here is the advertisement in which the new "slant" was announced:

GIMBLES

TELLS THE

WHOLE

TRUTH

... No, what we have ... is a lot of the truth, more of the truth than anybody expected Gimbels to tell, but not the whole truth. It is not in the nature of profit-motivated business to tell the whole truth. Gimbels is paid by its customers, but is responsible ultimately, not to its customers, but to its stockholders. Hence the pressure of the economic determinants is here as always and everywhere toward the exploitation of the customer up to the tolerance limit of the traffic....

Mr. Collins' demarche is designed to produce customers by manufacturing a "systematized illusion" to the effect that business is not business, and that the customer, on entering Gimbels, can safely put aside and forget the maxim, *caveat emptor*, which is the only ultimate protection of the buyer in a profit-motivated economy.

Suppose that Mr. Collins' readers are convinced; that they do stop worrying about whether they are being cheated or not. They would like to do this because it would certainly mean a great saving of time, money and energy. But what happens if they do? They find that Gimbels' stock in trade consists not merely of goods but of "systematized illusions" built up by decades of advertising and capitalized in trademarks which add a considerable percentage to the cost of the product and a still higher percentage to the price of the product. In the drug and cosmetics department they would find that the price of the products offered for sale frequently represents about 90% of advertising bunk and 10% of merchandize. Will Gimbels, which is pledged to tell the truth the whole truth, and nothing but the truth, tell them that....

The conclusion … in the minds of good citizens in and out of the advertising business is that the abuses of advertising should be corrected; that Congress should pass another law…. As a former advertising man, made familiar by years of practice with the various techniques of the profession, the naïveté of this conclusion leaves me groaning with despondency. Congress can and probably will legislate itself blue in the face, without changing an iota of the basic economic and cultural determinants, and so long as these determinants continue to operate the exploitation of the consumer will simply, in response to criticism, spin the kaleidoscope of technical adaptations. To put it more brutally, advertising will merely find new ways of manufacturing suckers and trimming them. Mendacity is a function of trade and observes no ethical limits just as military warfare observes no ethical limits. Advertising is an exploitation of belief. The raw material of this traffic is not merely products and services but human weakness, fear and credulity….

7. Humor Magazine Satirizes the Role of Advertising in Hard Economic Times, 1931

"Smile Away the Depression," *Ballyhoo* (November 1931), 6. Peter Newark American Pictures/Bridgeman Art Library.

ESSAYS

Both of these essays take up the changes needed in advertising, and in the culture, for consumption to become hegemonic. Sociologist Michael Schudson, professor of communication and adjunct professor of sociology at the University of California, San Diego, traces the social changes necessary before advertising and the culture of consumption could become taken for granted and locates the 1920s as a crucial decade for these changes. The late Roland Marchand, professor of history at University of California, Davis, examines both the advertising professionals and the advertisements they created to understand how advertising's ways of seeing and communicating became part of everyday life.

Defining and Locating Consumer Culture in the 1920s

MICHAEL SCHUDSON

In American society, people often satisfy or believe they can satisfy their socially constituted needs and desires by buying mass produced, standardized, nationally advertised consumer products. This was not always the case nor is it today a universal phenomenon. Why should it be so prominent a characteristic of contemporary American culture? ...

The department store, like the city street, like the railroad coach or compartment, was a new kind of public place. It changed the entire act and art of shopping. One did not simply enter a shop and ask the storekeeper to go to his shelves or backroom for an item. In the department store, things were displayed, and the shopper had a range of things to observe....

The department stores first, but then other retailers, began to change their business practices. *Speed* of sale became a factor it had never been before and the idea of "stock-turn" or, as we say today, turnover, became important.... Customers became relatively more anonymous. They were less part of a buyer-seller relationship, more part of an audience for a spectacle of sales. With goods made visible before them, "eye-catching" appeal became a more vital attribute of a product, and merchandising for the retailer began to be less a matter of knowing the stock and more a matter of presenting it well.

Indeed, department stores made themselves great stages. The clerks acted as friendly, but elegant, hosts. People thought of the stores as social centers and dressed up to go shopping....

Luxury was not democratized so much as made markedly more visible, more public, and more often articulate—through advertising—than it had been before. The department stores did less to provide equality in consumption than to encourage a democracy of aspiration and desire. They contributed to the democratization of envy....

Michael Schudson, "Historical Roots of Consumer Culture," in *Advertising, The Uneasy Persuasion: Its Dubious Impact on American Society* (New York: Basic Books, 1986).

[D]epartment stores could succeed at the end of the nineteenth century because at that time American cities became "riding" rather than "walking" habitations…. [E]asy access to transportation changed the spatial possibilities of daily life. People did not any longer have to live within walking distance of their place of work; suburbs developed and the middle class especially began to move out and to become commuters to work. People did not have to shop in their own neighborhoods any more. They could take the train to some other part of town or to "downtown" to do their shopping. Thanks to newspaper advertising, they could learn what goods were available at what prices in all parts of the city if there were stores that sought a city-wide clientele for their wares.

The department stores were just such stores and they were crucial to subsidizing the growth of urban newspapers…. Of the expanding use of advertising in the late nineteenth century, the most important by far was department store advertising…. Department store ads were important not only in size but in style. Wanamaker's, for instance, sought self-consciously to "journalize" advertising, to make ads more newsy, informationally accurate and up-to-date with copy changing daily….

Where people live and die in the same small community, the people they associate with as adults are the same people they grew up with as children…. People derive a sense of self as the self is reflected back in the opinions of other people. When "significant others" remain much the same throughout one's life, identity has a clear foundation…. Further, when a person's status in the community is established by birth or family, the consequences of one's own achievements or failures are not so far reaching. The ne'er-do-well son of the aristocrat is still an aristocrat. The peasant's son who learns to read and write and study the Bible is still a peasant and defers to the aristocrat. Status is no more problematic than identity.

No community was ever quite like the ideal I describe but many communities were more like it than almost any community has been since the industrial and democratic revolutions produced a highly mobile, urban, class society in which social mobility became a real possibility and a powerful ideology. Geographic and social mobility in modern society are especially potent forces for personal disruption….

In contemporary society, geographic or social mobility does not just happen, people *expect* it to happen, so the family exercises a different kind of control than it once did. The family provides a socialization process for its children that anticipates their mobility. Children learn to pay attention not just to their parents but to their peer group and to the mass media…. The family remains crucial, but more and more, a common culture, that includes advertising and the mass media, plays its part….

With a more mobile society and, to some extent, a more open social fabric, realms in which choice rarely figured become open to individual decision making. Most important decisions—who to marry, what career to enter, what religion to adhere to—become matters of selection. As the early 1900s brought improved systems of transportation and communication and a vastly improved system for the distribution of goods to rural parts of the country, consumer "lifestyle" and individual expression and identity-formation through lifestyle became more widely available. William Leiss has ably argued that a society of high-intensity consumption is not so much one in which new needs are manufactured and foisted upon consumers as one in which citizens lose a secure understanding of what their needs are and to what extent commodities can satisfy them. Needs become "ambiguous" as individual choices multiply.

The mass media help escort people into the wider world of choice, broadening horizons, blurring provincial demarcations. On the one hand, the media enlarge people's sense of their own and the world's possibilities; on the other hand, the media lead people to constantly compare themselves to others or to images of others....

In this world, external signs hold great importance and people leap at anything that can be used to signify.... In other words, they are symbols that people use as maps for charting a complex and uncertain world. People in the new mobile, urban world of the late nineteenth century required new symbol systems.... Most people needed to connect themselves to the wider world, the socially and geographically mobile, most of all.

There were various ways to find identity and placement in the larger world. Income was especially convenient because it provided a *ranked* identification, because it was subject to transformation, and because it tended to be a good, though by no means perfect, index of a variety of socially meaningful traits, including political power and social standing. It had the disadvantage of being, by itself, invisible. Increasingly, however, an index for income was visible and available in the status and quality ranking of consumer goods.... Consumer goods begin to be an index and a language that place a person in society and relate the person in symbolically significant ways to the national culture.

During the nineteenth century, more and more goods manufactured in factories rather than in homes poured onto the market. More and more necessities of life were bought outside the home and outside the neighborhood, too. An excellent example is clothing. In 1790, 80 percent of all clothing was made in the home for family use. A century later, for men and boys, 90 percent was made outside the home....

The availability of store-bought, ready-made clothing helped extend and democratize fashion....

Fashion in dress, better than any other example of consumption, is a material, externalized symbol system that connects people to social worlds and individualizes them in those worlds. For more and more people in the late nineteenth century and after, clothing came to be expressive and signifying. But so, too, did other material objects. Where buying replaced making, then looking replaced doing as a key social action, reading signs replaced following orders as a crucial modern skill. Shorthands for expression and signification became more and more desirable and useful to urbanites; manufacturers exploited the desires of people for social location and identity with the production of "brand name" goods. Brand name goods *appeared* at the end of the nineteenth century for a number of reasons; they were *accepted* for the reasons discussed here. In a mobile society, commercial products with familiar names provide people with some sense of identity and continuity in their lives. And in a society with a high concern for social mobility, material possessions of known and ranked standing provide statements of social status and may provide entry into desired social worlds.

But it will not do to hang everything on this "identity" argument by itself. It explains too much, I think, and therefore too little. It is exactly the kind of argument by sociologists that rightly raises the hackles of historians. It is notoriously difficult to make such an argument historically specific. People have used a growing number of manufactured consumer goods for some time, beginning at least in the eighteenth century…. At what point can it be said that people actively construct their identities from material things? If this is in some measure always true, when does it become predominantly true? And to what extent does it remain, even today, a rather modest truth, with people's surest sense of self and deepest foundation of social standing derived from family and occupation, not lifestyle? …

The growing importance of standard, identifiable products and brands may be conceived in a manner less dependent on psychological assumptions about identity. Some brand names, like "Yves St. Laurent," offer identity and status, but others, like McDonald's or Coca-Cola or Kentucky Fried Chicken, do not. Their promise is not identity but familiarity and reliability of product. Where consumers do not make their own goods and do not buy at neighborhood stores where they know and are known to the merchant, brand names become a form of consumer protection…. Brand-name goods and other standard products such as the "convenience foods" that it is fashionable to complain about have this quality…. A survey of five hundred house wives found that purchasing a major brand or a brand previously used is taken to be a better means of reducing risk in a purchasing situation than government reports or word-of-mouth information. The housewives are not seeking status or identity when they opt for the brand name; they are minimizing risk to their families. In the late nineteenth century, they were doing the same thing. The world was changing so that available products were less often local and known and local retailers were more often large institutions serving a wider public than before. Further, the consumers themselves were less often local and known. Geographic mobility was high and immigration was at a peak. There was plenty of incentive, then, for shoppers to seek the guarantee of predictability that brand names would provide….

For historian Daniel Boorstin, the goods of mass consumption are not to be denounced glibly. He refers to the relations people establish with one another through the insignia of mass consumption, through the sharing of Pierre Cardin shirts or Harley-Davidson motorcycles as "consumption communities." This is a tendentious phrase; it incorporates into a slogan the very question that needs to be addressed about a consumer society: *is* there any community of consumption? And if there is, what kind of community is it? Does the sharing of goods—not the sitting down at table and breaking bread together but the impersonal sharing, the fact that John Smith from Buffalo and Jill Jones from Santa Barbara both wear Jordache jeans—does that establish a sense of community between them?

The answer is no, it does not establish any kind of community a person could put much stock in. Boorstin here is ideologue more than analyst.... Goods themselves are not (only) the enemies of culture and not (only) the debasement of culture and not (only) something foisted unwillingly upon defenseless consumers. Goods are constituents of culture and the sharing of their names is a part of what it means to partake of culture....

But what kind of society is ours that produces the particular systems of naming we have? What is special about a system in which words like "Chevy," "polyester," and "Holiday Inn" take on importance? Who does the naming in our society, who has the power of words, and how is that power used? ....

The concepts of "identity" and "culture" and the changing needs of people in a mobile society do not suffice to explain the shift to a consumer society in the period 1850 to 1930. Nor do they explain "materialist" values. As Neil Harris points out, a consumer society is not the same thing as a materialist society; nineteenth-century Americans were regarded by most observes, including the trenchant Tocqueville, as archetypal materialists, even in 1830. But materialism was connected at that date to both consumption *and* production. People still made things at home and satisfied material longings that way. This became less true by the end of the nineteenth century. Industrialization displaced home industry and, in a rather short span of years, people found themselves unable "to match, in precision, variety, attractiveness, and especially cost, the provision of objects produced by American manufacturers, from clothing and furniture to food and drink." The changing nature and significance of consumption, then grew not from autonomous changes in the life of the citizen or the family but from the intersection of such changes with the emergence of large-scale consumer goods industries. I turn, then, to a consideration of changes on the production side of the economy.

Consumer Goods and the Production Side of the Economy

Whether it was Brandreth's Vegetable Universal Pills or Radam's Microbe Killer or Lydia Pinkham's Compound, nineteenth-century newspapers were covered with patent medicine advertising.... When *Press and Printer* of Boston tabulated advertisers who made regular use of advertising, they found that 425 of the 2,583 enterprises counted sold medicines and drugstore items, more than double the next leading category. It is hard to exaggerate the importance of patent medicines in the history of advertising....

Ads for patent medicines.... sought to establish a clear, memorable *identification* for their product. This was more important than the particular "promise" about what the medicine would do. It was most important to establish a name people could remember, feel comfortable with, and believe to represent an important or well-established firm. The identification would often be with something exotic as in Hayne's Arabian Balsam, Hoofland's Greek Oil, Osgood's Indian Cholagogue, or Jayne's Spanish Alternative....

Most patent medicine advertising was repetitious and dull. Many ads, all identical, would be placed in the same issue of the same newspaper.... There was great weight placed on establishing and maintaining product identification, by the continuity and repetition of a name or trademarked image....

The competition among medicines, carried out largely through advertising, was severe, and it has been estimated that less than 2 percent of remedies launched in New York had even modest success.

In the mid-nineteenth century, patent medicines were the most prominent advertised product. In the 1870s and 1880s, department store advertising came to match that of patent medicines. But, in retrospect, the development on the production and distribution side of the economy most important in creating an advertising-oriented consumer culture was the emergence of advertising for nationally branded goods. This was spawned by a relatively small group of new, technologically and organizationally innovative manufacturers. Nearly all of the first national advertisers were enterprises that used new continuous-process machinery to produce low-priced, packaged consumer goods. The massive increase in output made possible by the new machinery led manufacturers to build large marketing and purchasing networks and to engage in widespread advertising. These enterprises included many that remain to this day the leading advertisers in the country: Procter & Gamble, Colgate-Palmolive, H. J. Heinz, Borden, Eastman Kodak, Quaker Oats, Pillsbury, Campbell Soups, Carnation, Libby McNeil & Libby, and American Tobacco. They produced cigarettes, soap, canned foods, breakfast cereals, matches, and photographic film and equipment. These are, with a partial exception of photographic equipment, exclusively "experience" goods. Thus they are products whose advertising is likely to include very little direct information and is likely to focus on the reputability of the manufacturer....

The Quaker Oats Co. may be taken as an example. Oats were raised in quantity in the late nineteenth century, especially in Iowa, Ohio, and Illinois. Ferdinand Schumacher, a German immigrant, was the first to develop a branded oat product for human consumption. When he began milling in Ravenna, Ohio, he used the same techniques millers had used since the fifteenth century....

[O]ne of Schumacher's competitors, Henry Parsons Crowell, was quickly adopting all the latest innovations. His mill, also at Ravenna, by 1882 became "the first in the world to maintain under one roof operations to grade, clean, hull, cut, package, and ship oatmeal to interstate markets in a continuous process that in some aspects anticipated the modern assembly line." Crowell called his product "Quaker Oats." The development of highly efficient "continuous-process" methods was the first critical step in establishing a capacity for national advertising of cereals. The new technology expanded the industrial capacity of firms so that increasing production at little increased cost was no longer difficult. The main problem for the cereal manufacturers and others like them was "to move their goods quickly enough or to advertise them effectively enough to keep their high-volume production facilities operating steadily."

Henry Crowell registered the trademark of a "figure of a man in Quaker garb" in 1877, the first registered trademark for a breakfast cereal. Crowell ...

pioneered in packaging, promotion, and advertising. Crowell introduced a folding carton for Quaker oats packaging, a method that had been patented only ten years before. Because the unfolded package lay flat, it could be easily printed on and so the Crowell carton displayed the Quaker emblem in four-color printing with recipes printed on the package. This was the beginning of the end of selling cereal to the retailers in bulk (although in health foods stores, the old methods of retailing have been revived)....

The emphasis in advertising for nationally branded products, as for patent medicines, was more on identification than on identity. The advertising profession of the day "seemed to equate quality with quantity" and valued the ubiquity of a product name and trademark above all else. For Quaker Oats, making the Quaker symbol well known was the all-important task. Claims for the specific merits of Quaker oats varied and types of appeals changed. Ads at different times connected Quaker products to "love, pride, cosmetic satisfactions, sex, marriage, good health, cleanliness, safety, labor saving, and status seeking." But the Quaker Oats symbol was permanent and visible everywhere, on billboards, streetcars, newspapers, calendars, magazines, blotters, cookbooks, Sunday church bulletins, metal signs on rural fences, company-sponsored cooking schools, free samples given away house-to-house, booths at county fairs and expositions.

Quaker Oats did not limit itself to advertising as a tool, nor did the other early national advertisers. Advertising was but one aspect of a national marketing effort.... More crucial than advertising was the development of national and sometimes global organizations of managers, buyers, and salesmen that the early mass marketing firms created. The new technology of continuous-process production made possible a new social invention—not advertising but the organization chart, a regular hierarchy of responsibility, an administrative structure responsible for marketing as well as the production of the manufactured good....

By the turn of the century, advertising had become an important element in the American economy. Some of the reasons for the rise of advertising can be understood as "market driven": advertising provided information about what goods were available for sale in a society that no longer consisted of face-to-face economic relations. Some of the early informational advertising and the department store advertising was market driven, in this sense.... But some of the development of advertising is better thought of as "producer driven": for firms where technology had solved production problems, advertising arose as part of a marketing effort to sell goods whose supply could be increased easily at little additional production cost. In the case of the patent medicines, advertising was the main marketing tool. For nationally advertised, branded products that arose in continuous-process production industries after 1880, advertising was one important element in a marketing mix that included direct salesmanship, packaging, and the establishment of hierarchical, national marketing organizations.

The distinction between market-driven and producer-driven advertising bears on the controversy over whether advertising creates or simply responds to felt needs. To the extent that advertising arose in response to social and economic changes in a mobile market society, it is difficult to see it as an original or prime cause of consumer culture. To the extent, however, that technological developments in industrial manufacturing precipitated growing investment in distribution and sales and advertising, advertising can be seen as a somewhat independent, not solely reactive, force in American society. I do not think the historical record resolves the debate about advertising's role in creating "needs," but I do think it reveals some of the complexity of the issue and makes it hard for anyone to leap with unqualified certainty to one side ("advertising just responds to social trends") or the other ("advertising is the creator of consumer culture").

The Media and the Agencies as Promoters
of Promotion

Having considered, at least briefly, social changes that altered people's desires for goods and susceptibility to advertising and changes in manufacturing that led to markedly greater incentives for businesses to seek national distribution and the advertising that accompanies it, I have addressed the largest factors in the late nineteenth century that paved the way to a goods-intensive consumer culture. … Advertising is a relationship between a producer (or distributor) who advertises, an agency that creates the ad, a medium that carries the ad, and an audience of consumers to whom the ad is directed. I have thus far considered market-driven forces that enabled the rise of advertising (changes in the lives of the people who represent the market for consumer goods) and producer-driven forces (changes in the technology of industry and the social organization of retailing). There were also changes in the mass media and the emergence of advertising agencies—together these can be taken as "self-generating" sources of advertising. The media live off advertising revenue and the advertising agencies' reason for existence is advertising. The presence of these institutions in the economy has been a force for the growth of advertising.

The first advertising agents were more the servants of the newspapers than of the firms that bought advertising space…. Soon thereafter, the typical agent became a true middleman, a space jobber who sold newspaper space to advertisers and then bought the space to fill his orders. This was typical of agents in the 1850s.

As the agency system developed, agents moved from space jobbing to "space wholesaling." …

Nonetheless, the advertising agency remained for some time an institution of very limited scope. It bought and sold space. It did not produce ads. But its activities, however limited, provided businesses a real service, thanks to the growth of national markets and the developments in transportation and communication that made that growth possible. Merchants did not know much about the media for advertising outside their own town or region. Agents emerged to exploit business's ignorance of institutions that had become relevant for commercial success….

This is not to say that businesses all quickly recognized that advertising agencies would be useful—or that advertising itself would be useful to them….

The first promotional work of the agencies, then, was to sell the idea of advertising to business….

Only after this change did advertising art and copy become part of the responsibility of the agency. Between 1880 and 1900, agencies began to write copy for their clients. As the volume of advertising increased, skill in writing copy became more important. Buying more space or using heavier type or larger type sizes was not enough, and agencies that could offer services in writing more persuasive advertisements gained a competitive edge....

As agencies became established, they became an independent force promoting the idea of advertising, and so did their trade journals and trade associations.... In examining directories of advertisers, historian Daniel Pope found that 20 percent of firms listed as advertisers in New York in 1901 used advertising agencies, but that this increased to 35 percent in 1911. In Boston, similarly, the figure jumped from 20 percent in 1901 to nearly 50 percent in 1911.

The media, too, increasingly dependent on advertising revenue, actively promoted the use of advertising. The media try to convince businesses that it pays to advertise and that, in particular, it pays to advertise in one specific medium...

The advertising agencies, meanwhile, were growing not only larger and more important but more self-important. Agencies, especially the larger agencies with national advertisers as clients, sought to gain "professional" standing for advertising men. Thus they eagerly supported a move toward "scientific" advertising by sponsoring market research and by welcoming the language and literature of psychology into advertising work....

... [T]he first development of significance in market research was not to see the common elements in human nature but to see the obvious differences; especially to recognize that there are two sexes and that women, not men, are the primary consumers in American culture. "The proper study of mankind is MAN," said one ad in *Printer's Ink*, "...but the proper study of markets is WOMAN." It was a cliché among advertisers by the 1920s that women are the "purchasing agents" of their families; the trade journals cited the figure that 85 percent of all consumer spending is done by women....

If the difference between men and women came to be seen as important, so did the difference between the affluent and people of moderate means.... While the language of psychology, in the 1920s and again in the 1950s, attracted the greatest interest and controversy in advertising, sophistication about basic sociological variables like class and gender has had a more pronounced impact on advertising practice.

The advertising agencies by the 1920s were becoming institutions of considerable resources and confidence. But advertising agents were not only men of confidence; they were confidence men. Their livelihood depended on selling to business the idea that advertising was an effective marketing tool. It would be naive to read their sales pitches to the business community as honest accounts of the power of advertising....

The problem of advertising is more complex. Twentieth-century advertising and twentieth-century consumer culture have roots in the changing nature of the market in the late nineteenth century which developed along with changes in modes of transportation and communication, urban growth, and a cultural climate for and social fact of social and geographic mobility. In addition, changes in the manufacturing processes in various industries and the capacity to increase output without substantial increases in product costs encouraged a new emphasis in business on marketing and distribution; the growing independent influence on business of the media and advertising agencies also stimulated the development of advertising.

The social transformation that gave rise to advertising not only made mass-produced and advertised products more important to people but altered the criteria for consumption, the qualities in goods deemed desirable. The growth of a consumer society has been a qualitative as well as a quantitative change.

Early Advertising Methods

ROLAND MARCHAND

There were two mothers, and each had a sickly young son. The first mother summoned her son and said: "Thou art spindly and underweight. Verily, I fear for thy health. Here, take and eat these nutritious vegetables." But the boy sulked and put them aside with harsh words. And his mother said: "Trouble me not. Except as ye eat these bitter viands, which I have prepared for thine own good, ye shalt have no desserts nor any other good thing." The mother continued to coax and threaten, but the boy ate not the vegetables and he waxed exceedingly cranky. But the mother relented not, for she feared for his character.

The second mother observed this and she said to herself, "Verily, I will seek a better way." And she arose and went to the wise elders. As she drew near, the elders cried, "Behold, take and try this new substance which is named 'soup.' Receive it with gladness, for in it are nutritious vegetables, disguised and hidden, among mystic letters and other curious things." And she said to her son, "Do not fret, for the eating of this soup shall be fun, and for each bowl thereof thou shalt receive a gold star. And when thy chart overfloweth with stars, thou shalt arise and enter the great club and the elders will reveal unto you the secret handshake." And it came to pass that the boy waxed exceedingly robust and strong.

The first mother thought to condemn her child, for he was puny beside the other, he brought home ill news from school, and he desecrated the dinner hour with loud complaining. But the second mother chastised her, saying, "Blame not the child. Thou hast led him in the harsh olden ways, but at a cost that is not meet. Behold the new way which I have shown thee. My child partakes of what is best for the sake of fun, and there is no bitter cost. Fail no more. Go and do likewise."

Thus, had it been translated into biblical prose, might have read one of the great parables of American advertising in the late 1920s—the parable of the

Captivated Child. Didactic advertising tableaux may be called "parables" not because they conform to prevailing definitions of Jewish, New Testament, or secular parables in every respect, but because they attempt to draw practical moral lessons from the incidents of everyday life. Like the parables of Jesus, these advertising stories employed stark contrasts and exaggeration to dramatize a central message. And, like the parables of Jesus, they sought to provoke an immediate decision for action.

Of course, we must not ignore the important respects in which advertising tableaux like that of the Captivated Child did not conform to the model of the biblical parables. The advertising parables offered comfortable rather than distasteful truths. They usually sought to persuade more through insinuation than confrontation, and they sought unthinking assent rather than active thought or new insight. They encouraged readers to assimilate the product into their present lives…. Whereas the biblical parables have aptly been characterized as encounters with our sense of the limitations of reality, the parables of advertising promised readers no insurmountable limitations and offered a reality easily within the reach of their hearts' desires. In short, advertising parables bore much the same relationship to biblical parables as melodrama has traditionally been understood to bear to high art or tragedy.

Advertisers found themselves attracted to this form, which we might now characterize more strictly as the "melodramatic parable," for practical reasons. As a story without an identifiable author, often presented in such a manner as to suggest either distilled folk wisdom or suprahuman insight, the parable served to divert attention away from the advertiser as interested "seller" and toward the ad's message. Moreover, it was well adapted to the task of luring readers into active involvement….

The parable flourished in American advertising in the late 1920s and early 1930s. Several advertising parables were so frequently repeated and so effectively reduced to formulas that their entire story could eventually be suggested by a phrase or two. These I have designated the "great parables" of the age. They did not directly invite interpretation on more than one level or challenge the audience to accept a new moral logic. Yet they did, in spite of their narrow, practical intent, incorporate some wider dimension of meaning. They reinforced (and even encouraged conversions to) a modern, secular "logic of living."…

A flush of anticipation colored the cheeks of the beautiful young lady as her escort seated her at the elegant table. It was her first important dinner among the fashionables of the city's smart set. But as the butler served the first course, her thrilled excitement turned to terror. "From that row of gleaming silver on either side of her plate, which piece shall she pick up?" Suddenly she sensed, as a knowledgeable mother would have been able to advise, that her chance of being invited to such an affair again—in fact, her whole future popularity— would be determined by this crucial first impression of her "presence." As her social destiny hung in the balance, "She could feel every eye on her hesitating Hand." …

These … advertisements suggest the drama and pathos with which copywriters could recount the popular parable of the First Impression. According to such tableaux, first impressions brought immediate success or failure. Clearly, the scenarios were fantastical. Yet the parable of the First Impression, for all its exaggerated dramatics, drew much of its persuasive power from its grounding in readers' perceptions of contemporary realities. In a relatively mobile society, where business organizations loomed ever larger and people dealt far more often with strangers, many personal interactions were fleeting and unlikely to be repeated. In large organizations, hiring and promotion decisions now often seemed arbitrary and impersonal. No longer were they generally predictable on the basis of accumulated personal connections and past interactions. The reasons why one man gained a promotion or one woman suffered a social snub had become less explicable on grounds of long-standing favoritism or old family feuds. In the increasingly anonymous business and social relationships of the age, one might suspect that anything—including a first impression—had made the crucial difference....

Sensing its power in these circumstances, a variety of advertisers made use of the parable of the First Impression. Often they modified the basic formula of the tableau slightly to fit their particular product. Clothing manufacturers stressed overall appearance; gum, toothpaste, and toothbrush makers promised a "magic road to popularity in that first winning smile."...

Capitalizing on an increasing public uncertainty that true ability and character would always win out in the scramble for success, advertising parables of the First Impression stressed the narrowness of the line that separated those who succeeded from those who failed. Many men possessed relatively equal abilities. The intensity and evenness of the competition gave great import to every detail of one's appearance. Far from deploring the apparent trend toward judging people on superficial externals, advertising tableaux often suggested that external appearance was the best index of underlying character. People were always—necessarily and appropriately—looking for quick clues to your taste and character. If they found these in the cut of your clothes, the brightness of your teeth, the age and taste of your furniture, your inept choice of silverware, or the closeness of your shave, they judged appropriately in a world of quick decisions. If your outer appearance, and that of your home, failed to reflect your true qualities of taste and character, you had no one to blame but yourself....

The merchandising strategy underlying the parable of the First Impression was obvious. People would certainly display more concern for the details of their personal appearance and that of their home if they could be induced to scrutinize themselves through the eyes of other people and to conceive of every aspect of external appearance as an index to their true character. But such an appeal could only succeed in a society which had come to doubt that a person's true character and worth were adequately revealed and judged in other, less superficial, ways.

Advertising men knew from their personal experience in the business world that first impressions *did* make a difference. The shifting, uncertain relationships in the field of advertising, the processes by which advertisements gained approval from clients, and the apparently fickle tastes of consumers in response to various advertising appeals, all encouraged them to conclude that, in many aspects of life, externals counted for more than intrinsic qualities. Working in an urban, sophisticated milieu, and impressed by the increasing complexity and ambiguity of business and social relationships, advertising men sensed that the parable of the First Impression had become a plausible explanation for how things worked in this "new world" that they knew and that others were increasingly coming to encounter....

At most, advertising could only have acted as one of a number of forces in American society contributing to a tendency toward self-accusation. But it had obviously discovered a sensitive social nerve to stimulate and exploit. Whereas movies and soap operas often provided vicarious experiences of triumphs over society's false accusations, advertisements emphasized the power, validity, and pervasiveness of the world's judgmental scrutiny....

As they opened their September 1929 issue, readers of the *Ladies' Home Journal* were treated to an account of the care and feeding of young Livingston Ludlow Biddle III, scion of the wealthy Biddles of Philadelphia, whose family coat-of-arms graced the upper right-hand corner of the page. Young Master Biddle, mounted on his tricycle, fixed a serious, slightly pouting gaze upon the reader, while the Cream of Wheat Corporation rapturously explained his constant care, his carefully regulated play and exercise, and the diet prescribed for him by "famous specialists." As master of Sunny Ridge Farm, the Biddles' winter estate in North Carolina, young Livingston III had "enjoyed every luxury of social position and wealth, since the day he was born." Yet, by the grace of a modern providence, it happened that Livingston's health was protected by a "simple plan every mother can use." Mrs. Biddle gave Cream of Wheat to the young heir for both breakfast and supper. The world's foremost child experts knew of no better diet; great wealth could procure no finer nourishment. As Cream of Wheat's advertising agency summarized the central point of the campaign that young Master Biddle initiated, "every mother can give her youngsters the fun and benefits of a Cream of Wheat breakfast just as do the parents of these boys and girls who have the best that wealth can command."

While enjoying this glimpse of childrearing among the socially distinguished, *Ladies' Home Journal* readers found themselves schooled in one of the most pervasive of all advertising tableaux of the 1920s—the parable of the Democracy of Goods. According to this parable, the wonders of modern mass production and distribution enabled every person to enjoy the society's most significant pleasure, convenience, or benefit. The definition of the particular benefit fluctuated, of course, with each client who employed the parable. But the cumulative effect of the constant reminders that "any woman can" and "every home can afford" was to publicize an image of American society in which concentrated wealth at the top of a hierarchy of social classes restricted no family's opportunity to acquire the most significant products. By implicitly defining "democracy" in terms of equal access to consumer products, and then by depicting the everyday functioning of that "democracy" with regard to one product at a time, these tableaux offered Americans an inviting vision of their society as one of incontestable equality.

In its most common advertising formula, the concept of the Democracy of Goods asserted that although the rich enjoyed a great variety of luxuries, the acquisition of their *one* most significant luxury would provide anyone with the ultimate in satisfaction...

Thus, according to the parable, no discrepancies in wealth could prevent the humblest citizens, provided they chose their purchases wisely, from retiring to a setting in which they could contemplate their essential equality, through possession of an identical product, with the nation's millionaires....

The social message of the parable of the Democracy of Goods was clear. Antagonistic envy of the rich was unseemly; programs to redistribute wealth were unnecessary. The best things in life were already available to all at reasonable prices. But the prevalence of the parable of the Democracy of Goods in advertising tableaux did not necessarily betray a concerted conspiracy on the part of advertisers and their agencies to impose a social ideology on the American people. Most advertisers employed the parable of the Democracy of Goods primarily as a narrow, non-ideological merchandising tactic....

Most advertisers found the social message of the parable of the Democracy of Goods a congenial and unexceptional truism. They also saw it, like the other parables ... as an epigrammatic statement of a conventional popular belief. Real income was rising for nearly all Americans during the 1920s, except for some farmers and farm workers and those in a few depressed industries. Citizens seemed eager for confirmation that they were now driving the same make of car as the wealthy elites and serving their children the same cereal enjoyed by Livingston Ludlow Biddle III. Advertisers did not have to impose the parable of the Democracy of Goods on a contrary-minded public. Theirs was the easier task of subtly substituting this vision of equality, which was certainly satisfying *as a vision*, for broader and more traditional hopes and expectations of an equality of self-sufficiency, personal independence, and social interaction....

Incessantly and enticingly repeated, advertising visions of fellowship in a Democracy of Goods encouraged Americans to look to similarities in consumption styles rather than to political power or control of wealth for evidence of significant equality.... Freedom of choice came to be perceived as a freedom more significantly exercised in the marketplace than in the political arena. This process gained momentum in the 1920s; it gained maturity during the 1950s as a sense of class differences was nearly eclipsed by a fascination with the equalities suggested by shared consumption patterns and "freely chosen" consumer "lifestyles."...

In 1930 the pharmaceutical firm of E. R. Squibb and Sons sought to capture the attention of readers for a dramatized version of a now-familiar fable. Employing a touch of the popular "believe-it-or-not" mystique, it introduced a note of mystery and irony into its advertising headline: "The interesting story of how man outwitted nature—and *lost!*" The revelation it had to offer, Squibb boasted, would be "another of those thrilling stories from the annals of modern science," a story of "how man, in his struggle to be civilized, became his own arch-enemy." In the beginning, Nature had prudently placed essential vitamins in the "coarse, plain foods she intended us to eat." But man, captivated by new and tempting tastes, had sought to make such foods more appetizing. In the process, he had "cooked and refined out of them" the very vitamins that Nature had foreseen would be necessary for good health. "Today," Squibb sermonized, "we are paying the penalty for this mistake. 'Civilized ills' plague us—ills caused by an incomplete diet of highly refined foods."

Had the story ended there, the parable would have remained a simple jeremiad. It might even have suggested a return to the purer, less decadent practices of yore. But the fable contained a second irony. If Nature, in its instinctive wisdom, now sought to punish civilized mankind for its waywardness, then Civilization, in its own sophisticated wisdom, had found a way to regain Nature's intended gifts without sacrificing the fruits of progress. Squibb's Vitamin Products would lift the curse that Nature had unthinkingly sought to inflict on Civilization.

Such was the parable of Civilization Redeemed. A familiar theme in the advertising tableaux, it usually varied from version to version only in the extent of its elaboration and in the particular form taken by Nature's curse. In proclaiming the victories over threats to health and beauty that the products of civilization now made possible, these parables of Civilization Redeemed never sought to denigrate Nature. In an era when the suntan first became fashionable and the ultraviolet ray an object of veneration, the virtues of Nature were not lightly dismissed. The point of the parable was that Civilization, which had brought down the curse of Nature upon itself, had still proved capable of discovering products that would enable Nature's original and beneficent intentions to triumph. Since it was inconceivable that civilized traits or habits, once attained, would ever lapse or be renounced, it was necessary for progress that they not come accompanied by the unacceptable penalties that an uncomprehending Nature sought to impose. The parable of Civilization Redeemed taught that the advance of civilization, temporary afflictions notwithstanding, need never exact any real losses. Civilization had become its own redeemer....

Far from questioning the course of civilization, then, advertisers encouraged readers to indulge even more fully in those modern habits that invited Nature's curse. Rather than avoid soft foods or slacken their pace, men and women could pursue their civilized habits and tastes with abandon, confident in the capacity of the advertised product to save them from any ill consequences. Since advertising men worked amid the atmosphere of deadlines and conflicting pressures, they could vividly convey the deleterious qualities of a fast-paced, "overcivilized" social and business life. By raising the specter of civilization destroying the balance of nature, they gave dramatic and sometimes exaggerated expression to the uncertainties of a wider public. After this cathartic airing of anxieties, they offered assurances, through the parable of Civilization Redeemed, that the apparent costs of progress could be avoided. Civilization and Nature were not antithetic. No brakes need be applied to the wheels of progress.

Advertising stories do not have unhappy endings; nor do advertising parables preach hard lessons. The parable of Civilization Redeemed was no exception. It confirmed Americans in one of their treasured common beliefs—the belief in unequivocal progress, in the compatibility of technology with the most desirable qualities of Nature....

The ideology of advertising is an ideology of efficacious answers. No problem lacks an adequate solution. Unsolvable problems may exist in the society, but they are nonexistent in the world glimpsed through advertisements. Thus the parable of Civilization Redeemed simply stated explicitly the implicit message of all advertising....

Perhaps the consummate expression of the beliefs embodied in the parable of Civilization Redeemed appeared in advertisements in the early 1930s for Midol, a patent medicine for menstrual cramps. Warning that "Nature won't postpone her process to accommodate social engagements," Midol promised relief in seven minutes by working "directly on the organs themselves." In so doing, it proved the capacity of civilization's products to carry out the beneficent intentions of Nature. "The periodic process is natural," Midol explained, "but the painful part is not." That pain in any form—physical, social, or psychological—was "not natural" was a proposition that Americans most devoutly wished to believe. Advertising, and particularly advertising tableaux of the parable of Civilization Redeemed, offered only encouragement to such wishful thinking....

Mother was vexed, exhausted, almost driven to distraction. Bobby simply would not eat his carrots, even though mother had followed "all the suggestions laid down by authorities on child training." Her efforts to get him to eat the vegetables essential to his health had become a "pitched battle." This particularly disturbed mother since, as everyone now realized, forcing or strenuous coaxing would destroy her vital bond of companionship with her child.... Mother recognized her duty to shape Bobby's diet; yet angry confrontations and tearful refusals would prove her a failure as a mother. What to do!

Fortunately, just during Bobby's most difficult years—from 1929 through 1933—the Campbell Soup Company offered a strategy to solve mother's dilemma. Realizing the hopelessness of the "pitched battle," Campbell's Soup ads recommended enticement rather than confrontation.... Attractive home meals of Campbell's Soups would captivate Bobby's appetite, restrain his search for forbidden foods, and eliminate the exhausting need for coaxing. "It's not 'vegetables' to them," promised Campbell's, "it's just good soup!" By following the simple strategy proposed by this parable of the Captivated Child, all mothers could mold their "little outlaws" into happy, healthy youngsters without the harsh discipline that might turn them into willful, "sulky foes." Mothers could avoid the negative effects of irritable coaxing and still bring "the end of the great rebellion!"

In seizing upon the parable of the Captivated Child, Campbell's Soups and a score of other advertisers fashioned popular theories of child guidance into a cogent merchandising strategy. Child psychology was riding a wave of popularity as a behavioral science. As new appliances lessened the time required for other domestic tasks, doctors, dieticians, psychologists, and other "authorities" explained to women new standards of child nurture. Some of these involved painstaking expertise in establishing complex and rigid schedules; others required time-consuming devotion to the development of empathetic yet manipulative emotional relationships. All of the new responsibilities encouraged women to invest more emotional energy in their role as mothers and to recognize that they would be judged more heavily than ever by their successes or failures in the role. As child guidance authorities discerned more and more difficult "problems" in attaining the proper diet for children and in properly molding their behavior without destructive discipline, advertisers eagerly publicized those problems and offered their products as solutions....

Given ... three axioms—parents should be companions to their children; children do not choose what is best for them; and children should not be forced or coaxed—the final basic assumption of the parable of the Captivated Child emerged as the only apparent solution to the problem of child management. The mother must become a deft but loving manipulator. With the indispensable aid of enticing products, she should use her child's own tastes and interests to "guide him to thing he should do." Such captivation was easy when mothers could count on a product like Wheaties, which was "as alluring and enticing to a child as a French Confection...."

The parable of the Captivated Child, like the other parables, was not simply an invention of the advertising trade.... Before advertising elaborated the idea in its parables, leading psychologists had already prescribed the replacement of traditional discipline with psychological manipulation of the child's natural impulses for its own good....

Advertising parables of the Captivated Child did not simply mirror contemporary society. They promulgated a particularly indulgent version of current theories of child guidance and diffused it to a wide audience. And these tableaux provided the constant repetition that gave the new ideas the authority of omnipresence. Although women were probably most influenced by their own upbringing in their style of child care, still the advertisements enabled them to experience vicariously the failures and guilt feelings of mothers who ignored the new ways.

As an advertising tool, the parable of the Captivated Child gave special emphasis to certain aspects of the new child-guidance theories that the manuals and advice books had suggested with far less intensity. For obvious merchandising reasons, the ads advocated parental indulgence with far less qualification than the experts. Sensing that family democracy meant earlier and wider participation in the joys of consumerism, advertisers enthusiastically endorsed the idea of family conferences and shared decision-making. Advertising tableaux surpassed even the child-rearing manuals in placing total responsibility on the parents for every detail of the child's development, thus magnifying the potential for guilt. And they exaggerated the ease with which children might be manipulated. Psychologists occasionally argued that the mother might need to assert her domination in a direct contest of wills with the child, but the advertising parable portrayed a parent-child relationship in which open conflict was always unnecessary. Above all, it encouraged mothers to define their role as that of guarantors of a conflict-free home through their mastery of the new methods and the available products for manipulation.

The parables of the First Impression, the Democracy of Goods, Civilization Redeemed, and the Captivated Child were only four of many parables in 1920s and 1930s advertising tableaux.... In each case, the parable so succinctly and vividly encapsulated widely accepted ideas that it propelled them back into the society with a more compelling force and a more entrancing ambience. Advertising parables did not challenge the society to overturn conventional ideas, but they did facilitate the spread of those subtle reformulations of old ideas and values endorsed by the most "modern" segment of the population. Frequent reiteration of each parable by a number of advertisers gave the pattern of thinking it embodied such an aura of inevitability that fundamentally different points of view became increasingly difficult to imagine. Popularized for a widening audience, the parables acquired the status of social clichés—notions with the quality of "givens" that established the ideological framework within which other ideas would be explored.

Why did advertisers return again and again to the same "great parables"? We know that their measures of feedback were too rudimentary and defective to demonstrate that the audience responded to these particular fables. In the absence of such validation, copywriters fell back upon the expedient that had always served them in their creative decision-making—their own instinctive judgment, biased as it was by the conditions of their own lives. Advertising writers resorted again and again to the great parables and recited them with confidence because they found their lessons validated in their *own* lives. For instance, in their own careers—shifting and uncertain, constantly dependent upon the success of brief presentations to prospective clients—they had been forced to acknowledge the importance of appearances. What was more, the success of each of their creations, as the trade press constantly reminded them, was dependent on the first impression that it made upon a hurried, inattentive reader. The parable of the First Impression was preeminently a parable for the advertising trade itself.

So, too, in a metaphorical way, was the parable of the Captivated Child. Advertisers employed this parable to align themselves with the most up-to-date literature on child philosophy and to pursue good merchandising strategy. But their enthusiasm for it may also have stemmed from the way in which its admonitions to parents resonated with the advice that advertisers regularly exchanged among themselves about how to approach the consumer audience. Readers, they reminded each other, could not be forced or bullied into buying. They had to be tempted, subtly manipulated, given an image of the pleasures and rewards they would gain—in short, captivated. A parable that pointed the way to human betterment and increased pleasure through manipulation was likely to seem axiomatic to a practicing advertising man.

The parables of the Democracy of Goods and Civilization Redeemed also gained authority in the minds of advertising leaders because they served as parables of the function of advertising itself. The Democracy of Goods sought to define social standing in terms of the consumption of specific products rather than by broader measures of wealth or occupational and civic stature. By transferring all significant competition and achievement out of the realm of production and into the realm of consumption, it exalted the process of advertising and distribution as the solution to all problems. The parable of Civilization Redeemed offered a similar therapeutic approach in a way that particularly touched the social experience of advertising agents. Its admonitions about the nervous tension of modern society and the dangers of degenerate softness seemed to diagnose the endemic ills of the advertising profession—insecurity, the pressure of deadlines, and the temptations of overindulgence in the pleasure of affluent and sophisticated urban living. Yet the parable offered catharsis by promising that these particulars ills of civilization—and by implication, all perils arising from modernity—could be cured by advertised products.

Thus, although the great parables were employed on each occasion for a specific merchandising purpose, their cumulative effect was to educate consumers to the modernity epitomized by the advertising agent. In a manner far less radical than the biblical parables, they invited readers to a new "logic of living" in which the older values of discipline, character-building, self-restraint, and production-oriented achievement were subordinated to the newer values of pleasure, external appearance, and achievement through consumption. These were not the parables of a radical gospel, but of an optimistic and mildly therapeutic ministry. Rather than challenging entrenched values and ideas, they brought a modern cast to the American dream by subtly redefining the terms of its fulfillment....

FURTHER READING

Chan, Kara. *Advertising and Hong Kong Society* (2006).

Davila, Arlene. *Latinos, Inc.: The Marketing and Making of a People* (2001).

Frank, Thomas. *The Conquest of Cool* (1997).

Jhally, Sut. *The Codes of Advertising: Fetishism and the Political Economy of Meaning in the Consumer Society* (1987).

Lears, T. J. Jackson. *Fables of Abundance* (1994).

Leass, William, Stephen Kline, Sut Jhally, and Jacqueline Botterill. *Social Communication in Advertising* (2005).

Moreno, Julio. *Yankee Don't Go Home* (2003).

O'Barr, William M. *Culture and the Ad: Exploring Otherness in the World of Advertising* (1994)

————. "AdText: An Online Interdisciplinary Curriculum for Advertising in Society, Cultural and History." Retrieved from www.adtextonline.org

Ohmann, Richard M. *Selling Culture: Magazines, Markets, and Class at the Turn of the Century* (1996).

Pendergast, Tom. *Creating the Modern Man: American Magazines and Consumer Culture. 1900–1950* (2000).

Pope, Daniel. *The Making of Modern Advertising* (1983).

Scanlon, Jennifer. *Inarticulate Longings: The Ladies' Home Journal, Gender and the Promise of Consumer Culture* (1995).

————. *The Gender and Consumer Culture Reader* (2000).

Schor, Juliet B. *Born to Buy: The Commercialized Child and the New Consumer Culture* (2005).

Sivulka, Julian. *Soap, Sex, and Cigarettes: A Cultural History of American Advertising* (1997).

Strasser, Susan. *Satisfaction Guaranteed: The Making of the American Mass Market* (1989).

Sutton, Denise H. *Globalizing Ideal Beauty: How Female Copywriters of the J. Walter Thompson Advertising Agency Redefined Beauty for the Twentieth Century* (2009).

Swett, Pamela E. S. Jonathan Wiesen, Jonathan R. Zatlin, and Victoria De Grazia. *Selling Modernity: Advertising in Twentieth-Century Germany* (2007).

Turow, Joseph. *Breaking Up America: Advertisers and the New Media World* (1998).

CHAPTER 8

Cars as Popular Culture

Democracy, Racial Difference, and New Technology, 1920–1939

The introduction of affordable transportation, in the form of the automobile, coupled with the creation of the vacation, transformed pleasure travel in the 1910s and 1920s. Automobile manufacturer Henry Ford introduced mass production of his famous Model T in 1913, and lowered the price of buying a new car to about $300 by 1926. Although Ford commonly has gotten credit for the democratization of automobile ownership, he had many competitors and American consumers had a range of models and prices to choose from when buying cars. And buy cars they did; by the late 1920s car registrations exceeded 20 million and industry leaders declared the market saturated, meaning that the majority of native-born, white Americans owned at least one car. For rural Americans, the car became a necessity, a way to cover long distances between towns and cities more quickly and efficiently. The car also opened the door to a new pastime, the auto vacation. Although Americans of the upper classes had traveled for pleasure since the late nineteenth century by ship and by rail, the introduction of inexpensive and highly individualized means of transportation, with the car, meant that middle- and even some working-class Americans could travel more readily and with less expense. While some adventurers set off across country, driving coast to coast on a growing network of interstate highways after 1920, a week-long or even weekend trip to the country or nearby historical sites was more common. Writing about the effects of the automobile in Middletown, *their study of American culture in Muncie, Indiana, during the 1920s, sociologists Robert and Helen Lynd declared that the automobile was the most influential new invention of the early twentieth century. The Lynds and their subjects claimed that it had permanently shifted patterns of everyday life and "re-made leisure," particularly by spreading the "vacation habit."*

As historians Cindy Aaron and Margarite Schaffer have shown in their comprehensive histories of the vacation and the "See America First" movement, respectively, vacations and especially auto vacations were laden with ideology. Middle-class Americans wanted their time off to be a form of self-improvement, a way to restore their minds and bodies through physical exercise and escape from the city. Cultural critics of the time, among them Theodore Roosevelt and Henry Ford, saw the city as a necessary evil, a place where the middle class had to work, but also a place that made people soft and sapped their strength. Cities also seemed crowded with immigrants and culturally fragmented. Arguments promoting vacations took on a distinctly nativist cast in the years surrounding World War I. The automobile seemed like the most American form of travel— unlike the railroads, cars were individualized, privately owned, flexible, rugged, and supposedly democratic, or open to everyone who could afford one. But did this new transportation technology really democratize leisure? Although more people could buy cars, the car itself did not reconfigure social boundaries predicated on race in the 1920s and 1930s.

Early scholars of the automobile accepted the premise that automobiles made travel more democratic. More recent historical work has examined the ways in which the car reinforced social, gender, and racial segregation of the American landscape. The popular cultures constructed around automobility—a new kind of individualized mobility—and the auto vacation provide a wealth of evidence about the meaning of technology in American culture.

DOCUMENTS

The following articles discuss the cultural politics of automobility and debate whether the automobile democratized leisure travel. As the documents illustrate, automobility was built on prevailing ideas of nativism, anti-urbanism, and racial segregation. Document 1 argues that the car was an instrument of democracy in the 1920s. Who did Vanderbilt include in his vision of an automobile society? Who was excluded? The photograph in Document 2 shows that despite racial segregation the car still appealed to Native Americans and, indeed, almost all communities of Americans. Why? Document 3 was written by a white journalist observing Native American uses of the automobile. What assumptions does the writer make about Native Americans' technological know-how based on their race? Is this similar to how white observers saw African American drivers? How do these assumptions set up social hierarchies based on race and technology? Do they give whites a technological advantage? Document 4 provides a broader, sociological view of how the automobile changed life in *Middletown*. In Document 5, Lillian Rhoades provides a vital critique of the Lynds' study in *Middletown* and refutes the notion that the automobile democratized leisure travel for middle-class African Americans. In Document 6, Alfred Edgar Smith notes the benefits and the difficulties of travel by car for African American drivers.

1. Cornelius Vanderbilt Jr., Wealthy Writer and Movie Producer, Says Automobiles Democratize Leisure, 1921

... To-day, there are but few people in these United States who have not travelled in a motor car. And every clear thinking American, be he rich or poor realizes that in a measure, the automobile and its manufacturers are helping to solve the labor and social problems of the future....

In the western part of our great country, more especially does not notice the tendency of the automobile to bring into intimate and helpful contact sections of our population which normally would never meet. Thousands, I might almost say hundreds of thousands, are taking their vacations every summer in automobiles. The highways west of the Mississippi are daily filled with a motley of wheeled vehicles. The transcontinental routes abound with tourists, and home-seekers; and the wonderful roadways of the Pacific slope are alive with machines from every section of the country....

Last summer Mrs. Vanderbilt and I came west shortly after we were married, on another *newshunt*.... [W]e thought it would be amazing and interesting to follow the crowd in true western style, so we purchased, along with the car, a camping outfit. For nineteen weeks we camped every night and look the luck of the road as fate happened to bring it.

We brushed shoulders with every type of humanity imaginable, and many types unimaginable. We learned the love of the open road, the cheery campfire, the starry nights and the great north woods. We looked forward with pleasure and interest to the friends we would make each night; and many of those good friendships, brought to us by the fate which guides all those who travel the open road, will last forever.

In Washington Oregon, California or British Columbia, camping-a-la-motor is a most delightful form of amusement that a man can desire. One meets in the camping grounds every possible type of person in the world. At first one would think that a type could be told by the variety of car in which it travelled, but I quickly learned the fallacy of this point of view. Those possessing the greatest wealth are more often than not those who travel in the least expensive or in the oldest type of vehicle. A flashy, or highly decorative, car is usually owned by one who has made his money at some one's else

Cornelius Vanderbilt, Jr., "The Democracy of the Motor Car," *Motor* (December 1921), 21–22.

expense during the war, or is the property of one who shines behind the footlights....

... Four other cars were here also, and their occupants had gathered around a huge camp fire, coat and hat-less "swapping yarns." We joined the company and eagerly listened to the tales that were passed.

An elderly man who held the floor was calmly reciting a passage of Gungha Din, which he said would illustrate the story he had just told. A comely little miss, who said she had come alone, all the way from Kansas City, described her trip, claiming that a girl was safer on the prairies than on Fifth Avenue. A gaudily attired young man told tales of the movie studios in Los Angeles; while a very weary traveller from El Paso, Texas, wanted all the world to know that the worst roads in America were those within a radius of twenty miles. At the moment, the camp-fire group was joined by another traveller, more weary and foot-sore than the rest of us. He was a typical tramp, and the tales he told us that calm evening in the Syskiou, were enough to bring tears to the eyes.

I later learned that the gentleman imbued with Gungha Din was a United States Senator; the comely miss from Kansas City, the heiress of a large newspaper owner; the gaudily attired young man, a prominent silver screen actor; and the oathful gentleman from Texas, none other than a bishop. The wayside tramp whose narrative genius had brought the only tears of the night is still and probably always will be a "weary Willie."

Another time while crossing a range of mountains in eastern Oregon, we encountered very bad roads, with extensive detours. On one of the litter, stranded near the top of a dangerous ascent, we found a circus on wheels. The lion's cage-car had broken is front axle, and the snake charmer was doing her best to encourage the fat lady to place herself beneath the front wheels, as they had lost their jack. Behind us, puffing valiantly, came a heavily laden Chevrolet, in which we saw an old couple and two little girls. Their license plate bore the letters of Florida and we learned they had been travelling five months on wheels.

Everyone went to the rescue of the snake charmer and fat lady; and half an hour later extricated the lion's cage from the mass of debris, placing its chariot tenderly beside the road. At this moment two men in an expensive car blew loudly their electrical trumpet and came over the brow of the hill. Our little Buick and our friends from Florida blocked the path and halted the mad assault of those who were "too proud to work," and we did not get out of the way until we had forced them, after a long wait, to back up over the brow of the hill once more. And this is an instance of the rough and ready but poetic justice of the open spaces, for the ways of the road, customs without set creeds, are those of fair play and democracy for all.

2. Native Americans Take Control of the
Car and Their Image, 1916

3. Magazine Writer George H. Dacy Describes
the Symbolic Power of the Automobile for
Native Americans, 1922

If you were a motorist and were speeding along the Dixie Highway in central Missouri, the strangest procession of which you could possibly conceive would be a train of automobiles one hundred and fifty-two miles long carrying one hundred and seventy-five Indians of all sizes and ages diked out in their tribal splendor with bright-hued blankets and gaudy head-dresses. Now there is not one chance in a million that such a procession of redskin tourists will ever be assembled. However, if the thirty-five thousand Indians who own automobiles and live on the government reservations once got together for an automobile parade, the procession would be approximately as mentioned above. At present there are more than three hundred and fifty thousand red men living on the one hundred and fifty-five Indian

Frank Palmer/Library of Congress.

George H. Dacy, "Redskins and Red Roadsters," *Illustrated World* (August 1922), 862–864.

reservations in the United States. The automobile owners among the "Injuns" are adequate to provide cross-country transportation for one-half of the aborigines who now make their homes on Uncle Sam's reservations.

The Indians have taken to automobiles like street urchins take to circus parades and free ice cream. To the average redskin, the automobile is the banner prize. He covets a horseless carriage. Each red man now has one goal in view. It is to own an automobile. As soon as he saves enough money, he buys one of the "devil-wagons." It does not require the services of an expert salesman to close a deal with the Indian. The car sells itself—especially if it is gaudily painted and dolled up with glittering accessories. Do not think for a minute that the average Indians are content with the cheaper and more popular makes and models of cars. They want the biggest and best. The Indians that have money change cars frequently. Some of them buy a new car every three or four months. For the most part, they abuse their motor cars. They neglect to give the machines proper mechanical attention. As soon as the car halts or breaks down, the Indian is through with it. He will sell it for a mere fraction of what it is worth and will then seek the dealer again to purchase another car....

The Osage Indians of Oklahoma are the millionaires among the red men. Their former hunting grounds have been found to be prodigally rich oil lands. Some of the redskins receive royalties as great as the President's salary annually. Last year, the average income of every man, woman and child on the Osage Reservation was in excess of ten thousand dollars. With so much ready money at their command, it is no wonder that the Osages are the motorcar Magnates of their territory. Many of these Indian families own four or five cars among which red roadsters, yellow touring cars and light green sedans predominate. The majority of these automobiles are the high-powered, expensive made-in-America models.

The wealthy Indians like to outdo one another in the excellence and superiority of their motor cars. To the redskin, size counts more than efficiency in the use of oil and gas or smoothness of operation and ridability. When the small automobile bus first came on the market, the Indians immediately rushed to purchase these modern "prairie schooners" which were exactly what they wanted. Later on they took to buying panel body delivery cars. Big-powered trucks came next in popularity, but they soon went into discard as they were short on speed. Then a former chieftain stole away to the city one day and when he returned he was proudly driving one of the largest automobile hearses that ever was operated in the state of Oklahoma. For many months this hearse was the champion "devil-wagon" among the Indians of the Osage Reservation....

... A problem has arisen on several of the reservations to keep the red men from trading their lands for worn-out and useless automobiles. The arrangement is such that when the Indians have learned the fundamentals of civilization and business dealing, they are given full possession of their lands. Many of them sell these lands for little or nothing in order to buy automobiles. Ready money is what counts with the Indian. A dollar in hand is worth more than ten in the bank according to his way of reasoning. Hence he will always sell anything he owns for one-tenth or less of what it is worth when he wants spot cash.

Indian boys are interested particularly in gasoline tractors and automobiles, according to surveys that have been made at the different Indian trade schools.

A dozen of the leading manufacturers of automobiles in the United States have constant orders in with the Indian Service and the trade schools for young redskins to serve as apprentices in their factories and to learn the automobile business. They report that the Indians rank among the best mechanics that they employ. Although the Indians are rather slow to learn they are correspondingly slow to forget. They do not talk during working hours and do not waste as much time as some of the other motor mechanics....

4. Sociologists Robert S. Lynd and Helen Merrell Lynd Study How the Automobile Changed Leisure in Famous Study of *Middletown*, 1929

Although lectures, reading, music, and art are strongly intrenched in Middletown's traditions, it is none of these that would first attract the attention of a newcomer watching Middletown at play.

"Why on earth do you need to study what's changing this country?" said a lifelong resident and shrewd observer of the Middle West. "I can tell you what's happening in just four letters: A–U–T–O !"...

The first real automobile appeared in Middletown in 1900. About 1906 it was estimated that "there are probably 200 in the city and county." At the close of 1923 there were 6,221 passenger cars in the city, one for every 6.1 persons, or roughly two for every three families. Of these 6,221 cars, 41 per cent. were Fords; 54 per cent. of the total were cars of models of 1920 or later, and 17 per cent, models earlier than 1917. These cars average a bit over 5,000 miles a year. For some of the workers and some of the business class, use of the automobile is a seasonal matter, but the increase in surfaced roads and in closed cars is rapidly making the car a year-round tool for leisure-time as well as getting-a-living activities. As, at the turn of the century, business class people began to feel apologetic if they did not have a telephone, so ownership of an automobile has now reached the point of being an accepted essential of normal living.

Into the equilibrium of habits which constitutes for each individual some integration in living has come this new habit, upsetting old adjustments, and blasting its way through such accustomed and unquestioned dicta as "Rain or shine, I never miss a Sunday morning at church."... No one questions the use of the auto for transporting groceries, getting to one's place of work or to the golf course, or in place of the porch for "cooling off after supper" on a hot summer evening; however much the activities concerned with getting a living may be altered by the fact that a factory can draw from workmen within a radius of forty-five miles, or however much old labor union men resent the intrusion of this new alternate way of spending an evening, these things are hardly major issues. But when auto riding tends to replace the traditional call in the family parlor as a way of approach between the unmarried, "the home is endangered," and all-day Sunday motor trips are a "threat against the church"; it is in the activities concerned with the home and religion that the automobile occasions the greatest emotional conflicts.

Group-sanctioned values are disturbed by the inroads of the automobile upon the family budget. A case in point is the not uncommon practice of mortgaging a home to buy an automobile. Data on automobile ownership were secured from 123 working class families. Of these, sixty have cars. Forty-one of the sixty own their homes. Twenty-six of these forty-one families have mortgages on their homes. Forty of the sixty-three families who do not own a car own their homes. Twenty-nine of these have mortgages on their homes. Obviously other factors are involved in many of Middletown's mortgages. That the automobile does represent a real choice in the minds of some at least is suggested by the acid retort of one citizen to the question about car ownership: "No, sir, we've *not* got a car. *That's* why we've got a home." According to an officer of a Middletown automobile financing company, 75 to 90 per cent of the cars purchased locally are bought on time payment, and a working man earning $35.00 a week frequently plans to use one week's pay each month as payment for his car.

The automobile has apparently unsettled the habit of careful saving for some families. "Part of the money we spend on the car would go to the bank, I suppose," said more than one working class wife. A business man explained his recent inviting of social oblivion by selling his car by saying: "My car, counting depreciation and everything, was costing mighty nearly $100.00 a month, and my wife and I sat down together the other night and just figured that we're getting along, and if we're to have anything later on, we've just got to begin to save." The "moral" aspect of the competition between the automobile and certain accepted expenditures appears in the remark of another business man, "An automobile is a luxury, and no one has a right to one if he can't afford it. I haven't the slightest sympathy for any one who is out of work if he owns a car."...

Even food may suffer:

"I'll go without food before I'll see us give up the car," said one woman emphatically, and several who were out of work were apparently making precisely this adjustment.

Twenty-one of the twenty-six families owning a car for whom data on bathroom facilities happened to be secured live in homes without bathtubs. Here we obviously have a new habit cutting in ahead of an older one and slowing down the diffusion of the latter.

Meanwhile, advertisements pound away at Middletown people with the tempting advice to spend money for automobiles for the sake of their homes and families:

"Hit the trail to better times!" says one such advertisement....

Many families feel that an automobile is justified as an agency holding the family group together. "I never feel as close to my family as when we are all together in the car," said one business class mother, and one or two spoke of giving up Country Club membership or other recreations to get a car for this reason. "We don't spend anything on recreation except for the car. We save every place we can and put the money into the car. It keeps the family together," was an opinion voiced more than once. Sixty-one per cent. of 337 boys and 60 per cent. of 423 girls in the three upper years of the high school say that they motor more often with their parents than without them.

But this centralizing tendency of the automobile may be only a passing phase; sets in the other direction are almost equally prominent "Our daughters [eighteen and fifteen] don't use our car much because they are always with somebody else in their car when we go out motoring," lamented one business class mother....

An earnest teacher in a Sunday School class of working class boys and girls in their late teens was winding up the lesson on the temptations of Jesus: "These three temptations summarize all the temptations we encounter today: physical comfort, fame, and wealth. Can you think of any temptation we have today that Jesus didn't have?" "Speed!" rejoined one boy. The unwanted interruption was quickly passed over. But the boy had mentioned a tendency underlying one of the four chief infringements of group laws in Middletown today, and the manifestations of Speed are not confined to "speeding." "Auto Polo next Sunday!!" shouts the display advertisement of an amusement park near the city. "It's motor insanity—too fast for the movies!"...

The threat which the automobile presents to some anxious parents is suggested by the fact that of thirty girls brought before the juvenile court in the twelve months preceding September 1, 1924, charged with "sex crimes," for whom the place where the offense occurred was given in the records, nineteen were listed as having committed the offense in an automobile. Here again the automobile appears to some as an "enemy" of the home and society.

Sharp, also, is the resentment aroused by this elbowing new device when it interferes with old-established religious habits. The minister trying to change people's behavior in desired directions through the spoken word must compete against the strong pull of the open road strengthened by endless printed "copy" inciting to travel. Preaching to 200 people on a hot, sunny Sunday in midsummer on "The Supreme Need of Today," a leading Middletown minister denounced "automobilitis—the thing those people have who go off motoring on Sunday instead of going to church. If you want to use your car on Sunday, take it out Sunday morning and bring some shut-ins to church and Sunday School; then in the afternoon, if you choose, go out and worship God in the beauty of nature—but don't neglect to worship Him indoors too." ... If we except the concentrated group pressure of war time, never perhaps since the days of the campmeeting have the citizens of this community been subjected to such a powerfully focused stream of habit diffusion. To get the full force of this appeal, one must remember that the nearest lakes or hills are one hundred miles from Middletown in either direction and that an afternoon's motoring brings only mile upon mile of level stretches like Middletown itself....

But if the automobile touches the rest of Middletown's living at many points, it has revolutionized its leisure; more, perhaps, than the movies or any other intrusion new to Middletown since the nineties, it is making leisure-time enjoyment a regularly expected part of every day and week rather than an occasional event. The readily available leisure-time options of even the working class have been multiplied many-fold. As one working class housewife remarked, "We just go to lots of things we couldn't go to if we didn't have a car." Beefsteak and watermelon picnics in a park or a near-by wood can be a matter of a moment's decision on a hot afternoon.

Not only has walking for pleasure become practically extinct, but the occasional event such as a parade on a holiday attracts far less attention now....

Use of the automobile has apparently been influential in spreading the "vacation" habit. The custom of having each summer a respite, usually of two weeks, from getting-a-living activities, with pay unabated, is increasingly common among the business class, but it is as yet very uncommon among the workers. "Vacations in 1890?" echoed one substantial citizen. "Why, the word wasn't in the dictionary!" "Executives of the 1890 period *never* took a vacation," said another man of a type common in Middletown thirty-five years ago, who used to announce proudly that they had "not missed a day's work in twenty years." Vacations there were in the nineties, nevertheless, particularly for the wives and children of those business folk who had most financial leeway. Put-In Bay, Chautauqua, country boarding-houses where the rates were $5.00 a week for adults and $3.00 for children, the annual conference of the State Baptist Association, the Annual National Christian Endeavor Convention, the annual G.A.R. encampment, all drew people from Middletown. But these affected almost entirely business class people. A check of the habits of the parents of the 124 working class wives shows that summer vacations were almost unknown among this large section of the population in the nineties. In lieu of vacations both for workers and many of the business class there were excursions: those crowded, grimy, exuberant, banana-smelling affairs on which one sat up nights in a day coach, or, if a "dude," took a sleeper, from Saturday till Monday morning, and went back to work a bit seedy from loss of sleep but full of the glamour of Petoskey, or the ball game at Chicago. Two hundred and twelve people from Middletown went to Chicago in one week-end on one such excursion. One hundred and fifty journeyed to the state capital to see the unveiling of a monument to an ex-governor—"a statesman," as they called them in those days. Even train excursions to towns fifteen, twenty, and forty miles away were great events, and people reported having "seen the sights" of these other Middletowns with much enthusiasm....

5. African American Sociologist Lillian Rhodes Rebuts Middletown's Findings, 1933

... Between colored L_____ and Middletown's better working class group, we find some similarity. They both get up in the morning and go to work about the same hour, and they both return about the same time in the evening to about the same kind of homes. They go to church, to the movies and they send their children to the public schools. On the surface here are two groups of working

Lillian Rhodes, "One of the Groups Middletown Left Out," *Opportunity: The Journal of Negro Life*, 11(March 1933), 75–77, 93. Copyright © 1933, National Urban league. All rights reserved. Reproduced by permission.

class people apparently similar in many respects, but when we study the groups more closely, we find there are many differences....

If your skin is of the right hue, it is an open sesame to all the leisure time pursuits in L_____ If not, you keep within your own group and save yourself embarrassment. However, after the L_____ Theatre was built, its opening was looked forward to with eager anticipation by the school children of all ages. Free tickets had been distributed and on the big day when they were presented, the colored children were told they had the wrong tickets for admission. Later several adults were told very politely that the house was sold out. So taking the hint, colored L_____ dug down among its meagre pennies and rode into the city on Saturday nights to see its favorite show at the R_____ Theatre, Jewish owned, but with all colored employees. A year or so later the L_____ Theatre changed management and the new owners realized that white L_____ too continued to motor into the city for its movie shows. Receipts were falling off and expenditures mounting. In devious ways it was made known to colored L_____ that the new management welcomed colored patrons. For once those of a dusky hue felt the urge of race pride and refused to patronize the theatre that had once turned them down, and so continued their weekly trips to the city.

Every home has a radio and all but three have automobiles. Middletown and L_____ see the same shows, hear the same programs over the radio, and go to distant points in automobiles to parties, picnics, and "just to see the sights." It is an avenue of escape from the hum-drum of every day living.

Little Miss Colored L_____ comes back from the movies with new ideas of dress, of arranging the hair, of furnishing the home, and with new ideas of love making.

When white Middletown comes back from an extended auto trip, the talk is of the pleasant incidents connected with it. Colored L_____ talks, among other things, of the "Jim-Crowism" it encounters at times at rest camps and service stations, and long discussions ensue over the race problem and a probable way out....

6. Urban League Magazine Explains the Difficulties for African American Drivers, 1933

Good roads beckon to you and me, daily we grow more motor-wise. The nomad in the poorest and the mightiest of us, sends us behind the wheel, north, south, east, and west, in answer to the call of the road. And in addition to invitation, there in propulsion. The ever-growing national scope of modern business commands; pleasure suggests; and (in downright selfish frankness) it's mighty good to be the skipper for a change, and pilot our craft whither and when we will. We feel like Vikings. What if our craft is blunt of nose and limited of power and our sea is macadamized; it's good for the spirit to just give the old railroad Jim Crow the laugh.

Alfred Edgar Smith, "Through the Windshield," *Opportunity*, 11(May 1933), 142–144.

Nevertheless, with transcontinental and intersectional highways, with local roads growing nationally good, with good cars growing cheaper, and with good tires within the reach of everyone; there is still a small cloud that stands between us and complete motor-travel freedom. On the trail, this cloud rarely troubles us in the mornings, but as the afternoon wears on it casts a shadow of apprehension on our hearts and sours us a little. "Where," it asks us, "will you stay tonight?" An innocent enough question; to our Nordic friends, of no consequence. But to you and me, what a peace-destroying world of potentiality....

The Bugbear is the great uncertainty, the extreme difficulty of finding a lodging for the night,—a suitable lodging, a semi-suitable lodging, an unsuitable lodging, any lodging at all, not to mention an eatable meal. In a large city (where you have no friends) it's hard enough, in a smaller city it's harder, in a village or small town it's a gigantic task, and in anything smaller it's a matter of sheer luck. And, in spite of unfounded beliefs to the contrary, conditions are practically identical in the Mid-West, the South, the so-called North-east, and the South-southwest.

The typical confronting-condition and procedure is as follows: After a day of happy carefree meandering along good roads to the tune of from four to sixteen cylinders, a pleasant physical sense of tiredness makes itself felt and it is decided to stop at the next village, hamlet, or junction to seek a place to dine and to lay the weary head. Lights presently come to view, and assuming a look of confidence for the benefit of the wife, we search anxiously and somewhat furtively for a dark-hued face. Presently we spy one and make inquiry in a low voice as to the possibility of securing a night's lodging. This first individual invariably answers you with a blank stare, and you suddenly remember certain mannerisms of your long-lost boyhood in the South ... and we repeat the question slowly and in a way you know as well us I do. This elicits the information that there is no hotel for "us," there is no rooming or boarding house, but Mrs. X has a place where "folks stay sometimes." So away to Mrs. X's across the railroad tracks.

Mrs. X when aroused from dinner or from a rocker, regards our proposals with an expressionless stare, which we, being of kindred blood understand quite well. In our desperate need our early training again comes to the rescue and we disarm our hostess after a time and put her completely at her ease, so that it is guessed that we can be provided with a bed, and later under the influence of our overworked charm we are provided with a meal. It doesn't seem so hard in the telling; but remember we were lucky, any one of a number of things could have gone wrong forcing a continuation of the journey for twenty or thirty miles and n repetition of the procedure. And also, Mrs. X in the above case probably provides for us to the best of her ability, and her provisions, meals and otherwise, are without a doubt, the best to be had. But "best" is a relative thing....

In the light of personal experience and of questioning friends, it seems that the real motorists' nightmare is the uncertainty of finding a lodging, rather than the type of lodging itself. The more so, as I am led to believe that a traveller must inure himself to a certain amount of discomfort and hardship, be he in any section of the United States, Canada, Europe, or wherever he may be. So the first and major problem is how and where to be sure of a place to stay. Obviously the answer lies in the compilation of an authentic list of hotels, rooming houses, private homes catering to the occasional traveller, tourist camps, and every type of lodging whatsoever, including those run by members of other races and open to Negroes; and the availability of such a list to our growing army of motor-travellers. Such a list would if complete, be invaluable … for I am convinced that within the area of every fifty square miles of the more frequently travelled sections there are lodgings to be found at all times. If we just knew exactly where they were, what a world of new confidence would be ours.

Up to date there have been, to my knowledge, two efforts to supply this need. The preparation and sale of one such list, which included hotels, rooming houses and the like, resulted in a bankruptcy. The other list includes only hotels, Y.M.C.A.'s and Y.W.C.A.'s, but it is most complete and authentic. It was compiled by Mr. James A. Jackson who is now the director of the Small Business Section of the Marketing Service Division of the United States Department of Commerce, with offices in the new Commerce Building in Washington. This list contains some 120 hotels, 31 Y.M.C.A.'s and 14 Y.W.C.A.'s in 35 States, the District of Columbia and Canada. I heartily recommend this list to you. Also I live in hope that some individual, organization, or publication with unlimited publicity at his or its command will attempt a more inclusive and complete list. I am sure it would not lack contributors. I think with what great pleasure I could recommend a private home in small town in Ohio, one in Missouri, one in Tennessee, and a hotel in Virginia.

The summer past, we turned the blunt nose of our Viking craft westward on the concrete-asphalt seas, and sailed away for new conquests and adventures. Starting from Washington, D.C., the first half of our journey was punctuated with the usual very short or very long runs between Pittsburgh, Chicago, St. Louis, and Ft. Riley, to take advantage of the presence of known friends and accommodations. And pleasant are the memories of our stay with real friends at these objectives. But somehow it takes the joy out of gypsying about, when you have to be at a certain place by a certain time, and there are one or two unpleasant memories of way stops between stations.…

It would seem that our sensibilities would be somewhat dulled by the continuous hurts they receive in this land of ours; but not so. Every time that a camp manager announced his camp full for the night, or showed us to a cabin that was second rate in appearance, the thought persisted, "Is he doing this because I am a Negro?" Probably we imagined slights where none were intended. Certainly we have the pleasantest of memories of these camps, of the Mormons, of the Utah Indian (named Smith) who welcomed us royally and wanted to talk for into the night about Senator Smoot and things politic, of the Colorado hostess who insisted we would be more comfortable in her hotel than in a cabin, of cordial Californians, and others.…

[S]peaking of chain syndicates, a last word on this matter. As a group we have no reason to love these organizations as colored labor within their ranks is usually taboo. But having switched to a well known brand of gasoline because it could be found in any and all localities the length and breadth of this country and others, in all fairness let it be known that the employees were uniformly courteous, attentive, anxious to serve, and never failed to welcome us with a cherry good morning or evening, and to speed us on our way with well wishes and an invitation to revisit. And this regardless of locale (we returned through the South). Only the attendants at privately-owned stations were discourteous or apathetic. And yet, only the privately-owned stations employed an occasional Negro. A paradox, no? A typical example of a changing spirit in the cotton belt of the South, was the deft covering by an attendant at a chain station, of a sign on the drinking water fountain reading "For White Only," when the colored tourist drew up for gas and oil. This was three Summers ago, last summer the sign had disappeared.

 # ESSAYS

The essays pose the following questions: How do we study the diversity of experiences with regard to the automobile? What role did technology play in the formation of popular culture and struggles over public leisure space? Kathleen Franz, associate professor of history at American University and one of the editors of this volume, examines the racialized terrain of auto travel in the 1920s and 1930s and the contrasting experiences of white and black drivers. This historical discussion of African American drivers considers how black entrepreneurs and pleasure seekers built a separate system of auto travel in this period and grappled with contradictory discourses and expectations of African American automobility. In a similar vein but with a different subject, cultural historian Philip DeLoria, professor of history, American culture, and Native American studies at the University of Michigan, interrogates the cluster of ideas informing the intersection of Native American identity and the automobile in the early twentieth century. He asks: Why did the image and idea of Native American drivers seem strange to white Americans? What kinds of expectations and images did whites bring to the encounters with Native drivers, and how did the act of buying and driving cars by Native Americans unsettle if not restructure dominant ideas of technological progress and "Indianness"?

African-Americans Take to the Open Road

KATHLEEN FRANZ

… Racial divisions were central to the construction of what historians of technology have termed automobility, or individual spatial mobility. Racial discrimination on the open road and representations of African-Americans as technologically incompetent reinforced a belief in white superiority at a time when the white middle class was feeling the threat of cultural fragmentation and blacks had started gaining middle class status. In the 1920s, white motorists relied on

Kathleen Franz, "'The Open Road:' Automobility and Racial Uplift in the Interwar Years," in *Technology and the African American Experience*, ed. Bruce Sinclair. Copyright © 2004 Massachusetts Institute of Technology, by permission of The MIT Press.

ideologies of racial difference established in the nineteenth century to reinforce the boundaries between the races on the open road....

As ... members of the black middle class purchased the new machine and sought the freedom of movement it promised, they created a new site of racial contestation in the United States. For their part, black motorists developed a set of strategies that allowed them to access the new technology and its culture, and to challenge both segregation and white attempts to represent all blacks as unskilled drivers.

This essay investigates the automobile as an instrument of cultural power that offered black middle-class drivers access to both personal mobility and technological expertise. I argue that the emergent black middle class in the 1910s and the 1920s adopted the automobile not only as a means to circumvent segregation, but as a material expression of racial uplift ideology. This ideology held that African-Americans could assimilate into American culture through education, bourgeois morality, and a culture of self-improvement.... The concept of "race" progress in the early twentieth century focused on education and community action, but the ideology of uplift also had a material component, a cultural aesthetic that used material goods and, especially, the new technology of the automobile to demonstrate the achievement of a middle class lifestyle.

Cultural histories of technology, with their focus on users, material culture, and consumption, suggest two ways in which we can expand the scope of African-American history. First, a focus on material culture can help us broaden the study of the black middle class from the lives and ideas of intellectuals to the material practices of everyday life, such as consumption of new technologies and leisure travel. As historians of technology who study women have shown, consumption is a highly political form of technological use. Second, studies of how the black community appropriated technological artifacts can highlight the importance of technological skill and knowledge within larger arguments about racial progress. As an example, I will show how black narratives of progress used the automobile to insert African-Americans into dominant discourses of economic prosperity, leisured mobility, and technological know-how....

Between 1918 and 1939, automobility offered the small but growing black middle class an opportunity for greater spatial and social equality. Some scholars have asserted that blacks and whites used the automobile in similar ways, but most have emphasized the differences between the experiences of black and white motorists....

Car ownership among African-Americans grew more slowly during this period than it did among whites. Yet motor cars and the possibility of vacation travel became a material signifier of racial progress. Assessing the increase in automobile ownership among the black middle class in the 1920s, Robert Moton observed, "If motor cars are an index of prosperity there is significance in the fact that in every city of any considerable size Negroes are to be found in possession of some of the finest cars made in America." More black Americans purchased automobiles after 1918 than they did before the war, partly as a result of the growth of the resale market.

Black publications such as *The Crisis, Champion,* and *Opportunity* and newspapers such as the *California Eagle* promoted car ownership, provided vacation information, and defined the cultural meanings of automobility. Melnotte Wade, a contributor to *Champion,* encouraged her husband to buy a car in 1917, when "autos were the rarest of the rare in our community and no colored man had yet been the proud possessor of one." "I must confess," she wrote, "that it had long been the height of my ambition to travel some other way than by train or the monotonous jog-jog behind old Dobbins…. Shutting my eyes to all ideas of economy, I could see myself lolling back in a car of my own." The remainder of the article was a warning to potential car buyers who gave in to such impulses. Mrs. Wade and her husband had been sold a lemon by an unscrupulous white car dealer. Nevertheless her dream of enjoying the freedom afforded by the automobile resonated with others in her community.

The call of the "free car and open road" resonated in middle-class black communities in the 1920s. As Gaines has noted, the black elite shared the dominant culture's distaste for cities crowded with migrants from the rural South. Over several weeks in June 1924 the *California Eagle* ran a series entitled "Where Will You Spend Your Vacation?" The *Eagle* suggested that its readers cure their vacation fever by taking a "vacation of fifteen days or more" consisting of a motor trip to the woods. The paper urged readers to cut costs by camping: "… we would advise that you rough it…. This affords you an advantage that is to be appreciated only by a visit to this wonderful place and too it reduces your expense to a minimum."…

Most important, the automobile offered African-Americans [possible] escape from the Jim Crow segregation they encountered trains and street cars. In 1930, the writer George Schuyler observed that the main reason African-Americans bought automobiles was to avoid substandard segregated transportation. "All Negroes who can do so purchase an automobile as soon as possible," he wrote, "in order to be free of discomfort, discrimination, segregation and insult." He noted that buying an automobile was a "gesture of manliness and independence." Alfred Edgar Smith, a teacher from Washington, DC, confirmed this desire for independence in 1933. "It's mighty good," he testified, "to be the skipper for a change, and pilot our craft whither and when we will. We feel like Vikings. What if our craft is blunt of nose and limited of power and our sea is macadamized; it's good for the spirit to just give the old railroad Jim Crow the laugh."…

In the 1920s, however, black motorists were unable to escape the specter of Jim Crow even on the open road. Beginning with the outdoor recreation movement at the turn of the century, the open road came to symbolize individual freedom. The antithesis of the city, the open road represented a place where American urbanites could escape the degenerative effects of city life and re-create themselves in a community of "like-minded" Americans. Although white travelers constructed the open road as a technological democracy, open to anyone who owned a car, they simultaneously limited access to automobility through a system of discrimination and representation that positioned nonwhites outside the new motor culture.

In their rhetoric, white motor philosophers such as Elon Jessup declared driving and auto camping to be the "most democratic sport in America." For white travelers the social benefits of the new technology were clear: the car gave them a feeling of control over the space of public leisure and entitled them to membership in a national community of middle-class motorists. Observing the regional and class diversity of Americans driving and camping along the open road, Jessup concluded that the car had made pleasure travel available to a broader segment of Americans....

But rather than welcoming black motorists, the fraternity of the open road re-inscribed older forms of racial discrimination on the landscape of public leisure. When African-Americans traveled, they encountered not a feeling of national camaraderie but a contested terrain that was neither officially segregated nor completely welcoming. The growing numbers of white-owned hotels, resorts, and auto camps that grew up alongside the road often did not admit blacks. A writer for *Crisis* surveyed the landscape of travel in the United States from the perspective of the black elite: "The white [traveler], for instance, may choose from a thousand different places the one to which he will go with his family.... He has but to choose and pay his board. But you, if you are colored, will knock in vain at the farmhouse door for board and lodging. The beautiful, inexpensive, out-of-the-way places are out of your way, indeed."...

Even the National Parks, the epitome of the open road movement for many white Americans, perpetuated racial discrimination. In the early 1920s, the National Park Service debated whether it could openly exclude blacks. At the sixth National Park Conference, held in Yosemite in 1922, park superintendents "decided that, while colored people could not be openly discriminated against, they should be told that the parks have no facilities for taking care of them." Conference participants reasoned that the Department of the Interior was not at fault if blacks were denied accommodation because "the attitude of the help of the hotels (over whom the park has no jurisdiction) makes it difficult for [black motorists] to go through the park as they cannot be furnished service."

White journalists and travel writers reinforced the exclusion of nonwhites from the growing auto culture by representing them as primitive or nontechnological.... Tourist narratives, popular fiction, post cards, and automobile advertising all perpetuated minstrel images of blacks as lazy, boastful, and technologically backward. A common trope of tourist photography was the image of rural nonwhites (African-Americans, Hispanics, Native Americans) standing in front of dilapidated housing, lacking modern technologies such as indoor plumbing or birth control, and baffled by the sight of motor cars. Representing nonwhites as primitive—as noncontributors to modern progress—these images undermined African-Americans' claims to social and technological equality. Furthermore, during the 1920s and the 1930s, white travel writers clung to the image of blacks as reckless drivers and poor mechanics....

Although they had high hopes, members of the black [middle class] understood that simply owning an automobile would not free them from segregation or completely revise misrepresentations of blacks as reckless or primitive. In 1930, George Schuyler noted that the South was growing accustomed to the notion that blacks owned cars but "there was a time not long ago when in most sections of Dixie a Negro with a well-kept or expensive automobile was suspected of stealing it."

Black leaders used several strategies to overcome discrimination, counter minstrel images of black drivers, and ensure participation in the new motor culture. Middle-class blacks in the 1920s and the 1930s mounted a tripartite campaign for auto citizenship: they produced counter images of black drivers as inventive and respectable; they legally challenged discrimination by auto insurance companies and hotels; and they created separate systems of travel that protected the comfort and safety of black motorists....

Eager to demonstrate black mechanical expertise in a culture that valued automotive know-how, black journalists reported the activities of black automobile drivers, inventors, and entrepreneurs. Black newspapers appropriated the dominant discourse that portrayed test drivers as the epitome of masculinity, expressed both physically and technologically. For instance, when A. L. Headen drove his new car from Chicago to Kansas City in July 1922, the *Chicago Defender* lauded both the superior design of the car and Headen's technological expertise and physical prowess.... Headen was not only a skilled driver but also a successful inventor, and the *Defender* called his car design "a masterpiece of automobile engineering."... According to social psychologist and patent examiner Joseph Rossman, who challenged existing notions of racial inferiority in the late 1920s, any race that produced inventors could not be inferior, or at least had the potential to contribute to the progress of civilization. Technological skill could blur the lines of racial and class difference and underpin arguments for social equality....

Automobiles offered a springboard into the middle class for African-Americans both economically and culturally. Chauffeuring and, later, jitney services became a way for black mechanics and drivers to own their own businesses and achieve status comparable to, if not above, that of Pullman porters. Social commentators such as Charles Johnson argued in the 1940s that in the early days of automobility, "negroes were expected to operate automobiles for whites, but not to own them." Yet, historically, a small group of black inventors and entrepreneurs not only owned cars in the 1910s and the 1920s but took advantage of their automotive skill to run driving schools for chauffeurs and even start their own automotive companies. Lee Pollard, for instance, opened a garage and automobile school in New York City in 1901, which blossomed into a training institute for black chauffeurs in the 1910s. Pollard, who published a manual for chauffeurs in 1914 entitled "How to Run an Automobile," made a respectable income by teaching others how to drive. He also gained renown in New York's black community as an inventor of automobile accessories, including a convertible enclosure, and later as a builder of airplanes and owner of an African import business....

Automobile ownership provided material evidence that one segment of the black community had achieved a middle-class life style, while, at the same time, reinforcing class and color divisions among African-Americans. The *California Eagle* published news of the most elite strata of automobile owners in its "Automotive Section." In the early 1920s, the *Eagle's* "Exhaust" column functioned as a social register of automobile owners by recording who bought new cars and who took automobile vacations. Listing the occupations and leisure activities of automobile owners, the paper wove the automobile into portraits of black success. For instance, in December 1923 readers learned that "S. B. W. Mayo, besides steering the destinies of the Citizen's Investment Company also steers a Studebaker; Dr. Ruth Temple, besides being one of our leading medical lights is a believer and leader in automobiles; and Wm. Pickens and Bob Davis, who move folks for a livelihood, have two sport Durants, and believe us, when we say they sport some."…

As the car became part of the everyday life of more African-Americans, the black elite launched a series of legal challenges to discrimination on the road. With the help of the NAACP and the Urban League, black motorists attempted to end the discriminatory policies of auto insurance companies and hotels. Representations of blacks as reckless drivers had had material consequences for African-American motorist, who had great difficulty acquiring automobile insurance in the 1920s and the 1930s. Wendell Sayers, a real estate broker in Seattle, wrote to Thurgood Marshall, special counsel for the NAACP, in the fall of 1938 seeking a list of insurance companies that would accept blacks. "As a broker," Sayers wrote, "I have applications for automobile liability insurance and property damage insurance on an automobile owned and operated by Negroes and Orientals. In this section of the country, I am advised that insurance companies are refusing this risk because of prejudice, many of them stating frankly why they refuse the risk." Sayers added that he was black and that he considered it his duty to his race to help his clients find insurance companies. The NAACP hear the same story from several states, and both the NAACP and the Urban League eventually initiated legal challenges to insurance companies covering automobile liability. Marshall and others noted that the denial of liability insurance put an unnecessary burden on blacks by forcing them to prove their financial security, pay higher premiums and by denying them a driver's license if they could not acquire insurance.

Various members of the black community also brought suit against discriminatory policies at hotels in the 1930s. One lawsuit initiated by a Washington physician, Dr. B. Hurst, against a New York City hotel prompted a broader campaign against discrimination by hotels. Motoring from Montreal to New York City, Hurst's experiences fit a pattern all too familiar to blacks. Although the family made advance reservations at the Prince George Hotel in New York City, when the group arrived at midnight, the hotel night clerk refused them service. Saying that he never received a room reservation, the clerk turned Hurst and his party our onto the street. In a detailed letter to Walter White, secretary of the NAACP, Hurst described the nightmare of searching the dark city for rooms. After being refused at four different hotels he "elected to try [his] fortunes in the 'Y's' of Harlem."

Hurst's experience gave the NAACP the perfect upper middle-class subject to challenge racial discrimination at hotels…. Despite these early efforts, hotel discrimination persisted throughout the 1930s; landmark legislation did not come until 1964, when the *Heart of Atlanta Motel vs. United States* case made discrimination in the operation of public accommodations illegal under free-commerce laws.

Facing continued discrimination on the open road, African-Americans created separate systems of travel, including resorts, hotels, and travel agents. Fueled by a newly motorized black middle class, resorts such as those at Idlewild,

Michigan, and Elsinore, California, flourished in the 1920s. Although the Idlewild was founded by white developers, members of the black community, such as W. E. B. Du Bois, endorsed it as a haven of summer pleasure for African-Americans. In a 1921 review of possible tourist destinations for black travelers, Du Bois told the readers of *Crisis:* "I know the cost and prejudice and intriguing ugliness of Atlantic City. I have tasted the lovely beauty of the beach at Sea Isle and sat in the pretty dining room at Dale's, Cape May.... Beside Idlewild they are nothing. Not for one moment in fine joy of life, absolute freedom from the desperate cruelty of the color line ... not for one little minute can they rival or catch the bounding pulse of Idlewild."...

At the same time, there were some efforts to create protective associations for black motorists who wished to undertake trips of more than a day. For instance, black auto racing enthusiasts in Chicago formed the AAAA, the Afro-American Automobile Association, in 1924. Leaders in the black automobile community of Chicago included Headen, the automobile inventor, auto driver, and head of his own automobile manufacturing company, who wanted to create an organization that would promote black automobile racing. Recognizing the particular needs of black motorists in general, the organizers enlarged the mission of the AAAA to include assistance to travelers on a national scale....

In 1936, Victor Green, a black travel agent in New York City, answered the call for a national guidebook of hotels and other motor services that were either black-owned or catered to black tourists. He explained, "it has been our idea to give the Negro traveler information that will keep him from running into difficulties, embarrassments and to make his trip more enjoyable." The *Negro Motorist's Green Book* began as a local publication in 1936, but the desire for copies was so great that the booklet was sold nationally in 1937. Widening the scope of information provided, Charles McDowell, collaborator on Negro Affairs for the United States Travel Bureau (also created in 1937), contributed national information to the publication. The publication offered advice on automotive upkeep, but its primary duty was to survey the difficult terrain of the open road and provide accurate information on hotels and other accommodations that would accept black motorists. And at the end of the day, it helped answer the question, "Where will you spend the night?" In this way, the *Negro Motorist's Green Book* was a pioneering effort to make automobility possible for middle-class blacks. The travel guide, along with the auto-related services it contained, helped create a safe, if separate, road for African-American motorists in the period just before World War II, and on into the years after 1945....

This study of black motorists in the early twentieth century describes the world of automobility, and of the open road, as racially contested terrain. It also provides historical context for understanding the appropriation of the automobile in that period by African-Americans to challenge discrimination in spatial and technological terms.

Facing racial prejudice and hostile misrepresentation, black political leaders and newspaper editors used the automobile as an icon of the technological skill and the economic power of the African-American middle class, and to refute white stereotypes of black drivers. As they purchased, drove, and tinkered with cars in the 1920s, African-Americans inserted themselves into a larger national discourse of technological progress—claiming ingenuity, bourgeois responsibility, and, ultimately, equal citizenship in the technological democracy of the open road.

The Racial Politics of the Automobile

PHILIP DELORIA

Geronimo's Cadillac is a historical event. It is a song, an image, a story, a car. It is an idea—or, rather, a cluster of ideas.... A short ride in Geronimo's Cadillac can take us through an exploration of the unexpected juxtaposition of Indians and cars. We might start by splitting the person apart from the vehicle. If you had to pick a single person to stand for *Indianness*, you could do worse than Geronimo, the iconic Apache leader who stands in American popular memory for resistant warriors everywhere and the defeated prisoners we imagine they became.... Likewise, if you had to pick a single car to stand for a world of automobiles, you could do worse than the Cadillac. Its array of rich meanings encompasses, not only technical excellence and social aspiration, but also class and race critique and crossing.... Cars make one visible, asserting publicly that driver and riders are certain kinds of people; it would be hard to top the Cadillac in that regard.

To imagine Geronimo riding in a Cadillac then, is to put two different symbolic systems in dialogue with one another. Indians, we can assert confidently, have been central symbolic elements in American culture for a very long time. Nature and nation, violence and colonial conquest, race and race crossing, nostalgia and guilt—images of Indians have been used to make sense of these things and many more besides....

[I]n the explosion of mass cultural production that characterized the twentieth century, the automobile has been among our most evocative symbols. Mobility, speed, power, progress: these things matter, and Americans of every race, class, gender, and origin have found ways to express them in automotive terms.... As important as the moving of people from point A to point B, however, is the fact that automobiles express a driver's sense of self and of the nature of his or her power. The tough guy who needs a military-style sport utility vehicle, the customized cars emerging out of youth and ethnic cultures, advertisers' gendered invocations of truck-driving manliness and soccer-mom vanliness, the identities, adventures, and nostalgia we invest in the idea of the open road—all these are part and parcel of a culture imaginatively built around automobility.

Things get weird, however, when the symbolic systems built on cars and Indians intersect. Even as today's highways teem with Jeep Cherokees, Pontiac Azteks, Dodge Dakotas, and other "Indian cars," there still remains, for many Americans, something disorienting about Geronimo—and his real and metaphoric descendants—cruising around in Cadillacs. On the one hand, there is a palpable disconnection between the high-tech automotive world and the primitivism that so often clings to the figure of the Indian. At the same time, however, those very distinctions are constantly being squashed back together.... The imagined separation of Indians and cars, and the mixing together of meanings, gets even more estranging when you try to juggle the symbolic ambiguities while at the same time admitting that flesh-and-blood Indian people may own, drive, and like cars. How might one think about the uncertainties conjured up, for instance, when the non-Indian world turns to imagine a Cherokee in a Cherokee—or a Geronimo in a Cadillac?

What kinds of expectations cohered among white Americans when their enthusiasm for automotive technological advance intersected with their twentieth-century perceptions of Indians, newly visible in movies, music, and sporting events? How did Indian people deal with the possibilities Inherent in the automobile? And how did their actions appear in relation to the expectations being built around the unexpected meeting of technology and Indianness?... Over the course of the twentieth century, automotive Indians may not have appeared in American culture as often as warlike Indians did in Hollywood film, but they have lived behind the wheel in all kinds of powerful ways. It is worth pursuing a few of these in some detail....

"Getting civilized in a rush!" exulted a 1904 article in *The Indian's Friend*, a publication of the National Indian Association (NIA), a non-Indian missionary organization: "While settlers were pouring into Bonesteel, South Dakota in anticipation of the opening of the Rosebud reservation, no one's entry created such a sensation as that of Two John, a full blood Sioux, who, with his wife, dashed into town riding in a new $2000 automobile which he had recently purchased in Omaha."

If *The Indian's Friend* represents one strand of the early-twentieth-century perspective—excitement over Two John and his car—the Oklahoma poet Paul Eldridge took a different and darker view in his 1936 poem "Gray Roadster":

> I wonder what ditch in northeastern Oklahoma
> You will presently adorn, slim gray roadster.
> Will the slim young Osage who steers you
> Snuff you out some flaring night
> When the cars roar deep-throated
> Down the Bartlesville road?
> Or will he destroy you by day
> In a flowering plum thicket,
> Intoxicating in its sweet perfume?
> (There are plum trees at every curve of the road in his country.)
> Is your steel more sturdy
> Are your fibers more felted
> Than those of the eight Nashes and the Paige
> Who have preceded you in the hands of the indefatigable destroyer...
> The slim young Osage?

Texas country-folk singer Michael Murphey likely did not know about Two John and his 1904 model automobile but looked back to the same time, to stories he had heard about Geronimo. Living under house arrest at Fort Sill, Oklahoma, Geronimo had apparently once driven a Cadillac around the grounds. Perhaps Murphey had seen Ferguson's picture showing Geronimo in a top hat seated behind the wheel of a car. Or maybe he'd heard about how, in 1905, Geronimo had ridden in an automobile as it chased a poor bison around a rodeo ring in a Wild West spectacle labeled "The Last Buffalo Hunt." Looking, with a sense of irony and mild outrage, from the vantage point of 1972, Murphey wrote a song, "Geronimo's Cadillac," that suggests the extent to which the lives led by Geronimo, Two John, or slim young Osages would be understood as curiosities of the past, framed by expectations that left little room to imagine Indian people taking the wheel:

> Sergeant, sergeant don't you feel, there's something wrong with your automobile?
> Governor, Governor, don't you think it's strange, to see an automobile on the Indian range?
>
> Jesus tells me and I believe it's true; the red man is in the sunset too
> Ripped off his land, won't give it back; and they sent Geronimo a Cadillac.

Consider, finally, a Native critique of automotive expectation, a scene in the Spokane writer Sherman Alexie's 1998 film *Smoke Signals*: a wide shot of a bleak but beautiful western reservation. Two Native women roll up in an "ndn car," battered and worn and capable of being driven only in reverse. Arms crooked over the seat, bodies turned back, eyes fixed on the rear window as they drive, the women converse easily with the film's male protagonists, who sit in the rear. Alexie is offering viewers a reservation sight gag, to be sure, but his reverse-motion Indian car makes viewers think about what is and what is not natural at the crossroads where Automobile Avenue meets Indian Street. As the car rolls against the grain, its movement draws our attention to the idea of Indian *backwardness* and to the familiar expectation of *forward* motion, a white American ideal that connects technological advance with social progress. Placing an Indian at the wheel, the film asks its viewers to consider the ways in which Native people have been perceived to fit—or to be excluded from—a story of social-technological improvement. And so the car moves forward ... backward.

Michael Murphey's question—isn't it strange to see an automobile "on the Indian range," being driven by an Indian person?—framed a key expectation that emerged in the early-twentieth-century meeting of Indians, Anglos, and automobiles. The ironic unnaturalness to which Murphey gestured made sense, one suspects, to Paul Bldridge and his readers in the 1930s and to the Christian missionaries of the NIA in 1904. It is the same strangeness that fuels Sherman Alexie's car, a technology possessed but—in the non-Indian imagination—not really controlled or understood by its Native drivers. That strangeness developed historically, in ways that we can trace through these texts, among others.

There are, of course, important social and economic reasons that might help us account for the unexpectedness that Murphey, the NIA, Eldridge, Alexie, and others have sensed in the idea of an Indian driving a Nash, a Paige, a Ford, or a Cadillac. In 1904, it was rare enough to see an automobile anywhere on American roads, let alone on roads in the American west, where most Native people seemed to reside. How much rarer, then, to see an Indian at the wheel? After all, most Native people lacked the material resources that let one acquire an automobile. It was easy to imagine impoverished and primitive Indians along the roadside or beside the tracks, watching as white modernity passed them by. Two John's sensational entry into Bonesteel quite naturally impressed onlookers as a bizarre anomaly rather than an everyday commonplace. And Eldridge's slim young Osage wrecked his expensive cars within an entire social context that was thought to be anomalous: Indians with oil money.

But there is more to it than that. The sense of estrangement has persisted over the entire life of the automotive century itself, from 1904 through the present. Even as social and economic constraints have eased, the pairing of Indians and automobiles has continued to tweak non-Native anxieties about progress and its costs. Symbolic systems surrounding Indians (nature, violence, primitivism, authenticity, indigeneity) and automobiles (speed, technological advance, independence, identity, progress) continue to evoke powerful points of both intersection and divergence. If the estrangement can be tracked back in time, it can also be broadened beyond the question of cars. Indeed, automotive unexpectedness is part of a long tradition that has tended to separate Indian people from the contemporary world and from a recognition of the possibility of Indian autonomy in that world.

Technology has been a key signifier in that tradition, which has been nurtured since the dawn of Western colonialism and which, of course, reaches far beyond Native America. Every moment of contact in which Europeans sought to impress the natives by firing a gun, demonstrating a watch, predicting an eclipse, or intro-ducing mirrors and steel set expectations about the backwardness of indigenous peo-ple and their seemingly genetic inability to understand and use technology. Those European expectations emerged from (and then reproduced) representations of untutored primitives looking on in astonishment at the wonders of the West.

Within any expectation, of course, there is ample room for confusion and contradiction—*unevenness,* to borrow the literary critic Mary Poovey's word. Ideologies develop, mature, and decay historically, and they do so in tension with other ideological formations. In the case of Indian violence, as we have seen, one can trace rough trajectories of expectation, as well as moments of rhe-torical overlap, around *outbreak* and *pacification.* Expectations bleed together in any single utterance; it is the mingling that often proves most compelling. Such is the case with the ideas that non-Indians held about automobiles and Indians, which have been more uneven and multiple than a bare-bones colonial vision of indigenous technological backwardness....

But, if the very idea of Indian cars signified progress to some, to others it evoked a wholly different set of expectations, one frequently announced in terms of "mindless squandering." In a society that had often claimed to link progress, not only with technology, but also with thrift, automobile purchase (for Indians, at least) was irrational waste. Buying a car inverted, in current terms, the selling of Manhattan Island for twenty-four dollars in beads and trinkets—a little tragic, a little humorous, and all too revealing about an essential Indian inability. Unlike those who saw car purchases as evidence of techno-progress, then, critics of the "squandering school" thought that autos demonstrated the utter impossibility of Indian progress. For them, Indian use of technology revealed, as Paul Eldridge so eloquently suggested, that Indian difference was not evolving into modern sameness but was, instead, racial, essential, and unchanging. Eight Nashes, a Paige, a roadster—Eldridge's slim young Osage would destroy car after car after car after car. Such was his birthright. Indians, claimed even nastier critics, couldn't even *see* cars as progressive technology. Rather, they had always been attracted to "bright and shiny trinkets," of which automobiles were simply the latest fashion. Native people were supposed to be incapable of planning for the future or anticipating the consequences of their actions. They were, in a familiar metaphor, "like children"—or worse. "The Indian who purchases a flivver," observed Indian Office Inspector W. J. Endecott, "is held to be a spendthrift or of unsound mind or of dishonest habit."

These rather different expectations—social development as opposed to essential racial difference, progress as opposed to squandering—emerged from the same root, the idea that technology marked a key difference between the West and the globe's indigenous peoples. Not surprisingly, the expectations collided frequently, often within the same utterance....

Imagining Indians as technological primitives empowered an equal and opposite reaction—a celebration of the mechanical advance of a distinct white modernity. Unlike Geronimo, a white American driver of 1904 was pushing the envelope of history. Nor were such self-understandings confined to a story of social evolution, with whites always at the advanced edge of history and Indians and others destined to trail behind. Technological mastery also proved a racial endowment, a further measure of white superiority. And it was, of course, a gendered notion as well. Seeing technology in masculine terms suggested that Indian men—often feminized historically (and, more recently, in the terms of pacification)—were doubly or trebly unsuited to the automobile. Indian women, caught up the mingled terms of race and gender, might be imagined outside the automobile even more easily.

Indian women and men, one should note, were hardly alone in bringing up the imagined rear. Similar expectations grew up around other social groups as well. How odd, some thought, to see the sons and daughters of slaves driving cars! Wasn't it somehow inappropriate for a Mexican or an Asian immigrant to step behind the wheel? ... Mobility served as a form of empowerment, and it made Indians, African Americans, Latinos, Asians, workers, and all manner of women just a little more threatening. Automobility seemed an undeserved benefit that those lower down on the social ladder had no right to exercise....

In 1972, Michael Murphey had been struck by the freakishness, the irony, even the tragedy of Geronimo sitting in a car. Geronimo was supposed to be defeated but dignified. In a car, he looked incongruous, like something of a joke. It is possible that he was ordered to sit in the car for Ferguson's photograph, a colonial subject bowing to a command performance. But Geronimo was probably better acquainted with automobiles than most of his non-Indian neighbors. He had conducted a relatively lucrative business in personal appearances and autograph signings at several expositions, events that often displayed the latest in American technological progress. He had been in Omaha for the 1898 Trans-Mississippi and International Exposition. In Buffalo, at the 1901 Pan-American Exposition, he had seen the well-lit Electric Tower, 375 feet tall, not to mention airships and, of course, automobiles. More cars were on hand when he went to work at the 1904 Louisiana Purchase Exposition in Saint Louis. And, along with Quanah Parker, American Horse, Hollow Horn Bear, and others, he had ridden—on horseback—in Theodore Roosevelt's 1905 inaugural parade, which featured one of America's first presidential motorcades. Like the performers who accompanied Buffalo Bill Cody, Geronimo had, in fact, traveled widely and seen American technological innovations firsthand. He'd been painted and photographed countless times. So, when Oklahoma's Miller Brothers 101 Ranch decided to sponsor a "Last Buffalo Hunt" as entertainment for a group of visiting newspaper editors, he apparently had few qualms about riding in the car that chased a bison around the rodeo ring. Nor, we can easily imagine, was he quite so taken aback by the prospect of driving a Cadillac around Fort Sill or of sitting in the front scat to have his photograph taken.

Two John's story would seem to be somewhat different, and, perhaps, more typical, than Geronimo's. After all, Two John did not simply hop into an available car; he took the initiative to purchase one. Such was the case with Black Cloud and Billy Two Drinks, with Maria Martinez at San Ildefonso pueblo (she invested earnings from "craft performance" at the 1915 San Diego World's Fair in a car), with Marsie Harjo in Oklahoma, with John Bluebird (who got his through a crooked reservation teacher), with Charles Walking Bull (who traded borrowed Indian-issue cattle for his), with William White (who used his as an employee at the Crow reservation school), and with unknown first purchasers on reservations or in towns across the country. What enabled these people to evade the substantial social and economic restraints and use automobiles to imagine and create a new world on their own terms? ...

An economic window of opportunity and a clear realization of the usefulness of automobiles happened to coincide with sporadic infusions of cash on many reservations in the form of payments from claims cases, land and cattle sales, leasing, allotment sales, and Wild West income....

By far the most regular source of cash on many reservations came from the sale of individual allotments. Put into place by the Dawes General Allotment Act of 1887, the allotment policy sought to divide Indian land held in common and to force Native people to occupy individual homesteads. Allotment sought to impose forcibly a change in social evolutionary status, from hunter-gatherer (the default position for Indians in American popular thought) to sedentary farmer (or, at worst, semi-sedentary rancher). From there, Indians would have, in theory, only a few short steps up the ladder to modern industrial capitalism. Originally, the federal government was to hold the title to an individual's allotment in trust for twenty-five years in order to protect the Indian landholder.

Changes and amendments to the policy, however, rendered this provision stunningly ineffective....

The story of early-twentieth-century land loss is without doubt one of the vilest episodes in the long history of American colonialism—rendered even more so by the professed belief of at least some Indian reformers that they had done the right thing. We should not hesitate to mark it, not simply as classically tragic (though it was all that), but as a tragedy marked by a cold viciousness—and by the pain, damage, and distrust left in its wake. Indeed, the linked terms *tragedy* and *squandering* provided cover for those who contemplated the transactions....

As in the case of Two John, squandered money often went to automobile dealers. At Yankton, the agent noted: "The Indians found it hard to resist the temptation to own a car when they saw their neighbors riding in one." On the Crow reservation, 80 percent of the proceeds from allotment sales went for "cars and other luxuries." Another agent observed that, when the patents were delivered, Indians were dogged by "land buyers, auto agents and fakes of all kinds."...

There is no reason to believe that Indian people saw anything valid in the dismissive words of agents and bureaucrats, who insisted that capital—in the form of land or cash disbursements—should be reinvested into individual farms or ranches or perhaps small local stores. As many non-Indian homesteaders in the West would demonstrate, it took far more capital than that possessed by Indian people to succeed at most twentieth-century farming or ranching, particularly on the plains. And, by expanding the distance one could travel in a day, the car itself would, by the late 1920s, spell an end to the small stores that once dotted western reservations and surrounding homesteader areas. Given the disinclination of many tribes to farm, the abundant examples of non-Indian farm and ranch failure, and the uncertain future offered by government policymakers, buying a car seemed wasteful only to white Americans. For Native societies, automobile purchase and travel may have been a more sensible way to make a meaningful life than to take a horse-drawn plow to the soil.

And so many Indian people bought cars. In truth, automobile purchase often fit smoothly into a different logic—long-lived Indian traditions built around the utilization of the most useful technologies that non-Indians had to offer. Just as many plains people had eagerly adopted the horse, transforming their societies in the process, so too did Black Cloud, Billy Two Drinks, and other cultural experimenters of the early twentieth century explore the useful potential of the automobile. At the founding of the Rosebud and Pine Ridge reservations, for example, the leaders Red Cloud and Spotted Tail had insisted on negotiating freight-hauling contracts for reservation goods and government annuities, and freighting had become a small, culturally resonant industry on those reservations. It made good sense for Billy Two Drinks to consider moving from teams to automobiles, not only in terms of a capitalist service market, but also in terms of the cultural transformations and persistences that allowed horse nomads to become cowboys and freight drivers in the first place. Would Black Cloud or Two Drinks have seen their automobiles as capital investments? Hard to know. It would not be out of line, however, to suggest that their purchases made sense within the social and cultural frameworks in which they lived.

The auto and the mobility that made up the word automobile pointed exactly to the ways in which mobility helped Indian people preserve and reimagine their own *autonomy* in the face of the reservation system. Reservations, we know, functioned as administrative spaces, meant to contain Indian people, fixing them in place through multiple forms of supervision. Despite the assault on Native land bases, many Indian reservations, particularly in the west, remained landscapes characterized by great distances. Automotive mobility helped Indian people evade supervision and take possession of the landscape, helping make reservations into distinctly tribal spaces. Indeed, one might read in the antipathy toward Indian automobility a slight whiff of the nervousness surrounding outbreak and independence.... [L]ong-distance travel—and especially such travel between reservations—allowed Native people to imagine an even broader vision of Indian country, one that transcended individual tribes and places and helped create new expressions of the pan-Indian and the intertribal. It is no coincidence that the rise of an intertribal powwow circuit began at the same moment as Indian people were acquiring and using automobiles....

Automobiles must have seemed particularly useful for the ways they opened up the new while continuing to serve older cultural ideals. The car offered transportation for the frequent visits and gatherings so often part of Native life. On the plains, cars easily served as mobile housing, reprising the older functions of both horse and tipi. Indeed, one of the reasons why Native people seemed more inclined to buy cars than motorcycles may well lie in their ability to serve as both transportation and communal living space.... Within their cars, Indian families sometimes replicated the social arrangements of the tipi or other lodging, building blanket partitions in order to maintain the avoidance relations necessary to proper kinship behavior. A son-in-law at the wheel might thus avoid looking at his mother-in-law, who occupied her own compartment in the back seat. And, where plains people had once decorated and rubbed their horses with sage, they began to place the plant across the front dashboard....

Rather than succumb to the powerful temptation to imagine Indian automobility as anomalous, we might do better to see it in Indian terms—as a cross-cultural dynamic that ignored, not only racial categories, but also those that would separate out modernity from the Indian primitive so closely linked to it. Automobiles, in this sense, can be seen to stand for a broader history of Native use of technology. Indeed, cars made up only one prominent branch in a family tree of such engagements, which have ranged from horses and guns to cameras and computers.

FURTHER READING

Adas, Michael. *Machines as the Measure of Men: Science, Technology, and Ideologies of Western Dominance* (1990).

Allen, Michael Thad, and Gabrielle Hecht. *Technologies of Power: Essays in Honor of Thomas Parke Hughes and Agatha Chipley Hughes* (2001).

Aron, Cindy S. *Working at Play: A History of Vacations in the United States* (1999).

Belasco, Warren J. *Americans on the Road: From Autocamp to Motel, 1910–1945* (1997).

Clarsen, Georgine. *Eat My Dust: Early Women Motorists* (2008).

Flink, James J. *The Automobile Age* (1990).

Jackle, John J. *Motoring: The Highway Experience in America* (2008).

———. *The Tourist: Travel in Twentieth-Century North America* (1985).

Kline, Ronald. *Consumers in the Country: Technology and Social Change in Rural America* (2000).

McCannell, Dean. *The Tourist: A New Theory of the Leisure Class* (1999).

McShane, Clay. *Down the Asphalt Path: The Automobile and the American City* (1995).

Miller, Danieil, ed. *Car Cultures* (2001).

Oldenziel, Ruth. *Making Technology Masculine: Men, Women, and Modern Machines in America, 1870–1945* (2004).

Packer, Jeremy. *Mobility without Mayhem: Safety, Cars, and Citizenship* (2008).

Rothman, Hal K. *Devil's Bargains: Tourism in the Twentieth-Century American West* (2000).

Schaffer, Marguerite S. *See America First: Tourism and National Identity, 1880–1940* (2001).

Scharff, Virginia. *Taking the Wheel: Women and the Coming of the Motor Age* (1992).

Sieler, Cotton. *Republic of Drivers: A Cultural History of Automobility in America* (2008).

Wrobel, David M., and Patrick T. Long, eds. *Seeing and Being Seen: Tourism in the American West* (2001).

CHAPTER 9

Radio Enters the Home, 1920–1942

The beginnings of broadcasting help explain the role of the state in the production and dissemination of popular culture. Radio's beginnings show how the federal government and business worked together to shape entertainment. The commercialized format developed in radio and carried over into television and the Internet was not natural, but a construction that served the interests of business and government. Commercial radio, and the resistance to it, changed ideas of public and private, national audiences, citizenship, and the technological basis of popular culture.

Radio began with kids building radios out of spare parts in order to talk to each other across the country. As wonderfully described by historian Susan Douglas, the first "hams" (middle-class, urban, white men and boys) experimented with radio transmission and reception in the decade before World War I by using inexpensive crystals as detectors, oatmeal boxes wound with wire stolen from construction sites as tuning coils, and telephones as headsets. Even before broadcast radio was conceived, amateurs used radio to communicate across long distances. The active participation of these young, male hobbyists influenced the shape of the radio industry soon to be controlled by large corporations.

In 1919, one of the hams, Frank Conrad, a Westinghouse engineer, began airing a regular program of recorded music from a well-made transmitter in his Pittsburgh garage. Lots of folks wanted to listen so they sent sons, or the war veteran down the block who had learned about radio in the service, to buy the materials needed to build a radio receiving set. Westinghouse sold more equipment when Conrad broadcast. To further encourage sales, Westinghouse moved Conrad's transmitter to the top of their factory, applied for a federal license, set up regular transmitting hours, and named the station KDKA. Radio had changed from point-to-point communication into a potential mass medium.

Before the radio networks developed in 1926, listeners and the large radio companies explored other possibilities for programming and financing radio broadcasting. These experiments illustrated roads not taken in American media organization and proved that commercialized broadcasting was neither natural nor inevitable, but simply the easiest and most profitable solution for the corporations already involved in radio. Companies who manufactured radio equipment expected to profit from their radio operations, but options other than selling time on the air existed, as did nonprofit alternatives to commercial broadcasting. The particular commercial form American broadcasting took resulted from the interaction of several different decisions and predispositions, beginning with a desire, on the part of both ordinary people and the radio industry, for national radio service. As radio stations sprang up, built by newspapers, feed stores, municipalities, colleges, and radio equipment manufacturers, the hams (like the hackers who spread an interest in the Internet) helped others build receiving sets and, in the process, indoctrinated new audience members into the thrill of receiving signals from distant places.

By the time of the 1927 Radio Act (amended and extended in the 1934 Communications Act), radio networks existed, tying stations together into a national system by sending radio programs over telephone wires from New York for local rebroadcast. Broadcast advertising was also well-established, with advertisers overcoming their initial reluctance to using radio. But, while setting up the Federal Radio Commission (which became the Federal Communications Commission, still the regulator of broadcasting) and insisting that broadcasting operate for the "public convenience, interest and necessity," the two laws ignored networks and broadcast advertising. The corporations that controlled radio and advertised over the air pressured the federal government to narrowly regulate broadcasting and not challenge its commercial basis. Politicians found radio an important political tool, already recognizing broadcasters as key allies, and so ensured that radio continued with enough regulation to make it technologically possible but without any challenges to its commercial and centralized programming. Listeners remained fascinated and thrilled by the high-quality entertainment, news, and sports coming into their living rooms and radio played a crucial role in American culture through the Great Depression and World War II. Understanding the development of radio, which drew its programming and structure from minstrel shows and vaudeville, helps explain the commodified nature not only of television but of many other popular culture forms as well.

 # DOCUMENTS

These documents include the stories of all those involved in early radio, from broadcasters and listeners to critics and federal government regulators. Document 1, although written in 1937, is a memoir of an early broadcaster remembering the challenges of being first "on the air." Document 2 presents an article from a radio magazine that quoted listeners about their thoughts on radio programming. The humor magazine *Ballyhoo* ridicules broadcast advertising in Document 3. A Federal Communications Commission report, presented here in Document 4, recounted a range of opinions about commercial broadcasting, but in many ways this inquiry (and the report about it) substituted for any federal legislative action regulating broadcast advertising. President Franklin Roosevelt saw the importance of broadcasting for politics and governing and his Fireside Chats became an important way for the president to speak to the public. Document 5 is an excerpt from one of the early Chats, given at the beginning of Roosevelt's first term in office. Like all advertisers, radio broadcasters worried about what listeners thought. Paul Lazarsfeld was one of the first radio researchers, a precursor of those who compiled broadcast ratings and, in Document 6, Lazarsfeld carried over into radio the idea that women were the most important consumers.

1. Broadcaster Credo Fitch Harris Remembers
Early Radio Broadcasting, 1937

... The Department of Commerce controlled whatever radio affairs were astir at the time, for the Federal Radio Commission and the subsequent Federal Communications Commission were pleasures yet to be experienced....

Thus to that Department we wrote that I was coming for a license to operate. The law requiring such procedure seemed scarcely to have been printed long enough for the ink to dry. There was no question of denial, for what difference could a radio station make in the serenity of our national life? Who wanted to spend money for one of them, anyhow, when few people would go to the costly trouble of buying some mysterious kind of a contraption which might, or might not, enable them to listen? And listen to what? More particularly, for how long? The great American public knew little or nothing about it, and even those who did, conceived it to be a sort of glorified toy that would soon drop into disuse, like Christmas dolls and wind-up trains....

In the Department of Commerce a young man stated that our call letters were WHAS, our wave length 360 meters, except when broadcasting weather reports when we would use 485 meters.

"What does WHAS stand for?" I asked.

"Search me," he answered agreeably.

"But what does that mean about 360 meters for programs and 485 for weather?"

"I suppose you'll have to work it out for yourself. I'm just reading it off your license."...

"Please realize," I continued ... "that you're looking upon the neediest needy who ever came in here. Isn't there anyone who can shine a little more light on the situation?"

"Secretary Hoover is in a meeting and Mr. Carson's away on a government boat. I doubt if the President would know. You might ask Congress. Anyway," he added genially, "I was told to keep this for you. You'd better take it."

And thus our first license was literally thrust at me. Looking back, it seems unbelievable that there should have been no "hearings," no entanglements, nor even a pleasant little legal battle which today, in similar circumstances, would be fought out before a body of honorable gentlemen,—the Radio Division of the FCC—sitting in banc with the wisdom of Solomon stamped upon their patient faces, as they listen to a flow of technical nomenclature that fifteen years ago had not got into dictionaries....

In the beginning when 360 meters had been assigned to all stations, happily there were only a few and those widely scattered. For, although we did not become aware of it until later, it was impossible to tune those clumsy little transmitters with any reasonable degree of accuracy and, because of that, their mutual interference was negligible to the listener. Crystal sets, which remained constant

Credo Fitch Harris, *Microphone Memoirs of the Horse and Buggy Days of Radio* (New York: Bobbs-Merrill, 1937).

and only caught the nearest signal, were almost entirely used at first. But shortly more efficient types began to be manufactured which could "pull in" distant stations, and therefore if all transmitters were operating on a precisely fixed frequency, with no variations whatsoever, listening to any particular one would have been unpleasant because of heterodyning from the others. That gradual improvement in receivers, as well as correspondingly more efficient transmitters, resulted in the necessity of giving stations different wave lengths, as at present. But that came later....

Our license was good for ninety days. Before the end of those three short months we were told to file another application for a further ninety-day permission. That procedure continued until a few years ago, when licenses—or franchises—were extended to the noble length of six months.

Some future historian will write the surprising anomaly of these present day big businesses, which high powered stations have come to be, possessing faith enough to risk a fortune in an undertaking that holds no guarantee of continuance beyond half a year. For a station cannot own its wave length, as Congress had decreed that all radio channels belong to the public domain. I pray you, do not entertain the idea that our path is strewn with roses.

In recent hearings before the Federal Communications Commission, broadcasting during those first two years that we operated was twice referred to as "the prehistoric era." And, indeed, that expression fit it like a girdle. The dawning industry, compared to its present development, was tolerably suggestive of that first imaginary animalcule which emerged from ooze to become, in time, a mastodon—or man, if my fundamentalist friends will permit the simile....

To get back to our knitting! The largest transmitter then known was ordered, and a laboratory engineer came out ahead of time to select a place for its installation. We were becoming properly excited....

I do vividly recall his explanation of what a radio wave looked like:

"Throw a stone into a still pond, and the undulating circles, pressing outward, are an exact imitation."...

Since the station was formally established as a department of two daily papers, and their articles of incorporation were changed to embrace it, we became by law and mutual interests one of that large family—the baby, true enough, yet definitely creating a third factor in the organization which was now composed of: a morning newspaper, an afternoon newspaper, and WHAS....

Our first idea of locating the studios in the parent building was discarded when it became known that vibrations of the presses would work havoc with microphones and other delicate radio adjustments. So we were given space high up in an adjacent storage building, where silence was the only virtue, and the construction of quarters went forward.

I shall never forget that studio. To reach it you had to take the *Courier-Journal* elevator to its topmost limit. There, amid the unceasing noise of busy linotypes, you might gaze around more or less helplessly until directed to a solid iron door. Two feet beyond this you came upon an iron and asbestos fire door. We must have been expected to burst into flames at almost any moment, because the underwriters specified fire doors aplenty. Stepping then upon an iron platform which spanned a dizzy height between the two buildings, you would climb a narrow iron stairway. It was not uncommon to see visitors carefully avoid touching that iron hand-rail, lest they receive some kind of an electrical shock—for the average mind was obsessed by curiously superstitious fears concerning us.

At the top of these stairs stood a large porcelain drinking water affair which a janitor filled each morning with ice. A few paces farther, still overhanging the chasm, was the little motor generator. Then, turning left, you would pass another fire door and enter our reception room. To one side of this stood the transmitter behind a glass partition, with a large and threatening red sign: "DANGER." Straight through the reception room was my office, with a secretarial desk and typewriter. From this a door led into the music room—the studio in fact.

Perhaps that particular room was designed to be no more torturous than others of its kind throughout America.

Best acoustical engineering thought called for padded walls, padded ceiling and heavily carpeted floor. Not a whisper of sound could be tolerated from the outside. Within the room no slight reverberation of a musical note was supposed to bounce from any surface and distort microphonic reproduction. Our windows were small, very small, yet they must be tightly closed and covered with padded frames. Electric fans? O, horrors, no! Thus spoke the experts before experience taught them kinder ways, and as a matter of course their finished product looked and felt like an air-tight padded cell. It was a madhouse, too, upon occasions!...

A dynamic, wholesome looking cuss dashed into my office that pleasant October morning in 1925 as if he had only ten seconds to catch a train. He came from Chicago, and brought its stimulating breezes with him. Before he talked fifteen minutes I felt like I'd been taking a guaranteed tonic for six months. His idea was explained, adopted, and The Mid-Continent Broadcasters' Association became a fact. Five other stations besides our own, representing Chicago, St. Louis, Denver, Ft. Worth,—the sixth eludes me—would take an advertising program of one hour, which he was prepared to sell. In the order named, these would cover the week— that is, Chicago on Mondays, Louisville on Tuesdays, St. Louis on Wednesdays, Denver on Thursdays, Ft. Worth on Fridays, and the one I have forgotten on Saturdays. The client, a cigar manufacturer, would thereby get coverage from some mid-continent point with great regularity. Each station would charge him $400 an hour for time and music, and the contract would run ten weeks.

Parenthetically, that client, desiring to test the pulling power of this new advertising medium, included in his copy for these microphones an offer to mail, free of charge, three cigars to everyone who wrote him. During our third week he wired an urgent appeal to the six of us: "Please stop immediately. Am using twenty girls to mail cigars and four days behind already. We cannot stand it. No one can stand it. Stop immediately." So our first customer folded up because of too much advertising, and the Mid-Continent Associates, for some forgotten cause, dissolved. But we had launched into the selling of time.

Thus was borne to the ear what is now internationally known as "the American system." The irritability it soon stirred up has never been matched on land or water. Earlier contented listeners suddenly exploded and showered us with indignant letters. One wrote: "If it's the last act of my life, I'm going to invent something to turn my radio off during those advertising talks, and turn it on again when the music starts!"

But before this man's genius had had a chance to bloom he, like most of his countrymen, began to realize the advantage of the American system over the so-called "European system," where governments own the stations, prohibit advertising, and listeners pay a yearly tax on each receiver they own. A proportion of that levy goes for the buying of radio entertainers, and the programs are said to be inferior to ours. I do not mean that foreign countries lack artists entirely comparable to those in the States, but the broadcasts suffer from an absence of competition.

Here, large advertisers employ trained staffs to build the best available air shows, and cost means little when vieing with the standards, charm and interest of preceding and following periods. None can afford to suffer by comparisons. They pay staggering prices for Metropolitan Opera stars and choruses, symphony and dance orchestras, headliners from successful theatrical productions, tragedians, comedians, punch and punchinello, picked up from coast to coast upon a network of copper wires and brought to millions of firesides. So the American listener, in lieu of touching the nerve of his purse for another tax, rather prefers hearing a few words about some motor car or cigarette as payment for a snappier, better and greater variety of free entertainment....

After our return from Detroit, while waiting the arrival of the transmitter.... I found ... office space and began to write masses of letters.... I gathered a list of musical persons in Louisville and contiguous areas, and began my letters—explaining what a radio telephone broadcasting station was and inviting them to come and register their willingness to entertain for us—free of charge, as a matter of course. The idea of paying radio talent was then as remote as selling time to advertisers....

For it should be remembered there were no networks in those days, and no electrical wizard had devised a way of picking up entertainment by telephone lines at remote control points. Every program we broadcast had to originate within our own padded room, so it was necessary to have a long string of volunteers on call and for them to be dependable enough to cross our threshold promptly thirty minutes before starting time. Otherwise there would be no concert, or one that got off late. What those troubadors wished to sing or play I left to their own choosing, and half an hour was none too long in which to orientate their introductions, think up a few words about each musical selection and, if possible, some interesting fact concerning the life of its composer.

Although the Department of Commerce had granted us use of the entire twenty-four hours, should we want it, on the other hand there might be trouble afoot were we to remain entirely silent or even tardy in beginning periods which we had publicly committed ourselves to fill. So my letters, while meant to be subtly enticing, were emphatic.

You may think that the preparation of shows from four to five o'clock every afternoon, and seven-thirty to nine each night except Sundays, would be quite a simple undertaking. Comparing that weekly total of sixteen hours to our present schedule of one hundred and twenty-four, it is. But sometime when you've nothing else to do, try it for a few years, depending entirely upon unpaid amateur talent. First, however, accept a friendly tip and engage your room in a sanitorium....

As our opening night approached, citizens almost raided electrical stores to buy crystal sets and earphones. Tube receivers had scarcely come into the broadcasting picture. A scattered few were built by budding young engineers (without loud speakers, of course), yet they spread out over so much room—or rather so many rooms—that few homes were physically able to house them. Crystal sets were fairly good while they worked. On going dead, the frantic fan would wiggle his wire whisker to another part of the crystal, or another, and still another. Then he might dash to the medicine chest and give it a dab of rubbing alcohol. If that failed he might put it in the oven for a ten minute baking. Meanwhile the concert was probably over. Those were good recipes in their day and generation, and during our first year of broadcasting we must have repeated them by telephone to a thousand anxious inquirers.

Carefully I had gone over my talent list and picked out the choicest material for our first big night, announced to open Tuesday, July 18, 1922....

We were to open at seven-thirty o'clock.... By seven-twenty the studio was closed. There we waited as the clock ticked off minute after minute. Mercury in the thermometer was about the only other thing that moved. Then, one by one handkerchiefs appeared, but I frowned them back into their pockets. Handkerchiefs might make a noise.

Two minutes more to go! At the end of those torturous one hundred and twenty seconds a red signal light would flash on the studio wall, and we would be—on the air! I explained this quickly in a hoarse whisper, and once more warned the room to silence. No cough! No sneeze! My heart was pounding. Our star soprano was breathing painfully. I could see the contralto's pulse beating in her throat. All nerves were tuned to concert pitch. Suddenly the red light glowed! Someone gave a little gasp. I, also, wanted to gasp, but swallowed it and exclaimed in my best manly voice: "This is WHAS, the radio telephone broadcasting station of the *Courier-Journal* and the *Louisville Times,* in Louisville, Kentucky!"

It was the first cry of our infant broadcaster. A rather long cry, but a lusty one....

Going in town next day I passed a church. On the bulletin-board out front was the subject of the pastor's following Sabbath sermon: GOD IS ALWAYS BROADCASTING.

Broadcast had instantly taken its place in the public mind. At least, throughout our locality, it became an active and controversial subject of conversation, whereas two months earlier the word was scarcely mentioned....

2. Listeners Speak Out in *Radio Broadcast* magazine, 1927
Answers the Questionnaire Brought Forth

Since we prepare this department many weeks in advance of publication, at the time of writing the first responses to the questionnaire in the January issue have only just come in. And very painstakingly and drolly filled out they are! Of course we won't be able to deduce any general conclusions as to the tastes

John Wallace, "The Listener's Point of View," *Radio Broadcast*, 10(February, March, April, May, 1927).

of our clientele until all the replies are in…. But it seems only fair that we share with you the fun of reading the replies. Here are excerpts from the hundred or so answers we have at hand:

> Do you listen in your radio as you would to a regular show, or do you simply turn it on and use it as a background to other activities: (This was the first question asked).

I always listen to the radio as I would to a regular show. If conversation or other activities must be indulged in, I shut off the radio….

Every evening *Radio.* (Other activities are the background.)

Your suspicion is right. We smoke, drink our very old rye (at least two weeks old), and talk and talk, and when the radio interferes we turn it down, *or* shut it off altogether.

Usually as to a regular show. Select programs carefully. Do not listen to all the "bunk" on the air.

If something special, a feature worth while, we listen until the bitter end. Generally however radio is "background."

50.50

Listen about 25 per cent. Use as background 75 per cent. (Your suspicion is correct.)

Yes we give it our undivided attention, when programs are good— otherwise we choke it off.

For a good feature program we listen as though at the theater. Many programs aren't worth listening to, so the set is turned off to avoid competition.

Used as a background mostly, because the general program is of such quality that neither the artist nor the selection is such as to demand continuous attention….

> Do you regularly tune-in on distant stations or do you regularly rely on your local stations: [This was question two.]

Rely on local stations primarily because congestion has almost ruined DX reception.

I am emphatically a DX hound. I get more pleasure from a distant program or a new station than from any amount of locals, who are always with us.

The station from which the program sounds best regardless of location, DX means nothing to a sensitive receiver. All stations are locals.

Probably three fourths of our entertainment comes from the local or near-by broadcasters, *but,* the lure of distance still holds its charms. I have often seen the statement made that the DX hound is vanishing and this is all wrong. It is a natural error. Most radio writers are experimenters and the realization finally comes to all experimenters that we must as yet rely on the locals for *consistent good* reception. The new owner of a radio set demands distance … and if his set does not get distance regularly he is dissatisfied. The man who knows nothing of radio expects too much. The man who knows much of radio expects reception over great distances to be decidedly inferior to that of locals—nevertheless most of us still get a kick out of hearing that station two thousand miles away….

90 per cent, local, 10 per cent, distance.

Yes sir!! DX gives a thrill that locals, no matter how good they are, cannot produce. The man who says he only wants locals has a good reason for saying it. His set won't get anything else. If he could get DX easily he would be just as much of a fan as the real DX bug.

The writer is a DX hound. This comes after the program part of the family retires.

Rely on local (Cleveland) or near-by stations. DX in my opinion is a thing of the past.

I try regularly in spite of the advertisers, "hi-power," and the congested wave channels. What would the average receiving set be like to-day if there had never been any so called "DX hounds"?

What do you call distant stations: For clearness and volume our (Florida) best programs come from Chicago and New York....

Keep two complete sets in commission. One in living room for general entertainment and *quality* reproduction. One in den for fishing but the fishing has become almost impossible of late due to congestion of ether.

Confirmed DX hound of worst variety.

Not interested in DX. Bores me stiff to hear or read anything concerning DX. Rely entirely on local New York and Newark stations. (not more than 5 in all.)...

What are the six best broadcasts you have heard: [This was the last question.]

Answers to this question, as you may suspect, cover a lot of ground. Here are a few we come across oftener than others as we glance through the replies: Radio Industries Banquet; Dempsey-Tunney Fight: Victor concerts; National Broadcasting Company Inaugural program: McNamee's World Series 1925: Goldman Band; various Atwater Kent and Eveready Hours; Boston Symphony; New York Symphony; Balkite, Maxwell, Ipana, Goodrich, Royal, A & P, Clicquot, Whittall, and so forth, Hours; Ford and Glenn; Jones and Hare; President's Messages; Army-Navy Game; 1925 and 1926 Democratic National Convention; U. S. Marine Band; Damrosch Recitals; KDKA Little Symphony; WGN'S "Down the Mississippi"; Dr. Cadman; KDKA Westinghouse Band; "Roxy"; Penn. Railroad Hour, etc....

Herewith some of your own opinions, listeners, as culled from supplementary notes accompanying the questionnaire replies....

LINCOLN, NEBRASKA.

SIR:

Ah! Another questionnaire! I hasten to answer.... Now as to the questions. You need not apologize for that first one. I am a traveling man and I have been entertained in at least 200 private homes this year. I can not remember a single place in the bunch where the broadcasts were listened to as one would in a show. Even the prayers in the church services were interrupted with bright remarks, and other irresponsible and extraneous material. If I were sure Carl Drexer would get a peek at it I should call it "static," but it wasn't. I'll bet a quart of "snake juice" that there would not be so many church services broadcast if the parsons could sit around the garage stove with some of their audience....

SIR:

With a large and varied field of entertainment to choose from, I have no quarrel to pick with any of the broadcasters. Each is endeavoring to the best of his ability to attract customers, much in the same manner as the stage purveyors do. To me the element of chance is part of the fun. One night everything off color, the next an oriental dream. It's good and soul satisfying philosophy to take the good with the bad and mediocre in alternate doses.

Again I have no quarrel with direct or indirect advertising; at least I am satisfied to know, in a decent way, to whom I am indebted for the privilege of being entertained. I protest the present method adopted by the [New York] *Herald Tribune's* daily program, wherein it prints "Orchestra and Artists" 9:00 P.M. Worthless stuff. If it is the Eveready Hour, I am entitled to know it. I like them and when I see that name, and all others for that matter, I can make my own choice without prejudice, just as I choose rubber tires, perfumes, radio sets or batteries....

HARTFORD, CONNECTICUT.

SIR:

Our radio usually runs most of the time each evening when we are home and reception conditions are good. Dinner music during our evening meal. The local newspaper is scanned for programs of merit and we tune-in on those appealing to us as being most interesting and of best quality.

When any particular event of outstanding interest is advertised we generally plan to invite a few friends and make an evening of it....

POUGHKEEPSIE, NEW YORK

SIR:

We usually start the radio at 6 P.M. and keep it going while we carry on our other activities. Of course we follow the programs and pick out the numbers which we like best, changing from station to station. It usually takes a concert like the Victor Concert last evening to make us stop our bridge game and give our whole attention to the music. However we seem to hear everything that's going on even while we're concentrating on something else. A jazz concert, however, always means that we tune-in on another station or turn off the radio entirely. Some dance music is all right but most of it sounds like—well, I could make better music by dumping the kitchen utensils on the floor. We enjoy popular music as long as it is music. You may think we are inconsistent but we do enjoy banjo and Hawaiian music....

BISBEE, ARIZONA

SIR:

Now that you have given your readers an opportunity to tell what they do with their radio receivers, through the medium of your questionnaire, I would like to suggest that you give us another questionnaire to find out what the sentiment is about elimination or muzzling about ninety per cent of the broadcast stations of the country. I refer particularly to the broadcasters who are dishing out direct advertising and grinding out the most mediocre of programs. Radio is doomed as a source of entertainment unless something is done quickly to remedy the heterodyning nuisance. It is impossible to listen fifteen minutes to a satisfactory program without having the program ruined by some interfering station. With the many thousands of "better, cost less" bloopers, and the heterodyning of interfering stations, radio reception is nothing more than a horrible experience just now. As a partial remedy to the heterodyning trouble why not put all the broadcasters who do direct advertising on one wavelength, reducing their power, and then let them advertise and heterodyne each other to their hearts' content. It would try the patience of Job to try to tune-in a program these nights that did not have its infernal jazz background, or some advertiser dishing out the "dope" on the wares he has to sell. The radio advertiser is a Worse offender of decency than the billboard advertiser, whose only offense is to spoil part of the scenery. It is high time for some drastic action to curb these nuisances, and cut out some of the "tank town" broadcasting stations whose only excuse for being on the air is to sell something, or radio is going to pass out as a family entertainer. RADIO BROADCAST, being the outstanding radio publication of the Western Hemisphere, should "take the bull by the horns" and build a good sized fire under him. Otherwise our radio receivers are only fit to look at. Personally, I am just about through with mine if this messy situation is going to be a regular diet....

3. Humor Magazine *Ballyhoo* Makes Fun of Commercials, 1931

> Ballyhoo presents herewith a new departure that will revolutionize the Radio Industry, and isn't it about time?

Here you are, folks! Why pay out a lot of money for a radio set full of static, more money for electric current, tubes, and repairs, when, with our Home Correspondence Course, and a few simple gadgets, you can have exactly the same enjoyment! Yes, sir, exactly the same enjoyment!

This is all you need. An old set of dinner chimes, or a cow bell; an old Victrola and some old records, the older the better, and our specially prepared programs.

Get the family together some night and invite in some friends, then go in the other room, or hide behind the couch with your dinner chimes, your Victrola and one of our programs. All you have to do is read our program aloud. Why after you're through, they will say. "My Goodness Gracious! Where did you get that beautiful radio set!"

These Home Radio Programs are offered to readers of Ballyhoo for the amazingly small sum of five (5) cents a piece, and we have on hand over five thousand different programs!. Think of it! You may select from 5,000

"Be Your Own Broadcasting Station!" *Ballyhoo* (October 1931), 37.

programs! Send $5 for our booklet "What is Home Without a Radio," and select your own programs. Here, Program A—3689.

All set? All right, now hit the dinner gong, but not too hard, and read aloud as if you had a hot potato in your mouth. If you haven't got a hot potato, a handful of nails will suffice.

Station C. R. A. P.! Good evening, mugs! This is station C. R. A. P., broadcasting on an all too frequency of 3,657 killowats, and watt a killowat! When you hear the gong, it will be exactly one and one hundreth second past eight o'clock, Eastern standard time, and who the hell cares! (Smack the gong) This time ladies and gentlemen of the radio audience, is furnished by the Hellova Watch company, makers of fine shovels and bird cages. This is Percival P. Zilch, your station announcer, and if you don't like my voice go lay an egg.

At this hour, ladies and gentlemen of the radio audience, we bring you, Gawd help you, the Ducky Wucky Hour. Remember, ladies and gentlemen of the radio audience. Duckies are always KIND to the throat....

We'll say it again! ... In fact we'd keep on saying it all night, only we know you want to hear some music (Now turn on the victrola. Play "After the Ball is over," Or "Waltz me around again, Willie," but don't play more than a minute.) Now, ladies and gentlemen of the radio audience, Doctor Aloyisius Q. Zilch will tell you what he thinks of Ducky Wuckies! Remember, seventy-five thousand nine hundred and fifty-six physicians (we would have had seventy-five thousand, nine hundred and fifty-seven only he reached for an ankle instead of a Ducky, and her husband was home!). Ha! Ha! endorse Ducky Wuckies! Doctor Aloyisius Q. Zilch! All right Doctor!....

Ladies and gentlemen of the radio audience! Hoffen stohk du bista mockloffenpoop do shaney gazoggle!

Thank you. Doctor! The Ducky Wucky orchestra will now play "In the shade of the old apple tree!"

See how simple it is? And you ought to see our Fleishman Yeast Program! It's a honey! Order now!

4. Federal Radio Commission Reports on Commercial Broadcasting and Its Regulation, 1932

What Plans Might be Adopted to Reduce, to Limit, to Control, and Perhaps to Eliminate the Use of Radio Facilities for Commercial Advertising Purposes.

Answer.... Any plan the purpose of which is to eliminate the use of radio facilities for commercial advertising purposes will, if adopted, destroy the present system of broadcasting.

Any plan to reduce, limit, and control the use of radio facilities for commercial advertising purposes to a specific amount of time or to a certain per cent

Federal Radio Commission, *Commercial Radio Broadcasting: Report of the FRC in reply to Senate Resolution 129*, Seventy-second Congress, First Session (Washington, D.C.: Government Printing Office, 1932).

of the total time utilized by the station must have its inception in new and additional legislation which either fixes and prescribes such limitations or specifically authorizes the commission to do so under a general standard prescribed by that legislation. While the commission may under the existing law refuse to renew a license to broadcast or revoke such license because the character of program material does not comply with the statutory standard of public interest, convenience, and necessity, there is at present no other limitation upon the use of radio facilities for commercial advertising.

Such regulation, whether specifically undertaken by Congress or delegated by it to the commission, could extend both to the quality and the quantity of commercial advertising. While the quality of advertising might and probably would be difficult of adequate regulation, the quantity of such advertising could be limited to certain hours in the day or night and to a certain number of such hours; also, provision could be made limiting the advertising matter to a certain per cent of the time devoted to total programs or commercial programs....

[I]t will be observed from the matter collected in this report that while sales talks, etc., consumed 6.55 per cent of the total hours used during the sample week by the 582 stations of all classes and that such matters consumed 18.11 per cent of the total commercial hours of such stations, sales talks and related matters consumed only 11.27 per cent of the commercial programs of chain stations as compared to 20.03 per cent of the commercial programs of local stations. A flat restriction placed upon the amount of time used for sales talks without regard to the location, power, and activities of stations would, in all probability, work inequitable results. Moreover, and in any case or class, limitations upon the use of time for commercial advertising, if too severe, would result in a loss of revenue to stations which, in all probability, would be reflected in a reduction in the quantity and quality of programs available to the public.

The radio act of 1927 was obviously designed to permit the licensees of broadcasting stations the maximum of latitude in the matter of program material. Such licensees are in a singularly favorable position to learn what the audience wants to hear and to make the necessary changes in program material and in methods of presentation that will cause their programs to be favorably received by a substantial majority of the listeners. The adoption of regulation of the sort herein described should be undertaken only when it clearly appears that a majority or at least a considerable number of the licensees have failed to operate their stations in a manner acceptable to a majority of the listening public. If, in the opinion of Congress, that time has now arrived, we conceive it to be advisable to enact such legislation as will permit the commission to impose such regulations as the circumstances from time to time seem to warrant rather than legislation imposing specific restrictions and unflexible limitations.

WHAT RULES OR REGULATIONS HAVE BEEN ADOPTED BY OTHER COUNTRIES TO CONTROL OR TO ELIMINATE THE USE OF RADIO FACILITIES FOR COMMERCIAL ADVERTISING PURPOSES.

Answer. Broadcasting systems in foreign countries that are supported entirely by revenue derived by a tax or license fee for receiver set ownership or by government subsidy do not, as a rule, accept commercial advertising, whereas stations owned and operated by private interests are supported mainly from advertisements and subsidies paid voluntarily by the listening public.

A few of the foreign governments have rules and regulations to insure high-quality programs by simply restricting advertising matter to short announcements or according to the amount of time consumed—generally from 10 to 40 minutes daily.

In other countries there is no censorship on advertising, but they have rules and regulations to prevent the broadcasting of objectionable statements prejudicial to the government.

Ten of the thirteen foreign countries that were investigated permit commercial advertising, and with one exception have laws, rules, or regulations governing such advertising.

Austria, England, and Russia prohibit commercial advertising.

The Australian Government-controlled stations (class A) which are operated by the Australian Broadcasting Co. do not accept advertising of any kind, whereas the privately owned and operated stations (class B) derive their revenue entirely from advertising.

It appears from the information available that the French broadcasting system is similar to that type employed in Australia except that the Government prohibits all direct advertising over Government stations, whereas the privately owned and operated stations derive their revenue solely from commercial advertising....

WHETHER IT WOULD BE PRACTICABLE AND SATISFACTORY TO PERMIT ONLY THE ANNOUNCEMENT OF SPONSORSHIP OF PROGRAMS BY PERSONS OR CORPORATIONS.

Answer. It would not appear to be practicable and satisfactory at the present time, and in the ordinary case, to permit only the announcement of sponsorship of programs by persons or corporations.

The American system of broadcasting is predicated upon the use of radio facilities as a medium for local and national advertising. Upon this use depends the quantity and quality of commercial and sustaining programs. The competition between advertisers insures the employment of the best talent available and a variety in kind of commercial programs. The commercial programs furnish the principal source of revenue to stations. The quality and character of sustaining programs are dependent upon the revenue received from the sale of time for commercial advertising purposes. The daily newspaper furnishes a parallel: A newspaper can be sold to the subscriber at a cost greatly under the cost of production because it is used as a medium for advertising and what it contains of a news, educational, literary, and entertaining value depends almost entirely upon the revenue received from the sale of space for advertising purposes. Similarly, a radio broadcast station can present sustaining programs that are of great educational value and rich in entertainment only in a degree measured by the revenue derived from the sale of time for purposes of commercial advertising.

Information made available to the commission shows that sponsorship of programs by name would amount, in the ordinary case, only to good-will advertising. A few products and their uses may be so well and generally known as to permit this. On the other hand, and as to the majority of products, such advertising would involve an expense which national advertisers are not now willing and in a position to bear.

Many products have several uses which must be described to be understood and appreciated. New products frequently need to be explained. Nearly every manufacturer seeks to develop concerning his product special characteristics which set it off from competing products and make it more desirable. Identity of product, description of uses, and characteristics must be woven into and become a part of the program to make it of value to the sponsor. What applies to the national advertiser applies in even greater degree to the local advertiser. In such cases identity by name only would be of little value to the advertiser.

It should be borne in mind that if a restriction permitting sponsorship by name only should cause a number of advertisers to discontinue the use of radio facilities as a medium for commercial advertising, such nonuse would immediately and inevitably be reflected in a decrease both in the quantity and quality of programs available to the public. A serious loss in revenue to the stations could, under our system of broadcasting, have no other result....

In an effort to obtain information upon this subject, the commission addressed the ... letter to the advertising agencies who purchase time from the two major chain companies....

The replies to this letter ... give expression of opinions and ideas of men who use all kinds of advertising media and upon whose judgment manufacturers rely for the expenditure of many millions of dollars annually.

Because these letters contained only an expression of opinion, an effort was made to learn if facts could not be supplied to support the opinions. Such facts could not be obtained for the reasons described in a letter received from the executive secretary of the American Association of Advertising Agencies the text of which is quoted:

In answering your questionnaire, most agencies will tell you, I believe, that in their opinion radio advertising will not pay the advertiser if his commercial credits are limited to a simple statement of sponsorship of the program. Their answers will consist of opinions because there is no data available at present that would be conclusive for the following reasons:

1. Commercial announcements limited to sponsorship alone were used only in the very earliest days of radio broadcasting. There are probably no records available on this early period, and even if there were such information, it would not answer to-day's problem because conditions are entirely different.

   From a potential listening audience of a few thousand, radio has grown to attract the interest of millions. Early radio advertisers used the medium for novelty, with no analytical study of its effects. Other advertisers have been attracted to radio by the apparent satisfaction of earlier users and its great vogue with the public.

The fact that radio broadcasting started with simple sponsorship and rapidly developed more detailed advertising presentation shows, I believe, that in the opinion of advertisers and agencies, more detailed presentation is necessary.

2. We can not make a test of simple sponsorship because few if any would take the risk. It would be against their better judgment and experience.

3. Another reason why agencies can not furnish supporting data on what they believe would be the effect of simple sponsorship, is that they rely ordinarily on the registration of consumer reaction to advertising rather than upon sales as an indication of effectiveness. It is ordinarily impossible to separate sales secured and to credit them to the particular advertising which was responsible for them. Most advertisers use more than one kind of advertising media. Radio advertisers also advertise in newspapers, in magazines, and on outdoor boards and signs. They use business and trade papers, catalogs, direct mail, street-car and subway advertising, farm papers, and so on.

When sales are made, who can tell how much was due to radio, how much to newspapers, or to magazines? Advertising seeks to arouse interest and create good will as well as to make sales. Interest and good will are imponderable values, which are felt rather than measured. We get a registration of them through coupons and letters sent to the advertiser and from dealers, distributors, and the advertiser's salesmen. It is these cumulative registrations that point toward the need in radio broadcasting of identifying the product and describing its characteristics and uses.

All these variables and continually changing factors are what make advertising and selling an art. But they do not prevent advertisers and agencies from trying to get facts about the effectiveness of appeals and of various media. Among the fact-finding studies now being conducted are....

Studies of program popularity by individual advertisers and agencies. These are going on all the time. The most recent ones have been made by telephone during the time of the broadcasting....

This type of operation tends over a period of time to produce programs with greater popularity, because the sponsors are constantly seeking to swell their audiences by giving them what they like best to listen to. It is better, of course, to find out what the people actually do listen to than to ask them what kind of programs they prefer.

It is interesting in this connection to observe that among the most popular programs are many which carry the most advertising. For example: Chase & Sanborn, True Story, Literary Digest, Lucky Strike, Coca-Cola, Fleischman, Collier's, A. & P., Camel, Blue Ribbon Malt, Maxwell House, Cities Service, Pepsodent, Socony, Blackstone, Palmolive, and Cremo....

5. President Franklin Roosevelt Uses Radio to Calm Americans at the Beginning of the Great Depression, 1933

I want to talk for a few minutes with the people of the United States about banking—with the comparatively few who understand the mechanics of banking but more particularly with the overwhelming majority who use banks for the making of deposits and the drawing of checks. I want to tell you what has been done in the last few days, why it was done, and what the next steps are going to be. I recognize that the many proclamations from State Capitols and from Washington, the legislation, the Treasury regulations, etc., couched for the most part in banking and legal terms should be explained for the benefit of the average citizen. I owe this in particular because of the fortitude and good temper with which everybody has accepted the inconvenience and hardships of the banking holiday. I know that when you understand what we in Washington have been about I shall continue to have your cooperation as fully as I have had your sympathy and help during the past week.

First of all let me state the simple fact that when you deposit money in a bank the bank does not put the money into a safe deposit vault. It invests your money in many different forms of credit-bonds, commercial paper, mortgages and many other kinds of loans. In other words, the bank puts your money to work to keep the wheels of industry and of agriculture turning around. A comparatively small part of the money you put into the bank is kept in currency—an amount which in normal times is wholly sufficient to cover the cash needs of the average citizen. In other words the total amount of all the currency in the country is only a small fraction of the total deposits in all of the banks.

What, then, happened during the last few days of February and the first few days of March? Because of undermined confidence on the part of the public, there was a general rush by a large portion of our population to turn bank deposits into currency or gold. A rush so great that the soundest banks could not get enough currency to meet the demand....

It was then that I issued the proclamation providing for the nation-wide bank holiday, and this was the first step in the Government's reconstruction of our financial and economic fabric. The second step was the legislation promptly and patriotically passed by the Congress confirming my proclamation and broadening my powers so that it became possible in view of the requirement of time to emend (sic) the holiday and lift the ban of that holiday gradually.... I want to tell our citizens in every part of the Nation that the national Congress—Republicans and Democrats alike—showed by this action a devotion to public welfare and a realization of the emergency and the necessity for speed that it is difficult to match in our history.

The third stage has been the series of regulations permitting the banks to continue their functions to take care of the distribution of food and household necessities and the payment of payrolls.

Franklin Roosevelt, *Fireside Chat 1: On the Banking Crisis* (12 March 1933). Available at:
Presidential Speech Archive, Miller Center for Public Affairs, University of Virginia
http://millercenter.org/scripps/archive/speeches/detail/3298

This bank holiday while resulting in many cases in great inconvenience is affording us the opportunity to supply the currency necessary to meet the situation. No sound bank is a dollar worse off than it was when it closed its doors last Monday. Neither is any bank which may turn out not to be in a position for immediate opening. The new law allows the twelve Federal Reserve banks to issue additional currency on good assets and thus the banks that reopen will be able to meet every legitimate call....

A question you will ask is this—why are all the banks not to be reopened at the same time? The answer is simple. Your Government does not intend that the history of the past few years shall be repeated. WE do not want and will not have another epidemic of bank failures.

As a result we start tomorrow, Monday, with the opening of banks in the twelve Federal Reserve Bank cities—those banks which on first examination by the Treasury have already been found to be all right. This will be followed on Tuesday by the resumption of all their functions by banks already found to be sound in cities where there are recognized clearinghouses. That means about 250 cities of the United States.

On Wednesday and succeeding days banks in smaller places all through the country will resume business, subject, of course, to the Government's physical ability to complete its survey....

It is possible that when the banks resume a very few people who have not recovered from their fear may again begin withdrawals. Let me make it clear that the banks will take care of all needs—and it is my belief that hoarding during the past week has become an exceedingly unfashionable pastime. It needs no prophet to tell you that when the people find that they can get their money— that they can get it when they want it for all legitimate purposes—the phantom of fear will soon be laid. People will again be glad to have their money where it will be safely taken care of and where they can use it conveniently at any time. I can assure you that it is safer to keep your money in a reopened bank than under the mattress.

The success of our whole great national program depends, of course, upon the cooperation of the public—on its intelligent support and use of a reliable system.

I hope you can see from this elemental recital of what your government is doing that there is nothing complex, or radical in the process.

We had a bad banking situation. Some of our bankers had shown themselves either incompetent or dishonest in their handling of the people's funds. They had used the money entrusted to them in speculations and unwise loans. This was of course not true in the vast majority of our banks but it was true in enough of them to shock the people for a time into a sense of insecurity and to put them into a frame of mind where they did not differentiate, but seemed to assume that the acts of a comparative few had tainted them all. It was the Government's job to straighten out this situation and do it as quickly as possible—and the job is being performed....

We shall be engaged not merely in reopening sound banks but in the creation of sound banks through reorganization. It has been wonderful to me to catch the note of confidence from all over the country. I can never be sufficiently grateful to the people for the loyal support they given me in their acceptance of the judgment that has dictated our course, even though all of our processes may not have seemed clear to them.

After all there is an element in the readjustment of our financial system more important than currency, more important than gold, and that is the confidence of the people. Confidence and courage are the essentials of success in carrying out our plan. You people must have faith; you must not be stampeded by rumors or guesses. Let us unite in banishing fear. We have provided the machinery to restore our financial system; it is up to you to support and make it work.

It is your problem no less than it is mine. Together we cannot fail.

6. Radio Researcher Paul Lazarsfeld Presents Information about Women Listeners to Broadcasters and Advertisers, 1942

As the war goes on, the life of the nation will center increasingly about three groups: men in the armed services, defense workers, and housewives. The problem of communicating with these groups on subjects significant on the home front, therefore becomes a major concern for research people. Among women, daytime serials have by far the largest number of followers.

During the past year systematic research has been made into the nature of the serial, the nature of its audience, and the effect of the serial on the audience. The results of this research are now being made public. The first result shows that most criticism of the day-time serial has been seriously beside the point....

About 40 per cent of all women, including those who are employed, listen regularly to some daytime serials, which means that they have approximately 20 million devotees.

The average number of programs these women hear can be estimated at two to three a day.

Listening is somewhat more frequent in smaller towns than in cities, and is far more frequent in rural areas. It also increases in the lower income groups, but the differences are not very great. No consistent age differences have been established so far.

There is no *one* form or type of daytime serial. They vary from cheerful humor to tense drama. They deal with many kinds of men, and women....

[A]t the moment, one type dominates the field, and when people speak of the daytime serial, they … mean this fundamental type, which can be described as follows: the central characters are a group of people, one or two of whom get into a long series of troubles. The plot consists of getting them out of trouble. The dramatic technique is a skilful mixture of excitement interspersed with discussions among characters.

Paul F. Lazarsfeld, *What We Really Know about Daytime Serials* (New York: Columbia Broadcasting System 1943). Originally a speech given at "The Pulse of New York," 21 October 1942. Copyright © 1942 by Paul F. Lazarsfeld. Reproduced by permission.

The black-and-white technique of the older mass literature has been abandoned. Usually, you find in these stories three types of characters: the weak, the good and strong (who are often women), and the villain. The latter two fight out the case of the weak one, and his final salvation is assured. The stories of this type resemble one another, and all follow certain rules which can be discovered by systematic analysis.

Women, it appears, get two chief gratifications out of listening:

First, there is an escape, a day-dreaming, which carries them away from their daily lives.

Second—almost the reverse—women use the stories as a source of guidance in their private lives. About 40% of the listeners say that the serials helped them to solve their own problems; they give concrete and detailed instances in which they dealt with people more successfully because they had listened to these programs. The stories also provide women with a crude sort of psychological knowledge which carries beyond the limits of their own experience.

Here are a few examples of the way the women talk in interviews:

In "Women in White" *the brother was going off to war. She reconciled herself, that he was doing something for his country. When I listened it made me feel reconciled about my son—that mine is not the only one. In the story the brother is very attached to the family—he tells them not to worry, that he would be all right and would come back.*

I like Helen Trent. *She is a woman over 35. You never hear of her dyeing her hair. She uses charm and manners to entice men and she does. If she can do it, why can't I? I am fighting old age, and having a terrible time. Sometimes I am tempted to go out and fix my hair. These stories give me courage and help me realize I have to accept it.*

I think Papa David *helped me to be more cheerful when Fred my husband comes home. I feel tired, but instead of being grumpy I keep on the cheerful side. The* Goldbergs *are another story like that.* Mr. Goldberg *comes home scolding and he never means it. I sort of understand Fred better because of it....*

In spite of such testimony to the value of the daytime serial, a number of criticisms can be brought against it.

The problems in the stories and the solutions of the problems are both of a special kind. The problems do not rise because people strive for certain goals and have to overcome obstacles to succeed. Rather, the characters in the stories want things to remain as they are, and the stories tell how the old balance is restored after disturbing incidents have been overcome. This ties in with the fact that the "advice" derived from the stories seems often to lead to acceptance of one's fate, rather than to finding the cause of the problem and, by finding it, find also a way to basic betterment....

The disturbing incidents are usually introduced by individuals; individuals also solve the problems. Social forces, discords inherent in general economic conditions, are seldom introduced. People lose jobs, for instance, because of the jealousy of another person or other similar personal frictions. Non-personal factors come in only in terms of sickness or accidents. Up to the war, there was hardly ever a "cause" of major importance which the characters served. And conversely, nothing in the stories helped the listeners to a better understanding of our present society.

The philosophy implied in the plots tends to flatter the prejudices of the audience. For instance, men are discriminated against; about twice as often as women, men are the source of other people's troubles. Over and over again a difficult situation is solved by a woman who proves to be better than the man who really should have done the job. Special stress is laid on the fact that, for women, life is not over after forty. The majority of the principal characters belong to the middle class. Rich people are belittled; they usually do not know how to handle their own affairs, and are likely to be saved by some representative of the common middle-class. Manual workers hardly ever appear.

By thus highlighting with approval the groups to which the listening women themselves belong, these programs certainly do not build up self-criticism or an effort toward self-improvement. (On the other hand, they represent an interesting progress beyond the motion picture, which still deals mainly with wealthy people and with problems often far from the experience of the ordinary man.)...

On the other hand, there is so far no evidence that listening to these daytime serials has any bad effect. A considerable number of studies have shown little difference between listeners and non-listeners.

About 30 per cent of all women are available at home some time during the day, and still do not listen to daytime serials. If the serials do have any effect, I should be expected that after so many years those who listen and those who do not, would prove to be different in certain respects. The average daytime serial listener has somewhat less formal education than the woman who does not listen. But when we compare listeners and non-listeners in other respects, it is surprising to see how similar they are....

The two main concerns which have been expressed in regard to the effect of daytime serials were (1) that serials make women less responsible citizens, and (2) that they lead them into emotional difficulties....

In the audience of daytime stories, we have, then, almost half of all American women, and much more than half of all those who are available during the day. They seem to be a quite normal section of American citizenry.

The radio industry and the Office of War Information are perfectly justified in their effort to use these programs as a vehicle for war messages. Aside from casual references, or the weaving in of actual information, the war can enter the plots in two ways. It can either become an integral part of the stories, skilfully dealing with such problems as the home front, the post war world, the nature of the enemy. Or the war can become just another trouble against which the experiences of isolated individuals are enacted.

It is vitally important that the former alternative be taken. It would be unintelligent to obscure by happy endings the heroic tragedies of our war. We shall have to tell how personal losses should be borne, and can be overcome by work and understanding of higher purposes. We shall have to show the importance of real information, and the analysis of complex social situations. A future in which colored nations will play a much greater role can be anticipated by a realistic handling of domestic race problems. A world in which some interference of government with private matters is likely to remain, can be reflected in plots where the role of the individual in his community is constructively treated. The increasing importance of Labor can be shown by the introduction of characteristic types which have so far been entirely lacking from the stories....

By coming to grips with actuality, the daytime serial will not only serve the war: the stories, themselves, will benefit. Part of the criticism directed against the insignificance of these serials was due to the fact that until the war came, there were so few important things on which a large audience could agree. Now we live in a world where the ultimate criterion is no longer what we like to do, but what our duty is. If radio gets into the habit of telling this to large number of listeners now, it will acquire a tradition which will make it an even more important social instrument.

 # ESSAYS

This chapter asks questions about changing concepts of commercialism, community, and public and private. In the first essay, Susan Smulyan, professor of American civilization at Brown University and co-editor of this volume, examines how radio programming changed as the commercialization of radio increased. She shows both how advertisers needed to be convinced that radio would work to reach consumers and how radio drew on older forms of popular culture for its programming. Jason Loviglio, associate professor of American studies and director of media and communication studies at the University of Maryland, Baltimore County, makes a complex argument about how radio changed ideas of public and private by examining President Franklin Roosevelt's Fireside Chats as well as his wife Eleanor Roosevelt's radio broadcasts.

Paying for Radio by Selling Time

SUSAN SMULYAN

How do you do, everybody, how do you do?
How do you do, everybody, how are you?
Don't forget your Friday date,
Seven-thirty until eight,
How do you doodle doodle doodle doodle do?

Billy Jones and Ernie Hare, known as the "Happiness Boys," opened and closed their weekly, half-hour radio show for five and a half years in the early 1920s with their theme song, "How Do You Do?" Their program was different in several respects from other radio shows of the early 1920s: few early radio shows had sponsors, like Happiness Candy, or featured professional performers, like Jones and Hare. From 1923 to 1933 Jones and Hare enjoyed a huge success, but then had to scramble for radio jobs as the industry changed dramatically with the introduction of networks and fully commercialized national broadcasting. They remained on the air until Hare's death in 1939, but their popularity had peaked.

The rise and decline of the Happiness Boys illustrates the influence on broadcasting both of the network system and the advertising industry. Programming, performers, advertising, advertisers, and audience surveying all changed dramatically over the first twelve years of broadcasting. Some programming and personnel changes stemmed from social and cultural factors—among others, changing tastes, the Depression, and increased nationwide acceptance of the urban experience. But the push for national radio, the establishment of the wired network system, and the campaign to promote broadcasting to advertisers had even more immediate effects.

Relatively unknown recording artists such as the Happiness Boys, with their small-town humor, gave way to already celebrated urban vaudevillians; regional sponsors were replaced by national sponsors; listeners' letters ceded influence to the new art of audience surveys. These differences came about as a decentralized regional system, with small advertisers afraid of offending listeners, evolved into a centralized national system, with corporate sponsors largely in control of programming. As the promoters of broadcast advertising worked to make radio more closely match prior advertising media, station managers and performers simultaneously sought models for new programs and advertisements in their own short history.…

Most stations in the 1920s were desperate to fill the few hours a day they stayed on the air. Early radio listeners thus heard a somewhat chaotic jumble of different kinds of music, talks, poetry, children's stories, plays, and sports. Music predominated, performed by local amateurs with an occasional traveling professional or hotel dance band coaxed before the microphone by the lure of free publicity. Soloists such as singers, violinists, and pianists were most common. Many radio musicians showed little skill in their performances of traditional sentimental ballads or light classics, yet touring dance bands brought the best in popular music, brilliantly performed, to the airwaves.…

The very first broadcast radio stations had experimented with phonograph records—placing the microphone next to the phonograph's horn—but the poor quality of the transmission discouraged listeners. As a matter of prestige, therefore, early stations boasted that they used only live musicians. The U.S. Department of Commerce institutionalized the prejudice against recordings in 1922 by relegating stations transmitting recordings to less desirable frequencies. Even when improved technology permitted the electrical broadcast of recordings, regulations still favored live programming and thus the wealthier stations that could afford to pay performers.…

Most early radio stations lost money, partly because the station management had no clear purpose in broadcasting. Entertaining listeners was not always the top priority, with some stations programming for "uplift" or education. Controversies over programming seldom emerged, for it was difficult to determine what listeners wanted to hear, management was unsure what it wanted to broadcast, and performers were so scarce that stations put anyone willing on the air immediately. Station managers (who also usually acted as announcers) made the programming decisions. Often young men with some wartime radio experience, these early managers had little knowledge of the entertainment business, and expediency dictated the content of most programs. The manager of a Kentucky radio station wrote that "it was necessary to have a long string of volunteers on call and for them to be dependable enough to cross our threshold promptly thirty minutes before starting time." He reported that he left the choice of material to the artist, but that "half an hour was none too long in which to orientate their introductions, think up a few words about each musical selection, and, if possible some interesting fact concerning the life of its composer."…

As listeners tired of pursuing distant radio signals and sought better programming, radio magazines and stations became more interested in what programs listeners liked. Even before radio had much advertising, or stations thought of turning a profit, more systematic studies of listener preferences were attempted.…

[E]arly radio audience surveys reported that listeners enjoyed sponsored programs, largely because they featured consistent and professional performers.… By 1927 … long-distance listening remained popular only for those without access to high-quality local programming. Listeners enjoyed the sponsored programs best—this several months before the founding of NBC.…

Harried station managers were finding that sponsorship could fill radio time with little station effort and improve program quality by featuring professional performers. Sponsors were spending money on broadcasting, something most stations could not do, at a time when listeners were clamoring increasingly for better programs.… It was not surprising that listeners enjoyed the shows designed by sponsors to please them. While never in a majority, the pre-network sponsored shows of the mid-1920s became important models for later programming.…

In August 1923 Billy Jones and Ernie Hare first appeared on radio as the Happiness Boys to promote the Happiness Candy Company at a time when radio industry leaders and observers were heatedly debating the question, "who pays for broadcasting?" Jones and Hare presented a program different from almost anything else heard in 1923. The Happiness Candy Company's purchase of time on New York's WEAF could have happened only on a station owned, or licensed, by AT&T, as it then maintained the sole right to sell time over the air. Yet most companies remained reluctant to buy time on WEAF, making the candy company's sponsorship a daring move. Happiness Candy Company was thus one of the first American corporations to consider radio a regional selling tool; it approached WEAF because the station's advanced technology promised a strong signal to a large audience.

The Happiness Boys were also unusual in their regular weekly time slot: "your Friday date, seven-thirty until eight." Most radio programs of the early 1920s, sponsored or unsponsored, were one-time events. Because amateur performers, usually unreliable, could not be persuaded to appear regularly, a weekly entertainment program had never been tried before.…

The use of a theme song to identify the "Happiness Boys" show was also innovative and notable. Jones and Hare had worked in vaudeville but were earning their living as recording artists when Happiness Candy hired them. Their extensive experience in the entertainment industry, including specialized practice before a microphone, made them a rarity in early radio. On the show and on their records (which they continued to produce at a prodigious rate) they performed "song and patter," a mixture of comic songs and jokes commonly used by two-man minstrel and vaudeville acts. Besides introducing comedy to radio, the Happiness Boys brought to the airwaves their polished renditions of sentimental ballads, skillful harmonies, and an appealing manner....

Listener dislike of early radio advertising influenced the shape and form of the Happiness Candy Company's program, which followed the techniques of indirect advertising, including naming the performers after the product (hence the "Happiness Boys") as an inoffensive way of repeating the sponsor's name several times during a program. Other advertisements, however brief, usually brought complaints from listeners unused to any sales pitches over the air. The Happiness Boys also sang cheerful songs, since their employer believed that geniality reminded the audience of the product's name.

Sponsorship such as the Happiness Candy Company's had emerged shortly after the birth of broadcast radio. Small-town and rural stations presented a few sponsored shows, but the most popular originated from the urban stations. These programs went out to several stations on one of the pre-network chains, or were transmitted with a strong signal sent by the latest equipment....

The earliest sponsors in the 1920s were middle-sized firms that manufactured relatively inexpensive products consumers bought regularly and frequently, including candy (Happiness Candy Company, Smith Brothers cough drops), toothpaste (Ipana), groceries (A & P), soft drinks (Clicquot Club ginger ale), tires (B. F. Goodrich), and batteries (Eveready). Because many Americans still thought of radio as frivolous, and because of uncertainty about the size and composition of the radio audience, broadcast advertisers seldom tried to influence consumers to make expensive purchases....

Radio sponsors of the 1920s usually produced their programs themselves, with some help from station personnel. Performers often came from the recording industry, because they had experience before the microphone and because they believed broadcast work might help publicize their recordings. Recording companies warned that radio would cut into the sales of records and diminish the popularity of some artists, but the musicians themselves, including Jones and Hare, disagreed. Most vaudeville performers, on the other hand, ignored radio in the 1920s because it paid little or nothing and had microphones instead of live audiences; vaudeville traveling schedules also permitted little time for outside engagements.

Recording artists possessed another attribute that early radio advertisers looked for: anonymity. The type of advertising used on radio called for performers who could submerge their own identities to promote a product. Vaudeville stars would not and, as well-known figures, could not take a role that obliterated their personae. Jones and Hare, on the other hand, *were* the Happiness Boys, and while listeners knew their personal names, the sponsor's name remained far more important. Many radio performers remained completely unknown.... Announcers never mentioned the individual names of the Ipana Troubadours, the A & P Gypsies, or the Clicquot Club Eskimos. Advertisers in the 1920s and early 1930s wanted the emphasis placed on their brand names and looked to the performers not for prestige (as they would later), but for entertainment that would remind listeners of the product....

[T]he Happiness Boys thrived on early radio. The popularity of the team in the 1920s was reflected in the many articles written about them, mentions made of their act by other artists, their mail (often reported as 700 letters a week), and their large salaries (Hare claimed to be "working on my second million" at the time of the stock market crash)....

The first continuity for the "Happiness Boys" listed seven songs—three duets and four solos—with a "gag" following each song. A warning began the script: "Don't forget to mention after every song that it is the Happiness Boys from station WEAF entertaining." While later programs became more elaborate, the basic format probably varied only slightly. Jones and Hare began with a simple piano accompaniment, which was later replaced by a small orchestra; programs occasionally featured guests....

Radio programs did begin to sound different in the 1930s. Gone ... were the anonymous musicians playing nostalgic or semiclassical songs. Gone too were diffident advertisers favoring indirect appeals....

The technology of the network system, dependent (like vaudeville) on local outlets, helped bring established vaudeville stars to radio. That step helped convince many listeners that radio existed as an entertainment, rather than an educational, medium and therefore could be commercial. The relaxed, old-fashioned, small-town humor of the Happiness Boys gave way to the frenzy of Eddie Cantor. Cantor's national prominence and proven attraction made him a logical choice to star over a network system that now closely resembled a vaudeville circuit. By the early 1930s broadcast advertising had become accepted, national audiences were available, and small businesses, hit hard by the Depression, had stopped advertising and been replaced over the airwaves by large corporations and their advertising agencies.

In 1932 NBC had fewer advertisers than in 1931, but each spent more on radio. For example, Standard Brands (makers of Chase and Sanborn coffee, Fleischmann's yeast, and Royal Jell-o, among other products) sponsored three programs. Such large companies spent more on radio programs and often sought well-known performers for prestige. Radio's now comparatively generous salaries—combined with diminishing vaudeville opportunities—lured stars such as Cantor to network shows.

Broadcast advertisers, for their part, believed that radio audiences were now listening to specific favorite programs, and sponsors hoped that well-known entertainers would sustain interest.... Broadcast advertising thus became more direct, and unabashed commercials began asking consumers outright to buy products.

These changes in broadcast advertising convinced sponsors of the usefulness of advertising agencies.... Throughout the 1930s it was the agencies, with the assistance of the performers involved, that produced most network radio programs.

The new emphasis on advertising meant that programming became more rigid. As the cost of radio time rose, each program carefully allocated its precious minutes among commercial breaks and program content. Scripts became ever more elaborate and choreographed, so that advertisers could be assured of a professional rendition of their message and so that agencies could justify their high fees. By 1934 sponsored radio programs already differed considerably in form, content, and style from the "Happiness Boys" program of ten years earlier.

Many of these changes date from 1931, when Eddie Cantor became the host of the "Chase and Sanborn Hour," although the biggest transformation occurred during the 1932 radio season, when a host of new radio shows debuted featuring Ed Wynn, George Burns and Gracie Allen, Jack Benny, George Jessel, Jack Pearl, and Fred Allen.... [T]he star and host was often a comedian, and the shows emphasized comic sketches.

Cantor, born poor and Jewish on New York's East Side, had quit school early to play vaudeville (often as a black-faced juggler), work in the Ziegfeld Follies, and perform in nightclubs. He lost a great deal of money in the stock-market crash and, after having earlier decided to retire in 1929, instead found himself seeking work to support his family. Between 1929 and 1931 Cantor worked sporadically on Broadway and in films, and wrote a book before finding a well-paying radio job. Unlike earlier radio performers, Cantor had no formal musical training; but he did have an understanding, honed by years of touring, of the national audience. Already well-known when hired by Chase and Sanborn, he became enormously popular as a result of his radio show.

Earlier, Cantor had participated in the "New Humor" brought by immigrants to the vaudeville stage. Albert McLean has described vaudeville's urban and ethnic (mostly Jewish) humor as based on verbal misunderstandings, rooted in stories of family life and of the underdog, and with a compressed and frantic form built around the joke (a modern invention that flourished in vaudeville). The compression and verbal basis of this humor made it natural for radio. The radio performers of the 1920s had relied on music and on what McLean calls the "relaxed whimsy of the minstrel show." Cantor's programs, by contrast, featured jokes, skits, and stories about Ida Cantor and the couple's five daughters. Cantor's scripts, written by David Freedman (many of radio's new writers, as well as performers, now came from vaudeville), depended on a "joke factory" where young writers reworked old jokes to fit the week's subject.

The vaudevillians also chose subjects new to radio.... Broadcasters worried that while theater audiences might be willing to listen to vulgarity and ethnic humor in vaudeville houses, radio listeners would not want such subjects, language, or performing styles in their living rooms.

Vaudeville entertainers and broadcasters had to make other adjustments to each other. Although many radio shows had studio audiences, audience participation was not encouraged until vaudeville performers came to radio. Some programs even separated the audience from the performers with a glass curtain.... Radio's coldness shocked vaudevillians such as Cantor, who were accustomed to interaction between audience and performer.

Several radio stars later claimed to have been the first to invite on-air audience reactions, but it was Cantor's particular way of playing to the audience that made his program such a success.... His first experiment in audience participation occurred when he couldn't resist donning a woman's hat and fur scarf to enliven a routine. Cantor based many of his comic radio sketches on outrageous costumes, which the announcer would describe to the radio listeners. Vaudeville's reliance on such visual clowning posed problems when performers moved to radio. The response of the studio audience provided some justification for visual gags, but the performers who relied on word play and situation comedy lasted longer on radio than those who appeared in funny hats....

[N]ew methods of audience surveying provided more detailed information on the popularity of specific programs. These new audience surveys (forerunners of the postwar rating services) began in 1930 with a report prepared by Crossley, Inc.... for the Association of National Advertisers (ANA). The ANA Radio Committee decided to cooperate with other interested parties in financing a system of audience surveys to be undertaken by Crossley, Inc. The original subscribers to what was called the Cooperative Analysis of Broadcasting (CAB) project were radio sponsors, but within the first year advertising agencies began to participate as well....

The reports became increasingly elaborate, with charts and essays providing information gleaned from phone calls made four times daily. The CAB surveys, financed as they were by national advertisers, focused on national programs but, as the competition between NBC and CBS for affiliates heated up, station area surveys also began to measure the relative popularity of local radio stations....

The search for greater reliability and the continued application of the latest social science techniques to radio audience surveys reflected the increasing amounts of money being spent by advertisers on radio programming....

Experiments using radio as an advertising medium had deprived early performers of their names, and the money spent to ensure the success of those who came after reinforced the anonymity of the radio stars of the 1920s. Throughout the period programs continued to be produced in a variety of ways and for a variety of reasons, any of which might have served as a model radio system. But the triumph of sponsorship overshadowed other possibilities in the same way that the fame of radio stars of the 1930s eclipsed that of their predecessors.

As the networks established themselves and commercialized programming took over the airwaves, a diverse group of educators, publishers, and reformers voiced clear opposition to broadcast advertising. James Rorty summarized these protests against the growing commercialism of radio when he wrote that "in its essence, the charge levelled against the 'American System' of advertising-subsidized radio broadcasting is that it is drunk and disorderly." Rorty's phrase implied that commercialized broadcasting was socially unacceptable, morally bankrupt, and, in those waning days of Prohibition, subject to government regulation.... The protesters and the radio industry fought over federal regulation of broadcasting, each side seeking to have its vision or radio written into law.

Many observers of early broadcast radio had worried about the influence of commercialism. The protests in the early 1930s complained as well of the power of the networks to force competitors out of business. The opposition included educational and religious groups, political reformers, and newspaper publishers worried about competition from radio advertising.... This small and underfinanced group (especially when compared to the radio networks) nevertheless managed to call public attention to the problems inherent in a commercialized radio system, and to renew hope that fundamental change was still possible.

The Depression and the New Deal influenced both these protests and the responses to them. Concerns about competition in a tight business climate as well as a questioning of the efficiency and morality of capitalism underlay much of the criticism. The protesters turned to the federal government, then in an active phase of business regulation, for help in containing the radio monopoly. But the growing importance of broadcasting in politics and the huge profits made by broadcasters during difficult times gave the networks and the radio industry enormous leverage with legislators and federal officials.

Confusion over the best means for protecting the public from unfair or unethical business practices had a long history, and the protections most often had proven favorable to the businesses being regulated. In a manner reminiscent of earlier debates, Congress considered whether to regulate the results of the growing commercialism of radio or to strengthen the alternatives (in the form of local or nonprofit stations) to the networks. The result of these deliberations, the 1934 Communications Act, barely mentioned networks or advertising, and did not include any protections for educational, religious, farm, or labor stations. By ignoring the two most dynamic forces in radio, the Communications Act accepted and reinforced commercial broadcasting. In addition, it placed alternative nonprofit stations in such a weak position that they could never challenge a system financed through the sale of time to advertisers. The Communications Act continues to control American broadcasting today—not only because it serves as the primary legislation outlining the regulatory powers of the Federal Communications Commission, but also because it validated and strengthened the commercialized system of broadcasting that began in radio and then was transferred, almost without change, to television....

A number of factors moved educational, religious, and political leaders to protest the form and content of American broadcasting. As the commercialization of radio grew, as indirect advertising gave way to direct advertising, and as the programs presented on the radio became more formulaic, some listeners found themselves disappointed. The increasing strength of radio networks as competitors with newspapers and nonprofit stations spurred those particular groups into action. In addition, the federal reallocation of radio frequencies, which favored commercial stations at the behest of the industry, angered educational broadcasters. The growing power and influence of leftist political movements, which viewed capitalism skeptically, also contributed to the criticism. Finally, beginning in 1932, the New Deal climate that regarded business as an activity to be regulated in the public interest meant that the conflict between the radio industry and its detractors would be played out in the congressional battle over the 1934 Communications Act....

The protests against commercial radio did help to change the nature of ... radio legislation. Early congressional efforts at reform of the radio industry had concentrated on structure rather than content. As broadcast advertising grew, and as its critics began to complain, Congress took notice.... Sen. James Couzens ... introduced a resolution "calling for a report from the FRC on the use of radio facilities for commercial advertising purposes." The resolution, directly critical of the commercialism of American broadcasting, noted "there is growing dissatisfaction with the present use of radio facilities for the purposes of commercial advertising.".....

In public, both the radio industry and its detractors welcomed the FRC survey.... The behind-the-scenes maneuverings of the broadcasting industry, however, belied its public confidence. The NAB began a secret emergency fund-raising program to cover the cost of "providing the broadcasting stations with materials designed to present to the American public the real facts." NBC scrambled to give its affiliates information "with which to answer questions regarding network programs," as it "is to our best advantage" that the answers given to the FRC survey be "uniform."

Reformers saw the survey as a chance to show "the commercial radio monopoly" that "the American people are disgusted with the glaring evils which have been allowed to grow up in American radio by a negligent and commercially-minded Federal Radio Commission." As usual, they relied on volunteers to present their case to the FRC and the public, and never marshaled the same level of pressure as did the commercial broadcasters.... The educators did complain, after the fact, about the unfairness of the survey, noting that the FRC had chosen National Education Week, when networks broadcast more educational programs, as the sample period. Further, they argued that the FRC ignored the NCER and other educational organizations, while it did talk to advertisers' organizations.

The FRC's commitment to commercial radio pervaded its report, *Commercial Radio Advertising,* delivered and printed in 1932. To answer the Senate's questions, the FRC solicited information from stations about their programs and practices.... It also corresponded with individual advertising agencies, the American Association of Advertising Agencies, the Secretary of State, and with others who had knowledge of broadcasting in foreign countries. The report took the simple form of answers to the previously specified congressional questions, with the FRC presenting itself as a neutral purveyor of information. The responses to the questions about educational broadcasting were extremely detailed and quoted extensively from FRC dockets, but the FRC relied on opinion in its discussion of commercial radio. The commission contended that, at most, one-third of all radio broadcasts were commercial, while other programs, termed "sustaining," were "presented by the station without compensation and at its expense." The FRC explained this apparent altruism by noting that sustaining programs helped stations serve the public interest as mandated by the 1927 Radio Act, enlarging and holding an audience and thereby increasing the value of time available for commercial programs....

The FRC reminded Congress that if it restricted radio sponsorship to announcements only, advertisers might stop using radio and "such non-use would immediately and inevitably be reflected in a decrease both in quantity and quality of programs made available to the public." The report thus clearly outlined the perils to broadcasting if advertising disappeared, but it never addressed the other contingency: what would happen if sustaining programs vanished, victims to the growing demand by sponsors for airtime?

The report's conclusion emphasized the commission's own competence to regulate broadcasting.... The FRC existed from year to year, dependent on yearly legislation for its continuance. Yet by 1932 it had accumulated a staff and bureaucracy that used the Senate's questions to make a case for their own jobs. Throughout the report, the FRC presented solutions to radio's problems that maintained or increased the commission's power.

In the end, the 1934 Communications Act gave the Federal Communications Commission unrestricted discretionary powers in the matter of license granting. Left to the mercy of the new FCC, educational and other nonprofit stations faced continuing discrimination.

The FRC … emerged strengthened by its transformation into the FCC. Its own bureaucratic momentum, combined with congressional knowledge of administrative agencies' susceptibility to pressure, made its inclusion in the new regulatory framework practically a foregone conclusion. Additionally, radio's growing use as a political tool and its importance in everyday life made administrative regulation, usually little noticed outside the industry, more appealing to Congress than prescriptive legislation.…

[A]s in the rest of the New Deal era's legislation, a dialectic between regulation and competition can be found in the federal response to radio. At once concerned about the "radio trust" in manufacturing and the control of broadcasting by only a few companies, all three branches of the federal government also saw the need for a rationalization of the "natural monopoly" enjoyed by the networks. Federal planning and regulation, they hoped, might mitigate the drawbacks of a monopolistic system and increase competition. In the end, however, governmental regulation only strengthened the largest and commercialized broadcasting companies at the expense of the smaller and nonprofit broadcasters, and lessened competition, outcomes that mirrored most other interactions between the New Deal government and the economy.

The Influence of Broadcasting on Politics

JASON LOVIGLIO

Among the tens of thousands of letters and telegrams that poured into the White House in the days after Roosevelt's second Fireside Chat of May 7, 1933, one letter from a Louisiana listener included a clipping of a cartoon from the *New Orleans Times-Picayune* portraying the event. Underneath the caption, "Just Among Friends," a husband and wife sit on a comfortable pin-striped sofa, presumably their own, next to a smiling President Roosevelt. "And so," Roosevelt says (in a paraphrase of the chat's concluding lines), "with mutual confidence, we go forward!" The president is depicted as slightly oversized, handsome, and energetic, gesturing casually, a visual representation of the intimate tone that made the chats so affecting.… The couple beam at the president as the husband exclaims, "Boy! Does this beat the White House spokesman!"

The *Times-Picayune* cartoon's central image—a smiling, reassuring Roosevelt seated in the home of an American family—had, in the first two months of his administration, already become a well-recognized symbol of these special addresses, the president's persona, and, more broadly, the public philosophy of the New Deal. Roosevelt's mail reflected the public preoccupation with this image, and the intimacy, friendliness, and "open way" with which the new president communicated via the radio. After the first Fireside Chat, a New York City man wrote: "you are more than just another President, in that your willingness to put plain facts in a plain way before the people brings you real close to their fireside, and creates a warmth in their hearts for you, such as they have for a real good friends."…

In addition to mastering radio's intimate mode of address, Roosevelt also borrowed from a centrifugal force in radio address—beckoning to listeners to leave the privacy of domestic space for a broader, wider, and more public site of reception. Saul Bellow's recollection of listening to Roosevelt's voice as it issued from the radios in a line of parked cars along the Chicago Midway provides a particularly compelling example of the power of radio—and the Fireside Chats—to transform public space. The Fireside Chats were one of the most effective ways that Roosevelt articulated the public philosophy of the New Deal: an expansion of government's role in the everyday life of its citizens and a rhetorical embrace of a broader, more inclusive public sphere. The Fireside Chats, perhaps more than any other broadcasts of the early network era, made the most of the contradictory impulses in radio's construction of its own public. In examining the popular responses to the chats, it becomes clear that Roosevelt's intimate visits in the homes of his listeners were often experienced as invitations to transform the boundaries of domestic, political, and social space in the service of national renewal.…

The couple in the cartoon, dressed up for an evening at the theater but sitting in … their living room, is an apt … figure for the complicated public performance of radio reception. As this cartoon suggests, the Fireside Chats epitomized the immediacy, intimacy, and direct democracy that Americans associated with their new president and with the still-new phenomenon of national radio. Radio's installment into the family home promised an end to the circuitous routes of information through press secretaries, newspapers, and other media. The absence of a radio in the cartoon depiction of the couple's transformed living room makes clear the conflation of Roosevelt and the radio apparatus. Like Saul Bellow's account of listening to a Fireside Chat issuing from cars parked along Chicago's Midway, the cartoon connects the pleasure of radio listening to leisure, consumption, and the shifting boundaries of public and private space. The Fireside Chats invited listeners into a privileged realm of mobility that enabled them to feel as if they had crossed the boundary separating public and private, backstage and onstage. Roosevelt's audience was made to feel privy to the cultural work of defining a national identity by transgressing the border between public and private. These authorized transgressions—public speech in "intimate" spaces—were part of the unique allure of network radio.…

From the very start, the Fireside Chats were strikingly successful performances, as radio broadcasts and political speeches, two distinct categories that would overlap during Roosevelt's presidency. The popularity of the chats has to be considered within several related historical contexts, not the least of which is the rapidly developing radio industry. The chats, like the Roosevelt presidency of which they were a part, came on the scene during the most crucial period in the development of broadcasting. Between 1930 and 1937, the percentage of homes with a radio grew from 40 per cent to 80 per cent. A national network system was already in place by the early 1930s, and programs like *Amos 'n' Andy* and *The Goldbergs,* with national brand-name sponsors like Pepsodent and Oxydol, already commanded massive national audiences.

It is important to note that Roosevelt drew on radio's already established convention of the intimate mode of address. Prior to Roosevelt's Fireside Chats, several national and regional broadcast "personalities," including "Roxy" Rothafel, Will Rogers, and Father Coughlin, won large audiences who responded enthusiastically to the informality and intimacy of their speech. In the popular press, radio critics also called for a more intimate mode of address on the air. "Talk to me as if I were sitting in the room with you," one critic of the era pleaded, "not in an auditorium full of morons." Even political figures like Father Coughlin and Senator Huey Long had already used aspects of this folksy mode of address for broadcasts that sought to move a national audience on pressing matters of policy and politics. Indeed, early network radio actively "trained" its listeners in the late 1920s and early 1930s to participate in a reciprocal, "two-way" relationship with radio personalities by sending letters to favorite actors, announcers, even characters.

The Fireside Chats tapped into intimate modes of address established by such programs and revolutionized their political potential. From an average of about four hundred messages a day from the administration of Grover Cleveland through that of Herbert Hoover, the number of messages received at the White House soared during Roosevelt's presidency to between five thousand and eight thousand a day.... The chats also tapped into the national address inherent in network radio and in presidential oration itself. As in the cartoon, the president placed himself right beside his listeners on the threshold of a new social space, the intimate public of national radio.

At least part of the popularity of the Fireside Chats can be attributed to the elaborate planning that went into the details of the broadcasts. Although fifty-five of Roosevelt's speeches were carried over the radio in his first year in office, only four of them were considered Fireside Chats. Unlike speeches broadcast from public venues, the chats were delivered exclusively from the White House, that is, from Roosevelt's home. And although Roosevelt and his top staffers used radio, press conferences, newsreels, and personal appearances more than any other administration had, the Fireside Chats marked a qualitative departure from previous political uses of the mass media. Unlike most speeches carried by the networks, the chats were uniquely designed to suit the formal and ideological requirements of network broadcasting.

In addition to elaborate preparations in the writing of these addresses, great care was taken in the timing and aesthetics of the broadcasts. Scholars of speech have dissected Roosevelt's impressive radio performances from a myriad of perspectives, generally concurring … that he had "the best modulated radio voice in public life." Studies of his pitch (tenor), intonation ("vibrant with enthusiasm"), pronunciation ("eastern" mixed with elements of "general American"), cadence ("measured and deliberate"), and speaking rate (a comparatively slow one hundred words per minute) and volume (great dynamics) all bear out the general scholarly, journalistic and popular consensus that Roosevelt was a master public speaker.… A great deal of care went into the tuning of the chats as well. Nearly every one of them was delivered at a moment of strategic importance; nine were given on the same day as or within a day of an address, proposal, or proclamation to Congress. Typically broadcast between 9:45 and 10:45 p.m. eastern time (often on a Sunday evening), to reach the entire nation during the prime evening hours, the chats were brief, averaging thirty minutes apiece.

In these accounts and in popular historical memory, the chats came to stand in as a symbol for Roosevelt's persona, and to some extent for his physical person as well. It has often been remarked that the radio extended the president's limited mobility, compensating for his paralyzed legs and thus enabling him to reach corners of the country he could not possibly have reached otherwise. From the very beginning, the Fireside Chats were popularly figured as "intimate visits" from the president to the homes of his listeners. Roosevelt, as master of ceremonies, used the apparatus of network radio so skillfully that it seemed to disappear, leaving in its place the figure of Roosevelt himself. Clearly, Roosevelt was made for radio, right down to the special dental bridge custom-made to eradicate the faint whistling sound his voice made over the air. And, for the millions of Americans whose reception habits were being formed during the tumultuous days of the Depression and the early New Deal, radio was made for Roosevelt.…

The first chat, on March 12, 1933, came at the end of Roosevelt's first week in office, a week that began with the radio broadcast of his inaugural address. These two radio addresses together generated nearly half a million pieces of mail to the White House, launching the era of mass political mail and inaugurating Roosevelt's unprecedented mastery of the public opinion, mass media, and especially radio. National audiences for the subsequent chats remained high— breaking and rebreaking records for listenership.…

The Fireside Chars proved to be the ideal medium for Roosevelt to articulate the New Deal's rearrangement of public and private spheres in American life. The national public that Roosevelt hailed in the Fireside Chats was a broad one, collapsing distinctions between state authority, economic activity, citizenship, and the social world. Roosevelt's broadcasts were an apt medium through which to explain the New Deal's unprecedented expansion of the state's regulatory and administrative authority into the "private" economic spheres of industry, agriculture, labor, and the family.

The early Fireside Chats are remarkable in their ability to combine intimate gestures ("you and I know," "my friends," etc.) with often highly sophisticated and involved discussions of monetary policy, agricultural price controls, the history of the British welfare system, and so on. They were successful broadcasts in part because of Roosevelt's ability to translate the initiatives of and the impulses behind the New Deal into the informal patterns of radio speech. In particular,

Roosevelt used the chats to explain the unprecedented federal interventions into industrial and agricultural modes of production. He also used the chats as a way to sell his audience on the paradoxical notion that a new expert class of government planners would join "the people" in revitalizing participatory democracy.

The chats were successful because of the way they conflated radio listening with national identity, inviting listeners to participate in the invention of the new public realm of radio reception from the comfort of their own homes while also collaborating in the process of national recovery. Listening to the chats, Roosevelt implied, conferred on his audience the status of amateur brain truster, an active agent in the New Deal's reshuffling of the relationship between the government and the people, labor and management, public and private. In the intimate public of radio, Roosevelt invited his audience back and forth across the boundaries of public and private, retracing in words the authorized transgressions of the New Deal. In the process, the early Fireside Chats made themselves at home in the emerging patterns of radio reception.

Roosevelt's first Fireside Chat, on the severe nationwide banking crisis of February and March 1933, at the start of his presidency, provides an excellent example of how he used radio and New Deal interventions into "the private sector" to encourage listeners to see themselves as both members of and agents for the public his broadcasts called into being. Indeed, the very nature of the banking crisis—a radical loss of depositors' confidence in the nation's banks' ability to convert savings into currency—was an ideal first test for the administration's broad approach to the Depression and for Roosevelt's use of the radio to establish an intimate but authoritative rapport with his audience. The extraordinary success of this broadcast in restoring confidence in the nation's banks has been well documented. This episode is also, in some ways, an ideal one for demonstrating Roosevelt's conservative use of populist imagery to reinforce existing economic institutions. The specter of "incompetent or dishonest bankers" violating "the people's" trust becomes the setting in which the people—divided and afraid—are galvanized into unity and confidence in the system by Roosevelt, radio, and the promise of their own upward mobility.…

Roosevelt begins his first Fireside Chat by distinguishing two parts of his audience: "the comparatively few who understand the mechanics of banking" and "the overwhelming majority of you who use banks for the making of deposits and the drawing of checks." Drawing this distinction between the expert few and the uneducated many may seem an odd way to begin an appeal for national unity. But by the end of the chat it becomes clear that drawing, effacing, and redrawing distinctions between members of his audience is Roosevelt's main rhetorical strategy for forging a national public.

Roosevelt's explanation of the banking crisis begins by assigning blame to the "undermined confidence on the part of the public," part of a passage that deftly conflates bank depositors, his radio audience, and "the public." This may seem an unremarkable observation, yet this move accomplishes some important rhetorical and ideological work. First, like all subsequent chats, this one, by addressing the entire American public, announces itself, performative-style, as a quasi-official utterance. Roosevelt speaks with the voice of the government to the nation itself. A second important elision is that which links the government of the United States to the banking industry, a mixing of public and private authority that the present emergency requires. Third, by assuming that his audience—the American public—is divided between banking experts and depositors, he effectively excludes the millions of Americans too poor to own bank accounts. Participating in Roosevelt's unifying public requires listeners to abstract themselves from their own particular circumstances in order to join a larger imagined community....

Tacking back and forth between his two audiences, now divided into another, starker pairing, "the hysterical demands of hoarders" and "the intelligent support" of the more thoughtful, Roosevelt makes clear that the integrity of the banking system, like the government's reconstruction of the financial and economic fabric, requires a new definition of the public and a new mode of communicating to that public. By the end of the address, the ratios of these two audiences seem to have switched; the majority seems to understand banking and their important role as faithful depositors while the "very few who have not recovered from their fear" persist in "unfashionable" hoarding. This shift, Roosevelt implies, has been effected through the radio broadcast itself; the president, the radio, and the listeners together completed a circuit of communication in which words became performative utterances, conjuring the changes they described.... In exchange for their confidence, this address seems to offer the listener an opportunity to move out of class-bound identity as an uninformed depositor, or worse, a "hysterical" hoarder, into a new position of status and trust.

In his conclusion, Roosevelt made clear the link he saw between this broad, new public—educable and unafraid—national radio reception, and national recovery: "there is an element in the readjustment of our financial system more important than currency, more important than gold, and that is the confidence of the people themselves." In the case of the banking crisis, it becomes clear that the self-confidence of "the people" is the key to the recovery of the nation's banks; further, such a national spread of confidence depends on the nation's moving from the initial division of the uneducated many and the sophisticated few to the confident many and the hysterical few. In this move, Roosevelt replaces a distinction of expertise in the "mechanics" of government and industry with a distinction in a different kind of expertise: the confident and self-conscious knowledge of "the people" as the sovereign power behind national recovery and reconstruction....

Roosevelt's early Fireside Chats called for a unified national audience—an audience already hailed by network radio's national address—at the same time that they policed key distinctions within the audience. The rhetoric of "the people" worked to target a broad "popular elite" in his audience, the supporters of New Deal programs, as opposed to the "selfish few," "the hoarders," and "shirkers." In this way, Roosevelt explicitly invites his national audience to join in the production of public opinion and to abandon any notion of class solidarity and the particular fears, interests, and complaints that may have been part of that class-based identity....

In the chats of this era, defining public and private was a continuous process, one that Roosevelt mastered while still making overtures to his audience as necessary collaborators, whose new status replaces class-bound notions of identity....

"The development of our defense program makes it essential that each and every one of us, men and women, feel that we have some contribution to make toward the security of our nation," So begins the Fireside Chat of May 26, 1940. By early that year, the Fireside Chats had become part of a broader mobilization for war. Hailing a national public for "active duty," these wartime chats enforced conformity and discouraged "difference" by making the most of the link between listenership and citizenship. By celebrating the mass production of public opinion as a kind of "arsenal of democracy," these chats also helped to shape the contours of the public's opinions and participation, subordinating democratic processes to the exigencies of national emergency. In the process, a contradictory version of "the public" became ingrained both in the political culture and in the idea of broadcast reception; this public was intimate and national, sovereign yet passive, theoretically all-inclusive and yet sharply bounded by traditional exclusions.

Along with the shifting play of distinctions that characterized the earlier chats, the wartime chats articulated sharper, more fixed boundaries between "citizens" and "friends," on the one hand, and "enemies of democracy," "foreign agents," and "fifth columnists," on the other. Radio listening became, in the rhetoric of the chats, a component of a broader media mobilization that preceded the United States' entry into the war by more than a year. The chats of this period regarded radio listeners as the cultural equivalent of military and industrial defense workers, creating through their production of a unified public opinion a cadre of defense agents....

The Fireside Chats of 1940 and 1941 epitomized Roosevelt's masterful use of radio to galvanize the American people around powerful nationalist imagery, during a period of unprecedented need for industrial production. Roosevelt's vision of a productive, unified people laying aside all particular notions of identity (labor allegiance, pacifism, isolationism, etc.) is at the heart of his call for "a great arsenal of democracy." It is an arsenal, Roosevelt makes clear, in which the people produce not just war materiel but also an idealized version of themselves, a unified national public....

The nation emerges in these broadcasts as a historical actor, both an expression of popular will and the centralized force dictating how it is to be mobilized: "the nation expects." "the nation has a right to expect," "the nation will expect," and "The American people will not tolerate." This version of the nation connected the will of the people with the authority of the state and the industrial capacity of the market economy....

In her widely syndicated "My Day" column, Eleanor Roosevelt provided an interesting model for the process by which "private" citizens came to participate in the national public commanded by the Fireside Chats. Seated in the front row in the East Room of the White House for the National Emergency broadcast of May 1941, Roosevelt describes her feeling of alienation from the proceedings. Surrounded by diplomats from several South American republics, Mexico, and Canada, the first lady felt "strangely detached, as though I were outside.... I represented no nation, carried no responsibility." Out of this sense of public alienation, via her husband's words, comes a sense of belonging. Detached from the affairs of state and the goings-on in her own home, the first lady suddenly understands herself as "a part of the general public." From this vantage point, she is moved by the sight of her husband's face and the sound of his voice to a new sense of patriotic mission. "In my capacity of objective citizen, sitting in the gathering, I felt that I wanted to accept my responsibility and do my particular job whatever it might be. I think that will be the answer of every individual citizen of the U.S.A."

Alienating and isolating on a personal level, her husband's radio address becomes irresistible to the extent that she can adopt the subject position of "objective citizen." The first lady, like the rest of the 65 million Americans who listened to Roosevelt that night, had to be recruited from some residual private space into the self-consciousness and self-abstractedness of the national public of the Fireside Chats. The Fireside Chats, more than any other broadcasts of the period, made explicit the personal and political significance of the transformation from private person to citizen/listener.

Eleanor Roosevelt's frank account of her own response to the broadcast illustrates an idealized version of the process of becoming a member of the radio public. It also illustrates some of the ways her public persona came to represent a significant model of citizenship in the context of the contradictory demands of mass-mediated democracy. Her own radio persona, composed in several different commercially sponsored series of "chats" on a variety of national and international policy issues, represents a response to her husband's much more celebrated one....

Eleanor Roosevelt was a popular and well-paid radio personality in the 1930s and 1940s. Her commercially sponsored programs for Ponds Cream, Arch-Preserver Shoes, Sweetheart Soap, and the Pan-American Coffee Bureau garnered the first lady unprecedented money, sway, admiration, and criticism. Along with her speaking engagements and nationally syndicated column, "My Day," which she wrote continuously for more than twenty-five years, Eleanor Roosevelt became one of the most popular and influential figures in the Roosevelt administration and in American public life. In 1940 alone, she earned $156,000 for her sponsored radio work alone, making her one of the highest-paid performers on the radio and making her a lightning rod for criticism about impropriety. Curiously, most of this criticism stemmed from a perceived sense of the first lady violating traditional gender roles, rather than from questions about conflicts of interest, politicizing commercial speech, and so on. She used her radio platform to air these criticisms and to respond to them, including a letter from a woman taking her to task for being out in the public eye so much that she was neglecting her husband at home....

Despite ... relentless criticism, Mrs. Roosevelt forged a public persona that was influential and popular. In opinion surveys, her approval ratings were much higher than her husband's and cut across all sectors of the nation, but they were especially high among women....

Mrs. Roosevelt challenged the gendered logic of network radio that consigned women's voices to a purely private realm of domesticity, consumerism, and emotional relationships. That her contributions to radio have been largely forgotten says more about the continued power of such gender discrimination and perhaps the general amnesia that clouds over nearly all of our historical memory of radio....

Sponsored by makers of soap, hand lotion, shoes, and coffee, and encouraged to discuss recipes, and forced to donate all proceeds from her work to charity, Mrs. Roosevelt was, in many respects, cast into a stereotypically feminine role on the broadcast dial. In her 1940-41 program, she was introduced as the Coffee Bureau's "charming news analyst" and her discussion of domestic and international current events took place "over our coffee cups," evoking the metaphoric space of the home, even, more precisely, the kitchen, where women gab rather than debate. However, what she actually said on that program provides a fascinating example of one of the myriad ways women on the radio negotiated gendered boundaries of public and private discourse. In addition, her work on this program provides a fascinating contrast to the president's use of the radio, in its embrace of a radio public in which the particularities of national and religious differences, political disagreement, and, above all, class struggle are acknowledged and affirmed as necessary to a democratic society. Also worth noting is the striking way that the commercial system of radio provided so many opportunities over the years for Mrs. Roosevelt's progressive voice. Public-service broadcasting, in contrast, tended to treat women, and politically minded women in particular, as if they did not exist at all.

Her radio career began in the latter part of 1932, before her husband's inauguration, with her delivering commentary on child rearing and family relations. The job quickly exposed her to the particularly bizarre challenges of the job of first lady, a public role, which she likened to being in a fishbowl, but which required her to tread carefully outside of any but the most domestic sorts of activities. Criticized for using her name "for commercial purposes," and for an unguarded on-air comment in which she seemed blasé about the drinking habits of teenaged girls, Roosevelt conceded: "I suppose I have made some mistakes."...

By 1934, she was back on the air, earning five hundred dollars per minute, compensation reserved for only the highest-paid stars in radio. Sponsored by a roofing company and then by the Simmons Mattress Company, the first lady delivered weekly news commentaries. A short series on education, sponsored by a shoe company, followed shortly thereafter. In 1935, she broadcast a program focusing on "life in the White House," which tended to highlight the amusing, glamorous, and mundane aspects of the Roosevelts' daily life.... Through it all, Roosevelt fended off criticism that she was too highly paid, that she unfairly benefited the commercial prospects of one company over another, that she failed to disclose the precise details of her donations to charity, and in general that she brazenly transgressed the propriety of public and private modes of speech and conduct. And, of course, she was criticized by intellectuals and industry insiders for the triteness of her commentary and the shrillness of her voice, respectively....

Throughout the 1930s and into the early 1940s, Mrs. Roosevelt's radio broadcasts tended to focus on traditional women's issues relating to domesticity:

child rearing, wifely duties, and the social duties of modern debutantes.... The commercial dictates of daytime broadcasts sponsored by soap, lotions, and other household consumer items, and the controversies swirling around the first lady's active working life, worked together to make such topics the safest and most successful. But because of her own status as a working, dynamic personage, many of her broadcast topics tended to stretch the definition of domestic affairs to embrace questions about traditional women moving into public life—the very boundary that Mrs. Roosevelt transgressed. The *Pond's Program* featured programs on the topics "Married Women Working" and "Woman's Career vs. Woman's Home." With the *Pan-American Coffee Hour,* Mrs. Roosevelt began to take on more consistently serious matters of politics and policy. Although there were occasional digressions into lighthearted homemaking tips, the seriousness of the times seemed to have enabled her mobilization on behalf of New Deal programs and civilian defense, which she saw as inextricably connected. And although this would prove to be one of the most controversial periods in the first lady's tenure and evoked the most heated opposition to her transgression of the public/private boundary, it also produced some of the most impressive radio broadcasts of her career....

Following on the heels of the wartime chats, Eleanor's broadcasts, sponsored by the Pan-American Coffee Bureau, provide a striking set of contrasts to those of her husband.

Over Our Coffee Cups, a weekly Sunday evening program, aired from September 1941 through April 1942, a season in which the nation moved from the sidelines to the center of the global conflict. If this period was marked by the president and others in the administration as a time to circle the rhetorical wagons around an increasingly narrow definition of Americanism, Eleanor Roosevelt moved in a starkly different direction. In her first broadcast, she emphasized the warm relations between the United States and the nations of Central and South America, many of which constituted the Pan-American Coffee Bureau, her commercial sponsor. Americans, she observed, composed "twenty-one separate and individual nations, each with its own particular interests and individualities, each holding the same loyalties to their particular country that we hold to our United States."

In her gently chiding way, Roosevelt accused her countrymen of using terms like "Pan-Americanism" "rather meaninglessly" and cautioned that "we cannot generalize as freely as we've done." This move, away from meaningless generalizations and toward a multiplicity of differences among people, words, and countries, is characteristic of her broadcasts from this period. Her emphasis on the importance of differences stands in stark contrast to the tendency, in 1940 and 1941, of the president to emphasize unanimity and to warn against the dangers of dissent. Throughout the autumn of 1940, she returned again and again to the "thousand different meanings" of the word *defense.* For her, the term became an invitation to talk about a broad range of social problems and their solutions, which were as crucial to national defense as guns and soldiers. The rising cost of living, the dangers of wage controls, the quality of government-run homes for the aged, equality of opportunity—these became central issues in her expansion on the meaning of defense....

Mrs. Roosevelt fell victim to a coordinated campaign of attack designed to bring into high relief the inevitable contradictions between her public persona, her political work, and her essentially domestic figurehead role as first lady.

One letter demonstrated the power of this attack to reinscribe powerful gender boundaries that silence women's voices when they dare to speak outside of narrow channels of private discourse: "Mrs. Roosevelt, you would be doing your country a great service if you would simply go home and sew for the Red Cross. Every time you open your mouth the people of this country dislike and mistrust you more."… In her weekly broadcast for the Pan-American Coffee Bureau,… she struck back sharply at her critics, employing to very powerful effect the rhetoric of war to define an irreducible distinction between the values of "privilege or equality." Instead of seeking common ground through a shared recognition of the diversity of meanings and positions, Roosevelt makes clear that some distinctions cannot be eased or transformed through the rhetoric of unity, nor through the blandishments of radio oratory. Unlike President Roosevelt, the first lady does not seek to transform class and ideological divides into something more convenient and manageable; instead, she recognizes the attacks on her as the last front in "the age-old fight for the privileged few against the good of the many." She continues:

> There is not now and never will be in this country or anywhere else in the world unity between these two groups. Perhaps we must all stand up and be counted in this fight, the virtuous Westbrook Peglers [a conservative newspaper columnist and one of her chief critics] on one side, the boondogglers, so called, on the other. This is not a question of Republican or Democrat but privilege or equality. But if there has to be a fight, I'm glad I'm enlisted as common soldier with the many. There is nothing that matters in the least to me which those who have raised this hue and cry can give me or take away from me. What makes this country in the long run a better place in which to live for the average person, what makes us strong to win the war and the peace, because our needs are met and because we are given a sense of security. That matters. For that I intend to fight.

At the conclusion of the Pan-American Coffee Bureau program's season in April 1942, Eleanor Roosevelt did not broadcast on her own commercially sponsored program for the duration of the war. However, she continued to speak over the air as a guest on other programs, or as part of ad hoc presentations concerning vital wartime issues, on several dozen occasions over the next three years.…

For all her success and popularity on the radio, in print, and in her personal appearances, Eleanor Roosevelt remained deeply ambivalent about her status as a public personage, insisting that "I only like the part of my life in which I am a person."… Precisely because that transformation was always in process, and always in doubt, Eleanor Roosevelt was a powerful symbol for women's uncertain perch in public life in the 1930s and 1940s. In her movement from Victorian wife and mother urging women to stay at home, to her bold public criticism of legislation that would have restricted married women from working, she became adept at creating a personage at the intersection of domesticity and politics, while holding on to a sense of herself as essentially fractured between person and personage. "It is less difficult," she reflected in 1960, "for a woman to adjust to new situations than it is for a man."

Franklin and Eleanor Roosevelt each used radio to construct unprecedented political personages. In creating a nationalist discourse in the folksy strains of commercial radio speech, Franklin emphasized unity both as an ancestral given and as the never-ending work of the New Deal and wartime publics he hailed. In almost diametrical opposition, Eleanor's radio voice insisted on the "thousand meanings" that swirled around the words, people, and concepts of the administration, the nation, and the world. She addressed not "the nation," nor "the people," but instead "those who listen to my broadcast," a humbler sense of audience, which reflects the marketplace realities of commercially sponsored programming and her own marginal place in the national discourse. Emphasizing diversity and the often uncomfortable juxtaposition of military and civil-defense goals, Eleanor Roosevelt's radio public—ridiculed and forgotten—provides an alternative legacy for radio's potential as an apparatus for negotiating the shifting grounds of public and private performance on a national and international stage.

FURTHER READING

Craig, Douglas B. *Fireside Politics: Radio and Political Culture in the United States, 1920–1940* (2000).

Czitrom, Daniel. *Media and the American Mind* (1983).

Doerksen, Clifford. *American Babel: Rogue Radio Broadcasters of the Jazz Age* (2005).

Douglas, Susan J. *Listening In: Radio and the American Imagination, from Amos 'n' Andy and Edward R. Murrow to Wolfman Jack and Howard Stern* (1999).

———. *Inventing American Broadcasting, 1899–1922* (1987).

Fisher, Marc. *Something in the Air: Radio, Rock, and the Revolution That Shaped a Generation* (2007).

Goodman, David. *Radio's Civic Ambition: American Broadcasting and Democracy in the 1930s* (2011).

Hilmes, Michele. *NBC: America's Network* (2007).

———. *Radio Voices: American Broadcasting, 1922–1952* (1997).

Hilmes, Michele, and Jason Loviglio, eds. *Radio Reader: Essays in the Cultural History of Radio* (2002).

Horten, Gerd. *Radio Goes to War* (2003).

McChesney, Robert. W. *Telecommunications, Mass Media, and Democracy: The Battle for Control of U.S. Broadcasting, 1928–1935* (1993).

Nachman, Gerald. *Raised on Radio* (2000).

Neer, Richard. *FM: The Rise and Fall of Rock Radio* (2001).

Newman, Kathy. *Radio Active: Advertising and Consumer Activism, 1935–1947* (2004).

Russo, Alexander. *Points on the Dial: Golden Age Radio beyond the Networks* (2010).

Walker, Jesse. *Rebels on the Air: An Alternative History of Radio in America* (2004).

CHAPTER 10

Defining Popular Music
The Concept of Authenticity and the Role of Culture Brokers, 1935–1950

Like many of the genres under review in this textbook, the history of popular music deserves its own Major Problems volume. However, it would be difficult to survey the history of popular culture without some discussion of music. The authors have decided to include one slice of the musical pie by focusing on folk and blues music and questions of authenticity. A case study of collecting the blues and folk ballads by folklorists and music promoters offers a way to wrestle with questions of authenticity in popular culture and how music has been collected and sold by culture brokers. The chapter traces the transformation of folk forms, such as the blues, into popular, commercialized music in the period between the 1930s and the 1950s. The documents and essays also explore the murky, but politically charged distinctions between the categories of folk and popular culture.

Folklorists and cultural historians have written extensively on the history of folk and roots music, its formation, regional and musical forms, who collected the music and why. Historians of popular culture have been particularly interested in the complicated and often blurry distinctions between the folk and the popular, and how both scholars and culture brokers (those who sought to collect, promote, and, eventually, commercialize folk and roots music) actively constructed the cultural meanings of the "folk." As historian John Storey notes in his history of popular culture, Inventing Popular Culture, *definitions of the "folk" have been important in shaping how scholars have approached popular culture. He writes that intellectuals working in Europe and the United States in the nineteenth and early twentieth centuries created and defined popular culture in two ways, as a* "quasi-mythical rural folk" culture that represented culture of common people and "mass culture," the commercialized forms used by the urban, working class. For folklorists and middle-class intellectuals working in the United States, the folk represented examples of authentic and immutable American culture. Mass or popular culture, on the other hand, was subject to the market, changed with technologies and audiences, was commodified, and aimed at the masses.

Early interest among collectors in folk culture corresponded to a sense of cultural fragmentation, precipitated by immigration and the industrial revolution in the United States. Their interest in finding a true folk was linked to a sense of both nationalism and nostalgia for an imaginary Anglo American past. In the late nineteenth century, the search for an Anglo American folk took collectors or "ballad hunters," such as Harvard professor Francis James Child, on romantic quests to find communities isolated from and unchanged by urbanization, industrialization or immigration. Child produced a canon of folk ballads that shaped approaches to collecting and defined folk music well into the twentieth century. From the nineteenth century through the 1930s, folklorists in the United States followed in Child's footsteps and mined communities in Appalachia and other rural areas for their traditional music, calling these forms "folk."

In the 1930s, some folklorists became commercial promoters of folk music as part of what historian Benjamin Filene has termed the "cult of authenticity." As broadcast radio matured, it offered new venues for music and a new, mass market for roots and country music. Folk promoters reacted against the threat of commercial music and the spread of new technologies and instruments. They hoped to provide a counterweight to these changes by recording and preserving traditional forms of music and, eventually, entering the commercial world to promote these forms. Therein lay the paradox of folk music: culture brokers opened the door to commercialization as they tried to reach a wider audience, and at the same time they established definitions of what constituted authentic folk music.

The cult of authenticity had contemporary critics who commented on its contradictions. An historian David Whisnant has shown in his seminal work on the politics of culture in Appalachia, ethnomusicologist Charles Seeger (father of singer Pete Seeger) criticized the White Top Folk Festival held in Virginia in the 1930s as "reactionary" and exclusive. A more well-known debate, however, centers on the relationship between blues musician Lead Belly (Huddie Leadbetter) and ethnomusicologists John A. and, his son, Alan Lomax who collected and defined folk music in this period. Some contemporary critics and later scholars have claimed that Lead Belly suffered from stereotypical representations and unfair contracts that gave him little control over his image. In the later part of this period, Mexican American writer and folklorist Américo Parades provided a critique of culture brokers who sought to define, neutralize, limit, and even colonize the music and stories of ethnic and racial communities. Starting in the 1950s, his work on folklore and music of the Mexico-Texas boarderlands challenged the idea of a purely Anglo American past and gave political voice to Mexicans and Mexican Americans. In particular corridos, or narrative folk ballads of Mexico, memorialized Mexican heroes who challenged Anglo authority.

What were the differences between folk and popular culture in the period under discussion? How did scholars, collectors, and promoters construct a "cult of authenticity" and how did it impact popular music? What did the blues and corridos have in common? What are the musical descendents of blues and corridos? Is it important that certain forms of music maintain a sense of authenticity?

 DOCUMENTS

The documents in this chapter chart the influence of the blues on popular music from the 1930s to the 1950s, the work of culture brokers in shaping not only notions of authenticity but the image of musicians, and the political nature of both blues and corridos. The first three documents debate the controversial career of Lead Belly in the 1930s from different perspectives. They include reviews by a white journalist writing for a national magazine, well-known music critic and chief of the Music Division at the Library of Congress, Carl Engel and African American activist, Richard Wright. Why would white observers characterize Lead Belly as a minstrel? What are the connections between minstrelsy and the carefully-constructed public persona of Lead Belly? Document 4 discusses the fluid boundaries between musical forms and the transition from blues to rock and roll in the 1950s. Documents 5 and 6, examine the famous borderland corrido about Gregorio Cortez, documented by Américo Paredes. How did the ballad frame Cortez as a popular or folk hero? Are there any similarities between the corrido and blues music? How did Paredes give political voice to Mexicans and Mexican Americans in his analysis of the corrido?

1. *Time,* a National Magazine, Takes a Negative View of Lead Belly, 1935

In Texas a black buck known as Lead Belly murdered a man. He sang a petition to Governor Pat Neff and was granted a pardon. Back in the Louisiana swamplands, where he was born Huddie Ledbetter, his knife made more trouble. He was in State Prison at Angola when John A. Lomax, eminent ballad collector, stopped by last summer and asked the warden if he could please hear Lead Belly sing.

John Lomax arrived in Manhattan last week to lecture on ballads and with him was Lead Belly, wild-eyed as ever. The Negro had been pardoned again because Mr. Lomax had made a phonograph record of a second petition and taken it to Louisiana's Governor Allen. Lead Belly was released from prison on Aug. 1. [A] month later when Mr. Lomax was sitting in a Texas hotel he felt a tap on his shoulder. It was Lead Belly, saying: "Boss, here I is." His knife bulged in his pocket. In his hand was a rickety green-painted guitar held together by string.

Wearing overalls and a blue hickory shirt over a yellow one, Lead Belly sang in Manhattan last week for University of Texas alumni. And John Lomax was nervous. Theatrical agents and radio scouts insisted on hearing his protege, who had been out on a wild 24-hour rampage in Harlem. Until it was time for him to sing Lomax kept his hell-raising minstrel locked up in a coat room. But the performance went off without mishap. Lead Belly's voice is rich and clear. He plays and sings with his eyes closed, taps single time with one foot, triple with the other. He claims that most of his songs are his own. He sang about when "me and a bunch of cowboys had that famous battle on Bunker Hill," and again about the Negro who "throwed his jelly out of the window." The minstrel was proudest when he chanted the petition which won him his first pardon. The refrain:

I am your servant, composed this song;

Please, Governor Neff, let me go back home.

I know my wife will jump and shout When de train roll up and I come steppin' out.

Please, Governor Neff, be good an' kind, Have mercy on my great long time, I don't see to save my soul; If I can't get a pardon, try me in a parole....

Please, Governor Neff, be good and kind, And if I can't get a pardon, will you cut my time?

If I had you, Governor Neff, like you got me, I would wake up in the mornin' and set you free.

And I'm going home to Mary—po'

Mary.

2. Influential Music Critic Reviews the
Negro Folksongs as Sung by Lead Belly, 1937

Views and Reviews

Professor John A. Lomax has enriched our knowledge of the feathered fauna of our land with his discovery and detailed description of the singing jailbird—*Captus cantor lomaxius*—, and a lusty warbler it is. Its habitat stretches throughout [all] the states of the Union, but apparently it is most prevalent in the South. In color it varies between milk-chocolate and anthracite. Such migratory tendencies as it may show, are generally prompted by sudden impulses of flight which, however, are rarely crowned with success. Its nesting period is determined by the duration of brooding imposed by the nature of circumstances.

For several years now, Mr. Lomax has pursued his ornitho-musico-penological research and has tracked his bird in the penitentiaries of nine Southern states.... In

Carl Engel, "Views and Reviews," *The Musical Quarterly*, 23(3, July 1937), 388–395, by permission of Oxford University Press.

a recent publication ("Negro Folk Songs as Sung by Lead Belly"; New York, The Macmillan Co., 1936), Mr. Lomax has avoided the tumbling into musical pitfalls that marked his earlier venture, by having had recourse this time to the experience and skill of Dr. George Herzog, of Columbia University, in the transcribing upon paper of the bird's elusive notes. We have here a collection of Negroid "folktunes" that, in its visible presentation of the melodies, more closely approaches the actual rendition than has heretofore been the case....

What this music represents, even our pundits can not wholly agree upon. With respect to the tunes contained in Professor Lomax's latest volume, Dr. Herzog says that "more than half of these melodies and texts have been published in other collections, in some other version. Others are of white parentage, some are white tunes pure and simple." This seems to us good judgment. Mr. Lomax would have us feel "pretty sure" that the tunes he has gathered "are not precisely like other versions." But we are certain that "pretty sure" is not quite dependable enough a method for a scientific bird-catcher.

Once he had caught his prize-specimen, Mr. Lomax decided not only to tame it but to let the public in on this piece of domestication. How it began and how it ended, is the kernel of real interest in Mr. Lomax's latest story. We shall be able merely to give an outline here of what distinguished the most notable among the "charming vocalists" whom Mr. Lomax encountered in his visits to the great penitentiaries and convict farms of the South....

In essence, Mr. Lomax's collection consists of Mr. Lead Belly's vocal repertory, which is accompanied always by informative paragraphs of the collector's and often by some pithy or salty comment of the singer's. The whole is prefaced by the tale of Lead Belly's exploits, including those which brought him into conflict with the law, and by Mr. Lomax's entertaining account of the eventful six months during which he and his son Alan had Lead Belly for a travelling companion. Readers of this magazine have had occasion to become familiar with Mr. Lomax's enlivening style. He knows how to spin a colorful yarn....

It [was] in Angola prison that Professor Lomax, in quest of material for the Archive of American Folksong in the Library of Congress, came upon Lead Belly. From him, Mr. Lomax secured about one hundred "folky" songs. Mr. Lomax entertains the belief that long confinement in prison cells keeps the singer of folk-songs from influences which tend to contaminate and pervert the "folky" strains and thus rob these songs of their authenticity. We do not hold to this theory....

That poets and singers can be rogues, is nothing new; nor need enforced seclusion forbid admittance to the Muse.... Even Oscar Wilde, disgraced and incarcerated, rose to at least one excellent piece of poetry and some superlatively fine prose.

All of which should deceive no one into imagining for a moment that Mr. Huddie Ledbetter, alias Lead Belly, is in any form, shape, or manner comparable to this ... eminent and tragic culprit-poet. In Mr. Lomax's account of Lead Belly's Odyssey the note of tragedy is conspicuously missing. Tragedy invites pity. The tale of Lead Belly—intemperate, reckless, vicious black man—is curious but not affecting. His songs are blunt though often quaint; they seldom step out in more then pedestrian gait. Most of the time it is an egomaniac of inferior perceptivity and intelligence who is picking a good-humored brawl with fate and his own sins....

Lead Belly's crowning and chirping and warbling have been faithfully recorded by Mr. Lomax and his son Alan.... But Mr. Lomax was anxious to let the world know and appreciate Lead Belly not only from his records, but from his actual singing. The opportunity to do so came in the autumn of 1934, after Governor O. K. Allen had reprieved the convict. Mr. Lomax promptly seized it, with a courage and a spirit of adventure that would do credit to the most gallant explorer. The narrative of what occurred during the six months of this travelling association—especially in Mr. Lomax's incomparable telling—makes capital reading....

With a certain amount of native shrewdness, Lead Belly himself seems to have put the idea into Mr. Lomax's head.... Mr. Lomax succumbed to this beguiling prospect—which included the gratuitous unreeling of countless jingles to the twanging of a twelve-string guitar. The ultimate outcome was a sad rebuke to Mr. Lomax's kindness and optimism....

Undismayed, Mr. Lomax challenged all risks to life and limb, in the interests of art and learning. The grand tour began from Mr. Lomax's home in Austin, Texas, through Arkansas. At the large prison farm of that state, near Pine Bluff, Lead Belly showed the first signs of restlessness and dissatisfaction. He greatly enjoyed, though, two visits to the women's convict camp, where a noisy how-de-do was made over him, and where records were obtained of a few songs from the singing of a bunch of lively young Negro girls. But he often voiced his easily explicable and growing disgust with "lookin' at niggahs in the penitenshuh." He expressed the very natural wish to "go somewhere else." Mr. Lomax, with an over-indulgent regard for the demands of human urges, decided to take the road back to Shreveport and Fannin Street. There Lead Belly disappeared for two days and nights, and then cheerfully turned up again, as any straying tom-cat might do in certain seasons of the year. Then the trek north continued, and so did Lead Belly's occasional presumptions on Mr. Lomax's easy-going temper. New York was the shining goal, with fame and money beckoning.

A foretaste of things-to-come was had in Philadelphia, where Lead Belly on December 30, 1934, entertained the members of the Modern Language Association of America at their annual smoker. The delighted listeners filled his hat with silver and dollar bills. When, that same night, Lead Belly was asked to sing before a group of Bryn Mawr intellectuals and he was driving the car into the college campus, he confided to Mr. Lomax: "Well, maybe dey don't know it, but dey is about to hear de famousest niggah guitar player in de world." It had taken very little to turn Lead Belly's dusky head....

It was not long before reporters and publicity-hounds got on the scent of a news-story that savored of the sensational. A charming and modest university professor from Austin, Texas, was hoisted to the giddy pinnacle of Manhattan head-lines, hailed as the discoverer of a rank criminal who could sing tender blues as well as blood-curdling ballads. He cleaved his way to the front page with a double-edged sword. No wonder that William Rose Benét wrote a full page ballad about Lead Belly and that the magazine "Time" printed his picture and the story of his career. No wonder that the president of a college cancelled a contract already made by its music department after he had read one of Lincoln Barnett's accounts emphasizing the shady side of poor Lead Belly's past.

There was a struggle between admiration and condemnation. It could have but one issue. Lead Belly, with Professor Lomax as master of unceremonious ceremonies, played and sang his so-called "folk-tunes" for a while before a great variety of people, ranging from crowds of Negro convicts to groups of polite and socially eligible miscreants. They all listened absorbedly, they applauded and filled his hat. The Associated Press took him under its far-spreading wing; the radio gave him its precious "time" and felt rewarded at any price. For a fleeting moment, Lead Belly became "a national figure."...

Before long, Mr. Lomax admits, Lead Belly's attitude towards him and his son Alan began gradually to change: he grudgingly consented to meet engagements that had been made for him; for days he would gruffly refuse to give of his songs or stories; he began to neglect his household duties; his demands for extra money and his consumption of gin grew apace....

Mr. Lomax goes so far as to say that "through our own mistakes in dealing with him," the cankered minstrel assumed the part of "an arrogant person, dressed in flashy clothes, a self-confident boaster." The last glimpse we catch of this incorrigible wastrel and his woman, is to see them depart, in a Greyhound bus, for their beloved and more congenial Shreveport.

No doubt, Professor Lomax will consider his harvest of "sinful songs" worth all the trouble he took in the reaping. Indeed, they furnished him with the material for a most diverting extravaganza in Negroid folklore. But a critical examination of this assortment of "hollers," of "reels," of "work songs," and the rest, can lead any unbiased judge to only one conclusion: that real gems of pure water, touched with deep fervor and stark beauty, such as are found in such quantity among the Negro spirituals, were not in Huddie Ledbetter's repertory. Confinement and the chain-gang did not improve the native trend of his mind; freedom and the benefactions of Mr. Lomax could not alter his ways. It was not to be expected....

3. Richard Wright, an African American Novelist, Describes the Politics of Lead Belly's Image, 1937

When 50-year-old Huddie Ledbetter planks himself in a chair, spreads his feet and starts strumming his 12-stringed guitar and singing that rich, barrel-chested baritone, it seems that the entire folk culture of American Negro has found its embodiment in him.

Blues, spirituals, animal songs, ballads and work songs pour forth in such profusion that it seems he knows every song his race has ever sung.

Richard Wright, "Huddie Ledbetter, Famous Negro Folk Artist, Sings the Songs of Scottsboro and His People," *Daily Worker* (12 August 1937), 7.

Shaped and moulded by some of the harshest social forces in American life, Ledbetter admits that he knows 500 folk songs, "and maybe many more I can't count."

He makes his songs out of the day-to-day life of his people. He sings of death, of work of balked love, of Southern jails no better than hell-holes, of chain gangs, of segregation, and of his hope for a better life....

Wins Pardon

When Ledbetter won himself a pardon for the second time out of a Southern prison by composing folk songs, the Southern landlords exploited him, robbed him of his self-made culture and then turned him loose on the streets of Northern cities to starve.

John A. Lomax, collector of American folk sons for the Library of Congress, heard of Ledbetter and went to see him in prison.

And here begins one of the most amazing cultural swindles in American history. Lomax found in Ledbetter a mine of lore, songs, tunes and adages of the South. He persuaded Ledbetter to make a phonograph record. When finished, it contained two songs; one a love song, Irene, a haunting and tender melody; the other was called To O.K. Allen. It was a chanted plea to Governor Allen of Louisiana for a pardon. The plea was sung so successfully that exactly one month later Ledbetter was free.

Uses Ledbetter

Lomax then beguiled the singer with sugary promises, telling him that if he helped him to gather folk songs from other Negro prisoners in various prisons throughout the South, he would make him rich.

Lomax used the influence of his official position with the Library of Congress to get into prisoners and get songs. But he knew that a white man would have great difficulty in getting Negro prisoners to confide their folk culture in him, so he used Ledbetter as his guide and entree.

Ledbetter and Lomax traveled through Texas, Arkansas, Alabama, Louisiana, and gathered folk songs which later were compiled into a book, "American Ballads and Folk Songs." And the only credit Ledbetter got for that book was the "high honor" of seeing his name in print.

Begins Attacks

In addition Lomax, in order to make engagements and more profit, gave out a vicious tirade of publicity to the nation's leading newspapers about the Negro folk singer. Leadbetter was represented in the *New York Herald Tribune, Time Magazine* and over the radio as a half sex-mad, knife-totting, black buck from Texas. *Time Magazine, March of Time* and the newspapers generally featured him in such tones.

In due time Lomax toured the Northern and New England states with Ledbetter, charging $100 per night for each appearance and in addition sometimes took up collections which amounted to over $50.

When Leadbetter insisted upon a straight and legal contract, Lomax told him that he was saving his money for him, and that, "If I gave you your money you'd throw it away in Harlem."

When the tour ended Leadbetter received but $15 for his appearance in the March of Time; nothing for his extensive travels and work save a sum of $255 paid to him in skimpy installments: $55 in cash and the remaining $200 in checks which were so dated that he could not draw but $50 of it each month.

Goes South

Ledbetter, who had married in the meantime, took the checks and his wife and went to Shreveport, LA. He got what few jobs he could, but the Southern whites would have none of him.

Three years ago he came back to New York, this time alone save for his wife, a laundry worker, who since has become his manager.

Even if New York contracts were hard to get, and for the second time Ledbetter was victimized by a prejudiced white Southerner in a theatre engagement. Finally he joined the Worker's Alliance and applied for relief.

Threaten Songs

The relief authorities could not believe that Ledbetter did not have money saved from his extensive appearance on the stage and threatened to withdraw his food ticket. In return the folk singer threatened to write a song about the rotten relief methods and the relief authorities granted his demands.

"The folks in the Workers' Alliance are the finest I've even known," said Ledbetter. "I feel happy when I am with the boys here in the Workers' Alliance. They are different from those Southern white men."

Two of his latest compositions are on the methods of segregation used in Washington D.C., and his elation over the recent Scottsboro victory. The words of **Bourgeois Blues** are as follows:

> I was in Washington the other day
> And I heard a white man say,
>   "I am a bourgeois…"
>
>   Chorus:
>   Aw, bourgeois! Aw, bourgeois!
>   I got them bourgeois blues!
>   And I'm sure gonna spread the news!
>
> When I was in Washington
> I couldn't understand
> How them white folks treat the colored man…
>
> We went all over town
> Trying to find a place to stay
> Everywhere we went the white folks run us away…

★ ★ ★

Me and my wife was standing on a stair
And we heard a white man say,
"We don't want no niggers up there…"

★ ★ ★

I advise colored folks to listen to me
And stay away from Washington D.C.
'Cause it's a bourgeois town…

★ ★ ★

Them rich white folks in Washington
They sure know how
To throw you a nickel to see you bow…

4. Paul Ackerman, Journalist, Discusses the Political Potential of Music, 1956

Hard and fast cleavages between the country and western, pop, and rhythm and blues fields are rapidly breaking down. This is no sudden development, for all of us remember how tunes by the great late Hank Williams would go pop years ago. Today however, the evidence on all sides has piled up to indicate that there is much overlapping of categories. Whereas it was unusual years ago for a song in one field to make it in another, it is quite common today.

An examination of the record market in both the singles and package field will illustrate the truth of this….

Perhaps the most interesting example of the breakdown of categories, however, is the current overlapping of the country, rhythm and blues field. Today the diskeries are pushing out an increasing number of disks which are out by country artists, but which have a definite r&b quality about them. The outstanding example of this type of performer today is Elvis Presley, recently with Sun Records and now on the Victor label.

Presley skyrocketed to fame on Sun, via a souped-up vocal style remarkable for its r&b quality, and accompanied by a throbbing beat of guitar and bass. Meanwhile many other country artists, such as Marty Robbins on Columbia, Charlie Core on King, Johnny Cash on Sun have been doing an amazing amount of country blues disks—blues which have an r&b, quality….

Entering the sweepstakes, of course is Deceits c&w exec Paul Cohen who has quietly scouted around and has picked up a couple of young performers with the "Presley sound." One of these is Tommy Smith. Decca is expected to release sides by these artists soon.

Cohen, by the way, throws same interesting light on the whole c&w, r&b, trend. He notes that the fields were always taking that country singers, as evidenced by the songs of Jimmie Rodgers, have always had a feeling for the

Paul Ackerman, "Barriers Being Swept Away in C&W, Pop and R&B Fields," *Billboard*, 1956. Billboard article used with permission of Prometheus Global Media, LLC.

blues and that often the difference between a country side and an r&b side is merely the use of strings as against the use of horns. The Presley sound—it is pointed out, might be called r&b, without horns, but with strings.

There is one aspect of the c&w, r&b, overlapping which is often forgotten. This is the interesting manner in which r&b is influence in country seems to be running parallel to r&b's interest in pop. The latter came first, of course, and it will be interesting to see whether the r&b incursion into country will assume the same proportions.

Meanwhile Presley, a key figure in it all, has been getting a tremendous buildup via performances on national TV programs. He has also been breaking into the gossip columns—all indicative of the fact that neither he—nor the music he stands for—can be considered as strictly country....

In short, it may be said that today hillbillies and hillbilly music are where you find them. It could be Boston, or Frank Dailey's Meadowbrook, or the New York Palace Theatre. Similarly, pop music is where you find it. And this could be over a deejay show in Nashville, Tenn.; on a disk which couples Hugo Winterhalter and Eddy Arnold. And, of course, r&b enjoys a similarly wide geographical spread, for it has left its mark in pop and c&w.

It's getting harder to tell 'em apart.

5. Américo Paredes, Ethnographer and Culture Critic, Investigates the Political Meanings of El Corrido de Gregorio Cortez, 1958

... *Corrido,* the Mexicans call their narrative folk songs, especially those of epic themes, taking the name from *correr,* which means "to run" or "to flow," for the *corrido* tells a story simply and swiftly, without embellishments. *El Corrido de Gregorio Cortez* comes from a region, half in Mexico and half in the United States, known in this book as the Lower Rio Grande Border, the Lower Border, or simply the Border (with a capital B). Some people call it the Rio Grande Valley, but this name is also given a New Mexican area. In Texas, only the American side is usually called the Valley, and the name is associated with cotton, grapefruit, and the tourist industry.

El Corrido de Gregorio Cortez, then, is a Border Mexican ballad, "Mexican" being understood in a cultural sense, without reference to citizenship or to "blood." But we must stress "Border" too. It is as a border that the Lower Rio Grande has made its mark: in legend, in song, and in those documented old men's tales called histories.

Borders and ballads seem to go together, and their heroes are all cast in the same mold. During the Middle Ages there lived in some parts of Europe, especially in the border areas, a certain type of men whose fame has come down to us in legend and in song. On the Scottish-English border there were heroes like

Wallace, the rebel against English domination, like Jock o the Side, Hobie Noble, Willie Armstrong, and other Liddesdale and Teviotdale raiders, whose favorite occupation was defying the power of England....

People composed ballads about men like these; legends grew up about them, and they became folk heroes, to be studied and argued about by generations of scholars. To this same class belongs Gregorio Cortez, who lived not in Europe of the Middle Ages but in twentieth-century America. This is his story, the fact and the legend of it: Gregorio Cortez, who defended his right with his pistol in his hand.

The Border Mexican Against the Rinches
[Texas Ranges]

The *corrido* of border conflict assumes its most characteristic form when its subject deals with the conflict between Border Mexican and Anglo-Texan, with the Mexican—outnumbered and pistol in hand–defending his "right" against the *rinches*. The *corrido* of border conflict follows a general pattern, out of which emerges the Border concept of the hero. It is a concept that is reflected in other *corrido* themes as well, because border conflict dominated Border balladry for almost a century. Basically the pattern is that established with [Juan N Cortina, 1824–1892] Cortina in 1859. It is always expressed in the *corrido* form.

Pablo González is walking past the Rio Grande City court-house with his wife when she is insulted by the Anglo-American law. He shoots a *rinche* and takes to the brush with his rifle and his pistol, where he fights off numbers of *rinches* who come after him. Finally another Border Mexican, who he thinks is his friend, visits Pablo and unloads his rifle when Pablo is not looking. A little while later Pablo is attacked and shot down by the *rinches* while he is trying to load his rifle....

Ignacio Treviño is quietly drinking off a whiskey at the White Elephant Saloon in Brownsville when a whole army of Texas Rangers and deputies ride into town. They have come to wipe out the Brownsville police force, which is made up of Mexicans. One particular Ranger has come down with the special job of shooting police chief Joe Crixell in the back. Ignacio fights them all at the White Elephant and drives them away, but his victory is temporary. In the end he and other survivors of Crixell's force have to seek refuge across the river.

And so the pattern has been put together, that same pattern which finds expression in the ballads and stories about Gregorio Cortez. It is never the same in all its details, nor does it always correspond to fact, but it carries the real man along with it and transforms him into the hero. The hero is always the peaceful man, finally goaded into violence by the *rinches* and rising in his wrath to kill great numbers of his enemy. His defeat is assured; at the best he can escape across the border, and often he is killed or captured. But whatever his fate, he has stood up for his right.

The *Corrido* of Border Conflict
as a Dominant Form

The period of border conflict [1836 to 1930s] resulted in the gradual emergence of the *corrido* as the dominant form of Lower Border balladry. The conflict period was shorter than similar ones in medieval Europe. The Border *corrido,* by the time it entered its decadent period in the 1930s, had not assumed total hegemony over Border balladry, as did the *romance* in Spain. But the process is clearly evident, and because it was not completed it is easier to see in action. One can see the balladry of the Lower Border working toward a single type: toward one form, the *corrido;* toward one theme, border conflict; toward one concept of the hero, the man fighting for his right with his pistol in his hand....

Border conflict dominates as a theme. The old ballad subjects, dealing mostly with the everyday activities of the Rio Grande folk, lose much of their interest. Ballads are received from Greater Mexico, from Cuba, and even from the United States, but their themes, mostly proletarian, are not imitated. The local ballads all take on the complexion of conflict. The term *rinche* (Texas Ranger) is extended not only to possemen but to border patrolmen, immigration officers, prison guards, and even to Pershing's soldiers when they are in pursuit of the border raider Pancho Villa. In some cases, such as in *El Corrido de José Mosqueda,* a ballad with a purely outlaw background is transformed into a ballad of border conflict.

The concept of the hero as a man fighting for his right also becomes dominant. The proletarian ballad's concept of the hero as an outlaw who robs the rich to give to the poor does not gain acceptance, though Greater Mexican ballads containing it are sung and enjoyed. Nor does the Border outlaw repent, to furnish a moral for the crowd. The outlaw is either seen frankly as an outlaw, without sentimentalizing, or he is made an actor in border conflict. The hero, however, is not the highwayman or the smuggler, but the peaceful man who defends his right. The Border ballads that have been most widely accepted are those containing the three factors mentioned: *corrido* form, border-conflict theme, and a hero that defends his right.

In 1901 border conflict was sixty-five years old.... On a June day in 1901 Gregorio Cortez sat peacefully at home, far from the Border, relaxing after the noonday meal and watching his corn grow. Sheriff Brack Morris of Karnes County drew up beside Gregorio's gate in a surrey with fringe on top. The events that followed were told in legend and ballad. Gregorio Cortez came to epitomize the Border *corrido* hero, and his ballad brought the elements of the heroic Border *corrido* to a focus. *El Corrido de Gregorio Cortez* set the model for the twentieth-century heroic *corrido* of the Lower Border. It is not too much to suggest that it had an influence on the Greater Mexican heroic *corrido,* which began ten years after Cortez rode his famous ride.

The Mexico City Broadside

1
Como decimos, así es,
en mil novecientos uno,
el día veintidós de junio
fue capturado Cortés.

As we say, so it is;
In nineteen hundred and one,
On the twenty-second of June
Cortez was captured.

2
En junio día veintidós
por telégrafo supieron
que a Cortés lo aprehendieron
entre el Sauz y Palafox.

In June, on the twenty-second,
By telegraph it was known
That Cortez had been apprehended
Between El Sauz and Palafox.

3
Se aprehendió en Campo de Oveja,
de don Abraham de la Garza,
él perdió toda esperanza,
ya en la frontera de Texas.

He was captured in Sheep Camp,
Of Don Abraham de la Garza,
He lost all hope
When he was already on the Texas border.

4
Que viva nuestra nación,
aunque sufriendo revés,
Viva, Gregorio Cortés,
que ha honrado su pabellón.

Long live our country
Although suffering setback,
Long live Gregorio Cortez,
Who has honored his flag.

5
Murieron tres aprehensores,
por falta en determinar,
y así han podido pagar
los justos por pecadores.

Three captors died
For lack of discernment,
And thus there have paid
The just for the sinners.

6
Todito el Río Grande estaba,
resguardando el litoral,
parece que se esperaba,
conflicto internacional.

All the Rio Grande
Was guarding the shore;
It seemed that they were expecting
An international conflict.

7
La madre patria es hogar,
que hijo e hija ama,
pues México tiene fama,
disciplina militar.

The mother country is a home
That loves both daughter and son,
For Mexico has fame,
Military discipline.

8
Cortés a Morris mató,
la pistola que sirvió,
por otra luego cambió
a un amigo que encontró.

Cortez killed Morris;
The pistol that was used
He exchanged for another
With a friend that he met.

9

Su coche a tiro tomó,	His coach and team [?] he took,
toda esta advertencia tuvo,	He was careful to do all this;
tres millas y media anduvo	He rode three miles and a half
y allí se apeó y amarró.	And then got down and tied up.

10

De América su nación,	Of America her nation
ha sufrido este revés,	Has suffered this setback,
pues nuestro hermano Cortés	For our brother Cortez
ha honrado su pabellón.	Has honored his flag.

11

Se oyen de Cortés querellas	From Cortez are heard complaints,
lamentándose al Creador,	Lamenting to the Creator,
el pabellón tricolor	The tricolor flag,
idéntico a las estrellas.	Identical to the stars.

12

Gregorio Cortés venía	Gregorio Cortez was coming
de incógnito y lo entregaron,	In disguise and he was betrayed;
y así lo determinaron,	Thus it was arranged,
porque así les convenía.	Because it was to their interest.

13

La grande alarma que hoy pasa	The great alarm that now happens,
en San Antonio, Laredo,	In San Antonio, Laredo,
por el gran furor y miedo,	From the great fury and fear
querían acabar la raza.	They wanted to exterminate our People.

14

Llegó a casa de Robledo,	He got to Robledo's house,
allí con él conversó,	There he conversed with him;
nada de esto les contó,	He told them nothing of this,
porque no tuvieran miedo.	So they wouldn't be afraid.

15

Glover aquí lo asaltó,	Glover surprised him here,
descalzo salió de aquí,	Barefoot he went out of here;
volvió por calzado ahí,	He returned for his shoes
y a Glover muerto encontró.	And found Glover dead.

16

A Cortés llegan con fallos,	To Cortez they come with judgments,
siendo íntegro mexicano.	Being an upright Mexican,
Diciendo:—¿Cortés y hermano	Saying, "Cortez and brother
son ladrones de a caballo?	Are thieves on horseback?"

17

¡Dios de mí tenga clemencia	May God on me have mercy,
adiós, esposa, ay de míl	Farewell, wife, woe is me!

por cincuenta años salí
sentenciado, a penitencia.

18
Así difundió su amor,
nuestro Redentor Jesús.
Gracias mil, don Pablo Cruz,
Editor "DEL REGIDOR."

19
Pablo Cruz se distinguió
como íntegro mexicano,
este prominente hermano
que su ayuda me impartió.

20
Su indulgente Redacción
y su unión confraternal,
con su luz intelectual,
él abrió una suscripción.

21
Participo esta noticia,
a gente culta y honrada…
los de lista enumerada,
la suerte le sea propicia.

22
¡Y aquí acaba de una vez,
la desgracia lamentando!…
Aquí se acaba cantando
el Corrido de Cortés.

For fifty years I departed,
Sentenced to the penitentiary.

Thus did he diffuse His love,
Jesus, our Redeemer;
A thousand thanks, Don Pablo Cruz,
Editor of *El Regidor.*

Pablo Cruz distinguished himself
As an upright Mexican,
This prominent brother
Who gave me his help.

His indulgent Staff
And his confraternal union,
With his intellectual light,
He began a subscription.

I make this news known
To cultured and honest people;
Those on the numbered list—
May fortune be propitious to them.

And here ends at once,
The misfortune lamenting!…
This is the end of the singing
Of the ballad of Cortez.

6. Folk Ballad Remembers the Courage of Gregorio Cortez and Conflicts along the Mexico–Texas Border, 1958

In the county of El Carmen
A great misfortune befell;
The Major Sheriff is dead;
Who killed him no one can tell.

"El Corrido de Gregorio Cortez" in *With His Pistol in His Hand: A Border Ballad and Its Hero,* *translated by Américo Paredes.* Copyright © 1958, renewed 1986. By permission of the University of Texas Press.

At two in the afternoon,
In half an hour or less,
They knew that the man who killed him
Had been Gregorio Cortez.

They let loose the bloodhound dogs;
They followed him from afar.
But trying to catch Cortez
Was like following a star.

All the rangers of the county
Were flying, they rode so hard;
What they wanted was to get
The thousand-dollar reward.

And in the county of Kiansis
They cornered him after all;
Though they were more than three hundred
He leaped out of their corral.

Then the Major Sheriff said,
As if he was going to cry,
"Cortez, hand over your weapons;
We want to take you alive."

Then said Gregorio Cortez,
And his voice was like a bell,
"You will never get my weapons
Till you put me in a cell."

Then said Gregorio Cortez,
With his pistol in his hand,
"Ah, so many mounted Rangers
Just to take one Mexican!"

 # ESSAYS

The first essay by Benjamin Filene, associate professor of history at the University of North Carolina, examines the cult of authenticity in the 1930s and explores the role of the Lomaxes in popularizing folk music as part of a resurgent interest in the "common man." Filene offers a complex case study of the Lomaxes 'Should be Lomaxes' relationship to Huddie Leadbetter that illuminates the quest to promote and popularize authenticity in the 1930s. The second essay, by José David Saldivar, professor of Ethnic Studies and English at University of California at Berkeley, was part of a larger work on the "experimental and anti-imperialist" scholarship of Américo Paredes. Written for Amy Kaplan and Donald Peases', *Cultures of United States Imperialism*, the longer essay argued for the importance of studying borderlands as places where culture is mixed, hybrid, and important for de-centering our understanding of American culture, turning traditional notions of authenticity on their head.

Culture Brokers and Questions of Authenticity

BENJAMIN FILENE

Over the decade, John Sr. and Alan [Lomax] would travel tens of thousands of miles and make thousands of recordings. They did so not with the detachment of academics but with the zeal of proselytizers. Eager to promote their vision of America's musical past, they recognized early on the power of enlisting living vernacular musicians—"actual folk"—to aid their cause. In a pioneering move, the Lomaxes began to promote not just the songs they gathered but the singers who sang them. In doing so they produced a web of criteria for determining what a "true" folk singer looked and sounded like and a set of assumptions about the importance of *being* a "true" folk singer. In short, they created a "cult of authenticity," a thicket of expectations and valuations that American roots musicians and their audiences have been negotiating ever since....

In June, John Lomax had persuaded the Macmillan publishing company to contract for a book of folk songs. In 1933 Lomax used this contract to draw support for a collecting expedition. The American Council of Learned Societies and the Library of Congress's Archive of American Folk-Song contributed funds that enabled Lomax to order one of the first portable electronic recording machines for the trip. The archive, now leaderless, having dismissed Robert Gordon, agreed to be the official repository for the materials Lomax gathered. Having again enlisted Alan as his assistant, in June 1933 Lomax loaded his Ford with "two army cots and bedding, a cooking outfit, provisions, [and] an infinite number of 'etceteras.'" After a delay, the Lomaxes added to this miscellany the 350-pound "portable" Dictaphone recorder, which they built into the back seat. It came with two seventy-five-pound batteries, a microphone, cables, and piles of blank aluminum and celluloid disks. Carrying this load the Ford lumbered off, and the Lomaxes began their hunt for America's folk songs.

The Lomaxes had a complicated agenda for this expedition. Their collecting methods and attitude make the trip, from today's perspective, seem part talent search, part sociological survey, and part safari. Primarily they sought traditional folk music in the "eddies of human society," self-contained homogeneous communities cut off from the corrupting influences of popular culture. Mainstream communities, the Lomaxes feared, had lost touch with their folk roots.... The Lomaxes hoped to find the old styles "dammed up" in America's more isolated areas. They collected from remote cotton plantations, cowboy ranches, lumber camps, and, with particular success, southern segregated prisons. John Lomax believed that prisons had inadvertently done folklorists a service by isolating groups of informants from modern society. On their 1933 trip, the Lomaxes recorded in the penitentiaries of five states, as they sought to document "the Negro who had the least contact with jazz, the radio, and with the white man.... The convicts heard only the idiom of their own race."...

Early on in the 1933 trip the Lomaxes were convinced of the value of their efforts. One of the first people they recorded was an African American singer and guitarist named *Huddie Ledbetter, or "Lead Belly."* The Lomaxes "discovered" Lead Belly, roughly forty-four years old at the time, in Louisiana's Angola prison, where he was serving out a sentence for murder. Lead Belly astonished the Lomaxes with the variety of songs he knew and the verve and virtuosity with which he played them. He seemed to be a living link to traditions that were slipping away, a storehouse of old-time songs greater than they had thought possible to find in the twentieth century. John Lomax would later write, "From Lead Belly we secured about one hundred songs that seemed 'folky,' a far greater number than from any other person." Although Lead Belly did know some popular songs, the Lomaxes felt that "his eleven years of confinement had cut him off both from the phonograph and from the radio." The Lomaxes had stumbled upon the folk song find of their dreams.

Lead Belly inspired such excitement in the Lomaxes because he confirmed their most basic assumptions about American folk song, assumptions that may now seem commonplace but that in the early thirties represented decisive blows against the still powerful [James Francis] Child canon. The variety of songs that Lead Belly knew, for instance, nicely illustrated for the Lomaxes that America did have a folk song heritage independent of Britain. Even more so than Carl Sandburg and Robert Gordon, the Lomaxes were determined to praise America's indigenous music, refusing to apologize for its supposed inadequacy. In *Our Singing Country* (1941), they wrote that America's artists "have created and preserved for America a heritage of folksongs and folk music equal to any in the world."

As an exemplar of the African American song tradition, Lead Belly vividly illustrated that one need not be an English peasant to sing folk songs. On the 1933 trip, John Lomax was quite aware that in recording African American music he and Alan were displacing the Anglo-dominated folk music canon.... Setting aside for the moment Lomax's sensationalized style, for him to locate black songs in the center of America's folk song canon marked a significant step in the early thirties. In the book that resulted from their 1933 trip, *American Ballads and Folk Songs* (1934), the Lomaxes stated matter-of-factly that blacks created "the most distinctive of folk songs—the most interesting, the most appealing, and the greatest in quantity."

Beyond illustrating the richness of America's musical traditions, Lead Belly's immense repertoire lent credence to the Lomaxes' assertions that these traditions remained very much alive in contemporary America.... [T]hey dismissed notions that an authentic folk song must be hundreds of years old and that only fragments of true folk culture survived in contemporary society. The Lomaxes depicted a much more robust folk tradition. They argued that traditional American music remained vibrant, creative, and essential to American life. Alan Lomax urged

Americans to fight "the tendency ... to begin to regard [folk] culture as static—to leave out of consideration its living quality (present and past)."...

The Lomaxes succeeded as canon makers, though, not just because they embraced performers with the repertoire and style of Lead Belly. At least as important as how they defined the new American folk canon were the ways in which they preserved and popularized its exemplars. First of all, the Lomaxes rejected ... manuscript-based collecting and instead relied almost completely on fieldwork. A living oral tradition, they believed, could not be captured in a Harvard library....

In an extension of this desire to collect directly from folk sources, the Lomaxes turned to the recording machine. Folklorists such as Robert Gordon and John Lomax himself had used recorders before, but in the 1930s the Lomaxes employed superior technology, recorded far more widely, and embraced the recording medium with more passion than previous collectors. No written document, the Lomaxes felt, could capture the full flavor and intricacy of a folk performance, and the process of transcription relied too much on human skill and judgment to be accurate. Even dedicated transcribers like Sharp, they concluded, could not do justice to the subtlety and emotion that a Lead Belly brought to his songs. On their trips, the Lomaxes relied exclusively on the recording machine to take down songs, always experimenting with new techniques and technologies in the hope of achieving a less distorted sound. The recorder, they believed, removed the collector as a source of bias and captured all of a song's nuances. Instead of a scholar's representation of song, the machine preserved a folk singer's entire performance, unadulterated. As Alan Lomax recalled, using the recorder on the 1933 trip "meant that for the first time there was a way to stick a pipeline right down into the heart of the folks where they were and let them come on like they felt."

Aside from producing more lifelike renditions of songs, then, the recording machine enabled the Lomaxes to downplay their role in the collecting process. John Lomax accentuated this point, stressing that he was "innocent of musical knowledge, entirely without musical training."...

In idealizing the recording machine, the Lomaxes tapped into what historian William Stott has called the "documentary motive" of the thirties. As George E. Marcus and Michael M. J. Fischer explain, "There was a hunger for reliable information, a widespread suspicion that newspapers were manipulating the news,... and a simple unavailability of public facts." In this context, the recorder appealed as an incontrovertible source of truth. How could a recording machine lie?

In addition to making more effective use of the recording machine, the Lomaxes began to realize the potential of the Archive of American Folk-Song. Like Gordon, the Lomaxes had secured the archive as a repository for the recordings they collected. But the Lomaxes had a much stronger sense than their predecessor of the power and possibilities that the archive offered collectors. Gordon had used his position at the archive primarily as a base from which to pursue his own private collecting work. The Lomaxes, though, realized that government backing for their enterprise could give it added credibility. They used the archive not simply as a storage place for their recordings but as a credentializing institution, a way to link their personal musical tastes to a sense of national mission. Having the Library of Congress behind them made it easier for the Lomaxes to attract folk musicians to record and to secure a hearing for the music after they recorded it. When requesting permission to collect in prisons, for example, John Lomax always emphasized his position as honorary curator at the archive. His association with the nation's library gave him access that might otherwise have been denied....

Beyond the Lomaxes' considerable skill at collecting vernacular music, what truly separated them from their predecessors was their ingenuity at popularizing it. In the twenties, Ralph Peer and Carl Sandburg had been attentive to the possibilities of using publicity to generate interest in old-time music. But Peer, for all his influence, had not articulated a unified vision of American music—he had not tried to shape the way America remembered its musical past. And Sandburg, for all the hype he generated, had not recognized the fascination that folk figures could generate in a modern industrialized culture—he had chosen himself to be the star figure who would personify folk traditions. The Lomaxes were the first to use "actual folk" to promote a coherent vision of America's folk music heritage. To promote their canon they relied not on a popular interpreter of folk songs but on exemplars from the folk culture itself. They enlisted the full array of mass media—newspapers, radio, movie newsreels, concerts, and records—to transform rural folk musicians into celebrities. In effect they spread their vision of American music by integrating folk into mass culture.

The Lomaxes' efforts to popularize representatives from folk culture added an element that became central to the folk music revival of the thirties and to every burst of interest in roots music since then—an impression of authenticity. In some ways, of course, this appeal was nothing new. The supposed purity and simplicity of the music had been what attracted the earliest collectors of roots music and what interpreters like Sandburg had capitalized on. But by dispensing with the secondhand interpreters and foregrounding the rural musicians who created the folk music, the Lomaxes added a new source of authenticity—the performers themselves. Purity now was attributed not just to specific folk songs (e.g., Child ballads) but to the folk figures who sang them. Audiences and critics began to assess roots musicians with new standards.

The Lomaxes' handling of Lead Belly helped spur this fascination with a folk performer's authenticity. Lead Belly was released from prison in 1934. A popular story, spread widely by the Lomaxes in the thirties and forties, says that Lead Belly was freed because the Lomaxes delivered his stirring musical appeal to Louisiana's governor, who was moved to commute his sentence. The Lomaxes did make a second visit to Lead Belly in prison in June 1934, and they did record his "Governor O.K. Allen" song, but prison documents show that Lead Belly actually won his release for good behavior. Upon his release, Lead Belly was eager to pursue a postprison musical career, and the Lomaxes, having found a living example of the noncommercial tradition they prized, could not stand to allow their discovery to remain in the Louisiana backcountry. Early in 1935, therefore, the Lomaxes took Lead Belly to New York City. There they recorded scores of his songs for the Archive of American Folk-Song, booked appearances for him at concerts, took him on a lecture-recital tour of eastern colleges … and arranged commercial recording sessions for him.

Most striking, upon arriving in New York the Lomaxes launched a publicity blitz, promoting Lead Belly as the folk song find of the century. This media campaign essentially relied on two strategies to establish Lead Belly's authenticity—strategies seemingly at odds. On the one hand, the Lomaxes depicted Lead Belly as the living embodiment of America's folk song tradition, a time capsule that had preserved the pure voice of the people. Often this strategy involved counterposing Lead Belly's "pure" music to its inferior modern descendants.…

At the same time, though, that the Lomaxes ennobled Lead Belly as an authentic folk forefather, they thoroughly exoticized him. Their publicity campaign depicted him as a savage, untamed animal and focused endlessly on his convict past. Long after Lead Belly had been freed, Lomax had him perform in his old convict clothes, "for exhibition purposes,… though he always hated to wear them."…

In describing Lead Belly, John Lomax consistently stressed his rapacity. Shortly before taking Lead Belly to the North, Lomax wrote a letter previewing his coming attraction for the papers: "Leadbelly is a nigger to core of his being. In addition he is a killer. He tells the truth only accidentally…. He is as sensual as a goat, and when he sings to me my spine tingles and sometimes tears come. Penitentiary wardens all tell me that I set no value on my life in using him as a traveling companion. I am thinking of bringing him to New York in January."…

Others who worked with Lead Belly in the thirties and forties dispute this portrait of him. Most people who met him commented on his gentleness. Pete Seeger remembers him as soft voiced, meticulously dressed, and "wonderful with children." Seeger found it "hard to believe the stories we read of his violent youth." Producer Moses Asch recalls that his first impression was Lead Belly's "overall aristocratic appearance and demeanor." Lead Belly had enough of an "idea of money," moreover to demand that John Lomax give him control over the revenues from his concerts. For the first eight months or so that he was with the Lomaxes they used him as their chauffeur and house servant. He drove the car on their collecting expeditions and to and from concert engagements, and he did chores around the Lomax home in Wilton, Connecticut. The Lomaxes kept two-thirds of Lead Belly's concert earnings and deducted room and board from the remainder. Lead Belly angrily challenged this arrangement (brandishing a knife) in March 1935, and a shaken John Lomax put him on a bus back to Shreveport, Louisiana. Lead Belly promptly hired a lawyer to press for compensation. Lomax eventually paid a lump sum to settle the matter.

Regardless of the inaccuracies in their portrayal, the Lomaxes' emphasis on Lead Belly's "Otherness" seems to have been strikingly effective…. Routinely the press in the thirties described Lead Belly with epithets Like "two-time Dixie murderer," "[Lomax's] murderous protégé," or "two-time killer, who twice sang his way out of jail." In a typical story, the *Brooklyn Eagle* announced Lead Belly's wedding (a major media event organized by the Lomaxes) by reporting, "Lead Belly, the Louisiana swamplands Negro equally proficient with knife or guitar, is happy today in the knowledge that Martha Promise…, who sheltered him between prison sentences, is with him again." …

In his public persona, then, Lead Belly seems to have been cast as both archetypal ancestor and demon—and to have been convincing as the real thing in each role. These conflicting personas illustrate a dynamic that has characterized the cult of authenticity ever since. Revival audiences yearn to identify with folk figures, but that identification is premised on difference. Roots musicians are expected to be premodern, unrestrainedly emotive, and noncommercial. Singers who too closely resemble the revival's middle-class audiences are rejected by those audiences as "inauthentic" Generally, then, the most popular folk figures—those with whom revival audiences most identify—are those who have passed a series of tests of their "Otherness."

The Lomaxes' handling of Lead Belly resonated with a current of primitivism that ran through early-twentieth-century modernism. Avant-garde writers, artists, and intellectuals used "the primitive" as a source of imagery, metaphors, and behavior patterns that fulfilled personal longings and enabled cultural critiques. Picasso and the cubists incorporated the stark geometries of African sculptures in their work. Art collectors and intellectuals (including Freud) sought out these sculptures for their galleries and studies. In *Heart of Darkness* (1913), Joseph Conrad used a ride down the Congo to signify his exploration of the darkest depths of the human soul. Both the 1893 Columbian Exposition in Chicago and the 1904 World's Fair in St. Louis put "primitive" tribes on display. Beginning in 1912, Edgar Rice Burroughs masterfully moved the fascination with the primitive into popular culture with his wildly successful series of Tarzan novels. Often these appropriations of the primitive were based on extremely limited knowledge of non-Western societies. The modernists' representations of the primitive said as much about their own artistic visions and personal fantasies as about the people whose culture they purported to depict. "The primitive" became a symbol that could encompass violence, sex, irrationality, and, at the same time, noble innocence and childlike naïveté....

The Lomaxes, then, in pursuing culture in the "eddies of human society" (and in expressing both fascination and fear at what they found there), were engaging in an exploration of "Otherness" that had deep roots. Emerging from these antecedents, the search for the "primitive" took on an especially rich and idiosyncratic inflection during the Great Depression. Many Americans in the period mistrusted business and political leaders and blamed them for the hard times.... In this environment, the Lomaxes' depictions of Lead Belly as both everyman and outlaw tapped into what one might call the "outsider populism" of the period—a tendency in the thirties to locate America's strength and vibrancy in the margins of society. The depression had caused many Americans to reevaluate what forces in society were good, powerful, and sustaining. The economic collapse had led to speculations about weaknesses in the national character, questions about whether the country had lost touch with the spirit that had once, many Americans felt, made it great. Many romanticized a mythical time in the past when Americans were more vigorous, more honorable, and more self-sufficient....

There is, of course, an oxymoronic quality inherent to "outsider populism": how can one build populism around those outside "the people"? The outsiders appealed, though, because they reminded Americans of themselves—or of how they wanted to see themselves: independent, proud in the face of hardship, straightforward, beholden to no special interests. Images of the folk attracted Americans because they suggested sources of purity and character outside the seemingly weakened and corrupt mainstream of society. Ironically, then, to highlight a person's marginality in relation to the mainstream helped authenticate him or her as an exemplar of American grit and character. For the Lomaxes to depict Lead Belly as an exotic animal added to his appeal. They realized that if they wanted Lead Belly to achieve mainstream popularity his very incompatibility with mainstream society was his greatest asset.

This realization led the Lomaxes to manipulate not only Lead Belly's image but also his music. As the Lomaxes knew, Lead Belly's commercial strength depended on the perception that his songs were "pure folk." But they also recognized that popular audiences would not necessarily appreciate the folk style unadulterated. So, even as the Lomaxes worked to preserve Lead Belly's "authenticity," they encouraged him to make his singing more accessible to urban audiences. Alan Lomax recalled that white audiences found Lead Belly's southern dialect impenetrable until he "learned to compromise with Northern ways and 'bring his words out plain.'" The Lomaxes may also have urged Lead Belly to insert spoken comments in the middle of his songs, a technique for which he is famous. Spoken sections made a song easier for a neophyte to understand by outlining its plot, explaining obscure words and symbols, and providing transitions between verses....

A close look at one Lead Belly song, "Mister Tom Hughes' Town," illustrates how Lead Belly's musical style evolved in the years after he left prison. "Tom Hughes" was a signature piece in Lead Belly's repertoire, one that he recorded six times between 1934 and 1940 and twice more at his final recording sessions in 1948. He first recorded the song for the Lomaxes on July 1, 1934, while still an inmate in the Louisiana State Penitentiary in Angola. This version is a hard-edged, sometimes bawdy tale that recounts Lead Belly's desire as a youth to flee home and enjoy the illicit pleasures of Fannin Street, the red-light district of Shreveport, Louisiana, where Tom Hughes was sheriff. To an outsider, the song is stirring but can sound opaque, full of arcane slang and local references. Over the next six years, as Lead Belly moved from prison to freedom, from Louisiana to New York, and from field recordings to the commercial studio, he made a series of alterations to the song. Some changes were subtle and some dramatic. Some innovations surfaced just a few months after he left prison; others evolved gradually over years. Some reappeared in each subsequent version of the song, while others dropped away forever as soon as they were introduced. The changes to "Tom Hughes" do not, then, reflect a complete transformation in Lead Belly, but they do suggest a trend—a shift toward a less rough-edged style that, presumably, he hoped would attract wider audiences....

In addition to making more effort to explicate the song's story, Lead Belly's postprison versions of "Tom Hughes" considerably changed the story's outcome. In the first field recording, the narrator leaves for Shreveport, ignoring the pleas of his mother to stay at home, and adopts a licentious lifestyle about which he is remorseless, even boastful. Subsequent versions, though, add lyrics in which the narrator falls on his knees and begs his mother to forgive him for his past behavior. Most striking, most of Lead Belly's postprison renditions omit two suggestive verses that appear on the first field recording. In these verses Lead Belly refers to a woman who earns her living by "[workin] up her tail," and he exclaims that she has "somethin' lawd /I sure would like."

The taming of Lead Belly's narrator is also reflected in changes in his performance style. First of all, most of Lead Belly's subsequent versions of "Torn Hughes" are slower in speed than the original field recording, a change that makes the narrator sound less frenzied. Lead Belly has more time to sing the words, and they come out more clearly than in his first session, in which he runs many words together. Similarly, Lead Belly's voice is more emotive on his first recording of the song. While all the versions of "Tom Hughes" feature Lead Belly humming a melody in a moaning voice, in the first version he uses a sharper attack on the moans, giving them a piercing quality that most subsequent versions lack.

These transformations appear even more dramatically in a 1940 rendition of "I'm on My Last Go-Round," a song that uses the same tune and a variation of the Tom Hughes refrain. This recording session was Lead Belly's first with a major record company, and Alan Lomax arranged and supervised the session. In this version Lead Belly's singing has lost all the bite that it had on the initial field recording. The song is considerably slower than on earlier versions, and Lead Belly's usually rough voice sounds almost mellifluous. Light, delicate strummings have replaced his once fierce guitar work.

One can suppose that the Lomaxes and the commercial producers of Lead Belly's records played a direct role in reshaping "Tom Hughes," but it would be a mistake to presume that Lead Belly himself resented the advice. He had a notable interest in popularizing his music and a willingness to alter his songs. The evolution of "Tom Hughes" does not necessarily chart the crass exploitation of a "pure" folk artist. More accurately, the ebb and flow of his style illustrates how contact with the Lomaxes and the world of commercial recordings affected Lead Belly's sense of what would appeal to white audiences. In addition, the changes give us a glimpse of the musical dilemmas Lead Belly faced as he tried to find his niche in the folk revival. How much should he adapt his style, and in what direction? What appealed to audiences as an honest-to-goodness rough-edged sound and what struck them as abrasive? What was the boundary between "mysterious" and scary? Throughout his career, Lead Belly struggled to translate his persona as a musical throwback into popular success....

... Even with the adaptations [Lead Belly] made to his style, he never enjoyed significant popularity in his lifetime. His records, even those on commercial labels, sold little, and he forever struggled with financial hardship. For much of the thirties, in fact, he and his wife depended on assistance from the New York Department of Welfare. In 1949 when he died of amyotropic lateral sclerosis, or Lou Gehrig's disease, Lead Belly was well known enough to generate an obituary in the *New York Times* but not popular enough to have achieved a broad-based following or any kind of financial security. Americans found Lead Belly fascinating, it seems, but they kept him at arm's length.

Lead Belly's commercial career sputtered because of the contradictory demands placed on him by the folk revival. The outsider populism impulse that made Lead Belly and the other folk singers so intriguing to thirties Americans trapped them between the conflicting demands of purity and commercialism. Fundamentally, these singers' appeal depended on their folkloristic purity. They faced significant pressure, therefore, to sing only timeless songs that had been passed down (but not altered) through generations of oral transmission. This notion, though, of a pristine and unchanging traditional music fundamentally misrepresented the reality of folk culture. As the Lomaxes well knew, the folk tradition had always depended on its adaptability. Lead Belly himself, for example, continually altered his songs. In concert he often varied his lyrics to mention the city in which he was performing, and he adjusted his repertoire to the tastes of his audience.

No roots musician, moreover, was as isolated as the entrepreneurs of the folk revival wished. Although he had spent his whole life in the rural South, much of it confined in prison, Lead Belly was quite well versed in popular culture and saw no reason to shut himself off from it. He was renowned for his openness to all kinds of music, including Tin Pan Alley.… Similarly, Lead Belly did not share John Lomax's fears about the radio's corrupting influence on his repertoire. He so much enjoyed listening that while in New York he wrote a tribute song called "Turn Your Radio On," singing, "You listen into tell what's goin' on in the world."…

If selecting songs to play was so complicated, choosing the style in which to play them must have seemed especially bewildering to the folk revival singers of the thirties. The singers' appeal to the cult of authenticity depended on the notion that they had a "natural" sound—a style unsullied by the encroachments of popular culture. But, as the case of "Tom Hughes" suggests, a singer's style often was altered in an effort to reach popular audiences. Folk performers were encouraged to moderate the pitch of their voices, enunciate clearly, and slow down their songs. Singers like Lead Belly and Josh White took these lessons to heart in an effort to broaden their music's appeal.

Performers who did make stylistic adjustments, though, soon found that adapting their sound jeopardized their standing in the eyes of the folk revival's core following. Purists denounced them for selling out their pure heritage. Folklorist Charles Haywood thought Lead Belly a "sad spectacle" by the end of his career, charging that he had changed to fit "night clubs and popular taste."… In the place of strong rhythms the guitar was toying with delicate arpeggi and delightful arabesques, filling in between verses with swaying body movements, marching up and down the stage, swinging the guitar over his head, instrument upside down, or behind his back. This was a sad and tragic sight, cheap vaudeville claptrap." Lead Belly attempted to adapt to the commercial market, and as a result, says Sven Eric Molin, "folklorists shake their heads over his recordings and distinguish between an 'earlier' and a 'later' Leadbelly, for … the singing techniques and the choice of materials changed, and Tin Pan Alley had its perceptible influence."

The Lomaxes had encouraged Lead Belly to adjust his style, but they, too, spoke wistfully of his "purer" past. As early as January 1935, John wrote to his wife that he and Alan were "disturbed and distressed at [Lead Belly's] beginning tendency to show off in his songs and talk, when his money value is to be natural and sincere as he was while in prison. Of course, as this tendency grows he will lose his charm and become only an ordinary, low ordinary, Harlem nigger." Alan Lomax found that "Lead Belly recorded his songs for a number of companies though never so beautifully as he had first sung them for us in Louisiana." He described Lead Belly's 1940 recordings as "not complete authenticity, but ... the nearest thing to it that could be achieved away from the prison farms themselves."

Lead Belly did not have the same yearning for the purity of the prison farms, but he does seem to have internalized the confusing standards that the Lomaxes and folk song revivalists set for him. In a 1940 letter to Alan Lomax, Lead Belly wrote: "If your Papa come I would like for Him to Here me sing if He say i Have Change any whitch i Don't think i have and never will But to Be [sure] to get his ideas about it i would feel good over what ever he say about it." Lead Belly's predicament arose from the conflicting demands the folk revival placed on him. As Joe Klein writes, folk singers who tried to make it in urban society while remaining "true to their roots" ended up like "museum pieces, priceless and rare, but not quite marketable in the mass culture." The folk revival tried to use idealized conceptions of authenticity to achieve its dreams of reaching mass audiences. But the tensions in this agenda left performers like Lead Belly caught in limbo between folk and popular culture.

Like many roots musicians, Lead Belly found his way out of this limbo only after his death. Within months of his death at the end of 1949, the Weavers, a singing quartet featuring Pete Seeger, issued their version of Lead Belly's "Goodnight Irene." It eliminated from the song verse about taking morphine, changed the ominous-sounding lyric "I'll *get you* in my dreams" to "I'll *see* you in my dreams," and added lush vocal harmonies. It became a number one hit.

The Weavers' "Irene" was only one in a series of efforts by Lead Belly's allies in the folk revival to advance his legacy after his death. At the end of January 1950, Alan Lomax organized a tribute concert for him in New York's Town Hall. After Lomax moved to England that year, he produced a radio series that introduced British audiences to Lead Belly's music. (In 1956, Lonnie Donegan, a British banjo player, returned the favor by making Lead Belly's "Rock Island Line" a top-ten hit in America.) Moses Asch, who had recorded scores of Lead Belly songs for his Folkways label between 1941 and 1948, kept all of Lead Belly's albums in print and, in 1954, issued *Lead Belly's Last Sessions,* a set of three double albums featuring more than ninety songs and stories that Lead Belly had recorded in 1948 at the home of jazz historian Frederic Ramsey, Jr. A series of books, too, helped bring Lead Belly to new audiences. In 1959 Alan Lomax published a collection of Lead Belly songs, followed in 1962 by a songbook that he issued in collaboration with Asch. In 1965 Pete Seeger issued a manual on how to play twelve-string guitar in the style of Lead Belly. Meanwhile, in concert after concert, Seeger performed Lead Belly's music and recounted his story. As folk-styled music surged in popularity in the late 1950s and 1960s, a new generation found Lead Belly. His music became a staple at coffeehouses and folk festivals across the country. The 1960s folk revival did more to cement Lead Belly's reputation than had all his own efforts while he was alive.

Recent decades have witnessed a series of affirmations of Lead Belly's place in the canon of roots musicians. He was inducted into the Rock and Roll Hall of

Fame (1988), the Blues Hall of Fame (1986), and the Náshville Songwriters Association International's Hall of Fame (1980). In 1988 Columbia Records issued a tribute album, for which Beach Boy Brian Wilson, rock and roll pioneer Little Richard, and country legend Willie Nelson covered Lead Belly songs. In 1993, a few months before the suicide of lead singer Kurt Cobain, grunge-rock superstars Nirvana performed a Lead Belly tune for an MTV "Unplugged" album.

On the face of it, such tributes are the stuff of tragedy. If only Lead Belly had lived long enough to see his dreams fulfilled! At the same time, the posthumous nature of Lead Belly's success has an air of inevitability to it. It is questionable to what extent he could have reaped the fruits of fame even if he had lived. Lead Belly's renown in the decades after his death certainly derived in part from his considerable artistry, but it was equally driven by the same dynamics that had frustrated and constrained him while he lived—the romanticized (and racialized) life story that had been constructed for him, the primitive emotiveness attributed to his music, the notion that he somehow existed out of time, or at least before the time in which artifice and superficiality had permeated popular culture. In his day, these myths brought Lead Belly momentary popular attention, but they hamstrung his efforts to advance within popular culture, leaving him a folk-revival darling who struggled desperately to make ends meet. The real tragedy, perhaps, is that Lead Belly could flourish in public memory—as a posthumous folk forefather—in a way that he never could have as an active performer. With the "real" Lead Belly buried in Louisiana, each generation could "discover" him for itself, much as the Lomaxes had decades before. Successive cohorts of middle-class, almost exclusively white audiences could become entranced by the Lead Belly myth, revel in the bracing foreignness of his songs, and, eventually, reinterpret the songs as their own. After his death, then, Lead Belly himself became an authenticating agent, one who could bestow legitimacy on performers and fans searching for a sense of roots in the midst of ephemeral pop culture.

In his lifetime, Lead Belly was stymied by the tensions within the cult of authenticity—between rural African American traditions and an emerging set of white cultural brokers, between field recordings and the commercial record industry, between folklore and the modern mass media, between raw naturalism and calculated promotion. In the realm of memory, though, these oppositions that had trapped him became the source of his appeal and his achievement as a roots musician. Haltingly, often painfully, Lead Belly brought together forces that his successors would deploy to powerful advantage.

Collecting Culture on the Mexico–Texas Border

JOSÉ DAVID SALDIVAR

… [Americo] Paredes's antidisciplinary border project underscores the ways in which the dominant Anglo-centric discourse suppresses regional differences. In matters of

José David Saldivar, "Américo Paredes and Decolonization" in *Cultures of United States Imperialism,* eds. Amy Kaplan and Donald E. Pease. Copyright © 1993, Duke University Press. All rights reserved. Reprinted by permission of the publisher.

cultural description, Paredes shows that what is striking (in this Anglocentric context) is the steady discrimination of certain regions as in this limited sense "regional," which can only hold if certain *other regions* are not seen in this way. This discrimination is a function, he suggests, of centralization; a form of what Raymond Williams called the "city-country" opposition. It is clearly connected with the distinction between "metropolitan" (core) and "provincial" (peripheral) cultures, which became significant from the sixteenth century.... Paredes's bold deterritorializations thus serve as both tactical political strategies specifically designed to counter Anglocentric hegemony in border disputes as well as interdisciplinary fantasms designed to transgress rigidly "border patrolled" discursive boundaries.

Seen in this light, Paredes occupies a unique position among borderland writers today. No contemporary figure of the proto-Chicano Movement generation has so extensive an oeuvre to their credit. The range of this work, moreover, is probably unprecedented in either the United States or Latin America, including ethnographies on the people of Greater Mexico, literary criticism, analysis of ballads, collections of folktales, semantic inquiry, poetry, film scripts, short stories, and novels. Yet until recently sustained discussion of Paredes's work has been relatively wanting. Despite its increasing authority and influence in the field of Chicano Studies, there has so far been no attempt to analyze the border-defying work as a whole. The immense variety of Paredes's writing, crossing academic boundaries and confounding disciplinary expectations, has no doubt been one of the reasons for this quiet. It wasn't until the 1980s that the first assessment came, with the appearance in 1986 of two essays, "Mexican Ballads, Chicano Epic: History, Social Dramas and Poetic Persuasions" and "The Return of the Mexican Ballad" by José E. Limon, an anthropologist and former pupil of Paredes. Almost simultaneously, Paredes for his part addressed himself to major definitions and representations of spatial materialism and the politics of cultural identity, with the publication of *George Washington Gómez,* a novel he started writing in 1936, completed in 1940, but did not publish until the exemplary post-modern year of 1990....

Throughout these interventions, Paredes's focus on people's history, culture, and social class arrangements is powerfully personal and at times indulges in textual experimentation. *"With His Pistol in His Hand"* tells the story about the hegemonic border and the history of his ancestors in south Texas. Like many postcolonial Chicano/a writers, Paredes declares that he is not an immigrant. Neither his ancestors in the 1750s in Nuevo Santander nor he years later moved from the borderlands; instead U.S. military aggression transformed the Río Grande Valley from an organic class society (where a certain social order and relations made sense to a people) into a barbed wired and segregated society.

After discussing how the border was imposed on south Texas, Paredes focused on how Chicanos used *corridos* (ballads of border conflict) to counter Anglocentric hegemony. As literary scholar Ramón Saldívar puts it, "the nineteenth- and twentieth-century *corridos* served the symbolic function of empirical events (functioning as a substitute for history writing) and of creating counterfactual worlds of lived experience (functioning as a substitute for fiction writing)." To be sure, Paredes saw his project as participating in the cultural conversations of the Southwest borderlands, where border culture is a serious contest of codes and representations. More specifically, *"With His Pistol in His Hand"* inaugurates a Chicano artistic and intellectual response to the white supremacist scholars of the 1930s and 1940s such as Walter Prescott Webb and his followers who represented in their texts a popular, romanticized history....

To dramatize his sense of culture as a site of social contestation, Paredes's focus on *corridos* is "antisubjectivist" because in ballads of border conflict like "El Corrido de Gregorio Cortez" he located the sources of meaning not in individual subjectivities, but in social relations, communication, and cultural politics. While the *corrido* certainly points to border men such as Gregorio Cortez (who resisted arrest by Sheriff Morris and who defended himself "con la pistola en su mano"), the subject in this *corrido* is meant to stand not as an individual but as an epic-like construction of the south Texas society that interpellated him. As is well known, Cortez's fate, for Paredes, cannot be distinguished from communal fate.

Paredes's *"With His Pistol in His Hand"* concludes by bemoaning the "fall" of the *corrido* proper and its containment as a form of symbolic social resistance. "The period of 1836 to the late 1930's," he writes, "embraces the life span of the corrido of the Lower Border" (p. 132). The Civil war, the English-speaking invasion of the borderlands, and the French invasion of Mexico, however, "complicated the clash of peoples along the Border" (132). Additionally, after the 1930s, with the commercialization of popular music by both the Mexican and American mass cultural music industry, and with the dissolution and fragmentation of formerly organic Texas Mexican ranching communities by way of the effects of "world system" agribusiness and the green revolution, the need for alternative symbolic forms to express resistance became all the greater. Paredes himself acknowledges the fall of the *corrido* after it entered its "decadent" phase when he turns to another form of social resistance, namely, the Chicano novel. The transfiguration of the *corrido* hero and the decline of the utopian *corrido* epoch in south Texas is the subject of Paredes's historical bildungsroman, *George Washington Gómez*, written during the Great Depression. Indeed we can say without exaggeration that Paredes's novel is very precisely about the large and small dislocations in space that must occur before, at the novel's end, the hero George G. Gómez can completely assimilate. And that place itself is precisely located by Paredes at the center of competing local, national, and international interests, spanning the hemisphere. Formally, Paredes represents the Great Depression in south Texas—what he calls "La Chilla" (the Squeal)—as a structure of expansion and contraction. That is, he introduces the formal structure upon which many of the novel's sections will be patterned, for he gives the reader a generalized view of the plight of Mexican American men and women, followed by a close-up of his representative characters, the García and Gómez. This formal literary pattern, of course, echoes the structural features of one of the most sensational social protest novels of the period, namely, John Steinbeck's *The Grapes of Wrath*. Central to *George Washington Gómez*, then, is Paredes's preoccupation with cultural identity, representation, and the politics of location, for Mexican American identity is not as transparent as we have been taught to think....

With George G. Gómez we are far removed from the utopian collective concerns of border heroes like Gregorio Cortez. Paredes, however, in recreating the "border troubles" in his narrative opens the stage for the Chicano novel thirty years before the so-called Chicano Renaissance of letters in the 1960s. His focus, moreover, on *corridos* and on folklore and musical performance in his numerous writings forces us to look at folklore and pop culture as equally powerful, creative, and influential areas of counter-discourses. Paredes, indeed, dwells in his writings on the role of folklore as an instrument of the culture of conflict because it wages struggle itself in the forms of songs, legends, *dichos,* and proverbs. As anthropologist Richard Bauman argues, Paredes' "work is an exemplary vindication of that premise on which the best of folklore and anthropology is built: that a deep, detailed, nuanced understanding of the local will inspire a more global vision."

Paredes's novel (written in the late 1930s) … [r]elates among other things the encounter of the ethnographic field-worker with the native inhabitants of south Texas. In other words, Paredes begins to open up the question of how cultural analysis constitutes its objects—societies, traditions, knowable communities, subjectivities, and so on. Near the novel's end, he asks the following "postcolonial" questions about historical/anthropological fieldwork: Who is being observed? What are the political locations involved? How is one group's core another's periphery? Paredes deconstructs the ethnographic encounter in south Texas by sardonically describing the traveling culture collector, K. Hank Harvey:

> [H]e was considered the foremost of authorities on the Mexicans of
> Texas. Hank Harvey had been born in New York City some sixty years
> before. He had gone to grade school there and then worked in a
> delicatessen to make some money so he could come down to his
> dreamland, Texas…. After he had come to Texas with only a few
> years of schooling, he resolved to become an authority on Texas history
> and folklore. In a few years he had read every book there was on the
> early history of Texas, it was said, and his fellow Texans accepted him
> as the Historical Oracle of the State. There was a slight hitch, it is true.
> Most early history books were written in Spanish, and K. Hank didn't
> know the language. However, nobody mentioned this, and it didn't
> detract from Harvey's glory.

The striking part of this passage is Paredes's attempt to demystify the authority of the executive historical ethnographer and to open to discussion what James Clifford calls "ethnography's hierarchy and the complex negotiation of discourses in power-charged, unequal situations." If thinking of the observer as neither an innocent nor omniscient is striking, Paredes shakes things up a bit more by representing Harvey as a monological scholar incapable of fully inscribing his "native" subjects. Eventually Harvey learns a "few words of Spanish which he introduced into all of his later writings, somewhat indiscriminately," and his fame as a historian and folklorist grows "too big even for the vast Texas," and soon he becomes a "national and then an international figure." Paredes's wry description of Harvey, however, becomes full of rage, for Harvey's scholarly project occurs alongside a peculiar sense of mission—what used to be called the white man's burden…. For Paredes, what has come to be called the Spanish borderlands by ethnographic historians such as K. Hank Harvey is in fact an invention, an imperialist historical formation, an enactment, a political paradox, an ongoing (mis)translation. To be sure, Harvey functions in the novel as a symbol for scholars such as … J. Frank Dobie (*Flavor of Texas*) who claimed to have "discovered" and invented the Spanish Southwest for the Anglo-American popular readership…. Dobie … was instrumental in constructing disciplinary folklore societies in the Southwest and was the first to teach a course on the culture of the Southwest at the University of Texas at Austin. Paredes thus pegs the Harveys of the Southwest as representing the "Mexicans of south Texas" in the mode of what anthropologist Renato Rosaldo called "imperialist nostalgia," that longing on the part of imperialist agents such as missionaries, ethnographers, government officials, and others for the indigenous forms of life that they often had a hand in destroying. In this discourse, Paredes describes the Spanish borderlands as the site where men like Harvey can be real authorities, where they can lament the closing of the frontier….

Lurking behind the title of Paredes's novel, there is the haunting cultural symbology of George Washington, who in his Farewell Address proclaimed: "The name of American must always exalt [your] just pride … more than any appellation derived from local discriminations. With slight shades of difference, you have the same Religion, Manners, Habits, and political principle." For Américo Paredes, however, "the name of American" was an interpretative fiction. Doing the work of the dominant culture, Washington's address, like the rest of the classic American literary canon, interprets away differences between the religions, manners, habits, and political principles of the people from Our America. As Bercovitch suggests, "the name of American worked not only to displace the very real (and deepening) differences within the country, but equally—within the country's reigning liberal constituency—to display differences of all kinds of proof of a victorious pluralism." Paredes thus presents a counterdiscourse to the homemade discourses of U.S. imperialism: he articulates the experiences, the aspirations, and the vision of a people suffering colonial/postcolonial rule from the inside. What distinguishes him from his Anglocentric contemporaries lies not in his intellectual or aesthetic judgment but in the depth of his extraordinary understanding of the dynamics of empire….

FURTHER READING

Bendix, Regina. *In Search of Authenticity: The Formation of Folklore Studies* (1997).

Cantwell, Robert. *Ethnomimesis: Folklife and the Representation of Culture* (1993).

———. *When We Were Good: The Folk Revival* (1997).

Davis, Angela. *Blues Legacies and Black Feminism: Gertrude "Ma" Rainey, Bessie Smith, and Billie Holiday* (1999).

Fox, Aaron. *Real Country: Music and Language in Working Class Culture* (2004).

Garofolo, Reebee. *Rockin' Out: Popular Music in the USA* (1996).

Jones, Leroi. *Blues People: Negro Music in White America* (1999).

Kruin, Richard. *Reflections of a Culture Broker* (1997).

Leppert, Richard, and Susan McClary, eds. *Music and Society: The Politics of Composition, Performance, and Reception* (1989).

Lipsitz, George. *Dangerous Crossroads: Popular Music, Postmodernism and the Poetics of Place* (1997).

Middleton, Richard. *Pop Music and the Blues: A Study of the Relationship and Its Significance* (1972).

Peterson, Richard. *Creating Country Music: Fabricating Authenticity* (1999).

Saldívar, Ramón, and Donald E. Pease. *The Borderlands of Culture: Américo Paredes and the Cultural Imaginary* (2006).

Waksman, Steve. *Instruments of Desire: The Electric Guitar and the Shaping of Musical Experience* (2001).

Whisnant, David. *All That Is Native and Fine: The Politics of Culture in an American Region* (25th Anniversary Edition) (2008).

Wolf, Charles and Kip Lornell. *The Life and Legend of Leadbelly* (1999).

CHAPTER 11

Television Becomes Part of the Family, 1955–1965

In the years immediately following World War II, television became the consumer item of choice and a new, powerful medium of popular culture. Although the technology of television made a brief appearance at world's fairs in the 1930s, TV did not become a viable and affordable consumer product until the late 1940s. As historian Lynn Spigel notes: "Between 1948 and 1955, television was installed in nearly two-thirds of the nation's homes, and the basic mechanisms of the network oligopoly were set in motion. By 1960, almost 90 percent of American households had at least one receiver." In addition, television filled a deep-seated desire to return home. After living with dislocations caused by a long economic depression and World War II, Americans embraced an ideal of home and family togetherness. Television promised to fulfill these goals and satisfy the deferred desire to consume by bringing new products right into the living room.

One could argue that television was an outgrowth of earlier media technologies, movies and radio. But it challenged these forms and changed leisure practices in its own right. To be sure, television borrowed heavily from radio; it was also commercial broadcasting funded by sponsors who used programming to sell the image of corporations (public relations) and sell products. Programming, such as variety shows and soap operas, as well as stars transferred from radio to television. In addition, like radio, TV was part of the home, an intimate companion to one's daily activities. But the visual aspects of television and the eventual corporate cooperation between networks and Hollywood would make television more powerful than radio in terms of reinforcing consumer culture. Hollywood would eventually enter the business of producing shows for television, as with an early business deal between Disney and ABC in the mid-1950s to air Disney Programming that also promoted the studio's amusement park and its films. Television networks would also shift the relationship between networks and sponsors in the 1950s with broadcasters, NBC, CBS, and latecomer ABC, gaining more control over programming and advertising. For example, broadcasters, in a move to gain control over schedules, engaged multiple sponsors for shows. This shifted the power over programs and advertising away from sponsors and to networks.

Rather than delving into the business of television, however, this chapter examines the popular culture that blossomed around watching TV and debates about the social utility and impact of programming on everyday life. Television—as material culture, a set of viewing practices, and a form of mass communication—changed the private space of the home and inspired debate about mass communications and the common good. Television was introduced as a family medium, with the hope that it would knit together the ruptured fabric of family life after the war. The marketing of television and television programming reflected this mandate to speak to the family and improve domestic life in the 1950s and 1960s. Situation comedies dominated prime-time viewing and took family relations as their central focus. Advertising on and off the air situated the set within the domestic circle of living rooms, instructing purchasers how to incorporate the technology into their home décor. Nevertheless critics from different corners of the cultural landscape worried about the social effects of TV along two fronts, that too much TV viewing would harm children mentally and physically and that commercial TV contributed nothing to the improvement of society even though it used public airways. TV programming that included African Americans and coincided with the civil rights movement inspired public discussion about representations of race on TV and how the medium did or did not contribute to racial progress.

DOCUMENTS

All of the documents explore the domestic and social uses of television. Document 1, an advertisement from General Electric (manufacturer of televisions, and parent company of NBC), tells consumers that they need not just one but several televisions, one for each member of the household. Where much of the advertising of the time portrayed TV as the glue that held families together in the living room, this ad moved to new territory, suggesting that each family member should have his or her own set. Document 2 explores the sociology of television viewing within the contexts of family and neighborhood. Leo Bogart asserts that studies of television should move beyond its psychological effects because TV was most often viewed in social settings. The study traces the impact of the medium on daily routines, on participation in social activities and civic clubs, and on family relations. Document 3 demonstrates that family life was prime fodder for television programming through situation comedies. Mr. Adams and Eve are Hollywood stars asked to play a "normal" American couple in a new TV series. The humor stems from their inability to embody the "average, normal, typical American." Documents 4 and 5 offer critiques of television as dishonest, describing how stations aired fixed quiz shows and misleading advertising and call television a "wasteland" devoid of social benefits. In contrast, Documents 6 and 7 discuss the importance of television in advancing integration and civil rights in the 1960s through actors such as Bill Cosby, who co-starred in the popular program *I Spy* with white actor Robert Culp. Although the show had no overt racial message, the African American newspaper, the Chicago Daily Defender claimed the show presented a new image of African Americans and implied it contributed to the Civil Rights movement. This new technology would clearly have a revolutionary effect on everyday life. What did owning a TV set mean for

American families? How did consumers think about television and what did they worry about in terms of its impact on their routines, family, and social relations?

1. Advertisement Pictures Television in the Family Circle, 1955

2. Leo Bogart, Critic, Describes Television as a Social Medium, 1956

TV Viewing in Its Social Setting

Studies of television and other mass media generally present reports expressed in terms of aggregate activity.... [E]mphasis is usually on the total numbers of people in the audience or on the differences in the viewing patterns of various sections of the population. Often such studies seem reminiscent of a mechanistic school of psychological theory, in which a stimulus (the communications medium) acts on an inert subject (the audience) and elicits an appropriate response. Actually, this is far from being an accurate description of what takes place.

The mass media audience is never exposed to any communication in a vacuum. The audience invariably receives the message in a social setting which profoundly influences the way in which the message is perceived, interpreted and absorbed. Communication via the mass media is more than an individual communication multiplied a thousand or a million times.

The child sitting on his mother's lap and hearing a story read aloud is responding not merely to the abstract symbols on the printed page but to the many sensations of love, security and mystery evoked by this shared experience. In later life, the solitary reader finds pleasure in reading not only because he has absorbed the author's wisdom or art but because he in turn can pass something of this on to others.

The importance of the social setting is even more readily apparent for viewing television than for reading. Since the days of TV's first appearance, the social character of viewing has gone through at least three major stages.

1. *The tavern phase.* In the earlier days, television sets were most often found in public places, notably in the taverns of large cities. The tavern audience was predominantly a male fellowship, particularly in workingclass neighborhoods, where the local bar is a kind of club in which men are accustomed to spend their evenings. The "crowd" at the tavern might include a core of intimates, a wider circle of nodding acquaintances, and a relatively small number of itinerant strangers.

The advent of television gave a focus to tavern life. The noise of the loudspeaker probably reduced the flow of casual small talk. However, TV provided a common denominator of experience which may actually have stimulated some conversation among people with little in common to talk about. On the evenings when television presented some outstanding attraction—especially an athletic contest—the tavern acquired even more importance than usual as a center of neighborhood life.

2. *The pioneer phase.* The first families to acquire TV sets were drawn from a higher income level than those who made up the tavern audience. Their viewing was no longer a public act. It took place in the familiar setting of the home, and the entire family participated. The pioneer set owners found their lives profoundly

Leo Bogart, "TV Viewing in Its Social Gathering," in *The Age of Television: A Study of Viewing Habits and the Impact of Television on American Life*, ed. Leo Bogart. Copyright © 1956 by Leo Bogart. Reprinted with permission of the publisher, The Continuum International Publishing Group.

T A B L E 1   Distribution of Radio and TV Sets—By Location

	Location of All Television Sets	Location of All Radios
Living Room	85%	34%
Bedroom	3	29
Kitchen	—	22
All Other	12	15
	100%	100%

Source: 1954 ARF-Politz Survey

affected by the new medium. It kept them at home more, and cut down on outside activities like visiting or attendance at public events and meetings.

The singular aspect of TV viewing at this stage was that it was *more* than a family activity. The set-owning families were more frequently visited by friends and neighbors who had not yet acquired sets themselves. Their homes became social centers of a kind, though the sociability was sometimes superficial. This was the epoch of the "TV party," in which visitors gathered to see the programs, were fed beer and pretzels and left after only a minor exchange of amenities with the hosts.

3. *The mature phase.* In areas where television ownership has spread to the point of virtual universality, viewing reverts to a pattern which resembles that of radio listening in its prime. Viewing is now almost wholly within the family group, with outsiders not normally present. The television set remains the focal point of the family's typical evening activities. However, it probably no longer occupies the dominant position which it enjoyed in TV's earlier days, when other social activities slackened and even casual conversation was hushed in obedience to the set's demands. Television programs represent one of the family's principal shared experiences, and as such are a subject for small talk and occasionally for real discussion.

With a well-established habit of steady viewing night after night, it is not strange that the family which is suddenly deprived of television, through set breakdown or other circumstances, feels itself at a great loss.

The television set is typically located in the living room, at the heart of the family's life. A survey conducted by Alfred Politz for the Advertising Research Foundation in 1954 found 85% of the sets in the living room (Table 1).

There is no reason to believe that the nature of television viewing has now entered its final phase. As more families acquire several sets, and as the sets themselves become lighter and less cumbersome, TV will spread through the various rooms of the house, much as radio has done, and viewing may become more of an individual activity and less of a family affair.

What TV Does for People

How did television enter the home in the first place? The obvious answer that it was acquired for purposes of family entertainment is not necessarily the whole story. Melvin Goldberg, asking 102 pioneer TV owners in New York what had led them to buy a television set, found a third referring to sports events, and a fourth to home entertainment. 18% said their children had wanted a set. 15% commented that they had been viewing TV at friends' homes and now felt they wanted a set of their own.

In a study of 740 persons in a Boston neighborhood (1951), Bernard Fine and Nathan Maccoby asked TV owners, "What were your main reasons for buying the set?" 45% gave entertainment as the reason, 13% said it was for the children, and 8% mentioned companionship as the reason. People of below-average education were most apt to mention TV's value for the children, as though protesting (too much) their own lack of interest....

It is evident that "entertainment" means different things to different people. Once television entered a community, many people felt that they had to acquire a set in order to keep up with the Joneses. In a study of 784 set owners in Atlanta in 1951, Raymond Stewart quotes the following remarks:

> "Everyone expected us to have a set. I guess we wanted it because it was embarrassing not to have one."

> "I didn't want it but my husband did. He saw them in so many homes and thought we ought to have one."

On the other hand, the first persons to acquire a set enjoyed the prestige of their pioneer status, and the special privileges of sociability and social leadership:

> "It hasn't meant so much. I enjoyed it so much more when mine was new. I had one of the first anywhere around. Then so many friends came in to see it with me."

Television, Stewart found, also has a very special meaning for invalids, or for Southern Negroes who are similarly barred from public entertainments:

> "It provides pleasure for us, especially since my husband has arthritis. It's a medium for him to feel like he's keeping up with things and it passes the time."

> "It permits us to see things in an uncompromising manner. Ordinarily to see these things would require that we be segregated and occupy the least desirable seats or vantage point. With television we're on the level with everyone else. Before television, radio provided the little bit of equality we were able to get. We never wanted to see any show or athletic event bad enough to be segregated in attending it."

Television's Place in Family Life

Television viewing is characteristically a family activity, and as such it represents a kind of experience which is distinct from that of other media. Radio at one time had the same character, but radio listening appears increasingly to be something which people do by themselves, like reading. On the other hand, "going out" to the movies or to other forms of commercial entertainment is less likely to involve the whole family, and correspondingly more often occurs among persons of the same age group, whether this takes the form of teen-age dating or of adult socializing....

The family character of TV viewing has from the start aroused a good deal of social commentary and speculation. Television's appearance was heralded as the beginning of a resurgence of American family life. The forecast was made that it would bring children in from outdoors to join with their elders around the hearth. Clerics, concerned about the decline of the family in an age of innumerable distractions and temptations, expressed the hope that television would enhance the attractions of the home for those who were inclined to stray outside its shelter. Accompanying this pious optimism there were also some skeptical voices. The rise of television, it was pointed out, represented an even further intrusion of the impersonal influences of the mass media into the intimate circle of family life.

Which of these contradictory predictions has been shown to be correct? Certainly television has proved to be a strong attractive force for all members of the family. It has brought more family groups together in the living room, of an average evening, than radio was able to do a few years earlier—as appears evident from TV's larger audiences.

Television provides the unifying effect of a common activity or interest on lives in which there is a scarcity of meaningful shared experience. In quotations like the following (from Stewart's study) it is also apparent that TV fills a void of boredom.

> "It keeps us together more. Friends drop in when they probably wouldn't otherwise. It's an entertainment that we take part in that isn't affected by the weather."

> "It makes a closer family circle. It draws our interests together. Instead of all doing different things, we are enjoying something together now. Before my husband was out a lot at night or was reading. My aunt would read and the boy would be playing. My brother-in-law usually slept."

> "We are closer together. We find our entertainment at home. Don and her boy friend sit here instead of going out, now. We sit and eat popcorn. Before television, I sat around and went nuts at home while my husband worked. He is tired when he gets home and would go to sleep just sitting around."

> "It keeps us closer together. It keeps down that wonder of where we can go and what we can do. My husband is very restless; now he relaxes at home."

In relieving boredom, television may also alleviate family tension:

> "It seems that family life is not as monotonous as before TV. We disagreed a little more before. Then one of us would go out of the house for a while; now we turn on television."

> "It keeps us happier. My husband and I get along a lot better. We don't argue so much. It's wonderful for couples who have been married ten years or more. It has been very entertaining for the boy. Before television, my husband would come in and go to bed. Now we spend some time together."

In fact, in some cases, the purchase of a set may actually have been motivated by the desire to eliminate family conflicts over the use of leisure time:

"My husband did not like to go to shows. I did. He liked to go to ball games. I didn't. We decided this would be the answer for us."

It might be expected that television tends to be a unifying influence in those families which, to begin with, showed the highest cohesiveness, and a divisive influence in homes where individual interests were already most dispersed. In a home characterized by tension or where family members pursue their own bents, television might simply represent one additional distraction to keep people separate, and disagreement about programs might mean only one more bone of contention in a struggle for power.

TV's Effects on Visiting and "Going Out"

A number of surveys, most of them made under university auspices, have considered television's effects on family life. As in studies of TV's impact on other communications media, these researches have compared television families with families that had not yet acquired sets. In a number of cases the set owners have been asked their opinion of television's influence, comparing the present situation with the period before the set was obtained.

These studies agree completely that television has had the effect of keeping the family at home more than formerly, and has cut down a good many of its outside activities....

A mail survey made in the spring of 1950 by Fact Finders Associates, among 1800 readers of *TV Guide,* found two-thirds of those responding saying they went out less often than they had before television, but two in five said that they were doing more home entertaining. Similarly, a 1949 survey made for Duane Jones by Lawrence J. Hubbard found that of nearly 1600 television owners who returned questionnaires, three-fourths had more visitors than formerly—both children and adults....

TV and Conversation

Not every observer of television's effects agrees that it has enhanced the intimacy of family life, even though it has kept the family at home. Early comments often called attention to the inhibiting influence of television on conversation. In the New York *Herald Tribune* of June 9, 1948, John Crosby made this grim prediction:

"The impact of television on our culture is one of the liveliest little topics of discussion to come along in some time, much of it conducted between clenched teeth. The most obvious and dire effect, one that strikes everyone who has seen more than two television broadcasts, is on conversation. There isn't any. The moment the set goes on, conversation dies. I don't mean it languishes. It dies. Messages are transmitted back and forth by means of eye-rolling, eyebrow lifting and frantic wig-wagging of the hands. (Only high priority messages are permitted: You're wanted on the telephone. Could I have another drink? That sort of thing.) People who will venture an occasional whisper in church remain awed and silent in front of a television set."…

3. "Mr. Adams and Eve," an Early Program Represents Television on Television, 1957

Mr. Adams and Eve

Starring
Ida Lupino
and
Howard Duff
Network: CBS-TV
Producer: Frederick De Cordova
Assistant Producer: Warren Toub
Director: Dan Weiss
Writer: Sol Saks….

A small, foreign-looking night club.
Eve in stage costume with long black-net stockings, dancing on tiny floor. Howard, with unlighted cigarette hanging from lips, accompanies her on small-size piano. She ends dance leaning with back against the corner of the piano.

> EVE: I waited for you last night. Why didn't you call?
>
> HOWARD: Because you're common. (*plays chord*)
>
> EVE (*Pulls him to his feet facing her*): I hate you!
>
> HOWARD (*Quietly*): I hate you too.
> *They simultaneously slap each other. Stare at each other, the impulsively embrace and kiss, Eve backed against piano.*
>
> DIRECTOR (*Enters*): Cut! Print that.
>
> EVE (*Rubbing derriere*): Can't we get a round piano?
> *Wardrobe woman fusses with Eve's costume. Maid holds cup of coffee, giving Eve intermittent sips.*
>
> DIRECTOR: That's it for today, kids.
>
> HOWARD: Good. Then I can take this cigarette off.
> *Bustle of activity and ad-libbing in background.*

"Typical: Mr. Adams and Eve," in *Best TV Humor of 1957*, ed. Irving Settel (New York: Ballantine Books, 1957).

GAFFER: Let's wrap it up, boys.

ASSISTANT DIRECTOR: Come get your call sheets.
Howard and Eve walk towards dressing room, accompanied by Wardrobe Woman continuing to fuss with Eve's costume. Maid carrying coffee.

DIRECTOR (*Hands Howard script pages*): Here's the scene we're going to do Monday. You can study it over the weekend. It's a great scene.

HOWARD: What do they put these cigarettes on with, anyway?

EVE: Can we get Spike to get these eyelashes?

DIRECTOR (*Shouts*): Makeup!

HOWARD (*To Eve*): You were great in that scene, darling.

EVE: So were you, my pet.

HOWARD: Who's going to be looking at me when you're standing there with those beautiful legs?

EVE: Oh, sweetheart, you've got lovely legs, too.

HOWARD: That's true, but they're under the piano all the time.
Interior tiny portable dressing room.
Steve, the agent, a Dan Tobin type, slumps in chair with feet on lounge. Eve enters followed by Wardrobe Woman, followed by Maid, followed by Director, followed by Howard.

HOWARD: Alone at last.
Steve sips drink.

EVE (*Takes Steve's feet off lounge and puts them on chair*): Not overworking are you, Stevie, boy?

STEVE: Why should I work hard? You two are getting ninety per cent of my money.

EVE (*Sighs, Collapses on relaxboard*): Ohhh … it's good to have that piano off my back. *Maid puts cigarette in Eve's mouth and lights it.*

HOWARD (*Picks Steve's feet off chair. Lights cigarette*): What's on your mind, Steve?

STEVE: Johnson's got a deal he wants to talk to you about.

EVE: Wait a minute. We're taking it easy when we're through with this picture.

HOWARD: Get somebody else to help support you.

STEVE: I told him you wouldn't be interested. But he made me promise to ask.
All are now milling around, climbing over each other in the tiny dressing room.

WARDROBE WOMAN (*She's "grand lady," ex-character actress with precise English accent*): Do you want to give me your costume now, Eve?

EVE: No, thank you, Mrs. Caruthers Later.

DIRECTOR (*Ushering Wardrobe Woman and Maid out*): Let's get out and let them relax. See you Monday, children. You'll love that scene. (*Kisses fingers*) What beautiful writing!

SPIKE (*Enters*): Was somebody calling for me?

DIRECTOR: We've been calling make-up all over the place. (*Exit*)

SPIKE: I hate directors. (*Walks over to Howard*) What is it?

HOWARD (*Back to Spike as he looks over the script*): Take off the eyelashes. (*Spike reaches for Howard*) Not me, her!

SPIKE (*Moving to Eve, Irritably*): Well, I don't know. Everybody works differently.

EVE (*To Steve*): What kind of a script is it?

STEVE: It's a new TV series.

EVE (*Sits up*): Oh no!

SPIKE: *Please!* How can a person work?

EVE: We wouldn't do TV, would we, Howard?

HOWARD (*To Steve*): I promised my mother. (*Goes back to script*)

STEVE: I told him you wouldn't be interested. It's another one of those domestic comedies. You know, the average, normal, typical American couple who live halfway up the next block.

SPIKE (*Putting eyelashes in a bottle*): When you want your eyes, they'll be in this bottle. (*Exits*)

STEVE: And you and Howard just aren't the types. *Eve slowly sits up.*

HOWARD (*Reading pages and groaning*): Oh no! ... Oh, for pete's sake.... Isn't this awful?

EVE: Steve?

STEVE: Hm?

EVE (*Quietly*): Why aren't we the types?

STEVE: Well, you and Howard aren't ... well, you're not typical.

EVE (*Storming*): Who's not typical?

STEVE (*Jumps*): Well, I just ...

EVE (*Angry*): We're just as typical as ... Just because we're actors everybody seems to think ... How can you walk in here and say something like that?

HOWARD: Please, Eve, how can I concentrate on this crummy script?

EVE: You know what he said?

HOWARD: What's the difference what he said? Who listens to agents?

EVE: But you know what he said?

HOWARD: Okay ... what did he say?

EVE: He says we're not typical.

HOWARD (*Deliberately walks up to Steve and waves his finger under his nose*): I'm as typical as any jerk in Beverly Hills.

EVE: People think just because we're actors we're freaks or something.

HOWARD: Yeah.

EVE: And that we take baths in goat's milk.

HOWARD: Yeah. Remember the time I mowed the lawn? (*To Steve*) That typical enough for you?

EVE: When?

HOWARD: When what?

EVE: When did you mow the lawn?

HOWARD: The time the gardener was sick in April.

EVE: In April we were in Europe.

HOWARD: I mean a year ago April.

EVE (*Triumphantly*): That's right. I remember now. And last Thursday I set my hair *myself!* (*To Steve*) How typical can a person get? *Both turn and glare at Steve.*

STEVE (*Looks from one to the other. Throws down the last gulp of his drink*): Well, I think I'll be running along. Be seeing you around, kids. (*Tries to sneak out*)

HOWARD (*Blocks his way*): What's the idea coming around here telling us we're not typical?

EVE: Yeah.

STEVE: I didn't say that. It's the fellow at the network that said it. *I* think you're typical.

HOWARD: You know what you are? You're a typical agent, that's what you are.

STEVE: That's a nasty thing to say.

HOWARD: There, how do *you* like it, huh?

EVE (*Remonstrating*): Howard ...

HOWARD: He can dish it out, but he can't take it.

STEVE (*Angry*): Okay, you asked for it. Typical? There's nothing average, normal, or typical about either of you. You're not even real. Outside of getting out of bed and dressing there's not another thing you can do for yourselves. (*Howard starts to interrupt*) I'll bet you don't even know where the fuse box in your house is. (*This stops Howard. He doesn't*) And, Eve, if the restaurants were closed on your house-keeper's day off, you'd *starve*. (*Pauses. Quietly*) You're my best friends, and I'm crazy about both of you, and maybe I'm just an agent, but I got my self-respect, and there're times when a man's got to stand up and speak his mind no matter what the price. (*Glowering*) You two just ain't typical. (*Exits*)

HOWARD: I should have punched him in the nose.

EVE (*Grimly*): Howard … he's right.

HOWARD (*Pause*): Let's get dressed and go home. (*Looks up to see she is staring thoughtfully into space*) So we're not typical. Kill us, we're not typical.

EVE (*Thoughtfully walks to mirror*): Aren't we real? Who is that staring at me in the glass? (*Howard's head appears next to hers in mirror*) Is that a real human being there … flesh and blood?

HOWARD (*Kisses her shoulder*): It ain't chopped liver. (*Both stare into mirror*) They never even told me we had a fuse box, so how should I know where it is?

Adams' living room.
Eve standing at French window looking out.
Phone rings. She ignores it.

HOWARD (*Enters, wearing shower robe, rubbing hair with towel. Answers phone without seeing Eve*): Hello. Oh, sure … I think we can. Wait a minute —I'll ask her. (*Picking up phone walks toward door as far as extension allows. Calls*) Eve, we'll have time to pick up Sheila, won't we? (*Eve doesn't answer. Howard crosses back. Speaks into phone*) Yeah, I'm sure we'll have time to … (*Sees Eve*) Eve, we'll have time to pick up Sheila, won't we?

EVE (*Absently*): Hm?

HOWARD: Eve, what are you doing?

EVE: Just thinking—(*Saunters toward mirror. Looks at herself searchingly*)

HOWARD (*Into phone*): Sheila, hang on a minute. (*Resignedly settles himself comfortably in a chair, holding receiver in lap*)

EVE: Howard, you know what I've been thinking? (*Howard shakes his head "no"*) Howard, are you listening to me? (*Howard shakes his head "yes"*) You know what I've been thinking? (*Howard shakes his head "no"*) We have been missing the real things in life!

HOWARD (*In phone*): Sheila, this may take a little time. Do you want me to call you back? (*Pause*) All right then, hang on.

EVE (*Crosses to window*): We keep so busy with interviews, parties, premieres. But the basic real things in life are right out there waiting for us.

HOWARD (*Sets phone down on table and walks to window*): What things?

EVE: Just to take a walk ... nowhere special. Just to take a walk like the average normal typical American couple.

HOWARD (*Gets it*): Ohhhh.

EVE: To hear the first Robin in spring. To say "Hi" to your neighbor. To ... watch a baseball game. To eat mother's homemade apple pie.

HOWARD: Your mother never made an apple pie in her life.

EVE: It's a figure of speech. The only things of real value are the simple things, the basic pleasures ... my home ... my husband ... sitting in our own living room next to a fire. Me in my negligee, you reading *Variety*.
We hear indistinguishable voice from phone.
Howard picks it up. Listens.

HOWARD (*In phone*): Okay, I'll try again, Sheila. (*To Eve*) Sheila wants to know if we can pick her up.

EVE (*Lost in reverie at window*): Howard, remember that day we were first married? We went walking in the rain?

HOWARD (*In phone*): Better let me call you back. (*Shrugs resignedly*) All right, hang on. (*Places receiver on desk. Walks over to Eve*) Eve, it's a quarter to eight. Either let's...

EVE: We got all wet and we found shelter in that abandoned barn. Remember, Howard?

HOWARD: *Yeah*, I remember.

EVE (*Snuggles up to him, head on his shoulders*): And afterwards...

HOWARD (*Softly*): Yeah, afterwards.

EVE: Howard, are those times gone ... lost ...?

HOWARD (*With feeling*): I don't think so. (*Kisses the back of her neck and ear. Suddenly remembers the phone*) Excuse me. (*Bends down to speak into the phone*) You better call a cab, Sheila. (*Hangs up, puts his arms around Eve as before*) Now what were you saying, darling?

EVE: Howard, the simple, real, *typical* things are the only things worth having.

HOWARD (*Kissing her*): You said it, kid.

EVE: Howard, let's try to get back to those things.

HOWARD: Okay.

EVE: What time does the average, normal, typical American get up when he's not working on a picture?

HOWARD (*Still busy*): About seven-thirty.

EVE (*Dismayed*): Seven-thirty (*Determinedly*) Howard we're going to start being typical at seven-thirty tomorrow morning.

HOWARD: I started ten minutes ago.
Adams' bedroom at dawn
Sounds of birds out of window. Eve and Howard peacefully sleeping in luxurious bed. Alarm rings.

EVE (*Sits bolt upright*): What, what, what, what … ? (*Pause*) Howard!

HOWARD (*reaches over and picks up phone*): Sheila, you better take a cab.

EVE: Howard, time to get up.

HOWARD (*In phone*): Eve, where are you?

EVE (*Looks around bleary-eyed*): I'm home … in bed.

HOWARD: Then where am *I?*

EVE: Home in bed.

HOWARD (*Hangs up phone. Peers around room*): By golly, she's right. (*Goes back to sleep*)
Alarms rings again.

EVE (*Half climbs over Howard and turns alarm off. This awakens Howard again. He peers closely at her*): What's the matter?

HOWARD: Some silly dame just called up and said she was you.

EVE (*Sleepily*): Howard, time to get up. It's seven-thirty.
They both go back to sleep.

EVE (*Bolts up in bed. Puzzled*): Why did we have to get up at seven-thirty? (*Nudges Howard. Howard*) Howard!…

HOWARD (*Sleepily*): Huh?

EVE: Why did we have to get up at seven-thirty?

HOWARD: I don't know. Go to sleep. (*Goes back to sleep*)

EVE: I can't sleep. It must have been something important. I wouldn't have set the alarm. (*Racks her brain for a moment, shrugs, then goes back to sleep*)

HOWARD (*Sits bolt upright*): Now *I* can't sleep. (*Racks his brain*) Eve, why did we have to get up at seven-thirty?

EVE (*Sleepily*): I don't remember any more.

HOWARD (*Disgruntled, lying down*): If that isn't typical! *Both sleep for a moment*

EVE (*Sits up again*): Typical! That's it! (*Shakes Howard*) Howard, this is the morning we were going to start being typical. (*Howard clutches pillow with both hands*) You promised, Howard.

HOWARD (*Resignedly gets up. Sits at side of bed in stunned immobility. Raises his head suddenly*): The basement!

EVE: What about the basement?

HOWARD: I'll bet that's where the fuse box is. It's the logical place.

EVE: (Throws switch to intercom beside bed): Elsie … Elsie.

HOWARD: Why aren't you getting up?

EVE: You know I can't get up until I have my coffee. (Into intercom) Elsie … *Elsie!*

ELSIE'S VOICE: What, what, what, what!

EVE: Elsie, we're up.

HOWARD: Eve, you can't bother Elsie. She was up till three serving the company we brought home from the party.

EVE: Oh, of course. (*Into intercom*) Elsie, dear, I'm sorry. You just go right on sleeping.

ELSIE'S VOICE (*dryly*): Thanks.

HOWARD (*Putting on robe*): Well, get up.

EVE (*Tragically*): Without coffee?

HOWARD: If you want coffee you'll have to get up, go into the kitchen, and make it.

EVE (*As if they were the Seven Tasks of Ulysses*): Get up, go into the kitchen, and make coffee. (*Looks at him bravely*) I'll try. (*Painfully gets out *of bed, Howard helping, and stands there as Howard helps her on with robe)*

HOWARD: That's the girl. You just gotta get to the kitchen. You'll make it. It's all downhill.

Interior of kitchen.
Howard and Eve enter, Howard supporting her.

EVE (*Very jittery*): I'll be all, right in a minute, Howard, just as soon as I have my coffee.

HOWARD (*Concerned*): Sure, sure you will, honey. We'll have it in a minute.

EVE (*Getting panicky*): You know how I am, Howard, until I have my coffee.

HOWARD: Sure, we'll make some instant coffee.

EVE: I have to have coffee, and as soon as I have coffee I'll be all right.

HOWARD (*Looking through cupboards*): Let's see, where is that coffee? I can't seem to find it.

EVE (*Frantic*): You can't find it? (*Tragically*) There isn't any coffee!

HOWARD (*Still looking*): Sure there is. I'll find it.

EVE: What if there isn't any?

HOWARD: Now, honey, we'll find it. (*Flicks on intercom*) Elsie.

EVE: What if there isn't any coffee in the whole house?

HOWARD (*Loudly*): Elsie!

ELSIE'S VOICE: What, what, what, what!

HOWARD: Elsie, where's the coffee?

ELSIE'S VOICE: Well, where are you?

HOWARD: In the kitchen.

ELSIE'S VOICE: That's where it is.

HOWARD: But *where* in the kitchen?

ELSIE'S VOICE: First shelf from the corner next to the waffle iron.

EVE (*Opens cupboard*): I can't find the waffle iron.

HOWARD (*Into intercom*): She can't find the waffle iron.

ELSIE'S VOICE: Up above and to the left of the lower shelf where I keep the spices.

EVE: Where is the lower shelf where she keeps the spices?

HOWARD (*Into intercom*): Where is the lower shelf where you keep the spices?

ELSIE'S VOICE: Where is she standing?

HOWARD: Facing the refrigerator.

ELSIE'S VOICE: The coffee is Up Stage Left.

EVE: Oh. Here it is.

HOWARD (*Into intercom*): We found it. (*Puts water on to boil*)

EVE (*Proudly. Into intercom*): Elsie, we're making coffee!

ELSIE'S VOICE: When I get up at noon I'll call the Associated Press and give them the scoop.

Howard and Eve having coffee.

EVE: Look, it's a quarter to eight and we've had our coffee and we have the whole blessed day before us.

HOWARD: Okay, it's a quarter to eight. Now what do we do? (*Eve looks at him blankly*) I've got an idea.

EVE: What?

HOWARD: Let's go back to bed. We've been typical for a half hour. We don't want to go into this suddenly—we may get the bends. A half hour today, an hour tomorrow—by Wednesday we can stay up all day.

EVE: You're not taking this seriously, are you?

HOWARD: Should I?

EVE: Howard, this is important. I'm trying to find myself. I want to be able to do what every normal average typical woman does ... I want to stand on equal footing with all of them. I want to be able to meet them face to face—(*walks to window*) and say Hello out there! I'm Mrs. Eve Adams, housewife and woman. How do you do!

WOMAN'S VOICE How do you do!
(*From backyard*):

4. *The New Republic*, Leftist Magazine, Objects to Television, 1959

Deception on TV

There was collusion between contestants and producers on TV quiz shows. *Twenty-One* and *Tic-Tac Dough*, neither of which is now seen, were rigged. For which stale news the reading public is indebted to the House Subcommittee on Legislative Oversight. The disclosures are a comfort to many whose self-esteem had been deflated by watching the case with which common folk, with only a rubbing of forehead and a wetting of lips, could remember so many dull facts.

NBC's response has been interesting, recalling earlier days when the possibility of scandal sent executives racing for cover, the network did not wait for charge to be preferred, let alone proved, against its employee Charles Van Doren before taking him off the air. It had no idea people cheated.

The whole affair is riddled with deceit, and not just the small deceit of quiz contestants being briefed in advance. Misrepresentation has long been rationalized as unavoidable in this competitive society where one plays the game to win. Did the producer and players think they were doing wrong? If they did, they quickly suppressed the thought. "I didn't think of it in terms of fraud," one contestant testified. "The excitement appealed to me." "I really didn't," another said. "I was perfectly blithe about it. They were having a happy time, I was, everybody was." The amorality has not shocked the public, for it is assumed that similar deceptions are practiced elsewhere. What would business be without deals, private understandings, faintly false claims? In what business are people expected to look gift horses in the mouth?

They came to a contestant's home in Forest Hills and asked: "How would you like to earn $25,000?"

"I said: 'Who wouldn't?' "

Forty-four million out of 51 million American households own one or more TV sets. On these sets were shown programs paid for by advertisers who last year, it is reported, spent $1,344,200,000. How honest is most of that advertising? It is a question that needs but has not had study by the Federal Communications Commission, the agency that is officially responsible for regulating the broadcasting industry. One may agree with the FCC Chairman, John Doerfer, that "there are many things that are fraudulent, deceitful and reprehensible that law cannot reach," but it would be helpful were the FCC to inform Congress and the public exactly what those "many things" are.

Or is it assumed that the public wants to be fooled, demands the illusion that plain girls can be transformed into Botticelli beauties by hair rinses and deodorants? Or that millions who have been smoking more and enjoying it less can enjoy it more by smoking more of another brand, perhaps one that offers a new high porosity cigarette paper? Or that the real joy of living is contained in a can of beer? Or that after the beer, relief is just a swallow away? Television needs investigating, but not by a Subcommittee or an FCC that strains at gnats and swallows camels.

A real investigation would center on a simple question: why is television so bad, so monotonous? The change over the past few years from Elvis Presley to Pat Boone is progress from the obscure to the insipid. But is that the best TV can do? Must the majority of TV time be given to the romance of river boats and prairies, the adventures of dead-pan but hurting-inside detectives, the banalities of the "family shows," the weary insouciance of the Bings and the Frankies, the smiling but vacuous going on of Gale Storm, Donna Reed, Ernie Ford, Betty Hutton, June Allyson, Mickey Rooney, Ozzie and Harriet?...

Someday some Congressman ... who feels strongly enough that the involuntary servitude of the TV viewer has gone on long enough will contest the claim of the television industry that American people should be grateful they have "free" TV. He will point out that it means freedom to choose for the most part among the bad and the mediocre, or to turn the set off. He will acknowledge that TV can do great things; it has done them on news events and on such rare programs as *Playhouse 90*. Still, he will insist that in reaching for the largest possible audience at all times, television has betrayed its legal obligation to serve the public "interest, convenience and necessity."

The Congressman who asks the right questions will make enemies. The networks, ad agencies and sponsor will show him they can shoot faster than Wyatt Earp. But what a hero he would be to 44 million American households!

5. Federal Regulator Newton Minow Criticizes Television as "A Vast Wasteland," 1961

Delivered 9 May 1961—NAH Ass. of Broadcasters Conference

When you work in broadcasting you volunteer for public service, public pressure, and public regulation. You must compete with other attractions and other investments, and the only way you can do it is to prove to us every three years that you should have been in business in the first place.

I can think of easier ways to make a living.

But I cannot think of more satisfying ways.

I admire your courage—but that doesn't mean that I would make life any easier for you. Your license lets you use the public's airwaves as trustees for 180 million Americans. The public is your beneficiary. If you want to stay on as trustees, you must deliver a decent return to the public—not only to your stockholders. So, as a representative of the public, your health and your product are among my chief concerns.

Now as to your health, let's talk only of television today. 1960 gross broadcast revenues of the television industry were over 1,268,000,000 dollars.... So the percentage increase of total revenues from '59 to '60 was 9 per cent, and the percentage increase of profit was 9.7 per cent. This, despite a recession throughout the country. For your investors, the price has indeed been right.

So I have confidence in your health, but not in your product. It is with this and much more in mind that I come before you today.

One editorialist in the trade press wrote that "the FCC of the New Frontier is going to be one of the toughest FCC's in the history of broadcast regulation." If he meant that we intend to enforce the law in the public interest, let me make it perfectly clear that he is right: We do. If he meant that we intend to muzzle or censor broadcasting, he is dead wrong. It wouldn't surprise me if some of you had expected me to come here today and say to you in effect, "Clean up your own house or the government will do it for you." Well, in a limited sense, you would be right because I've just said it.

But I want to say to you as earnestly as I can that it is not in that spirit that I come before you today, nor is it in that spirit that I intend to serve the FCC. I am in Washington to help broadcasting, not to harm it; to strengthen it, not weaken it; to reward it, not to punish it; to encourage it, not threaten it; and to stimulate it, not censor it. Above all, I am here to uphold and protect the public interest.

Newton Minow, "Television and the Public Interest," speech delivered 9 May 1961, National Association of Broadcasters, Washington, D.C. Available at: http://www .americanrhetoric.com/speeches/newtonminow.htm

Now what do we mean by "the public interest?" Some say the public interest is merely what interests the public. I disagree. And so does your distinguished president, Governor Collins....

... [I]n today's world, with chaos in Laos and the Congo aflame, with Communist tyranny on our Caribbean doorstep, relentless pressures on our Atlantic alliance, with social and economic problems at home of the gravest nature, yes, and with the technological knowledge that makes it possible, as our President has said, not only to destroy our world but to destroy poverty around the world—in a time of peril and opportunity, the old complacent, unbalanced fare of action-adventure and situation comedies is simply not good enough.

Your industry possesses the most powerful voice in America. It has an inescapable duty to make that voice ring with intelligence and with leadership. In a few years, this exciting industry has grown from a novelty to an instrument of overwhelming impact on the American people. It should be making ready for the kind of leadership that newspapers and magazines assumed years ago, to make our people aware of their world.

Ours has been called the jet age, the atomic age, the space age. It is also, I submit, the television age. And just as history will decide whether the leaders of today's world employed the atom to destroy the world or rebuild it for mankind's benefit, so will history decide whether today's broadcasters employed their powerful voice to enrich the people or to debase them.

If I seem today to address myself chiefly to the problems of television, I don't want any of you radio broadcasters to think that we've gone to sleep at your switch. We haven't. We still listen. But in recent years most of the controversies and cross-currents in broadcast programming have swirled around television. And so my subject today is the television industry and the public interest.

Like everybody, I wear more than one hat. I am the chairman of the FCC. But I am also a television viewer and the husband and father of other television viewers. I have seen a great many television programs that seemed to me eminently worthwhile and I am not talking about the much bemoaned good old days of "Playhouse 90" and "Studio One."

I'm talking about this past season. Some were wonderfully entertaining, such as "The Fabulous Fifties," "The Fred Astaire Show," and "The Bing Crosby Special"; some were dramatic and moving, such as Conrad's "Victory" and "Twilight Zone"; some were marvelously informative, such as "The Nation's Future," "CBS Reports," "The Valiant Years." I could list many more programs that I am sure everyone here felt enriched his own life and that of his family. When television is good, nothing—not the theater, not the magazines or newspapers—nothing is better.

But when television is bad, nothing is worse. I invite each of you to sit down in front of your television set when your station goes on the air and stay there, for a day, without a book, without a magazine, without a newspaper, without a profit and loss sheet or a rating book to distract you. Keep your eyes glued to that set until the station signs off. I can assure you that what you will observe is a vast wasteland.

You will see a procession of game shows, formula comedies about totally unbelievable families, blood and thunder, mayhem, violence, sadism, murder, western bad men, western good men, private eyes, gangsters, more violence, and cartoons. And endlessly commercials—many screaming, cajoling, and offending. And most of all, boredom. True, you'll see a few things you will enjoy. But they will be very, very few. And if you think I exaggerate, I only ask you to try it....

Why is so much of television so bad? I've heard many answers: demands of your advertisers; competition for ever higher ratings; the need always to attract a mass audience; the high cost of television programs; the insatiable appetite for programming material. These are some of the reasons. Unquestionably, these are tough problems not susceptible to easy answers. But I am not convinced that you have tried hard enough to solve them.

I do not accept the idea that the present over-all programming is aimed accurately at the public taste. The ratings tell us only that some people have their television sets turned on and of that number, so many are tuned to one channel and so many to another. They don't tell us what the public might watch if they were offered half-a-dozen additional choices. A rating, at best, is an indication of how many people saw what you gave them. Unfortunately, it does not reveal the depth of the penetration, or the intensity of reaction, and it never reveals what the acceptance would have been if what you gave them had been better—if all the forces of art and creativity and daring and imagination had been unleashed. I believe in the people's good sense and good taste, and I am not convinced that the people's taste is as low as some of you assume....

Certainly, I hope you will agree that ratings should have little influence where children are concerned. The best estimates indicate that during the hours of 5 to 6 P.M. sixty per cent of your audience is composed of children under twelve. And most young children today, believe it or not, spend as much time watching television as they do in the schoolroom.

I repeat—let that sink in, ladies and gentlemen—most young children today spend as much time watching television as they do in the schoolroom. It used to be said that there were three great influences on a child: home, school, and church. Today, there is a fourth great influence, and you ladies and gentlemen in this room control it.

If parents, teachers, and ministers conducted their responsibilities by following the ratings, children would have a steady diet of ice cream, school holidays, and no Sunday school. What about your responsibilities? Is there no room on television to teach, to inform, to uplift, to stretch, to enlarge the capacities of our children? Is there no room for programs deepening their understanding of children in other lands? Is there no room for a children's news show explaining something to them about the world at their level of understanding? Is there no room for reading the great literature of the past, for teaching them the great traditions of freedom? There are some fine children's shows, but they are drowned out in the massive doses of cartoons, violence, and more violence. Must these be your trademarks? Search your consciences and see if you cannot offer more to your young beneficiaries whose future you guide so many hours each and every day.

Now what about adult programming and ratings? You know, newspaper publishers take popularity ratings too. And the answers are pretty clear: It is almost always the comics, followed by advice to the lovelorn columns. But, ladies and gentlemen, the news is still on the front page of all newspapers; the editorials are not replaced by more comics; and the newspapers have not become one long collection of advice to the lovelorn. Yet newspapers do not even need a license from the government to be in business; they do not use public property. But in television, where your responsibilities as public trustees are so plain, the moment that the ratings indicate that westerns are popular there are new imitations of westerns on the air faster than the old coaxial cable could take us from Hollywood to New York. Broadcasting cannot continue to live by the numbers. Ratings ought to be the slave of the broadcaster, not his master. And you and I both know that the rating services themselves would agree....

You must provide a wider range of choices, more diversity, more alternatives. It is not enough to cater to the nation's whims; you must also serve the nation's needs. And I would add this: that if some of you persist in a relentless search for the highest rating and the lowest common denominator, you may very well lose your audience. Because, to paraphrase a great American who was recently my law partner, the people are wise, wiser than some of the broadcasters and politicians think.

As you may have gathered, I would like to see television improved. But how is this to be brought about? By voluntary action by the broadcasters themselves? By direct government intervention? Or how?

Let me address myself now to my role not as a viewer but as chairman of the FCC. I could not if I would chart for you this afternoon in detail all of the actions I contemplate. Instead, I want to make clear some of the fundamental principles which guide me.

First: the people own the air. And they own it as much in prime evening time as they do at six o'clock Sunday morning. For every hour that the people give you—you owe them something. And I intend to see that your debt is paid with service.

Second: I think it would be foolish and wasteful for us to continue any worn-out wrangle over the problems of payola, rigged quiz shows, and other mistakes of the past. There are laws on the books which we will enforce. But there is no chip on my shoulder. We live together in perilous, uncertain times; we face together staggering problems; and we must not waste much time now by rehashing the cliches of past controversy. To quarrel over the past is to lose the future.

Third: I believe in the free enterprise system. I want to see broadcasting improved, and I want you to do the job. I am proud to champion your cause. It is not rare for American businessmen to serve a public trust. Yours is a special trust because it is imposed by law.

Fourth: I will do all I can to help education television. There are still not enough educational stations, and major centers of the country still lack usable educational channels. If there were a limited number of printing presses in this country, you may be sure that a fair proportion of them would be put to educational use. Educational television has an enormous contribution to make to the future, and I intend to give it a hand along the way. If there is not a nation-wide educational television system in this country, it will not be the fault of the FCC.

Fifth: I am unalterably opposed to governmental censorship. There will be no suppression of programming which does not meet with bureaucratic tastes. Censorship strikes at the tap root of our free society.

Sixth: I did not come to Washington to idly observe the squandering of the public's airwaves. The squandering of our airwaves is no less important than the lavish waste of any precious natural resource. I intend to take the job of chairman of the FCC very seriously. I happen to believe in the gravity of my own particular sector of the New Frontier, There will be times perhaps when you will consider that I take myself or my job *too* seriously.

Frankly, I don't care If you do. For I am convinced that either one takes this job seriously—or one can be seriously taken.

Now how will these principles be applied? Clearly at the heart of the FCC's authority lies its power to license, to renew or fail to renew, or to revoke a license. As you know, when your license comes up for renewal, your performance is compared with your promises. I understand that many people feel that in the past licenses were often renewed *pro forma*. I say to you now: renewal will not be *pro forma* in the future. There is nothing permanent or sacred about a broadcast license.

But simply matching promises and performance is not enough. I intend to do more. I intend to find out whether the people care. I intend to find out whether the community which each broadcaster serves believes he has been serving the public interest. When a renewal is set down for a hearing, I intend, whenever possible, to hold a well-advertised public hearing, right in the community you have promised to serve. I want the people who own the air and the homes that television enters to tell you and the FCC what's been going on. I want the people—if they're truly interested in the service you give them—to make notes, document cases, tell us the facts. And for those few of you who really believe that the public interest is merely what interests the public, I hope that these hearings will arouse no little interest.

The FCC has a fine reserve of monitors—almost 180 million Americans gathered around 56 million sets. If you want those monitors to be your friends at court, it's up to you.

Now some of you may say, "Yes, but I still do not know where the line is between a grant of a renewal and the hearing you just spoke of." My answer is: Why should you want to know how close you can come to the edge of the cliff? What the Commission asks of you is to make a conscientious, good-faith effort to serve the public interest. Every one of you serves a community in which the people would benefit by educational, and religious, instructive and other public service programming. Every one of you serves an area which has local needs—as to local elections, controversial issues, local news, local talent. Make a serious, genuine effort to put on that programming. And when you do, you will not be playing brinkmanship with the public interest....

Another and perhaps the most important frontier: Television will rapidly join the parade into space. International television will be with us soon. No one knows how long it will be until a broadcast from a studio in New York will be viewed in India as well as in Indiana, will be seen in the Congo as it is seen in Chicago. But as surely as we are meeting here today, that day will come; and once again our world will shrink.

What will the people of other countries think of us when they see our western bad men and good men punching each other in the jaw in between the shooting? What will the Latin American or African child learn of America from this great communications industry? We cannot permit television in its present form to be our voice overseas.

There is your challenge to leadership. You must reexamine some fundamentals of your industry. You must open your minds and open your hearts to the limitless horizons of tomorrow. I can suggest some words that should serve to guide you:

Television and all who participate in it are jointly accountable to the American public for respect for the special needs of children, for community responsibility, for the advancement of education and culture, for the acceptability of the program materials chosen, for decency and decorum in production, and for propriety in advertising. This responsibility cannot be discharged by any given group of programs, but can be discharged only through the highest standards of respect for the American home, applied to every moment of every program presented by television.

Program materials should enlarge the horizons of the viewer, provide him with wholesome entertainment, afford helpful stimulation, and remind him of the responsibilities which the citizen has towards his society.

Now those are not my words. They are yours. They are taken literally, verbatim, from your own Television Code. They reflect the leadership and aspirations of your own great industry. I urge you to respect them as I do.... I urge you at this meeting and, after you leave, back home, at your stations and your networks, to strive ceaselessly to improve your product and to better serve your viewers, the American people.

I say to you ladies and gentlemen—I remind you what ... President [Kennedy] said in his stirring inaugural. He said: "Ask not what America can do for for you; ask what you can do for America." I say to you ladies and gentlemen: Ask not what broadcasting can do for you; ask what you can do for broadcasting. And ask what broadcasting can do for America.

I urge you, I urge you to put the people's airwaves to the service of the people and the cause of freedom. You must help prepare a generation for great decisions. You must help a great nation fulfill its future....

6. Robert de Koos, *TV Guide* Writer, Views Bill Cosby as an Upwardly Mobile Individual, 1965

Bill Cosby is the co-star of *I Spy,* an adventure comedy redolent of heroin, huggermugger, karate, mayhem and understated humor, which appears in color on the NBC network every Wednesday night.

Robert de Roos, "The Spy Who Came in for the Gold," *TV Guide* (23 October 1965).
Courtesy of TV Guide Magazine, LLC © 1965.

Note must be made that Bill Cosby is a Negro—the first to be starred in a network drama series in the United States.

This comes as no surprise to Bill Cosby, who gained fame as a comedian. He's been a Negro for 28 years.

But the starring of a Negro may say something about the NBC network and the State of the Union, coming as it does 102 years after the signing of the Emancipation Proclamation.

Asked why he signed a Negro for the part of a CIA undercover agent, Sheldon Leonard, executive producer of *I Spy,* says:

"There was no motivation. The part was conceived for a white man—but a whole man, a man of humor, physical fitness and competence.

"I had signed Robert Culp and I looked around for his counterpart. Then I saw Cosby on one of the variety shows and a bulb lit up. I was sure he was the man I wanted.

"I make an intensive underground investigation before choosing a person for a long-range project of this sort. From every source I learned Bill Cosby was a tireless worker, a man striving to do his best.

"I called Grant Tinker of NBC and told him I had found a young comedian who had every quality we were looking for. 'In one way he is different,' I said. 'He is colored.'

" 'That's just great,' Tinker said. 'I think I speak for everyone at NBC when I say that.' "

Later, Tinker said, "We did not set out to get a Negro to star in a feature. We think it is right and proper, but it was not planned in any sense."

"Cosby comes on as an engaging, warmhearted, intelligent man," Leonard adds. "If anyone takes exception to this man because of his color, it will have to be some nut."

As for Bill Cosby, a former track star with a highly mobile face and a voice with many tricks, the most important thing is the chance to get rich. "Money is of the utmost importance to me," he says.

Cosby has no visions of sugar plums, low-slung, high-powered motorcars, yachts, penthouse apartments or other trappings of the rich. "If this series goes five years, I will be only 33 and rich," Bill says. "Then I can stop and do something I'd enjoy more. I want to be a schoolteacher. That would be a real challenge."

Three years ago, Cosby was tending bar in a cellar saloon to supplement "no income" as a sophomore at Temple University, Philadelphia.

There he probably would have stayed except for a fortuitous sense of humor. Bill entertained his customers with bits of dialog which were so successful that a friend suggested, "Get out from behind that bar and get on a stage."

Bill moved next door as a comedian at $12.50 a night. Today, three years later, he is one of the fastest-rising comedians in the business. He is a $15,000-a-week comic at the Nevada resorts and commands smaller, but still not paltry, sums from night clubs and college concerts.

His third record, "Why Is There Air?," was released in August. His first two, "Bill Cosby Is a Very Funny Fello ... Right!" and "I Started Out as a Child" won a Grammy award. "He's had a remarkable career for a man who doesn't tell jokes," said Norman Cornyn of Warner Bros. Records.

In a sense, Bill is ad-libbing his autobiography on stage, displaying a sharp comic sense as he rambles on. He talks about life in a poor family in Philadelphia, street football and teen-age dating, and takes off on some remarkable flights of fancy: Noah's colloquy with the Lord; a referee setting up conditions for the American Revolution; the plight of saber-toothed tiger, Ralphie, who lisps because he has only one saber.

Cosby does not banter about racial issues. "I started with some of that stuff, but I wasn't comfortable with it," he says. "The whole question about Negro comics is this: If they colored us white would we still be funny?"

"I realized how strong we would be as a team," Culp says, "but at first the other writers couldn't find the relationship. They all tried to put me in the front seat and Cosby in the back seat and that isn't the idea. We are actually almost mirror images of each other. Sometimes I take the back seat and sometimes Bill does."

As to Cosby the actor, Culp says, "He is the fastest natural study I've ever seen. He is cramming 10 years of education into a few months. No novice, no matter how talented can come up with performances like Bill.

"Of course, he's not a novice. He is involved in his comedy as an actor. But to become another guy and have another guy's emotions with a bit of hero juice thrown in—that is painfully hard to learn."

Sheldon Leonard, the executive producer, says, "I defy anyone to say Bill's not been acting all his life."

As for Bill himself, he is working very hard at his new craft.

"This is a job an actor could have had," he said. "I do feel a bit guilty about that because there are very few—a minute number—of Negro actors working or making money. I want them to say at least, 'He's not an actor but he did try.' I don't want them to say, 'He's not an actor and didn't even try to be.'"…

So in his first few months before the camera, Bill Cosby seems to have met every test. He likes the work. "It's just like college here," he says. "I know all the people. It's like a family."

And if everything continues well and if several million people like Cosby, Culp & Co some lower-class neighborhood school in Philadelphia can expect a new physical education teacher along about 1973.

His name will be Bill Cosby, ex-comedian, ex-actor.

7. *The Chicago Daily Defender,* an African American Newspaper, Views Bill Cosby as Presenting a New Image for African Americans, 1965

The most interesting new face on TV this season belongs to actor-comedian Bill Cosby.

"New Negro Image Created In Cosby's 'I Spy' Role," *The Chicago Daily Defender* (28 September 1965).

Cosby, the Negro government agent in "I Spy." is the first of his race to portray a hero-image in a weekly TV series.

The tall, laconic performer projects a style free of the underlying bitterness, chip-on-the shoulder racial intensity common in many Negro stars. Neither does he play the color of his skin for humor.

The result is a thoroughly likeable, relaxed performance of a well-educated hippie who moves through his role with no reference to the fact that he is a Negro.

Cobsy shares many of the same attitudes with the character he plays. But off-screen he is acutely aware of what is happening and, in a sense, the responsibility he bears.

He admits a degree of bitterness for the second class status he has lived with for all his 28 years, adding that he tries to keep it hidden—especially on screen for the NBC-TV series.

"I watch the scripts very carefully," he said in his dressing room during a lunch break. "They slipped some racial gags into some of the stories, but at my request they took them out."

"I am the first Negro ever cast as Captain Marvel or Superman. So I don't think the jokes are appropriate. But neither have I lost my identity as a Negro or attempted to turn white."

Much of Cosby's success is due to his co-star, Robert Culp, who is also a close personal friend.

Culp is a remarkably bright and articulate man, and in Cosby's words, "The best acting coach in the world."

Cosby was strictly a stand-up night club comedian until he began the series. But he has studied Culp's every move and expression to gain the necessary poise and know-how.

"I was afraid when we first started," Cosby said. "I was afraid of the camera, the crew and of making mistakes. I hurried through my lines and recited them instead of swinging into the part."

The easy camaraderie of the show's characters is a natural extension of the Cosby-Culp friendship, a warm relationship that evidences itself on the screen.

He believes Negro youths will be inspired by the educated, dignified image he presents. He also thinks that Caucasian viewers may see the Negro in a new light, an acceptable citizen to be admired and respected on his own merits.

"What viewers see on the screen is our message," Cosby said. "It might offend the average bigot, but I hope it will give warmth to many people who are mixed up about race relationships."

ESSAYS

These two foundational pieces take different approaches to the study of television: Lynn Spigel, Frances E. Willard Professor of Screen Cultures at the School of Communication at Northwestern University, makes a case for studying the material culture and viewing practices of television within the home, but Herman

Gray, professor of sociology at University of California–Santa Cruz, argues that scholars must look at programming and how television represented larger social, and in particular racial, relations during the network era. Where Spigel is concerned with audiences, Gray studies representations and the role of networks and producers in shaping the meaning of TV. Spigel examines the "ideological and social contradictions concerning the construction of gender and the family unit" and where televisions fit into these differing ideals of family unity and the realities of everyday life in the 1950s. She draws on sociological studies and print advertising to think about how Americans situated television within the home and the family circle. What can advertising tell us about the cultural ideas surrounding television during this era? How does advertising distort the picture of television within the domestic circle? What were the dominant hopes for and concerns about television among the average American consumer? In contrast, Gray studies the representations of African Americans on television and argues that these portrayals were constrained, disciplined, and constructed by and around the white point of view of network executives. Despite these limitations, he claims a small group of black actors, writers, and directors in this early period "forced open creative spaces within the productive apparatus of television" to revise representations of black Americans and introduce their points of view. How did Cosby fit into this argument? Did actors like Cosby ultimately overturn white representations of African Americans and older stereotypes taken from minstrelsy?

Each of these authors has written extensively on the social implications of television since these essays. Their work has inspired other scholars to examine both representations and viewing practices, creating an interdisciplinary field of television studies that draws on cultural studies, sociology, and history.

Television in the Family Circle

LYNN SPIGEL

… [I]n postwar years the television set became a central figure in representations of family relationships. The introduction of the machine into the home meant that family members needed to come to terms with the presence of a communication medium that might transform older modes of family interaction. The popular media published reports and advice from social critics and social scientists who were studying the effects of television on family relationships. The media also published pictorial representations of domestic life that showed people how television might—or might not—fit into the dynamics of their own domestic lives. Most significantly, like the scene from *Rebel without a Cause,* the media discourses were organized around ideas of family harmony and discord.

Indeed, contradictions between unity and division were central to representations of television during the period of its installation. Television was the great family minstrel that promised to bring Mom, Dad, and the kids together; at the same time, it had to be carefully controlled so that it harmonized with the separate gender roles and social functions of individual family members. This meant that the contradiction between unity and division was not a simple binary opposition; it was not a matter of either/or but rather both at once. Television was supposed to bring the family together but still allow for social and sexual divisions in the home. In fact, the attempt to maintain a balance between these two ideals was a central tension at work in popular discourses on television and the family.

The Family United

In 1954, *McCall's* magazine coined the term "togetherness." The appearance of this term between the covers of a woman's magazine is significant not only because it shows the importance attached to family unity during the postwar years, but also because this phrase is symptomatic of discourses aimed at the housewife. Home magazines primarily discussed family life in language organized around spatial imagery of proximity, distance, isolation, and integration. In fact, the spatial organization of the home was presented as a set of scientific laws through which family relationships could be calculated and controlled. Topics ranging from childrearing to sexuality were discussed in spatial terms, and solutions to domestic problems were overwhelmingly spatial: if you are nervous, make yourself a quiet sitting corner far away from the central living area of the home. If your children are cranky, let them play in the yard. If your husband is bored at the office, turn your garage into a workshop where he'll recall the joys of his boyhood. It was primarily within the context of this spatial problem that television was discussed. The central question was, "Where should you put the television set?" This problem was tackled throughout the period, formulated and reformulated, solved and recast. In the process the television set became an integral part of the domestic environment depicted in the magazines.

At the simplest level, there was the question of the proper room for television. In 1949, *Better Homes and Gardens* asked, "Where does the receiver go?" It listed options including the living room, game room, or "some strategic spot where you can see it from the living room, dining room and kitchen." At this point, however, the photographs of model rooms usually did not include television sets as part of the interior decor. On the few occasions when sets did appear, they were placed either in the basement or in the living room. By 1951, the television set traveled more freely through the household spaces depicted in the magazines. It appeared in the basement, living room, bedroom, kitchen, fun room, converted garage, sitting-sleeping room, music room, and even the "TV room." Furthermore, not only the room, but the exact location in the room, had to be considered for its possible use as a TV zone.

As the television set moved into the center of family life, other household fixtures traditionally associated with domestic bliss had to make room for it. Typically, the magazines presented the television set as the new family hearth through which love and affection might be rekindled. In 1951, when *American Home* first displayed a television set on its cover photograph, it employed the conventionalized iconography of a model living room organized around the fireplace, but this time a television set was built into the mantelpiece. Even more radically, the television was shown to replace the fireplace altogether, as the magazines showed readers how television could function as the center of family attention. So common had this substitution become that by 1954 *House Beautiful* was presenting its readers with "another example of how the TV set is taking the place of the fireplace as the focal point around which to arrange the seating in the room." Perhaps the most extreme example of this kind of substitution is the tradition at some broadcast stations of burning Yule logs on the television screen each Christmas Eve, a practice that originated in the 1950s....

As the magazines continued to depict the set in the center of family activity, television seemed to become a natural part of domestic space. By the early 1950s, floor plans included a space for television in the home's structural layout, and television sets were increasingly depicted as everyday commonplace objects that any family might hope to own. Indeed, the magazines included television as a staple home fixture before most Americans could even receive a television signal, much less consider purchasing the expensive item. The media discourses did not so much reflect social reality; instead, they preceded it. The home magazines helped to construct television as a household object, one that belonged in the family space. More surprisingly, however, in the span of roughly four years, television itself became *the* central figure in images of the American home; it became the cultural symbol par excellence of family life.

Television, it was said, would bring the family ever closer, an expression which, in itself a spatial metaphor, was continually repeated in a wide range of popular media—not only women's magazines, but also general magazines, men's magazines, and on the airwaves In its capacity as unifying agent, television fit well with the more general postwar hopes for a return to family values. It was seen as a kind of household cement that promised to reassemble the splintered lives of families who had been separated during the war. It was also meant to reinforce the new suburban family unit, which had left most of its extended family and friends behind in the city.

The emergence of the term "family room" in the postwar period is a perfect example of the importance attached to organizing household spaces around ideals of family togetherness. First coined in George Nelson and Henry Wright's *Tomorrow's House: A Complete Guide for the Home-Builder* (1946), the family room encapsulated a popular ideal throughout the period....

But one needn't build a new room in order to bring the family together around the television set; kitchens, living rooms, and dining rooms would do just as well. What was needed was a particular attitude, a sense of closeness that permeated the room. Photographs, particularly in advertisements, graphically depicted the idea of the family circle with television viewers grouped around the television set in semicircle patterns.

As Roland Marchand has shown with respect to advertising in the 1920s and 1930s, the family circle was a prominent pictorial strategy for the promotion of household goods. The pictures always suggested that all members of the family were present, and since they were often shot in soft-focus or contained dreamy mists, there was a romantic haze around the family unit. Sometimes artists even drew concentric circles around the family, or else an arc of light evoked the theme. According to Marchand, the visual cliché of the family circle referred back to Victorian notions about domestic havens, implying that the home was secure and stable. The advertisements suggested a democratic model of family life, one in which all members shared in consumer decisions—although, as Marchand suggests, to some extent the father remained a dominant figure in the pictorial composition....

Much like the advertisements for radio and the phonograph, advertisements for television made ample use of this reassuring pictorial convention—especially in the years immediately following the war when advertisers were in the midst of their reconversion campaigns, channeling the country back from the wartime pressures of personal sacrifice and domestic upheaval to a peacetime economy based on consumerism and family values. The advertisements suggested that television would serve as a catalyst for the return to a world of domestic love and affection—a world that must have been quite different from the actual experiences of returning GIs and their new families in the chaotic years of readjustment to civilian life....

The transition from wartime to postwar life resulted in a set of ideological and social contradictions concerning the construction of gender and the family unit. The image of compassionate families that advertisers offered the public might well have been intended to serve the "therapeutic" function that both Roland Marchand and T.J. Jackson Lears have ascribed to advertising in general. The illustrations of domestic bliss and consumer prosperity presented a soothing alternative to the tensions of postwar life. Government building policies and veteran mortgage loans sanctioned the materialization of these advertising images by giving middle-class families a chance to buy into the "good life" of ranch-style cottages and consumer durables. Even so, both the advertising images and the homes themselves were built on the shaky foundations of social upheavals and cultural conflicts that were never completely resolved. The family circle ads, like suburbia itself, were only a temporary consumer solution to a set of complicated political, economic, and social problems.

In the case of television, these kinds of advertisements almost always showed the product in the center of the family group. While soft-focus or dreamy mists were sometimes used, the manufacturers' claims for picture clarity and good reception seem to have necessitated the use of sharp focus and high contrast, which better connoted these product attributes. The product-as-center motif not only suggested the familial qualities of the set, but also implied a mode of use: the ads suggested television be watched by a family audience....

Even families that were not welcomed into the middle-class melting pot of postwar suburbia were promised that the dream of domestic bliss would come true through the purchase of a television set. *Ebony* continually ran advertisements that displayed African-Americans in middle-class living rooms, enjoying an evening of television. Many of these ads were strikingly similar to those used in white consumer magazines—although often the advertisers portrayed black families watching programs that featured black actors. Despite this iconographic substitution, the message was clearly one transmitted by a culture industry catering to the middle-class suburban ideal. Nuclear families living in single-family homes would engage in intensely private social relations through the luxury of television.

Such advertisements appeared in a general climate of postwar expectations about television's ability to draw families closer together. In *The Age of Television* (1956), Leo Bogart summarized a wide range of audience studies on the new medium that showed numerous Americans believed television would revive domestic life. Summarizing the findings, Bogart concluded that social scientific surveys "agree completely that television has had the effect of keeping the family at home more than formerly." One respondent from a Southern California survey boasted that his "family now stays home all the time and watches the same programs. [We] turn it on at 3 P.M. and watch until 10 P.M. We never go anywhere." Moreover, studies indicated that people believed television strengthened family ties. A 1949 survey of an eastern city found that long-term TV owners expressed "an awareness of an enhanced family solidarity."…

Typically also, television was considered a remedy for problem children. During the 1950s, juvenile delinquency emerged as a central topic of public debate. Women's magazines and child psychologists such as Dr. Benjamin Spock, whose *Baby and Childcare* had sold a million copies by 1951, gave an endless stream of advice to mothers on ways to prevent their children from becoming antisocial and emotionally impaired. Not only was childrearing literature big business, but the state had taken a special interest in the topic of disturbed youth, using agencies such as the Continuing Committee on the Prevention and Control of Delinquency and the Children's Bureau to monitor juvenile crimes. Against this backdrop, audience research showed that parents believed television would keep their children off the streets. A mother from the Southern California survey claimed, "Our boy was always watching television, so we got him a set just to keep him home."…

Seducing the Innocent

More than any other group, children were singled out as the victims of the new pied piper. Indeed, even while critics praised television as a source of domestic unity and benevolent socialization, they also worried about its harmful effects, particularly its encouragement of passive and addictive behavior. In 1951, *Better Homes and Gardens* complained that the medium's "synthetic entertainment" produced a child who was "glued to television." Worse still, the new addiction would reverse good habits of hygiene, nutrition, and decorum, causing physical, mental, and social disorders. A cartoon in a 1950 issue of *Ladies' Home Journal* suggests a typical scenario. The magazine showed a little girl slumped on an ottoman and suffering from a new disease called "telebugeye." According to the caption, the child was a "pale, weak, stupid looking creature" who grew "bugeyed" from sitting and watching television for too long. Perhaps responding to these concerns, some advertisements presented children spectators in scenes that associated television with the "higher arts," and some even implied that children would cultivate artistic talents by watching television….

As the popular wisdom often suggested, the child's passive addiction to television might itself lead to the opposite effect of increased aggression. These discussions followed in the wake of critical and social scientific theories of the 1930s and 1940s that suggested that mass media injects ideas and behavior into passive individuals. Adopting this "hypodermic model" of media effects, the magazines circulated horror stories about youngsters who imitated television violence….

Of course, the controversy surrounding television was simply a new skirmish in a much older battle to define what constituted appropriate children's entertainment. Such controversies can be traced back to the turn of the century when reformers, most notably Anthony Comstock, sought to regulate the content of dime novels. Similar battles were waged when middle-class reformers of the early 1900s debated film's impact on American youth, and later these reform discourses were given scientific credence with the publication of the Payne Fund Studies in 1933. Broadcasting became the subject of public scrutiny in that same year when a group of mothers from Scarsdale. New York, began voicing their objections to radio programs that they considered to be harmful to children. The public outcry was taken up in special interest magazines—especially the *Christian Century, Commonweal, New Republic, Outlook, Nation,* and *Saturday Review.* In all cases, childhood was conceived as a time of innocence, and the child a blank slate upon whom might be imprinted the evils of an overly aggressive and sexualized adult culture. In her work on *Peter Pan,* Jacqueline Rose has argued that the image of presexual childhood innocence has less to do with how children actually experience their youth than it does with how adults choose to conceptualize that experience. The figure of the innocent child serves to facilitate a nostalgic adult fantasy of a perfect past in which social, sexual, economic, and political complexities fade into the background.

In the postwar years, the urge to preserve childhood innocence helped to justify and reinforce the nuclear family as a central institution and mode of social experience. Parents were given the delicate job of balancing the dividends and deficits of the ever-expanding consumer culture. On the one hand, they had to supply their youngsters with the fruits of a new commodity society—suburban homes, wondrous toys, new technologies, glamorous vacations, and so forth. Early schooling in the good life would ensure that children continued on a life trajectory of social mobility based on the acquisition of objects. On the other hand, parents had to protect children from the more insidious aspects of the consumer wonderland, making sure that they internalized the ability to tell the difference between authentic culture and synthetic commercial pleasures. According to Helen Muir, editor of the *Miami Herald's* children's books section, there was a difference between the "real needs and desires of children" and "the superimposed synthetic so-called needs which are not needs but cravings." In this context, mass media provided parents with a particularly apt target. More than twenty years before Marie Winn called television "the plug-in drug," Muir and others likened mass media to marijuana and other narcotics that offered children a momentary high rather than the eternal pleasures of real art.

The most vocal critic was psychiatrist Fredric Wertham, whose *Seduction of the Innocent* (1953) became the cornerstone of the 1950s campaign against comic books. For Wertham, the tabula rasa conception of the child was paramount; the visual immediacy of comics, he argued, left children vulnerable to their unsavory content. Although most social scientists and psychologists had a more nuanced approach to mass media than Wertham had, his ideas were popularized in the press and he even served as an expert witness in Estes Kefauver's 1954 Senate Subcommittee hearings on juvenile delinquency. The war that Wertham waged against mass culture struck a chord with the more general fears about juvenile delinquency at the time, and parents were given armor in what popular critics increasingly defined as a battle to protect the young from the onslaught of a hypercommercialized children's culture.

Indeed, discussions about children and mass culture typically invoked military imagery. One woman, who had read Wertham's 1948 article in the *Saturday Review,* wrote a letter that explained how her children had become "drugged" by mass media: "We consider this situation to be as serious as an invasion of the enemy in war time, with as far-reaching consequences as the atom bomb." One year later, anthropologist Margaret Mead expressed similar fears to her colleagues, worrying about children who grew up in a world where "radio and television and comics and the threat of the atomic bomb are every day realities." If in the late 1940s television was seen as just one part of the threatening media environment, over the course of the 1950s it would emerge as a more central problem.

As Ellen Wartella and Sharon Mazzarella have observed, early social scientific studies suggested that children weren't simply using television in place of other media; instead, television was colonizing children's leisure time more than other mass cultural forms had ever done. Social scientists found this "reorganization hypothesis" to be particularly important because it meant that television was changing the nature of children's lives, taking them away from school work, household duties, family conversations, and creative play. This hypothesis was also at the core of early studies conducted by school boards around the country, which showed that television was reducing the amount of time children spent on homework. Researchers and reformers were similarly concerned with television's effects on children's moral and physical welfare. As early as 1949, PTA members voted at their national convention to keep an eye on "unwholesome television programs." Religious organizations also tried to monitor television's unsavory content. In 1950, the National Council of Catholic Women counted violent acts in television programs while Detroit's Common Council (which was composed of religious groups and city officials) drew up a three-prong plan to make the new medium safe for children and teenagers. By 1951, the National Council of Catholic Men had joined the fray, considering a system of program ratings, while Catholic teachers were urging the formation of a Legion of Decency at their annual conference in Washington. Even Wertham, who devoted most of his energy to comic books, included in his book a final chapter on television (appropriately titled "Homicide at Home"), which warned parents that programs such as *Captain Video* and *Superman* would corrupt the potential educational value of the new medium and turn children into violent, sexually "perverse" adults.

Such concerns were given official credence as senators, congressmen, and FCC commissioners considered the problem. Commissioner Frieda Hennock championed educational television, which she believed would better serve children's interests. Thomas J. Lane, representative from Massachusetts, urged Congress to establish government censorship of television programs, claiming that teachers and clergymen "have been fighting a losing battle against the excess of this one-way form of communication," and praising parents who were demanding that the "'juvenile delinquent called television'" be cleaned up "before it ruins itself and debases everybody with whom it has contact." Largely in response to such concerns, the NARTB (following the lead of the film industry and its own experience with radio) staved off watchdog groups and government officials by passing an industry-wide censorship code for television in March 1952, a code that included a whole section on television and children. But the debate persisted and even grew more heated....

While scholarship has centered around the question of how television affects children, little has been said about the way adults have been taught to limit these effects. What is particularly interesting here is the degree to which discussions about television and children engaged questions concerning parental authority. Summarizing parents' attitudes toward television, Bogart claimed, "There is a feeling, never stated in so many words, that the set has a power of its own to control the destinies and viewing habits of the audience, and that what it 'does' to parents and children alike is somehow beyond the bounds of any individual set-owner's power of control." In this context, popular media offered solace by showing parents how they could reclaim power in their own homes—if not over the medium, then at least over their children. Television opened up a whole array of disciplinary measures that parents might exert over their youngsters.

Indeed, the bulk of discussions about children and television were offered in the context of mastery. If the machine could control the child, then so could the parent. Here, the language of common sense provided some reassurance by reminding parents that it was they, after all, who were in command. As the *New York Times'* television critic Jack Gould wrote in 1949, "It takes a human hand to turn on a television set." But for parents who needed a bit more than just the soothing words of a popular sage, the media ushered in specialists from a wide range of fields; child psychologists, educators, psychiatrists, and broadcasters all recommended ways to keep the problem child in line.

One popular form of advice revolved around program standards. Rather than allowing children to watch violent westerns such as *The Lone Ranger* and escapist science-fiction serials such as *Captain Video,* parents were told to establish a canon of wholesome programs....

In many ways this canon recalled Victorian notions of ideal family recreation. Overly exciting stimuli threatened to corrupt the child, while educational and morally uplifting programs were socially sanctioned. In response to these concerns, magazines such as *Reader's Digest, Saturday Review,* and *Parents* gave their seal of approval to what they deemed as culturally enriching programs.... In all cases, critical judgments were based on adult standards. Indeed, this hierarchy of television programs is symptomatic of the more general efforts to establish an economy of pleasure for children spectators that suited adult concepts about the meaning of childhood....

Meanwhile, for their part, children often seemed to have different ideas. As numerous surveys indicated, youngsters often preferred the programs that parents found unwholesome, especially science-fiction serials and westerns. Surveys also indicated that children often liked to watch programs aimed at adults and that "parents were often reluctant to admit that their children watched adult shows regularly." Milton Berle's *Texaco Star Theater* (which was famous for its inclusion of "off-color" cabaret humor) became so popular with children that Berle adopted the persona of Uncle Miltie, pandering to parents by telling his juvenile audience to obey their elders and go straight to bed when the program ended. Other programs, however, were unable to bridge the generation gap. When, for example, CBS aired the mystery anthology *Suspense,* numerous affiliates across the country received letters from concerned parents who wanted the program taken off the air. Attempting to please its adult constituency, one Oklahoma station was caught in the cross fire between parents and children. When the station announced it would not air "horror story" programs before the bedtime hour 9:00 P.M., it received a letter with the words "We protest!" signed by twenty-two children....

In part, anxieties about parental control had to do with the fact that television was heavily promoted to families with children. During the 1950s, manufacturers and retailers discovered that children were a lucrative consumer market for the sale of household commodities. An editor of *Home Furnishings* (the furniture retailer's trade journal) claimed, "The younger generation from one to twenty influences the entire home furnishings industry." As one of the newest household items, television was quickly recognized for its potential appeal to young consumers. Numerous surveys indicated that families with children tended to buy television more than childless couples did. Television manufacturers quickly assimilated the new findings into their sales techniques. As early as 1948, the industry trade journal *Advertising and Selling* reported that the manager of public relations and advertising at the manufacturing company, Stromberg-Carlson, "quoted a survey ... indicating that children not only exert a tremendous amount of influence in the selection and purchase of television receivers but that they are, in fact, television's most enthusiastic audience." Basing their advertisements on such surveys, manufacturers and retailers formulated strategies by which to pull parents' purse strings—and heart strings as well. In 1950, the American Television Dealers and Manufacturers ran nationwide newspaper advertisements that played on parental guilt. The first ad in the series had a headline that read, "Your daughter won't ever tell you the humiliation she's felt in begging those precious hours of television from a neighbor." Forlorn children were pictured on top of the layout, and parents were shown how television could raise their youngsters' spirits. This particular case is especially interesting because it shows that there are indeed limits to which even advertisers can go before a certain degree of sales resistance takes place. Outraged by the advertisement, parents, educators, and clergymen complained to their newspapers about its manipulative tone. In addition, the Family Service Association of America called it a "cruel pressure to apply against millions of parents" who could not afford television sets. In the midst of this controversy, the American Television Dealers and Manufacturers discontinued the ad campaign. Although this action might have temporarily quelled the more overt fears of adult groups, the popular media of the period continued to raise doubts that often surfaced in hyperbolic predictions of the end of patriarchal family life....

A House Divided

In a home where patriarchal authority was undermined, television threatened to drive a wedge between family members. Social scientists argued that even while families might be brought together around the set, this spatial proximity did not necessarily translate into better family relations. As Eleanor MacCoby observed in her study of families in Cambridge, Massachusetts, "There is very little interaction among family members when they watch TV together, and the amount of time family members spend together exclusive of TV is reduced, so it is doubtful whether TV brings the family together in any psychological sense."

Popular periodicals presented exaggerated versions of family division, often suggesting that television would send family members into separate worlds of pleasure and thus sever family ties, particularly at the dinner table. In 1950, Jack Gould wrote, "Mealtime is an event out of the ordinary for the television parent; for the child it may just be out." In that same year a cartoon in *Better Homes and Gardens* showed parents seated at the dining room table while their children sat in the living room, glued to the television set. Speaking from the point of view of the exasperated mother, the caption read, "All right, that does it! Harry, call up the television store and tell them to send a truck right over!" In 1953, *TV Guide* suggested a humorous solution to the problem in a cartoon that showed a family seated around a dining room table with a large television set built into the middle of it. The caption read, "Your kids won't have to leave the table to watch their favorite programs if you have the Diney model....

Harmony gave way to a system of differences in which domestic space and family members in domestic space were divided along sexual and social lines. The ideal of family togetherness was achieved through the seemingly contradictory principle of separation; private rooms devoted to individual family members ensured peaceful relationships among residents. Thus, the social division of space was not simply the inverse of family unity; rather, it was a point on a continuum that stressed ideals of domestic cohesion. Even the family room itself was conceived in these terms. In fact, when coining the phrase, Nelson and Wright claimed, "By frankly developing a room which is 'entirely public' ... privacy is made possible. Because there's an 'extra room,' the other living space can really be enjoyed in peace and quiet."

This ideology of divided space was based on Victorian aesthetics of housing design and corresponding social distinctions entailed by family life.... [T]he middle-class homes of Victorian America embodied the conflicting urge for family unity and division within their architectural layout. Since the homes were often quite spacious, it was possible to have rooms devoted to intimate family gatherings (such as the back parlor), social occasions (such as the front parlor), as well as rooms wholly given over to separate family members. By the 1950s, the typical four-and-one-half room dwellings of middle-class suburbia were clearly not large enough to support entirely the Victorian ideals of socio-spatial hierarchies. Still, popular home manuals of the postwar period placed a premium on keeping these spatial distinctions in order, and they presented their readers with a model of space derived in part from the Victorian experience.

The act of watching television came to be a central concern in the discourse on divided spaces as the magazines showed readers pictures of rambling homes with special rooms designed exclusively for watching television. Sets were placed in children's playrooms or bedrooms, away from the central spaces of the home. In 1951, *House Beautiful* had even more elaborate plans. A fun room built adjacent to the home and equipped with television gave a teenage daughter a "place for her friends." For the parents it meant "peace of mind because teenagers are away from [the] house but still at home."

It seems likely that most readers in their cramped suburban homes did not follow these suggestions. A 1954 national survey showed that 85 percent of the respondents kept their sets in the living room, so that the space for TV was the central, common living area in the home. Perhaps recognizing the practical realities of their readers, the magazines also suggested ways to maintain the aesthetics of divided spaces in the small home. While it might not have been possible to have a room of one's own for television viewing, there were alternate methods by which to approximate the ideal. Rooms could be designed in such a way so that they functioned both as viewing areas and as centers for other activities. In this sense, television fit into a more general functionalist discourse in which household spaces were supposed to be made "multi-purposeful." In 1951, *Better Homes and Gardens* spoke of a "recreation area of the living room" that was "put to good use as the small fry enjoy a television show." At other times such areas were referred to specifically as "television areas." While in many cases the television area was marked off by furniture arrangements or architectural structures such as alcoves, at other times the sign of division was concretized in an object form—the room divider.

In some cases the television receiver was actually built into the room divider so that television literally became a divisive object in the home. In 1953, for example, *Better Homes and Gardens* displayed a "living-dining area divider" that was placed behind a sofa. Extending beyond the sofa, its right end housed a television set. As the illustration showed, this TV/room divider created a private viewing area for children. In 1955, one room-divider company saw the promotional logic in this scenario, showing mothers how Modernfold Doors would keep children spectators at a safe distance. The ad depicts a mother sitting at one end of a room, while her child and television set are separated off by the folding wall. Suggesting itself as an object of dispute, the television set works to support the call for the room divider—here stated as "that tiresome game of 'Who gets the living room." Moreover, since room dividers like this one were typically collapsible, they were the perfect negotiation between ideals of unity and division. They allowed parents to be apart from their children, but the "fold-back" walls also provided easy access to family togetherness.

The swiveling television was another popular way to mediate ideals of unity and division. In 1953, *Ladies' Home Journal* described how John and Lucille Bradford solved the viewing problem in their home by placing a large console set on a rotating platform that was hinged to the doorway separating the living room from the play porch. Lucille told the magazine, "The beauty of this idea … is that the whole family can watch programs together in the living room, or the children can watch their own special cowboy programs from the play porch without interfering with grownups' conversation."

This sociosexual division of space was also presented in advertisements for television sets. In 1955, General Electric showed how its portable television set could mediate family tensions. On the top of the page a cartoon depicts a family besieged by television as Mother frantically attempts to vacuum up the mess created by her young son who, sitting on his tricycle, changes the channel on the television console. Father, sitting on an easy chair in front of the set, is so perturbed by the goings-on that his pipe flies out of his mouth. The solution to this problem is provided further down on the page where two photographs are juxtaposed. The photograph on the right side of the page depicts Mother and Daughter in the kitchen where they watch a cooking program on a portable TV while the photograph on the left side of the page shows Father watching football on the living room console. This "split-screen" layout was particularly suited to GE's sales message, the purchase of a second television set. The copy reads: "When Dad wants to watch the game … Mom and Sis, the cooking show … there's too much traffic for one TV to handle."

The depiction of divided families wasn't simply a clever marketing strategy; rather, it was a well-entrenched pictorial convention. Indeed, by 1952, advertisements in the home magazines increasingly depicted family members enjoying television alone or else in subgroups. At least in the case of these ads, it appears that the cultural meaning that were circulated about television changed somewhat over the course of the early years of installation. While television was primarily shown to be an integrating activity in the first few years of diffusion, in the 1950s it came to be equally (or perhaps even more) associated with social differences and segregation among family members.

It is, however, important to remember that the contradiction between family unity and division was just that—a contradiction, a site of ideological tension, and not just a clear-cut set of opposing choices. In this light, we might understand a number of advertisements that attempted to negotiate such tensions by evoking ideas of unity and division at the same time. These ads pictured family members watching television in private, but the image on the television screen contained a kind of surrogate family. A 1953 ad for Sentinel TV shows a husband and wife gently embracing as they watch their brand new television set on Christmas Eve. The pleasure entailed by watching television is associated more with the couple's romantic life than with their parental duties. However, the televised image contains two children, apparently singing Christmas carols. Thus, the advertisement shows that parents can enjoy a romantic night of television apart from their own children. But it still sustains the central importance of the family scene because it literally *represents* the absent children by making them into an image on the screen. Moreover, the advertisement attaches a certain amount of guilt to the couple's intimate night of television, their use of television as a medium for romantic rather than familial enjoyment. The idea of guilty pleasure is suggested by the inclusion of two "real" children who appear to be voyeurs, clandestinely looking onto the scene of their parents' pleasure. Dressed in pajamas, the youngsters peek out from a corner of the room, apparently sneaking out of bed to take a look at the new television set, while the grownups remain unaware of their presence.

The tensions between opposing ideals of unity and division were also expressed in material form. Manufacturers offered technological "gizmos" that allowed families to be alone and together at the same time. In 1954, *Popular Science* displayed a new device that parents could use to silence the set while their children watched. As the magazine explained, "NOBODY IS BOTHERED if the children want to see a rootin'-tootin' Western when Dad and Mother want to read, write or talk. Earphones let the youngsters hear every shot, but the silence is wonderful." DuMont had an even better idea with its "Duoscope" set. This elaborate construction was composed of two receivers housed in a television cabinet, with two chassis, two control panels, and two picture tubes that were mounted at right angles. Through polarization and the superirmposition of two broadcast images, the set allowed two viewers to watch different programs at the same time. Thus, as the article suggested, a husband and wife equipped with polarized glasses were able to watch television together but still retain their private pleasures.

While the Duoscope never caught on, the basic problem of unity and division continued. The attempt to balance ideals of family harmony and social difference often led to bizarre solutions, but it also resulted in everyday viewing patterns that were presented as functional and normal procedures for using television. Popular discourses tried to tame the beast, suggesting ways to maintain traditional modes of family behavior and still allow for social change. They devised intricate plans for resistance and accommodation to the new machine, and in so doing they helped construct a new cultural form.

Television as Representation
HERMAN GRAY
The Historical and Discursive Formation of Television Treatments of Blackness

… Alone, the argument that television representation of blackness is primarily shaped by changing industrial and market conditions that enabled a small number of black producers, directors, and writers to tell stories about black life from the perspective of blacks is reductionist. To avoid such reductionism, I want to argue also for a reading of the social meaning and cultural significance of television's representations of blackness in terms of their political, historical, and aesthetic relationship to earlier generations of shows about blacks. I contend that contemporary television representations of blacks depend heavily on shows about families, the genre of (black) situation comedy, entertainment/variety programming, and the social issue traditions of Norman Lear.…

Ultimately, then, I argue that our contemporary moment continues to be shaped discursively by representations of race and ethnicity that began in the formative years of television…. The formative period of television and its representation of race and ethnicity in general and blacks in particular is central to my argument in two crucial ways: first, together with dominant representations of blacks in film, radio, the press, and vaudeville, this inaugural moment helped to shape the cultural and social terms in which representations of blacks appeared in mass media and popular culture …; second, as illustrated by Marlon Riggs's … documentary film, *Color Adjustment,* this formative period is a defining discursive

and aesthetic moment that enabled and shaped the adjustments that black representations continue to make. It remains the moment against which all other television
representations of blackness have reacted. And it is the defining moment with which
subsequent representations … remain in dialogue.

In the early 1950s, programs such as *Amos 'n' Andy, Beulah, The Jack Benny
Show*, and *Life with Father* presented blacks in stereotypical and subservient
roles whose origins lay in eighteenth- and nineteenth-century popular forms.…
Blacks appeared primarily as maids, cooks, "mammies," and other servants, or
as con artists and deadbeats. These stereotypes were necessary for the representation and legitimation of a racial order built on racism and white supremacy.
Media scholars and historians have clearly established the formative role of
radio in the institutional and aesthetic organization of early television.… [T]he
networks, first with radio and later with television shows such as *Beulah, Amos
'n' Andy*, and *The Jack Benny Show*, played an active and crucial role in the
construction and representation of blacks in American mass media. In the televisual
world of the early 1950s, the social and cultural rules of race relations between
blacks and whites were explicit: black otherness was required for white subjectivity; blacks and whites occupied separate and unequal worlds; black labor was
always in the service of white domesticity (*The Jack Benny Show, Life with Father,
Beulah*); black humor was necessary for the amusement of whites.

Culturally, because blackness served whiteness in this way, the reigning
perspective of this world was always staged from a white subject position; when television did venture inside the separate and unfamiliar world of blacks—in, say, *Amos
'n' Andy*—viewers found comforting reminders of whiteness and the ideology of
white supremacy that it served: here was the responsible, even sympathetic, black
domestic in *Beulah*; there were the responsible but naive members of the world of
Amos 'n' Andy. But seldom were there representations of the social competence and
civic responsibilities that would place any of the black characters from these shows on
equal footing with whites.… Black characters who populated the television world of
the early 1950s were happy-go-lucky social incompetents who knew their place and
whose antics served to amuse and comfort culturally sanctioned notions of whiteness,
especially white superiority and paternalism. These black folk could be trusted to
manage white households, nurture white children, and "restore balance and nor-
malcy to the [white] household,"… but they could not be trusted with the social
and civic responsibilities of full citizenship as equals with whites.

In the racially stratified and segregated social order of the 1950s United
States, there was enough about these representations to both comfort and offend.
So pervasive and secure was the discourse of whiteness that in their amusement
whites were incapable of seeing these shows and the representations they presented as offensive. At the same time, of course, many middle-class blacks
were so outraged by these shows, particularly *Amos 'n' Andy*, that the NAACP
successfully organized and engineered a campaign in 1953 to remove the show
from the air.… As racist and stereotypical as these representations were, the cultural
and racial politics they activated were far from simple; many poor, working-class,
and even middle-class blacks still managed to read against the dominant discourse
of whiteness and find humor in the show. However, because of the charged racial

politics between blacks and whites, as well as the class and cultural politics within black America, the tastes, pleasures, and voices in support of the show were drowned out by the moral outrage of middle-class blacks. To be sure, although blacks and whites alike may have found the show entertaining and funny, these pleasures meant different things. They were situated in very different material and discursive worlds. The social issues, political positions, and cultural alliances that shows such as *Amos 'n' Andy* organized and crystallized, then, were powerful and far-reaching in their impact, so much so that I believe that contemporary representations remain in dialogue with and only now have begun to transcend this formative period.

By the late 1950s and throughout the 1960s, the few representations of blacks that did appear on network television offered more benign and less explicitly stereotypical images of African Americans. Shows such as *The Nat "King" Cole Show* (1956–57), *I Spy* (1965–68), and *Julia* (1968–71) attempted to make blacks acceptable to whites by containing them or rendering them, if not culturally white, invisible. In these shows the social and cultural "fact of blackness" was treated as a minor if not coincidental theme—present but contained. In the racially tense and stratified United States of the middle 1960s, Diahann Carroll and Bill Cosby lived and worked in mostly white worlds where whites dare not notice and blacks dare not acknowledge their blackness. Where the cultural and social "fact of blackness" was irrepressible, indeed, central to the aesthetics of a show, it had to be contained. (Whiteness also operated as the dominant and normative place of subjectivity both on and off the screen. In this racialized world of television common sense neither whites nor blacks had any need to acknowledge whiteness explicitly.)

This strategy of containment was used with Nat Cole, the elegant and sophisticated star of *The Nat "King" Cole Show*. An accomplished jazz—read black—pianist, Cole was packaged and presented by NBC to foreground his qualities as a universally appealing entertainer. Cole was the host of a television variety show that emphasized his easy manner and polished vocal style, and the containment of his blackness was clearly aimed to quell white fears and appeal to liberal white middle-class notions of responsibility and good taste. In the social and cultural climate of the times, NBC thought it necessary to separate Cole from any association with the black jazz life (an association made larger than life with the sensational press coverage of Billie Holiday, Charlie Parker, Charles Mingus, and Miles Davis), equating black jazz artists with drugs, sex, rebellion, and social deviance. Despite this cautious strategy, the network's failure to secure national sponsors for the show, especially in the South, resulted in cancellation of *The Nat "King" Cole Show* after only one season. Sanitized and contained representations of blacks in the late 1950s and the 1960s developed in response to the stereotypical images that appeared in the early days of television. They constitute signal moments in discursive adjustment and readjustment of black representations in commercial television....

Against this discursive backdrop as well as the social rebellions of the 1960s, the representations of black Americans that appeared throughout the 1970s were a direct response to social protest and petitions by blacks against American society in general and the media in particular for the general absence of black representations.... Beginning in 1972, television program makers and the networks produced shows that reached for "authentic" representations of black life within poor urban communities. These programs were created as responses to angry calls by different sectors of the black community for "relevant" and "authentic" images of black people.

It is easy to see now that both the demand for relevant shows and the networks' responses were themselves profoundly influenced by the racial and cultural politics of the period. The new shows offered were designed to contain the anger and impatience of communities on the move politically; program makers, the networks, and "the community" never paused to examine critically the notions of relevance or authenticity. As a visible and polemical site of cultural debate, television moved away from its treatment of blacks in the previous decade. The television programs involving blacks in the 1970s were largely representations of what white liberal middle-class television program makers assumed (or projected) were "authentic" accounts of poor black urban ghetto experiences. *Good Times* (1974–79), *Sanford & Son* (1972–77), and *What's Happening!!* (1976–79), for example, were all set in poor urban communities and populated by blacks who were often unemployed or underemployed. But more important, for the times, these black folk were good-humored and united in racial solidarity regardless (or perhaps because) of their condition. Ironically, despite the humor and social circumstances of the characters, these shows continued to idealize and quietly reinforce a normative white middle-class construction of family, love, and happiness. These shows implicitly reaffirmed the commonsense belief that such ideals and the values they promote are the rewards of individual sacrifice and hard work.

These themes appeared in yet another signal moment in commercial television representations of African Americans—in the hugely successful miniseries *Roots*. Inhabiting the televisual space explored three years earlier in the miniseries *The Autobiography of Miss Jane Pittman, Roots* distinguished itself commercially and thematically as one of the most-watched television shows in history. Based on Alex Haley's book of the same name, *Roots* presented the epic story of the black American odyssey from Africa through slavery to the twentieth century. It brought to millions of Americans, for the first time, the story of the horrors of slavery and the noble struggles of black Americans. This television representation of blacks remained anchored by familiar commitments to economic mobility, family cohesion, private property, and the notion of America as a land of immigrants held together by shared struggles of hardships and ultimate triumph.

There is little doubt that the success of *Roots* helped to recover and reposition television constructions and representations of African Americans and blackness from their historic labors in behalf of white racism and myths of white superiority. But the miniseries also contributed quite significantly to the transformation, in the popular imaginary, of the discourse of slavery and American race relations between blacks and whites. That is to say, with *Roots* the popular media discourse about slavery moved from one of almost complete invisibility (never mind structured racial subordination, human degradation, and economic exploitation) to one of ethnicity, immigration, and human triumph. This powerful television epic effectively constructed the story of American slavery from the stage of emotional identifications and attachments to individual character family struggles, and the realization of the American dream. Consequently, the social organization of racial subordination, the cultural reliance on human degradation, and the economic exploitation of black labor receded almost completely from the story. And, of course, this quality is precisely what made the television series such a huge success.

From the distance of some seventeen years, I also want to suggest another less obvious but powerful effect of *Roots,* especially for African American cultural struggles over the sign of blackness. My criticisms of the dominant labors of the series notwithstanding, I want to propose that for an entire generation of young blacks, *Roots* also opened—enabled, really—a discursive space in mass media and popular culture within which contemporary discourses of blackness developed and circulated. I think that it is possible to locate within the media discourse of blackness articulated by *Roots* some of the enabling conditions necessary for the rearticulation of the discourse of Afrocentric nationalism. In other words, I would place *Roots* in dialogue with the reactivation and renewed interest in black studies and the development of African-centered rap and black urban style, especially their contemporary articulation and expression in popular culture and mass media. It seems to me that *Roots* enabled and facilitated the circulation and saturation of the popular imaginary with television representation of Africa and blackness. Finally, relative to the televisual construction of African Americans and blackness in the 1950s and 1960s, *Roots* helped to alter slightly, even momentarily interrupt, the gaze of television's idealized white middle-class viewers and subjects. However minimal, with its cultural acknowledgment of black viewers and subjects, the miniseries enabled a temporary but no less powerful transitional space within which to refigure and reconstruct black television representations.

In black-oriented situation comedies of the late 1970s and early 1980s, especially the long-running *The Jeffersons,* as well as *Benson, Webster, Diff'rent Strokes,* and *Gimme a Break,* black upward social mobility and middle-class affluence replaced black urban poverty as both setting and theme…. Predictably, however, the humor remained. Even though these situation comedies were set in different kinds of "families"—single-parent households, homes with cross-racial adoptions—that were supposed to represent an enlightened approach to racial difference, in the end they too were anchored by and in dialogue with familiar themes and emblems of familial stability, individualism, and middle-class affluence…. Although blackness was explicitly marked in these shows, it was whiteness and its privileged status that remained unmarked and therefore hegemonic within television's discursive field of racial construction and representation…. As with their predecessors from the 1950s and 1960s, blacks in the shows from the 1970s and early 1980s continued to serve as surrogate managers, nurturers, and objects of white middle-class fascination…. Furthermore, as conventional staples of the genre, they required unusual and unfamiliar situations (e.g., black children in white middle-class homes) for thematic structure and comedic payoff. In appearance, this generation of shows seems more explicit, if not about the subject of race, at least about cultural difference. However, because they continued to construct and privilege white middle-class viewers and subject positions, in the end they were often as benign and contained as shows about blacks from earlier decades.

The Cosby Moment

Discursively, in terms of television constructions of blackness, *The Cosby Show* is culturally significant because of the productive space it cleared and the aesthetic constructions of black cultural style it enabled. Pivotal to understanding the social position and cultural significance of contemporary television representations of blackness is what I shall call the Cosby moment. Like the miniseries *Roots*, *The Cosby Show* reconfigured the aesthetic and industrial spaces within which modern television representations of blacks are constructed.

Indeed, under Bill Cosby's careful guidance the show quite intentionally presented itself as a corrective to previous generations of television representations of black life. In countless press interviews, Cosby voiced his frustrations with television's representation of blacks. Here is just one:

> Run down what you saw of black people on TV before the Huxtables.
> You had "Amos 'n' Andy," one of the funniest shows ever, people say. But who ever went to college? Who tried for better things? In "Good Times,"
> J. J. Walker played a definite underachiever. In "Sanford & Son," you have a junk dealer living a few thousand dollars above the welfare level. "The Jeffersons" move uptown. He owns a dry-cleaning store, lives in an integrated neighborhood. Where are the sociological writings about this....

Positioning *The Cosby Show* in relation to the previous history of programs about blacks helps explain its upper-middle-class focus. More significantly, the show's discursive relationship to television's historical treatment of African Americans and contemporary social and cultural debates (about the black underclass, the black family, and black moral character) helps to explain its insistent recuperation of African American social equality (and competence), especially through the trope of the stable and unified black middle-class family....

In *The Cosby Show*, blackness, although an element of the show's theme, character, and sensibility, was mediated and explicitly figured through home life, family, and middle-classness. Cosby explained the show's treatment of race: "It may seem I'm an authority because my skin color gives me a mark of a victim. But that's not a true label. I won't deal with the *foolishness* of racial overtones on the show. I base an awful lot of what I've done simply on what people will enjoy. I want to show a family that has a *good* life, not people to be jealous of."... The Huxtable family is universally appealing, then, largely because it is a middle-class family that happens to be black....

In an enactment of what Stuart Hall (1981b) calls the "politics of reversals" in black-oriented shows from the 1970s, the merger of race (blackness) and class (poverty) often provided little discursive and textual space for whites and many middle-class blacks to construct meaning for the shows that was not troubling and derisive. *The Cosby Show* strategically used the Huxtables' upper-middle-class status to invite audience identifications across race, gender, and class lines. For poor, working-, and middle-class African Americans, Asian Americans, latinos, and whites it was impossible simply to laugh at these characters and make their blackness an object of derision and fascination.

Rather, blackness coexisted in the show on the same discursive plane as their upper-middle-class success....

In this respect, *The Cosby Show* is critical to the development of contemporary television representations of blacks. The show opened to some whites and affirmed for many (though by no means all) blacks a vast and previously unexplored territory of diversity within blackness—that is, upper-middle-class life....

Discursively, the show appropriated the genre of situation comedy and used it to offer a more complex representation of African American life than had been seen previously.

This ability to organize and articulate different audiences together successfully through televisual representations of upper-middle-class African Americans accounts for *The Cosby Show's* popularity as well as the criticisms and suspicions it generated.... If, to its credit, the program did not construct a monolithic and one-dimensional view of blackness, then ... its major drawback was its unwillingness to build on the very diversity and complexity of black life that it brought to television. That is to say, the show seemed unwilling to critique and engage various aspects of black diversity that it visually represented. In particular, *The Cosby Show* often failed even to comment on the economic and social disparities and constraints facing millions of African Americans outside of the middle class.

The show seemed unable, or unwilling, to negotiate its universal appeals to family, the middle class, mobility, and individualism on the one hand and the particularities of black social, cultural, political, and economic realities on the other. While effectively representing middle-class blackness as one expression of black diversity, the show in turn submerged other sites, tensions, and points of difference by consistently celebrating mobility, unlimited consumerism, and the patriarchal nuclear family.... Notwithstanding its political and cultural desires, *The Cosby Show* seemed nevertheless underwritten by the racial politics of "unity," which comes at the cost of subordinating key differences within that unity. In the social climate of the Reagan and Bush years and amid debates about affirmative action and the urban underclass, the show as [Michael] Dyson (1989) puts it,

> presented a black universe as the norm, feeling no need to announce the imposition of African American perspectives since they arc assumed. Cosby has shown us that we need not construct the whole house of our life experience from the raw material of our racial identity. And that black folk are interested in issues which transcend race. *However, such coming of age progress should not lead to zero-sum social concerns so that to be aware of race-transcending issues replaces or cancels out concerns about the black poor or issues which generate interracial conflict.* (emphasis added)

As Dyson suggests, *The Cosby Show's* strategic stance on the "foolishness of racial overtones" has its limits. This was made painfully obvious in April 1992 with the entirely coincidental, but no less poignant, juxtaposition of the show's final episode with news coverage of the Los Angeles riots. The televisual landscape that evening dramatically illustrated that no matter how much television tries to manage and smooth them over, conflict, rage, and suspicion based on race and class are central elements of contemporary America. Next to the rage that produced pictures or Los Angeles burning, the representations and expressions of African American life and experience on *The Cosby Show* ... seemed little more than soothing symbolic props required to affirm America's latest illusion of feel-good multiculturalism and racial cooperation.

Many of the same contradictions and labors of blackness found in the representations of African Americans on *The Cosby Show* were also present in other black-oriented shows that appeared in the aftermath of the show's success. *Amen, Homeroom, 227, Snoops, Family Matters,* and *True Colors*, provided familiar (and comfortable) renderings of black middle-class family life in the United States. The cultural traditions and social experiences and concerns of many African Americans, although much more explicit, nevertheless functioned in these programs as comedic devices, to stage the action or signal minor differences. Although often staged from a black normative universe, these shows seldom presented black subjectivities and cultural traditions as alternative perspectives on everyday life. That is to say, as a cultural and experiential referent, blackness was seldom privileged or framed as a vantage point for critical insights, guides to action, or explanations for what happens to African American people in modern American society....

The *Cosby Show's* most significant contribution to television's representations of blacks and the ongoing discursive adjustments that are central to such a project has been the way that it repositioned and recoded blackness and black (middle-class) subjectivity within television's own discursive and institutional practices. To be sure, the limitations and criticisms of the show, especially the cultural labors it performed in the rearticulation of a new, more "enlightened" racism, as well as the consolidation of Reaganism on the question of race and morality, must be registered.... However, coming as it did in the midst of neoconservative assaults, African American cultural debates, and the transformation of the television industry, the show has also had an enabling effect within television. Indeed, *The Cosby Show* itself became the subject of parody and imitation. In its last few seasons the show turned its thematic gaze away from its narrow preoccupation with familial domesticity to pressing social issues, including education and employment, affecting urban black youth.

For most of its run I remained ambivalent about *The Cosby Show*. As a regular viewer, on many occasions I found pleasures in the predictable humor and identified with the idealizations of family, mobility, and material security represented on the show. I took particular delight in the program's constant attempt to showcase black music and such musicians as John Birks (Dizzy) Gillespie, B. B. King, Mongo Santamaria, and Betty Carter. On the other hand ... I have criticized the show for its idealization of the middle class and its failure to address issues that confront a large number of African Americans. I have often regarded this ambivalence as my unwillingness to stake out a position on the show, to make up my mind. But this unwillingness, I am increasingly convinced, is part of the show's appeal, its complexity in an age of racial and cultural politics where the sign of blackness labors in the service of many different interests at once. As I have been arguing, *The Cosby Show* constructed and enabled new ways of representing African Americans' lives. But within black cultural politics of difference the strategy of staging black diversity within the limited sphere of domesticity and upper-middle-class affluence has its costs....

FURTHER READING

Allen, Robert C. *Channels of Discourse, Disassembled* (1992).

Baughman, James L. *Same Time, Same Stations: Creating American Television, 1948–1961* (2007).

Boddy, William. *Fifties Television: The Industry and Its Critics* (1992).

Classen, Steven. *Watching Jim Crow: The Struggles over Mississippi TV, 1955–1969* (2004).

Doane, Mary Ann. *The Desire to Desire: The Woman's Film of the 1940s* (1987).

Jhally, Sut, and Juston Lewis. *Enlightened Racism:* The Cosby Show*, Audiences, and the Myth of the American Dream* (1992).

MacCabe, Colin. *High Theory/Low Culture: Analysing Popular Television and Film* (1986).

Murray, Susan. *Hitch Your Antenna to the Stars: Early Television and Broadcast Stardom* (2005).

Murray, Susan, and Laurie Ouellette, eds. *Reality TV: Remaking Television Culture* (2004).

Newcomb, Horace. *Television: The Critical View*, 6th ed. (2000).

Penley, Constance, Elisabeth Lyon, et al. *Close Encounters: Film, Feminism and Science Fiction* (1991).

Press, Andrea. *Women Watching Television* (1991).

Spigel, Lynn, and Michael Curtin, eds. *The Revolution Wasn't Televised: Sixties Television and Social Conflict* (1997).

Spigel, Lynn, and Denise Mann, eds. *Private Screenings: Television and the Female Consumer* (1992).

Torres, Sasha. *Black, White and in Color: Television and Black Civil Rights* (2003).

———. *Living Color: Race and Television in the United States* (1998).

CHAPTER 12

Youth and Popular Culture during the Cold War, 1952–1960

In explaining the cold war, the period after World War II when the United States and the Soviet Union struggled for global supremacy, many historians have used the idea of "containment." A foreign policy first described by George Kennan, an advisor to President Harry Truman, containment referred not to a simple military victory over an enemy, but to political, diplomatic, and military maneuvers to keep the enemy within their "sphere of influence." Cultural historians have pointed out that the idea of containment also applied to social arrangements inside the United States.

Historian Elaine Tyler May wrote that "in the domestic version of containment, the 'sphere of influence' was the home. Within its walls, potentially dangerous social forces of the new age might be tamed." Domestic containment, like its international counterpart, offered security and stability in the face of greater threats, including the atomic bomb, than Americans had ever imagined. Despite these insecurities, and perhaps in response to the security brought by the ideology of containment, the end of World War II saw a huge "baby boom." Returning soldiers and their wives started families, bought homes, and enjoyed better economic circumstances than families had during the Depression.

The so-called Kitchen Debate of 1959, when Vice President Richard Nixon and Soviet leader Nikita Khrushchev toured an American home on display in Moscow, showed the intersection of international policy and domestic ideology. During a conversation, the first in several years between leaders of the two countries, Nixon lectured Khrushchev on the consumption opportunities available to American families. Nixon remarked, "Would it not be better to compete in the relative merits of washing machines than in the strength of rockets?" confident of capitalism's ability to supply the domestic sphere. Americans saw this intertwining of American foreign policy, democratic political ideals, and domestic arrangements as natural.

By the late 1950s, the youngest of the baby boomers were teenagers and worries about their behavior took on huge cultural importance. Many of the activities of these young people challenged domestic containment, whether ideas of proper behavior in a social hierarchy where "parents know best," gender roles in which women worked only in the home, or sexual norms that prescribed chastity for unmarried young people and mandated heterosexuality. Television situation comedies focused on white, suburban families, increased in popularity and demonstrated domestic containment at work. Each episode contained a challenge to the family and its form and each conflict resolved in the allotted half-hour. One way to understand these shows is to think of their parody. On a more recent television program, The Simpsons, *nothing is as it is supposed to be: the father is not the smartest and the strongest; the kids don't obey; home is not a sanctuary; and there is no security.*

Parental protests over popular culture provided another place to see how domestic containment operated. Entertainment producers created products aimed at the expanding and profitable youth market. Parents worried that new forms of mass media subverted their authority and introduced their children to sex and violence. Trying to contain experimentation and protest, parents blamed popular culture for the messages it carried and the uses made of it by restless young people. Arguments in the late 1950s over comic books, films, and music (particularly rock and roll) took place in the larger context of domestic and international containment. The experimentation, the protests, and the conflict over the ideas presented in popular culture provided the impetus for the social movements of the 1950s and 1960s, particularly the civil rights and women's movements.

 # DOCUMENTS

These documents illustrate popular culture's perceived bad influence on young people and, in particular, a fear of juvenile delinquency that arose after World War II. When popular culture became more important in the lives of teenagers, it also became a focus for parental anxieties and subject to state-mediated censorship. At the same time, some teenagers found in these cultural forms a chance to consider and express opposition to the rigid racial and gendered categories of cold war America. Document 1 shows the comic book violence that so shocked middle-class parents and caused Frederic Wertham, in Document 2, to blame comics for a range of social evils. Document 3 shows the role race played in defining normal family life as a mainstream magazine expressed surprise at Asian Americans' proper behavior. This article also paved the way for the construction of Asian Americans as a "model minority" especially when contrasted with the supposedly deviant behavior of African American families. The reviews of popular culture in Documents 4, 5, and 6 express suspicion of popular culture as a possible cause for juvenile delinquency, particularly in boys. Document 7 shows how young women used song lyrics to recognize themselves as a group facing specific problems, here in the management of their sexuality.

1. Horror Comics Challenge Middle Class Norms, 1952

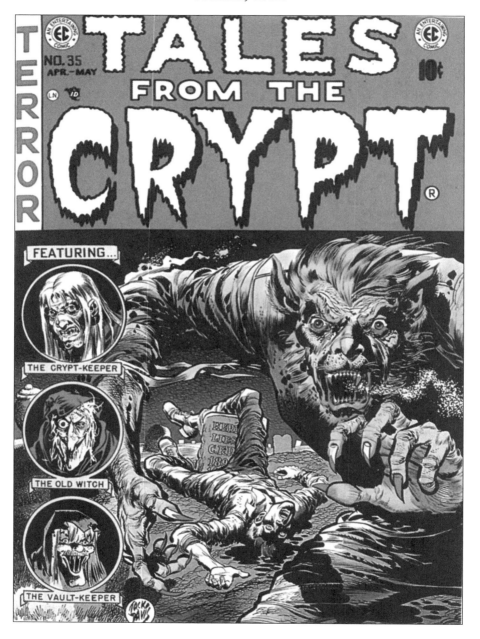

Tales From the Crypt, April–May, 1952, Image courtesy of *The Advertising Archives.*

2. Frederic Wertham, Crusader against Comics, Makes His Case to Parents, 1953

… Many adults think that they know all about crime-comic books because they know mystery and detective novels, comic strips in newspapers, and have cast an occasional glance at a comic book at a newsstand or in a child's hand. But most adults really have no idea of the details and content of the majority of crime-comic books.

Children, however, do know what comic books are. Comic books featuring crime are read primarily by children and are intended for them. The whole crime-comic book trade is designed for them and is dependent on them, even though there are adults, too, who read such comics.

Of course there are people who still fall for the contention of the comic-book industry that their products deal not with crime, but with the punishment of crime. Is not the very title of one of these books "CRIME does not pay"? Here, too, adults are more readily deceived than children. Children know that in quite a number of crime-comic books there is in the title some reference to punishment. But they also know that just as that very reference is in small letters and inconspicuous color, the parts of the title that really count are in huge, eye-catching type and clear sharp colors: CRIME; CRIMINALS; MURDER; LAWBREAKERS; GUNS….

The keynote of crime-comic books is violence and sadism. This is featured in the illustrations and in the text. In one typical crime comic with a catchy crime title, one story alone has ten pictures of girls getting smacked in the face, beaten with a whip, strangled, choked by hand, choked with a scarf. In addition, two men are killed and one man is crippled….

Juvenile delinquency has increased about 20 per cent since 1947. It is, however, not the number but the kind of delinquency that is the salient point. Younger and younger children commit more and more serious and violent acts. Even psychotic children did not act like this fifteen years ago. Here are some random samples of what today's "delinquents" actually do:

1. —Three boys, six to eight years old, took a boy of seven, hanged him nude from a tree, his hands tied behind him, then burned him with matches. They could not find their first choice for this treatment—a girl of six. Probation officers investigating found that they were re-enacting a comic-book plot.

2. —A boy of eleven killed a woman in a holdup. When arrested, he was found surrounded by comic books. His twenty-year old brother said, "If you want the cause of all this, here it is: It's these rotten comic books. Cut them out, and things like this wouldn't happen."…

I could continue this almost indefinitely. There is nothing in these "juvenile delinquencies" that is not described in comic books. These are comic book plots.

In comic books usually these crimes remain unpunished until the criminal has committed many more of them. Children are not so lucky. They face severe punishments whenever they are caught. Educated on comic books, they go on to a long postgraduate course in jails (with the same reading matter)....

The average parent has no idea that every imaginable crime is described in detail in comic books. That is their main stock in trade. If one were to set out to teach children how to steal, rob, lie, cheat, assault and break into candy stores, no more insistent method could be devised. It is of course easy and natural for the child to translate these crimes into a minor key; stealing from a candy store instead of breaking into a bank; stabbing and hurting a little girl with a sharp pen if a knife is not handy; throwing stones into windows of trains and cars instead of payroll robberies and holdups; beating and threatening younger children instead of Superman heroics, following the simple formula of older child against younger child instead of Superman against man.

Taking into account every conceivable possibility, comic books present the details of how to commit crimes, how to conceal evidence, how to evade detection, how to hurt people....

What is the relationship of crime-comic books to juvenile delinquency? If they would prevent juvenile delinquency, there would be very little of it left. And if they were the outlet for children's primitive aggressions, this would be a generation of very subdued, and controlled children. After all, at times the output of comic books has reached 950,000,000 a year, most of them dealing with crime. The whole publicity-stunt claim that crime comics prevent juvenile delinquency is a hoax. I have not seen a single crime-comic book that would have any such effect, nor have I ever seen a child or young adult who felt that he had been prevented from anything wrong by a comic book. Supposing you wanted to prevent promiscuous illegitimate sexual relations; would you publish millions of comic books showing in detail where and how the man picks up the girl, where they go, the details of their relationships in bed and then the next morning showing somebody breaking into their room, tossing them out of bed, beating them and/or killing them?

The role of comic books in delinquency is not the whole nor by any means the worst harm they do to children. It is just one part of it. Many children who never become delinquent or conspicuously disturbed have been adversely affected by them.

My investigations and those of my associates have led us, very unexpectedly at first, but conclusively as the studies went on, to the conclusion that crime comics are an important contributing factor to present-day juvenile delinquency. Not only are crime comics a contributing factor to many delinquent acts, but the type of juvenile delinquency of our time cannot be understood unless you know what has been put into the minds of these children. It certainly is not the only factor, nor in many cases is it even the most important one; but there can be no doubt that it is the most unnecessary and least excusable one.

I saw many kinds of children: normal ones; troubled ones; delinquents; those from well-to-do families and from the lowest rung of the economic ladder; children from different parts of the city; children referred by different public and private agencies; the physically well and the physically ill and handicapped; children with normal, subnormal and superior intelligence. My research (with associates at the Lafargue Psychiatric Clinic and the Queens Mental Hygiene Clinic) involved not only the examination, treatment and follow-up study of children, but also discussions with parents, relatives, social workers, psychologists, probation officers, writers of children's books, camp counselors, physicians—especially pediatricians—clergymen....

When judging the effect of comic-book reading, it must be kept in mind that many children read the same comic book over and over again, and that many comic books are read and reread by many different children. Comic books have no rival as the greatest publishing success in history. One crime-comic book announces on its cover that it is read by 6,000,000 readers. This is one of the worst comic books, a veritable primer for teaching Junior juvenile delinquency....

Crime-comic books represented about one tenth of the total of all comic books in 1946–47. In 1948–49 they increased to one third of the total. To these must be added the many horror, jungle, interplanetary, Superman and Superwoman types which are nothing but crime comics in a different setting.

At the end of 1948, the 60,000,000 comic books a month were split-up among over 400 comic-book titles of assorted types. All through 1948 the trend of the industry was toward crime comics. Experts of the industry were busy explaining to credulous parents that the industry was only giving to children what they needed and wanted, that scenes of crime and sadism were necessary for them—even good for them—and that the industry was only supplying a demand. But in the meantime parents had begun to look into crime-comic books and different groups and local authorities started to contemplate, announce, attempt—and even to take—steps.

Suddenly the industry converted from blood to kisses, from crime to love. They tooled up the industry for a kind of comic book that hardly existed before: love-confession type.

It is a mistake to think that love comics are read only by adolescent and older young people. They are read by very young children as well. An eight-year-old girl living in a very comfortable environment on Long Island told me, "I have lots of friends and we buy about one comic book a week and then we exchange. I can read about ten a day. I like to read the comic books about love because when I go to sleep at night I love to dream about love."

One comic book changed from a super-sadistic jungle book to the new-style love comic, with the title I LOVED: *True Confession Stories*. Another confession-comic book is the reincarnation of a previous teen-age book with an innocuous title. That one was, despite its title, one of the most sexy, specializing in highly accentuated and protruding sweater breasts in practically every illustration. Adolescent boys call these "headlights comics." The repetitiousness of the emphasis on breasts can be expressed psychologically only as breast fetishism. In other comic books, other secondary sexual characteristics of women—for example, the hips—are played up in the drawing....

Such comic books lead to temptation and to confusion. It is unreasonable to regard all kinds of sex play between children and adolescents as delinquency, but there are forms of serious sex delinquency among children nevertheless. Before the comic-book era the sexual play of children was rarely characterized by brutality, violence and sadism. Nowadays this is all too frequent. If sexual fantasies are stirred in hundreds of thousands of children, it is inevitable that some of them will carry out their fantasies in fact. The general comic-book view of girls as luxury prizes, sexual objects and "molls" to be physically maltreated at will reinforces the association of sex with force....

But what about all the "good" comic books?

Among the "good" comic books whose quantity counts at all are usually reckoned the animal comics, the Disney comics and their imitators, classical books in comic-book form, comic books that are reprints of newspaper comic strips, some teen-age girl comics and some boys' sport comics. The mainstay of the "good" comic books are the animal comics and a few of the relatively innocuous related comics. How many of these are there?

At the present time the number of comic books fluctuates around 90,000,000 a month. There are estimates which are lower; there are others of 100,000,000 a month and more. According to the *Wall Street Journal* there are 840,000,000 units a year, 20 per cent more than four years ago. If one figures carefully, from all available reliable data, the numbers printed, published, distributed and actually read, the animal and related comics amount to less than one length of all comic books. This is a liberal estimate, for crime comics are traded so often and for so many years, and handed around to so many people, and read so repeatedly, that the actual proportion is much smaller. But even if one leaves out the reading and distributing and does not count the fact that the bad comics have much larger editions of each title than the "good" ones—even then the number of the "good" comics is less than two tenths. This is what all the fuss about "good" comics boils down to....

The industry regards selling books to children as its prerogative—that is to say, as a right to be exercised without external control. To use constitutional rights against progressive legislation is, of course, an old story. "We are allowing ourselves," said Vindlia Peterson, "in the name of free speech (oh, fatal misuse of a high principle), to be bamboozled into buying or letting our children buy the worst propaganda on the market. It is a tyranny by a handful of unscrupulous people. It is as much a tyranny as any other on the face of the earth."

What is censorship? The industry has obscured that by claiming that the publisher exercises a censorship over himself. That is not what censorship means. It means control of one agency by another. The social fact is that radio, movies, stage plays, translations do function under a censorship. So do newspaper comic strips, which all have to pass the censorship of the newspaper editor who sometimes rejects advance proofs. But comic books for children have no censorship.

It is a widely held fallacy that civil liberties are endangered or could be curtailed by the censorship of children's books. But freedom to publish crime comics has nothing to do with civil liberties. It is a prevention of the idea of civil liberties. It has been said that if comic books for children were censored on account of their violence "you couldn't have a picture of Lincoln's assassination in a text book?" Would that be such a calamity? There are many other pictures of Lincoln's time and life that would be far more instructive in a textbook. But the whole inference is wrong, in any case. A picture of Lincoln's assassination would be incidental to a book expounding large themes....

Legal control of comic books for children is necessary not so much on account of the question of sex, although their sexual abnormality is bad enough, but on account of their glorification of violence and crime. In my attempts to formulate the principles of a crime-comic book law I realized that it is necessary to introduce more public-health thinking for the protection of children's mental health. In the reaction to my proposals I found an interesting fact: People are always ready to censor sex. But they have not yet learned the role of temptation, propaganda, seduction and indoctrination in the field of crime and violence.

Laws in the service of public health do not necessarily deal with criminal intent. They cope with what the lawyers call public-welfare offenses, dealing with food, drugs and sanitation. What I wanted to accomplish was to add mental health to those categories….

Whenever you hear a public discussion of comic books, you will hear sooner or later an advocate of the industry say with a triumphant smile, "Comic books are here to stay." I do not believe it. Parents will realize that comic books are not a necessary evil. I am convinced that in some way or other the democratic process will assert itself and crime-comic books will go, and with them all they stand for and all that sustains them. But before they can tackle Superman, Dr. Payn and all their myriad incarnations, people will have to learn that freedom is not something that one can have, but is something that one must do.

3. *Saturday Evening Post* Explains Why Chinese American Youth Are Not Juvenile Delinquents, 1955

Not long ago, a New York City judge wrote to the *New York Times* saying that not in the seventeen years he had been on the bench had a Chinese-American teen-ager been brought before him on a juvenile delinquency charge. The judge said that he queried his colleagues on the matter and they too, expressed their astonishment. They said that not one of the estimated 10,000 Chinese-American teen-agers, to their knowledge, had ever been haled into court on a depredation, narcotics, speeding, burglary, vandalism, stickup, purse-snatching or mugging accusation. A check with San Francisco, where there is a large colony of Chinese-Americans, tells the same story. The same holds true of Chicago, where the police report "excellent" behavior on the part of Chinese-American youngsters.

P. H. Chang, Chinese consul-general in New York City, was asked to comment on this warm and amazing return. He said simply, "I have heard this story many times from many judges. They tell me that none of our people are ever brought before them for juvenile delinquency. They were surprised, but I was not, Why?"

"I will tell you why I think this is so. Filial piety, the love for parents, is a cardinal virtue my people have brought over from the China that was once free.

A Chinese child, no matter where he lives, is brought up to recognize that he cannot shame his parents. To do so would relegate him to worse than oblivion, for his parents would disown him and he would be cast free and alone from our traditions that go back many, many centuries."

"Before a Chinese child makes a move, he stops to think what the reaction on his parents will be. Will they be proud or will they be ashamed? That is the sole question he asks himself. The answer comes readily, and thus he knows what is right and wrong."

"Above all other things, the Chinese teen-ager is anxious to please his parents before he pleases himself. Our family households work on the theory that the parents are wise and seasoned, and if the children follow the same course, they can do no wrong."...

4. *New York Times* Film Reviewer Bosley Crowther Worries about Young People in *The Blackboard Jungle,* 1955

M-G-M's "Blackboard Jungle," now showing at Loew's State, is one of the toughest, hardest hitting social dramas the screen has had in years. In picturing the shocking experiences of a young man teacher in a city vocational high school, where he is up against a classroom full of rowdies, hoodlums and out-right juvenile crooks, it creates a terrifying notion of the undiscipline and rebelliousness of slum-area youth and the almost complete inability on the part of teachers to handle them.

It is not just an unrelenting drama of juvenile delinquents in the pattern of "Dead End," with the hooligans set against a background of general society. Neither is it a drama of a limited segment of lawless youth such as the motorcycle ruffians in "The Wild Ones," who were reflective of an anti-social cult. It is a story of an evident cross-section of so-called underprivileged teen-age boys and their virtual capture and paralyzation of one of those most significant of democratic institutions, a public school.

Teacher's Gethsemane

There is nothing pretty about it. Under the direction of Richard Brooks, who also wrote the screen play from the novel of Evan Hunter, published last fall, this picture of a teacher's Gethsemane is brutally realistic in style and it is charged with such violences and humiliations as make the blood run cold.

Insolence and defiance toward the teachers are commonplace in the crowded school that is presumably offered as typical of many in our cities today. More startling to comprehension are the criminal and terroristic acts committed by some of the pupils and apparently condoned by all. An attempted rape of a woman teacher, a vicious assault on two men teachers outside the school, the vandalistic destruction of some phonograph records belonging to one of these men and an attack on the other right in the classroom by a boy with a switch-blade knife are among the more shocking depredations that the pupils commit.

And "pupils" is barely the word for them, for learning is what they do least in this school. There appears little hope or effort for it, either by the teachers or the boys. The one teacher who seems to have some idea of imparting knowledge is the hero, played by Glenn Ford. The others range from bursts of fitful fervor to attitudes of cynicism and despair. Survival in this brutish "blackboard jungle" would seem to depend on never turning one's back to the boys.

Take it from us, this is a staggering and morbidly fascinating film!

But is it a true and valid picture of conditions in any schools today—even in those metropolitan high schools that draw their pupils from the crime-breeding slums. Indeed, are there any schools where pupils are so completely arrogant and out-of-hand, so collectively devoted to disorder, as are the hoodlums in this film?...

If so, then, of course, this picture is tragically justified, and it is time for some drastic social action. But if it isn't—if the details in this film are "stacked" and exaggerated, even with the most sincere intent of causing a "public awareness" of problems and inadequacies in schools—then it seems to us irresponsible and fraught with peril.

For what are the likely impressions it will leave in the public mind? One is that the vocational high schools are full of insolent, bad boys who are highly unreliable. This can go hard for graduates seeking jobs. Another is that the teachers are sloppy and ineffectual, which can hurt—not help—the current movement for higher teacher pay. Young people also may be discouraged from wanting to teach in city schools when they think they may be confronted with horrible conditions such as these. And, of course, some boys may be emboldened to imitate the hoodlums in this film, no doubt to their eventual misfortune, and to the passing distress of all concerned.

Certainly juvenile delinquency is a problem today. But it will not help to have it misrepresented and sensationalized.

5. *New York Times* Film Reviewer Bosley Crowther Considers Juvenile Delinquency in *Rebel Without a Cause,* 1955

The recognized increase in the number of youngsters in our society who are emotionally disturbed and who manifest their disturbance in various manners, including delinquency and crime, offers a strong temptation to film makers to move in on that theme. Goodness knows, it is infinitely dramatic and full of possibilities. But it is also exceedingly delicate and subject to easy abuse by those who, either willfully or blindly, might misrepresent or sensationalize.

Certainly there was no intention on the part of Metro-Goldwyn-Mayer to make its "Blackboard Jungle" an exaggeration of the general nature of the boys and the conditions that prevail in a typical big-city vocational high school in a low-class area. But some of the critical reactions to that picture were almost as strong as the resentments and violences in it. The feeling was that it had gone overboard.

So, we suspect, many people will feel that Warner Brothers' "Rebel Without a Cause" is a desperate and dangerous distortion of another aspect of modern disturbed youth. For there is a tendency in this picture to toss every bit of the blame for the insecurity and rebelliousness of its three key youngsters upon their parents and the police—the former for not "understanding" and the latter for being dull and dumb.

No "Chicken"

The main character in this item at the Astor is a handsome teen-age lad who has a phobia about being tagged a "chicken" (a coward) by his unstable friends. This is because his well-off father, whom he apparently once loved, has lacked the "guts" to stand up to his nagging mother in the forcible manner the boy thinks he should. And so our restless, mumbling misfit, played intensely by the late James Dean, is indecisive himself and is groping for security and an understanding love.

The person from whom he gets it, all in the course of one mad day, is a girl his own age of good background who is also emotionally disturbed. Her trouble is that her father stopped kissing her when she was 16 and this has filled her with such a sense of not belonging in her family that she has taken up with high school "cowboys" and "goons."

In the course of proving he isn't "chicken," by fighting a switch-blade knife duel with one of these lads and then by vying with him in a desperate and suicidal game with automobiles, Mr. Dean wins the admiration of the young lady, played prettily by Natalie Wood. Together they seek a lonely exile, from which they are soon returned home when a young friend, also a misfit, tragically is killed by the police. Fortunately, at this point, dawn breaks in the parents' minds.

There is a great deal in this picture that does reflect the attitudes of certain teenage elements, particularly in their bullying braggadocio and their mania for pointless violence. But the insistence with which the scriptwriter and director address sympathy to the youngsters at the expense of their parents and others who represent authority (even an innocent schoolteacher also comes in for a passing knock) renders this picture's likely influence upon real youngsters with emotional disturbance questionable. There is a deception in its pretense of "understanding" that can gravely mislead.

Little Egos

We certainly would not want to argue for the prohibition of such films, but we continue to insist that producers be more careful and responsible in what they say. To paraphrase an old axiom, little egos have big eyes....

6. *Time* Magazine Describes Objections to Rock 'n' Roll, 1956

In Boston Roman Catholic leaders urged that the offensive music be boycotted. In Hartford city officials considered revoking the State Theater's license after several audiences got too rowdy during a musical stage show. In Washington the police chief recommended banning such shows from the National Guard Armory after brawls in which several people were injured. In Minneapolis a theater manager withdrew a film featuring the music after a gang of youngsters left the theater, snake-danced around town and smashed windows. In Birmingham champions of white supremacy decried it as part of a Negro plot against the whites. At a wild concert in Atlanta's baseball park one night, fists and beer bottles were thrown, four youngsters were arrested.

The object of all this attention is a musical style known as "rock 'n' roll," which has captivated U.S. adolescents as swing captivated prewar teen-agers and ragtime vibrated those of the '20s. It does for music what a motorcycle club at full throttle does for a quiet Sunday afternoon.

Rock 'n' roll is based on Negro blues, but in a self-conscious style which underlines the primitive qualities of the blues with malice, aforethought. Characteristics: an unrelenting, socking syncopation that sounds like a bull whip; a choleric saxophone honking mating-call sounds; an electric guitar turned up so loud that its sound shatters and splits; a vocal group that shudders and exercises violently to the beat while roughly chanting either a near-nonsense phrase or a moronic lyric in hillbilly idiom.

Samples:...

Long tall Sally has a lot on the ball Nobody cares if she's long and tall

Oh, Baby! Yeh-heh-heh-hes, Baby Whooooooo,

Baby! I'm havin' me some fun tonight, yeah....

The fad began to flame a couple of years ago, when pop music was so languid and soupy that kids could no longer dance to it—and jazz headed farther out. Rock 'n' roll got its name, as it got some of its lyrics, from Negro popular music, which used "rock" and "roll" as sexy euphemisms. It caught on with the small record companies, e.g., Dot, King, Sun, that flourish in the Southern, Central and Western states, and soon it grew too big for the majors to ignore.

Strangely enough, a group of nonmusicians became the objects of teen-age adulation—the rock-'n'-roll disk jockeys....

When their names appear on theater and dance-hall marquees announcing a stage show or "record hop," the stampede is on. The theater is jammed with adolescents from the 9 a.m. curtain to closing, and it rings and shrieks like the jungle-bird house at the zoo. If one of the current heroes is announced—groups such as Bill Haley and His Comets or The Platters, or a soloist such as Elvis Presley—the shrieks become deafening. The tumult completely drowns the sound of the spastically gyrating performers despite fully powered amplification. Only the obsessive beat pounds through, stimulating the crowd to such rhythmical movements as clapping in tempo and jumping and dancing in the aisles. Sometimes the place vibrates with the beat of music and stamping feet, and not infrequently kids have been moved to charging the stage, rushing ushers and theater guards....

Does rock-'n'-roll music itself encourage any form of juvenile delinquency? Illinois' Cook County Sheriff Joseph D. Lohman, who was a professional sociologist and criminologist before becoming sheriff, says: "I don't think there's any correlation between juvenile delinquency and rock 'n' roll, but rock 'n' roll is a symptom of a condition that can produce delinquency." Even Boston's fired-up anti-r. & r. campaigners concede that "it is a fad that has been adopted by the hoodium element, and that's where the trouble starts."... Pop Record Maker Mitch Miller, no rock 'n' roller, sums up for the defense: "You can't call any music immoral. If anything is wrong with rock 'n' roll, it is that it makes a virtue out of monotony." For the prosecution, the best comment comes indirectly from Actress Judy Holliday in Born Yesterday: It's just not couth, that's all.

7. Songwriters Carole King and Gerry Goffin Reproduce Girls Talking, 1960

Carol King and Gerry Goffin, "Will You Still Love Me Tomorrow?" performed by The Shirelles, 1960.

Tonight you're mine completely
You give your love so sweetly
Tonight the light of love is in your eyes
But will you love me tomorrow?

Is this a lasting treasure
Or just a moment's pleasure?
Can I believe the magic of your sighs?
Will you still love me tomorrow?

Tonight with words unspoken
You say that I'm the only one

But will my heart be broken
When the night meets the morning sun?

I'd like to know that your love
Is love I can be sure of
So tell me now, and I won't ask again
Will you still love me tomorrow?

(INSTRUMENTAL)

So tell me now, and I won't ask again
Will you still love me tomorrow?
Will you still love me tomorrow?
Will you still love me tomorrow?

 # ESSAYS

These essays consider domestic containment from the two sides of the gender divide in the 1950s and 1960s. James Gilbert, professor of history, University of Maryland, examines the construction of ideas about proper masculinity and juvenile delinquency in popular films. Gilbert writes that the congressional hearings into the causes of juvenile delinquency, led by Senator Estes Kefauver, maintained that "the mass media stood between parent and child" and "provoked youthful misbehavior and juvenile delinquency." In particular, Gilbert describes the reactions to two important films, *The Blackboard Jungle* and *Rebel without a Cause,* and the worries that such films, rather than discouraging juvenile delinquency, might glamorize it. Parents had the same worries about the ways in which girl groups sang about sexual relationships. But Susan J. Douglas, professor and chair of the communications department, University of Michigan, focuses on how the young women themselves, the singers and their listeners, used the music to think through the contradictions raised by social rules about female sexuality. These groups sang about issues that mattered to young women, particularly the double standard (that boys could have sex without trouble and that girls who had sex faced not only physical complications such as pregnancy but cultural ones, such as being thought promiscuous) and they sang as if a like-minded community of young women were listening. In the girl groups, we see the beginnings of the women's liberation movement and maybe the end of cold war culture and domestic containment.

Boy Culture/Bad Boys

JAMES GILBERT

The enormous outpouring of concern over juvenile delinquency in the mid-1950s presented the movie industry with dangerous but lucrative possibilities. An aroused

---

James Gilbert, "Juvenile Delinquency Films," in *A Cycle of Outrage: America's Reaction to the Juvenile Delinquent in the 1950s.* Copyright © 1986 by Oxford University Press. Reproduced by permission.

public of parents, service club members, youth-serving agencies, teachers, adolescents, and law enforcers constituted a huge potential audience for delinquency films at a time when general audiences for all films had declined. Yet this was a perilous subject to exploit, for public pressure on the film industry to set a wholesome example for youth remained unremitting. Moreover, the accusation that mass culture caused delinquency—especially the "new delinquency" of the postwar period—was the focus of much contemporary attention. If the film industry approached the issue of delinquency, it had to proceed cautiously. It could not present delinquency favorably; hence all stories would have to be set in the moral firmament of the movie Code. Yet to be successful, films had to evoke sympathy from young people who were increasingly intrigued by the growing youth culture of which delinquency seemed to be one variant.

The industry therefore moved slowly and hesitantly at first, expending time, money, and public relations on several exploratory efforts such as *The Wild One, Blackboard Jungle, Rebel Without a Cause,* and, later, *Blue Denim.* These films broke new ground for Hollywood because each simultaneously generated a good deal of controversy (including the accusation of prompting delinquent behavior) and each stimulated enormous interest in, and perhaps participation in, a new youth culture. Seeing this, studios quickly produced remakes and denatured versions of these early successes for the burgeoning teenage, drive-in audience. By the end of the 1950s, such studios as American International and Allied Artists were cranking out benign youth-culture films vaguely based upon these early explorations. By this time delinquency films emerged as a genre catering to young people. The issue of delinquency shown in the movies evolved into an occasional sideways glance at drugs, sex, and beatnik crime. But the most lucrative productions stressed the innocence of youth culture in such films as the Bikini Beach series or the endless variants on the theme that parents misunderstood rock and roll.

This transformation was significant because it paralleled, and perhaps accelerated, a simultaneous shift in public attention away from the evils of delinquent culture toward the end of the 1950s to a celebration of youth culture in the 1960s. Thus, in the long run, the accusation that movies contributed to delinquency probably benefitted the industry, for it persuaded them to make several films that capitalized on this controversial subject. It also suggested a means for catching and holding the teenage segment of an otherwise vanishing family audience....

... [D]elinquency, as a separate topic for attention, both in theory and popular culture, absorbed and refracted new postwar theories and controversies. Just at the time Hollywood began to view its audience as segmented into groups whose tastes and attitudes were different, American society had begun to stress the important gaps of generation and subculture. In this age of integration, counter-tendencies of disintegration and privatism were also strongly expressed, and nowhere more so than around problems of adolescence. These contradictory tendencies, emergent in the 1950s and focused—perhaps even formulated—around such issues as delinquency, multiplied rapidly in the 1960s and 1970s. The result was a cacophony of competing demands and strongly articulated identities.

Stanley Kramer's picture, *The Wild One,* released in 1953, stands in transition from the somber realism of "film noir" pessimism and environmentalism to the newer stylized explorations of delinquent culture that characterized the mid-1950s. Shot in dark and realistic black and white, the film stars Marlon Brando and Lee Marvin as rival motorcycle gang leaders who invade a small California town. Brando's character is riven with ambiguity and potential violence—a prominent characteristic of later juvenile delinquency heroes. On the other hand, he is clearly not an adolescent, but not yet an adult either, belonging to a suspended age that seems alienated from any recognizable stage of development. He appears to be tough and brutal, but he is not, nor, ultimately, is he as attractive as he might have been. His character flaws are appealing, but unnerving. This is obvious in the key symbol of the film, the motorcycle trophy which he carries. He has not won it as the townspeople assume; he has stolen it from a motorcycle "scramble." Furthermore, he rejects anything more than a moment's tenderness with the girl he meets. In the end, he rides off alone, leaving her trapped in the small town that his presence has so disrupted and exposed. The empty road on which he travels leads to similar nameless towns; he cannot find whatever it is he is compelled to seek.

Brando's remarkable performance made this film a brilliant triumph. Its moral ambiguity, however, and the very attractiveness of the alienated hero, meant that the producers needed to invoke two film code strategies to protect themselves from controversy. The first of these was an initial disclaimer appearing after the titles: "This is a shocking story. It could never take place in most American towns—but it did in this one. It is a public challenge not to let it happen again." Framing the other end of the film was a speech by a strong moral voice of authority. A sheriff brought in to restore order to the town lectures Brando on the turmoil he has created and then, as a kind of punishment, casts him back onto the lonesome streets.

Aside from Brando's stunning portrayal of the misunderstood and inarticulate antihero, the film did not quite emerge from traditional modes of presenting crime and delinquency: the use of black and white; the musical score with its foreboding big-band sound; the relatively aged performers; and the vague suggestions that Brando and his gang were refugees from urban slums. Furthermore, the reception to the film was not, as some might have predicted, as controversial as what was to come. Of course, there were objections—for example, New Zealand banned the film—but it did not provoke the outrage that the next group of juvenile delinquency films inspired.

The film that fundamentally shifted Hollywood's treatment of delinquency was *The Blackboard Jungle,* produced in 1955, and in which traditional elements remained as a backdrop for contemporary action. The movie was shot in black and white and played in a slum high school. But it clearly presented what was to become the driving premise of subsequent delinquency films—the division of American society into conflicting cultures made up of adolescents on one side and adults on the other. In this film the delinquent characters are portrayed as actual teenagers, as high school students. The crimes they commit are, with a few exceptions, crimes of behavior such as defying authority, status crimes, and so on. Of most symbolic importance is the transition in music that occurs in the film. Although it includes jazz numbers by Stan Kenton and Bix Beiderbeche, it is also the first film to feature rock and roll, specifically, "Rock Around the Clock" played by Bill Haley.

The story line follows an old formula of American novels and films. A teacher begins a job at a new school, where he encounters enormous hostility from the students. He stands up to the ringleader of the teenage rowdies, and finally wins over the majority of the students. In itself this is nothing controversial. But *Blackboard Jungle* also depicts the successful defiance of delinquents, who reject authority and terrorize an American high school. Their success and their power, and the ambiguous but attractive picture of their culture, aimed at the heart of the film Code and its commitment to uphold the dignity of figures and institutions of authority.

Despite a redemptive ending, plans to produce the film by Richard Brooks provoked opposition from the MPAA Code Authorities and interference from executives in the parent company, Metro-Goldwyn Mayer. The Code Authority was particularly upset about the "general brutality" of the script and the insistence of the authors on showing an attempted rape of one of the female school teachers. Ultimately, however, the film achieved a seal without significant changes.

The most important objections came from the studio and within the industry. Brooks had to search for several months to find an actor willing to play the lead of the schoolteacher, until he secured the services of Glenn Ford. Then he explored the possibility of filming in New York, but the city school system denied him permission. Finally, in the midst of his shoot, he received a letter from the New York offices of MGM, from Nicholas Schenck. Enclosed was a two-page script for a new scene with instructions to include it in the movie. The addition pictured a riot in a Moscow high school. Brooks was appalled by this interference and, after discussions with Dore Schary, proceeded without the scene.

Still cautious, the studio opened the film with a disclaimer. It also used a policeman as a voice of authority who explained postwar delinquency in this way: "They were six years old in the last war. Father in the army. Mother in a defense plant. No home life. No Church life. No place to go. They form street gangs.... Gang leaders have taken the place of parents."

Despite this protective sermonizing, the film aroused substantial opposition. It did so for many reasons, but principally because it pictured a high school with unsympathetic administrators and teachers in the grip of teenage hoodlums. Given contemporary fears of just such a situation, and the belief that such was the case throughout the United States, the film's realistic texture was shocking. But other elements distressed some audiences. For example, the leading adolescent character is a black student, played with enormous sympathy and skill by Sidney Poitier. And the clash of cultures and generations, which later became standard in juvenile delinquency films, was in this its first real expression, stated with stark and frightening clarity....

Public response to *Blackboard Jungle* provided a glimpse of the audience division between generations and cultures. Attending a preview of the film, producer Brooks was surprised, and obviously delighted, when young members of the audience began dancing in the aisles to the rock and roll music. This occurred repeatedly in showings after the film opened. But other reactions were more threatening. For example in Rochester, New York, there were reports that "young hoodlums cheered the beatings and methods of terror inflicted upon a teacher by a gang of boys" pictured in the film. But box office receipts in the first few weeks indicated a smash hit, and in New York City the first ten days at Loew's State theater set a record for attendance.

Nevertheless, the film caused an angry backlash against the film industry. Censors in Memphis, Tennessee, banned it. It was denounced by legal organizations, teachers, reviewers like Bosley Crowther of the *New York Times,* and even by the Teenage Division of the Labor Youth League (a communist organization). The National Congress of Parents and Teachers, the Girl Scouts, the D.A.R., and the American Association of University Women disapproved it. The American Legion voted *Blackboard Jungle* the movie "that hurt America the most in foreign countries in 1955." And the Ambassador to Italy, Clare Booth Luce, with State Department approbation, forced the film's withdrawal from the Venice Film Festival.

Such attention and controversy generated considerable discussion inside the MPAA about the merits of such films, particularly for display in foreign markets where, it was feared, any negative portrayal of the United States would incite anti-American feelings. Foreign representatives of the MPAA were particularly troubled by government bans on the film in India, Italy, and Indonesia. To smooth its exhibition elsewhere, the MPEAA (the export wing of the trade association) spliced in special prologues and epilogues for markets such as Great Britain.

Following swiftly on this commercial success was *Rebel Without a Cause,* a very different sort of film, and perhaps the most famous and influential of the 1950s juvenile delinquency endeavors. Departing from the somber working-class realism of *Blackboard Jungle, Rebel* splashed the problem of middle-class delinquency across America in full color. Moreover, its sympathy lay entirely with adolescents, played by actors James Dean, Natalie Wood, and Sal Mineo, who all live wholly inside the new youth culture. Indeed, this is the substantial message of the film: each parent and figure of authority is grievously at fault for ignoring or otherwise failing youth. The consequence is a rebellion with disastrous results....

When it approved the film, the Code Authority issued two warnings. Geoffrey Shurlock wrote to Jack Warner in March 1955: "As you know, we have steadfastly maintained under the requirements of the Code that we should not approve stories of underage boys and girls indulging in either murder or illicit sex." He suggested that the violence in the picture be toned down. Furthermore, he noted: "It is of course vital that there be no inference of a questionable or homosexual relationship between Plato [Sal Mineo] and Jim [James Dean]." A follow-up commentary suggested the need for further changes in the area of violence. For example, Shurlock noted of the fight at the planetarium: "We suggest merely indicating that these high-school boys have tire chains, not showing them flaunting them."

Despite these cautions, the film, when it was released, contained substantial violence: the accidental death of one of the teenagers in a "chickie run"; the shooting of another teenager; and Plato's death at the hands of the police. Furthermore, there remained strong echoes of Plato's homosexual interest in Jim.

The film also took a curious, ambiguous position on juvenile delinquency. Overtly, it disapproved, demonstrating the terrible price paid for misbehavior. Yet the film, more than any other thus far, glorified the teenage life-styles it purported to reject. Adult culture is pictured as insecure, insensitive, and blind to the problems of youth. Teenagers, on the other hand, are portrayed as searching for genuine family life, warmth, and security. They choose delinquency in despair of rejection by their parents. Indeed, each of the three young heroes is condemned to search for the emotional fulfillment that adults deny: Dean for the courage his father lacks; Natalie Wood (as his girlfriend) for her father's love; and Plato for a family, which he finds momentarily in Dean and Wood. Instead of being securely set in adult society, each of these values must be constructed outside normal society and inside a new youth-created world. What in other films might have provided a re-conciling finale—a voice of authority—becomes, itself, a symbol of alienation.…

By using middle-class delinquency to explore questions of existence, this film undeniably contested the effectiveness of traditional family and community institutions. There is even the hint that Dean, Wood, and Mineo represent the possibility of a new sort of family; but this is only a fleeting suggestion. In the end it is family and community weakness that bring tragedy for which there can be no real solution. Without the strikingly sympathetic performances of Dean, Wood, and Mineo, this picture might have fallen under the weight of its bleak (and pretentious) message. As it was, however, *Rebel Without a Cause* was a box office smash, and Dean's short, but brilliant career was now assured.

As with *Blackboard Jungle,* the MPAA was the focus of furious reaction to the film. Accusations of copycat crimes, particularly for a stabbing in Indiana, Pennsylvania, brought condemnations and petitions against "pictures which depict abnormal or subnormal behavior by the youth of our country and which tend to deprave the morals of young people." The MPAA fought back against this accusation in early 1956 as Arthur DeBra urged an investigation to discover if the incident at the Indiana, Pennsylvania, high school had any rela-tionship to the "juvenile delinquency situation in the school and community." As one writer for the *Christian Science Monitor* put it, "the new Warner Brothers picture will emerge into the growing nationwide concern about the effects on youth of comics, TV, and movies." This prediction was based upon actions already taken by local censors. The Chicago police had ordered cuts in the film, and the city of Milwaukee banned it outright.

On the other hand much of the response was positive.… [F]an letters had poured into Hollywood.…

Quite clearly, the film became a milestone for the industry. It established youth culture as a fitting subject for films, and created some of the most pervasive stereotypes that were repeated in later films. These included the tortured, alien-ated, and misunderstood youth and intolerant parents and authority figures. It did not, however, lead to more subtle explorations of the connections between youth culture and delinquency. If anything, the opposite was true. For one thing, Dean was killed in an auto accident shortly after this enormous success. Furthermore, it was probably the seriousness of *Blackboard Jungle* and *Rebel* that provoked controversy, and the movie industry quickly learned that it could attract teenage audiences without risking the ire of adults if it reduced the dosage of realism. Thus the genre deteriorated into formula films about teenagers, made principally for drive-in audiences who were not particular about the features they saw.…

This visual depiction of delinquency and its spread from the slums and working-class sections of cities into the middle class coincided with developing notions of the cultural transmission of delinquency. But generally, by the end of the 1950s, Hollywood had ceased to treat the subject with any seriousness. Instead, youth culture films relied on stereotypes developed from more serious films, but voided of any content. Formulaic explanations took the place of complex or ambiguous portrayals. The generation gap and parental misunderstanding or inflexible authority figures were blamed for transforming the legitimate behavior of youth into criminality. As a result of the industry's gradual abandonment of the concept of the family film, studios began to use the delinquency-youth culture theme as a subject exclusively for teenagers. Notions that had at one time been developed in serious films were reduced to formulas pitched to gain attention from younger audiences who delighted in the music, dancing, and daring of young film stars, and the apologetic behavior of parents and school officials. By the early 1960s the delinquency or youth-culture film had become a genre like the Western with expected elements that could be varied or reformulated to sustain interest....

There were other indications in the film industry that delinquency had lost some of its controversy, even for adults. In 1961 United Artists released *West Side Story,* one of the most successful musicals ever produced. Based on Leonard Bernstein's 1957 Broadway hit, the film closely followed the original play with some significant casting changes. The most essential element of that story is the theme, borrowed from Shakespeare's *Romeo and Juliet. West Side Story* divides the ill-starred lovers by ethnicity and gang, not family. Tony and Maria fall in love but cannot overcome the hatred and misunderstanding of the rival ethnic gangs, the Jets and the Sharks. Ultimately, Tony is swept into a fight that sets off a rumble that destroys him....

The most pleasing part of the film was the singing and dancing. The action—even the violence—was highly stylized. The two gangs sang of their hatred for each other. But when Bernstein set this action to music, he avoided the current teenage idiom of rock and roll; instead he used jazz. It was as if he chose to pitch the film to adults, not teenagers. Perhaps most important, the whole issue of juvenile delinquency is satirized—even the notion that crime comics caused delinquency. Thus, as the Jets wait for a rumble, one of them sprawls on a concrete stoop to read a comic book. Another remarks:

> See them cops; they believe everything they read in the papers about us cruddy J.D.'s. So that's what we give 'em. Something to believe in.

Then follows the hilarious song, "Gee, Officer Krupke," which satirizes the leading theories of delinquency. First claiming, "We ain't no delinquents. We're misunderstood," the gang moves through a mocking presentation of popular theories. The final reprise sums up these explanations of why a gang member is delinquent:

> Judge: The Trouble is he's crazy.
> Psychiatrist: The Trouble is he drinks.
> Social Worker: The Trouble is he's lazy.
> Judge: The Trouble is he stinks.
> Psychiatrist: The Trouble is he's growing.
> Social Worker: The Trouble is he's grown!

Krupke, we got troubles of our own. Gee,
Officer Krupke. We're down on our knees,
'Cause no one wants a fellow with a social disease—
Gee Officer Krupke, What are we to do?
Gee Officer Krupke, Krup you!

Thus Bernstein undercut one of the most powerful attacks upon youth culture: the therapeutic model of explanation. However, the contentious issue of delinquency and the media did not end with the film *West Side Story* in 1961. There were still serious juvenile delinquency films made, and still accusations that movies and other elements of the media triggered delinquent behavior. The nation was still appalled by the level and frequency of adolescent violence. Yet the film industry, which had been caught in the maelstrom of accusations during the mid-1950s, had weathered the storm and, indeed, profited from it. Using the Code as well as various forms of public relations, the industry exploited the intense public concern about the behavior of youth while protecting itself from severe criticism. By the end of the 1950s and into the 1960s, however, Hollywood rarely treated the subject seriously. Instead, it developed the teenage genre film to appeal to a younger audience. In effect, filmmakers had identified the significance of a new youth culture which it attributed to a new teenage audience. Echoes of delinquency stereotypes remained in many of these films, but the major impulse was to sanitize delinquency and praise youth culture as good clean fun.

Whether or not Hollywood influenced audiences to agree with this perception is hard to determine, but it is surely true that the question of delinquency by the early 1960s seemed far less important than it had once been. In its stead, the public gave new, and often positive, attention to American youth culture, of which delinquency now appeared to be a minor subset. This reorientation suggests that much of the dispute surrounding juvenile delinquency and the media following World War II was in fact a misunderstanding or the expression of distaste for the development of youth culture. Social disapproval certainly intensified the initial belief that new patterns of behavior, including language, dress, and music, signified growing criminality. But, as the public in the early 1960s discovered, youth culture was not necessarily something to bemoan; it could be an innovation to be celebrated. This moment of recognition signaled a profound change in the role of adolescent culture in American society.

Girl Culture/Bad Girls

SUSAN J. DOUGLAS

In December 1960, something new happened in American popular music. A girl group, composed of four black teenagers, had the number-one hit in the

Susan Douglas, "Will You Love Me Tomorrow? Changing Discourses About Female Sexuality in the Mass Media, 1960–1980," in *Ruthless Criticisms: New Perspectives in U.S. Communication History* eds. William S. Solomon and Robert W. McChesney. Copyright © 2005 by University of Minnesota Press. Reproduced by permission.

country. The song featured an adolescent female voice deliberating plaintively about whether or not she should succumb to the seductive promises of love from her boyfriend. Should she give in and have sex with him, or heed the advice she had heard all her life, that if she did so, he would lose all respect for her and jilt her once he had gotten what he wanted? The lyrics of the song, written by Carole King and Gerry Goffin, poignantly evoked the girl's struggle. In "Will You Love Me Tomorrow," Shirley Owens, lead singer for the Shirelles, wondered whether the tender looks, longing sighs, and declarations of love, so seemingly genuine that night, were actually to be trusted.

The song represented a pivotal cultural moment. It inaugurated that era in popular music when girl groups, as well as individual girl singers, became a regular feature of, and often topped, the top-forty charts. In the mid-1950s, when Elvis Presley dominated the charts—in 1956, five of the nine top singles of the year were by Elvis—there would be weeks, and sometimes months, when no women or female groups had hits among the top fifteen records. By the early 1960s, it was not unusual for five of the top fifteen hits to be by female artists. Although songs and movies by Elvis continued to be released while he was in the army, his forced removal from the rock scene signaled a sea change in the music industry and, in fact, in the culture industry at large. By the early 1960s, Elvis's brand of raw, sexually aggressive masculinity, which resonated with other male rockers such as Chuck Berry, Jerry Lee Lewis, and Little Richard, had to compete with a new sound and a new "female-centered pop sensibility." Usually these singers were still girls, often they were African American, and many sang in groups. And they were not singing about doggies in windows or old Cape Cod.

In 1960, the year of the Shirelles' first number-one hit, there were approximately 11.7 million girls between the ages of twelve and eighteen in the United States, and they were exerting increasing economic clout. The average of four dollars a week a girl received as an allowance was spent on cosmetics, magazines, movies, records, and clothes. In an effort to tap into this flow of discretionary income, executives in the culture industry, from film producers to admen, sought to produce music, films, TV shows, ads, and magazines that these girls would buy, both literally and figuratively. The goal, of course, was to cash in on this newly identified market of female "baby boomers."

One unintended and ironic result was that all of this marketing attention helped cultivate a highly self-conscious sense of importance and difference among these girls. The rise of so much popular culture addressed to teenage girls was key to an emerging, prefeminist sense of their own power and autonomy. All these media products conveyed the message, despite the retrograde images of beach bunnies, pliant girlfriends, and aspiring brides, that as a generation these girls really mattered, economically and culturally. This new, female-centered pop sensibility gave this huge cohort of girls and young women a sense, however inchoate and apolitical, of historical destiny. They sensed they were freer of constraints than their mothers had been, that they were modern, "with it," riding a wave of progress, less old-fashioned; they sensed that anything was possible. Such a message, reworked over and over in books, films, TV shows, and popular music, helped set the stage for the feminist revolution of the early 1970s.

What gave rise to this sensibility? Most obvious, and probably most important, was the coming of age of that huge demographic bulge in the population subsequently labeled the baby boom, those children born between 1942 and 1964. While the segregation of adolescents into a distinctive "youth culture" had begun to emerge gradually in the United States since the turn of the century it was in the 1950s and 1960s that this culture became huge, formidable, and distinctive. In the late 1950s and early 1960s, the growth rate of the teenage population took off at four times the average of all other age groups. Above all, and forged especially by the rise of rock and roll, was this cohort's sense of itself as a group to be reckoned with. This was true for girls as well as for boys.

This [essay] examines the proliferation of pop culture texts geared to young women in the 1960s.... These now are regarded either with amusement, as the ultimate in high kitsch, or with contempt for promoting trivializing, objectifying, sexist images of women. I intend to reclaim these texts, and to argue that they had important historical consequences. At first blush it might seem that a movie such as *A Summer Place* or a song such as "He's So Fine" has absolutely nothing to do with feminism, except that it contributed to an ideology many young women would ultimately react against. I would like to suggest that such texts played a different and much more complicated role in women's history, and that by rereading them we can come to a richer understanding of feminism's immediate prehistory. Embedded in much of the popular culture of the time were changing discourses about what constituted female sexuality, which included critiques of the double standard, an acceptance that girls' sexual desires were normal and healthy, and images of girls acting on those desires without suffering dire consequences. We need to consider these media texts as profoundly serious cultural documents that addressed the percolating aspirations, frustrations, and conflicts within young women that ultimately would lead them to reject the gender ideology of the 1950s and to seek out something new.

This popular culture hardly was progressive in any feminist sense of the word, yet neither was it as monolithic and oppressive as we might think. Rather, much of this popular culture was marked by major rifts, major fault lines within its ideological terrain. One of the principal rifts is a representation of patriarchy in crisis. Because these texts contained major contradictions about the proper balance between female passivity and agency, they problematized the young girl's stance toward her place within American patriarchy and within a culture obsessed by consumerism. These simmering criticisms, embodied in new images of young girls with some agency in the world, marked the beginning of a prefeminist sensibility that eventually led to the rise of the women's liberation movement in the United States.

My project, then, is to extend the existing historiography of the women's movement, and to argue that this prehistory of the second wave of feminism, with its beach movies, girl groups, and flying nuns, is a cultural history too long dismissed and overlooked, both by male cultural critics and by feminists. The standard accounts of the women's movement look to the experiences of young women in the civil rights movement and the New Left in the 1960s, document what they learned and how they were patronized, and then recount how these disaffected, usually radical women began organizing the foundational groups of the women's liberation movement. These same histories also track the organizational history of liberal feminism, beginning with the Kennedy Commission's 1963 *Report on the Status of Women* and then reviewing the establishment of NOW and WEAL and the push for congressional passage of the ERA.

While these are, of course, essential and important histories, they also are the histories of a relatively small group of women and are, therefore, incomplete. As primarily political histories, they do not examine in depth the convergence of a range of cultural and social factors that made a huge cohort of mostly anonymous and apolitical young women move from prefeminism to some version of feminism over a ten- to fifteen-year period. By reviewing the evolution of this upheaval from a cultural perspective and analyzing how it played out in the mass media, I hope to add to our understanding of the myriad factors that affected—and were affected by—the changing identities of teenage girls in the 1960s. Without those millions of anonymous young women, the women's liberation movement would not have had the enormous impact it did. The mass media played a central, if often inadvertent, role in this shift from prefeminism to feminism.

By the early 1960s, there was no longer simply a teen culture, defined as it was in the 1950s primarily by male voices and male performers. Now there was a distinctive teen girl culture, with teenage girl performers directly addressing teenage girl listeners. These voices sang about the pull between the need to conform and the often overwhelming desire to rebel, about the tension between restraint and freedom, and about the rewards—and the costs—of prevailing gender roles. They foregrounded, in other words, teen female ambivalence in the face of the major cultural contradictions surrounding gender roles in the early 1960s. In between songs about going to the chapel or wanting to be Bobby's girl were other tunes, songs about rebel boyfriends, defiant daughters, and new, sexually aggressive young women.

At the core of most of this female pop culture, then, was a discourse of ambivalence and contradiction. Visual representations of freedom, power, and sexual liberation were counterbalanced by admonitions about the dangers of assertiveness, license, and letting go. More than ever, girls were presented with "on the one hand, on the other hand" positions, since there were so many appealing points of identification to inhabit simultaneously....

THE MUSIC OF GIRL GROUPS

It was in the popular music of the era, ... that the contradictory messages about female sexuality, agency, and rebelliousness received the widest array of expression. Tin Pan Alley, jolted out of complacency by the runaway success of rock and roll in the 1950s, began in the early 1960s to pursue the teen market much more aggressively. Music publishers and producers hired teenage songwriters such as Carole King and Ellie Greenwich, cultivated many teen girl singers, and organized a host of new labels, all to produce records they hoped to sell to adolescent girls. As a result, pop music was the one area of popular culture in which the broadest range of adolescent female voices could be heard, producing what has come to be called "girl-talk" music. The main buyers of girl-talk records were, not surprisingly, young girls.

While much has been written about the cultural significance of Elvis Presley, Bill Haley, and other male rockers to the baby-boom generation, the girl groups have received little serious scholarly attention. Any music performed and favored by adolescent girls is routinely considered to be lightweight, formulaic, overly commercialized fluff of only fleeting import because female singers and their audiences are considered to have only a rudimentary understanding of what constitutes "real," authentic, artistically serious music. In addition, the music of teenage girls is not thought to have any long-term influence, either on other music or on social change. When the music of girl groups has been considered by historians of popular music, it has been condemned for feminizing, and therefore ruining, rock and roll.

Yet, recent feminist analyses of girl music—most notably the work of Susan McClary and Barbara Bradby—challenge such interpretations, and urge us to consider how "girl-talk" music has functioned in shaping the identities of its listeners. Central to this process of identification, and to the success of such music, is the way these songs automatically assume, and give voice to, the ambivalent position of adolescent girls within patriarchal society. Both scholars focus on how such music provides multiple subject positions for the girl singers and their audiences, so that the listener can be, by turns, an active subject in pursuit of her man and a passive object, waiting and yearning to be noticed. Both women suggest that it can be empowering for young women to be able to try on such different personas, especially those that defy patriarchal norms and expectations. Then Bradby goes further. She suggests that such feminine discourses, filled with these kinds of contradictions, may have had some historical effectivity, since they are an integral part of the "historical process of conflict and change." She notes provocatively that "certainly it is striking that the name of the form 'girl groups' prefigures the main organizational form of the women's movement, the 'women's group,' which was also a form for the development of talk."

One of the reasons popular music is so critical to women's history is that music is the cultural form most open to highly personalized readings and the form most closely tied to sexual expression and rebellion. As Susan McClary notes, because music is "often concerned with the arousing and channeling of desire," and because it "can cause listeners to experience their bodies in new ways," certain types of music can "influence and even constitute the way listeners experience and define some of their most intimate feelings." Thus, such music can and does "participate actively in the social organization of sexuality." As young people embraced rock and roll, McClary continues, "their notions of sexuality— their perceptions of their own most intimate dimensions of experience—split off irrevocably from those of their parents." One key departure, and an important one, was the articulation of a position of active sexuality by schoolgirls.

The question listeners were confronted with was this: Should she or shouldn't she? By extrapolation, of course, the question quickly became, Should I or shouldn't I? These questions were not only about sex, they were also about the degree to which girls should be assertive with boys, about how much agency it was proper for a girl to have in the world. They were also asking about whether girls should listen to their mothers, or rebel against them, especially when it came to obeying bourgeois codes of morality. Circumscribed within the confines of heterosexual love and marriage were images of rebellion, agency, defiance, and power, driven by an upbeat, usually danceable, and almost always euphoric music that seemed to promise transcendence and change.

Sexuality emerged, in these songs, as an eternal ache, a kind of irresistible, unquenchable state of constant tension. It involved "both desire and its prohibition." The undeniable push for outlet clashed with the pull for containment; the need for expression collided with the need for sublimation; and the desire to seduce merged with a fear of seduction. The pleasures and pains of vulnerability comingled. The understanding that male-female relationships were necessarily masochistic, particularly for the girl, circulated with rejections of female victimization and passivity.

The discourse of girl group music was private, confidential, confessional, and knowing, and, either openly or furtively, it often was about sex. Through these songs, which were, by turns, boastful, rebellious, and self-abnegating, girls could assume a variety of female subject positions, some of them empowering and others masochistic. The songs were about escaping from yet acquiescing to the demands of American patriarchy. In them, girls enjoyed being looked at with desire; but they also enjoyed looking with desire themselves. They were surveyors, not just of themselves and their girlfriends, but of boys too. They were totally confident; they were abjectly insecure. Some songs said, "Do," and others said, "Don't." Sometimes the voices were those of an active subject out to get the guy or showing off her boyfriend to her friends. At other times, the voice was that of the passive object, yearning patiently to be discovered and loved. Most interesting, and most frequently, the girl played an active role in both her imaginary and real construction of herself as the object of the boy's desire. As girls listened to their radios and record players, they could be martyrs to love, telling their former boyfriends to "walk on by," authorities who "know something about love," sexual aggressors, pursuing boys and urging them to call "any ole time," or, occasionally, prefeminists, as in such songs as "You Don't Own Me" and "Don't Make Me Over."

But it was not just that a song such as "I Wanna Be Bobby's Girl" offered a very different subject position from "You Don't Own Me." What is so interesting about so many girl-talk songs is the way contradiction is embedded within individual songs. As Barbara Bradby argues, girl-talk songs are different from male rock songs because "the female subject in the performance is divided against herself." In the same song, a girl can be both passive and active, a victim and an agent, a duality encouraged by the structure of lead singer and chorus in most girl-group songs. By singing these songs to themselves, girls could imagine conforming and rebelling at the same time.

In all these songs, however, it was young girls who were speaking subjects, and, fanned by high sales, the proliferation of so much girl talk legitimated adolescent female subjectivity as having a rightful and necessary place in pop culture discourses. In these songs, girls were tied to each other by a special, exclusive knowledge of the pains and joys of narcissism and masochism. They knew things about boys and love that they shared with each other, and this shared knowledge—smarter, more deeply intuitive, more worldly wise than any locker-room talk—provided a powerful bonding between girls.

Female rebellion was expressed in a variety of ways. Most noteworthy were those songs that celebrated the rebel hero, the boy who rejected the moral codes of bourgeois society, the boy every girl's parents loved to hate. By allying herself romantically and morally with the rebel hero, the girl singer and listener proclaimed her independence from the safe, predictable expectations about being domesticated within a tame, respectable marriage. He was the motorcycle rider the girl's parents were always putting down in "Leader of the Pack"; the social misfit who never did what he was supposed to do in "He's a Rebel"; the boy who cannot afford nice presents for his girlfriend because he is living on unemployment in "He's Sure the Boy I Love." But also of critical importance to these and other songs in which girls confided to each other about their boyfriends was the fact that the girls were knowing, active, speaking subjects while the rebel heroes and other boys were the objects of the girls' gaze and of their talk.

Because there is not space here to analyze all these personas or songs, I would like to discuss briefly how the contradictions between female agency and passivity were both managed and exacerbated in certain categories of songs. In "tell him" songs, such as "Wishin' and Hopin'," "Easier Said Than Done," and "Tell Him," the girl is advised to abandon the time-wasting and possibly boy-losing stance of passively waiting for *him* to make the first move. She is warned that passivity may cost her her man and is urged to act immediately and unequivocally. Yet the form of this action is to state her undying devotion to the boy, to do her hair exactly the way *he* likes it, to do what he wants to do, and to tell him she would die for him. The girl makes the first move, but only so she can quickly assume a more compliant and passive role. Nonetheless, in "Tell Him" and "Easier Said Than Done," the pulsing, exuberant dance rhythms of the songs, with their euphoric feel, reinforce the liberating sense of transcendence from old gender restrictions, at least in the area of courting. In "Da Doo Run Run," the lead singer of the Crystals asserts that she will indeed make that boy hers, while the Chiffons in "He's So Fine" sing about picking out the right boy and going straight after him. Should a girl make the first move or not? The question was asked in girl-talk songs many times, and often the answer was yes.

In songs about teen desire, girls clearly responded with sexual pleasure to their boyfriends; for instance, in "And Then He Kissed Me," the girl describes a new kind of kissing that she clearly wants more of. And in many advice songs, which warned about playboys, advised how to identify true love, and acknowledged that "you can't hurry love," the message that girls knew a thing or two, and that they would share that knowledge with each other to beat the odds in a man's world, circulated confidently from song to song. The fact that many of these songs explored the inner feelings of the girl singer herself provided easy and instant identification for the introspective female listener eager to latch onto any glamorized public representation of female subjectivity. Also key to this identification was something the already-fragmented teen subject recognized and took great comfort in: the division of the girl singer into two equally compelling voices—active and passive views of herself....

CONCLUSION

All of the texts discussed here, while seemingly silly and inconsequential, together constituted an important and breakaway "on the one hand, on the other hand" discourse about girls taking action that not only revealed, but also accelerated, the dissolution of 1950s gender codes. In an attempt to cash in on the burgeoning teen girl market of the 1960s, a market that included conformists, rebels, and millions of girls who were both, the culture industry created a range of texts with many, often conflicting, points of identification for young girls. The films, songs, and TV shows of the period provided girls with different personas to inhabit, and while some were just as conforming, passive, and sexually restrained as any 1950s stereotype, others were not: they rejected mom's advice, they took up with the wrong kind of boy, they went all the way, and they had superhuman powers their husbands didn't.

No single film or TV show or book changed history. But the way their various representations overlapped, reinforced, and even contradicted each other had a cumulative effect on what young girls thought might be possible for them in the future. Instead of viewing the emergence of feminism in 1968 as a break with the past, we should see the women's liberation movement as, simultaneously, a reaction against and a product of this prefeminist pop culture imagery. Considering the way popular culture heightens our own internal contradictions, our fragmented subjectivity, is not interesting only theoretically; it helps us understand that at certain points in history, as young people wrestle with the implications of their increasingly ambivalent stances toward establishment culture, they can and do change history. And this is exactly what young girls in the 1960s did.

Many of these texts and the female personas they offered to young girls glamorized a new mind-set, a liberation from the rigid sexual dogmas of the past. We cannot know how young girls appropriated the meanings of all these texts, but it is clear that some of the positions offered to them were, in fact, prefeminist. Because teenage girls were invited to assume subject positions that were rebellious, that rejected the double standard, that provided girls with permission, even encouragement, to have some agency in the world, they gradually, over time, became more emboldened, more questioning of the status quo, and more desirous of liberation, first from minor constraints and then from very large ones indeed. After nearly a decade of trying on the personas of the rebel, the sexual sophisticate, the knowing girl who was bonded to other girls in a group, and the witch with larger-than-life powers, some girls—certainly enough girls—decided they did not want to imagine, fantasize, or pretend anymore. By the early 1970s, they wanted this power for real.

FURTHER READING

Altschuler, Glenn. *All Shook Up: How Rock 'n' Roll Changed America* (2003).

Austin, Joe, and Michael Nevin Willard, eds. *Generations of Youth* (1998).

Bailey, Beth L. *Sex in the Heartland* (1999).

Breines, Wini. *Young, White, and Miserable: Growing Up in the Fifties* (2001).

Cohen, Lizabeth. *A Consumer's Republic: The Politics of Mass Consumption in Postwar America* (2003).

Couvares, Francis G., ed. *Movie Censorship and American Culture* (1996).

Douglas, Susan J. *Where the Girls Are: Growing Up Female with the Mass Media* (1994).

Dudziak, Mary. *Cold War Civil Rights: Race and the Image of American Democracy* (2002).

Graebner, William. *Coming of Age in Buffalo: Youth and Authority in the Postwar Era* (1989).

Guralnick, Peter. *Last Train to Memphis: The Rise of Elvis Presley* (1995).

Horowitz, Daniel. *The Anxieties of Affluence: Critiques of American Consumer Culture, 1939–1979* (2004).

Maira, Sunaina. *Desis in the House: Indian American Youth Culture in New York City* (2002).

May, Elaine Tyler. *Homeward Bound: American Families in the Cold War Era* (1988).

CHAPTER 13

Popular Culture and Globalization

Beyond Imperialism

American popular culture has been global in scope since the nineteenth century and has played a complicated and integral role the economic and political expansion of the nation. As Chapter 4 demonstrated, beginning in the nineteenth century, showmen such as Buffalo Bill Cody and the Ringling Brothers performed across Western Europe. At the same time, American factories churned out consumer products that made their way not only to Britain and Europe but also to various American territories. The reach of American consumer capitalism continued to grow in the twentieth century as cultural commodities—whether movies, Ford cars, jazz, Disney products, or McDonald's hamburgers—expanded American markets and influence around the world.

This chapter argues that some of these products became powerful and sometimes volatile symbols of Americanization. Popular commodities have been intentionally or unintentionally loaded with ideologies; they perform cultural work suggesting how audiences should think about and embody or resist prevailing notions of race, gender, age, ethnicity, class, and nationalism. Much like the reenactments of the maritime battles of the 1898 war, later forms of popular culture were crafted with a particular interest in promoting American foreign policy abroad. Historians such as Penny von Eschen, among others, have studied the deployment of American popular culture as a weapon in cold war diplomacy. Soft diplomacy included sending movies to occupied Japan and later jazz musicians to places that might be sympathetic to the spread of communism. These efforts were intended to promote ideas of American democracy and showcase the benefits of consumer capitalism. State Department officials sent jazz greats such as Dizzy Gillespie, Louis Armstrong, Dave Brubeck, and Duke Ellington on goodwill tours to highlight American liberty. Jazz presented the perfect answer to charges of racial oppression in the United States, it was uniquely American, had a freeform style, and an African American lineage. The jazz ambassadors, as they were known, especially Louis "Satchmo" Armstrong, proved a huge success abroad, but in unexpected ways. Armstrong, for instance, found common ground with his listeners through a sense of shared struggle for equality. Addressing these contradictions, the Brubecks and Armstrong wrote and performed a jazz musical entitled the Real Ambassadors *(1962) that commented on the power of music as a diplomatic tool and satirized the overtly ideological goals of the State Department.*

Despite the intentions of the State Department, popular culture was and is a two-way street; audiences have been and still are critical to the production of meaning. The government could not control the meaning of the jazz tours, just like Disney cannot determine what audiences think of its movies. While producers can design products to appeal to the needs and desires of audiences, what consumers do and what they think is negotiated on the ground and within historical and cultural contexts that are often quite distinct from the United States. Therefore, scholars of popular culture such as John Storey have critiqued arguments about the homogenizing power of American popular culture as overly simplistic. Storey and others have noted that marketing success—the effective selling of goods or forms—does not equal the acceptance of ideas. American popular culture forms may effect change in other cultures but those changes often come from the bottom up rather than from the outside in. Storey proposes a model of glocalization rather than homogenization wherein audiences localize or appropriate American commodities and make sense of them according to their own cultural priorities. In addition, more recently, scholars have begun to study how the United States has become a market for media products from other places. Certainly part of Disney's success is its use of not only universal themes but also fairy tales and myths from a variety of cultures, its creation of hybrid characters and stories that are not particularly American. So, not only is popular culture deeply embedded in consumer capitalism, it is mobile, hybrid, and it challenges a sense of cultural authenticity based on geographic location since it moves across cultural and national borders.

This chapter asks: How did popular culture continue to inform and aid American foreign policy well into the twentieth century? Do American cultural forms—whether jazz, Disney, or McDonald—promote Americanization, or do local cultures appropriate, resist, and rework popular culture in a process known as glocalization? Or are American products hybrids? For instance, how can McDonald's become part of local cultures but also stand as an icon of American culture? Alternatively, how has the United States become a market for cultural commodities created aboard? Finally, how can historians and cultural anthropologists collaborate in studying circulation of cultural commodities and the creation of popular culture? What do historians bring to the project of understanding the globalization of American products?

DOCUMENTS

The documents take varying positions on the cultural and ideological power of American cultural commodities, but most call into question the ability of cultural products to impose American ideals on other cultures. In Document 1, jazz musician Dave Brubeck supports the "unifying influence" of jazz on audiences and argues that it had wide appeal around the world. In Document 2, cartoonist Andy Singer illustrates common perceptions of the hegemonic and imperial power of American corporations storming native cultures with American products. Documents 3 and 4 bring an anthropological perspective to the study of globalization. In Document 3, as part of a massive project, media scholars studied the impact and use of Disney products on consumers around the world, finding in favor of Storey's idea of glocalization, that most of their subjects made sense of these products within their own local contexts. In a similar vein, David Wu, an anthropologist, examined the incorporation of fast food giant McDonald's into daily life in Taiwan. Document 5 provides a counter-example of how a Japanese media company strategized the marketing of Pokemon to appeal to an American market. One final example looks not only at the entrance of American musical forms into Turkey but also their active appropriation and reworking by musicians who wish to retain a distinct cultural identity.

1. Dave Brubeck, a Jazz Musician, Describes His Role in American Diplomacy, 1958

Between 5:30 P.M. on Feb. 8, at the Royal Festival Hall in London, and midnight of May 10, in the Khayyam Theatre in Baghdad, four American jazz musicians—Paul Desmond (alto saxophone), Joe Morello (drums), Eugene Wright (bass) and myself (piano)—traveled better than halfway around the world and played above seventy concerts in Great Britain, Germany, Holland, Belgium, Sweden, Denmark, Poland, Turkey, India, Ceylon, Pakistan, Afghanistan, Iran and Iraq. I give the itinerary in this much detail for the most relevant of reasons: it is illustrative of both fact and symbol, the one hardly less tangible than the other.

The fact is that jazz, our single native art form, is welcomed—not simply accepted—without reservation throughout the world and is felt to be the most authentic example of American culture. It would be fatuous of me to pretend to correlate its importance with the billions of dollars we have spent in restoring nations ravaged by war and in raising the living standards of underdeveloped countries, or the day-to-day spadework of statesmen and diplomats. But there is no mistaking its effect: it arouses a kinship among peoples; it affords them flashes of recognition of common origins, because of its basic relationship to folk idioms; and the forthrightness and directness of its appeal are grasped alike by the naive and the sophisticated. More of it is being heard abroad today than ever before. Even more heartening to me is the knowledge that occasionally, as was the case with the major portion of our tour, it is being sent overseas under official auspices. From Warsaw to Baghdad, we were financed by President Eisenhower's Special International Program for

Cultural Presentations, as administered by the American National Theatre and Academy.

To me the symbol is uncomplicated. It is one of unity and of uninhibited, if sometimes wordless, communication, but I think it has to be examined on two levels, sociologically as well as musically. In the first place, the range of language, culture and race between London and Baghdad is wide, so very wide. But there are three white men in our quartet and Gene Wright is a Negro. A number of other bands that have toured foreign countries come to mind. There have been white instrumentalists in all of Louis Armstrong's bands, and in those of Dizzy Gillespie and Lionel Hampton; there have been Negroes in those of Benny Goodman and Stan Kenton, to say nothing of Norman Granz' big troupe, "Jazz at the Philharmonic."

Jazz is color blind. When a German or a Pole or an Iraqi or an Indian sees American white men and colored in perfect creative accord, when he finds out that they travel together, eat together, live together and think pretty much alike, socially and musically, a lot of the bad taste of Little Rock is apt to be washed from his mouth. Obviously, a similar effect is produced by the best of our serious music, our theatre and our literature, but I am concerned here specifically with jazz.

The United States assumes the most moral role of all internationally. A greater demand is placed on us for human decency than on any other country, and while the sight and sound of a mixed band improvising on "Love Walked In," for example, is not to be compared with a summit conference in Geneva, Washington or Moscow, it is not to be ignored. Louis symbolizes even more than he understands. He is in life what you find more frequently in fiction—the uneducated American Negro who, through his genius, has overcome all possible obstacles and who is loved universally, Love walks in, all right, when Louis plays....

Musically, by its very nature, [jazz] is the most creative, the freest and most democratic form of expression I know. What is the essence of jazz? It is music freely created before listeners (watchers, too) by a group of instrumentalists, each of whom is afforded a maximum of individual expression in a democratically agreed on framework of rhythms, harmonies and melodies....

Furthermore, jazz is music whose sources are world-wide—African, European, Asian, American—and therefore may be understood almost instantly, whether by a provincial group of Indians 500 miles inland from Bombay or a cosmopolitan audience in West Berlin....

I will make one or two more generalizations about jazz and then I will attempt to prove the truth of them. I don't like to use the word "propaganda" in connection with it, although it is the easiest one to explain its value. Maybe it is and maybe it isn't "America's secret weapon," as a *New York Times* correspondent once said in describing Louis Armstrong's effect in Europe. But I do know this—and I believe it to be more than coincidence—generally, wherever there was dictatorship in Europe, jazz was outlawed. And whenever freedom returned to those countries, the playing of jazz invariably accompanied it....

Everywhere we went—in the free nations, in dictatorships, in undeveloped countries—the unifying influence of our kind of music was brought home to us....

The editor of an anti-Western magazine sat next to my wife during one of our two concerts in Ankara and she noticed he seemed pretty agitated all during the performance. We found out later why. "For the first time in my life," he told me backstage, "you have made me forget that I am a Moslem and that you are Christians."

I am not a little proud of the fact also that one of the Ankara performances was heard by Cevat Menduk Altar, Turkey's General Director of Fine Arts. I was told by Patricia Randles, assistant cultural officer of the U. S. I. S. in Ankara, that she had "been here fifteen months and this is the first time I've been able to get him to attend any United States function." (Two days after the band got back to New York, we read that Miss Randles had been killed in an automobile accident in Ankara.) Altar, I learned afterward, is a friend of Hindemith and an expert on Chopin, and he had lectured on the latter in Poland.

What made Altar a jazz fan was nothing more mysterious than the circumstance that his two daughters were enthusiasts. And that brings me around to what I suppose I can call the coda of this piece. The understanding that comes out of jazz begins with the musician. It doesn't make much difference whether a man plays traditional style, or Dixieland, or bop, cool, modern or progressive, and it doesn't matter much what he thinks he is playing, as long as that ensemble understanding exists among the players. That's the first circle.

The second circle is that of the fans who have bought tickets to a performance. Somewhere in a set of program notes I wrote is this sentence: "I think of an audience as a co-creator, the fifth instrument to our quartet. How an audience chooses to play its part is determined anew each time musicians and listeners gather together." The third circle consists of those people who read the reviews of our jazz concerts and are prompted to come either to the next one or to one staged by another group. And the fourth circle is that of people who, all charged up by the third, finally become members at the second themselves.

Let me take one more chorus. In Kabul, I was met by an ex-policeman from Berkeley, Calif., Al Riedel, who is helping organize Afghanistan's forces. He pointed to this huge mountain around Kabul and at its top a wall. "For 5,000 years," he said, "people have been fighting over that wall—Tameriane, Genghis Khan, Alexander the Great, the Indians, the English, who knows who. If a small fraction of what they spent had gone into education instead of defense, that wall would have come down long ago. At best, defense is a temporary thing."

That night, lying awake in my hotel room, I heard three or four nomads— shepherds—passing under my window, playing their flutes. The music they made was the same they had made for 5,000 years. And the music had survived. How many of the things that were fought for over the wall on that mountain have?

2. Cartoonist Satirizes Disney as Leading Force of U.S. Imperialism, 1998

Reprinted from *The Funny Times*.

3. Media Scholars Assess the Results of the Global Disney Audiences Project, 2001

The Global Disney Audiences Project has only scratched the surface in our attempt to understand the significance of the Disney phenomenon. While it is dangerous and foolish to draw generalized conclusions across cultures, especially based on such limited and narrow samples, the Project's results do tell us quite a lot about Disney's pervasiveness and symbolic ubiquity, as well as the ambiguities and contradictions that exist among Disney audiences.

Disney's Pervasiveness: It's (Almost) Everywhere

It was obvious before we started this research that the Disney company had expanded its global marketing in recent decades. While Disney characters and products have been distributed and recognized in many countries since the early 1930s, the company's more recent corporate expansion has further reinforced the global recognition of the Disney brand. The research not only bolstered these initial suspicions but also provided some convincing evidence of Disney's global pervasiveness.

Perhaps the most telling evidence is the study itself, in which over 1250 respondents in eighteen different countries not only recognized and discussed the Disney brand but also reported a relatively high degree of interaction with the company's products. Access to and use of Disney products by college educated populations is clearly extensive, to the point of being virtually universal among our respondents. If these groups are indicative of the rest of their nations, and if the range of Disney products and prices are replicated, then we expect that the great majority of populations recognize, have access at least to inexpensive products, and use such materials.

From this perspective, the recognition of Disney seems to be a global phenomenon. Of course, marketing wizards and industry pundits might well respond, "We could have told you so!" However, this study provides information regarding Disney's presence that is not tainted by the usual distortions associated with commodifying and commercializing the production of information.

From the respondents, we confirmed that Disney is typically first experienced at a young age (first contact was generally between 4 and 5 years of age), and the experience is usually positive. More specifically, the questionnaires indicated that nearly 98 percent of the respondents had seen a Disney film, nearly 82 percent were familiar with Disney books, and around 79 percent had experienced Disney television programs and merchandise. In addition, we found that people generally tend to underestimate their exposure to Disney products, selectively reporting only a few examples until confronted with a specific list of the many Disney products and services that are available.

While the respondents generally felt most positive (or "liked") Disney products at a younger age, by and large they still like Disney products as young adults and continue to come into contact (or consume) these products. Further, they generally imagine a future in which they will introduce their own children to Disney products. In this way, most of our respondents incorporate Disney into their life cycles, treating the products as naturally attractive to children, enjoyable enough for adults, and important parts of the happy childhood that all parents want for their children.

Of course, there are certainly variations in the familiarity with and popularity of Disney in different countries. The most common experiences are with films and television programing, and various kinds of merchandise. However, some countries and geographic regions have incorporated Disney into cultural rituals such as the ritualized reading of Disney comics in Scandinavia, or visits to theme parks for Brazilians marking their passage into adulthood. But even where Disney products are not as pervasive or ubiquitous, respondents report a sense that "Disney products are everywhere."

This general sense of Disney's ubiquity is undiminished even when Disney products are less available: whether due to undeveloped markets within a country (as in Appalachia in the U.S.A.), national underdevelopment of markets (as in Greece and South Africa), or continental underdevelopment (as in Africa generally), respondents in such areas not only recognized the Disney brand but also demonstrated familiarity with the products. As one … South African respondent explained, "Everyone has heard of it. Everyone has a Disney product."

This theme surfaced routinely in the national profiles indicating, as Ingunn Hagen notes, "children's everyday lives are saturated with Disney products." In this sense, Disney's drive for corporate synergy has succeeded in creating a commercial intertext that connects Disney characters, stories, and merchandise across all media, saturating not only markets but lives. This constitutes Disney's symbolic ubiquity and raises questions about the relationship between this ubiquity, individual consciousness, and culture.

Some respondents and researchers are troubled by those questions. Respondents generally used two tactics to resolve such concerns. Some divided Disney into the good provider of fun and the bad overcommercializer. While enjoying the good Disney, they criticize the bad Disney's high prices and merchandising. Others sought comfort in the possibility of a general backlash against Disney, vowing to exercise selectivity in purchasing Disney products, or displaying uncertainty about introducing children to Disney. Such reflections formed the basis for the ambiguous or even negative positions taken by some respondents to Disney. Overall, however, the multitude think positively about Disney, as well as quite a few ardent fans who were definitely dazzled….

The multitude not only favors Disney but also often considers as taboo any serious examination—never mind any criticism—of Disney's meaning and impact. Resistance to study or criticism of Disney was especially marked in the U.S.A. and Japan. This strong affirmation may well lie in the connection between Disney and childhood—a connection that confers a special status to Disney products. Overall, Disney was linked to strong and positive memories of childhood, family, and ritualized activities—even by those who criticized the company. For Americans, of course, Disney's role in childhood is legendary. However, this also is true for children in other countries. In both Norway and Denmark, where printed material is especially popular, Disney is part of the ritual of reading, as well as being associated with the Christmas holidays, when a special Disney program was broadcast each year. Thus, … for Norwegian adults, Disney is associated with "an annual ritual embroidered with nostalgic feelings," as well as being integrated into children's everyday life in various ways. In Brazil, visiting Walt Disney World represents another kind of ritual—a rite of passage—for some Brazilian teenagers. While in Mexico, birthday parties are often celebrated with a plethora of piñatas, decorations and presents with Disney themes. Along the same lines, in Greece, some respondents thought there was something wrong with those not "touched by Disney films," and view Disney products as necessary for children.

Whether it was the link between the *Donald* books and grandparents in Denmark, birthday parties with Disney themes and presents in Mexico, or the family fun experienced at one of the theme parks for Brazilians, the association with childhood and memories seems to place Disney in a special, almost sacred, category. This connection with childhood may seem obvious given Disney's product line. But this association also played into the contradictions and ambiguities that were evident in many cases, as will be discussed further below.

There are other reasons why people think positively about Disney. The products often are viewed as high-quality and well-made entertainment. Many respondents told us that Disney products were especially appropriate and positive for children, and even explained how they were harmless and often educational. These students essentially argued the case for using Disney products based on rational appeals of quality, innocence, and educational value, thus separating themselves from those who embraced Disney because of its significance in familial rituals.

Others taking the approach of the rational consumer found Disney's intense marketing problematic. They were troubled by the commercialism that transformed a Disney film into a product line and that touted the product line over every available medium. Often they described Disney products and the Disney parks as overpriced and too expensive for the average family. Some ascribed the success and popularity of Disney to the company's marketing, which was described as pervasive and effective. They connected such marketing power with concerns about overcommercialization, aggressive merchandising, and expense.

While some of these respondents separated the good Disney that provides us with imaginative fun from the bad Disney that saturates markets with merchandise, others rejected Disney, critiquing both the company and its products. Researchers offer various explanations for this, attributing it to "adult reflections on childhood" … or respondents "constructing their own identities."… Nevertheless, the negative responses or forms of resistance to the Disney "magic" are worth further explanation.

For some Disney resisters, the company epitomized all that is negative about the U.S.A.: commercialism, materialism, mass production. The groups interviewed by Buckingham were especially cynical, as they discussed Disney as a "bad object," consistent with American culture and consumerism. Indeed, many respondents agreed that Disney teaches consumerism, which encourages conflicts between parent and child. Some interviewees recalled how they themselves had pressured their parents for Disney products. In other groups, respondents discussed the difficulty of dealing with the demands of their children ... for expensive Disney merchandise....

Besides criticizing Disney's corporate synergy and pricing, many resisters found fault with both Disney's narratives and its depiction of women. The moral content of Disney's tales was often described as heavy-handed and the treatment of romance stereotypical. This was especially important in the depiction of female protagonists, whose primary tasks were usually centered on romantic relationships. Adding in the tendency for recent Disney heroines to resemble Mattel's Barbie dolls, some of those interviewed found a negative subtext to Disney heroines. They noted that, although Esmeralda or Pocahontas were supposed to be more independent than classic heroines like Cinderella or Snow White, the Barbie-body type and emphasis on romance undercut any independence the new heroines might aspire to and relegated them to the status of sexual object. This suggests that some respondents recognized that Disney's new heroines were supposed to be read in a certain way—as independent women—but resisted that reading. Instead, they deconstructed the apparently progressive message of Esmeralda's or Pocahontas' independence to discover the same old sexism lurking underneath as a latent message. These resisters read against the grain, not to produce an oppositional reading, but rather to uncover an oppressive subtext. In this process, we may see some clues regarding the degrees of freedom and the constraints of cultural expectation that shape the work of resistant audiences as they negotiate a text.

Balancing this resistance, however, were respondents who also recognized problems with Disney's moralistic tales and stereotyped heroines, but who avoided criticizing Disney by arguing that the company was simply reflecting human nature or social institutions. While strong resisters easily critiqued the company's current operations, they became more ambiguous when recalling their own childhood experiences with Disney, assessing its ultimate value through that lens of personal memory and shared experience, as we shall see in the next section.

Disney's Influence: Cultural Identity/Imperialism Revisted

Beyond the points that emerged directly from the questionnaires and interviews, the project researchers pursued inquiries in six related areas: cultural industries, consumer culture, Americanization, global culture, cultural identity and cultural imperialism....

Americanization

Undoubtedly, Disney contributes to consumerism, but does it contribute to Americanization? Some countries and individuals have historically been attracted to various aspects of American culture, including such core values as rugged individualism, movie icons like James Dean or Jerry Lewis, products like Levi Strauss jeans, and entertainment bearing the Disney brand. Yet, that attraction does not predict national or individual responses to Americanization or American policy. One can embrace Disney while still resisting Americanization or critiquing American policies. This inconsistency is manifested differently in different cultures and is influenced by historical, cultural, economic, and political factors. The fact that, historically, Walt Disney and the Disney company have participated in U.S. efforts to Americanize other nations must also be taken into account.

Unsurprisingly, the Disney brand is associated with Americanization in many countries. While this has been more recent in some countries (such as South Africa), in many countries, it has a much longer history and quite complex roots. For instance, ... cultural Americanization in Japan, which dates back to the 1920s: "During this process, the world of Disney was introduced and gradually became accepted as the core of what people in Japan perceive as Americanism." With the success of Tokyo Disneyland and the expansion of cultural Americanization in Japan since the 1970s, Yoshimi has detailed how Disney has contributed to the transformation of "America" as symbol to "America" as system.

In contrast, ... the attitudes of Koreans are "intermingled with their feelings about the U.S.A. ... the ambivalent feelings towards, as well as the trust of, Disney products, is associated with the historical context of modernization in Korea." This interweaving of a corporate brand, Americanization, and modernization takes on greater significance in the context of globalization, as we shall see below....

As some of the discussions reveal, Disney is not always associated exclusively with Americanization, but with a growing global culture, often strongly influenced by American products and values.... [M]any of the French respondents were well aware of Disney's contribution to a "globalization of culture." This analysis was echoed in many other settings, as respondents found "Disney culture" to be either universal or at least consistent with the Western values of many other cultures. As one of the Australians interviewed noted, "The Disney movies do not promote American culture as such, but promote the standards of any wealthy Western culture." In other words, Disney contributes to a cultural standardization or cultural hybridity, as discussed by Morley and Robins.

This raises the issue of cultural hegemony and media imperialism: in the so-called "American Century" or "Pax Americana," which stretches from the end of World War II to the downfall of the Soviet Union to the current day, to what degree are the "standards of any wealthy Western culture" determined by the standards of the nation that dominates the world's political economy? And, to what extent can local audiences "denature, redefine, and appropriate"—as Molina observes in Mexico—the media products bearing these implicit values? Both processes are clearly at work and further research is necessary to map the extent of each and the interactions between each dynamic.

One approach to these issues was undertaken by [scholars in Australia and Japan], and others, who examined Disney texts within the national economic and cultural environment. In the Australian context, for example, ... the Disney formula became the national standard in media productions [and] respondents had a "broad acceptance of the stereotyping conventions of mass culture" and that few missed anything distinctly "Australian" in these globally oriented cultural products. If the future holds a global system of distribution where production remains oligopolized and formulae remain rooted in the model of U.S. commercial culture, then one has to wonder if and how localities, regions, and nations will maintain identities adjacent to the identities provided in global commercial media....

Indeed, many authors addressed the issue of identity. [In Mexico] ... local audiences might use Disney products in ways that foster cultural diversity.... [In the U.K.] Disney and other cultural objects serve as a means by which audience members construct identities and define themselves.... [R]espondents' ambiguity over Disney was a form of social action—or, a process of forming their own identities in relation to cultural products like Disney—and needs to be evaluated accordingly.

On the other hand, ... many Japanese have accepted American culture, and Disney. [One Author] suggests that Disney is used as a form of self-identification: "they can see no distance between themselves and the world of Disney." For example, this phenomenon has contributed to a cutesification trend ("*kawaii* culture") that is well known in contemporary Japanese society....

CULTURAL IMPERIALISM

For some respondents and researchers, these concerns regarding globalization, identity, and Americanization were interrogated through the lens of cultural imperialism. Some respondents made the connection specifically and voluntarily. Others used language that evokes the work of dependency theorists as well as researchers tracing the extent of media imperialism. For example, French respondents linked Disney with words such as "propaganda, manipulation, domination, and influence."

Across nations, and regardless of whether respondents affirmed or resisted Disney, many related Disney's business practices and cultural products to the imperialist and expansive logics of capitalism. Yet, frequently respondents and researchers reminded us of the need to balance the local with the global....

While Disney is not directly imposing its products and values on the rest of the world, its business practices make those products ubiquitous. This ubiquity, the incorporation of Disney products in family rituals, and the early contact with Disney products in childhood combine in complex and often contradictory ways to communicate Disney's core values and to set the terms within-which audiences evaluate Disney. Clearly, this process is what [Marxist theorist Antonio] Gramsci meant by the term "hegemony." [One scholar] describes it as the "soft, friendly side of globalization, whose penetration is so intense and persistent that it resounds in all local ambits and generates specific forms of appropriation.... Disney is accepted because its products and values appear innocent and compatible with local culture." [He] suggests Disney and other brands of commercial culture "don't appear as an imposition from outside the local system, but rather as a prolongation or continuation, as something that naturally adheres to fit within local culture. The perception of global culture thus remains partially veiled by its soft interaction with local culture."

Thus, through its domination of children and family entertainment; through its insinuation into family rituals, Disney promotes consumer culture, as well as specific tastes and values. Because of its special links to childhood and family, Disney and its products take on a nearly sacred status. That status makes criticism difficult, although, as we have seen, not impossible.

Significantly, criticism seems to be easier when directed at the company's market saturation and commercialism. The contradictions between Disney's core values and its aggressive merchandising provide the ground upon which individuals can achieve a more critical consciousness about Disney, and perhaps more generally about cultural industries operating in a global, capitalist system. Could the contradictions of capitalism ultimately unravel on a matter as simple as Disney's exploitation of children?...

4. David Y.H. Wu, Anthropologist, Believes Taiwanese McDonald's Is a Local Institution, 1997

McDonald's reception in Taiwan tells us a great deal about the Taiwanese people and their attempts to forge new cultural identities in a world characterized by globalism and postindustrial realignments. In Taiwan today ... eating is a political act....

McDonald's and the Revival of Taiwanese Localism

In 1984 the first McDonald's restaurant opened in east Taipei, on a street that sported hundreds of nouvelle shops, including supermarkets, clothing boutiques, and restaurant chains serving Korean barbecue, Hong Kong–style seafood, Italian pasta, and Japanese-style coffee. These commercial outlets constituted the leading edge of a global, cosmopolitan culture that entered Taipei in the wake of the economic boom of the 1970s.

The foreign food invasion was an obvious feature of Taipei's dramatic physical transformation, yet it did not signal the elimination or even the decline of native Taiwanese cuisine. In fact, a countercurrent was evident: the revival of the island's indigenous food traditions. On one of our trips home in the mid–1980s, my wife and I were presented with a visual metaphor for the two cultural traditions that coexist in contemporary Taiwan. On our way from the Chiang Kai-shek International Airport to Taipei (a journey that usually takes more than an hour), the driver made a detour to avoid the traffic jams on the motorway. We drove down a dusty road lined with used-car lots, junkyards, and cargo-storage hangars. Passing a truck depot near the motorway on-ramp, we saw dozens of colorful kiosks sporting neon signs that advertised betel nuts for sale. At the time I was struck by the seeming incongruity of this image: betel nuts, a traditional stimulant, for sale along a modern superhighway? It was not until later that I made a connection between these betel-nut stalls and the appearance of McDonald's. In my mind, they represent the two poles of ethnic consciousness and cultural identity in Taiwan today.

Whereas McDonald's is a reflection of the globalization process that has transformed Taiwan into a modern industrial power and a center of world business, betel-nut chewing is associated with the symbolic revival of a "Taiwanese" rural lifestyle among people who are searching for ways to construct a new national identity. Eating hamburgers is perceived as cosmopolitan, a way to connect with the world beyond Taiwan, while the people (mostly men) who chew betel nuts wish to connect with their Taiwanese roots and think of themselves as down-to-earth Taiwanese natives. The politics of Chinese nationalism (mainlander versus Taiwanese) is also reflected in this culinary confrontation....

McDonald's in Taiwan: The First Decade

Many Taipei residents were already familiar with hamburgers when McDonald's opened its first outlet in 1984. I remember vividly my first hamburger, eaten in a Western-style restaurant located in the Taipei theater district. The year was 1964, and the Chinese menu described what I was eating as a "German Hamburg minced beef cake"; I also had an "ice-cream soda" (a scoop of ice cream in a glass of soda water).

During the early 1980s I noticed that hamburgers served as a meal in themselves were available in tourist hotels, and hamburger-style dishes were sold by indigenous fast food outlets. However, hamburgers (*han bao* or *han bao bao,* literally meaning Hamburg or Hamburg meat dumpling) did not become a household term in Taipei until the arrival of McDonald's. The company first called itself Mai-Dang-Lao in Chinese, a phonetic rendering that captured the English name but confused many early consumers. The three Chinese characters literally mean "wheat-must-labor." In Hong Kong and some other places, the name Mai-Dang-Nu, or "wheat-become-slaves," was also found. Later the Chinese name was standardized as Mai-Dang-Lao, now used in Hong Kong, Beijing, and Chinese communities in the United States.

The McDonald's company had targeted the Taiwan market in 1980, when government restrictions still prohibited foreign enterprises from entering the food or food-processing business. According to company representatives, three factors contributed to McDonald's decision to open restaurants in Taiwan. First, there was still a U.S. military base in Taipei and a sizable American community. Second, there was an increasingly large Taiwanese population who had firsthand experience of the United States. Many Taiwanese had worked or studied in the States and had returned with a family. Third, there was an increasing number of upper-middle-class children with cross-cultural exposure and plenty of spending money. This group of youngsters typically had at least one parent who had been educated in the United States. In addition, the McDonald's survey noted the growth of a Taiwanese middle class who had been exposed to international cultures.

As noted above, McDonald's was the first foreign food enterprise allowed in Taiwan. This was a signal achievement, recognized as such by the local business community. The company was chosen for this honor in part because of its record of high standards in hygiene and production. David Sun served as McDonald's local partner during the first decade of operation. In 1994 Bill Rose, an American with international experience, took over as Chairman of McDonald's Taiwan.

There were 131 McDonald's restaurants in Taiwan by June 30, 1996. In an interview, Chairman Rose predicted that by the end of the century, Taiwan would have up to 500 outlets if the business kept pace with demand. A Taiwanese commercial newspaper quoted the Managing Director of McDonald's as stating that the company's turnover was NT$2 billion (approximately US$80 million) during the first half of 1994. By September 1994, turnover had exceeded US$110 million. Rose maintained that, "In terms of real dollars, among worldwide McDonald's organizations, Taiwan had the highest growth in 1994."…

McDonald's phenomenal success has attracted a great deal of media attention in Taiwan, not all of it favorable. During the 1970s, radical writers and intellectuals had accused the government of exploiting the cheap labor market in Taiwan and conspiring with foreigners, especially Americans and Japanese, to oppress its own people. In the 1980s McDonald's was often equated with the "invasion" of American culture and values. By the 1990s, the growth of indigenous business giants appears to have overshadowed the new foreign companies and the public outlook has changed accordingly. The anti-American sentiments that affect McDonald's operations in Korea are less apparent in Taiwan of the mid-1990s. Nor is McDonald's an unambiguous symbol of cultural imperialism.

On April 29, 1992, bombs exploded in McDonald's restaurants in Taipei and Kaohsiung, killing a policeman and injuring two employees. All 57 outlets then open in Taiwan were closed for the day. The incidents garnered worldwide attention, arousing conjectures that the McDonald's bombings reflected Third World resentment over American domination of the business world. It later became clear, however, that the bombings were the work of extortionists and local racketeers. Such incidents had occurred before, directed at Taiwanese businesses and wealthy families. McDonald's no doubt became a target after media reports publicized the "amazing story" of how in that year McDonald's in Taiwan had become one of the most profitable centers of McDonald's worldwide business. In a sense, therefore, the bombing shows that McDonald's is now treated like any other business in Taiwan, more a target of opportunity than a symbol of oppression.…

McDonald's as Sanctuary: Home Away from Home

In a study of McDonald's in the United States, the anthropologist Conrad Kottak describes how family members go through the rituals of ordering and eating food; it is clear from their actions that Americans feel comfortable and safe in McDonald's. We can almost say that the Golden Arches offer the promise of security and safety—a kind of sanctuary, removed from the uncertainties of life outside. I must admit that I was surprised to find a similar set of attitudes prevailing in Taipei, where many consumers treat McDonald's as a home away from home. Furthermore, in many neighborhoods Taiwanese have transformed the essentially "foreign" setting of McDonald's into a place at once familiar and indigenous.

During the summer and autumn of 1994, my wife and I concentrated our field research on one McDonald's restaurant in a Taipei suburb. It has in recent years become a kind of community center for students, teachers, parents, and grandparents. This particular McDonald's is a place for people of all ages to visit, eat, gossip, and otherwise pass the time. It also became clear to us that the restaurant offered a sanctuary from family tension, a respite from loneliness, and relief from the heat. This establishment has become "localized" in that it plays a key role in the routines of everyday life for many people who live in the neighborhood. The atmosphere here is very different from that which prevailed in Taiwan's first McDonald's restaurant, which was located in an elegant district and frequented primarily by yuppies, foreigners, and thrill-seeking teenagers.

As the same customers frequent the same McDonald's outlet day after day, they become acquainted with one another; they not only exchange greetings, but sometimes tell one another stories about themselves and their family life. The following accounts will give readers the flavor of these encounters....

McDonald's as a Temple Bazaar

When I first walked into the McDonald's restaurant discussed above, I could not believe how crowded it was. It was early afternoon on a weekday during the hot summer of 1994. Every seat was occupied; booths were packed with entire families, representing three generations in many cases. People moved in and out of the restaurant constantly, making the two glass doors resemble a merry-go-round. The lines in front of the counter never cleared. There were people walking in all directions; young children ran around, screaming loudly to show their excitement and pleasure. The noise level rivaled the old fashioned tea-houses I remembered from my younger days when I first visited Hong Kong.... This Taipei McDonald's had the same basic décor as a McDonald's in the United States, right down to the slogans painted on the wall (in English), but the customers were behaving quite differently.

On the following Saturday afternoon when I walked to this restaurant, I noticed a block away that something unusual was happening. A crowd had gathered, motor bikes were parked on the sidewalks nearby, and smoke was rising from a whole array of food vendors' carts clustered just outside the restaurant. Food hawkers sold sausages, roast squid, fishcakes, and traditional herbal drinks (*qingcaocha*) only inches from McDonald's glass windows. This particular restaurant was located on the ground floor of a five-story building, across the street from a primary school (with 6,500 students) and a city park. In front of McDonald's, along the elevated sidewalks, dozens of people stood chatting, eating, waiting, or just watching. The crowds, the constant flow of people, and the assembled vendors all helped to create, in my mind, the atmosphere of a temple festival or rural market. This festive atmosphere was the closest thing I had seen in modern Taipei to the "heat and noise" (Mandarin *renao*, Taiwanese *lauze*) of an old-fashioned temple bazaar.

Thus, it is not the food alone that draws people to McDonald's; rather it is the "action" unfolding in the surrounding neighborhood. Here people can count on seeing friends, hearing gossip, finding snacks (not just hamburgers), and making business contacts. In the past, Taiwanese temples were often flanked by snack stalls and food hawkers; this is still true in some parts of Taiwan, but in the major cities fast food outlets now play the role of social magnet. McDonald's is particularly important in this respect because local management is always careful to place the restaurants in central locations, fronting a plaza or adjoining a large school. It should not be surprising, therefore, that the Golden Arches has more symbolic meaning for many youngsters than does the local temple.

Space and Time: Life in McDonald's

Consumers in the Taipei McDonald's under investigation tend to spend much more time on the premises than do their counterparts in the United States or Hong Kong. As noted earlier, single individuals often treat McDonald's as a place to read, think, or simply kill time—often for over an hour at a sitting.

I observed many older people who ordered a cup of tea and sat, quietly by themselves, for an entire morning. Business people frequently arrived with brief-cases and used the restaurant for meetings lasting for over an hour. Young people treated McDonald's as a meeting place and a convenient setting for courtship. In no instance did I observe McDonald's staff trying to eject any of these customers; nor were efforts made to make lingerers feel uncomfortable. It is clear that from the local perspective, McDonald's is public space, much like a park or library. As long as customers do not disrupt business or disturb others, they are allowed to occupy seats and use facilities.

Young mothers with children came in for breakfast or a snack, and might leave their toddlers in the playroom at the back of the restaurant. On holidays and weekends, this space is used for birthday parties, with a woman employee acting as hostess for the group. Around lunchtime on weekdays, the restaurant was jammed with school children wearing their characteristic uniforms, arriving in groups of three or four, sometimes accompanied by a mother or grandmother. These youngsters chatted and ate like adults, with an air of sophistication and command that would not have been thinkable one generation ago....

Conclusion: Globalization and Localization

The arrival of McDonald's in Taiwan set new standards for operation, competition, and management within the local catering industry. "From raw material, to processing, to distribution, we are upgrading the standards of the food industry in Taiwan. We set the standard, others follow," said Bill Rose. A tour of modern Taipei confirms his view; McDonald's is clearly the leader in the fast food sector, along with Hardee's, Wendy's, and Pizza Hut. But its unquestioned success does not mean that McDonald's has, in any real sense, replaced "traditional" cuisines in Taiwan. The competition the company has engendered may have had the ironic and unintended effect of helping to revitalize indigenous foodways.

Transnational food chains have placed local (and once ubiquitous) street vendors under intense competitive pressure; many food hawkers have disappeared. Meanwhile, local food companies have responded to the challenge by setting up fast food-style restaurants that serve fried rice, steamed dumplings, congee, spring rolls, and turnip cakes (a Taiwanese snack made of rice flour, once sold primarily by hawkers). By the early 1990s, restaurant chains were introducing Taiwanese-style dishes that were reputed to have medicinal effects, such as duck soup with ginger root. These "local" foods appeal to people who do not enjoy Western-style fast foods but do appreciate convenience, cleanliness, and speedy delivery.

One of the hallmarks of the worldwide McDonald's system is attention to sanitation and hygiene. In East Asia, as Watson notes in his Introduction to this volume, McDonald's is commonly regarded as having started a revolution in consumers' awareness of public sanitation. This certainly appears to have been the case during the first few years of the McDonald's franchise in Taiwan. The provision of clean toilets was much discussed in middle-class circles and soon became the general expectation in Taipei. Prior to McDonald's entry into the Taiwanese market, local restaurants did not consider it a high priority to provide customers with clean toilets. Standards in the mid-1990s have improved greatly in major urban areas; however, the "revolution" in consumer expectations has not yet affected smaller cities or towns. It is also clear, from my own observations, that the vigilance of McDonald's own staff may have slipped. Many toilets in Taipei outlets were far from clean (by any standard) during the summer of 1994.

By the mid-1990s McDonald's had become a routine feature of "ordinary" life among the growing number of upper-middle-class families that identify with the cosmopolitan culture emerging in urban Taiwan. An entire generation of young people have grown up eating hamburgers, fries, pizza, fried chicken, and hot dogs—together with Coke, Pepsi, 7-Up, and Sprite. To Taiwanese youth, these products are most assuredly "local."

Meanwhile, other forms of consumption that have no connection to transnational firms are also flourishing in Taiwan. Perhaps the best example is betel-nut chewing, which has if anything increased during the past decade.... A taste for betel nuts has come to be equated with Taiwaneseness—expressed in its most down-to-earth form. It is therefore ironic that the betel nut and the Big Mac have emerged as symbols of "local" culture for different, but not necessarily opposed, categories of consumers in Taiwan. The two symbols represent the need to be at once Taiwanese and cosmopolitan, to be of this place—the island of Taiwan—but also part of the world beyond. To outsiders (and to many insiders as well) the two modes of consumption—hyperlocal versus transnational—appear irreconcilable. But in today's Taiwan, they coexist and, to a surprising extent, reinforce each other. Both the betel nut and the Big Mac are expressions of Taiwan's pursuit of a national identity in a political environment that has never encouraged such concerns.

Until the politics of identity cease to be an urgent matter for local people, food will never be just food in Taiwan. Meanwhile, the choices consumers make will continue to provide us with important clues to the competing symbols that constitute identity in Taiwan.

5. Executive Producer Discusses Why Japanese Animation Captured American Market, 2000

Pokemon, the breed of Japanese video-game and cartoon creatures whose name is short for "Pocket Monsters," is creating a sensation in the United States. The cute characters' first full-length feature *Poketto Monsuta: Myutsu no gyakushu*, released in the United States in November 1999 as *Pokemon: The First Movie— Mewtwo Strikes Back*, topped the U.S. box-office charts—if momentarily—and broke every overseas record for Japanese movies. Until recently anime (animation) and manga (comic book) culture, although considered one of Japan's few cultural industries that can compare with those of the rest of the world, had enjoyed the attention of only a small number of Japanimation buffs. Kubo Masakazu, known as the mastermind of the Pokemon craze, recounts how Pokemon succeeded in breaking this jinx....

Kubo Masakazu, "Why Pokemon Was Successful in America," *Japan Echo,* 27(2, 1 April 2000), 59–62. Translated from "Pokemon' wa naze Beikoku de Seiko shita ka," in *Ronza* (February 2000), 78–86; slightly abridged. (Courtesy of Asahi Shimbun.) Reprinted by permission from the author.

Although the Pokemon television series was popular in the United States, frankly we were not sure how well the movie would do there until just before it was released. We started negotiations on producing and distributing a U.S. version in February 1999, and after talking with nearly every major studio we chose Warner Brothers. The company must have run a survey beforehand and known for sure that the movie would be a hit, since it decided to show *Pokemon: The First Movie* in some 3,000 theaters nationwide.

It was at the time of the advance screening, held at Mann's Chinese Theater in Los Angeles a week before the actual release, that we really got the feeling that the movie was going to be successful. So many people had shown up for the event that the police had to block off part of Hollywood Boulevard. I have never seen such a sight in Japan. That was when I first sensed what I might call a real "tug on the line"—by no means were we full of confidence from the outset.

What greatly encouraged me in the project of exporting this movie to the United States, actually, was a contact I had with Kurosawa Hisao, the president of Kurosawa Production. Recently we at Shogakukan launched a new comic magazine, *Gotta*, using the same media-mix strategy as Corocoro Comics—which carries serials geared for lower elementary school children based on video-game characters but targeting an older age group. I visited Kurosawa to ask for his permission to make a series for the magazine combining elements of the movies Yojimbo and Tsubaki Sanjuro (Sanjuro), both directed by his father, Kurosawa Akira.

The junior Kurosawa immediately agreed. But at the same time, he gave me some words on what we could not do. The gist of what he said was that we should not alter the basic essence; but that aside, he gave us the freedom to do as we liked.

As everyone knows, Kurosawa Akira's films have been imitated in countries all over the world and in many ways, including by George Lucas and Steven Spielberg. These people, moreover, do not even try to hide the fact. Usually in a contract-oriented society like the United States, the moment someone says that you are copying another person's work, you have a lawsuit on your hands. But that does not happen with Kurosawa movies. Not only does it not cause trouble, but the fact that someone imitated the work results in heightening the value of the original Kurosawa film.

What Kurosawa said to me that day was precisely the approach we aimed for in the U.S. production of the Pokemon movie. With Norman Grossfield, who used to work for CBS, as the producer, the U.S. version was thoroughly adapted for the local market. The essential theme—respect for life, whether friend or foe and regardless of species—was not to be tampered with. But other than that, we trusted the U.S. staff, the sole consideration in remaking the movie being how best to make it appeal to American children. This, I think, is the main reason for the movie's success in the United States.

In the U.S. version, the music was all changed and the story was partially altered, and the running time grew slightly longer as a result. The lines, too, were not simply translated but were rewritten to make them more accessible to

American viewers. And about Y70 million went into adding even more punch to the pictures, including the computer graphics....

In talking about cultural barriers, the first thing that comes to my mind is Disney's animated screenplays. Most people are surprised when I say this. Disney animations are wonderful, and they exemplify a highly successful case of American cultural exports, so why do you say that? they ask me. But while Disney videos sell fairly well, there actually have not been many box-office hits in Japan. I believe the reason lies in the problem of localization. When bringing a movie to Japan, Disney does not think about adapting the work for Japanese audiences; it simply translates the lines from one language to another. In other words, pulling off a theater hit requires reworking a film according to the recipient country's sentiments, but Disney does not do that for quality-control reasons.

The same can be said of Japanese cultural exports to the United States. If the exporters are too strict about changing the content when marketing a work in a foreign culture, it is difficult to sell it to the masses....

Once we actually started looking at the requests of Warner Brothers, however, it often gave us headaches. Especially regarding the music, we even checked with them a number of times whether that was really what they wanted. They would reply, "Sure, this is perfect, no problem." As opposed to the Japanese version, which uses a lot of stirring orchestral music, the U.S. version mainly uses dance and rap music, and there were many scenes where we thought, Are they seriously going to play such driving music here?" Some sad scenes would be accompanied by very upbeat sounds, for instance. But when you listen carefully, you find that the lyrics actually match the scene. Considering that the soundtrack has already sold over a million copies on compact disc, I guess that what they did was right for the United States. They replaced the orchestral music with the kind of songs that American teenagers prefer, and they were right on the mark.

The people at Warner also gave us some hassle over the script. According to them, the Japanese original does not distinguish clearly enough between the good guys and the bad. Such a movie would not be successful in a multiethnic country like the United States, they insisted, because the viewers would not know who to identify with and who to cheer on. In other words, the heroes and villains needed to be identified clearly. They accomplished this by revising the various characters' lines.

There is proof that their insight was correct. Pokemon T-shirts have been sold in the United States since before the movie was released, and while in Japan the most popular by far are those with Pikachu, the main Pokemon featured in the series, in the United States those of Ash, the boy hero known in Japanese as Satoshi, sell better. I think this demonstrates how much American children revere heroes....

While we allowed considerable liberty in remaking the film, we made sure the theme and essential features were not changed, as I have already said. The two versions are the same in that they conclude with the message that the lives of both the protagonists and antagonists are equally valuable. This may have been unpopular with some Americans, particularly critics....

On the other hand, we also received positive comments from some who noted that the movie brought back feelings that they had forgotten. It seems that people with children tend to rate it more highly.

One thing that still makes me happy every time I think about it is that the audience applauded and cheered at key points in the story during the Hollywood preview screening, such as after the hero dies and Pikachu's tears bring him back to life, and also when the "good" Pokemon strike back. Just as in Japan, parent and child would rejoice together. I hear that people usually do not react like this at previews in the United States, so this was an indication that our work had been successful.

That is not to say that everything went perfectly well. I did feel the difficulty of exporting a cultural product without losing its Japanese character, and was forcibly reminded of some of the differences between Japan and other countries. Recently it was reported that some Pokemon cards had been taken off store shelves in the United States because a symbol resembling the Nazi swastika was printed on them. This is a sticky issue of international cultural understanding. Even though it is a highly familiar symbol that represents temples on maps for the Japanese, once it begins circulating overseas, it can evoke an entirely different response.

Another Japanese export that has done well in the United States is the Power Rangers TV series. In this series Japanese footage was used only for the fighting scenes between robots, and all scenes containing people were made anew with American characters in place of the Japanese ones. The show did well, and the toys sold very well, too. But I do not know of any other case like Pokemon where the nucleus was preserved so faithfully even while adjusting the cultural content for a foreign audience....

On thoroughly reviewing the work in this way, I think that the characters of Pokemon world are very well made. I would give them all full marks....

6. Turkish Journalists Interview Hip-Hop Star Ceza on Cultural Difference, 2008

Ceza's musical career began with his album *Yeralti* and it continues with *Bomba Plak*. In his words, he has been punishing the system since ten years. But he is not like the American rappers. Just as in his song, Ceza says: "There is a Difference Between [50 Cent] Us."...

Since When Have You Been Ceza?

I first discovered rap in 1980s. Then, as I started to write lyrics I used the name Ceza. Then I founded the group Nefret. We made albums in 1999 named as Yeralti, Meclisi Ala Istanbul in 2000 and then in 2001, Anahtar. Then Medcezir, Rapstar, Yerli Plaka and finally Bomba Plak.

Kubra and Busra Sonmezisik, "There Is a Huge Difference Between 50 Cent and Us," *Yeni Safak-Pazar* (8 February 2009).

What Kind of a Life Lies in Ceza's Past?

My dad was a government employee. We were living in a shanty house in Uskudar. We had a lot of financial problems. I listened to rap in those years. I was always a picky child.

Rap Is the Music of the Suppressed Blacks Who Were Seen as "The Other" in the Society. What is Your Reason?

It all started with the treatment in the school. I was an introvert, silent kid. I couldn't even talk even if I was right. This music enabled me to resist the things that were wrong. I opened myself, and I was able to share my feelings.... With this music, I was able to produce something that belong[s] to me....

Were You Criticized and Scorned?

After I started making this music I was scorned more. Because people were prejudiced. They said this is American music, American culture. Yet, they didn't want to hear what we wanted to tell. I always tried to speak the truths....

There is a Standard School of Rap, Baseball Hat, Baggy Pants, Earring, Cars, Women.... How Much Do You [Participate] in This?

It doesn't have to be like this. I never imitated American culture. I don't always wear baggy pants. There are great differences between us.

What [Are the] Differences?

They use humiliating words for women, they talk about drug dealing, beating and killing men on the streets. They boast about these. Someone who is called 50 Cent comes to Turkey. The song he sings means "I am a hustler." Acun2 invited him to his TV program and whole nation cheered his appearance. I'm embarrassed [by] such things, my faith and manners do not allow these. There are great differences in both my appearance and what I tell. I am a responsible person. I produce rap that fits in my own society, not the kind as you see in the Western world.

ESSAYS

The two essays reflect differing scholarly points of view and theoretical positions on the influence of American cultural commodities on non-U.S. audiences. John Storey, professor of cultural studies and director of the Centre for Media and Cultural Studies, University of Sunderland, England, examines the current scholarly debates about the impact of American culture abroad and questions assumptions about the hegemony of American popular culture, positing that popular culture is not embodied in products directly but made by audiences who buy and incorporate these products into their everyday lives. He argues for a model of glocalization. In contrast Gülriz Buken, professor of history at Bilkent University, Ankara, Turkey, takes the position that American cultural products have invaded and almost completely subsumed or displaced traditional Turkish culture. How do we reconcile these to evaluations of American popular culture and its influence around the world? Is there a definable American popular culture in the twenty-first century or are all cultural commodities hybrids?

Americanization or Glocalization: Studying American Culture's Place in the World

JOHN STOREY

Globalization is the name given to the complex relations which characterize the world in the twenty-first century. It refers to the relentless global flow of capital, commodities, and communications across increasingly porous territorial boundaries. National borders are becoming less and less important as transnational corporations, existing everywhere and nowhere, do business in a world economy.

Globalization also describes what is called "time–space compression" … the way in which the world appears to be shrinking under the impact of new electronic media, like satellite television and the internet, which facilitate the extending of social relations across time and space. Time and space no longer dictate the range of my relationships. Being near or being distant no longer organizes with whom I communicate. Electronic media (fax, telephone, e-mail, the internet) give me access to a world well beyond my "local" community. I may communicate more with people in Taiwan, Australia, Germany, the US, via e-mail, than I do with neighbors who live within 200 meters of my house. In this sense, the global may be more local than the local. Similarly, television news provides me with images and information about events that are taking place thousands of miles away from where I live. Unless I watch the "local" news or read the "local" paper, it is likely that I will be better informed about "global" events than I am about "local" events.

Time–space compression brings into close contact images, meanings, ways of life, cultural practices, which would otherwise have remained separated by time and spaces. This can produce a certain homogeneity of cultural experience or resistance in defense of a previous way of life, or it can bring about a mixing of cultures, producing forms of "hybridization." Nor should hybridization be seen as another name for coping with cultural imperialism; western societies also absorb and adopt cultural practices from elsewhere.

This aspect of globalization may be experienced by simply walking down the "local" high street, where "local" goods are displayed alongside "global" goods gathered in from around the world. We encounter the global in the clothes we wear, the music we listen to, the television programs and films we watch. Perhaps it is most visible in the food we eat. The culinary pluralism of, for example, most British towns and cities, where fish and chips compete with curries, kebabs, chilies, stir fries, pizzas and pasta, is clearly the sign of the globalization of the High Street menu. It is easy to object that we are not being given access to "authentic" cuisine, but authentic or not (and how much cuisine is really authentic?), it is understood as, for example, Indian, East African, Thai, Turkish, Mexican, Chinese, and Italian. It has certainly changed the cultural experience of eating out (and eating in via takeaways), so much so that chicken tikka masala is now regarded as the most popular *British* dish.

John Storey, "Globalization vs. Glocalization" in *Inventing Popular Culture*. Copyright © 2003 by Blackwell Publishing. Reproduced with permission of Blackwell Publishing Ltd.

Globalization also refers to the increasing global mobility of people. It may force workers to travel thousands of miles in search of paid employment. Think of something as everyday as football. Over the last few years the English Premier League has featured professional players from around the world: Algeria, Argentina, Australia, Austria, Belgium, Bermuda, Bosnia, Brazil, Bulgaria, Cameroon, Canada Chile, China, Colombia, Congo, Costa Rica, Croatia, Czech Republic, Denmark, Eire, Ecuador, Estonia, Finland, France, Germany, Greece, Holland, Iceland, Israel, Italy, Jamaica, Japan, Latvia, Liberia, Morocco, Nigeria, Northern Ireland, Norway, Peru, Poland, Portugal, Russia, Scotland, South Africa, Spain, Sweden, Switzerland, Trinidad, Turkey, Ukraine, Uruguay, United States, Venezuela, Wales, and Yugoslavia. Professional footballers who travel the globe in search of paid employment are certainly the glamorous and wealthy end of labor migration but they are, nevertheless, a sign of a global economy....

One dominant view of globalization is to see it as a process of homogenization, that is, as the reduction of the world to an American "global village," where everyone speaks English with an American accent, wears Levi jeans and Wrangler shirts, drinks Coca-Cola, eats at McDonald's, surfs the net on a computer overflowing with Microsoft software, listens to rock or country music, and watches a mixture of MTV, CNN news broadcasts, Hollywood movies, reruns of Dallas, and discusses the prophetically named World Series, while drinking a bottle of Budweiser or Miller and smoking Marlboro cigarettes. In this scenario globalization is the successful global imposition of Americanization, in which the economic success of US capitalism is underpinned by the ideological work that its commodities supposedly do in effectively destroying indigenous cultures and imposing an American way of life on "local" populations.

American sociologist Herbert Schiller (1979), for example, claims that the ability of American transnational companies to successfully unload commodities around the globe is producing an American global capitalist culture. The role of media corporations, he claims, is to make programs which "provide in their imagery and messagery, the beliefs and perspectives that create and reinforce their audiences' attachments to the way things are in the system overall" (30). In terms of the commodities which circulate as global culture there can be little doubt that the majority of these commodities originate from the US: While this establishes a clear case for the economic power of the US, it does not prove that global culture is increasingly American culture.

There are fundamental problems with the argument that the cultural complexity of the world is being reduced to an American global village. For example, globalization as Americanization works with a very discredited account of the flow of influence: it simply assumes that it is possible to inject the dominant globalizing culture into a weaker local culture and in so doing replicate a version of the dominant culture. Now it is one thing to point to the successful ways in which capitalism as a global system has organized the world in terms of the commodity and the market, but it is quite another to then claim that the result is a homogenized world culture. It is only possible to think this if you already think that commodities equal culture in an obvious and straightforward way.

Globalization as Americanization is reductive in the particular sense that economic success is assumed to be the same as cultural imposition: the recognition of the obvious success of US multinationals at placing products in most of the markets of the world is understood as self-evidently ideological success. Success in the economic sphere equals success in the cultural sphere; in this way, the cultural is flattened into the economic, as if it were nothing more that a manifestation of an always reliable effect. Globalization as Americanization assumes that commodities are the same as culture; establish the presence of the former and you can predict the details of the latter. But as John Tomlinson (1999: 83) points out, "if we assume that the sheer global presence of these goods is *in itself* token of a convergence towards a capitalist monoculture, we are probably utilising a rather impoverished concept of culture—one that reduces culture to its material goods." It may be the case that certain commodities are used, made meaningful, and valued in ways which promote capitalism as a way of life, but this is not something which can be established by simply assuming that market penetration is the same as ideological penetration. Such a claim depends on an argument which maintains that commodities have inherent values and meanings which are imposed on passive consumers. But if culture is the making and communication of meanings in contexts, then it is difficult to see how meanings made in one context can survive to be imposed in quite different contexts.

Another significant problem with globalization as Americanization, therefore, is that it operates with an extremely simplified notion of consumption. That is, it is assumed that audiences are the passive consumers of the cultural meanings which supposedly flow directly and unproblematically from the goods they consume. Hegemony is a complex and contradictory process: it is not the same as injecting people with "false consciousness." It is certainly not explained by the adoption of the assumption that "hegemony is prepackaged in Los Angeles, shipped out to the global village, and unwrapped in innocent minds," ... What are we to make of the global success of "hip hop"? Are South African, French, or British rappers the victims of American imperialism, the cultural dupes of a transnational music industry? This seems like a very difficult argument to sustain. A more interesting approach would be to look at how South African, French, or British youth have "appropriated" hip hop to meet their local needs and desires.

This is not to deny that capitalism is working—selling, goods, making profits—but it is to deny that its success is the result of people being too stupid to realize that if they drink Coca-Cola of wear Levi jeans their indigenous culture will be destroyed and they will become Americanized. A better way to understand the processes of globalization is one which takes seriously not just the power of global forces but also those of the local. This is not to deny power but to insist that a politics in which ordinary people are seen as mute and passive victims of a process they can never hope to understand, a politics which denies agency to the vast majority (or at best recognizes only certain activities as signs of agency) is a politics which can exist without causing too much trouble to the prevailing structures of global power.

Now it is certainly true that we can travel around the world while never being too far from signs of American commodities. What is not true, however, is that commodities equal culture. Globalization is not simply the production of a homogenized American global village in which the particular is washed away by the universal. The process is much more contradictory and complex, involving the ebb and flow of both homogenizing and heterogenizing forces and the meeting and mingling of the "local" and "global" in new forms of hybrid cultures, Roland Robertson (1995) uses the term "glocalization" (a term borrowed from Japanese business) to describe globalization as the simultaneous interpenetration of the global and the local. In other words, what is exported always finds itself in the context of what already exists; that is, exports always become imports as they are incorporated into an indigenous culture.

To see globalization as Americanization ... assumes that cultural commodities carry a monolithic message of manipulation, easily imposed on a passive audience, and thus winning them to the world view of the producers. Fortunately, consumption is not that straightforward: the global commodities of the culture industries always encounter people situated in local cultures. Consumption, therefore, is always an encounter between the materiality of a cultural commodity and the cultural formation of a consumer, which takes place in a particular context. Whether the outcome is manipulation or resistance, or a complicated mixture of the two, is a question which cannot be answered in advance of the actual encounter.

Globalization as Americanization also assumes that cultures can be lined up as distinct monolithic entities, hermetically sealed from one another until the fatal moment, of the globalizing injection. Against such a view, Ien Ang ... maintains that

> the global and the local should not be conceived as two distinct, separate and opposing realities, but as complexly articulated, mutually constitutive. Global forces only display their effectivity in particular localities; local realities today can no longer be thought outside of the global sphere of influence, for better or for worse....

Globalization is producing two contradictory effects, sameness and difference—that is, a sense that the world is becoming similar as it shrinks under the pressure of time–space compression, but also that it is characterized by an increasing awareness of difference. What on the surface may look like the export of sameness always involves the global being articulated with the local, and in the process having to compromise with local culture and tradition. Moreover, the processes of sameness may provoke the articulation of difference. Globalization is making the world smaller, generating new forms of cultural hybridity, but also bringing into collision and conflict different ways of making the world mean. While some people may celebrate the opening up of new global routes, other people may resist globalization in the name of local roots. Resistance in the form of a reassertion of the local against the insistent flow of the global can be seen in the increase in religious fundamentalism ... and the re-emergence of nationalism....

Rejecting the claim that globalization is really Americanization in disguise is not the same as saying that globalization is without power relations. The world is made up of many changing centers of power. Therefore, cultural flows can no

longer be understood as moving from the American imperial center to the colonial periphery. Although this means that globalization may lack an obvious
center, it is still marked by what Doreen Massey … calls "power geometry."
Some people travel, some do not, and others travel because they are forced to
move in search of work or away from political repression. Similarly, some people
have the power to make things happen, while others seem to be always those to
whom things happen, their lives continually shaped and structured by the powerful
actions of unknown people from a distant elsewhere….

There is a great temptation to think of the local as authentic and the global as
an inauthentic imposition. I think we should be careful to avoid romanticizing the
local as the organic expression of a more "real" way of life. If we listen carefully it
is possible to hear in the debates on the impact of the global on the local, echoes
of earlier debates about folk culture being destroyed by industrialism and urban-
ism. It is as if the local is an authentic folk culture and the global is a homogenizing mass culture. But it is always more complicated than this: the global is always
pan of the local; the local is what resists the global. As Edward Said … observes,
"all cultures are involved in one another; none is single and pure, all are hybrid,
heterogeneous, extraordinarily differentiated, and unmonolithic."…

Globalization offers the possibility of cultural mixing on a scale never before
known. This can of course produce resistance to difference, but it can also produce the fusing of different cultures and the making of new and exciting forms
of cultural hybridity.

Globalization is perhaps the final unwinding of the idea that for popular cultures to be truly authentic they have to be organically grounded in and bounded
by a locality, the culture of Yorkshire or California. Globalized culture is clearly
undermining what had been a key aspect in intellectual discussions of folk culture, that is, that being embedded in a particular space—the rural—and separated
by both time and space from the development of modern urban and industrial
life guaranteed "authenticity." The movement of people and commodities
around the globe, bringing the global into the local, clearly challenges the idea
that locality can fix the boundaries of a culture. The nomadic nature of global
cultures suggests we are witnessing a shift in how we see cultures, a shift from
culture as "roots" to culture as "routes."

To celebrate hybridity and forget about global power relations would be to
miss even more than those who see globalization as homogenization. Cultural
hybridity is not without its relations of power. As Nederveen Pieterse … observes,
"hybridity raises the question of the *terms* of mixture, the conditions of mixing and
mélange." He argues that the key factor in globalization as hybridity is that territorial
cultures are being gradually overshadowed by translocal cultures (see Table 1)….

Although globalization changes or even destroys the conditions which had
sustained previous modes of culture, it also supplies new resources for new forms
of culture. To see this as a significant cultural development does not mean that
we must first embrace the myth of folk culture and see the local as having previously existed in isolation from other localities, global or otherwise. As we saw in
chapter 1, there are no such cultures: all cultures have appropriated what was at
first "foreign," which was gradually absorbed as "second nature."

T A B L E 1   **Territorial cultures and translocal cultures (from Nederveen Pieterse, 1995: 61).**

Territorial Cultures	Translocal Cultures
Endogenous	Exogenous
Orthogenetic	Heterogenetic
Societies, nations, empires	Diasporas, migrations
Locales, regions	Crossroads, borders, interstices
Community-based	Networks, brokers, strangers
Organic, unitary	Diffusion, heterogeneity
Authenticity	Translation
Inward-looking	Outward-looking
Community linguistics	Contact linguistics
Race	Half-caste, mixed-breed, métis
Ethnicity	New ethnicity
Identity	Identification, new identity

Perhaps there will never be a global culture shared horizontally by all peoples of the globe; local circumstances, including local traditions, may always preclude it. But is that the kind of global culture worth working towards? Better, I think, to build a world culture that is not a monoculture, marked only by hierarchical distinctions, but a world culture which values plurality, in which diversity and difference exist in horizontal relations, equally valued as legitimate ways of living our relation to nature (including our own human nature) and, perhaps more important, ways of living our relations to each other. We would all become cosmopolitans, citizens of the world. And, as John Tomlinson … observes, "The first characteristic of cosmopolitanism … is a keen grasp of a glocalized world as one in which 'there are no others.'" This is not a denial of difference but an insistence on seeing difference within the context of a shared humanity: in effect, to live in both the local and the global and share a "glocalized" culture. This would be a truly popular culture.

An Argument against the Spread of American Popular Culture in Turkey

GÜLRIZ BÜKEN

The intensification of the export of American popular culture was as indispensable facet of America's economic expansionist policy during the post–World War II years. America had ample opportunity to boost its market economy by

Gülriz Büken, "Backlash: An Argument Against the Spread of American Popular Culture in Turkey," in *Here, There, and Everywhere*, eds. Reinhold Wagnleitner and Elaine Tyler May. Copyright © 2000 by University Press of New England, Lebanon, NH. Reprinted with permission pages 242–249.

disseminating consumerism by way of establishing the hegemony of its popular culture over many parts of the globe. This missionary undertaking was facilitated even more by the disintegration of the Soviet Block in the 1980s. In the 1990s, American, consumer sustained cultural hegemony, and the adaptation of the American lifestyle globally, is detectable not only in Western Europe but all over the world....

Eastern Europe, as well as Turkey, also manifest the Americanizing trends creeping across the European continent. As with European societies infected by the lure of American culture, influential segments of Turkish society—especially the upper middle class and the rich—have adopted American consumer habits and cultural values, regardless of the serious social problems and cultural erosion this will inevitably create. The Americanization process, however, should not be interpreted as complete erosion of cultural identity or wholesale alteration of Turkish notions of national identity but as a serious threat to the retainment of cultural heritage by the younger generation. Similarly, modernization should be distinguished from blindfolded imitation of the American way of life and the adopting of cultural values that negate Turkish mores and moral values.

Americanization of Turkey was expedited during Turgut Özal's presidency when private enterprise and consumerism were revitalized by state economic policies; nevertheless, Turkey was introduced to the American way of life as early as the mid-nineteenth-century.... Several writers of the period drew attention to the potential of this encounter for social and cultural transformation; nevertheless, consumer ideology and the American way of life were imported into Turkey with the first Frigidaire.... [E]conomic aid under the Truman Doctrine coupled with admiration for the superpower of the world facilitated the internalization of American popular culture by the nouveau-riche that was created by the devaluation of 1946. During the Democrat Party period new economic policies foregrounding free enterprise and capitalism were adopted. While inflation soared on the one hand, free trade led to the exhaustion of foreign currency reserves on the other; these were spent on importing cars and household items. American-made consumer products, sold in small shops collectively called the American Bazaar, met the needs of the nouveaux-riches, who could afford to emulate the American way of life. Turkish magazines designed after American models ... played an important role in the diffusion of American popular culture.

Nowadays, McDonald's, Pizza Hut, Kentucky Fried Chicken, Open Buffet, Supermarket, Hypermarket, Shopping Centre/Mall, Suburb, Townhouse, Sports Centre, Disneyland are names Turkish people recognize. According to some, these are signs of the annexation of Turkey to the global village; according to others, they are the milestones of American cultural and economic hegemony over the global village. For those surviving in the peripheries of the metropolitan centers or in underdeveloped hinterland Anatolia, they are the symbols of a virtual way of life beyond their reach. Indeed, they are the milieu by which American popular culture is internalized, no matter how it is labeled—Americanization cocacolonization, or mcdonaldization....

Nowadays, American popular culture is lived and consumed most of the time in Turkey, unconsciously and often quite naturally. Its consumption is facilitated by the variety and availability of consumer products the growth of consumer credit, the accessibility of radio and TV to all corners of the country, the increase in the number and services of advertising agencies, and the rapid spread of communications technology. Under the direction of the leading class and the captains of industry, it is generated by the mass media promoting prescribed worldviews and ideologies that come as a package along with commercialism, capitalism and consumerism. However, the hidden cost of embracing American consumerism was that Turkey began to trade in its own authentic cultural traditions and autonomy for a disconcerting homogenization and standardization of its culture.

Mass media was the key force in cultivating the atmosphere in which American popular culture could flourish and exert its pervasive and corrosive effect on Turkish popular culture. American movies projected fake or idealized images of an affluent society, soap operas concentrated on image-making, entertainment programs promoting American values made their way into Turkish homes.… In Turkey, as in the rest of the world, TV has also widened the gap between those who can afford to participate in commercial television's world of affluence and those who may only observe it from the outside.…

Affluent Turkish youth of the 1960s were … exposed to American popular culture when they were children through comic books and movies. Since their upper-middle-class parents could afford to send them to private schools, they learned English, danced to rock 'n' roll, listened to the Platters and Pat Boone, and wore bobby-sox, loafers, and sweaters. In the 1990s the younger members of this cohort, known as the TV generation, have grown up watching *The Muppet Show* or Disney cartoons and consuming the products of Walt Disney industries. Thus, at early ages, they are exposed to the mentality and way of life Disney's cartoons reflect: the reconstructions of world folklore and children's literature highlighted with American images and values. The older ones watch American-made movies or spend hours at home playing computer games such as Mortal Combat. It is not surprising that their constant exposure to American cultural icons has bred more familiarity with Pocahontas, Ninja Turtles, Batman, and Terminator than with Deli Dumrul, the Turkish Robin Hood of Dede Korkut Stories.…

The spread of American popular culture, primarily among the upper-middle-class and peripherally among the lower-class Turkish population, has created in its wake an opposition to the ideology behind it. The resurgence of fundamentalism in recent years which poses a serious threat to secularism, is responsible for creating the rift that has opened up between the Americanized privileged class and the lower middle class and poor. The fundamentalist Welfare Party has increased its power by claiming to be able to procure equality, well-being, and prosperity for all, as opposed to the capitalistic system, which, according to them, caters to the ambitions for success and prosperity of the privileged few. After the demise of the Welfare Party in January 1998, the newly founded Virtue Party continued to preach "just order" over and against "imitative order." The major issue they have brought forward is the headscarf that all the Muslim women should wear in public according to the fundamentals.…

Another significant reaction to American popular culture is the phenomenology of *kitsch* or *arabesque,* which emerged as a socioeconomic side effect of the Americanization process. From 1975 and into the eighties, *arabesque* came to define a lifestyle, generally of people who emigrated from rural areas to urban centers and faced certain—primarily economic—problems of adapting to the new urban bourgeois lifestyle: they could neither conserve their own cultural values and systems in this setting nor melt into the upper-middle class. Caught midway between, they developed their own version of popular culture. Certain kinds of objects, furniture, and costume became the signatures of their new way of life as, unable to afford the accoutrements of the upper middle class, they found refuge and cultural identification in reproductions of them.

This, the internalization of American popular culture by the influential segment of the Turkish population has had some undesirable consequences: the dissolution of moral norms and social values, the disintegration of traditional lifestyles that define cultural identity, the creation of cultural discrepancy between the Americanized and the traditionally oriented groups/classes, and the drastic modification of the nature of Turkish popular culture. Traditional popular culture was a bulwark against the hegemony of pressure groups of wealth and power. It expresses the hopes of the oppressed for a better world and of their struggles to achieve it.... [Now, however] the oppositional nature of Turkish popular culture has been corroded, and that culture has been transformed into an instrument of class hegemony. The United States, self-proclaimed champion of individualism, independence and democracy, has, through its spread of global consumerism, quite undemocratically contributed to the erosion of distinctive national cultures.

FURTHER READING

Allen, Matthew. *Popular Culture, Globalization and Japan* (2008).

Atkins, Taylor E. *Blue Nippon: Authenticating Jazz in Japan* (2001).

Bell, Philip, and Roger Bell. *Implicated: The United States in Australia* (1994).

Borgwardt, Elizabeth. *A New Deal for the World: America's Vision for Human Rights* (2007).

Crothers, Lane. *Globalization and American Popular Culture* (2006).

de Grazia, Victoria. *Irresistible Empire: America's Advance through 20th Century Europe* (2005).

Hammond, Andrew. *Popular Culture in the Arab World* (2007).

Horowitz, Daniel. *The Anxieties of Affluence: Critiques of American Consumer Culture, 1939–1979* (2004).

Iwabuchi, Koichi. *Recentering Globalization: Popular Culture and Japanese Transnationalism* (2002).

Kaplan, Amy, and Donald E. Pease, eds. *Cultures of United States Imperialism* (1993).

Kato, M.T. *From Kung Fu to Hip Hop: Globalization, Revolution, and Popular Culture* (2007).

LaFeber, Walter. *Michael Jordan and the New Global Capitalism* (2002).

McAlister, Melanie. *Epic Encounters: Culture, Media, and U.S. Interests in the Middle East, 1945–2000* (2001).

Mitchell, Toni, ed. *Global Noise: Rap and Hip-Hop Outside the USA* (2001).

Ramet, Sabrina P., and Gordana P. Crnkovic. *Kazaam! Splat! Ploof!: The American Impact on European Popular Culture since 1945* (2003).

Raz, Avaid E. *Riding the Black Ship: Japan and Tokyo Disneyland* (1999).

Rosenberg, Emily S. *Spreading the American Dream: American Economic and Cultural Expansion 1890–1945* (1982).

Tomlinson, John. *Globalization and Culture* (1999).

Wasko, Janet. *Understanding Disney: The Manufacture of Fantasy* (2001).

CHAPTER 14

New Media, New Networks, New Content, New Methodologies

Popular Culture's Past Illuminates Its Future

Are the issues raised by the history of American popular culture still important as new media change the popular culture landscape? The Internet can be described as a simple expansion of radio, television, and film or as an information revolution. When the medium changes, when the delivery system changes, popular culture itself changes. Radio programs built on vaudeville routines but had different technological imperatives; radio characters moved to television and changed as a result. Is the change brought by the Internet a change like the change from radio to television or is it something new? All agree on the importance of technology and technological change to popular culture's future just as it always influenced popular culture forms and content in the past. But some scholars see a continuous series of changes and some see a big break as the digital takes over all forms of popular culture. Because the Internet is so new, scientists and other social scientists join historians in examining its impact and importance.

To help scientists share information worldwide, Tim Berners-Lee of the European Organization for Nuclear Research (abbreviated as CERN, in French) and his colleagues invented the World Wide Web in 1989. Working collaboratively, scientists around the world contributed to the system, which still operates on an open standard, free for anyone to use. Not until the first widely available browser (Mosaic) was developed early in 1993, however, did the public find a way to go "online." As the CERN website explains, "1994 really was the 'Year of the Web'. The world's First International World Wide Web conference was held at CERN in May. It was attended by 400 users and developers, and was hailed as the 'Woodstock of the Web'.... By the end of 1994, the Web had 10,000 servers, of which 2,000 were commercial, and 10 million users.

Traffic was equivalent to shipping the entire collected works of Shakespeare every second." The first websites resembled the first radio stations—no one knew how to make money from them. The speed of adoption for the World Wide Web (10 million users in its first year) was repeated as e-commerce (despite the fact that the web had been developed by and for nonprofits) and social networking became important extensions of the original web.

Proponents argue that social networking turns passive consumers into active participants, helping unlock the political potential of popular culture. Much has been written about how Twitter and YouTube have strengthened political opposition and enabled organizing under oppressive regimes. At the same time, scholars, parents, and teachers worry about the impact on young people of computer games and Facebook, much as they did about movies in 1920 or comic books in 1950. The formation of personal and group identities, often reinforced through, or in opposition to, popular culture continue to play an important role in new media as Facebook groups, blogs, and podcasts both bring disparate groups together and separate groups based on race, gender, and political ideology. Critics worry that the web is not a public space where you might bump into people who don't necessarily share your views, but rather a set of self-identified and reinforcing small groups within which you can avoid anyone with different ideas. On the other hand, the globalized nature of popular culture seems to be reinforced when people can read instantly not only about what is happening around the world, but how ordinary people feel about the events.

Historians of twenty-first century popular culture face rapid change in their subjects, their way of working, and the texts available. For one quick example: blogs might be a great way to understand how ordinary people think, particularly about their on-line lives. But, while historians of the twentieth century often had to sample a few of the many documents available, on-line writing has become overwhelming. How can you write a history of blogging when the number of blogs available (in 2006, one guess was 50 million) far exceeds any historian's ability to look at even a small percentage? How can we write the history of the twenty-first century when all information is available all the time? Or is it? In 1996, the Internet Archive (a non-profit, on-line group) first began collecting old websites (and other born digital and digitized texts) to ensure that they would be available to future historians. One of their slogans is: "Archiving the Internet for Future Generations: Collect it, Manage it, Search it, Archive it." Historians may need new tools to help organize and analyze the huge amounts of information available on-line.

Faced with new technologies with such potent possibilities, scholars have joined fiction writers in thinking about what the future holds. Will commercialization of the Internet and of social networking affect what's possible to do or even to imagine? Are the new possibilities liberating or repressive? In their important 2006 work, Digital History, Roy Rosensweig and Dan Cohen divided historians, and others who write about new media, into three groups: cyber-enthusiasts, techno-skeptics and techno realists, in language that very much mirrors the cultural "pessimists" or "optimists" identified in Chapter 1. As you read the documents and essays in this chapter, it's a good time to think about your own views. Are you optimistic or pessimistic about the future of popular culture? Are you a skeptic, an enthusiast, or a realist about what new technologies bring to our lives and leisure?

DOCUMENTS

The documents in this section start with a look to the future, written just as the World Wide Web began. Document 1, by science fiction and cyber-punk novelist Neal Stephenson, appeared in *Wired* magazine (founded in 1993, just a year before this short story) and considers how entertainment, advertising, and the Internet could combine to control audience behavior, as well as how some consumers might rebel against such control. Futurist literatures, including science fiction, have long been part of popular culture, as both explanations and critiques, because so much of popular culture depends on technology. Karen Valby, in an article for a popular weekly magazine, points out one aspect of the "digital divide" and thus takes a different point of view in Document 2. In August, 2006, residents of Utopia, Texas, could only recently access a larger range of films, music, and books because of the Internet, and they were divided over whether more popular culture was a good thing. In Document 3, long-time *Newsweek* technology reporter, Steven Levy, considers why the iPod was so successful and ties its introduction and triumph to the attacks of September 11, 2001. Finally, in Documents 4 and 5, a musician with a PhD from the School of Oriental and African Studies at London University, living in London, writes (in March and May of 2009) for her hometown newspaper the *Singapore Straits Times* about her use of Facebook and why she loves and hates it. Shzr Ee Tan, a scholar of the Chinese diaspora, comments as both an analyst of social networking and as a global citizen, able as an intellectual to move among world capitals. How would the essays be different if written by a worker in an Asian sweat shop making the iPods and the computers on which scholars do their work?

1. Neal Stephenson, Science Fiction Writer, Envisions a Negative Future for Popular Culture, 1994

Yeah, I know it's boring of me to send you plain old Text like this, and I hope you don't just blow this message off without reading it.

But what can I say, I was an English major. On video, I come off like a stunned bystander. I'm just a Text kind of guy. I'm gambling that you'll think it's quaint or something. So let me just tell you the whole sorry tale, starting from the point where I think I went wrong.

I'd be blowing brown smoke if I said I wasn't nervous when they shoved in the needles, taped on the trodes, thrust my head into the Big Cold Magnet, and opened a channel direct from the Spew to my immortal soul. Of course they didn't call it the Spew, and neither did I—I wanted the job, after all. But how could I not call it that, with its Feeds multifarious as the glistening strands cascading sunnily from the supple scalps of the models in the dandruff shampoo ads.

I mention that image because it was the first thing I saw when they turned the Spew on, and I wasn't even ready. Not that anyone could ever *get ready* for the dreaded Polysurf Exam. The proctors came for me when *they* were ready, must have got my address off that job app yellowing in their infinite files, yanked me straight out of a fuzzy gray hangover dream with a really wandering story arc, the kind of dream concussion victims must have in the back of the ambulance. I'd been doing shots of vodka in the living room the night before, decided not to take a chance on the stairs, turned slowly into a mummy while I lay comatose on our living-room couch—the First Couch Ever Built, a Couch upholstered in avocado Orlon that had absorbed so much tar, nicotine, and body cheese over the centuries that now the centers of the cushions had developed the black sheen of virgin Naugahyde. When they buzzed me awake, my joints would not move nor my eyes open: I had to bolt four consecutive 32-ounce glasses of tap water to reconstitute my freeze-dried plasma.

Half an hour later I'm in Television City. A million stories below, floes of gray-yellow ice, like broken teeth, grind away at each other just below the surface of the Hudson. I've signed all the releases and they're lowering the Squid helmet over me, and without any warning BAM the Spew comes on and the first thing I see is this model chick shaking her head in ultra-slow-mo, her lovely hairs gleaming ... and in voice-over she's talking about how her dandruff problem is just a nasty, embarrassing memory of adolescence now along with pimples and (if I may just fill in the blanks) screwing skanky guys who'll never have a salaried job. And I think she's cute and everything but it occurs to me that this is really kind of sick—I mean, this chick has *admitted* to a history of shedding *blizzards* every time she moved her head, and here she is *getting down* under eight megawatts of color-corrected halogen light, and I just *know* I'm supposed to be thinking about *how much head chaff* would be sifting down in her personal space right now if she hadn't ditched her old hair care product lineup in favor of—

Click. Course, it never really clicks anymore, no one has used mechanical switches since like the '50s, but some Spew terminals emit a synthesized click— they wired up a 1955 Sylvania in a digital sound lab somewhere and had some old gomer in a tank-top stagger up to it and change back and forth between Channel 4 and Channel 5 a few times, paid him off and fired him, then compressed the sound and inseminated it into the terminals' fundamental ROMs so that we'd get that reassuring *click* when we jumped from one Feed to another. Which is what happens now; except I haven't touched a remote, don't even *have* a remote, that being the whole point of the Polysurf. Now it's some fucker picking a banjo, *ouch* it is an actual *Hee Haw* rerun, digitally remastered, frozen in pure binary until the collapse of the Universe.

Click. And I resist the impulse to say, "Wait a minute. *Hee Haw* is my favorite show."

Well, I have lots of favorite shows. But me and my housemates, we're always watching *Hee Haw.* But all I get is two or three twangs of the banjo and a glimpse of the eerily friendly grin of the banjo picker and then *click* it's a '77 Buick LeSabre smashing through a guardrail in SoCal and bursting into a fireball *before it has even touched the ground,* which is one of my favorite things about TV. Watch that for a while and just as I am settling into a nice Spew daze, it's a rap video....

And so it goes. Twenty clicks into the test I've left my fear behind, I'm Polysurfing like some incarnate sofa god, my attention plays like a space laser across the Spew's numberless Feeds, each Feed a torrent, all of them plexed together across the panascopic bandwidth of the optical fiber as if the contents of every Edge City in Greater America have been rammed into the maw of a giant pasta machine and extruded as endless, countless strands of polychrome angel hair. Within an hour or so I've settled into a pattern without even knowing it. I'm surfing among 20 or so different Feeds. My subconscious mind is like a retarded homunculus sacked out on the couch of my reptilian brain, his thumb wandering crazily around the keypad of the world's largest remote control. It looks like chaos, even to me, but to the proctors, watching all my polygraph traces superimposed on the video feed, tracking my blood pressure and pupil dilation, there is a strange attractor somewhere down there, and if it's the right one....

"Congratulations," the proctor says, and I realize the chilly mind-sucking apparatus has been retracted into the ceiling. I'm still fixated on the Spew. Bringing me back to reality: the nurse chick ripping off the handy disposable self-stick electrodes, bristling with my body hair.

So, a week later I'm still wondering how I got this job: patrolman on the information highway. We don't call it that, of course, the job title is Profile Auditor 1. But if the Spew is a highway, imagine a hard-jawed, close-shaven buck lurking in the shade of an overpass, your license plate reflected in the quicksilver pools of his shades as you whoosh past. Key difference: we never bust anyone, we just like to watch.

We sit in Television City cubicles, VR rigs strapped to our skulls, grokking people's Profiles in n-dimensional DemoTainment Space, where demographics, entertainment, consumption habits, and credit history all intersect to define a weird imaginary universe that is every bit as twisted and convoluted as those balloon animals that so eerily squelch and shudder from the hands of feckless loitering clowns in the touristy districts of our great cities. Takes killer spatial relations not to get lost. We turn our heads, and the Demosphere moves around us; we point at something of interest—the distinct galactic cluster formed by some schmo's Profile—and we fly toward it, warp speed. Hell, we fly right through the middle of it, we do barrel rolls through said schmo's annual mortgage interest statements and gambol in his urinalysis records....

Through the Demosphere we fly, we men of the Database Maintenance Division, and although the Demosphere belongs to General Communications Inc., it is the schmos of the world who make it—every time a schmo surfs to a different channel, the Demosphere notes that he is bored with program A and more interested, at the moment, in program B. When a schmo's paycheck is delivered over the I-way, the number on the bottom line is plotted in his Profile, and if that schmo got it by telecommuting we know about that too—the length of his coffee breaks and the size of his bladder are an open book to us. When a schmo buys something on the I-way it goes into his Profile, and if it happens to be something that he recently saw advertised there, we call that interesting, and when he uses the I-way to phone his friends and family, we Profile Auditors can navigate his social web out to a gazillion fractal iterations, the friends of his friends of his friends of his friends, what they buy and what they watch and if there's a correlation....

2. Karen Valley, *Entertainment Weekly* Writer, Describes Technological Changes in Popular Culture, 2006

There was a time when if you wanted to watch television in Utopia, a no-stoplight ranching community nestled in a green swath of Texas Hill Country 80 miles west of San Antonio, you'd better have liked what was playing on CBS or NBC. They were the only two channels that people here could get, unless the wind in the canyon wasn't blowing, and then you might twist the rabbit ears just right and luck into ABC. There was one honky-tonk radio station, there were no book or music stores, and the closest movie theater was a 50-minute drive to the Forum 4 in Uvalde. Diane Causey, the elegant manager of the antiques store in Utopia, spoke somewhat wistfully of her hometown's former cocoon from the outside world. "If we didn't see it on the old black-and-white TV or hear about it on the San Antonio radio station, we didn't know it existed," she said. Because Utopia has no mayor or local government, there is no one to record the official population, but locals guess that around 1,000 residents call the town home.... Rock & roll fans still can't buy a CD in Utopia, or a drink for that matter, and you can't go see a movie or a reading or a pop band. And if you want to rent a DVD, you're still stuck picking from a shelf of new releases and old Westerns at the gas station. But in the last few years, satellite TV and the Internet have swept through Utopia and remote small towns like it, and while crystal meth has yet to twist its grip around this middle American town, the kids are hooked on the thrilling instant gratification of MTV and MySpace.

There are 190 students, from prekindergarten through 12th grade, who go to the Utopia School, and they are the first generation of residents raised with any broad access to pop culture. Some of them casually enjoy it, the way someone in New York City might appreciate a dishwasher or a seat on the subway, and some of them are so nourished and sustained by entertainment that burning through half a tank of gas to go see a movie is a necessary investment. Not that that makes much sense to the folks in town who get driving so far to go to a Wal-Mart or a Spurs game or a stock show, but a movie?? The older generations can understand the appeal of *Lost* or *The Tonight Show* (though some complain of Jay Leno's too-frequent cracks at President Bush), but they still view Hollywood as a potential predator on their traditions and values.

So what happens when pop culture, a loud and messy and demanding new neighbor if ever there was one, moves into a town without entertainment? A sign in the middle of Utopia, next to the senior activity center and the Wash Tub laundromat, is both touchingly straightforward and vaguely threatening:

"Welcome to Utopia
A Paradise
Let's Keep It Nice"

Whoever put up that sign—an earnest plea, an impossible ideal—must yearn for the simpler days of his fuzzy black-and-white TV.

When I showed up in Utopia this summer, one of the first people to welcome me to town was 14-year-old Lexi Pittman.... Lexi and her half sister Ashley had been living with their grandparents, who run the four-room Sabinal River Lodge. After I checked in, Lexi, who's 4'9" and wore her MP3 player roped around the neck of her Abercrombie T-shirt, followed me into my room and proceeded to deliver a prim course on appropriate celebrity behavior. Smoothing her pretty brown hair in the bathroom mirror, she admonished young Hollywood stars like Lindsay Lohan, "I don't like her as much as I used to. Did you see what she was wearing in her 'Rumors' video? Ahem, and she says she doesn't want to be talked about!" Lexi sighed wearily. "These girls pretty much all turn out the same, don't they?"...

Nobody locks their trucks in town. Outside the Lost Maples Café, not only were the vehicles all unlocked, the keys dangling from the ignitions, but one pickup was still running while its owner calmly finished up his coffee inside....

... [A]fter the breakfast rush, Tacy Redden got on the phone to place her meat order—five T-bones, four chop sirloins, one longhorn, six rib eyes—before sitting down to explain her own beef with pop culture. Redden, 49, in jean capri pants and a denim blouse, was married and had her first of three children by the time she was 18. "I didn't have a big dream to go off," she said. "Now when kids get to high school, all they want to do is get the hell out of here.... Things were different when I was younger. When we were little—this was in the '60s—well, at night you ate supper and then we got in the old pickup and we drove over to Aunt Erma's house or Aunt Annie's and you went and visited for an hour and then you went home and went to bed. We didn't watch TV, because you couldn't hardly get it. Now you can get any channel you want, and it's changed that type of gathering for the worse. Fellowship is probably the main thing a small community has over a big city."...

"Our pop culture has gotten us away from our basic nature stuff," she said worriedly. "Everybody should raise an animal, even just a chicken, or grow a squash or a tomato plant. There's no cooking classes anymore. Kids don't know how to clean. If the commode's running, they don't know how to fix it! They don't know what a pilot light is. And it used to be that there were dances everywhere, country dances or the waltzes or the chicken dance or just the two-step. And last year, the [high school] seniors realized they couldn't dance. Well, you're going to get married and you don't know how to dance?... I don't know, maybe the dances didn't change enough to fit their needs and they got tired of the country stuff. Maybe there's no room for the two-step when you have pop culture at your fingertips."

At this point, even her own mother was a slave to the TV. "Oprah and Martha," Redden said with an exasperated laugh. "When they put Martha in jail, she about had a stroke! She was so upset that she put all of her savings in Martha's stock."

At the Utopia general store, like at any other supermarket in the country, there was a rack of magazines by the cashier. And here, alongside the issues of *Texas Horse* and *Outdoor Life,* there were tabloids like *The National Enquirer* and *In Touch.* On the agenda this week were whether Brad Pitt is really Angelina

Jolie's baby's father and whether Camilla has demanded a divorce from Prince Charles. Sixteen-year-old Kelli Rhodes, who was working her first summer job as the store's cashier, said customers are unmoved by the splatter of celebrities' private lives, and the screeching stories of their misery and upheaval are rarely purchased. "I may love Johnny Depp and Ewan McGregor, but I don't care what their love lives are like," she later e-mailed.

Kelli, whose homemaker mother is white and father, a registered nurse in Uvalde, is black, is one of two African-American kids at school....

In her *Simpsons* T-shirt, Xbox rubber bracelet, and Yoda watch, Kelli looked like the type of girl who was really going to love college, where she might find a group of fellow Quentin Tarantino and vampire-movie fans. While she's not much interested in hunting or the rodeo or church camp, she's nuts for the IFC network and graphic novels like Garth Ennis' *Preacher* (though if she wants to read the series' next installment, she'll have to make the drive into San Antonio to the nearest comic-book store)....

Kelli was the only person in Utopia who admitted to being a fan of the movie *Brokeback Mountain*. ("Just don't tell my mother," she said.) She and her best friend Perla fell hard for the movie after they rented it from Blockbuster Online, and though she runs the trailer on her Myspace page, she doesn't push the film on folks around town. When I asked one high schooler if any of his classmates in Utopia had ever come out, he looked surprised by such a naive question before responding no. "You'd get the crap beat out of you if you did," he said softly, sounding both amused and resigned.... "I suppose I'm a bit of a hypocrite for loving this movie and not supporting it like I should," admitted Kelli. "But around here, it's just seen as a joke, and I understand, because most people come from a strong Christian faith. They just don't get that nowadays being gay has almost become a part of pop culture. *Will & Grace, Queer Eye,* the gay movies—it's just not as big of a deal with kids today."

During Kelli's shift, her friend Grant Potter stopped into the store to buy some water softener. Grant, who scored a 1580 on his SATs, is off to Yale in the fall to study astronomy; he is the first Utopia student to get accepted to an Ivy League school. An affable 18-year-old wearing a driving cap and a Save Darfur bracelet, Grant loves Kelly Clarkson, the *Lord of the Rings* movies, Roger Ebert, and the TV shows *Battlestar Galactica* and *Scrubs*.... When I asked Kelli and Grant if rising gas prices ever kept them home from the movies, another old cowboy in line laughed. "It's entertainment!" he teased. "They don't care how much gas costs. There's nothing to do here."

Actually, a lot of kids in Utopia seemed perfectly happy spending their nights cruising a dirt road or parking at the bank or the Church of Christ with a case of Keystone Light. Then there were people like Kelli and Grant and 20-year-old Colter Padgett who make the trip each weekend into Uvalde to go see a movie.... The point is just getting out of town for a few hours, so he tries to see everything. Some of his favorite movies are *Eternal Sunshine of the Spotless Mind, Lost in Translation, Super Size Me,* and, though he had yet to see it, *Snakes on a Plane*. "Everyone on the Internet is predicting how awesomely bad it's going to be!"...

"There's no culture in Utopia," he said. "It's country music, country dances, country everything. That gets real old real fast, especially if you hate country like me."…

… But for all his complaints about life in a small town, he also could appreciate its reservoirs of warmth and compassion. After his mother was diagnosed with brain cancer, the women of Utopia took turns driving her the 80 miles each way to San Antonio for radiation treatments five times a week. Last year, when Grant Potter was accepted to summer classes at Harvard, his mother was short on the tuition fees. So the town put together an elaborate bake sale and raised the $2,000 he needed. And at the Utopia prom last year, the students settled on a "Hollywood" theme and everybody threw themselves into creating the set of a movie premiere. There were sequined letters of the famous Hollywood sign taped to the ground and spindly boas for the girls and sunglasses for the boys as they emerged from the limousines. On the sidelines, the parents posed as paparazzi, and one particularly game mother camped out at the top of the carpet so that she could ask the women about their dresses. Here the generations of Utopia gathered in celebration, around a red carpet duct-taped to the hot street, embracing the fluffiest fantasy of pop culture with smiles on their faces.…

During lunch, talk turned to the weather and gas prices and, briefly, to the war and the more than one dozen young men and women of Utopia fighting overseas.…

… Utopia lost its first of those kids when 23-year-old Army Sgt. Jeffery Wiekamp's helicopter crashed in Afghanistan.…

After news of Jeffery's death hit town, people immediately rallied around the family, taking meals over to the house, cleaning out their garages and camper trailers so … out-of-town relatives would have a comfortable place to sleep. Two long weeks later, Wiekamp's body was returned home. When the hearse rolled down Highway 187 into Utopia, every child in school, from pre-K through the 12th grade, those whose idea of paradise is small-town Texas and those who prefer the worlds revealed in a punk rock song or a darkened movie theater, stood silently on the sides of the road holding up American flags. It's such an affecting image, of grief and solidarity and respect, that it almost seemed like a scene from a Hollywood movie. Would that it had been.

3. *Newsweek* Writer Steven Levy Explains the Appeal of the iPod, 2006

Just what is it about the iPod?

It weighs 6.4 ounces and consists of a few layers of circuit boards and electronic components, covered by a skin of white polycarbonate and stainless steel. It's slightly smaller than a deck of cards. On the front is a screen smaller than a Post-it note, perched over a flattened wheel. It doesn't have an on-off switch. If

Steven Levy, *The Perfect Thing: How the iPod Shuffles Commerce, Culture, and Coolness* (London: Erbury, 2000). Copyright © Steven Levy. Reprinted by permission of The Random House Group Ltd. and SLL/Sterling Lord Literistic, Inc.

you didn't know what it was, you might guess that it was a sleek, high-priced thermostat, meant to control temperature in a high-priced condominium. A very sexy detached thermostat that feels very good when you palm it. But you almost certainly *do* know what it is—a portable digital music player that holds an entire library of tunes—because it is the most familiar, and certainly the most desirable, new object of the twenty-first century.

You could even make the case that it *is* the twenty-first century.

It arrived in October 2001, bringing the promise of pleasure to a world in transformation from its comforting analog roots to a disruptive digital future. The world did not fete it with parades. In October 2001, the world had its own problems. The newcomer was welcomed by fans of Apple Computer, the company that makes the iPod, and there was a generalized feeling that a new twist in gadgetry had arrived. There were some glowing reviews in newspapers and magazines. But ... *this?* No one expected *this.*

Here's what *this* is. The triumph of the iPod is such that the word "success" falls far short of describing it. Its massive sales don't begin to tell the story.... But none of the wizards at Apple headquarters in Cupertino, California, could know that the iPod would become the most important product in Apple's history since 1984's trailblazing Mac computer (if not more important). No one thought that within four years it would change Apple from a computer company to a consumer electronics giant deriving almost 60 percent of its income from music-related business. No one thought the iPod would change the music business, not only the means of distribution but even the strategies people would use to buy songs. No one envisioned subway cars and airplane cabins and street corners and school lounges and fitness centers where vast swathes of humanity would separate themselves from the bonds of reality via the White Earbud Express. No one expected that there would be magazine covers and front-page newspaper stories proclaiming this an "iPod Nation." No one predicted that listening to the iPod would dethrone quaffing beer as the most popular activity for undergraduate college students. And certainly no one thought that the name of this tiny computer *cum* music player would become an appellation to describe an entire generation or a metaphor evoking any number of meanings: the future, great design, short attention span, or just plain coolness.

But that's what happened....

... [Y]ou do not have to own an iPod, or even see one, to fall within its spell. The iPod is a pebble with tsunami-sized cultural ripples.

It changed the high-tech industry, particularly Apple. By the end of 2005, Apple Computer had sold more than 42 million iPods, at prices ranging from $99 to $599 (most sold in the middle range). What's more, at that time the iPod had about 75 percent market share of the entire category of digital music players. Its online digital music emporium, the iTunes Music Store, has sold more than a billion songs at 99 cents each, representing about 85 percent of all legal paid downloads, a market that barely existed before Steve Jobs herded the nasty cats running record labels and got them to agree to his way of selling music. The success of the iPod also created a "halo effect" that boosted the sales of Macintosh computers. Since the age of iPod began, Apple's stock price has increased more than 700 percent....

It's the symbol of media's future, where the gates of access are thrown open, the reach of artists goes deeper, and consumers don't just consume—they choose songs, videos, and even news their way. Digital technology gathers, shreds, and empowers, all at once. Mix, mash, rip, burn, plunder, and discover: these are the things that the digital world can do much more easily than before—or for the first time. The iPod, and the download dollar-store that accompanies it, makes sense of those things without making our brains hurt.

It's a six-ounce entanglement of cultural signifiers, evoking many things to many people. Headline writers and cultural critics talk of an "iPod Generation." This can mean a number of things—sometimes its just a shorthand way of saying "young people"—but generally it's used to depict a mind-set that demands choice and the means to scroll through ideas and ideologies as easily as a finger circles the wheel on the iconic front panel of an iPod. "It seems to me that a lot of younger listeners think the way the iPod thinks," wrote Alex Ross in *The New Yorker*. "They are no longer so invested in a single way of seeing the world."...

The title of this book, you may have noticed, is *The Perfect Thing*. The iPod is not perfect, of course.... But I use the word "perfect" for two reasons. The first is that the iPod's astounding success has come from a seemingly uncanny alignment of technology, design, culture, and media that has thrust it into the center of just about every controversy in the digital age. In each area, the iPod has made a difference. So don't think "perfect" as in flawless—more in the spirit of a perfect storm (in a good way, of course).

The second reason is that just about anyone who owns an iPod will at one point—usually when a favorite tune appears spontaneously and the music throbs through the earbuds, making a dull day suddenly come alive—say or think the following: "Perfect."

How did all this happen?

I had gotten the Apple letter the week before, an invitation to another one of Steve Jobs's carefully choreographed, exquisitely casual shows. It was to be held at Apple's headquarters in Cupertino on October 23, 2001. The most interesting thing about the invitation was the teasing addendum: "Hint: It's not a Mac." Usually, I would have hopped on the plane to see the latest wrinkle in the consistently fascinating saga of Jobs....

Those days I wasn't traveling. It was, after all, little more than a month after 9/11, and I, like just about everyone else in New York City, was depressed. My eleven-year-old son had seen the collapse of the Trade Center towers from the roof of his school before my wife rushed to pick him up. And now the gap where the towers had stood loomed larger than the towers ever had....

By the time of Apple's iPod press conference in October, the plane crashes had been followed by a wave of anthrax attacks. We even had a scare at *Newsweek;* someone came down with flu symptoms and recalled having opened a strange letter the week before....

Although I did not fly across the country for the Apple announcement, I did follow the news carefully....

Over the next few days, I began to play with the iPod Apple had sent me. I loaded a lot of my music into my black PowerBook G3.... The sound was excellent, though the white earbuds didn't fit me too well.... I must have spent the better part of a night pulling CDs from my shelves and loading songs. I walked everywhere with my iPod—the subway, the streets, down the halls of *Newsweek* to get my mail.

Then I discovered shuffle.

There were lots of different ways to sequence music on the iPod....

But the best way, I discovered, was to find the setting that said "shuffle," click through the menus till you got to a list of all your songs, pick a starting place, and go. From that point, your whole collection would resequence itself in glorious chaos. It was like my own private radio station that played only songs that I liked—after all, I had put them there.

I also began to cultivate a nice relationship with the actual device. It felt very good to hold. Spinning my thumb on the scroll wheel was satisfying. The smooth silvery back felt so sensual that it was almost a crime against nature....

Something odd began to happen. As the days passed and I bonded with my iPod, my spirits lifted somewhat. Maybe it was just a recovery process that would have happened anyway, but it seemed hastened by the daily delights of the music that appeared on my iPod.... I wasn't exactly *forgetting* about 9/11, but I was getting excited—once more—about technology and its power to transform our world.

This meant a lot. I am a technology writer. What had compelled me in the first place to devote my career to chronicling the digital revolution was my belief that this was the biggest story of our time. I have often expressed the thought, to the point of boredom to those close to me, that hundreds of years from now, if humanity survives its penchant for self-destruction, people will look back at these decades and wonder what it was like at the time everything changed. Now, living in a city where an awful smell still wafted uptown into my apartment window from the World Trade Center site, that condition about survival was suddenly looming larger....

Now I wondered. How could you devote your energies to documenting the Internet, cool gadgets, and the future of music when all this darkness was afoot? Interrupting those bleak questions came iPod, and in those days and the years since its introduction—despite not much good happening in the gloabal arena—I regained my confidence that technology is still the hallmark of our era.

4. Columnist Shzr Ee Tan Describes Why She Leaves Facebook, 2009

On the first day of the Year of the Ox, I unplugged myself from that delightfully evil time-sucker of a life-support system: Facebook....

Two days before my self-exile, I gave about 300 "friends" advance warning in the form of a status update.

Shzr Ee Tan, "Facebook, about-face: I've turned my back on the addictive website and its too real, too close for comfort world," *The Straits Times* (Singapore), (5 March 2009). The Straits Times © Singapore Press Holdings Ltd. Reprinted with permission.

Within seconds, the words, in screaming capitals "WHY, WHY?" railed themselves against my virtual wall. I felt obliged to reply there and then.

"A social experiment"—I scrawled back.

But then came the conspiracy theories, as I discovered through old-school e-mail messages over the next few days....

Did something nasty happen to me? Why was I not "friends" with X anymore? Had I sold out into the real world?

Hurt, confused and congratulatory texts beeped into my phone from various parts of the world.

I was pleasantly bemused: Perhaps these "friends", who had otherwise just been silent, show-off statistics all these months, were genuinely concerned after all.

The influx made me wonder about the gimmicky nature of the stunt I had pulled off.

All right, I admit "social experimentation" was not the only factor for my going cold turkey.

True, I had pulled the Facebook plug out of personal and academic curiosity as to what would change in my life as a result, and how other channels of (more human?) communication, such as receiving real chocolates, poking a real, random person in the street or developing a real obsessive-compulsive disorder, might actually manifest themselves.

But of course, what happened was I had become addicted.

"Welcome to the rest of your life"—a friend warned when I signed up to the social-networking site 18 months ago. He was not too wrong.

I became a status-update freak. I could not start each day without playing my Scrabulous moves in all seven of my simultaneously losing games.

I became an "Apps" and "Quiz" queen until it dawned on me that "friends", including deceptively innocent colleagues, could discover my secret serial-killer identity and—gasp—castigate me for joining a cause for the protection of Swedish underwear models.

So, of course I had to fiddle with the privacy settings to rectify all this....

I read and re-read the site's controversial terms-of-service agreement—currently the hot debate among members of this newly formed republic intent on fighting for privacy rights—and was furious for a while.

I shuddered and empathised with a "friend" who had to "fade" out his old Facebook existence after breaking up with his girlfriend and not knowing how to advertise the matter delicately online.

In the end, he was forced to create a completely new, parallel identity and "re-make" all his friends and bachelor's existence.

As recent reports of a murder sparked off by a Facebook break-up announcement in the United States came to light, I began thinking his cowardly act may not have been such a bad idea after all.

So let us get this straight once and for all: Facebook is not just a virtual world.

True, you could say it is a "simulation", giving us constantly changing pointillist views of the big, wide world constructed according to our chosen "friends".

But even the virtual drop-kicks, knee-jerk reactions to random posts and electronic signatures you happily dash off on Gaza petitions require you to push your fingertips against computer keyboard buttons in a room of some sort—whether it is the bedroom, office, cafe or study carrel.

These Internet actions have ultimately solid impacts—from the arenas of political activism to the frivolity of flash mobs and the oh-so-tactile real emotions....

But I digress. The logic of my Facebook withdrawal was not that the network had sucked me into a virtual or disintermediated world, but that it had become too real, too human and too close for comfort.

Of course, there is a safety net involved in my act of unplugging. I intend to get back on Facebook eventually. Who would not?

It would be akin to giving up air-conditioning and Bakelite: You do not really need it, but you also do.

I am not sure when my Facebook rehabilitation might ultimately take place.

Meanwhile, I have just signed up with the miniaturised version of Facebook, Twitter....

5. Columnist Shzr Ee Tan Describes Why She Rejoins Facebook, 2009

Three months to the day I exiled myself from that timesucker of an Internet cosmos, I finally caved in. I rejoined Facebook.

"Welcome to the rest of your life again," chimed a friend as he tut-tutted at my failed cold-turkey stint.

My withdrawal had been a social experiment embarked in the wake of a dawning fear that my right ear and left toe had become all but grafted onto the site.

But rather than simply save myself from a virtual meltdown, I figured I could also pretend I was doing "research". How might my world change as a result of this enforced hermitage?

Not very much—and for that very same reason, I am now back.

But first, some statistics:

Three days was all it took for a flurry of calls from concerned friends to die down. They assumed I had excommunicated them for forgetting to feed my virtual pet. Indeed, I was revealed to be still alive.

My e-mail volume doubled. For once, it was nice to receive words that were just that slightly more personalised than a status update.

Somebody actually poked me, with a real chopstick.

This is what happened: Even as I tried to leave Facebook, that long-tentacled media platform would not leave me be. The network of friends and friends-of-friends within spawned secondary offshoots in the form of e-mail and text messages as well as Twitter-feeds that kept me umbilically linked to the mothership. Cold turkey? If there wasn't much of a real withdrawal, where, then, were the withdrawal symptoms?

Shzr Ee Tan, "Facebook, I'm Back: I rejoined the social networking site after a hiatus because it's the wallpaper of my life," *The Straits Times* (Singapore), (28 May 2009). The Straits Times © Singapore Press Holdings Ltd. Reprinted with permission.

To be sure, there was a loss of an outlet for virtual voyeuring: Where I had once spent hours clicking on X's sister-in-law's best friend's toe-clipping photographic extravaganza for no significant reason, I was now blissfully unaware of her daily routine and wondering about the structure of my own. Did people really read my status updates anyway? Did anyone care?

The thing about Facebook is that a reality-Internet super-network can be too much of a good thing. Once we had the pleasure of not knowing what happened to the Ex-Girlfriend or School Geek until the joy of being surprised in the street or at reunion parties took over.

Today, such mysteries have become an instantly gratifiable click or, at the other extreme, a case of multiple indentities. I know of individuals who, rather than announcing an official change in "relationship status" or resorting to "unfriending" friends, simply went on to create new versions of themselves, with new user IDs.

But all this isn't just unique to Facebook. It is, if anything, part of the reality of today's over-projected world. The only way of escaping from your past, your life, your identity and that of others is to simply re-invent. And really, we have been doing this for ages already.

Multiple identities on Facebook? In actual fact, we have been "performing" different versions of ourselves long before—to our parents versus our school-mates, and to our bosses vs our cubicle partners….

Where the platform was once a novel toy which offered and, still offers, everything from ultra-nerd quizzes to virtual potted plants that grew leopard-print origami, it has also become a vehicle for social mobilisation and activism.

The rise of civil society and remarkable turnout at recent events such as Pink Dot and the Aware Extraordinary General Meeting would not have been possible, one suspects, without Facebook.

So now, I am back, not so much because I cannot do without it but because it is, simply, there. I receive updates from 90 different groups on the site. I post photographs, links and announcements that are so mundane I actually fall asleep while penning them down.

It is hardly exhibitionism or voyeurism here, simply because everyone else is running the same routine: The kick of intentionality is no longer potent.

Facebook, indeed, is no longer an object of fascination, no longer the flavour of the month. It has become the furniture and wallpaper of our lives. We almost even have the right to take it for granted.

Its newsfeed page has become my personalised newspaper-turned-grapevine. But even as I log on to the site every morning to find out what has been happening to my friends and their extended circles, I know that the platform can just as easily be replaced, if not by a more advanced format, then at least by just that slightly more old-fashioned mechanism.

A friend, who has more than 2,000 unread messages and 300 electronic requests yet to be dealt with on his profile, puts it this way: "Big deal, it's only Facebook."

In so many ways, he is absolutely correct. Facebook is a big deal. But Facebook, at the end of the day, is only Facebook.

ESSAYS

In the first essay, three scholars working in Canadian universities (Stephen Kline, is professor and director of the Media Analysis Laboratory, School of Communication, Simon Fraser University, where Greig de Peuter is a PhD candidate; Nick Dyer-Witheford is associate professor in the Faculty of Information and Media Studies at University of Western Ontario) describe the problems with a commodified and interconnected communications industry by focusing on computer games. While the idea that technological progress is always good has a long history, the authors worry about the narrowing of possibilities within the Internet's rhetoric of choice and interactivity. Henry Jenkins, director of Comparative Media Studies Program and professor of literature, Massachusetts Institute of Technology, remains more optimistic. A scholar of "fan culture" and a believer in the idea that audiences make and remake popular culture, Jenkins sees the "convergence" enabled by new technologies as presenting possibilities for popular culture forms to flourish and for people to have an impact on popular culture.

Scholars Posit New Media as Commodified, Not Liberatory, 2005

STEPHEN KLINE, NICK DYER-WITHEROD, AND

GREIG DE PEUTER

... Is it wicked chance or synchronicity that made *Titanic* one of the blockbuster movies of the twentieth century? That great ship was, after all, not just an impregnable vessel but a much-heralded communication medium symbolizing all that was progressive in an era of industrialization in which the conquest of space and time had become essential to the expansionary economies of trade and the global circulation of knowledge and people. So much so that the accelerating speed of travel became the obsession of its builders, who bragged about their superior engines as much as about the scale and opulence of their ship. Throwing caution to the wind, the White Star Line's owners and operators came to believe that they had triumphed over nature and eliminated all risk and unforeseen danger from transatlantic travel. Their arrogance expressed itself in a blind faith in the power of technology and a cheery optimism that they had transcended history at the dawn of a new age. The Hollywood love-boat story of ill-starred romance on that fatal voyage was promoted to bring teenagers into the cinema to defray the enormous costs of a lavish production. But the melodramatic tale of star-crossed lovers would not have distracted all the viewers from the spectacular but class-divided catastrophe brought about by the technological arrogance of those who designed and sailed the Titanic. The same technological arrogance permeates the euphoric descriptions of the contemporary "information age."…

In the so-called information age, each new series of computer chips, each smart appliance, and each domestic communication technology is successively celebrated by the captains of wired capitalism as ways of shrinking our world while expanding our freedom…. In the writings of futurists … the computer is an icon of technologically driven social change—an emblem of the more participatory, democratic, creative, and interactive world that is allegedly being delivered to us just by the power of the silicon chip.

For all the breathless excitement of such statements, their vision is in fact quite old. It is not just that faith in technological progress has been a main theme of Western, and particularly North American, culture from the era of railways to the age of nuclear power: the most recent version of this technocreed, celebrating the new world created by digitization—the "computer revolution," the "information society," the "wired world," the "global village"—has been around for a surprisingly long time….

Invoking a modernist conception of progress, the idea that digital-technology is bringing in an entirely new and better social order is familiar, not to say stale. In its basic form it is rooted in a version of what is called "technological determinism"—the idea that new machines drive social, political, and cultural change. The plough gave us agricultural society, the steam engines the industrial society, the computer the information society, and so on. This is a pretty simple idea—too simple, say many critics, who point out that it neglects the way political, economic, and cultural factors in turn shape the capacity for and direction of technological change….

As we look more closely at those leading the headlong charge to realize the "freedom," dignity, and efficiencies buried deep in the circuitry of digital media—whether Sun and Oracle, Microsoft and AOL, or Nintendo and Sony—we notice that their optimistic promotional discourse elides the interests of corporations and consumers in their vision of the information highway…. Yet we are not so much experiencing a "revolution" in domestic media as a corporate battle over the provision of services to consumers…. To the vanguard of this revolution, … the Internet is first and foremost a corporate battleground wherein the future patterns of communication will be set and won or lost at great profit. "No blood will be shed in this revolution," but certainly a lot of dollars will be diverted as more and more of our culture is commodified….

What … technological hyperbole have in common is a failure to account for historical context and social forces. For *Wired*'s promise of peace and prosperity ultimately depends not just on the wonders of computers but on the ways technological possibility is conceived, appropriated, designed, and, most importantly, sold. But what distinguishes current new media boosterism from earlier information age rhetoric is that our faith is being grounded in raw technological determinism as well as in a new social theory whereby communication media and free markets are a *determinative unity*. Communications technology and free markets make up the dancing dialectic of a new corporate millennialism that will allegedly galvanize our consumer economy, revive our flagging democratic culture, and repair our wounded environment....

Searching for a case study on which to test the digerati's claims, we might remind ourselves that in the closing years of the twentieth century the film industry was not the only megamedia complex telling the story of the Titanic's fatal voyage. Another, more futuristic entertainment business was already exploring the saga. *Titanic: Adventure in Time*, a computer game by the multimedia developer CyberFlix, promised its purchasers not merely the spectacle of nautical disaster but virtual immersion in it, as a British secret agent seeking to retrieve priceless stolen documents on the doomed ship.... Launched in 1996, the game actually preceded the movie. *Titanic: Adventure in Time* found a spot among the top-selling ten computer games for 1997 and 1998; worldwide rights were bought by a software sales and consultation firm called, appropriately enough, Barracuda; copies of the game could still be found on store shelves in 2002.

This might seem a mere footnote to a movie success story. But the interactive game industry, comprising video and computer games, rivals film in terms of its global revenues and impact on popular culture.... In fact, the US interactive-play business now matches Hollywood in economic power. According to the high-tech business journal *Red Herring,* the interactive game industry's revenues for 1999 topped $8.9 billion, compared to US movie box office receipts of $7.3 billion. The journal notes, however, that this figure is somewhat deceptive, since Hollywood generates far larger revenues thanks to various "synergetic" linkages such as pay-per-view TV, video and DVD rentals and sales, etc. Once these are taken into account, the global film industry took in some $47.9 billion; even if home and arcade gaming were added together, worldwide gaming revenue would only be $30 billion. On the other hand, the game industry is growing much faster than the film business; a typical prediction is that in the US alone it will climb from eight billion dollars in 2000 to twenty-nine billion dollars in 2005, these numbers roughly doubling worldwide.

Four decades have seen the digital game transformed from whimsical invention of bored Pentagon researchers, computer science graduate students, and nuclear research engineers into the fastest expanding sector of the entertainment industry.... No longer produced in garages by youthful geeks, a video game can now take a team of up to fifty specialized artists, writers, designers, animators, and programmers—working on expensive game engines with a commitment of financial resources of up to ten million dollars spread over two or three years. Hit titles like *Doom, Mortal Kombat,* and *Tomb Raider,* though less expensive to produce than blockbuster movies, reap profits on an even larger scale, potentially generating revenues in the hundreds of millions.

Interactive games are now viewed as the leading edge of a significant entertainment industry spanning very different technological platforms: home video game consoles, personal computers, Internet play, portable and wireless devices, arcade and virtual reality theme parks. Digital play practices have gradually colonized our homes, pockets, and cyberspace, becoming a daily habit for millions of people. According to a study supported by the Interactive Digital Software Association (IDSA), the industry's major promotional organization, over sixty percent of Americans, or about 145 million people, "play interactive games on a regular basis." Traditionally, youthful males under eighteen have been most attracted to this exciting form of entertainment, a pattern that our own research suggests still prevails, many boys playing on average one hour a day, and some heavy players languishing up to three hours a day at their consoles. IDSA, however, claims recent dramatic breakouts from this traditional young male market niche, both in terms of age, the reported average age of an interactive game player now being twenty-eight, and in terms of gender, females allegedly making up forty-three percent of players. Whatever the precise composition of the gaming audience, it is large, with the more than two hundred million games sold in 2000 equivalent to two for every household in America. Some years ago Allucquère Rosanne Stone suggested that "it is entirely possible that computer-based games will turn out to be the major unacknowledged source of socialization *and* education in industrialized societies before the 1990s have run their course." As we enter the third millennium, this prophecy seems well on the way to being realized.

The video and computer game industry also exemplifies the globalizing, transnational logic of twenty-first-century capital. Although founded in North America, many of its major corporate contenders are Japanese companies—Nintendo, Sega, Sony. The market for interactive games is today almost equally divided between North America, Europe, and Japan. Although the bulk of industry revenues comes from these bastions of advanced capital, games are now disseminated all around the world, booming digital play cultures appearing in countries such as South Korea and Malaysia, and gaming networks beginning to link contestants across continents....

[I]n the work of silicon utopians, video and computer games are hyperbolically celebrated for their "interactivity."

This is a term loosely applied to any media in which the audience technologically intervenes to structure its own experience. The claims are by now familiar: digital games are interactive media *par excellence* because their entertainment value arises from the cybernetic loop between the player and the game, as the human attempts, by the movement of the joystick, to outperform the program against and within which he or she competes. This feedback cycle is often represented as a dramatic emancipatory improvement over traditional oneway mass media such as television and its so-called "passive" audiences. Against mass culture's hegemonic embrace through its broadcast technologies, digital media devices and content will liberate us because their audiences structure their own experience in a triple sense: through technological empowerment, consumer sovereignty, and cultural creativity. The digerati, at their most celebratory, use interactivity to declare the mass media model, and the mass culture and system of corporate power that go with it, overthrown. The subject at the centre of it all, the interactive gamer, becomes the apogee of consumer sovereignty....

Young people's growing fascination with interactive play is itself one of the clearest signs that the digital era is well underway.... No longer submitted to the whims of television moguls, children's virtual drives down the information highway anticipate a future where popular culture will be accommodated to their own deepest desires. They would lead us to believe that the demassified media lead inexorably to the democratization of cultural production, as media corporations are plugged into youthful consumer wants, and as gamers define their own paths through the narratives of interactive games....

For many of the silicon utopians, there is a certain glee in viewing the generational divide that is beginning to appear between the young, who understand and adapt to interactive media more quickly, and the older generation, who foolishly resist the inevitable wiring of the world....

... [M]any silicon apostles speak of the empowerment of global youth culture as "connectivity" and "interactivity" begin to reverse the passivity, alienation, and isolation created by the mass broadcast technologies of the past. New media challenge authority and promote entrepreneurial attitudes, they claim, making the generational divisions the stepping-stone into the future of globally wired capitalism....

And so in the rhetoric of digital futurists, video games promise to transform the very basis of our centralized culture of the mediated mass market into a decentralized, connective, and populist republic of technology....

Over the last couple of decades a growing number of voices have dissented from such technological euphoria. They point out that far from levelling and democratizing, the coming of the information age has been marked by growing disparities in income, global unrest, and economic instability, along with increasing corporate control and waning accountability in the cultural industries. In a reaction against the inflated hyperbole of information revolutionaries, neo-Luddite perspectives have become prominent. Writers of this camp revive the image of early-nineteenth-century insurrectionists who smashed the machines of early industrial capital. Today's neo-Luddites present these early radicals not as ignorant obscurantists but as intelligent and justified opponents of the dehumanizing technologies that concentrated power in the hands of commercial owners. They warn that we should exercise a similar scepticism towards rhetoric about the necessity, promises, and inevitability of societywide digitalization. In the wake of the recent economic meltdown of Internet industries these critiques have attracted renewed attention....

We too reject the hyperbolic optimism that believes democracy is inherent in all information technology. But we are not content with a revival of Luddism, if it amounts only to nostalgia for a predigital era. We believe that digital technologies and global markets, as well as struggles in and against both, will indeed shape the future. But understanding the process requires an understanding of paradox and contradiction, not blind faith and a deterministic bent. We set out to avoid both technophilia and technophobia and attempt a more historical, more complex, hence more balanced account of the information revolution. We do so by turning a critical eye towards the video game as just one digital invention that is already in the hands of millions of young people.

Our critique begins with a rejection of the digital euphoria of technological determinism. Arguments ... conveniently ignore the process of the design and construction of gaming experiences as the transmission of meaning from "producers" to "consumers" in the context of the power relations of a market society, which are not escaped by this entertainment industry. Blindness to the complex corporate institutions, technical constraints, design processes, and marketing calculations that generate the game experience, and to the "negotiations" that take place between producers and consumers of digital games in the context of a for-profit cultural industry, leads the enthusiasts to conclude that the players construct the possibilities of their own cultural narratives and fantasies. In such one-eyed visions of interactive gaming the player is seen as defining the very rules of the game.

We also are not so quick to pit the mass media against the digital, or the supposed "passivity" of television audiences against the alleged "activity" of digital ones. Interactive gaming did not fall from the sky ready-made but rather emerged on the basis of the very mass-mediated markets and culture it supposedly surpasses. Video gaming is in many ways an offspring of television—technically, in so far as game consoles depend on the television screen for their visual display; culturally, as an extension of the privatized in-home acrion-adventure entertainment forms TV provided; and promotionally, as television advertising was a central element in selling the concept of gaming to children and youth. Furthermore, both television and video gaming are channels of commercialized culture, carrying a flow of commodified entertainment to youthful media audiences. Put simply, the new media are built on the foundations of the old.

So in our view the claims made by the digerati are only partially true. There is a real difference, of course, between interactive gaming and the flow of television programming: choice and responsiveness have been programmed into digital play. Critics of high-technology culture err if they fail to acknowledge the dynamism of youthful entertainment audiences or the ways media producers recognized and responded to them. The gamer chooses their characters and their teams and explores in those virtual spaces. In navigating the game's branching paths and deciding on the course of the narrative, video game players do indeed engage the virtual world as "active" audiences. Playing games is a complex psychological engagement that blends creative exploration with narrative in a form of mediated communication that infuses young people's engagements with participatory intensity. It is a dynamic cognitive activity and cultural practice that elicits a variety of audience responses: selection, interpretation, choice, strategy dialogue, and exploration characterize the player's relationship to the symbolic contents they manipulate on the screen. Clearly, there is an important cultural shift taking place from spectators to players.

But the interactive enthusiasts need to take a closer look at the degree and kind of "active" participation of young audiences in the construction of their "own" digital culture. Choosing a corridor, character or weapon—a rail gun or a chainsaw in a *Quake* death match—can be very absorbing. But it is hardly a matter of radical openness or deep decision about the content of play. Though gamers navigate through virtual environments, their actions consist of selections (rather than choices) made between alternatives that have been anticipated by the game designers. Gaming choice usually remains a matter of tactical decisions executed within predefined scenarios whose strategic parameters are preordained by the designers.

This preprogramming is implanted at a number of levels: technologically, in the capacities and valences of the machines players access; culturally, in the nature of the scenarios and storylines chosen for development; and commercially, in the price point of the software and hardware and in the marketing strategies that shape the trajectory of the industry as a whole. Indeed, to talk about "choice" in interactive games we must also address the market processes that have an impact upon what games are made available in the first place. When young gamers sit down to play ... entering an imaginary world that has been programmed to respond to their fascinations and desire for entertainment, they are at the point of convergence for a whole array of technical, cultural, and promotional dynamics of which they are probably, at best, only very partially aware.

Indeed, one of the main objectives of the game industry is to make sure that the player does not reflect on these forces. The *sine qua non* of game designers is described by some as the "disappearance of technology." They have learned that the enthusiasm of the gamer dissipates when characters or weapons act inappropriately, when players experience the boundary of the game space, when they are forced to interact with avatars in cumbersome ways, or when they are too quickly killed by an enemy. That is why the disappearance of the interface with computers is among the chief goals of gaming....

Immersed in the game, the player becomes an imaginary subject who is fighting virtual monsters in the catacombs of an infernal planet or plotting the overthrow of the simulated leaders of the Egyptian dynastic order. Precisely in that moment of suspended disbelief, the system of interactive play becomes most fetishized. The construction of that willing delusion by which the players imagine they are controlling their own fantasy defines the magic of gaming. Digital designers devote a lot of energy to understanding its mysteries....

There is nothing wrong, of course, with designing an absorbing virtual play environment: we too like to get lost in a game. Neither are we advocating clumsy video games. But given that game designers devote such attention to erasing the interface from players' awareness, eliminating every trace of the produced nature of the game experience, and promoting gaming as the zone of the superfantastical where we go to be entranced, it is hardly surprising that the average video gamer remains innocent of the reasons it takes two years to research and program an updated version of *Star Wars*, and how a single game can require millions of dollars in direct investment.... The gamer is unlikely to think much about the engineering wizardry or the history of this cultural form while he or she sits in front of the screen. At that moment, gamers are extensions of their virtual technology, unlikely to be aware of how that play was constructed for them in the mediated entertainment marketplace, or of how complex cultural biases came to be inscribed in the game.

They are also unlikely to think much about how energetically game developers have sold the play experience to them—despite the fact that marketing a game may account for up to one-third of the costs of production, or that the promotional campaigns devoted to the launch of new consoles—Microsoft Xbox, Sony PlayStation 2, and Nintendo GameCube—will probably amount to $1.5 billion worldwide. As with television, game makers had to learn not only to design and sell a new medium but also to construct the very audience for that medium. Here our account focuses attention on the growing cadre of digital "cultural intermediaries" (e.g., designers, marketers) who manage the flow of digital play culture to youthful consumers. The point is not that interactive games are now a crucial node in a web of synergistic advertising, branding, and licensing practices that spread throughout contemporary popular culture. It is also that these promotional practices work their way back into game content—so that considerations of market segmentation, branding, franchising, licensing, and media spin-offs are now present at the very inception of game characters, scenarios, and plotlines....

The paradox that is lost in ... visions of digital progress is that genuinely new technocultural innovations, from cellular phones to interactive games, are being shaped, contained, controlled, and channelled within the long-standing logic of a commercial marketplace dedicated to the profit-maximizing sale of cultural and technological commodities. While interactive games are in many ways genuinely "new" media, their possibilities are being realized and limited by a media marker whose fundamental imperative remains the same as that which shaped the "old" media: profit. While this encounter between digital media and capitalist markets may in part ... be reshaping markets, it is also constraining and channelling the directions taken by new media. Moreover, the demassified digital media do not necessarily mark a hard break with the symptoms of a mass-mediated culture, leading automatically to cultural diversification. We have to see the disturbances and frictions created by the intersection of new potentialities with old logics. Only by understanding the play of paradoxes—the discontinuities and continuities in economic, cultural, and technological spheres—that is structuring digital capital can we estimate the probable trajectory and possible alternatives for digital play culture. But this is the contradiction that the digerati cannot come to terms with. By shutting their eyes to the constraints that circumscribe interactive media, they blind themselves to actual, rather than merely notional, possibilities for change. It is against this reduction of possibility that our analysis takes aim. Our argument is not that multimedia systems are intrinsically oppressive, vacuous, or malign. It is rather that their potential is being narrowed and channelled in ways that betray their promise, even as that potential is promoted with the rhetoric of choice, interactivity, and empowerment.

Scholar/Fan Sees New Convergence Culture as Full of Potential

HENRY JENKINS

The story circulated in the fall of 2001: Dino Ignacio, a Fillipino-American high school student created a Photoshop collage of *Sesame Street*'s ... Bert interacting with terrorist leader Osama Bin Laden as part of a series of "Bert Is Evil" images he posted on his homepage.... It was all in good fun.

In the wake of September 11, a Bangladesh-based publisher scanned the Web for Bin Laden images to print on anti-American signs, posters, and T-shirts.... The publisher may not have recognized Bert, but he must have thought the image was a good likeness of the al-Qaeda leader. The image ended up in a collage of similar images that was printed on thousands of posters and distributed across the Middle East.

CNN reporters recorded the unlikely sight of a mob of angry protestors marching through the streets chanting anti-American slogans and waving signs depicting Bert and Bin Laden.... Representatives from the Children's Television Workshop, creators of the *Sesame Street* series, spotted the CNN footage and threatened to take legal action.... Coming full circle, amused fans produced a number of new sites, linking various *Sesame Street* characters with terrorists.

From his bedroom, Ignacio sparked an international controversy. His images crisscrossed the world, sometimes on the backs of commercial media, sometimes via grassroots media.... Welcome to convergence culture, where old and new media collide, where grassroots and corporate media intersect, where the power of the media producer and the power of the media consumer interact in unpredictable ways.

This book is about the relationship between three concepts—media convergence, participatory culture, and collective intelligence.

By convergence, I mean the flow of content across multiple media platforms, the cooperation between multiple media industries, and the migratory behavior of media audiences who will go almost anywhere in search of the kinds of entertainment experiences they want. Convergence is a word that manages to describe technological, industrial, cultural, and social changes depending on who's speaking and what they think they are talking about....

This circulation of media content—across different media systems, competing media economies, and national borders—depends heavily on consumers' active participation. I will argue here against the idea that convergence should be understood primarily as a technological process bringing together multiple media functions within the same devices. Instead, convergence represents a cultural shift as consumers are encouraged to seek out new information and make connections among dispersed media content....

The term *participatory culture* contrasts with older notions of passive media spectatorship. Rather than talking about media producers and consumers as occupying separate roles, we might now see them as participants who interact with each other according to a new set of rules that none of us fully understands. Not all participants are created equal. Corporations—and even individuals within corporate media—still exet greater power than any individual consumer or even the aggregate of consumers. And some consumers have greater abilities to participate in this emerging culture than others.

Convergence does not occur through media appliances, however sophisticated they may become. Convergence occurs within the brains of individual consumers and through their social interactions with others. Each of us constructs our own personal mythology from bits and fragments of information extracted from the media flow and transformed into resources through which we make sense of our everyday lives. Because there is more information on any given topic than anyone can store in their head, there is an added incentive for us to talk among ourselves about the media we consume. This conversation creates buzz that is increasingly valued by the media industry. Consumption has become a collective process—and that's … collective intelligence…. None of us can know everything; each of us knows something; and we can put the pieces together if we pool our resources and combine our skills. Collective intelligence can be seen as an alternative source of media power. We are learning how to use that power through our day-to-day interactions within convergence culture. Right now, we are mostly using this collective power through our recreational life, but soon we will be deploying those skills for more "serious" purposes…. I explore how collective meaning-making within popular culture is starting to change the ways religion, education, law, politics, advertising, and even the military operate….

The media industries are undergoing a … paradigm shift. It happens from time to time. In the 1990s, rhetoric about a coming digital revolution contained an implicit and often explicit assumption that new media was going to push aside old media, that the Internet was going to displace broadcasting, and that all of this would enable consumers to more easily access media content that was personally meaningful to them…. Sometimes, the new media companies spoke about convergence, but by this term, they seemed to mean that old media would be absorbed fully and completely into the orbit of the emerging technologies….

The popping of the dot-com bubble threw cold water on this talk of a digital revolution. Now, convergence has reemerged as an important reference point as old and new media companies try to imagine the future of the entertainment industry. If the digital revolution paradigm presumed that new media would displace old media, the emerging convergence paradigm assumes that old and new media will interact in ever more complex ways. The digital revolution paradigm claimed that new media was going to change everything. After the dot-com crash, the tendency was to imagine that new media had changed nothing. As with so many things about the current media environment, the truth lay somewhere in between: More and more, industry leaders are returning to convergence as a way of making sense of a moment of disorienting change. Convergence is, in that sense, an old concept taking on new meanings….

Political economists and business gurus make convergence sound so easy; they look at the charts that show the concentration of media ownership as if they ensure that all of the parts will work together to pursue maximum profits. But from the ground, many of the big media giants look like great big dysfunctional families, whose members aren't speaking with each other and pursue their own short-term agendas even at the expense of other divisions of the same companies….

Several forces, however, have begun breaking down the walls separating … different media. New media technologies enabled the same content to flow through many different channels and assume many different forms at the point of reception…. At the same time, new patterns of cross-media ownership that began in the mid-1980s, during what we can now see as the first phase of a longer process of media concentration, were making it more desirable for companies to distribute content across those various channels rather than within a single media platform. Digitization set the conditions for convergence; corporate conglomerates created its imperative....

... [W]e are in an age of media transition, one marked by tactical decisions and unintended consequences, mixed signals and competing interests, and most of all, unclear directions and unpredictable outcomes. Two decades later, I find myself reexamining some of the core questions ... about how we maintain the potential of participatory culture in the wake of growing media concentration, about whether the changes brought about by convergence open new opportunities for expression or expand the power of big media.

It is beyond my abilities to describe or fully document all of the changes that are occurring. My aim is more modest. I want to describe some of the ways that convergence thinking is reshaping American popular culture and, in particular, the ways it is impacting the relationship between media audiences, producers, and content.... Writing this ... has been challenging because everything seems to be changing at once and there is no vantage point that takes me above the fray....

I can't claim to be a neutral observer in any of this. For one thing, I am not simply a consumer of many of these media products; I am also an active fan. The world of media fandom ...has been a central theme of my work for almost two decades—an interest that emerges from my own participation within various fan communities as much as it does from my intellectual interests as a media scholar. During that time, I have watched fans move from the invisible margins of popular culture and into the center of current thinking about media production and consumption. For another, through my role as director of the MIT Comparative Media Studies Program, I have been an active participant in discussions among industry insiders and policymakers; I have consulted with some of the companies discussed in this book; my earlier writings on fan communities and participatory culture have been embraced by business schools and are starting to have some modest impact on the way media companies are relating to their consumers; many of the creative artists and media executives I interviewed are people I would consider friends. At a time when the roles between producers and consumers are shifting, my job allows me to move among different vantage points.... [R]eaders should also keep in mind that my engagement with fans and producers alike necessarily colors what I say. My goal here is to document conflicting perspectives on media change rather than to critique them. I don't think we can meaningfully critique convergence until it is more fully understood; yet if the public doesn't get some insights into the discussions that are taking place, they will have little to no input into decisions that will dramatically change their relationship to media....

[H]istory teaches us that old media never die—and they don't even necessarily fade away. What dies are simply the tools we use to access media content—the 8-track, the Beta tape. These are what media scholars call *delivery technologies*.... Delivery technologies become obsolete and get replaced; media, on the other hand, evolve. Recorded sound is the medium. CDs, MP3 files, and 8-track cassettes are delivery technologies.

To define media, let's turn to historian Lisa Gitelman, who offers a model of media that works on two levels: on the first, a medium is a technology that enables communication; on the second, a medium is a set of associated "protocols" or social and cultural practices that have grown up around that technology. Delivery systems are simply and only technologies; media are also cultural systems. Delivery technologies come and go all the time, but media persist as layers within an ever more complicated information and entertainment stratum.

A medium's content may shift (as occurred when television displaced radio as a storytelling medium, freeing radio to become the primary showcase for rock and roll), its audience may change (as occurs when comics move from a mainstream medium in the 1950s to a niche medium today), and its social status may rise or fall (as occurs when theater moves from a popular form to an elite one), but once a medium establishes itself as satisfying some core human demand, it continues to function within the larger system of communication options. Once recorded sound becomes a possibility, we have continued to develop new and improved means of recording and playing back sound. Printed words did not kill spoken words. Cinema did not kill theater. Television did not kill radio. Each old medium was forced to coexist with the emerging media. That's why convergence seems more plausible as a way of understanding the past several decades of media change than the old digital revolution paradigm was. Old media are not being displaced. Rather, their functions and status are shifted by the introduction of new technologies....

Much contemporary discourse about convergence starts and ends with what I call the Black Box Fallacy. Sooner or later, the argument goes, all media content is going to flow through a single black box into our living rooms (or, in the mobile scenario, through black boxes we carry around with us everywhere we go).... Part of what makes the black box concept a fallacy is that it reduces media change to technological change and strips aside the cultural levels we are considering here.

I don't know about you, but in my living room, I am seeing more and more black boxes. There are my VCR, my digital cable box, my DVD player, my digital recorder, my sound system, and my two game systems, not to mention a huge mound of videotapes, DVDs and CDs, game cartridges and controllers, sitting atop, laying alongside, toppling over the edge of my television system. (I would definitely qualify as an early adopter, but most American homes now have, or soon will have, their own pile of black boxes.) The perpetual tangle of cords that stands between me and my "home entertainment" center reflects the degree of incompatibility and dysfunction that exist between the various media technologies. And many of my MIT students are lugging around multiple black boxes—their laptops, their cells, their iPods, their Game Boys, their BlackBerrys, you name it....

Media convergence is more than simply a technological shift. Convergence alters the relationship between existing technologies, industries, markets, genres, and audiences. Convergence alters the logic by which media industries operate and by which media consumers process news and entertainment. Keep this in mind: convergence refers to a process, not an endpoint. There will be no single black box that controls the flow of media into our homes. Thanks to the proliferation of channels and the portability of new computing and telecommunications technologies, we are entering an era when media will be everywhere. Convergence isn't something that is going to happen one day when we have enough bandwidth or figure out the correct configuration of appliances. Ready or not, we are already living within a convergence culture....

Fueling this technological convergence is a shift in patterns of media ownership. Whereas old Hollywood focused on cinema, the new media conglomerates have controlling interests across the entire entertainment industry. Warner Bros. produces film, television, popular music, computer games, Web sites, toys, amusement park rides, books, newspapers, magazines, and comics.

In turn, media convergence impacts the way we consume media. A teenager doing homework may juggle four or five windows, scan the Web, listen to and download MP3 files, chat with friends, word-process a paper, and respond to e-mail, shifting rapidly among tasks. And fans of a popular television series may sample dialogue, summarize episodes, debate subtexts, create original fan fiction, record their own soundtracks, make their own movies—and distribute all of this world wide via the Internet.

Convergence is taking place within the same appliances, within the same franchise, within the same company, within the brain of the consumer, and within the same fandom. Convergence involves both a change in the way media is produced and a change in the way media is consumed....

Convergence doesn't just involve commercially produced materials and services traveling along well-regulated and predictable circuits. It doesn't just involve the mobile companies getting together with the film companies to decide when and where we watch a newly released film. It also occurs when people take media in their own hands. Entertainment content isn't the only thing that flows across multiple media platforms. Our lives, relationships, memories, fantasies, desires also flow across media channels....

... [A]nother snapshot: Intoxicated students at a local high school use their cell phones spontaneously to produce their own soft-core porn movie involving topless cheerleaders making out in the locker room. Within hours, the movie is circulating across the school, being downloaded by students and teachers alike and watched between classes on personal media devices.

When people take media into their own hands, the results can be wonderfully creative; they can also be bad news for all involved.

For the foreseeable future, convergence will be a kind of kludge—a jerry-rigged relationship among different media technologies—rather than a fully integrated system. Right now, the cultural shifts, the legal battles, and the economic consolidations that are fueling media convergence are preceding shifts in the technological infrastructure. How those various transitions unfold will determine the balance of power in the next media era.

The American media environment is now being shaped by two seemingly contradictory trends: on the one hand, new media technologies have lowered production and distribution costs, expanded the range of available delivery channels, and enabled consumers to archive, annotate, appropriate, and recirculate media content in powerful new ways. At the same time, there has been an alarming concentration of the ownership of mainstream commercial media, with a small handful of multinational media conglomerates dominating all sectors of the entertainment industry. No one seems capable of describing both sets of changes at the same time, let alone showing how they impact each other. Some fear that media is out of control, others that it is too controlled. Some see a world without gatekeepers, others a world where gatekeepers have unprecedented power. Again, the truth lies somewhere in between....

Convergence, as we can see, is both a top-down corporate-driven process and a bottom–up consumer-driven process. Corporate convergence coexists with grassroots convergence. Media companies are learning how to accelerate the flow of media content across delivery channels to expand revenue opportunities, broaden markets, and reinforce viewer commitments. Consumers are learning how to use these different media technologies to bring the flow of media more fully under their control and to interact with other consumers. The promises of this new media environment raise expectations of a freer flow of ideas and content. Inspired by those ideals, consumers are fighting for the right to participate more fully in their culture. Sometimes, corporate and grassroots convergence reinforce each other, creating closer, more rewarding relations between media producers and consumers. Sometimes, these two forces are at war, and those struggles will redefine the face of American popular culture.

Convergence requires media companies to rethink old assumptions about what it means to consume media, assumptions that shape both programming and marketing decisions. If old consumers were assumed to be passive, the new consumers are active. If old consumers were predictable and stayed where you told them to stay, then new consumers are migratory, showing a declining loyalty to networks or media. If old consumers were isolated individuals, the new consumers are more socially connected. If the work of media consumers was once silent and invisible, the new consumers are now noisy and public.

Media producers are responding to these newly empowered consumers in contradictory ways, sometimes encouraging change, sometimes resisting what they see as renegade behavior. And consumers, in turn, are perplexed by what they see as mixed signals about how much and what kinds of participation they can enjoy....

The decreasing value of the thirty-second commercial in an age of TiVos and VCRs is forcing Madison Avenue to rethink its interface with the consuming public. This new "affective economics" encourages companies to transform brands into what one industry insider calls "lovemarks" and to blur the line between entertainment content and brand messages. According to the logic of affective economics, the ideal consumer is active, emotionally engaged, and socially networked. Watching the advert or consuming the product is no longer enough; the company invites the audience inside the brand community. Yet, if such affiliations encourage more active consumption, these same communities can also become protectors of brand integrity and thus critics of the companies that seek to court their allegiance....

... [E]ntrenched institutions are taking their models from grassroots fan communities, and reinventing themselves for an era of media convergence and collective intelligence—the advertising industry has been forced to reconsider consumers' relations to brands, the military is using multiplayer games to rebuild communications between civilians and service members, the legal profession has struggled to understand what "fair use" means in an era when many more people are becoming authors, educators are reassessing the value of informal education, and at least some conservative Christians are making their peace with newer forms of popular culture. In each of these cases, powerful institutions are trying

to build stronger connections with their constituencies and consumers are apply-
ing skills learned as fans and gamers to work, education, and politics....

A core claim[is] that convergence culture represents a shift in the ways we
think about our relations to media, ... we are making that shift first through our
relations with popular culture, but ... the skills we acquire through play may
have implications for how we learn, work, participate in the political process,
and connect with other people around the world....

You are now entering convergence culture. It is not a surprise that we are
not yet ready to cope with its complexities and contradictions. We need to find
ways to negotiate the changes taking place. No one group can set the terms. No
one group can control access and participation.

Don't expect the uncertainties surrounding convergence to be resolved any-
time soon. We are entering an era of prolonged transition and transformation in
the way media operates. Convergence describes the process by which we will
sort through those options. There will be no magical black box that puts everything in order again. Media producers will find their way through their current
problems only by renegotiating their relationship with their consumers.
Audiences, empowered by these new technologies, occupying a space at the
intersection between old and new media, are demanding the right to participate
within the culture. Producers who fail to make their peace with this new participatory culture will face declining goodwill and diminished revenues. The resulting struggles and compromises will define the public culture of the future.

FURTHER READING

Chun, Wendy Hui Kyong, and Thomas Keenan. *New Media, Old Media: A History and Theory Reader* (2006).

Cohen, Dan, and Roy Rosenweig. *Digital History* (2006).

De Sola Pool, Ithiel. *Technologies of Power* (1983).

Garrelts, Nate, ed. *The Meaning and Culture of Grand Theft Auto: Critical Essays* (2006).

Gibson, William. *Neuromancer* (1984).

Gibson, William, and Bruce Sterling. *The Difference Engine* (1991).

Gittleman, Lisa. *New Media, 1740–1915* (2004).

Jenkins, Henry. *Fans, Bloggers and Gamers: Media Consumers in the Digital Age* (2006).

Liu, Alan. *The Laws of Cool: Knowledge Work and the Culture of Information* (2004).

Marvin, Carolyn. *When Old Technologies Were New: Thinking about Electric Communication in the Nineteenth Century* (1990).

Shirkey, Clay. *Here Comes Everyone: The Power of Organizing without Organizations* (2008).

Stephenson, Neal. *Snow Crash* (2002).

Thompson, John B. *Books in the Digital Age* (2005).

Vaidhayanathan, Siva. *Copyrights and Copywrongs: The Rise of Intellectual Property and How It Threatens Creativity* (2001).

Wright, Alex. *Glut: Mastering Information through the Ages* (2007).